# MECHANICAL ESTIMATING GUIDEBOOK

# MECHANICAL ESTIMATING GUIDEBOOK

## John Gladstone
*Editor, Engineer's Press*

## Kenneth K. Humphreys, PhD PE CCE
*Consulting Engineer*

**Sixth Edition**

**McGraw-Hill, Inc.**

New York   San Francisco   Washington, D.C.   Auckland   Bogotá
Caracas   Lisbon   London   Madrid   Mexico City   Milan
Montreal   New Delhi   San Juan   Singapore
Sydney   Tokyo   Toronto

**Library of Congress Cataloging-in-Publication Data**

Gladstone, John.
   [Mechanical estimating guidebook]
   Mechanical estimating guidebook.—6th ed. / editors, John Gladstone,
Kenneth K. Humphreys.
       p.    cm.
   Rev. ed. of: Mechanical estimating guidebook for building construction.
5th ed. 1987.
   Includes bibliographical references and index.
   ISBN 0-07-024227-5 (book).—ISBN 0-07-852846-1 (disk).—
ISBN 0-07-023620-8 (book and disk)
   1. Air conditioning—Equipment and supplies—Estimates.
I. Gladstone, John.  II. Humphreys, Kenneth King.  Mechanical estimating
guidebook for building construction.  III. Title.
TH7687.5.G556  1995
697'.0029'9—dc20                        95-19732
                                            CIP

1 2 3 4 5 6 7 8 9 0  AGM/AGM  9 0 9 8 7 6 5 4


ISBN 0-07-023620-8


The sponsoring editor for this book was Robert W. Hauserman, the editing supervisor was Caroline R. Levine, and the production supervisor was Suzanne W. B. Rapcavage. This book was set in Baskerville by Renee Lipton of McGraw-Hill's Professional Book Group composition unit.

*Printed and bound by R. R. Donnelley & Sons Company.*

McGraw-Hill books are available at special quantity discounts to use as premiums and sales promotions, or for use in corporate training programs. For more information, please write to the Director of Special Sales, McGraw-Hill, Inc., 11 West 19th Street, New York, NY 10011. Or contact your local bookstore.

 This book is printed on acid-free paper containing a minimum of 10% postconsumer waste.

# CONTENTS

# CONTRIBUTORS

In the preparation of this edition of *Mechanical Estimating Guidebook* several persons have contributed chapters or portions of chapters. Their contributions and their affiliations at the time of manuscript preparation were:

**Russel P. Fleming, PE**  *National Fire Sprinkler Association, Patterson, New York*

**John Gladstone**  *Engineer's Press, Coral Gables, Florida*

**Kenneth K. Humphreys, PhD, PE CCE**  *Consulting Engineer, Granite Falls, North Carolina*

**Kerry L. Kost**  *Project Time & Cost, Atlanta, Georgia*

**Harold E. Marshall, PhD**  *National Institute of Standards and Technology, Gaithersburg, Maryland*

**Stephen R. Petersen**  *National Institute of Standards and Technology, Gaithersburg, Maryland*

**David Rosoff, CCE**  *Building Economics Research Limited, Alexandria, Virginia*

Chapters written by Mr. Fleming, Mr. Kost, Dr. Marshall, and Mr. Petersen are identified as to authorship. The remaining chapters were prepared by the editors with the assistance of Mr. Rosoff who contributed to 14 of the 28 chapters in the book.

# PREFACE

When the first edition of the *Mechanical Estimating Guidebook* reached the market in 1960, it was essentially a pricing book; the author intended to update it every year. By the time the second edition was published (1962) and reader responses flowed back, he came to understand that what was needed (and didn't exist) at the point of production was not a pricing book but a solid estimating manual—a handbook. Subsequent editions reflect this concept.

The information contained herein has been accumulated over the years with great care and precision. Most of the workhours are based on actual time-motion studies done in the early years and refined, where necessary, in the later editions. In the last three editions, experts from various disciplines have been consulted and, in some cases, have written specific chapters.

Although thousands of pricing data are listed in this book, the time between gathering the data and writing the book and the actual marketing of the new edition is usually between one-and-a-half to two-and-a-half years. Pricing also varies greatly by geography, local conditions, time of year, etc. Published pricing has no universal validity. Cost data become obsolete very quickly. While it is true that rule-of-thumb cost data averages out quite reliably over a broad spectrum, no responsible estimator would submit a bid without an accurate takeoff and firm quotation from every supplier and subcontractor for each project. The cost data in *Mechanical Estimating Guidebook*—or any estimating book—should not be used for actual estimates without verification and adjustment to current price levels.

*Material Cost Adjustments.* Material prices have varied widely since 1985 when the last edition was prepared. Price indexes for various equipment items increased on the order of 50 percent for boilers and 25 percent for ductwork. Air conditioning equipment ranged from a decrease of 15 percent to increases of over 60 percent, while pumps increased anywhere from 10 to 120 percent, and fasteners ranged between decreases and increases of 60 percent. In general, trade prices since 1985 have increased approximately 5 percent per year.

Where future indexing is required, see *Producer Prices and Price Indexes* published monthly by the U.S. Government Printing Office, Washington, DC 20402, ISSN 0161-7311, compiled by the U.S. Department of Labor, Bureau of Labor Statistics. These indexes are highly detailed, and individual indexes exist for most specific types of equipment.

*Labor Cost Adjustments* The labor cost basis of this edition as compared to the last edition has increased by 26 percent. Labor figures in this edition are based on $24.65 per hour; to convert labor dollar figures from the fifth edition, use a multiplier of 1.26. Current labor costs can also easily be estimated by using the workhour figures in this book and multiplying the prevailing labor rates in the area of the job. No indexing is required in this case.

*Productivity Levels* Workhours and production rates have generally remained stable between the two editions. Readers who have annotated workhours and production rates in the last edition need not make any revisions unless otherwise stated. Excepting a few corrections, revisions, and additions, the labor workhour units are unchanged from the preceding edition.

Task times vary with each company. Shops that fare better than others may reflect increased productivity owing to coil-sheet ductwork fabrication, better utilization of new tools and equipment, well-developed in-house training programs, etc. Shops suffering from high costs and decreased productivity may have inefficient management, undetected blue-collar and/or white-collar theft, poorly selected and improperly organized work crews, poor scheduling, and so on. Classic treatises on economics indicate that productivity in modern industry is a function of mechanization, automation, modernization, and management, rather than worker sloth, indolence, cunning, or other built-in attitudinal traits commonly attributed to the work force. Complaints against workers goofing off and goldbricking, while often justified, are mainly management problems. Where the production schedule is free-flowing and unhampered and the project manager and supervisory workers are experienced, high-caliber personnel, productivity is high. But, of course, poorly trained and inexperienced men and women are a ubiquitous problem in both the blue-collar and white-collar sectors.

*General Revisions*   Technological advances in the industry have always been rapid, but the nineties have seen the most dramatic changes. Currently, the main concerns are *indoor air quality* (IAQ), *energy conservation, alternative refrigerants, and codification of standards*. All of these strongly affect cost. The authors have, therefore, expanded Chap. 4, "Mechanical Cooling and Refrigeration Equipment"; changed the focus in Chap. 22, "IAQ and Antipollution Filtration"; completely rewritten Chap. 25, "Energy Management"; and added a new chapter, 28, called "Codes, Standards, and Laws." To accomplish this and yet keep the work within acceptable publishing and marketing parameters, we were forced to drop two chapters that appeared in the previous editions—"Residential" and "Solar." For that we ask your indulgence.

Every chapter has been revised and updated to reflect current prices and new technologies. Wherever possible, tables and illustrations from the fifth edition have been used again to keep this new edition familiar and user-friendly to the many thousands of readers who have come to depend on this work for the last 35 years.

*Design Data*   Because the design and estimating functions are so closely intertwined, design information and brief discussions regarding tanks, etc., have always been included in *Mechanical Estimator's Guidebook*. Throughout the years, readers of this handbook have requested more design data illustrations and tables giving the physical dimensions of pipe, sheet metal, etc. Responding to this consensus, this sixth edition features additional design details.

We have tried to give this undertaking a breadth and depth that will meet the exacting needs of the professional estimator and cost engineer. It should be immediately useful to architects, building managers, and plant executives for its detailed, up-to-date information as well as its conceptual approach. We hope that engineers will find its "engineering style" and tightly organized format in step with their own ideas. And, finally, keeping mindful of the practical needs of the thousands of HVAC and mechanical contractors—the backbone of the industry—for *quick*, accurate access to vital information, we have tried to keep our work free of theoretical jargon and unburdened by lengthy discourse.

The computer disk accompanying this edition covers most of the tables in the book. They are presented as *Lotus 1-2-3*[1] spreadsheets compatible with any MS-DOS computer system.

*John Gladstone*
*Kenneth K. Humphreys*

---

[1] *Lotus* and *1-2-3* are trademarks of Lotus Development Corporation.

# BIBLIOGRAPHIC NOTES

Professional estimators must have access to pertinent reference sources to reinforce their own data files and feedback. Relevant articles appearing in the trade and professional journals should be filed in a good information retrieval system, and standard estimating handbooks should be kept within easy reach for ready reference. It is also valuable to augment the in-house database with the electronic versions of the standard estimating handbooks. Such electronic databases are available from the R.S. Means Co., Kingston, Mass. and Richardson Engineering Services, Mesa, Ariz., among others.

A short list of recommended literature appears at the conclusion of some chapters as back-up material for the particular crafts or tasks discussed. The following is a suggested personal working library. Some of the works cited deal directly with cost estimating; others deal with systems, procedures, application, techniques, tables of weights and dimensions, etc., all affording a better understanding of specific tasks and general operations. This is a basic "at hand" library, and it should be considered minimal.[2]

*AACE Transactions*, AACE International, Morgantown, W.Va. (Published annually.)

*AACE Recommended Practices and Standards*, AACE International, Morgantown, W.Va. (Updated and expanded periodically.)

*AACE Cost Engineers' Notebook*, AACE International, Morgantown, W.Va. (Updated and expanded periodically.)

*ASHRAE Handbook & Product Directory*, American Society of Heating, Refrigerating and Air Conditioning Engineers, Atlanta, Ga. (Four volumes: *Fundamentals, Equipment, Systems*, and *Applications*; updated every few years.)

*Building Construction Cost Data*, R.S. Means Co., Kingston, Mass. (Published annually.)

*Building Estimator's Reference Book*, Frank R. Walker Co., Lisle, Ill. (Updated every few years.)

Cohen, H. R., *HVAC Systems Evaluation*, R.S. Means Co., Kingston, Mass. 1990.

Cook, P. J., *Bidding for the General Contractor*, R.S. Means Co., Kingston, Mass. 1985.

Cook, P. J., *Estimating for the General Contractor*, R.S. Means Co., Kingston, Mass., 1982.

Cook, P. J., *Quantity Take-Off for the General Contractor*, R.S. Means Co., Kingston, Mass., 1989.

*Cost Engineering*, AACE International, Morgantown, W.Va. (A monthly journal of cost estimating, cost control, and project management.)

*Engineering News-Record* "Cost Roundup," McGraw-Hill, New York. (Published quarterly.)

*General Construction Estimating Standards*, Richardson Engineering Services, Inc., Mesa, Ariz. (Published annually.)

Gupton, G. W., Jr., *HVAC Controls: Operation and Maintenance*, Fairmont Press, Lilburn, Ga., 1987.

*Handbook of Air Conditioning, Heating and Ventilation*, 3d ed., Industrial Press, New York, 1979.

Horsley, F. W., and B. J. Cox, *Square Foot Estimating*, R.S. Means Co., Kingston, Mass., 1983.

Humphreys, K. K., and L. M. English (eds.), *Project and Cost Engineers' Handbook*, 3d ed., Marcel Dekker, New York, 1993.

---

[2]The majority of these publications are available to members of AACE International (formerly the American Association of Cost Engineers) at substantial discounts. For information concerning these books, as well as membership in AACE, contact the Association at PO Box 1557, Morgantown, WV 26507-1557, USA. Phone (800)858-COST or (304)296-8444.

*Local Climatological Data Annual Summary with Comparative Data*, National Climatic Data Center, Asheville, N.C.

*Manual for Construction Cost Estimating*, Frank R. Walker Co., Chicago, Ill., 1981.

McDonald, P. R., and R. Lamb, *Mechanical Contractor's Handbook of Claims Avoidance and Management*, Reston Publishing Co., Reston, Va., 1986.

*Means Assemblies Cost Data*, R.S. Means Co., Kingston, Mass. (Published annually.)

*Means Electrical Cost Data*, R.S. Means Co., Kingston, Mass., (Published annually.)

*Means Labor Rates for the Construction Industry*, R.S. Means Co., Kingston, Mass. (Published annually.)

*Means Man-Hour Standards for Construction*, 2d ed., R.S. Means Co., Kingston, Mass., 1988.

*Means Mechanical Cost Data*, R.S. Means Co., Kingston, Mass. (Published annually.)

*Monthly and Seasonal Weather Outlook*, U.S. Government Printing Office, Washington, D.C.

Moylan, J. J., and M. Mossman (eds.), *Means Mechanical Estimating: Standards and Procedures,* 2d ed., R.S. Means Co., Kingston, Mass., 1992.

*National Plumbing and HVAC Estimator*, Craftsman Book Co., Carlsbad, Calif., (Published annually.)

Ottaviano, V. B., *National Mechanical Estimator*, Fairmont Press, Lilburn, Ga. (Updated regularly.)

Page, J. S., *Estimators Man-Hour Manual on Heating, Air Conditioning, Ventilating, and Plumbing*, 2d ed., Gulf Publishing Co., Houston, Tex., 1978.

*Producer Price Indexes*, U.S. Department of Labor, Bureau of Labor Statistics, Washington, D.C. (Issued monthly.)

Rowe, W. H., III, *HVAC: Design Criteria, Options, Selection*, 2nd ed., R.S. Means Co., Kingston, Mass., 1994.

*Weather Data Handbook*, Ecodyne Cooling Products Division, McGraw-Hill, New York, 1980.

# ACKNOWLEDGMENTS

An estimating handbook is not a creative work of fiction by one individual; its authors cannot "invent" or think up its contents. Essentially its contents are the accumulation of many facts, the work of many people and groups. It is a task of harvesting, organizing, and synthesizing the myriad data (published and obscured) that reflects the common experience and history of all those who are related to the profession or craft and who have come before. To paraphrase Billy Manning's centennial theme for 1994-1995 (when he was president of the American Society of Heating, Refrigerating and Air-Conditioning Engineers), John Gladstone and Kenneth Humphreys have "built on the shoulders of giants."

Since 1959, Gladstone, and his collaborator, Dr. Humphreys, who joined him in 1983, have consulted dozens of experts in the field and drawn heavily on numerous sources of information. These sources include trade associations, labor unions, technical magazines and journals, industrial and engineering catalogs, and published standards by engineering societies and code bodies. Many of these sources have been cited in the references or bibliography or credited in the various chapters, but it is not possible to mention them all.

Particular thanks and credit are due to David Rosoff, Building Economics Research Ltd., Alexandria, Va. who made substantial contributions to and assisted in the preparation of half of the chapters in this book.

Specific trade associations, firms, and publications which were extremely helpful in supplying data for the various chapters of the book include the R.S. Means Co.; *Heating, Piping and Air Conditioning*; McGraw-Hill, Inc.; *Engineering News Record; Chemical Engineering*; National Automatic Sprinkler and Fire Control Association; National Fire Protection Association; National Insulation Manufacturers' Association; Rawlplug Company; Marley Company; Carrier Corporation; The Trane Company; York International; Ingersoll-Rand; Goulds Pump Co.; Crane Company; American Society of Heating, Refrigerating and Air-Conditioning Engineers; American Society of Mechanical Engineers; Sheet Metal and Air Conditioning Contractors' National Association, National Electrical Contractors Association; Air Movement and Control Association; and Manufacturers' Standardization Society.

Individuals who made major contributions to the preparation of some chapters of this sixth edition include Hugh T. Sharp, senior vice president (retired) of R.S. Means Co., Kingston, Mass.; Earl Hagood, Earl Hagood Inc., Miami, Fla.; and Alvaro Cadenas, Filbert Company, Miami, Fla. Also deserving the authors' thanks are John Tighe and Joey Abeledo of the Miami office of The Trane Company; Bob Harden, Spot Coolers of Miami; Scott Gordon, Tropic Air Conditioning; Cesar Montano, K.C. Air Conditioning Corp; Charles del Vecchio and Mark McHugh of Tropic Supply of Florida; and Lucas Cuadrano.

The authors also remain indebted to Dr. B. K. Lunde, George Gall, and Otto Mendel, who helped make the fifth edition the success it was and whose inimitable marks remain apparent in this sixth edition.

Usually a major creative effort requires the support of a cooperative and patient spouse. Betsy Humphreys and Ideal Gladstone have lent that support and displayed that patience during the creation of this work. But more, Betsy contributed much of her time assisting Ken with editing and inputing computer data that could not have been done without her. Ideal worked into the long hours of the night at the word processor making deadlines for John and attending to the business of rights and permissions, proofreading, and general correspondence.

# MECHANICAL ESTIMATING GUIDEBOOK

# CHAPTER 1
# ESTIMATING CRITERIA

## GENERAL DISCUSSION

When the first edition of this book was written in 1960, computer technology was in its infancy, and mechanical estimating was done manually. Even today, many air-conditioning, heating, and ventilating contractors rely on manual methods, and while they generally have access to computers, small contractors often use them primarily for word processing and accounting purposes, not for maintaining a database of estimating information. When doing estimates, the estimator treats the computer essentially as an electronic "pencil and paper"— the computer speeds up the estimating process, but the small contractor seldom maintains or uses a comprehensive database of historical cost information, in contrast to the general practice of large engineering and construction firms that rely on computer technology for project estimates. Recognizing this reality, we have written the present edition of this book to serve the needs of those who rely heavily on computers for mechanical estimates and those who do not. The format of the book is similar to prior editions in that the book relies heavily on tables to aid in manually preparing estimates. However, the data presented can also be utilized in electronic form by those using computers. All major tables are reproduced on disk as *Lotus 1-2-3\** spreadsheets for use in computer applications as desired by the reader.

David Chick (1992) discusses the rapid evolution of estimating practice from primarily manual to heavily computer-dependent. He states, however, that

> project estimating *techniques* have not changed, but the ability to store, retrieve, and present this information (with computers) has enhanced our ability to control projects....Those firms that invest in these resources are the winners.

Why has computer dependence evolved so rapidly? One reason is that contracting is a very risky business and computer applications can aid in minimizing some of the risk. Sanders and Cooper (1991) cited the fact that in 1987 contractors accounted for 11% of total U.S. business failures. They noted

> The construction industry is by its very nature extremely fragmented and highly competitive. Contractors must competitively bid for at least part of their work and then must deal with adverse weather conditions, fluctuating interest rates, inflation, change orders, and governmental regulations concerning hiring, wages, and job safety. All the while the contractor is attempting to construct a facility unlike any other ever built.

It is true that no two projects, even similar installations of heating, ventilation, and air-conditioning (HVAC) equipment, are exactly alike. Prices, labor productivity, working conditions, etc. are never constant nor fully predictable. Therefore, estimating is as much an art as it is a science.

---

*Lotus* and *1-2-3* are trademarks of Lotus Development Corporation. The disk provided with this book is compatible with Release 2.2 and higher of *1-2-3*. The *Lotus 1-2-3* file names are similar to the table numbers in this book, with a hyphen substituted for the decimal point in the table number. For example, Table 1.5 has a file name of TAB1-5, Table 2.3 has the name TAB2-3, etc.

Despite this complexity, many air-conditioning, heating, and ventilating contractors operate without formal estimating policies or standardized procedures. In these shops the estimating may be done by a mechanic, a sales engineer, a salesperson, a bookkeeper, or the owner. The larger shop may have a full-time estimator, a sales manager who doubles as an estimator, an engineer who doubles as an estimator, or a supervisor or service manager who is responsible for estimating.

Most skilled estimators in the trade have come upon their knowledge through years of experience and study, and many steadfastly consider it a breach of professional etiquette to be questioned as to the source of their knowledge. Often, when more than one estimator was employed, each estimator would have a private notebook from which to surreptitiously snatch estimating facts. These attitudes have been rendered obsolete by the computer. Historical cost information can no longer be kept in one's head or private notebook. The successful company, big or small, records this information from job to job in a computer database and retrieves and adjusts it as necessary for future estimates. Just as there is no substitute for estimating experience, there is also no substitute for the fact that historical data is not an estimate—it is reality, and computers can use that information and process it on future jobs with far greater speed and accuracy than can any human being using manual techniques. While computers do not ensure against errors in estimates, they are now a necessary business tool to increase the probability that estimates are accurate. The company that does not use them is far more likely to be one of those business failures than is the firm that uses them to best advantage.

## DEFINITION

*Estimating* is essentially an accumulation of details; the act of calculating all the costs that will enter into a particular job and arriving at a total. Because the estimate is made a priori, even with the use of computers, it can be only an educated guess. It is this educated guess—or estimate—that sets the production cost on which the profit and selling price are based. The estimator, who takes the first shot at the profit potential in any job, is in control where profit begins.

The attributes of the professional estimator must be many, of which perhaps the most important is visualization. A major qualification is the ability to visualize each operation incorporated in a job—first as a separate element and then the whole gestalt—and finally to translate these into accurate cost terms. Mechanical aptitude, production experience, application engineering, speed, accuracy, patience, and ability to get along with people are other requirements—in addition to a good sense of judgment and a bent toward organization. The mechanical estimator must be an avid reader of trade publications and must keep abreast of rapid advances, new tools, methods, new equipment and machinery, and product changes as they take place.

Because a warehouse of information must be readily available, the estimator must collect and classify continuously all pertinent data and check figures and enter them into the database, and is also responsible for taking notes on specific job problems, performing time and motion studies, and checking actual costs of each job to keep the estimating database up to date.

American National Standards Institute (ANSI) Standard No. Z94.2 (AACE International Standard No. 10S-90) recognizes three types of estimates:

**1.** *The order-of-magnitude estimate.* This is an estimate made without detailed engineering data. It is often developed using cost capacity curves, scaleup factors, or approximate factors. In mechanical estimating practice, the order-of-magnitude estimate is often referred to as an approximate, "horseback," or "ballpark" estimate. Such estimates are used for preliminary negotiating or decision making and for creative selling. Typically, it is made on the basis of cost per square foot or meter, cost per seat, cost per room, cost per ton, cost per cubic foot per minute (cfm), etc. These estimates are normally expected to be accurate within a range of $+50\%$ to $-30\%$.

**2.** *The budget estimate.* This estimate is prepared with the use of flowsheets, rough layouts, and equipment details. Budget in this case refers to the owner's budget, not that of the contractor. Also called the *preliminary estimate,* it is not used for submitting bids. It is used for appropriation of funds and for checking bids that are eventually received. Accuracy of a budget estimate should be in the range of $+30$ to $-15\%$.

**3.** *The definitive estimate.* This estimate requires very defined engineering data, including complete, or nearly complete, plans, piping and instrument diagrams, one-line electrical diagrams, equipment data sheets and quotations, and a complete set of specifications. Also called a *complete estimate* or *detailed estimate,* it covers all the cost factors relating to the work preparatory to submitting a bid. It must be very accurate. ANSI Standard Z94.2 specifies an accuracy range of $+15$ to $-5\%$ for this type of estimate. The successful estimator will achieve a far better level of accuracy than this. The final agreement between the estimated job and the actual cost will reflect the skill of the estimator, the validity of the database used, and the efficacy of the production department.

In addition to these three types of estimates, the mechanical estimator must make *progress* or *monthly estimates* as the job proceeds in order to determine the amount of progress payment due from the owner or general contractor on the job under construction.

Beyond this, the estimator will also be required to make estimates for the purposes of determining extras; appraising properties, damage claims, and insurance premiums; and performing feasibility studies.

The estimator is also advised to remember the following tongue-in-cheek definitions:

*Construction Definitions*

*Contractor*—a gambler who never gets to shuffle, cut, or deal
*Bid Opening*—a poker game in which the losing hand wins
*Bid*—a wild guess carried out to two decimal places
*Low Bidder*—a contractor who is wondering what he left out
*Engineer's Estimate*—the cost of construction in heaven
*Project Manager*—the conductor of an orchestra in which every musician is in a different union
*Critical Path Method*—a management technique for losing your shirt under perfect control
*Delayed Payment*—a tourniquet applied at the pockets
*Completion Date*—the point at which liquidated damages begin
*Liquidated Damages*—a penalty for failing to achieve the impossible
*Auditor[s]*—people who go in after the war is lost and bayonet the wounded
*Lawyer[s]*—people who go in after the auditors and strip the bodies
—*Author Unknown*

A sense of humor is a necessary prerequisite to being a good estimator.[1]

## FORMS AND METHODS

For accurate estimating and timed production, well-designed standard forms must be used. Good forms provide standardization, continuity, and a permanent record, and they reduce the workload as well as the chance of error. Whether forms are individually tailored to the requirements of a particular company, are ordered from a publisher who prints forms on the basis of a universal standard, or are obtained from a software supplier for computer printing, they should be selected with great care. Whenever possible, a form should serve a multiple purpose and eliminate the need for duplicating figures. All forms must be integrated to standard operating procedure and flow easily between departments. Figures 1.1 to 1.7 illustrate some typical forms.[2]

[1] The editors thank Administrative Controls Management, Inc., Ann Arbor, Mich., for bringing these definitions to our attention.

[2] *Editor's note:* Figures 1.1 through 1.7 have been printed in full-page size and may be reproduced by the reader as desired.

| ESTIMATE TABULATION & COST ANALYSIS SHEET | Job. No. |
|---|---|
| Project | Sheet No. |
| Address | Of |
| Date In   Date Due   Estimator | Total Tons |
| | Total C.F.M. |
| | Net Sq. Ft. |
| | Population |

| GROUP | ITEM | MANUFACTURER OR SUPPLIER | ESTIMATED MATERIAL | ACTUAL MATERIAL | ESTIMATED LABOR | ACTUAL LABOR |
|---|---|---|---|---|---|---|
| A | Compressor or Chiller Units | | | | | |
| | Vibration Rails | | | | | |
| | Pumps | | | | | |
| | Starters | | | | | |
| | Self-Contained Package | | | | | |
| | **SUB TOTAL A** | | | | | |
| B | Condensers, Air Cooled | | | | | |
| | Condensers, Water Cooled | | | | | |
| | Condensers, Evaporative | | | | | |
| | Receivers | | | | | |
| | Starters | | | | | |
| | Refrigerant (Lbs.) | | | | | |
| | Oil | | | | | |
| | **SUB TOTAL B** | | | | | |
| C | Air Units | | | | | |
| | Vibration Rails | | | | | |
| | Heating Coils | | | | | |
| | Reheat | | | | | |
| | Filter Section | | | | | |
| | Filters | | | | | |
| | Motors | | | | | |
| | Starters | | | | | |
| | Room Units | | | | | |
| | **SUB TOTAL C** | | | | | |
| D | Cooling Towers | | | | | |
| | Pumps | | | | | |
| | Starters | | | | | |
| | Grillage | | | | | |
| | **SUB TOTAL D** | | | | | |
| E | Hot Water Boiler | | | | | |
| | Pumps | | | | | |
| | Starters | | | | | |
| | Compression Tank | | | | | |
| | Hot Water Storage Tank | | | | | |
| | Oil Storage Tank | | | | | |
| | Chimney | | | | | |
| | **SUB TOTAL E** | | | | | |

Figure 1.1  ESTIMATE FORM—TABULATION AND COST ANALYSIS

| GROUP | ITEM | MANUFACTURER OR SUPPLIER | ESTIMATED MATERIAL | ACTUAL MATERIAL | ESTIMATED LABOR | ACTUAL LABOR |
|---|---|---|---|---|---|---|
| F | Piping, Chilled Water | | | | | |
| | Piping, Hot Water | | | | | |
| | Piping, Condenser Water | | | | | |
| | Piping, Refrigerant Lines | | | | | |
| | Piping, Steam | | | | | |
| | Piping, Condensate | | | | | |
| | Piping, Oil | | | | | |
| | Piping, Gas | | | | | |
| | **SUB TOTAL F** | | | | | |
| G | Hand Valves | | | | | |
| | Refrigeration Specialties | | | | | |
| | Heating Specialties | | | | | |
| | Heat Exchanger | | | | | |
| | Oil Separator | | | | | |
| | **SUB TOTAL G** | | | | | |
| H | Packaged Controls | | | | | |
| | Thermostats | | | | | |
| | Humidistats | | | | | |
| | Solenoids | | | | | |
| | 3 - Way Valves | | | | | |
| | Motorized Assemblies | | | | | |
| | **SUB TOTAL H** | | | | | |
| I | Ventilation Fans | | | | | |
| | Ventilators, Relief | | | | | |
| | Fan Motor Starters | | | | | |
| | **SUB TOTAL I** | | | | | |
| J | Air Purification, 1 | | | | | |
| | Air Purification, 2 | | | | | |
| | **SUB TOTAL J** | | | | | |
| K | Air Distribution: | | | | | |
| | Sidewall | | | | | |
| | Ceiling | | | | | |
| | Return | | | | | |
| | Dampers | | | | | |
| | Aspirator Mixing Boxes | | | | | |
| | Sound Attenuators | | | | | |
| | **SUB TOTAL K** | | | | | |
| L | Equipment Room Construction | | | | | |
| | Structural Cement, Pads | | | | | |
| | Structural Steel | | | | | |
| | Cutting Holes | | | | | |
| | Painting, Shop | | | | | |
| | Painting, Field | | | | | |
| | Trenching | | | | | |
| | Backfill | | | | | |
| | **SUB TOTAL L** | | | | | |

**Figure 1.1** (*Continued*)  **ESTIMATE FORM—TABULATION AND COST ANALYSIS**

| GROUP | ITEM | MANUFACTURER OR SUPPLIER | ESTIMATED MATERIAL | | | | ACTUAL MATERIAL | | | | ESTIMATED LABOR | | | | ACTUAL LABOR | | | |
|---|---|---|---|---|---|---|---|---|---|---|---|---|---|---|---|---|---|---|
| M | Sub Contracts | | | | | | | | | | | | | | | | | |
| | Electrical | | | | | | | | | | | | | | | | | |
| | Sheet Metal | | | | | | | | | | | | | | | | | |
| | Insulation, Sheet Metal | | | | | | | | | | | | | | | | | |
| | " C.W. Piping | | | | | | | | | | | | | | | | | |
| | " H.W. Piping | | | | | | | | | | | | | | | | | |
| | " Vessels | | | | | | | | | | | | | | | | | |
| | " Condensate Drain | | | | | | | | | | | | | | | | | |
| | " Ceilings, Roofs | | | | | | | | | | | | | | | | | |
| | " Acoustical | | | | | | | | | | | | | | | | | |
| | SCHEDULE ▶ SUB TOTAL M | | | | | | | | | | | | | | | | | |
| N | Special Equipment | | | | | | | | | | | | | | | | | |
| | Crane | | | | | | | | | | | | | | | | | |
| | Scaffolding | | | | | | | | | | | | | | | | | |
| | Ladders | | | | | | | | | | | | | | | | | |
| | Welding Machine | | | | | | | | | | | | | | | | | |
| | Others, 1 | | | | | | | | | | | | | | | | | |
| | Others, 2 | | | | | | | | | | | | | | | | | |
| | SCHEDULE ▶ SUB TOTAL N | | | | | | | | | | | | | | | | | |

| ENTER LABOR ITEMS HERE (Groups A thru N) | | LABOR GROUP | | | | | | % |
|---|---|---|---|---|---|---|---|---|
| Compressor or Chiller | A | | | | | | | |
| Condensers, Receivers | B | | | | | | | |
| Air Units | C | | | | | | | |
| Tower | D | | | | | | | |
| Boiler | E | | | | | | | |
| Piping | F | | | | | | | |
| Specialties | G | | | | | | | |
| Controls | H | | | | | | | |
| Ventilation | I | | | | | | | |
| Air Purification | J | | | | | | | |
| Air distribution | K | | | | | | | |
| Non-mechanical | L | | | | | | | |
| (Do not enter if labor is sub contract) ———▶ | M | | | | | | | |
| (Do not enter if labor is rental) ———▶ | N | | | | | | | |
| (If check, start, test, balance, etc., is not included in any of above, enter additional labor here ———▶ | | | | | | | | |
| TOTAL PRODUCTIVE LABOR  SCHEDULE ▶ | | | | | | | | 100% |

| ENTER MATERIAL ITEMS HERE | | MATERIAL SUB-TOTALS | | | | | | % |
|---|---|---|---|---|---|---|---|---|
| Compressors or Chiller | A | | | | | | | |
| Condensers, Receivers | B | | | | | | | |
| Air Units | C | | | | | | | |
| Tower | D | | | | | | | |
| Boiler | E | | | | | | | |
| Piping | F | | | | | | | |
| Specialties | G | | | | | | | |
| Controls | H | | | | | | | |
| Ventilation | I | | | | | | | |
| Air Purification | J | | | | | | | |
| Air Distribution | K | | | | | | | |
| Cement, Steel, Paint, etc. | L | | | | | | | |
| (Do not enter if material is sub-contract) ———▶ | M | | | | | | | |
| TOTAL MATERIAL COST  SCHEDULE ▶ | | | | | | | | 100% |

Figure 1.1   (*Continued*)   ESTIMATE FORM—TABULATION AND COST ANALYSIS

| | ITEM | % |
|---|---|---|
| Enter Here - Schedule 1 from Page 3 (Labor) | | |
| " " Schedule 2 from Page 3 (Materials) | | |
| " " Schedule 3 from Page 3 (Subs) | | |
| " " Schedule 4 from Page 3 (Rentals) | | |
| TOTAL JOB COST ▶ | | 100% |

| | |
|---|---|
| Non-Productive Labor | |
| Traveling Expenses | |
| Contingencies | |
| Clean-Up | |
| Supervision | |
| Engineering | |
| Service Reserve | |
| Interest | |
| Permits | |
| Bonds | |
| Insurance | |
| Tax | |
| Freight | |
| Diagrams under glass | |
| (If equipment in Schedule 4 is owned, not rented, show depreciation here) ▶ | |
| TOTAL JOB OVERHEAD ▶ | % |

| | |
|---|---|
| Enter total job overhead from above (Do not mark-up) | |
| Enter any sales commissions here (Do not mark-up) | |
| Enter here Schedule 1 from Page 3 (Labor) ___% Mark-Up | |
| Enter here Schedule 2 from Page 3 (Materials) ___% Mark-Up | |
| Enter here Schedule 3 from Page 3 (Subs) ___% Mark-Up | |
| Enter here Schedule 4 from Page 3 (Rental) ___% Mark-Up (Do not duplicate this item) | |
| CASH CONTRACT PRICE ▶ | |

| CHECK DATA FIGURES | REMARKS |
|---|---|
| $_____ Job Cost / Tons = $_____per Ton Cost | |
| $_____ Contract Price / Tons = $_____per Ton Selling | |
| $_____ Contract Price / C.F.M. = $_____per C.F.M. Selling | |
| $_____ Contract Price / Population = $_____per Person  Theatre, Church, Restaurant | |
| $_____ Contract Price / Square Feet = $_____per Square Foot | |
| _____ C.F.M. / Sq. Feet = _____C.F.M. per Sq. Foot | |
| _____ Square Feet / Tons = _____Square Feet per Ton | |

Figure 1.1  (*Continued*)   ESTIMATE FORM—TABULATION AND COST ANALYSIS

**ESTIMATE** PACKAGE UNIT SHORT FORM

JOB NO. _____

SHEET ____ OF ____ SHEETS

PROJECT_____

ADDRESS_____

_____

DATE IN_____ DATE DUE_____ ESTIMATOR_____

CHECKED BY _____

| QUAN. | ITEM / IDENTIFICATION | ESTIMATED MATERIAL | ACTUAL MATERIAL | ESTIMATED LABOR | ACTUAL LABOR |
|---|---|---|---|---|---|
| | Package Unit | | | | |
| | Package Unit | | | | |
| | Plenum | | | | |
| | Heating Coil | | | | |
| | Other Accessory | | | | |
| | " " | | | | |
| | Cooling Tower | | | | |
| | Air Cooled Condenser | | | | |
| | Pump | | | | |
| | Sleepers - Pads | | | | |
| | Thermostat | | | | |
| | Starter | | | | |
| | Other Controls | | | | |
| | Piping, Refrigeration | | | | |
| | " Condenser Water | | | | |
| | " Hot Water - Steam | | | | |
| | " Gas - Oil | | | | |
| | " Drain | | | | |
| | Pipe Insulation | | | | |
| | Sheet Metal | | | | |
| | Sheet Metal Insulation | | | | |
| | Supply Grilles | | | | |
| | Return Grilles | | | | |
| | Exhausters - Blowers | | | | |
| | Electrical Work | | | | |
| | Structural Work | | | | |
| | Plumbing Work | | | | |
| | Rigging Work | | | | |
| | Other | | | | |

| | | | |
|---|---|---|---|
| TOTAL MATERIAL | | | |
| SALES TAX | | | |
| LABOR | | | |
| MARK-UP | | | |
| PERMITS | | | |
| CONTINGENCY | | | |
| SERVICE RESERVE | | | |
| SALES COMMISSION | | | |
| TOTAL CASH CONTRACT PRICE | | | |

Figure 1.2 ESTIMATE FORM—PACKAGE UNIT SHORT FORM

**Figure 1.3   ESTIMATE FORM—PIPE TAKEOFF**

ESTIMATE    *BOILER WORK*

PROJECT_____

ADDRESS_____

_____

DATE IN_____ DATE DUE_____ ESTIMATOR_____

JOB NO. _____

SHEET    OF    SHEETS

_____

_____

CHECKED BY _____

| QUAN | ITEM | MATERIAL | ACTUAL | WORK-HRS | ACTUAL |
|---|---|---|---|---|---|
| | BOILERS | | | | |
| | BOILERS | | | | |
| | PUMPS, CONDENSATE | | | | |
| | PUMPS, FEEDWATER | | | | |
| | PUMPS, CIRCULATING | | | | |
| | PUMPS, OIL | | | | |
| | TANKS, BLOWDOWN | | | | |
| | TANKS, EXPANSION | | | | |
| | TANKS, WATER STORAGE | | | | |
| | TANKS, OIL STORAGE | | | | |
| | PACKAGED CONTROLS | | | | |
| | SPECIALTIES (From Schedule A) | | | | |
| | PIPING (From Schedule B) | | | | |
| | INSULATION | | | | |
| | BREECHING, STACK WORK | | | | |
| | SPECIAL EQUIP, CRANE | | | | |
| | "    WELDING MACHINE | | | | |
| | FREIGHT | | | | |
| | EQUIP. ROOM VENTILATION | | | | |
| | SUBCONTRACT,RIGGING | | | | |
| | "        ELECTRICAL | | | | |
| | "        PLUMBING | | | | |
| | TRENCHING AND BACKFILL | | | | |
| | START-UP AND TEST | | | | |
| | CUT, PATCH,AND PAINT | | | | |
| | CLEAN UP | | | | |
| | NON-PRODUCTIVE LABOR | | | | |
| | SERVICE RESERVE | | | | |
| | ENGINEERING | | | | |

OVERHEAD MARGIN, %    _____

DESIRED PROFIT MARGIN, %   _____

DESIRED GROSS MARGIN, %   _____

1. DIRECT MATERIAL, $_____

2. $\dfrac{\text{DIRECT MATERIAL, \$}\underline{\hspace{2cm}}}{1-\text{ GROSS MARGIN, \%}}$ = $_____  SUB TOTAL, MATERIAL

3. WORK HOURS_____ x LABOR RATE_____ = $_____ DIRECT LABOR

4. $\dfrac{\text{DIRECT LABOR, \$}\underline{\hspace{2cm}}}{1-\text{ GROSS MARGIN, \%}}$ = $_____  SUB TOTAL, LABOR

5. TOTAL MATERIAL_____ + TOTAL LABOR_____ = $_____ SELLING PRICE

6. SELLING PRICE _____ + SALES TAX _____ + PERMITS _____ =

GRAND TOTAL, CONTRACT PRICE $_____

Figure 1.4    ESTIMATE FORM—BOILER WORK

| QUAN. | DESCRIPTION | LABOR | | MATERIAL | | EXTENSION |
|---|---|---|---|---|---|---|

**ESTIMATE**  PRICING MATERIAL & LABOR

PROJECT_____

ADDRESS_____

DATE IN_____ DATE DUE_____ ESTIMATOR_____

JOB NO. _____

SHEET    OF    SHEETS

CHECKED BY _____

| QUAN. | DESCRIPTION | LABOR UNIT | LABOR TOTAL | MATERIAL UNIT | MATERIAL TOTAL | EXTENSION |
|---|---|---|---|---|---|---|

Figure 1.5   ESTIMATE FORM—PRICING MATERIAL AND LABOR

| ESTIMATE WET HEAT | JOB NO. |
|---|---|
| PROJECT | SHEET OF SHEETS |
| ADDRESS | |
| | CHECKED BY |
| DATE IN DATE DUE ESTIMATOR | |

| QUAN. | ITEM | MATERIAL | LABOR |
|---|---|---|---|
| | Boiler | | |
| | Burner | | |
| | Oil Tank, Pipe, and Fittings | | |
| | Combustion Chamber | | |
| | Pump | | |
| | Thermostat | | |
| | Low Limit Control | | |
| | Reverse Control | | |
| | Extra Controls | | |
| | Draft Regulator | | |
| | Flow Control Valve | | |
| | Pressure Reducing Valve | | |
| | Relief Valve | | |
| | Air Cushion Tank | | |
| | Domestic Water Heater and Tank | | |
| | Mixing Valve | | |
| | Pipe, Valves, Fittings, Hangers | | |
| | Pipe Covering | | |
| | Heating Units | | |
| | Radiator Enclosures | | |
| | Sets — Radiator Brackets | | |
| | Radiator Valves | | |
| | Radiator Union Elbows | | |
| | Radiator Air Valves | | |
| | Main Air Vents | | |
| | Floor and Ceiling Plates | | |
| | Smoke Pipe | | |
| | Foundation | | |
| | Electric Wiring | | |
| | Asbestos Cement | | |
| | TOTAL MATERIAL | | |
| | SALES TAX | | |
| | LABOR | | |
| | MARK-UP | | |
| | SERVICE RESERVE | | |
| | SALES COMMISSION | | |
| | PERMITS | | |
| | CONTRACT PRICE | | |

Figure 1.6  ESTIMATE FORM—WET HEAT

```
┌─────────────────────────────────────────────────────────┐
│                  VALVES AND SPECIALTIES                   │
│  ┌──────────────────────────────────────────────────┐    │
│  │ PROJECT_____JOB #    │    │
│  │ ADDRESS_____  │    │
│  │ DATE_____                          │    │
│  └──────────────────────────────────────────────────┘    │
│                                                           │
│  PRESSURE RELIEF VALVES_____                    │
│  CHECK VALVES_____                    │
│  GATE VALVES_____                    │
│  GLOBE VALVES_____                    │
│  ANGLE VALVES_____                    │
│  COCK VALVES_____                     │
│  STRAINERS_____                     │
│  PRESSURE REDUCING VALVES_____                    │
│  THERMO-STEAM REGULATORS_____                    │
│  COMBINATION PRESSURE GAGE AND THERMOSTATS____            │
│  FLOAT AND THERMOSTATIC TRAPS_____                    │
│  BUCKET TRAPS_____                    │
│  VACUUM BREAKERS_____                    │
│  CONTROL VALVES_____                    │
│  OTHER_____                     │
│  _____                      │
│  _____                      │
│  _____                      │
│  _____                      │
│                                   TOTAL                   │
└─────────────────────────────────────────────────────────┘
```

Figure 1.7    **ESTIMATE FORM—VALVES AND SPECIALTIES**

Only after the estimator has a feel for the job and a complete understanding of the scope of work should the takeoff begin. At this point, the accuracy of the check-data figures and the validity of the estimator's judgment are put to the test as the estimator sets forth an order-of-magnitude estimate that will later be corrected and go into the permanent database.

It is not at all unusual for killer clauses to be hidden in an obscure paragraph of the general conditions; the specifications must be carefully scrutinized for them, as well as for guarantees, service period, instructions, testing, etc. A short deadline is never an acceptable excuse for mere skimming of the specifications or failing to physically inspect the site.

Although the hourly wage rate for any craft is constant at any given time and place, labor productivity never is. It is labor productivity that places the greatest demands on the estimator's judgments. The validity of the estimate depends on how well the estimator can forecast the rise and fall of the rate of productivity for each craft and activity. Consequently, job preplanning and scheduling are part of the discipline. The estimator must be familiar with flowcharts, process charts, and the critical path method (CPM) as well as general construction practices and methods engineering.

The world is steadily moving to a unified metric system of measurement. The United States is one of the few countries still relying on the English measurement system. This is changing, however, and full metrication of construction projects is only a matter of time. The estimator must be aware of this fact and be ready to meet the challenge when full metrication does come. The estimator also must be capable of converting units within either measurement system (e.g., cubic feet to gallons in the English system and cubic meters to liters in the metric system). The Appendix provides a listing of conversion factors for the two measurement systems.

## ESTIMATING LABOR

The small commercial or residential installation using two workers will almost always agree in actual and estimated time, and it need not be considered from the social or organizational perspective. The larger mechanical construction involving several teams must be examined in the light of supervision, leadership, group behavior, organization, and communication. An individual's productivity can be dramatically altered in a team cluster setting.

Team formation may be prescribed by an agreement with a union and may specify a ratio of apprentices to experienced journeymen and supervisors. Table 1.1 lists a typical plumbing crew consisting of one plumber supervisor, two plumbers, and one apprentice; the weighted average hourly labor rate is $27.01, including fringe benefits based on the crew daily rate of $864.40 and base workhours per day of 32.

Throughout this text the unit of labor used is the workhour, and it is assumed that wherever the condition requires, two or more persons are working together as a team. Where a table indicates 6 workhours for a particular task, it follows that a two-person team will perform that task in 3 hr. Table 1.2 shows the prevailing labor rates around the country.

**TABLE 1.1**   Typical Plumbing Crew Pay Schedule

30-city average costs in 1994 dollars.

| Worker classification | Hourly base* | Daily cost |
|---|---|---|
| Plumber supervisor (inside) . . . . . | $28.80 | $230.40 |
| Plumber . . . . . . . . . . . . . . . . . . . . . | 28.30 | 226.40 |
| Plumber . . . . . . . . . . . . . . . . . . . . . | 28.30 | 226.40 |
| Plumber apprentice . . . . . . . . . . . . | 22.65 | 181.20 |
| Daily total . . . . . . . . . . . . . . . . . . | — | $864.40 |
| Average cost per workhour . . | — | 27.01 |

\*Including fringe benefits.

SOURCE: *Means Mechanical Cost Data 1994*, R.S. Means Co., Kingston, MA.

**TABLE 1.2**  Prevailing Hourly Wage Rates for Principal U.S. Cities, in Dollars

Based on craft wages including fringes, as of January 1, 1994. These data are intended for general reference only and should not be considered reliable for bid estimating.

| City | Asbestos workers | Electricians | Pipe-fitters and steam-fitters | Plumbers | Sheet-metal workers | Sprinkler fitters |
|---|---|---|---|---|---|---|
| Atlanta | 20.92 | 23.16 | 23.01 | 23.01 | 23.09 | 23.75 |
| Baltimore | 23.32 | 28.23 | 27.17 | 25.78 | 23.99 | 30.97 |
| Boston | 31.32 | 37.65 | 35.20 | 35.50 | 35.63 | 34.46 |
| Chicago | 31.60 | 32.95 | 31.42 | 31.30 | 31.01 | 32.17 |
| Cincinnati | 24.95 | 23.99 | 25.97 | 26.09 | 23.50 | 29.13 |
| Cleveland | 29.87 | 29.37 | 30.71 | 30.08 | 29.04 | 30.71 |
| Dallas | 19.14 | 20.63 | 19.98 | 19.98 | 20.43 | 25.98 |
| Kansas City, Mo. | 25.95 | 26.71 | 26.21 | 25.61 | 25.50 | 28.10 |
| Minneapolis | 28.98 | 30.04 | 28.86 | 28.14 | 27.67 | 29.70 |
| New Orleans | 20.13 | 20.45 | 19.84 | 19.84 | 20.81 | 24.27 |
| New York | 44.92 | 40.62 | 44.84 | 50.45 | 42.71 | 44.84 |
| Philadelphia | 33.82 | 35.91 | 34.67 | 34.67 | 35.59 | 36.71 |
| St. Louis | 31.36 | 31.41 | 32.63 | 29.28 | 28.57 | 33.33 |
| San Francisco | 36.52 | 44.13 | 53.15 | 53.15 | 42.91 | 53.15 |
| Seattle | 27.70 | 28.85 | 33.04 | 33.04 | 28.36 | 35.13 |
| Average | 28.70 | 30.27 | 31.11 | 31.06 | 29.25 | 32.83 |

SOURCE:  *Means Labor Rates for the Construction Industry,* R.S. Means Co., Kingston, Mass., 1994.

## WORKHOUR CORRECTION FACTORS

All workhour estimating tables assume a set of average working conditions, in an average area, performed by average workers, under average supervision, and so forth. These base workhours are always subject to conditions; they must be corrected accordingly.

There are four groups of conditions that will affect the rate of production on any construction job:

Weather conditions

Area conditions

General conditions

Task or operation conditions

Some conditions will affect the entire job, and the total workhours are subject to these conditions. Other conditions affect only one task, several tasks, one phase, one location, and so on. It is therefore necessary to analyze the job carefully, determine where the conditions require correction factors, and isolate the portion of the work affected.

If the estimator is using a sophisticated system such as CPM, the application of workhour correction factors is made much simpler because the entire job has already been divided into tasks; task conditions can be easily analyzed, and the corrected workhours become part of the network. If the takeoff or quantity survey is made by craft, say, piping or ductwork, then a subtotaling system must be used and each task affected must be isolated into a subtotal of workhours.

Tables of correction factors, like workhour tables, may be refined to a good degree of accuracy, but it is only the intelligence and judgment of the estimator that make such data meaningful. These figures can serve only as a guide; if used arbitrarily by an unskilled person, they become unreliable.

As presented in this text, the correction-factor tables are based on the loss of labor efficiency when the labor is subjected to certain conditions. These conditions may be psychological or physiological or a combination of both; or they may be complexity factors or delay factors or a combination of all.

In a few instances a condition may increase the efficiency of a task; hence the factor becomes a credit. Again, the estimator's judgment is required to make the proper application. For example, Table 1.3 shows credit factors for repetitive work. Assuming four multizone air handlers with identical runs of ductwork on four floors, a credit factor of 0.97 may be a fair assumption for ductwork erection. For the air-balancing team, on the other hand, the credit factor could go to 0.75. The estimator must break out those portions of the task that are substantially reduced—or perhaps even totally eliminated—because of typicality.

**TABLE 1.3**  Task Conditions—Correction Factors

Repetitive task occurs in typical floor, multistory construction. Based on buildings of five or more stories with average of 8,000 to 15,000 sq ft per floor.

| Type of building | Factor |
|---|---|
| Apartment house | 0.94 |
| Hotel | 0.95 |
| Office | 0.97 |
| School | 0.98 |
| Hospital | 0.98 |

In some cases a project may suffer a double penalty, such as overtime work that has an efficiency loss concurrent with an increase in hourly dollar rate.

Overtime in fact can cause a net loss in productivity with no net gain from the overtime hours. Numerous studies have shown that prolonged overtime schedules cause marked decreases in worker productivity.

Bromberg (1988) reported that on a 5-day workweek with 15 hr of scheduled overtime, actual productive gain was the equivalent of less than 5 hr on a regular schedule, a minimal gain for the investment of 22½ to 30 hr of additional labor cost at premium rates. At greater levels of overtime, net productive losses actually occurred.

Similarly, with a 6-day workweek and 8-hr workday, the added 20% of workhours (30 to 40% in terms of cost), resulted in a productive gain of only a few percent.

Moylan and Mossman (1992) reported similar declines in production efficiency with overtime schedules.

Classic studies of the Construction Users Anti-Inflation Roundtable (now the Business Roundtable) long ago reached similar conclusions about scheduled overtime (Blough, 1973; McGlaun, 1973).

Obviously, while overtime may occasionally be a practical necessity to correct problems that may be encountered on a job and job completion cannot be delayed because of contract or other provisions, it should never be a regular modus operandi, and the estimator should not include scheduled overtime in the estimate. It should be treated as an unusual situation and be covered as a project contingency cost item.

## Weather Conditions

It is usually possible to forecast seasonal and temperature conditions with a reasonable degree of accuracy based on average mean temperatures for a given area. The U.S. National Oceanic and Atmospheric Administration (NOAA), National Climatic Data Center (at Asheville, NC 28801) publishes a bulletin, *Local Climatological Data Annual Summary with Comparative Data,* listing 30-year average temperature and total precipitation by month, as well as a monthly bulletin showing the hourly observations for each day. The estimator can develop a suitable factor based on the nature of the work—whether it is inside or outside—and the degree of adverse weather expected.

In considering temperature effects on productivity for outside work, the wind-chill factor must be taken into consideration to determine the effective working temperature. The National Electrical Contractors Association (NECA) conducted an extensive study of the effect of relative humidity and effective temperature on craftworker productivity. NECA concluded that, at high relative humidity levels and extremes of effective temperature, productivity is severely impaired. Table 1.4 shows effective temperature as a function of wind speed and actual temperature, and Table 1.5 shows productivity as a function of effective temperature and relative humidity as determined by the NECA.

**TABLE 1.4**   Wind-Chill Factor

| Wind speed, mph | Effective or equivalent temperatures, °F, when actual thermometer readings, °F, are as follows: | | | | | | | | | |
|---|---|---|---|---|---|---|---|---|---|---|
| | 50 | 40 | 30 | 20 | 10 | 0 | −10 | −20 | −30 | −40 |
| Calm | 50 | 40 | 30 | 20 | 10 | 0 | −10 | −20 | −30 | −40 |
| 5 | 48 | 37 | 27 | 16 | 6 | −5 | −15 | −26 | −36 | −47 |
| 10 | 40 | 28 | 16 | 4 | −9 | −21 | −33 | −46 | −58 | −70 |
| 15 | 36 | 22 | 9 | −5 | −18 | −36 | −45 | −58 | −72 | −85 |
| 20 | 32 | 18 | 4 | −10 | −25 | −39 | −53 | −67 | −82 | −96 |
| 25 | 30 | 16 | 0 | −15 | −29 | −44 | −59 | −74 | −88 | −104 |
| 30 | 28 | 13 | −2 | −18 | −33 | −48 | −63 | −79 | −94 | −109 |
| 35 | 27 | 11 | −4 | −20 | −35 | −49 | −67 | −82 | −98 | −113 |
| 40 | 26 | 10 | −6 | −21 | −37 | −53 | −69 | −85 | −100 | −116 |

SOURCE:  National Safety Council.

**TABLE 1.5**   Craft Productivity Percentages at Various Environmental Conditions

| Relative humidity, percent | −20 | −10 | 0 | 10 | 20 | 30 | 40 | 50 | 60 | 70 | 80 | 90 | 100 | 110 | 120 |
|---|---|---|---|---|---|---|---|---|---|---|---|---|---|---|---|
| 90 | ? | 55 | 71 | 82 | 89 | 93 | 96 | 98 | 98 | 96 | 93 | 84 | 57 | 0 | ? |
| 80 | ? | 57 | 73 | 84 | 91 | 95 | 98 | 100 | 100 | 98 | 95 | 87 | 68 | 15 | ? |
| 70 | ? | 59 | 75 | 86 | 93 | 97 | 99 | 100 | 100 | 99 | 97 | 90 | 76 | 50 | ? |
| 60 | ? | 60 | 76 | 87 | 94 | 98 | 100 | 100 | 100 | 100 | 98 | 93 | 80 | 57 | ? |
| 50 | ? | 61 | 77 | 88 | 94 | 98 | 100 | 100 | 100 | 100 | 99 | 94 | 82 | 60 | ? |
| 40 | ? | 62 | 78 | 88 | 94 | 98 | 100 | 100 | 100 | 100 | 99 | 94 | 84 | 63 | ? |
| 30 | ? | 62 | 78 | 88 | 94 | 98 | 100 | 100 | 100 | 100 | 99 | 93 | 83 | 62 | ? |
| 20 | ? | 62 | 78 | 88 | 94 | 98 | 100 | 100 | 100 | 100 | 99 | 93 | 82 | 61 | ? |

Effective temperature, °F

SOURCE: "The Effect of Temperature on Productivity," *Test Report,* National Electrical Contractors Association, Washington, D.C., 1974. Reprinted by permission.

Rain must also be considered the greatest delaying agent in a construction operation. A study of the climatological data for most areas will quickly reveal the difficulty in relying on historical precipitation patterns; although the yearly averages seem to hold up fairly well, the possibility of extremes is disastrous. A number of weather forecasts are available that can help ease the risk. The *Monthly and Seasonal Weather Outlook* is available from the U.S. Government Printing Office.

In any case, a correction factor for workhours, or an allowance in dollars, must be made for any job having a possible weather range.

## Area Conditions

When a job is going into an area away from home base, the estimator must become familiar with the general economy as well as the amount of construction activity in the area. As a rule, a very active area enjoying a healthy economic climate will have a poor labor pool, poor in both quantity and quality. Other conditions can add up to high-complexity factors. A careful inspection of the area is a must for the professional estimator. Correction factors for area conditions are given in Table 1.6.

**TABLE 1.6**   Area Conditions—Correction Factors

| *Description* | *Factor* |
| --- | --- |
| Quality of available supervisors | 0.90–1.25 |
| Quality of available labor | 1–1.20 |
| Quantity of available labor | 1–1.25 |
| Harsh local working rules | 1–1.20 |
| Difficult living conditions | 1–1.05 |
| Heavy traffic congestion, poor unloading facilities | 1–1.15 |
| Poor transportation facilities | 1–1.05 |

## General Conditions

General conditions cannot always be predetermined and crashing, overtime, night shifts, etc. may become necessary at any point along the network if the job is lagging because of unpredicted delays or a change of target date. However, available correction factors for these conditions are fairly reliable; and if the original workhour estimate is plotted on a good bar chart or CPM network, or accurately subtotaled by task, the correction is a simple matter. Table 1.7 gives these factors.

## Task or Operation Conditions

Task conditions are subject to great variations of refinement; again, it becomes necessary for the estimator to make a judgment based on an understanding of the conditions. Table 1.8 shows a factor of 1.1 for *work in crawl space*. That is a fair consideration for average crawl-space conditions, but a crawl space could be tight enough to require a 1.75 factor. A sheet-metal shop may have an exceptionally fast worker who is 5 ft 4 in. tall. This person—working in a low-overhead, tight crawl space—would have a smaller efficiency loss than would an equally fast worker who is 6 ft 2 in. at 255 lb.

All factors could theoretically have subfactors ad infinitum, and any factor might be challenged, depending on the degree of the condition. Within this logic, the task-condition Tables 1.3, 1.8, and 1.9 and Figs. 1.8 to 1.10 are presented.

**TABLE 1.7**  General Conditions—Correction Factors

| Description | Factor |
|---|---|
| Crashing—overstaffing | 1.25 |
| Overtime: | |
| To 50 hr | 1.10 |
| To 54 hr | 1.12 |
| To 60 hr | 1.15 |
| To 65 hr | 1.20 |
| To 70 hr | 1.26 |
| To 84 hr | 1.33 |
| Over 84 hr | 1.44 |
| Night shift: | |
| Commencing at end of regular day shift | 1.10 |
| Commencing after 10 P.M. | 1.20 |

**TABLE 1.8**  Task Conditions—Correction Factors

| Description | Factor |
|---|---|
| Work in crawl space | 1.10 |
| Work in cramped shaft | 1.75 |
| Work in secret plan | 1.05 |
| Work with special care (merchandise, furniture, etc.) | 1.20 |
| Work and maintain quiet (local ordinances, hospitals, etc.). | 1.15 |
| Work in foul air | 1.10 |
| Interference by occupants | 1.15 |
| Interference by uncooperative GC. | To 1.30 |
| Interference by consulting engineer or inspector. | To 1.20 |

**TABLE 1.9**  Task Conditions—Correction Factors

Activity occurs on more than one floor.

| Number of floors | Factor |
|---|---|
| One, above or below ground | 1.02 |
| Two | 1.03 |
| Three | 1.05 |
| Four | 1.07 |
| Five | 1.09 |
| Six | 1.11 |
| Seven | 1.13 |
| Eight | 1.15 |
| Nine | 1.17 |
| Ten | 1.19 |
| Eleven | 1.21 |
| Twelve | 1.23 |
| Thirteen | 1.25 |
| Fourteen | 1.28 |
| Fifteen | 1.31 |
| Sixteen | 1.34 |
| Seventeen | 1.37 |

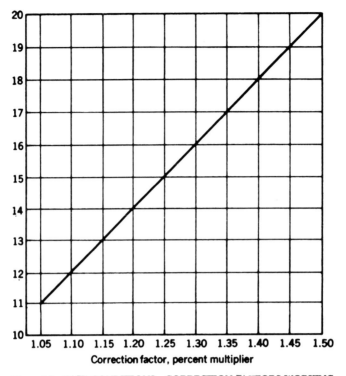

**Figure 1.8  TASK CONDITIONS—CORRECTION FACTORS WORKING FROM LADDER AT HEIGHTS ABOVE 10 FT**
*(Note: These factors are based on working height from standing level using a ladder suitable to the nature of the task. The height of the ladder is not considered.)*

**Example 1.1  Applying Correction Factors**  Assume a pipe-erection job, the total base estimated workhours to be 3,200, and the work subject to the following conditions:

1. Work from 10-ft scaffold. Task affects 70% of total job, or 2,240 base hours.
2. Night shift commencing at midnight. Task affects 20% of total job, or 640 base hours.
3. Interference by government inspectors. Affects all portions of the job.
4. Work in secret plan. Affects all portions of the job.

**solution**

Factor for work from 10-ft scaffold: from Fig. 1.9, select factor 1.10
Factor for night shift commencing at midnight: from Table 1.7, select factor 1.20
Factor for interference by government inspectors: from Table 1.8, select factor 1.20
Factor for work in secret plan: from Table 1.8, select factor 1.05
   2,240 base hours subject to conditions 1, 3, and 4
    640 base hours subject to conditions 2 to 4
    320 base hours subject to conditions 3 and 4

So,

| | | |
|---|---|---|
| $2{,}240 \times 1.10 \times 1.20 \times 1.05$ | $=$ | 3,104.6 |
| $640 \times 1.20 \times 1.20 \times 1.05$ | $=$ | 967.7 |
| $320 \times 1.20 \times 1.05$ | $=$ | 403.2 |
| 3,200 base hours | | 4,475.5 corrected workhours |

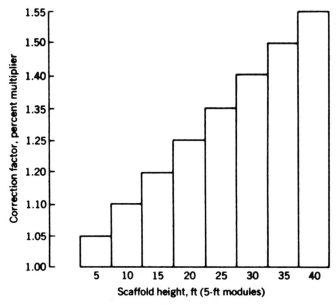

**Figure 1.9  TASK CONDITIONS—CORRECTION FACTORS, WORKING ON SCAFFOLD**
*(Note: These factors are not based on floor or ceiling elevation; they are based on the height of the scaffold, in 5-ft increments, from standing level. See Chap. 21 for information on scaffolding setup and dismantling labor and rental costs.)*

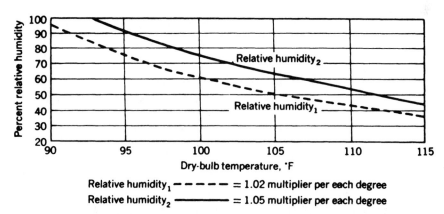

Relative humidity$_1$  - - - - -  = 1.02 multiplier per each degree
Relative humidity$_2$  ————  = 1.05 multiplier per each degree

**Figure 1.10   CORRECTION FACTORS FOR WORKING IN AREA TEMPERATURES ABOVE 90°F**
*(Note: For each degree rise above 90°F, multiply the base workhours by the appropriate factor. Enter the grid at the abscissa of dry-bulb temperature; if the intersection with the established relative humidity (RH) line falls at, or below, the broken-line curve, use the RH$_1$ factor. The zone above the solid-line RH$_2$ is marginal; activity in this environment proceeds for only brief periods and under extreme stress.) Ample drinking water must be made available for those working at these conditions; fans directed at the subject causing airstreams of 500 feet per minute fpm or more could lower the effective temperature by 3°F and substantially reduce the efficiency loss.*

## *ESTIMATING THE COST OF ESTIMATING*

The larger the organization, the easier it is to peg estimating costs. An *Engineering News-Record* article, "Fluor Ranks Estimating as Big Business," reported that Fluor Corp., Ltd engineers and constructors, using a staff of 22 estimators, spent $500,000 to get $100 million worth of contracts. Fluor's cost of estimating was running about 0.5% of sales.

Although it can be most difficult to assign true estimating costs for the small contractor or dealer type of operation—because of loose organization and overlapping duties—it seems reasonable to assume that the estimating costs are between 3 and 10% of sales. It is therefore not surprising that when the elusive cost of estimating was finally tracked down (in a private survey) for one company doing $300,000 sales, estimating was pegged at $21,000. This represented 7% of sales and 34% of the total operating expenses, considerably more than net profit.

Most contractors pay particular attention to the need for billing out all construction and service labor without omission, yet they appear in the Yellow Pages offering "free estimates...cheerfully." For those who have a more sober approach to estimating and are not very cheerful about giving it away free, the schedules given in Tables 1.10 to 1.12 may be of some help. Table 1.12 shows workhours required for preparation of drawings manually. Computer-aided drafting (CAD) on average reduces the workhour per mechanical drawing by almost 50%. The *Cost Engineers' Notebook* reported engineering costs for large mechanical installations in a range of 15 to 275 workhours per drawing and an average of 130 workhours with manual drafting. Using CAD the range reduced to 20 to 120 workhours with an average of 70 workhours. Note that for the simpler drawings requiring a minimum amount of time, manual drafting was more efficient in terms of workhours than CAD, because of setup time, etc. However, for all except the simplest drawings, substantial savings can be gained using CAD, and for all drawings accuracy is equal or better than with manual techniques.

**TABLE 1.10**    Fees for Professional Services

These are approximate figures and are subject to wide variation by geography and local economic conditions (1994 dollars).

| *Description* | *Fee per hour, $* |
|---|---|
| Sketcher | 40 |
| Mechanic | 50 |
| Service technician | 60 |
| Drafter | 60 |
| Estimator | 75 |
| Balancing technician | 75 |
| Service engineer | 85 |
| Construction engineer | 85 |
| Balancing engineer | 85 |

**TABLE 1.11**  Survey Estimates

Cost and fees to prepare cost estimate for commercial application, using DX air- or water-cooled packaged unit.

| Description | Workhours |
|---|---|
| Allowance for traveling time | 1.5 |
| Physical survey of buildings | 1.5 |
|    1. Pace off dimensions | |
|    2. Measure glass, etc. | |
|    3. Check equipment and duct location | |
|    4. Check roof construction | |
|    5. Check for plumbing connections | |
| Complete heat gain and plot psychrometer chart | 2.0 |
|    1. Sensible, latent, and total | |
|    2. Fresh air and recirculation cfm | |
|    3. Dehumidification requirements | |
| Lay out air distribution and select equipment | 2.0 |
|    1. Size ducts and sketch in single line | |
|    2. Select grilles, etc. | |
|    3. Select all equipment | |
|    4. Indicate piping and controls location | |
| Prepare cost estimate and proposal | 1.0 |
|     Total workhours for basic survey estimate | 8.0 |
| Survey fee @ $75 per hour: $600 | |
| For projects of 2 to 15 tons, use basic fee | 8.0 |
| From 16 to 40 tons | 12.0 |
| From 41 to 75 tons | 18.0 |
| For residential application | 10.0 |
| For sales engineer making initial presentation plus second visit, traveling time, and miscellaneous time to sign contract | 6.0 |
| To prepare econograph, plotting total owning and operating cost of any installation over estimated life of equipment | 4.0 |

**TABLE 1.12**  Shop Drawings and Permit Drawings

On 24 × 18 quality vellum using ¼-in scale.

| Description | Workhours |
|---|---|
| Package units: | |
|    2–5 tons | 6.0 |
|    6–10 tons | 7.0 |
|    11–30 tons | 8.0 |
|    31–75 tons | 12.0 |
| Applied equipment: | |
|    To 15 tons | 9.0 |
|    16–30 tons | 12.0 |
|    31–60 tons | 18.0 |
|    61–80 tons | 22.0 |
| Addenda: $65 per hr (1994 costs) | |

## *ESTIMATING MATERIALS*

The general procedure for estimating materials is to list all materials on quantity sheets and carry forward the tabulated totals to the summary or final estimate sheet.

Although most material estimates show only the first cost of material plus freight for job-site delivery, it is standard practice to estimate some materials as *installed* or *erected* or *set in place.* Pipe, for example, may be taken off on a quantity sheet, tallying all pipe footages and showing each fitting. The total is then brought forward to the summary sheet, and labor is shown as a separate item. In such cases labor is figured by the number of joints per hour. Another method is to set down one figure for pipe that includes labor and material. When the cost reflects the pipe erected, the estimator generally totals all the pipe footages, fittings, valves, and hangers for each size and type of pipe.

Ductwork is generally estimated on a cost-per-pound basis. Insulation for ductwork and vessels is generally estimated at a cost-per-square-foot-installed basis, whereas insulation for pipes is generally estimated on a cost-per-linear-foot-installed basis by using the same method as for the pipe itself.

## *ESTIMATING JOB OVERHEAD*

Job overhead is often included in general overhead and not treated as a separate item; however, many contractors break overhead down into two parts: job overhead and general overhead. Because job overhead is more variable with each job and general overhead is relatively fixed, job overhead is often treated as a separate item by the estimator to reach maximum accuracy.

Job overhead costs vary considerably, depending on

1. *Prejob costs*—preliminary expenses
2. *Through-job costs*—difficulties in performing the work
3. *Postjob costs*—cost of settling up and collecting

These costs may total from 3 to 15%; and, as a rule, smaller jobs allow a smaller job overhead percentage.

### Partial List of Job Overhead Costs

Salesperson's commissions
Contingencies
Tool and material sheds
Shop drawings and wiring diagrams
Surveys
Transportation
Wages of engineers
Wages of general supervisors
Fire, property, and police protection
Permits
Interest
Taxes
Insurance
Bonds

When owned by the contractor, special machinery and equipment should be shown as job overhead and may be estimated from a depreciation schedule. When such equipment is rented, it is usually entered as a direct cost and as such may be marked up to cover the cost of processing. For new construction work, *cleanup costs* are usually entered in job overhead at ¼ of 1% and for existing construction at ¾ of 1%.

## CONTINGENCY

All estimates should include an allowance for contingency. *Contingency* is an amount added to an estimate to allow for items that can't be defined in advance but that experience shows will likely be required. Unscheduled overtime to correct a problem is a good example of such an item. It must be recognized that contingency is not an allowance for errors in the estimate and should not be used as such. According to Zaheer (1988), "Contingency is a cost element...to cover statistical probability of occurrence of foreseeable elements of cost within the defined project scope." Zaheer goes on to say, "Contingency reflects a management judgmental allowance to avoid...project cost overruns" and "Contingency should not be too high to create a 'fat' estimate."

The latter statement is critical, particularly in bid preparation. Adequate contingency must be included in the estimate to avoid cost overruns, *but* it must not inflate the estimate; otherwise, the bid will be lost.

The level of contingency necessary is dependent on many factors and can't be generalized. It is a management decision based on experience, project risks, etc. A well-maintained historical project cost database showing actual versus estimated past costs is vital as a guide to selecting an appropriate, but not excessive, contingency amount.

## LARCENY

Suite crime and street crime (white-collar and T-shirt crime) first came to light as a major construction job cost around 1970. Presently, hundreds of millions of dollars in larceny costs are estimated around the country. One news article reported that New York City contractors were "increasing their bids by as much as 8% to offset anticipated losses due to jobsite crimes and *other forms of dishonesty.*" The *Miami Herald* reported that "in South Florida the loss through theft and vandalism runs to nearly 5 percent." In another article, *Newsweek* concluded that "employees steal anywhere from $40 billion to $100 billion from their companies every year, costs that invariably get passed on to the consumers."

Many contractors may feel that it is their inalienable right to move tools and materials—and even labor—to their new homes, garages, or boat docks, but this, in fact, is stealing. Executive conduct must be exemplary if employee theft is to be discouraged. Larceny includes onsite theft of fan sets, air conditioners, heating units, and pipe, fittings, and tools; truck hijacking; vandalism; and petty theft from shops and trucks by outside thieves, mechanics, and bosses themselves. Organized gangs are stealing pumps, condensing units, and pipe from jobsites, and mechanics sometimes siphon gas out of company trucks into private cars. Mechanics sometimes establish small moonlighting businesses on the side, and much of the materials for these private enterprise ventures comes from regular jobs. Security personnel should be posted at every jobsite. The more careful the estimate and the tighter the equipment and material control, the more effective internal security can become. Table 1.13 shows how one major firm treats suite crime and street crime in the overhead tabulation.

Security guards are increasingly necessary to patrol and protect construction sites from theft and vandalism. If guards are not provided by the general contractor, depending on the size of the job, the mechanical estimator should include the cost of guard service in the estimate. Kiley and Moselle (1993) quote a 1993 cost of $17.50 per hour for short-term use (one week or less) of construction site uniformed security guards, unarmed. This figure includes

**TABLE 1.13**  Job Overhead as Percentage of Labor

| Item | Percent |
| --- | --- |
| 1. Service reserve | 25.0 |
| 2. Supervision | 20.0 |
| 3. Engineering and drafting | 20.0 |
| 4. Insurance and taxes | 20.0 |
| 5. Larceny and security | 10.0 |
| 6. Tool removal and cleanup | 1.5 |
| 7. Field office and shed | 1.5 |
| 8. Timekeeper | 2.0 |
| 9. Temporary phone and power | 0.7 |
| 10. Clerk | 0.3 |
|  | 100.0 |

two-way radio contact, a backup patrol car, bonding, and liability insurance. For medium durations (one week to one month), the cost drops to $14.50 per hour and for longer terms, to $13.00 per hour. A 50% premium applies to holidays.

## ESTIMATING GENERAL OVERHEAD

All costs necessary to maintain and organize the business, independent of any particular job, may be considered as general overhead. These costs may vary from ½ to 10%, depending on the size, scope, and efficiency of the contractor organization, but will remain fixed for each contractor.

### Partial List of General Overhead Costs

Rent
Air conditioning
Furniture
Office supplies
Light
Telephone and telegraph
Wages of bookkeepers, secretaries, clerks, etc.
Wages of estimators and drafters
Legal and auditing expenses
Entertainment, promotion, and advertising
Automobile expenses
Dues and trade journals
Officers' salaries
Consulting fees
Insurance
Traveling expenses
Library

## PORTAL-TO-PORTAL

Although portal-to-portal expense must always be treated as a cost, it should not be considered as nonproductive labor. Traveling to and from the jobsite is a function of transporting means of production, and the precedent for paying workers for this time was set prior to World War II.

From the viewpoint of both pure economics and practical estimating, portal-to-portal transportation and traveling time should be treated as an overhead cost and therefore not marked up.

## ESTIMATING PROFIT

How profit will be estimated is the decision of the executive department and not of the estimator. Once the total costs have been tabulated, the estimator's job is concluded. If an estimator could estimate a job total cost to 100% accuracy, the profit would then not be estimated but rather would be a fixed amount based on the truth of the estimate.

Profit is usually expressed as a percent of the sum of the total costs of a mechanical construction, but it is frequently split up into several percents of different subtotals. For example, the executive department may instruct the estimating department to mark up all materials 30%, labor 40%, and subcontractors 5%, or materials 110%, labor 50%, and subcontractors 10%.

Although profit is fixed by the executive department, the estimator must understand markup and profit margins. *Markup* is the amount added to cost in order to arrive at a selling price.

**Example 1.2**   A mechanical construction cost totals $60,000; the selling price is to be computed at 25% markup. What is the selling price?

**solution**

$$\frac{\$60,000}{1} \times \frac{25}{100} = \$15,000$$

$$\$60,000 + \$15,000 = \$75,000 \text{ selling price}$$

or

$$\$60,000 \times 125\% = \$75,000 \text{ selling price}$$

The markup of $15,000 in this example is equal to 25% profit on the cost price.

If 25% profit on the selling price is desired, the markup on cost will have to be 33⅓% (Table 1.14).

**Example 1.3**   A mechanical construction cost totals $60,000; the selling price is to be computed so that a profit of 25% will be made on the sale. What is the selling price?

**solution**   Let

$$100\% = \text{selling price}$$
$$25\% = \text{margin}$$
$$75\% = \text{cost price or } \$60,000$$

$$100\% = \frac{\$60,000}{75\%} = \$80,000 \text{ selling price}$$

leaving a markup of $20,000 or $60,000 × 1.333% = $80,000.

**TABLE 1.14**   Profit Percentage Conversion

| % Markup on cost | = | % Profit on selling price | % Markup on cost | = | % Profit on selling price |
|---|---|---|---|---|---|
| 5.00 | | 4.75 | 31.58 | | 24.00 |
| 7.50 | | 7.00 | 33.33 $\frac{1}{3}$ | | 25.00 |
| 10.00 | | 9.00 | 35.00 | | 26.00 |
| 11.11 | | 10.00 | 37.50 | | 27.25 |
| 12.36 | | 11.00 | 40.00 | | 28.50 |
| 12.50 | | 11.125 | 42.86 | | 30.00 |
| 13.63 | | 12.00 | 45.00 | | 31.00 |
| 14.95 | | 13.00 | 47.00 | | 32.00 |
| 16.28 | | 14.00 | 50.00 | | 33.33 $\frac{1}{3}$ |
| 16.43 | | 14.25 | 53.85 | | 35.00 |
| 17.65 | | 15.00 | 55.00 | | 35.50 |
| 19.05 | | 16.00 | 60.00 | | 37.50 |
| 20.00 | | 16.66 $\frac{2}{3}$ | 65.00 | | 39.50 |
| 20.49 | | 17.00 | 66.66 $\frac{2}{3}$ | | 40.00 |
| 21.96 | | 18.00 | 70.00 | | 41.00 |
| 23.46 | | 19.00 | 75.00 | | 42.75 |
| 25.00 | | 20.00 | 80.00 | | 44.50 |
| 26.58 | | 21.00 | 85.00 | | 46.00 |
| 28.21 | | 22.00 | 90.00 | | 47.50 |
| 29.88 | | 23.00 | 100.00 | | 50.00 |

## AVOIDING ERRORS IN ESTIMATING

The greatest hazards in estimating are working under pressure and with interruptions. The exigencies of the trade will, of course, demand a certain amount of pressure on the estimator at all times, but not every job is an emergency. Each job should be properly qualified, and a maximum of time should be allowed. Experience bears out the general sentiments of the industry—that most emergencies are simply not emergencies. Most deadlines can be easily extended if all parties involved are calmly informed of the time requirements and whether the individual responsible asks for more time.

Interruptions break the continuity of thought which the estimator requires to develop an accurate tally. The working space provided for the estimator should be quiet and well illuminated, and suppliers and agents should be interviewed on an organized time schedule so that interruptions may be kept at a minimum.

The *complete estimate* (Fig. 1.1) form provides the best reminder list against omissions, and each item appearing on the list should be checked off. Items listed on the sheet but not required for a particular job should show the words *none* or *by others* in the space provided.

To avoid errors, here are some areas that require special scrutiny and notation:

Scale of drawing, for total linear feet of pipe, insulation, etc.

Height of structure, for vertical lifts, cranes, etc.

Equipment-room dimensions and air unit space limitations, for agreement with selected equipment

Electrical characteristics

Elevations for scaffold and ladder work

## DISCOUNTS

Often a manufacturer or jobber will show a list price in a catalog or descriptive bulletin and will issue a periodic discount sheet to the trade that reflects fluctuating market conditions. Such trade discounts are usually *chain discounts.*

Several methods of computing chain discounts and converting into one multiplier may be used; the simplest method is to subtract each discount from 100% and multiply the remainders.

**Example 1.4**   A boiler is listed in a manufacturer's catalog at a price of $24,000; the trade chain discount is 50% − 15% − 5% − 5%. What is the single discount? What is the multiplier factor? What is the net price of the boiler?

**solution**

$$
\begin{array}{cccc}
100\% & 100\% & 100\% & 100\% \\
\underline{-50\%} & \underline{-15\%} & \underline{-5\%} & \underline{-5\%} \\
50\% & 85\% & 95\% & 95\%
\end{array}
$$

$$0.50 \times 0.85 \times 0.95 \times 0.95 = 0.3835, \text{ or } 38.35\%$$

$$100\% - 38.35\% = 61.65\% \text{ single discount}$$

$$
\begin{array}{l}
\$24,000 \text{ boiler list price} \\
\underline{\times\ 0.3835} \text{ multiplier factor} \\
\$\ 9,204 \text{ net trade price}
\end{array}
$$

## BIDDING AND COMPETITION

A major purpose of contractors' estimates, of course, is to guide the preparation of bids for construction jobs. Most contracts, particularly large ones, are usually awarded on the basis of competitive bids. When preparing a bid, it is usually best to avoid projects that do not have detailed plans and specifications. Leave these to your competitors because a poorly specified project will invariably receive a bid or bids that have been underestimated or that sacrifice quality for price. Siddens (1992) recommends striving to get on the bidding lists of architects, who are known to produce detailed drawings and tight specifications and who stick to them. In these cases the responsibilities of the contractor are clearly defined, and the estimate and bid are much easier to prepare in an accurate manner, thus enhancing the probability of getting the job if the bid is low. Siddens goes on to state that public work competition is not well defined and that the contractor "must be certain his organization can bring to the project unique experience and efficiencies. Otherwise, he most certainly will be underbid by those desperate enough for work to bid without profit just to get a job."

## RECOMMENDED READING

*AACE Recommended Practices and Standards,* AACE International, Morgantown, W.Va. (Published periodically.)

*ASHRAE Handbook, Equipment,* American Society of Heating, Refrigeration and Air Conditioning Engineers, Atlanta, Ga. (Published periodically.)

*ASHRAE Handbook, Systems,* American Society of Heating, Refrigeration and Air Conditioning Engineers, Atlanta, Ga. (Published periodically.)

Blough, R. M., "Effect of Scheduled Overtime on Construction Projects," *AACE Bulletin,* **15,** 5 (1973), p. 155.

Borcherding, J. D., and D. F. Gainer, "Motivation and Productivity of Craftsmen and Foremen on Large Projects," *1980 Transactions of the American Association of Cost Engineers,* Morgantown, W.Va., Paper No. I.2.

Bough, P. E., "An Overview of US Labor Burden Rates," *Cost Engineering,* **35,** 1 (1993), pp. 9–12.

Bromberg, I., "Impact of Overtime on Construction," *1988 Transactions of the American Association of Cost Engineers,* Morgantown, W.Va., Paper No. H.3.

Chick, D., "The Changing Role of the Estimator," *Cost Engineering,* **34,** 7 (1992), pp. 23–25.

Cilensek, R., "Understanding Contractor Overhead," *Cost Engineering,* **33,** 12 (1991), pp. 21–23.

"The Effect of Temperature on Productivity," *Test Report,* National Electrical Contractors Association, Washington, D.C., 1974.

"Engineering Costs," *Cost Engineers' Notebook,* AACE International, Morgantown, W.Va., 1992.

"Fluor Ranks Estimating as Big Business," *Engineering News-Record,* April 17, 1961, pp. 110–111.

Gladstone, J., "Identify, Analyze Low Visibility Items in Mechanical Estimates," *Heating/Piping/Air Conditioning,* May 1972, pp. 76–80.

Humphreys, K. K., and L. M. English (eds.), *Project and Cost Engineers' Handbook,* 3d ed., Marcel Dekker, New York, 1993.

Kiley, M. D., and W. M. Moselle (eds.), *National Construction Estimator,* 41st ed., Craftsman Book Co., Carlsbad, Calif., 1993.

*Labor Rates for the Construction Industry,* R.S. Means Co., Kingston, Mass. (Published annually.)

Laufer, A., and J. D. Borcherding, "Using Pay to Motivate Construction Job Performance," *1981 Transactions of the American Association of Cost Engineers,* Morgantown, W.Va., Paper No. I.6.

McGlaun, W., "Overtime in Construction," *AACE Bulletin,* **15,** 5 (1973), p. 141.

Moylan, J. J., and M. Mossman (eds.), *Means Mechanical Estimating: Standards and Procedures,* 2d ed., R.S. Means Co., Kingston, Mass., 1992.

Rapier, C. P., "How to Deal with Accuracy and Contingency," *1990 Transactions of the American Association of Cost Engineers,* Morgantown, W.Va., Paper No. K.8.

Sanders, S. R., and T. E. Cooper, "Analyzing Construction Company Profitability," *Cost Engineering,* **33,** 2 (1991), pp. 7–14.

Siddens, R. S. (ed.), *Walker's Building Estimator's Reference Book,* 24th ed., Frank R. Walker Co., Lisle, Ill., 1992.

Zaheer, S. H., "Contingency and Capital Cost Estimates," *Cost Engineers' Notebook,* American Association of Cost Engineers, Morgantown, W.Va., 1988.

# CHAPTER 2
# CHECK DATA

## GENERAL DISCUSSION

In estimating, rule-of-thumb cost figures are extremely useful as a guide to quickly obtain an order-of-magnitude cost figure for a project and for checking more refined estimates for reasonableness. Many an otherwise well-done estimate has yielded a totally unrealistic answer because of a faulty assumption or a simple mathematics or data error. Such faulty estimates can be made to stick out like a sore thumb if checked by using rule-of-thumb figures (pun intended).

Good rule-of-thumb or check-data figures can save countless hours of design, drafting, and estimating time. Although estimates made using check data and budget prices can at times be exceptionally accurate, if misused, check data can lead to disastrous results. Check data must be used with care and with full awareness that it is no substitute for a detailed estimate and/or firm price quotations. As explained in Chap. 1, order-of-magnitude estimates, when properly performed, have an expected accuracy of only −30 to +50%. Clearly this level of accuracy is not adequate for anything more than preliminary decision making or for checking the reasonableness of an estimate prepared using more accurate techniques. As the term *check data* suggests, such data should be used as a check on estimates; it should not be used indiscriminately in lieu of a proper estimate.

Obviously, wage rates, production rates, freight costs, and material prices vary widely around the country. The data offered in this chapter are generally based on the average trade wage rate for 30 major U.S. cities as of January 1, 1994, which, including fringes, falls at about $24.65 per hour. This includes all direct fringe benefits such as health care, insurance, vacation, and pensions, but not the contractor's overhead. For a look at some prevailing wage rates for principal cities, see Table 1.3. The cost-in-place curves shown in the figures cited below should be viewed as a broad ribbon rather than a thin line, and adjustments should be made for specific local conditions.

A discussion of local conditions affecting job costs is presented in Chap. 1. Check data for cooling towers and other major components may be found in particular chapters.

The cost-in-place figures shown in Figs. 2.1 to 2.17 are based on the mechanical contractor's selling price to the owner and include labor, material, overhead, and profit, but they do not include sales tax, fees, commissions, etc.

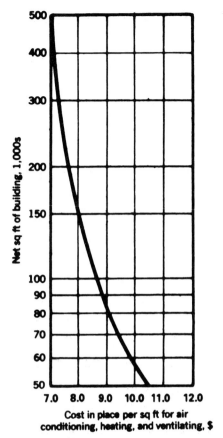

**Figure 2.1 COST IN PLACE**
**Size/Cost Ratio—Multistory Buildings**
*Relation of cost per square foot to total square feet of project, based on average costs for induction or fan-coil systems applied to multiroom, multistory structures.*

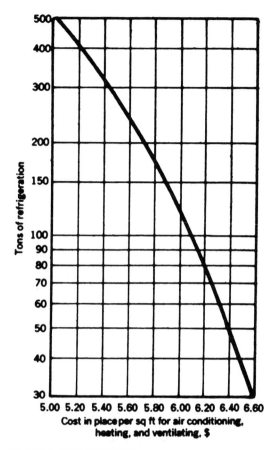

**Figure 2.2 COST IN PLACE**
**Size/Cost Ratio—Low-Silhouette Buildings**
*Relation of cost per square foot to required tonnage for comfort cooling in open-spaced buildings, such as shopping centers, stores, and manufacturing plants. To convert tons to square feet, multiply by 300.*

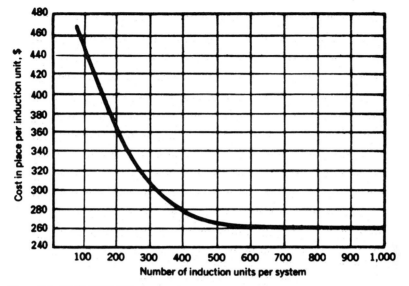

**Figure 2.3   COST IN PLACE**
**Induction Systems—Secondary-Water Circuit**
*Includes pump, heat-exchanger expansion tank, and piping materials, plus labor to erect the unit coils as well as all the above. Does not include unit control valves or pipe clusters.*

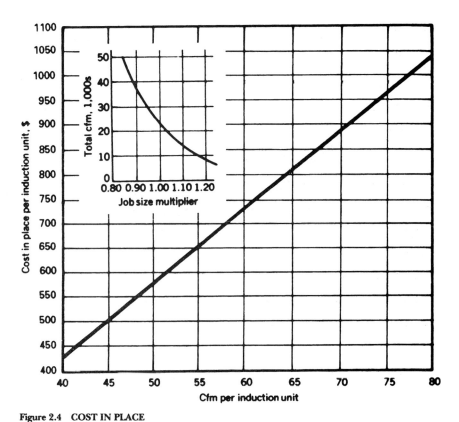

**Figure 2.4  COST IN PLACE**
**Induction Systems—Primary-Air Side**
*Includes: (1) Base unit with cabinet, accessories, and coils (erecting unit coils is included in the secondary-water-circuit curve). (2) Floor-to-floor air risers, air takeoff headers, air runouts, and two fire dampers. (3) Primary-air fan, motor and starter, casing coils, sound absorber, filters, outside-air louvers, dampers and screen, outside-air dampers, recirculation pump and starter, and two 30-ft lengths of return-air duct. (4) Supervision, erection, leak test, balance, and cleanup. Does not include controls, insulation, drains, runout enclosures, or book shelves.*

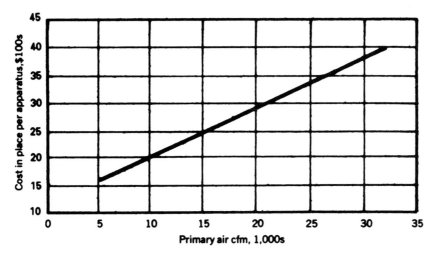

**Figure 2.5    COST IN PLACE**
Induction Systems—Primary-Air Insulation Apparatus Covering

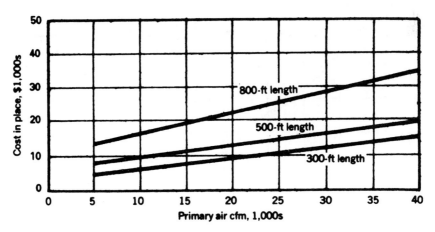

**Figure 2.6    COST IN PLACE**
Induction Systems—Primary-Air Insulation; Primary-Air Header Covering

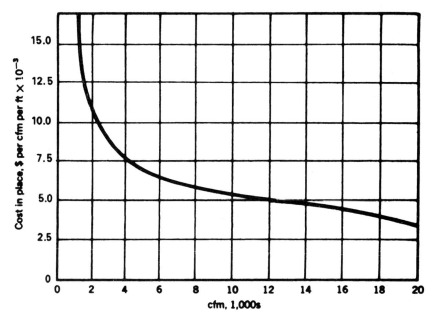

**Figure 2.7   COST IN PLACE**
**Low-Pressure Systems—Return-Air Ducts**
*For return-air grilles, add $0.15 per cfm. For fire dampers, add $425 per each; includes access door, ceiling panel, and erection.*

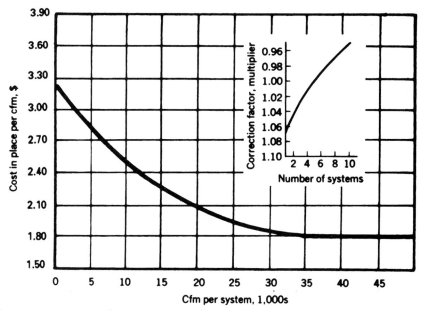

**Figure 2.8   COST IN PLACE**
**Low-Pressure Systems—Air-Side Supply**
*Includes (1) Apparatus casing with six-row coil, two-row hot-water coil, bypass section, filters, motor, and drive. (2) Outside air screen, louvers, and dampers. (3) Supply-system ductwork and connections. (4) All air distribution at 300 cfm per outlet. (5) Supervision, erection, and cleanup. Does not include controls, insulation, reheat coils, heating section, return-air-side ductwork and connections, fire dampers, vibration isolators, test and balance.*

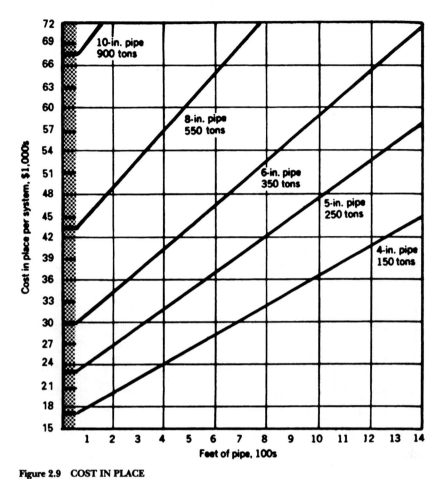

**Figure 2.9   COST IN PLACE**
**Main Chilled-Water Piping**
*Includes pumps, motors, valves, fittings, specialties, etc. Based on physical distance between main machine room and interconnecting apparatuses. The shaded area represents equipment room costs.*

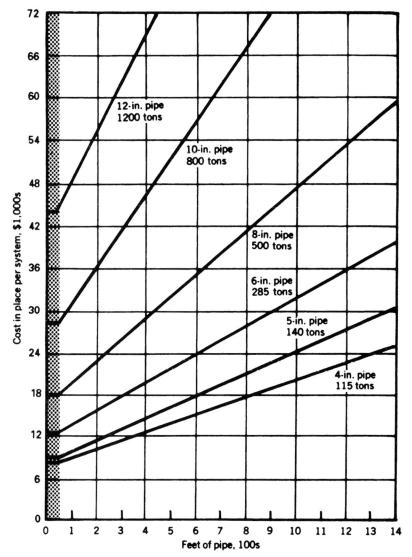

**Figure 2.10   COST IN PLACE**
**Condenser Water Piping**
*Includes pumps, motors, valves, fittings, specialties, etc. Based on centrifugal chiller; for absorption systems, use 1.33 multiplier. The shaded area represents equipment room costs.*

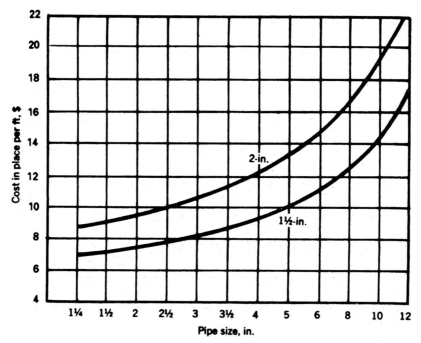

**Figure 2.11    COST IN PLACE**
Insulation—Chilled-Water Pipe Covering for Aboveground Application

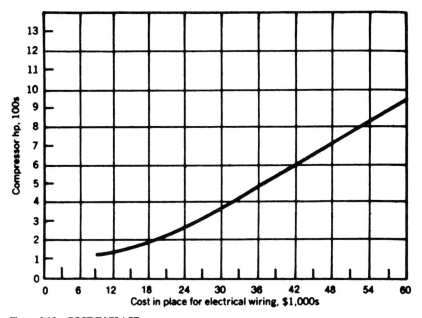

**Figure 2.12   COST IN PLACE**
**Electrical Wiring—Centrifugal Compressors**
*For absorption machines, pumps, and fan motors for cooling towers, etc., allow $120 per horsepower (hp) per motor.*

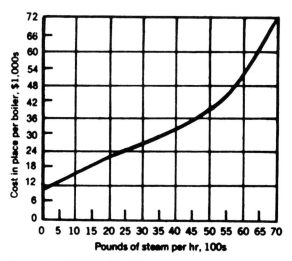

**Figure 2.13   COST IN PLACE**
**Boilers**
*Low-pressure Scotch-packaged fire tube, natural-gas-fired. Includes erecting, final pipe connections, and start-up.*

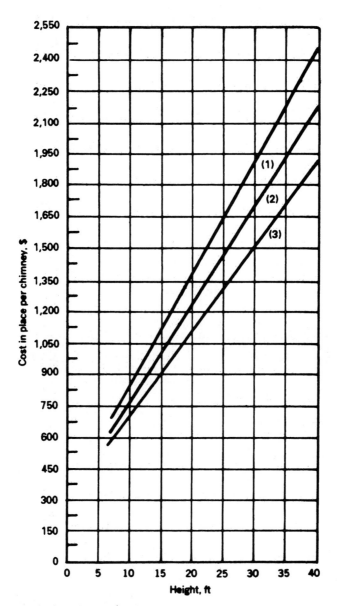

**Figure 2.14    COST IN PLACE**
**Brick Chimneys—with Flue Linings and Foundation**
*(1) 20 × 24 in. with two 8 × 12-in. flues. (2) 16 × 24 in. with two 8 × 8 in.*
*flues; also 20 × 20 in. with one 12 × 12 in. flue. (3) 16 × 24 in. with one 8 ×*
*12-in. flue.*

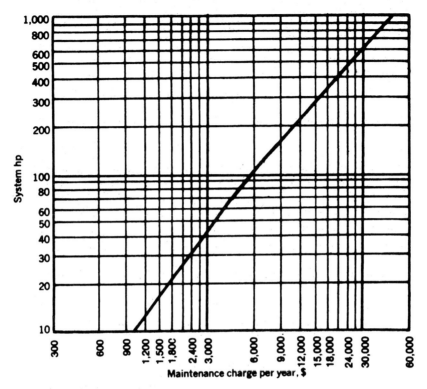

**Figure 2.15   COST OF SERVICE**
*Annual charges for full maintenance service. Based on single refrigerating machine; for more than one machine, use multiplier 0.75 per each additional machine.*

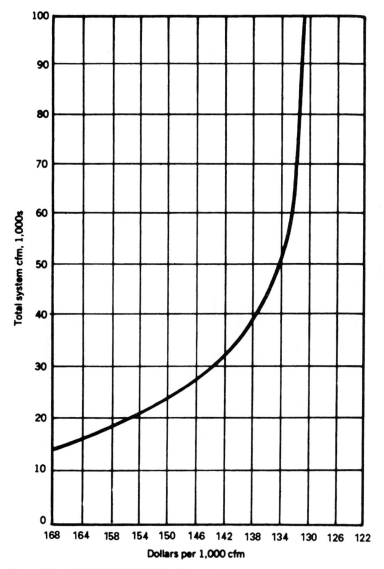

**Figure 2.16   COST OF BALANCING AND TESTING**
*Based on average for low-pressure multizone face and bypass systems; includes complete balance and certified report on all components for both hot and cold deck. Air-conditioning (AC) contractor credits the estimate when an independent balancing agency is specified.*

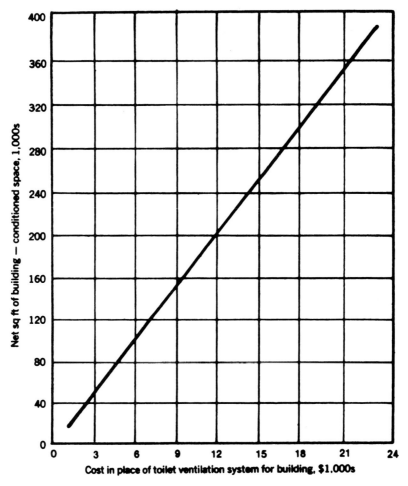

**Figure 2.17 COST IN PLACE**
**Exhaust Systems for Public Toilets in Office Buildings**
*Based on an average population of one person per 100 sq ft of conditioned space, minimum facilities per National Plumbing Code, and 10 air changes per toilet.*

## CHECK FIGURES

Speed estimates for qualifying projects are presented in Table 2.1. These are based on broad averages derived from analysis of thousands of jobs using standard application. Square feet per ton is an average figure; dollar *cost per ton* is approximate only. Actual costs, depending on the system selected, can vary substantially from these figures. Early-1994 roundup costs as reported from several sources showed air-conditioning selling prices to be as follows: residences, $800 to $1,200 per ton; rooftops, $1,300 per ton; mixed TX equipment on cooling tower condenser water, $1,500 to $1,800 per ton; chilled-water systems, $2,000 to $2,300 per ton.

As a percent of total building cost, the mechanical proportion for *hospitals* is considerably higher than that in most buildings, and in some cases it exceeds 40%.

**TABLE 2.1**  Speed Check Data—Comfort Cooling

Based on minimum cost for basic system.

| Application | sq ft per ton | Cost per ton, $* |
|---|---|---|
| Apartments | 500 | 1,800 |
| Banks | 240 | 2,200 |
| Bars and taverns | 90 | 1,700 |
| Barbershops | 250 | 1,700 |
| Beauty shops | 180 | 1,800 |
| Bowling alleys | 175 | 2,100 |
| Churches | 20† | 1,600 |
| Department stores | 350 | 1,700 |
| Drugstores | 150 | 1,600 |
| Hospitals | 280 | 2,800 |
| Hotels—guest rooms | 275 | 2,500 |
| Hotels—public spaces | 220 | 2,200 |
| Libraries, 50% relative humidity | 240 | 1,900 |
| Office buildings, multistory | 275 | 2,800 |
| Office buildings, single- or two-story | 340 | 2,800 |
| Offices, executive, small suites | 280 | 3,000 |
| Retail stores | 250 | 1,700 |
| Restaurants | 200 | 1,700 |
| Shoe stores | 220 | 1,700 |
| Specialty stores | 200 | 1,800 |
| Supermarkets | 350 | 2,000 |
| Theaters and auditoriums | 18† | 1,700 |

*These costs vary significantly with building size.
†Persons per ton.

Tables 2.2 to 2.5, for *apartment buildings, schools,* and *hospitals,* provide median cost information for those types of buildings. The data provided are taken from *Means Mechanical Cost Data 1994,* R.S. Means Co., Kingston, Mass. The cost figures are 1994 median figures, not averages; in other words, of the projects analyzed and reported by Means, 50% had lower costs and 50% had higher costs. In these tables, the individual median figures will not normally total up exactly to the sums and percents shown as averages would. Nevertheless, this information furnishes excellent check data for evaluating estimates.

**TABLE 2.2**  Check Data for Apartments—Square Foot Costs

| Application | Median cost per sq ft, $ | Percent of total building cost |
|---|---|---|
| Low-rise (1–3 story): | | |
| Plumbing | 3.87 | 9.0 |
| HVAC | 2.33 | 5.8 |
| Electrical | 2.93 | 6.7 |
| Total mechanical and electrical | 8.05 | 18.3 |
| Mid-rise (4–7 story): | | |
| Plumbing | 4.67 | 7.4 |
| Electrical | 4.52 | 7.2 |
| Total mechanical and electrical | 11.7 | 20.1 |
| High-rise (8–24 story): | | |
| Plumbing | 4.97 | 9.1 |
| Electrical | 5.05 | 7.6 |
| Total mechanical and electrical | 14.25 | 22 |

**TABLE 2.3** Check Data for Apartments—Unit Costs

| Application | Median cost, total $ per apartment unit | Mechanical and electrical cost per unit, $ |
|---|---|---|
| Low-rise (1–3 story) | $44,200 | $8,000 |
| Mid-rise (4–7 story) | 56,400 | 13,000 |
| High-rise (8–24 story) | 61,900 | 14,700 |

**TABLE 2.4** Check Data for School Buildings—Square Foot and per Pupil Costs

| Application | Median cost per sq ft, $ | Percent of total project cost | Per pupil cost, $ |
|---|---|---|---|
| Elementary schools: | | | |
| Plumbing | 4.74 | 7.1 | — |
| Heating and ventilating | 8.00 | 10.8 | — |
| Electrical | 6.60 | 10.0 | — |
| Total mechanical and electrical | 17.45 | 26.0 | 2,285 |
| Total project costs | 69.50 | — | 9,700 |
| Junior high and middle schools: | | | |
| Plumbing | 4.28 | 6.9 | — |
| HVAC | 8.35 | 11.5 | — |
| Electrical | 6.85 | 9.3 | — |
| Total mechanical and electrical | 17.15 | 26.8 | — |
| Total project costs | 71.20 | — | 8,400 |
| Senior high schools: | | | |
| Plumbing | 5.35 | 6.5 | — |
| HVAC | 8.15 | 11.5 | — |
| Electrical | 7.95 | 10.0 | — |
| Total mechanical and electrical | 20.05 | 24.3 | — |
| Total project costs | 71.05 | — | 9,950 |
| Vocational schools: | | | |
| Plumbing | 4.90 | 6.9 | — |
| HVAC | 8.35 | 12.1 | — |
| Electrical | 7.30 | 11.3 | — |
| Total mechanical and electrical | 18.05 | 28.3 | — |
| Total project costs | 68.35 | — | 18,500 |

**TABLE 2.5** Check Data for Hospitals

| Item | Median cost per sq ft, $ | Percent of total cost |
|---|---|---|
| Total Cost | 1.30 | — |
| Plumbing | 12.20 | 9.1 |
| HVAC | 17.60 | 13.8 |
| Electrical | 15.25 | 12.0 |
| Total mechanical and electrical | 42.60 | 34.0 |
| (Median total cost per bed = $54,200) | | |

**TABLE 2.6**  Check Data for Typical Heating and Cooling Costs, 1994

| Heating systems | $ per sq ft |
|---|---|
| Small hydronic, electric boiler, steam heat, fin-tube baseboard radiation (1,480 sq ft) | 8.81 |
| Large hydronic, electric boiler, hot-water heat, unit heaters (9,280 sq ft) | 4.35 |
| Hydronic, fossil fuel (gas) fired boiler, hot-water heat, unit heaters (1,070 sq ft) | 10.82 |
| Hydronic, fossil fuel (gas) fired boiler, hot-water heat, fin-tube radiation (1,070 sq ft) | 15.50 |
| Residential oil-fired, forced hot water, fin-tube radiation (1,000 sq ft) | 8.54 |
| Factory or commercial, oil-fired, forced hot water, fin-tube radiation (1,000 sq ft) | 16.60 |
| Apartment corridor air conditioning | |
| Fan-coil unit and packaged chiller, air-cooled (3,000 sq ft) | 8.27 |
| Packaged chiller, water-cooled, fan-coil unit (4,000 sq ft) | 9.38 |
| Rooftop, single-zone (500 sq ft) | 6.08 |
| Rooftop, multizone (3,000 sq ft) | 10.08 |
| Self-contained, water-cooled (500 sq ft) | 4.52 |
| Self-contained, air-cooled (500 sq ft) | 6.29 |
| Split system, air cooled condensing units (1,000 sq ft) | 3.05 |

**TABLE 2.7**  Typical Costs for Heating, Ventilation, and Air Conditioning (1994)

| Structure | Total sq ft | Floors high | Total bldg. cost, $ | Cost of HVAC, $ | Percent total bldg. cost | HVAC cost, $/sq ft |
|---|---|---|---|---|---|---|
| Hospital (HVAC only) | 50,000 | 3 | 6,500,000 | 900,000 | 13.8 | 18.00 |
| (complete mechanical) | | | | 2,210,000 | 34.0 | 44.20 |
| Bank | 16,000 | 1 | 1,570,000 | 112,800 | 7.2 | 7.05 |
| Church | 10,000 | 1 | 690,000 | 69,000 | 10.0 | 6.90 |
| Library | 40,000 | 3 | 3,400,000 | 375,000 | 11.0 | 9.38 |
| Shopping center | 140,000 | 1 | 6,600,000 | 574,000 | 8.7 | 4.10 |
| Motel | 70,000 | 4 | 4,600,000 | 257,600 | 5.6 | 3.68 |
| Retail store | 10,000 | 1 | 439,000 | 38,200 | 8.7 | 3.82 |
| Office buildings | 10,000 | 2 | 553,000 | 57,500 | 10.4 | 5.75 |
| | 300,000 | 6 | 21,000,000 | 1,950,000 | 9.3 | 6.50 |
| Apartment | 80,000 | 6 | 3,650,000 | 200,800 | 5.5 | 2.51 |
| Elementary school | 30,000 | 1 | 2,220,000 | 240,000 | 10.8 | 8.00 |

Table 2.6 provides information on typical costs of heating and air-conditioning systems. Table 2.7 provides typical 1994 selling prices for HVAC systems installed in a variety of building types and locations. Information provided in both of these tables is also taken from *Means Mechanical Cost Data 1994*.

Tables 2.8 to 2.10 provide unit cost speed check data for hospitals, schools, and some miscellaneous special applications.

Table 2.11[1] gives both engineering design data and budget cost estimating data for a wide range of commercial and industrial air-conditioning applications. For each item, engineering

---

[1] Table 2.11 does not appear on the computer disk provided with this book.

is shown first; cost pricing follows. As with all budget data and rule-of-thumb tables, the estimator must apply these data with caution. Prices may vary greatly by geography, building orientation, overall design, capacity, local wage scales, and other market variables. The risk of oversimplification is always present; however, if intelligently applied and judiciously used, the information in this table can save many hours of work and can be extremely helpful for preparing conceptual and preliminary estimates.

**TABLE 2.8**   Speed Check Data for Hospitals

| Item | Unit | $ per unit |
|---|---|---|
| Refrigeration system, including condensing circuit and interconnecting pipe | ton | 1,350 |
| Duct system, including fans, filters, and insulation | cfm | 4.48 |
| Kitchen and fume hood exhaust | cfm | 5.13 |
| Cooling system, complete | ton | 3,000 |
| Cooling system, complete | sq ft | 13.75 |
| Direct radiation | sq ft | 11.00 |
| Boiler plant, complete | lb/hr steam | 14.95 |

**TABLE 2.9**   Speed Check Data for School Buildings

| System type | $/sq ft |
|---|---|
| Package units | 5.25 |
| All air, single duct | 6.15 |
| All air, multizone | 6.50 |
| All air, single duct with reheat | 6.60 |
| Double duct, low velocity | 7.00 |
| Dual conduit, high velocity | 7.35 |
| Unit ventilators | 7.50 |
| Dual duct, high velocity | 8.25 |

**TABLE 2.10**   Speed Check Data—Special Applications

| Application | Sq ft/ton | $/ton cost |
|---|---|---|
| Data processing rooms, 50% relative humidity | 240 | 2,625 |
| Medical offices, waiting rooms | 150 | 1,950 |
| Printing and lithography shops, 50% RH | 240 | 2,000 |
| Textile mills, 50% RH | 275 | 1,800 |
| Skating rinks, indoors, refrigeration (excluding floor) | 100 | 1,900 |
| Chicken-house air conditioning, 50% RH | 200 | 2,000 |
| Cold storage warehouse, 35°F (1.7°C) | 500 | 3,000 |

**TABLE 2.11**  Detailed Budget Estimating Data

| Engineering and pricing | |
|---|---|

Engineering
**1. Load calculations**

| | |
|---|---|
| People—people/ton refrigeration | = 30 |
| Lights—kW/ton refrigeration | = 3.53 |
| Motors—hp/ton refrigeration | = 4.7 |
| Heat gain—sq ft/ton refrigeration (walls, floor, ceiling) | = 2,000 @ 20°F $\Delta T$ |
| Heat gain—sq ft/ton refrigeration (glass, single pane) | |
| North exposure | 375 |
| NE and NW exposure | 91 |
| E and W exposure | 71 |
| SE and SW exposure | 94 |
| South exposure | 150 |
| Circulated air—cfm/ton refrigeration | = 400 |
| Refrigeration service factor | = 20% of heat gain |
| Refrigeration product factor | = 50% of heat gain |
| Tons/person | = 0.033 |
| Tons/kW | = 0.283 |
| Tons/horsepower (hp) | = 0.213 |
| Tons/1,000 sq ft (walls, floor, ceiling) | = 0.50 |
| Tons/1,000 sq ft (glass, single pane) | |
| North exposure | 2.7 |
| NE and NW exposure | 11.0 |
| E and W exposure | 14.1 |
| SE and SW exposure | 10.6 |
| South exposure | 6.7 |
| Tons/1,000 cfm | = 2.50 |

**2. Compressor horsepower per ton at various temperature levels**

| Evaporator temperature, °F | Bhp per ton |
|---|---|
| 40 | 1.0 |
| 25 | 1.25 |
| −5 | 2.0 |
| −35 | 3.0 |
| −65 | 4.5 |
| −95 | 6.0 |

**3. Approximate turbine steam rates—lb water/hp/hr**

| | |
|---|---|
| 125-psi inlet—5-psi exhaust | 40 lbs/hp/hr |
| 125-psi inlet—26-in. vacuum condensing | 15 lbs/hp/hr |
| 5-psi inlet—26-in. vacuum condensing | 30 lbs/hp/hr |

**4. Approximate condenser water rates**

| | |
|---|---|
| Ammonia applications with cooling towers | 4–5 gpm/ton |
| Ammonia applications with city water | 3 gpm/ton |
| Refrigerants R-12 and R-22 with cooling towers | 2–3 gpm/ton |
| Refrigerants R-12 and R-22 with city water | 2 gpm/ton |
| With 55°F well water, use 1 gpm/ton for all refrigerants | |
| Lithium bromide absorption with cooling towers | 3–3.6 gpm/ton |
| For condenser operation, use 30 gal. degrees/min/evap. ton at about 40°F evaporator | |

(*Continued*)

**TABLE 2.11** Detailed Budget Estimating Data   (*Continued*)

---

### Engineering and pricing  (*Cont.*)

**Engineering**  (*Cont.*)

**5. Approximate condenser heat rejection rates**

| Evaporator temperature, °F | Approx. rejection per 1,000 Btu evaporator load |
|---|---|
| +50 | 1,200 |
| 0 | 1,500 |
| −50 | 1,800 |
| −100 | 2,100 |
| −150 | 2,400 |
| −200 | 2,700 |
| −250 | 3,000 |

$$\text{Actual gallon degrees/ton} = \frac{30 \times \text{approx. rejection above}}{1,250}$$

**6. Approximate condensing surface per ton refrigeration**

| | |
|---|---|
| Evaporative condensers for ammonia | 12–20 sq ft/ton |
| Horizontal condensers for ammonia | 5–10 sq ft/ton |
| Vertical condensers for ammonia | 10 sq ft/ton |
| Evaporative condensers for refrigerants R-12 and R-22 | 8–11 sq ft/ton |
| Horizontal condensers for refrigerants R-12 and R-22 | 6–10 sq ft/ton |

**7. Approximate chilled-water and brine flow rates**

| | |
|---|---|
| Chilled water for air conditioning | $1\frac{1}{2}$–3 gpm/ton |
| Brine for general-purpose refrigeration | 4–7 gpm/ton |
| Brine for skating rinks | 10–14 gpm/ton |
| For chilled water, use | 24 gal. degrees/min/ton |
| For brine, use | 28 gal. degrees/min/ton |

**8. Approximate cooling surface per ton refrigeration**

| | |
|---|---|
| Horizontal coolers for ammonia | 8–10 sq ft/ton |
| Horizontal coolers for refrigerants R-12 and R-22 | 6–10 sq ft/ton |

**9. Pump brake horsepower (based on 70% efficiency)**

$$\text{Bhp} = \frac{\text{gpm} \times \text{ft head} \times \text{specific gravity}}{2,800}$$

**10. Fan brake horsepower (based on 61% efficiency)**

$$\text{Bhp} = \frac{\text{cfm} \times \text{total pressure (in. of } H_2O)}{4,000}$$

**11. Cooling tower size**
Forced draft
For refrigerants R-12 and R-22, use 1.28 sq ft floor area per ton refrigeration
For ammonia, increase floor area by 50%

---

### Budget cost estimating

**Definition of terms used in budget estimating**

*Refrigeration system* (reciprocating or centrifugal) includes high-side and low-side equipment, interconnecting mains and installation

*High-side equipment* includes compressor, prime mover and controls, water-cooled condenser and receiver

*Low-side equipment* includes water cooler, brine cooler, direct expansion conditioner, or room piping. Interconnecting mains include refrigerant mains, insulation, and refrigerant charge

*Installation* includes freight, cartage, rigging, and erection
Evaporative and air-cooled condensers are priced as an addition

**TABLE 2.11**  Detailed Budget Estimating Data  (*Continued*)

1994 Dollars per ton refrigeration on delivered and erected basis

| Refrigeration system range, tons | Evaporator temperature, °F | | | | | |
|---|---|---|---|---|---|---|
| | 50 | 40 | 30 | 20 | 0 | −20 |
| 2–9 | 1,400 | 1,600 | 1,900 | 2,400 | 3,400 | 5,000 |
| 10–49 | 1,000 | 1,150 | 1,450 | 1,800 | 2,400 | 3,300 |
| 50–249 | 700 | 800 | 950 | 1,200 | 1,200 | 2,500 |
| ≥250 | 350 | 400 | 450 | 200 | 1,100 | 1,600 |

*Note:* These figures based on field-installed components. For small tonnages, look at packages such as plug refrigeration units and produce and frozen storage units.

### 1. Apparel stores
*Engineering:* 200–300 sq ft floor area per ton refrigeration
$1,200–$1,600/ton for complete bill of material

### 2. Bakeries
**(a) Dough mixers**
*Engineering:* 2 tons refrigeration per 1,000 lb bread/hr, 400 lb water/1,000 lb bread/hr for ingredient water delivered at 35°F
$2,400–$3,000/ton, 10–25-ton capacity for complete bill of material
**(b) Fermentation rooms**
*Engineering:* 1,000 sq ft/ton refrigeration; 78–80°F dry bulb (db) and 80% RH

### 3. Banks
*Engineering:* 200–350 sq ft floor area/ton
$1,400–$2,400/ton for complete bill of material

### 4. Barber shops
*Engineering:* 150–300 sq ft floor area/ton
$1,200–$1,800/ton for complete bill of material

### 5. Beauty shops
*Engineering:* 100–200 sq ft floor area/ton
$1,200–$1,800/ton for complete bill of material

### 6. Beverages
Soft drinks
*Engineering:* 33–40°F final chilled-water temperature
$2,000–$3,000/ton for 25–50-ton-capacity R-22 system
$1,200–$1,800/ton for 50–150-ton-capacity R-22 system
$1,200–$1,800/ton for 100–200-ton-capacity R-717 system
$1,100–$1,600/ton for 200–300-ton-capacity R-717 system

*Note:* 30–40% of above budget prices is for customer-furnished evaporator

(*Continued*)

**TABLE 2.11**   Detailed Budget Estimating Data   (*Continued*)

**7. Breweries**

*Engineering:* beer and wort coolers operate at approximately 45-psig (pounds per square inch gauge) suction ($NH_3$)

Storages operate at approximately 20-psig suction ($NH_3$)

**(a) Up to 500 barrels/day output**

*Engineering:* 2.16 barrels/ton refrigeration

$450/barrel for refrigeration system

$1,150/ton for refrigeration system

**(b) From 500 to 1,500 barrels/day output**

*Engineering:* 2.50 barrels/ton refrigeration

$350/barrel for refrigeration system

$1,000/ton for refrigeration system

**(c) From 1,500 to 3,000 barrels/day output**

*Engineering:* 3.00 barrels/ton refrigeration

$250/barrel for refrigeration system

$750/ton for refrigeration system

**8. Chemical chlorine**

*Engineering:* chlorine condensing requires 1.00 ton refrigeration per ton of chlorine condensed per day

$1,000–$1,600/ton for refrigeration system

**9. Cold-storage warehouses** (limited to 500,000 cu ft room volume)

*Engineering:* Figure 1 ton refrigeration/350 sq ft floor area or 5,000 cu ft room volume based on 4-, 6-, and 8-in. insulation for 35, 0, and −20°F rooms, respectively

Figure 75% total volume available for storage space and 25% for aisle and air-circulation spaces

Dollars/ton vary depending on central station vs. packages:

  35°F room, central station $2,700 per ton of refrigeration; packages $2,300/TR

  0°F room, central station, $3,400/TR; packages $3,000/TR

  −20°F room, central station $4,200/TR; packages $1,600/TR

**10. Dairies**

**(a) Ice flakes**

*Engineering:* 8 lb/iced crate; ice every other crate

$2,650/TR for refrigeration system

$3,775/ton ice for refrigeration system

**(b) Ice cream**

*Engineering:* 13 TR for complete plant/1,000 gal. ice cream per day

3.5 TR/100 gal. ice cream frozen/hr

0.33 TR/100 gal. ice cream hardened/day

Size of hardening room determined at 3 times peak load based on 16 gal./sq ft floor area which includes allowance for aisle space

$3,000–$3,800/ton

$6,200–$7,600/100 gal. ice cream frozen/hr

$600–$800/100 gal. ice cream hardened/day

**(c) Milk storage rooms**

*Engineering:* 100 sq ft floor area/ton (33°F ±1°)

75% useful room volume; 25% for unit, aisle, and air distribution

$3,500/ton for refrigeration system

**(d) Plate-type exchangers, raw-milk cooling**

*Engineering:* None

$500/1,000 lb milk/hr for plate unit

**(e) Plate-type pasteurizers**

**TABLE 2.11**  Detailed Budget Estimating Data    (*Continued*)

Cut 1 Duty: high-temperature short time

  Includes

    Frame, connections, and plates
    Panel board and controls
    Brine controls (if required)
    Holder tube
    Balance tank
    Hot-water set, bypass, and ejector
    Metering milk pump
    Centrifugal milk pump (>10,000 lb)
    Thermometers

  Controls
    Taylor cold-milk recorder
    Taylor brine recorder

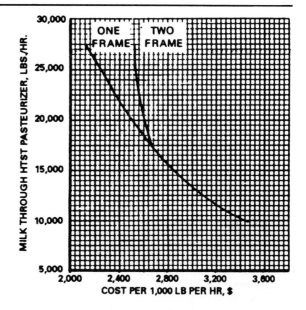

**(f) Receiving plants**
*Engineering:* 40 gal. milk (4 cans) cooled 72–38°F/hr = 1 TR
Brine instantaneous system, $750/ton for refrigeration system
Brine storage system, $\frac{3}{7}$ of the instantaneous load
$1,800/ton for refrigeration system
$450/can for refrigeration system

**11. Department stores**
*Engineering:*
Main floor—225–300 sq ft/ton refrigeration
Upper floors—275–400 sq ft/ton refrigeration
$2,000–$2,400/ton complete HVAC
$2,400–$3,000/ton plumbing, electrical, and mechanical

**12. Drugs and pharmaceuticals**
**Drying**
*Engineering:* batch process—modern trend is to start at 50 microns (−50°F) and finish at 18 microns (−65°F); some products start at 18 microns (−65°F) and finish at 4 microns (−85°F); 60% of load first 5 hr, and 40% next 15 hr for 24-hr cycle
Water vapor condensing load including losses figured at 1,500 Btu/lb
Refrigeration system—$5,000–$7,000/ton depending on temperature level

**13. Drug stores**
*Engineering:* 200–300 sq ft floor area/TR
$1,200–$1,700/ton for cooling
$400–$800/ton addition for heating

(*Continued*)

**TABLE 2.11**   Detailed Budget Estimating Data   (*Continued*)

14. **Factory air conditioning**
    *Engineering* (*based on rooftop units*): 150–300 sq ft floor area/ton
    Total circulated air 2–3 cfm/sq ft floor area
    Ventilation ½–1 cfm/sq ft floor area
    *Air conditioning and heating:* $440–$500/ton or $2.20–$2.50/sq ft floor area
    Installation:
    $350–$500/ton or $2.30–$3.30/sq ft floor area
    (Power wiring and architectural work not included)

15. **Fast-food places**
    **Air conditioning**
    *Engineering:* 12–15 cfm/outside air/person
    150–300 sq ft floor area/TR
    $800–$1,400/ton complete bill of material

16. **Fish**
    **Fishing boats—tuna clippers**
    *Engineering:* size 120–200 ft long; assume 100 tons catch over 1–3-week period
    Storage capacity 400–1,400 tons catch; actual refrigeration load ≤240 tons for a 250-ft clipper
    Cost of refrigeration approximately 10% of cost of ship

17. **Food stores**
    **Air conditioning**
    *Engineering:* 400–500 sq ft floor area/TR
    $300/hp for complete bill of material

18. **Foods, other**
    **(a) Candy**
    *Engineering:*
    Manufacturing—hard candy 65–75°F dry bulb (db), 40–50% RH
    Chocolate candy 60–75°F db, 40–50% RH
    Use 150–225 sq ft/TR
    Enrobing—75–80°F db, 17–19% RH
    Tunnel
       Hard candy—55°F db, 55°F dewpoint
       Chocolate candy—45°F db, 45°F dewpoint
    Storage—68 ± 3°F db, 45°F RH ± 5%
    250–400 sq ft/ton depending on size
    Starch curing rooms—some products at 72°F db and 45% RH; other products at 115°F db and 25% RH
    Cost/ton is normally 30–50% higher than standard air-conditioning cost
    **(b) Shrimp freezing (shipboard)**
    *Engineering:* 1 ton product/day equals 1.5 TR
    150–170 Btu to freeze 1 lb shrimp from seawater temperature to −5°F
    1,000–2,000-W generator for controls, pumps, fans, etc.
    11,000–14,000 Btuh/trawler
    $20,000–$40,000/trawler depending on whether a single or double compressor unit is utilized
    **(c) Fruits and vegetables**
    *Engineering:* use unit coolers; 5,000–7,500 sq ft; 250–300 sq ft/ton; above 7,500 sq ft, 400–500 sq ft/ton
    $10–$14/sq ft for 5,000–7,500 sq ft
    $8–$12/sq ft above 7,500 sq ft

**TABLE 2.11**   Detailed Budget Estimating Data   (*Continued*)

**19. Hospitals**
*Engineering:*
**(a) Contagious wards, nurseries, and operating rooms**
Can recirculate with provisions for dual filtering, 30% efficient filter upstream and 80% efficient filter downstream of air unit
Figure 12 total recirculations of air per hour, of which a minimum of 5 of these recirculations are to be outside air
**(b) Private rooms**
Figure 2 outside air changes per hour per room
**(c) Air-conditioning load**
275–350 ton/sq ft for entire building
Central system installed including ducts and pipes and terminal units, $2,800/ton
For breakout on ducts, figure $2.40/lb sheet metal
For ice requirements, figure 6 total ice makers per 120-bed hospital at $2,500/ice machine (a mixture of flakers and cubers)
**(d) Domestic hot-water requirements**
14½ gal./hr per bed for hospital with laundry
10½ gal./hr per bed for hospital without laundry
**(e) Domestic cold-water requirements**
Figure ½ domestic hot-water requirements listed in **(d)** above; this includes water for drinking fountains which utilize unitary cooling apparatus
**(f) Kitchen (dietary areas)**
Figure minimum of 6 outside air changes per hour
Figure 100 cfm of induction air for range hoods per sq ft range hood area

**20. Hotels**
**Air conditioning**
*Engineering:* 275–300 sq ft/ton refrigeration (public spaces treated separately)
$2,000–$2,600/ton for complete HVAC

**21. Meat packing**
**(a) Bacon-slicing room**
*Engineering:* 200 sq ft floor area/TR
45–50°F db—inside condition
$1,600–$2,400/ton for refrigeration system including ductwork
**(b) Chill room**
*Engineering:* 4000 lb meat/ton/24 hr including heat leakage
Air units sized and selected for 1 air change/min for beef, and 1–1¼ air changes/min for pork are advisable and will usually balance load requirements
$1,600–$2,400/ton for refrigeration system including ductwork
**(c) Quick freezing**
*Engineering:* 1 ton product/day = 2.0 TR
$2,400–$3,200/ton for refrigeration system ≤200 tons
$2,000–$2,400/ton for refrigeration system, >200 tons

**22. Offices**
**(a) Private**
*Engineering:* standard comfort conditions—low noise level; 180–200 sq ft floor area/ton
$3,000–$3,500/ton
**(b) General**
*Engineering:* standard comfort conditions, 200–400 sq ft floor area/ton
$1,000–$1,600/ton for complete bill of material
**(c) Medical**
*Engineering:* standard comfort conditions—50% outside air; 150–200 sq ft floor area/ton
$4,000–$5,600/ton for complete bill of material
*Note:* outside air depends on medical requirements

(*Continued*)

**TABLE 2.11** Detailed Budget Estimating Data  (*Continued*)

23. **Office buildings**
    *Engineering:* 100 sq ft/person net internal air-conditioned area
    *Note:* toilet rooms, stair tower, elevators, etc., are not in air-conditioned area
    Lights—6 W/sq ft
    200–340 sq ft/ton (5.0 tons/1,000 sq ft)
    $25/sq ft (total building area) plumbing, electrical, and mechanical
    $15/sq ft (total building area) heating, ventilating, and  air conditioning
    $2,400–$3,000/ton complete HVAC
    $2,800–$3,600/ton complete plumbing, electrical, mechanical

24. **Natural-gas processing plants**
    *Engineering:* average plant sized for 100 million cubic feet gas processed/day (100 M cu ft/day); a
    100-M-cu-ft/day plant may require 2,000–3,000 hp of compression for large field-erected refrigera-
    tion systems
    Figure at $250 per hp including drivers for centrifugal compression; other system components such
    as chillers and condensers must be figured separately according to specific requirements of each
    job
    Gas-compression requirements are a function of field pressures, processing pressures, and pipeline
    pressures

25. **Petrochemical and refining plants**
    Typical petrochemical plants are sized for 300–600 tons product/day; plant costs vary widely from
    $30,000/ton/day to as high as $60,000/ton/day
    Refining plants may be sized for 10,000–20,000 barrels product/day at $500–$900 per barrel initial
    plant cost
    For both petrochemical and refining plants, figure, as a rule of thumb, that 50% of all plants
    require some refrigeration and that 5% of plant cost is refrigeration cost
    Gas-compression requirements vary too widely to predict, depending on pressures and flow require-
    ments
    Figure $250 per hp for centrifugal compressor sets with drivers in the 2,000–3,000-hp range for
    either gas compression or as parts of large field-erected refrigeration systems

26. **Printing and lithography**
    *Engineering:* 75–77°F db; 45–50% RH close tolerances; year-around conditions
    Figure 200–250 sq ft floor area/ton
    $1,800–$2,400/ton for complete bill of material ($2,700–$1,900/ton in large metropolitan areas)
    $1,400–$1,900/ton for smaller and simpler installations

27. **Residences—apartment buildings**
    *Engineering:*
    Small apartment (3-room) 1 ton/apt.
    Large apartment (5-room) $1\frac{1}{2}$ tons/apt.
    $1,700–$2,000/ton, 2-pipe fan-coil unit, no automatic unit control
    $2,200–$2,600/ton, 2-pipe fan-coil unit with automatic unit control

28. **Ships**
    **(a) Marine ship's service (35°F)**
    *Engineering:* 1,000 cu ft room volume/TR ($\leq$ 2,000 cu ft)
    1,500 cu ft room volume/TR (> 2,000 cu ft)
    $7,500/ton above 1 ton (per U.S. Maritime specifications, which call for spare equipment for all
    movable parts plus 100% reserve)
    **(b) Marine cargo space (35°F)**
    *Engineering:* 1,000 cu ft room volume/TR
    $3,200/ton fob (free-on-board) shipping point; does not include seawater piping or pumps, brine
    piping or pumps, or insulation
    **(c) Marine cargo space (0°F)**
    *Engineering:* 2,000 cu ft room volume/TR
    $4,000/ton for refrigeration system, fob  shipping point in accordance with maritime specifications;
    does not include seawater piping or pumps, brine piping or pumps, or insulation

**TABLE 2.11**   Detailed Budget Estimating Data   (*Continued*)

**29. Shoe stores**
*Engineering:* 200–300 sq ft floor area/ton
$700–$1,200/ton for cooling
$400–$800/ton for heating

**30. Theaters (or auditoriums)**
*Engineering:* air circulation 25 cfm/person; outside air—6 cfm/person; 6 tons/100 seats; 18
seats/TR; low noise level in church auditoriums; desirable to have multiple recirculating fans (1 for
each zone) with zone temperature control of return-air bypass; lobby to be treated as separate air-
conditioned area
$25–$40/seat for refrigeration system
$90–$120/seat for complete HVAC system

**31. Variety stores**
*Engineering:*
With lunch counter—150–250 sq ft floor area/ton
Without lunch counter—250–350 sq ft floor area/ton
$800–$1,200/ton for cooling
$300–$500/ton for heating

**32. Cold test rooms (automobile)**
*Engineering:*
Minimum operating temperature        −40°F
Pulldown range  +85 to −40°F
Pulldown time   8 hr
Type condensing medium  85°F tower water
Type insulation   aluminum sheets
Design temperature of insulation        −65°F
Termination of services      equipment room—within 25 ft
Design data
Pulldown
Heat from walls and ceiling            1.1 tons/1,000 sq ft
Heat from floor  9.4 tons/1,000 sq ft
Heat from objects in room  0.33 ton/2,000 lb
Electrical load    0.5 ton/1,000 cu ft
Air load          0.55 ton/1,000 cu ft
No-engine load   not running during pulldown
Holding
Transmission      1.05 tons/1,000 sq ft
Electrical        0.5 ton/1,000 cu ft
Combustion air  52 Btuh/#
Engine (no dynamometer) 1.25 tons/# fuel
Engine (with dynamometer)          1.1 tons/# fuel

$10,000–$12,500/low-stage TR; total installation turnkey including refrigerating equipment, insulation,
piping, room construction inside building, fire protection, carbon monoxide and combustible-gas
detection system, engineering, and control system

SOURCE:   This table has been adapted from the *York Budget and Data Book,* copyright 1971, used by permission of York
International Corporation. Cost figures have been adjusted to 1994 by the authors to reflect current practice and typical pricing. Data for cooling requirements have, in some cases, been adjusted to reflect changes in building design and
requirements since 1971. No adjustments have been made for R-123, R-134A, or any other new refrigerants that have
come into use since the publication of *ASHRAE Standard 34-1992.* York International, McGraw-Hill, and the authors
assume no responsibility for the use of any of these data.

# CHAPTER 3
# MECHANICAL COOLING AND REFRIGERATION EQUIPMENT

## GENERAL DISCUSSION

The installation and erection of mechanical equipment such as compressors, air units, air-cooled condensers, blowers, pumps, and tanks, as measured in workhours, will depend on the weight, physical dimensions, and type of crate. It will be necessary to know how the final pipe connections are to be made, as well as the working heights, confinements of space, and the required vibration elimination.

In most cases the unloading and moving of heavy equipment is handled through rigging and trucking subcontractors, with cranes, gin poles, derricks, winches, and jacks. Helicopters are finding increasing use in rigging, particularly in placing rooftop units. Smaller package units, warm-air furnaces, pumps, small boilers, etc. may be handled directly.

Varying job conditions will dictate how detailed the breakdown must be, and this must, of course, be left to the final judgment of the estimator. For a complete discussion on rigging, see Chap. 19.

The 1994 air-conditioning system selling prices were reported as follows:

| Item | $ per ton |
|---|---|
| Residential | 800–1,200 |
| Rooftops | 1,200–1,400 |
| Direct expansion, with cooling tower | 1,500–1,800 |
| Chilled water, with cooling water | 2,000–2,300 |

## ESTIMATING

The estimating data do not include air balancing. For a discussion of this activity, see Chap. 15. Workhours for installing and ringing out remote controls not self-contained in the equipment may be found in Chap. 13.

Equipment and material prices shown are average net to the air-conditioning contractor, freight allowed. If the equipment must be hauled from a local warehouse to the jobsite within a 10-mile radius, add $8.33 per cwt (hundredweight).

## SELF-CONTAINED PACKAGE WATER-COOLED UNITS

Data in Table 3.1 is based on factory-assembled floor-standing models completely piped and ready for cooling-tower or single-pass water hookup.

### Self-contained Water-Cooled Units—Condenser Hookups

Final connections at the condenser are based on the schematic in Fig. 3.1. A pump is used for either cooling-tower or well operation, and it may be located at the condenser or at the cooling-water source. Straight cooling costs about $350 per ton; heat pumps, $400 per ton.

**TABLE 3.1**   Self-Contained Water-Cooled Units

**Materials**

| Nominal tons | Number of compressors | Cooling unit, $ | Heat pump, $ | One-row steam coil, $ | Two-row steam coil, $ |
|---|---|---|---|---|---|
| 5 | 1 | 2,490 | 3,980 | 90 | 120 |
| 7½ | 1 | 3,460 | 4,560 | 105 | 180 |
| 10 | 2 | 4,890 | 5,880 | 190 | 240 |
| 15 | 2 | 6,780 | 7,660 | 230 | 260 |
| 20 | 2 | 7,690 | 8,390 | 240 | 280 |
| 25 | 3 | 9,330 | 10,960 | 280 | 320 |
| 30 | 2 | 11,640 | 13,180 | 290 | 340 |
| 35 | 3 | 12,550 | 14,280 | 310 | 410 |
| 40 | 1 | 15,580 | 16,960 | 360 | 430 |
| 50 | 1 | 18,440 | 19,880 | 380 | 460 |
| 60 | 4 | 21,960 | 23,480 | 410 | 490 |

**Erection workhours**

*Start and check* based on number of compressors given above. Remove and replace average-size plate glass window to bring unit into store; allow $400. Remove and replace door jamb; allow $300.

| Nominal tons | Weight, lb | Unload from truck | Move within 40 ft | Uncrate, set, and align | Start and check | Total workhours |
|---|---|---|---|---|---|---|
| 5 | 850 | 0.85 | 0.68 | 0.93 | 2.9 | 5.36 |
| 7½ | 1,200 | 1.10 | 1.15 | 1.44 | 3.8 | 7.49 |
| 10 | 1,900 | 1.70 | 1.81 | 2.28 | 5.8 | 11.59 |
| 15 | 2,450 | 2.20 | 2.33 | 2.95 | 7.6 | 15.08 |
| 20 | 3,000 | 2.70 | 2.85 | 3.60 | 7.6 | 16.75 |
| 25 | 4,000 | 3.60 | 3.80 | 5.75 | 9.8 | 22.95 |
| 30 | 4,800 | 3.80 | 4.80 | 8.20 | 10.5 | 27.30 |
| 35 | 5,000 | 4.05 | 5.00 | 9.50 | 11.6 | 30.15 |
| 40 | 5,500 | 4.40 | 5.55 | 10.55 | 10.0 | 30.15 |
| 50 | 6,400 | 5.20 | 6.40 | 12.40 | 12.8 | 36.80 |
| 60 | 7,700 | 6.70 | 7.75 | 14.60 | 17.5 | 46.55 |

For setting small package units on other than main deck where no elevator is available, allow the following workhours:

| Nominal tons | 3 | 5 | 7½ |
|---|---|---|---|
| Set on balcony of store | 8.0 | 11.0 | 13.5 |
| Set on second floor | 3.4 | 4.1 | 5.5 |
| Set on third floor | 5.2 | 6.7 | 8.4 |
| Set in basement | 2.3 | 4.3 | 7.0 |

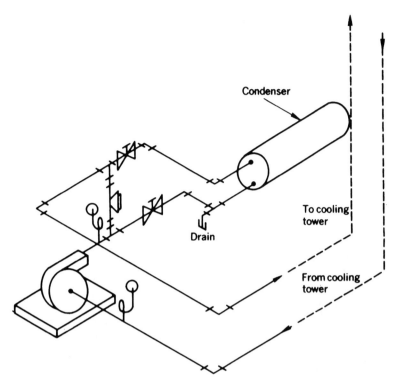

**Figure 3.1 CONDENSER WATER HOOKUP—SELF-CONTAINED PACKAGE UNIT**

Labor shown in Tables 3.2 and 3.3 includes handling pipe and fittings to within 40 ft from the truck to the equipment location, measuring, cutting, cleaning, soldering, and placing. It does not include hangers.

Material includes one 20-ft length of DWV drainage tube, three tees, six ells, two gate valves, one balancing cock, two gage cocks, one angle drain valve, and the necessary solder and flux for making up 29 joints.

**TABLE 3.2**  Water-Cooled Units—Condenser Hookups, Copper Tubing

| Nominal tons . . . . . . . . | 5 | 7½ | 10 | 15 | 20 | 25 |
|---|---|---|---|---|---|---|
| Pipe diameter, in. . . . . | 1½ | 1½ | 2 | 2 | 2½ | 2½ |
| Material, $ . . . . . . . . . . | 145 | 145 | 215 | 215 | 345 | 345 |
| **Workhours** . . . . . . . . . | 19.0 | 19.0 | 21.0 | 21.0 | 26.0 | 31.0 |
| Nominal tons . . . . . . . . | 30 | 35 | 40 | 50 | 60 | |
| Pipe diameter, in. . . . . | 3 | 3 | 3 | 3½ | 3½ | |
| Material, $ . . . . . . . . . . | 500 | 500 | 500 | 750 | 750 | |
| **Workhours** . . . . . . . . . | 34.0 | 34.0 | 34.0 | 42.0 | 42.0 | |

**TABLE 3.3** Water-Cooled Units—Condenser Hookups, Polyvinyl Chloride Tubing

| Nominal tons | 5 | 7½ | 10 | 15 | 20 | 25 |
|---|---|---|---|---|---|---|
| Pipe diameter, in. | 1½ | 1½ | 2 | 2 | 2½ | 2½ |
| Material, $ | 95 | 95 | 135 | 135 | 220 | 220 |
| Workhours | 10.5 | 10.5 | 13.0 | 13.0 | 18.0 | 18.0 |

| Nominal tons | 30 | 35 | 40 | 50 | 60 |
|---|---|---|---|---|---|
| Pipe diameter, in. | 3 | 3 | 3 | 3½ | 3½ |
| Material, $ | 350 | 350 | 350 | 550 | 550 |
| Workhours | 24.0 | 24.0 | 24.0 | 30.0 | 30.0 |

## Air and Water Requirements for Condensing Units

Air requirements of air-cooled condensing units may be estimated at 750 cfm/hp for refrigeration and 1,000 cfm/hp for air conditioning. For either application, air requirement is approximately 1,000 cfm/ton.

Water requirements for water-cooled condensing units may be estimated at 1.5 gpm/ton when using city water and 3 gpm/ton with a cooling tower.

## ROOFTOP PACKAGE UNITS

Rooftop units have accounted for a sizable portion of the market in recent years. In small sizes, self-contained, air-cooled package units may be attic-, transom-, or wall-mounted. For small sizes (3- to 5-ton systems) the standard procedure is to mount the unit flat on the roof on a pair of sleepers set in pitch pans. When the roof is constructed in an odd configuration or on more than one level, the sleepers are supported level on stanchions or angle iron. On existing gypsum roofs, the roof must be cut and vertical members must be supported from the structure below. Particularly for use with larger rooftop units, most manufacturers offer factory-built roof curbs. Depending on the size of equipment, roof curbs may be available in one price or be knocked down for assembly on the jobsite. Factory-shipped roof curbs are supplied with the necessary gasket material and screws.

Figure 3.2 shows a typical curb mounting with proper flashing and one of several available supply and return-air arrangements. Labor workhour data is based on uncrating, raising to a one-story roof with a high jack or truck-mounted forklift, setting the roof curb and unit, aligning and securing with bolts or guywires, and starting and checking. Wiring and condensate piping are not included. For costs of sleepers and pitch pans as well as skinning old roofs, see Chap. 17. To estimate standard rigging or helicopter rigging, see Chap. 19.

Table 3.4 covers material and erection labor for the complete line of rooftop units. For VAV terminal units compatible with rooftops, see Chap. 11.

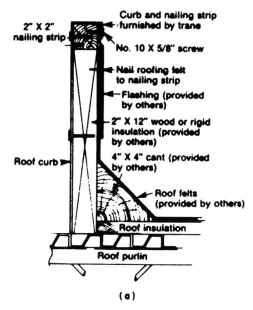

2" X 2"
nailing strip

Curb and nailing strip
·furnished by trane

No. 10 X 5/8" screw

Nail roofing felt
to nailing strip

Flashing (provided
by others)

2" X 12" wood or rigid
insulation (provided
by others)

4" X 4" cant (provided
by others)

Roof felts
(provided by others)

Roof curb

Roof insulation

Roof purlin

(a)

Note: Use 1-in. thick,6-lb-density fiberglass duct linear material.
Lined duct should be used for all returns.

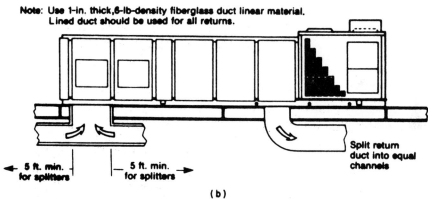

5 ft. min.
for splitters

5 ft. min.
for splitters

Split return
duct into equal
channels

(b)

**Figure 3.2   ROOFTOP PACKAGE UNIT, TYPICAL CURB MOUNTING AND AIR ARRANGEMENT**
*(Reproduced by permission of the Trane Company, LaCrosse, Wisc.)*

**TABLE 3.4** Self-Contained Rooftop Units

**2 to 5 tons—material**
Includes compressor, condenser, evaporator and associated piping, thermostat, filters, and 5-year compressor warranty. Side discharge.

| Nominal tons | 2 | 2½ | 3 | 3½ | 4 | 5 |
|---|---|---|---|---|---|---|
| Nominal cfm | 800 | 1,000 | 1,200 | 1,400 | 1,600 | 2,000 |
| Cooling only, $ | 1,380 | 1,441 | 1,890 | 1,865 | 2,133 | 2,487 |
| Add for electric heat, $ | 152 | 152 | 160 | 160 | 190 | 190 |
| Kilowatts | 5 | 5 | 5 | 5 | 10 | 10 |
| Heat pump, $ | 1,530 | 1,790 | 1,980 | 990 | 2,360 | 2,710 |
| Includes gas heat, $ | — | 1,860 | 2,140 | 2,280 | 2,450 | 2,915 |
| Accessories: | | | | | | |
|   Wall brackets, $ | 40 | 40 | 40 | 40 | 40 | 40 |
|   Roof curb, $* | 320 | 320 | 350 | 350 | 350 | 380 |

*Roof curb package includes provisions for 25% outside air.

**2 to 5 tons—hookups**

| Nominal tons | 2 | 2½ | 3 | 4 | 5 |
|---|---|---|---|---|---|
| Weight, lb | 300 | 350 | 380 | 475 | 675 |
| Ductwork, $ | 675 | 725 | 825 | 975 | 1,030 |
| Air distribution, $ | 125 | 170 | 180 | 205 | 275 |
| Insulation, $ | 395 | 430 | 450 | 500 | 550 |
|   Total material, $ | 1,195 | 1,325 | 1,455 | 1,680 | 1,855 |
| Erect and start, workhours | 4 | 4 | 4 | 4.5 | 6 |
| Extra to cut holes and flash on existing roof, $ | 241 | 241 | 241 | 276 | 276 |

**7½ to 17½ tons—material**
Includes compressor, condenser, evaporator and associated piping, thermostat, filters, 5-year compressor warranty, and packaged roof curb with provisions for 25% outside air. Side or downflow optional.

| Nominal tons | 7½ | 8½ | 10 | 12½ | 15 | 17½ |
|---|---|---|---|---|---|---|
| Nominal cfm | 3,000 | 3,400 | 4,000 | 5,000 | 6,000 | 7,000 |
| Cooling only, $ | 4,000 | 4,420 | 4,850 | 6,290 | 6,600 | 8,540 |
| Add for electric heat, $ | 265 | 352 | 352 | 352 | 352 | 519 |
| Kilowatts | 13 | 18 | 18 | 18 | 18 | 27 |
| Heat pump, $ | 4,660 | 5,320 | 5,890 | 7,330 | 7,810 | 9,690 |
| Electric heat supplement, $ | 230 | 230 | 230 | 230 | 310 | 310 |
| Kilowatts | 13 | 13 | 13 | 13 | 20 | 20 |
| Includes gas heat, $ | 4,260 | 5,120 | 5,330 | 7,120 | 7,450 | 9,420 |

**7½ to 17½ tons—hookups**

| Nominal tons | 7½ | 8½ | 10 | 12½ | 15 | 17½ |
|---|---|---|---|---|---|---|
| Weight, lb | 900 | 1,040 | 1,300 | 1,600 | 1,685 | 1,695 |
| Erect and start, workhours | 7.5 | 8 | 10 | 10 | 10 | 12 |
| Extra to cut holes and flash on existing roof, $ | 320 | 320 | 320 | 400 | 530 | 600 |

**TABLE 3.4**   Self-Contained Rooftop Units  (*Continued*)

**20 to 75 tons—material**

Includes refrigeration controls, thermostat, and filters.

| Nominal tons | 20 | 25 | 30 | 40 |
|---|---|---|---|---|
| Cooling only, $ | 11,680 | 12,690 | 16,660 | 19,590 |
| Includes electric heat, $ | 12,320 | 13,440 | 17,510 | 20,470 |
| Kilowatts | 30 | 30 | 30 | 50 |
| Includes gas heat, $ | 13,960 | 18,220 | 19,460 | 22,970 |
| Includes hot-water coil, $ | 12,960 | 13,890 | 18,220 | 21,680 |
| Includes steam coil, $ | 13,130 | 13,940 | 18,380 | 21,960 |
| Accessories: | | | | |
|    25% outside air, $ | 350 | 385 | 445 | 490 |
|    Fully automatic economizer, $ | 960 | 1,025 | 1,145 | 1,220 |
|    Modulating 100% exhaust fan, $ | 2,280 | 2,495 | 2,882 | 2,960 |
|    Downflow roof curb, $ | 520 | 520 | 580 | 585 |
|    Horizontal roof curb, $ | 1,490 | 1,490 | 1,530 | 1,630 |
|    VAV control, hot-gas bypass, | | | | |
|      inlet vanes and control, $ | 2,660 | 2,775 | 2,815 | 3,390 |

| Nominal tons | 50 | 55 | 60 | 75 |
|---|---|---|---|---|
| Cooling only, $ | 23,780 | 24,970 | 27,790 | 33,230 |
| Includes electric heat, $ | 24,880 | 25,890 | 29,160 | 34,980 |
| Kilowatts | 70 | 70 | 90 | 90 |
| Includes gas heat, $ | 27,690 | 29,280 | 31,970 | 38,730 |
| Includes hot-water coil, $ | 25,760 | 26,970 | 29,950 | 36,620 |
| Includes steam coil, $ | 25,200 | 26,260 | 29,630 | 35,920 |
| Accessories: | | | | |
|    25% outside air, $ | 480 | 480 | 520 | 610 |
|    Fully automatic economizer, $ | 1,380 | 1,380 | 1,465 | 1,525 |
|    Modulating 100% exhaust fan, $ | 2,460 | 2,910 | 3,465 | 4,100 |
|    Downflow roof curb, $ | 490 | 490 | 540 | 560 |
|    Horizontal roof curb, $ | 1,860 | 1,860 | 1,860 | 1,920 |
|    VAV control, hot-gas bypass, | | | | |
|      inlet vanes and control, $ | 3,675 | 3,675 | 3,780 | 3,990 |

**20 to 75 tons—hookups**

| Nominal tons | 20 | 25 | 30 | 40 |
|---|---|---|---|---|
| Nominal unit weight, lb | 4,000 | 4,800 | 5,550 | 7,500 |
| Roof curb weight, lb | 355 | 355 | 355 | 420 |
| Erect and start, workhours | 14 | 14 | 16 | 20 |

| Nominal tons | 50 | 55 | 60 | 75 |
|---|---|---|---|---|
| Nominal unit weight, lb | 8,850 | 8,900 | 9,200 | 10,000 |
| Roof curb weight, lb | 440 | 440 | 450 | 450 |
| Erect and start, workhours | 22 | 23 | 26 | 27 |

**TABLE 3.4** Self-Contained Rooftop Units (*Continued*)

**90 to 130 tons—material**
Includes fully automatic economizer with 100% outside air and complete VAV package with hot-gas bypass, inlet valves, and controls.

| Nominal tons | 90 | 105 | 115 | 130 |
|---|---|---|---|---|
| Cooling only, $ | 49,965 | 56,860 | 59,980 | 62,750 |
| Roof curbs, $ | 1,225 | 1,225 | 1,225 | 1,225 |

**90 to 130 tons—hookups**

| Nominal tons | 90 | 105 | 115 | 130 |
|---|---|---|---|---|
| Equipment weight, lb | 15,140 | 15,690 | 16,050 | 16,520 |
| Curb weight, lb | 720 | 770 | 770 | 770 |
| Erect and start, workhours | 32 | 35 | 40 | 45 |

## SPLIT AIR-COOLED PACKAGES

Split-system air-cooled equipment is available in a heavy-duty line for commercial and industrial application, and also in a small-tonnage range for light-duty residential application (Table 3.5). Table 3.6 includes the basic two-piece system of one high-side condensing unit and one low-side air-handler companion piece, factory-matched and ready for field piping.

**TABLE 3.5** Split-System Air-Cooled Package—Material

Includes condensing unit, evaporator, thermostat, filter box, filters, and 5-year compressor warranty.

| Nominal tons | 2 | 3 | 4 | 5 | 6¼ |
|---|---|---|---|---|---|
| Cooling only, $ | 1,380 | 1,640 | 2,290 | 2,490 | 2,895 |
| Add for electric heat, $ | 75 | 75 | 133 | 133 | 215 |
| kW | 5 | 5 | 10 | 10 | 10 |
| Heat pump, $ | 1,510 | 1,800 | 2,360 | 2,790 | 3,060 |
| Electric heat supplement, $ | 75 | 75 | 133 | 133 | 215 |
| kW | 5 | 5 | 10 | 10 | 10 |
| Nominal tons | 7½ | 10 | 12½ | 15 | |
| Cooling only, $ | 3,820 | 4,990 | 6,510 | 7,360 | |
| Add for electric heat, $ | 288 | 295 | 385 | 460 | |
| kW | 15 | 20 | 24 | 30 | |
| Heat pump, $ | 4,180 | 5,340 | — | 7,890 | |
| Electric heat supplement, $ | 215 | 245 | — | 260 | |
| kW | 10 | 18 | — | 20 | |
| Nominal tons | 20 | 25 | 30 | 40 | 50 |
| Cooling only, $ | 10,260 | 11,470 | 13,680 | 17,860 | 22,680 |
| Heat pump, $ | 10,930 | 12,140 | 14,490 | 18,990 | 24,960 |

*Note:* For sizes 20 through 50 tons, most manufacturers do not offer unit-mounted electric heat. However, duct-mounted heaters may be estimated at approximately **$30/kW.**

**TABLE 3.6**  Split-System Air-Cooled Packages

**Erection, workhours**

| Nominal tons | 3 | 5 | 7½ | 10 | 15 |
|---|---|---|---|---|---|
| Weight, lb. . . . . . . . . . . . . . . . | 550 | 750 | 900 | 1,600 | 2,100 |
| Unload from trailer . . . . . . . . . . | 0.85 | 1.16 | 1.40 | 2.50 | 3.25 |
| Move within 40 ft . . . . . . . . . . . | 0.66 | 0.90 | 1.08 | 1.90 | 2.51 |
| Uncrate, set, and align  . . . . . . . . | 1.00 | 1.36 | 1.64 | 2.90 | 3.82 |
| Hang air handler . . . . . . . . . . . . | 3.50 | 4.20 | 4.50 | 5.00 | 7.00 |
| **Total workhours** . . . . . . . . . . . | 6.01 | 7.62 | 8.62 | 12.30 | 16.58 |
| Nominal tons | 20 | 25 | 30 | 40 | 50 |
| Weight, lb. . . . . . . . . . . . . . . . | 3,200 | 3,700 | 4,500 | 5,200 | 7,100 |
| Unload from trailer . . . . . . . . . . | 5.00 | 5.75 | 7.00 | 8.10 | 11.00 |
| Move within 40 ft . . . . . . . . . . . | 3.84 | 4.45 | 5.40 | 6.25 | 8.50 |
| Uncrate, set, and align  . . . . . . . . | 5.80 | 6.70 | 8.20 | 9.45 | 12.90 |
| Hang air handler . . . . . . . . . . . . | 9.75 | 11.00 | 16.00 | 21.00 | 23.00 |
| **Total workhours** . . . . . . . . . . . | 24.39 | 27.90 | 36.60 | 44.80 | 55.40 |

**Piping hookups**

| Nominal tons . . . . . . | 3 | 5 | 7½ | 10 | 15 |
|---|---|---|---|---|---|
| Liquid line, in. . . . . . | ½ | ½ | ⅝ | ⅝ | ¾ |
| Suction line, in. . . . . | ⅞ | 1⅛ | 1⅛ | 1⅜ | 1⅝ |
| Material, $ . . . . . . . . | 114 | 168 | 180 | 204 | 276 |
| Workhours . . . . . . . | 15.0 | 16.5 | 17.0 | 19.5 | 21.5 |
| Nominal tons . . . . . . | 20 | 25 | 30 | 40 | 50 |
| Liquid line, in. . . . . . | ⅞ | ⅞ | ⅞ | 1⅛ | 1⅜ |
| Suction line, in. . . . . | 1⅝ | 2⅛ | 2⅛ | 2⅛ | 2⅝ |
| Material, $ . . . . . . . . | 288 | 456 | 468 | 480 | 648 |
| Workhours . . . . . . . | 22.5 | 24.0 | 24.0 | 25.0 | 32.5 |

Figure 3.3 shows the schematic upon which the workhours are based. The condensing unit is assumed to be set on a prepared concrete slab on the ground alongside the exterior structure wall. The air handler is suspended from a typical 10-ft ceiling, and normal working conditions are assumed.

## SPLIT-SYSTEM PIPING HOOKUPS

As shown in Fig. 3.3, the suction and liquid lines leave the condensing unit, rise vertically 10 ft, and then run laterally another 10 ft. An additional allowance of 10 ft of pipe is made in the estimate for the suction-line loop and final connections at the air handler.

The typical design is based on Refrigerant-22 and total equivalent length of 55 ft (pressure drop) for each line. Both liquid and suction lines are calculated at 30 ft physical length plus elbows. Type L copper is assumed, and the necessary refrigerant charge, brazing rod, and liquid sight glass are worked into the material cost. Pipe covering is not included. Labor includes handling pipe and fittings from truck to equipment location within 40 ft, measuring, cutting, cleaning, brazing, and placing hangers.

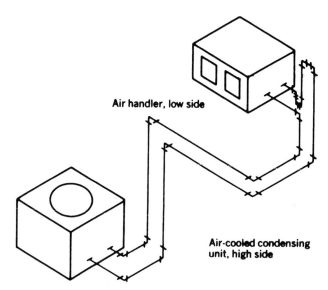

**Figure 3.3   SPLIT-SYSTEM AIR-COOLED PIPING HOOKUP**

## AIR-HANDLING UNITS

For either direct expansion or chilled-water application, the standard units shown in Table 3.7 include the insulated steel cabinet, blower, blower motor, and drive, filter rack (no filters), and four-row cooling coil, based on 500 fpm at 40°F suction. If more than a four-row coil, add $40 per 400 cfm for each additional row.

**TABLE 3.7**   Air-Handling Apparatus

**Material cost**

| Nominal tons | 10 | 15 | 20 | 25 | 30 | 35 | 40 | 45 | 50 | 60 |
|---|---|---|---|---|---|---|---|---|---|---|
| Nominal cfm | 4,000 | 6,000 | 8,000 | 10,000 | 12,000 | 14,000 | 16,000 | 18,000 | 20,000 | 24,000 |
| Nominal fan hp | 1 | 1½ | 2 | 3 | 5 | 8 | 10 | 10 | 15 | 15 |
| Base cost, $ | 2,260 | 2,580 | 3,460 | 3,920 | 4,460 | 4,820 | 5,290 | 5,950 | 6,550 | 8,100 |
| Two-row steam coil, $ | 385 | 435 | 465 | 532 | 598 | 610 | 654 | 713 | 713 | 785 |
| Bypass section, $ | 435 | 498 | 525 | 560 | 625 | 625 | 625 | 742 | 795 | 910 |

**Workhours**

| Nominal tons | 10 | 15 | 20 | 25 | 30 | 35 | 40 | 45 | 50 | 60 |
|---|---|---|---|---|---|---|---|---|---|---|
| Weight, lb | 700 | 900 | 1,300 | 1,400 | 2,200 | 2,500 | 2,700 | 3,000 | 3,300 | 3,700 |
| Unload from trailer | 1.08 | 1.40 | 2.00 | 2.20 | 3.40 | 3.90 | 4.20 | 4.65 | 5.10 | 5.75 |
| Move to 40 ft | 0.84 | 1.08 | 1.56 | 1.67 | 2.74 | 3.00 | 3.25 | 3.60 | 3.95 | 4.45 |
| Uncrate and erect | 4.58 | 5.52 | 5.94 | 6.63 | 10.36 | 11.10 | 12.05 | 12.75 | 13.95 | 15.80 |
| Workhours; base unit | 6.50 | 8.00 | 9.50 | 10.50 | 16.50 | 18.00 | 19.50 | 21.00 | 23.00 | 26.00 |
| Add for | | | | | | | | | | |
| Erect bypass section | 1.00 | 1.50 | 1.50 | 1.50 | 2.25 | 2.25 | 2.25 | 2.50 | 2.50 | 3.00 |
| Erect heating coil | 1.00 | 2.00 | 2.00 | 2.50 | 3.00 | 3.00 | 4.00 | 4.50 | 4.50 | 5.00 |
| Suspend from ceiling | 2.50 | 2.50 | 2.75 | 3.00 | 3.60 | 3.90 | 4.20 | 4.40 | 4.80 | 5.25 |

Workhours shown include uncrating, assembling, aligning, and bolting down on the foundation, as well as erecting the fan motor, drives, and guard. The average cost for an air-handling apparatus-base unit is $35 per 100 cfm.

## FAN-COIL UNITS FOR CHILLED-WATER MULTIROOM SYSTEMS

Standard equipment includes a four-row coil, three-speed fan motor, and three-speed switch with remote wall plate for ceiling-mounted units. The floor-standing unit is complete with steel cabinet and discharge panel. The ceiling unit less cabinet is chassis only, designed for concealed application; it includes the return-air plenum. The ceiling unit with cabinet is the same as above but includes a completely insulated enclosure with inlet and outlet duct connectors for exposed in-space application. For a complete discussion of available control packages, see Chap. 13. Tables 3.8 to 3.10 give material and labor for floor and ceiling models.

**TABLE 3.8**  Fan-Coil Units—Material Cost

| Nominal tons......... | ½ | ¾ | 1 | 1¼ | 1½ | 1¾ | 2 | 2½ | 3 | 3¾ |
|---|---|---|---|---|---|---|---|---|---|---|
| Nominal cfm......... | 200 | 300 | 400 | 500 | 600 | 750 | 800 | 1,000 | 1,250 | 1,500 |
| Floor convector, $ .... | 270 | 290 | 300 | 330 | 340 | — | — | — | — | — |
| Ceiling less cabinet, $ .......... | 210 | 230 | 240 | 250 | 260 | 320 | 370 | 410 | 450 | 580 |
| Ceiling with cabinet, $ .......... | 180 | 210 | 220 | 220 | 230 | 260 | 300 | 320 | 350 | 460 |

**TABLE 3.9**  Fan-Coil Units, Floor-Standing Convectors—Erection, Workhours

Does not include bringing units up to floor in multistory buildings, laying out, piping hookups, or outside-air connections.

| Nominal tons | ½ | ¾ | 1 | 1¼ | 1½ |
|---|---|---|---|---|---|
| Nominal cfm . . . . . . . . . . | 200 | 300 | 400 | 500 | 600 |
| Weight, lb. . . . . . . . . . . . | 90 | 105 | 110 | 115 | 125 |
| Unload from truck  . . . . . . . | 0.15 | 0.15 | 0.20 | 0.20 | 0.30 |
| Move to 40 ft  . . . . . . . . . . | 0.13 | 0.14 | 0.15 | 0.18 | 0.20 |
| Uncrate and align  . . . . . . . . | 0.72 | 0.75 | 0.80 | 0.87 | 1.00 |
| Total workhours  . . . . . . . | 1.00 | 1.04 | 1.15 | 1.25 | 1.50 |

**TABLE 3.10**  Fan-Coil Units, Ceiling-Suspended, in-Space—Erection, Workhours

| Nominal tons | ½ | ¾ | 1 | 1¼ | 1½ | 1¾ | 2 | 2½ | 3 | 3¾ |
|---|---|---|---|---|---|---|---|---|---|---|
| Nominal cfm . . . . . . . | 200 | 300 | 400 | 500 | 600 | 750 | 800 | 1,000 | 1,250 | 1,500 |
| Weight, lb. . . . . . . . . . | 51 | 62 | 70 | 75 | 85 | 165 | 185 | 195 | 205 | 225 |
| Unload from truck. . . . . | 0.13 | 0.13 | 0.13 | 0.13 | 0.15 | 0.28 | 0.32 | 0.35 | 0.37 | 0.40 |
| Move to 40 ft. . . . . . . . | 0.12 | 0.12 | 0.12 | 0.12 | 0.13 | 0.25 | 0.28 | 0.30 | 0.32 | 0.35 |
| Uncrate and suspend  . . . | 0.75 | 0.75 | 0.90 | 0.90 | 1.00 | 1.90 | 2.10 | 2.30 | 2.45 | 2.65 |
| Total workhours . . . . | 1.00 | 1.00 | 1.15 | 1.15 | 1.28 | 2.43 | 2.70 | 2.95 | 3.14 | 3.40 |

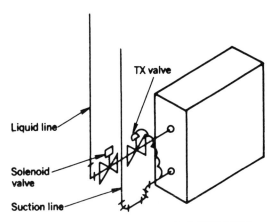

**Figure 3.4  AIR-HANDLING UNIT—PIPING HOOKUP**
*Direct-expansion evaporator with compressor above, single circuit.*

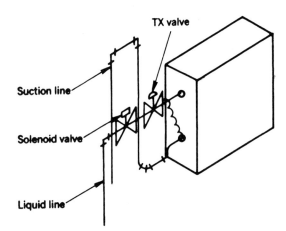

**Figure 3.5  AIR-HANDLING UNIT—PIPING HOOKUP**
*Direct-expansion evaporator with compressor below, single circuit.*

## AIR-HANDLING UNIT—PIPING HOOKUPS

Four common piping hookups are shown in Figs. 3.4 to 3.7. The line sizes and piping design are generally based on the discussion and recommendations in Chap. 3 of the *Handbook of Air Conditioning System Design, Carrier Corporation.*[1]

Workhours in Tables 3.11 to 3.15 (see also Fig. 3.8) include handling pipe and fittings from truck to equipment location within 40 ft, measuring, cutting, cleaning, brazing, and placing. Material costs are based on type L copper and include the brazing material as well as the pipe, fittings, and specials listed.

---

[1] McGraw-Hill, New York, 1965.

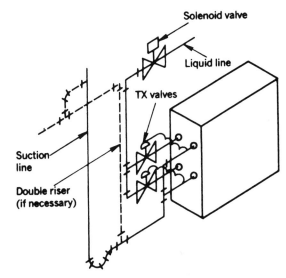

**Figure 3.6  AIR-HANDLING UNIT—PIPING HOOKUP**
*Direct-expansion evaporator with compressor above, twin circuit, with or without double riser.*

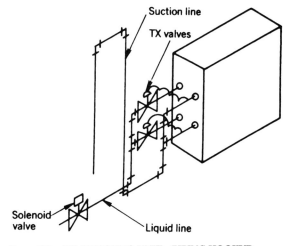

**Figure 3.7  AIR-HANDLING UNIT—PIPING HOOKUP**
*Direct-expansion evaporator with compressor below, twin circuit.*

**TABLE 3.11** Air-Handling Apparatus—Piping Hookup

DX evaporator with compressor above, single circuit, as shown in Fig. 3.4. Based on 10-ft suction line, two 45° street ells, and one 90° street ell; 10-ft liquid line, one 90° ell, one TX valve, one solenoid.

| Nominal tons. . . . . . . | 10 | 15 | 20 | 25 | 30 | 35 | 40 | 45 | 50 | 60 |
|---|---|---|---|---|---|---|---|---|---|---|
| Suction line, in. . . . . . . | 1⅝ | 1⅝ | 2⅛ | 2⅛ | 2⅛ | 2⅝ | 2⅝ | 2⅝ | 2⅝ | 3⅛ |
| Liquid line, in. . . . . . | ⅞ | ⅞ | ⅞ | ⅞ | 1⅛ | 1⅛ | 1⅜ | 1⅜ | 1⅜ | 1⅜ |
| Total material, $. . . . . | 216 | 264 | 324 | 450 | 500 | 550 | 562 | 600 | 600 | 720 |
| Total workhours . . . . . | 8.40 | 8.60 | 9.25 | 9.50 | 9.80 | 11.0 | 11.5 | 11.5 | 12.25 | 13.5 |

**TABLE 3.12** Air-Handling Apparatus—Piping Hookup

DX evaporator with compressor below, single circuit, as shown in Fig. 3.5. Based on 20-ft suction line, two 45° street ells, one 90° standard ell; 10-ft liquid line, one 90° ell, one TX valve, one solenoid.

| Nominal tons. . . . . . . | 10 | 15 | 20 | 25 | 30 | 35 | 40 | 45 | 50 | 60 |
|---|---|---|---|---|---|---|---|---|---|---|
| Suction line, in. . . . . . . | 1⅝ | 1⅝ | 2⅛ | 2⅛ | 2⅛ | 2⅝ | 2⅝ | 2⅝ | 2⅝ | 3⅛ |
| Liquid line, in. . . . . . | ⅞ | ⅞ | ⅞ | ⅞ | 1⅛ | 1⅛ | 1⅜ | 1⅜ | 1⅜ | 1⅜ |
| Total material, $. . . . . | 250 | 300 | 360 | 360 | 480 | 640 | 670 | 670 | 670 | 825 |
| Total workhours . . . . | 11.25 | 11.50 | 12.25 | 12.65 | 13.00 | 14.85 | 15.00 | 15.00 | 16.00 | 18.00 |

**TABLE 3.13** Air-Handling Apparatus—Piping Hookup

DX evaporator with compressor above, twin circuit, as shown in Fig. 3.6. Based on 16-ft suction line, two 45° street ells, one 90° street ell, one reducing tee, one 90° standard ell, two expansion valves, one solenoid. Extra for double riser: 10-ft pipe, two reducing tees, three 90° ells.

| Nominal tons. . . . . . . . . . | 10 | 15 | 20 | 25 | 30 | 35 | 40 | 45 | 50 | 60 |
|---|---|---|---|---|---|---|---|---|---|---|
| Suction-line main, in. . . . . | 1⅝ | 1⅝ | 2⅛ | 2⅛ | 2⅛ | 2⅝ | 2⅝ | 2⅝ | 2⅝ | 3⅛ |
| Liquid-line main, in. . . . . . | ⅞ | ⅞ | ⅞ | ⅞ | 1⅛ | 1⅛ | 1⅜ | 1⅜ | 1⅜ | 1⅜ |
| Total material, $. . . . . . . . | 250 | 260 | 372 | 372 | 454 | 645 | 575 | 680 | 680 | 755 |
| Total workhours . . . . . . . | 15.50 | 16.00 | 18.25 | 18.25 | 19.50 | 20.50 | 22.25 | 22.25 | 23.75 | 25.50 |
| Extra for double riser: | | | | | | | | | | |
|   Material, $ . . . . . . . . . . . | 25 | 30 | 30 | 30 | 42 | 52 | 52 | 52 | 88 | 95 |
|   Workhours . . . . . . . . . . . | 11.00 | 11.60 | 12.75 | 13.75 | 15.85 | 15.85 | 15.85 | 15.85 | 16.65 | 18.00 |

**TABLE 3.14** Air-Handling Apparatus—Piping Hookup

DX evaporator with compressor below, twin circuit, as shown in Fig. 3.7. Based on 26-ft suction line, two 45° street ells, one 90° street ell, one reducing tee, three 90° standard ells; 15-ft liquid line, one reducing tee, two 90° standard ells, two expansion valves, one solenoid.

| Nominal tons. . . . . . . . . . | 10 | 15 | 20 | 25 | 30 | 35 | 40 | 45 | 50 | 60 |
|---|---|---|---|---|---|---|---|---|---|---|
| Suction-line main, in. . . . . | 1⅝ | 1⅝ | 2⅛ | 2⅛ | 2⅛ | 2⅝ | 2⅝ | 2⅝ | 2⅝ | 3⅛ |
| Liquid-line main, in. . . . . . | ⅞ | ⅞ | ⅞ | ⅞ | 1⅛ | 1⅛ | 1⅜ | 1⅜ | 1⅜ | 1⅜ |
| Material, $ . . . . . . . . . . . | 285 | 300 | 430 | 430 | 516 | 624 | 670 | 755 | 815 | 880 |
| Total workhours . . . . . . . . | 18.50 | 19.00 | 21.50 | 21.50 | 22.75 | 24.50 | 26.00 | 26.00 | 27.50 | 30.00 |

**TABLE 3.15**   Air-Handling Apparatus—Chilled-Water Piping Hookup

Based on piping scheme illustrated in Fig. 3.8. Black-iron pipe sizes through 2 in. are screwed; 2½-in. up are welded and flange-fitted. Assume total 40-ft pipe of listed size and 1-in. diameter dirt legs.

*Workhours* includes handling pipe and fitting from truck to equipment location within 40 ft, measuring, cutting, making up joints, and placing. Erecting three-way valve is included in workhours, but three-way valve is not included in material cost.

Material cost includes 40-ft pipe, one gate valve, one globe valve, one plug cock, five unions, seven tees, three ells, two gage cocks, two air vents, one drain valve.

| Pipe size, in. | 1 | 1¼ | 1½ | 2 | 2½ | 3 | 4 | 6 |
|---|---|---|---|---|---|---|---|---|
| Material, $ | 240 | 300 | 360 | 625 | 940 | 1,400 | 1,610 | 2,450 |
| Total, workhours | 17 | 20 | 23 | 29 | 40 | 56 | 69 | 130 |

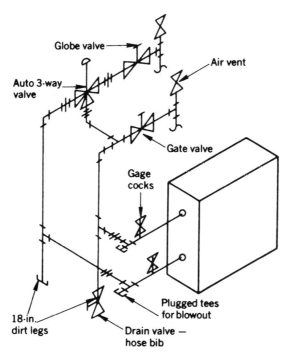

**Figure 3.8   AIR-HANDLING UNIT—PIPING HOOKUP**
*Chilled-water system.*

## AIR-COOLED CONDENSERS

Tables 3.16 to 3.18 are based on factory-assembled equipment shipped in one piece, with mounting legs attached, for outside application. The listed sizes are based on Refrigerant-12 at 96°F entering air, 115°F condensing temperature, and 40°F suction. Liquid receivers are not generally included and must be separately selected. The receivers listed in Table 3.16 as

**TABLE 3.16**  Air-Cooled Condensers—Material

| Nominal tons | 7½ | 10 | 15 | 20 | 25 | 30 | 35 | 40 | 50 | 60 |
|---|---|---|---|---|---|---|---|---|---|---|
| Horsepower | ¾ | 1 | 1½ | 1½ | 2 | 3 | 3 | 3 | 5 | 5 |
| Unit cost, $ | 1,690 | 2,660 | 3,190 | 3,410 | 4,320 | 4,790 | 6,120 | 6,580 | 7,580 | 8,510 |
| Extra for receiver, $ | 380 | 520 | 520 | 675 | 690 | 710 | 745 | 820 | 980 | 1,160 |
| Total material, $ | 2,070 | 3,180 | 3,710 | 4,085 | 5,010 | 5,500 | 6,865 | 7,400 | 8,560 | 9,670 |

**TABLE 3.17**  Air-Cooled Condensers—Erection, Workhours

Includes setting condenser and receiver but not special rigging, roof flashing, or tie-down cables.

| Nominal tons | 7½ | 10 | 15 | 20 | 25 | 30 | 35 | 40 | 50 |
|---|---|---|---|---|---|---|---|---|---|
| Unit weight, lb . . . . . . . | 500 | 600 | 650 | 900 | 1,000 | 1,100 | 1,350 | 1,550 | 1,875 |
| Receiver weight, lb . . . . | 120 | 120 | 150 | 225 | 280 | 375 | 480 | 480 | 550 |
| Unload from truck . . . . | 1.00 | 1.15 | 1.25 | 1.90 | 2.15 | 2.35 | 2.85 | 3.20 | 3.75 |
| Move to within 40 ft . . . | 0.75 | 0.85 | 0.95 | 1.35 | 1.65 | 1.75 | 2.15 | 2.75 | 3.00 |
| Uncrate, set and align . . . | 1.10 | 1.30 | 1.45 | 2.00 | 2.50 | 2.70 | 3.30 | 3.75 | 4.50 |
| Total, workhours . . . . . | 2.85 | 3.30 | 3.65 | 5.25 | 6.30 | 6.80 | 8.30 | 9.70 | 11.25 |

**TABLE 3.18**  Air-Cooled Condensers—Piping Hookup

Pipe shown in this table is based on type L copper using Refrigerant-12, sized for equivalent lengths of 100 ft. Condensate lines to receiver are one size greater than liquid line. Figure 3.9 illustrates design on which this table is based; it is assumed that the receiver is directly below condenser. Material includes 10 ft each hot-gas, condensate, and liquid lines, plus seven elbows and one valve to hot-gas entrance. Labor includes handling pipe and fittings from truck to equipment location (40 ft), measuring, cutting, cleaning, and brazing.

| Nominal tons . . . . . . . . . . . . . | 7½ | 10 | 15 | 20 | 25 | 30 | 35 | 40 | 50 |
|---|---|---|---|---|---|---|---|---|---|
| Hot-gas-line size, in. . . . . . . . | 1⅛ | 1⅜ | 1⅝ | 1⅝ | 1⅝ | 2⅛ | 2⅛ | 2⅛ | 2⅝ |
| Condensate-line size, in. . . . . | ⅞ | 1⅛ | 1⅛ | 1⅜ | 1⅜ | 1⅝ | 1⅝ | 1⅝ | 2⅛ |
| Liquid-line size, in. . . . . . . . . | ⅝ | ⅞ | ⅞ | 1⅛ | 1⅛ | 1⅜ | 1⅜ | 1⅜ | 1⅝ |
| Workhours. . . . . . . . . . . . . . . | 9.50 | 10.75 | 11.50 | 12.50 | 12.50 | 14.75 | 14.75 | 14.75 | 18.00 |
| Material, $. . . . . . . . . . . . . . . | 162 | 228 | 270 | 288 | 288 | 414 | 414 | 414 | 630 |

"extra" have been selected to allow 25% volume over the total system for expansion and hold additional charge for pressure control. See also Fig. 3.9.

## MAJOR COMPONENTS

Material and workhours for compressor units, condensing units, and piping hookups are given in Tables 3.19 to 3.22, and those for water-cooled condensers and receivers are given in Tables 3.23 and 3.24. No typical gas piping hookups are offered for the latter. Condenser piping hookups may be found in Table 3.2 as illustrated in Fig. 3.1. See also Figs. 3.10 and 3.11.

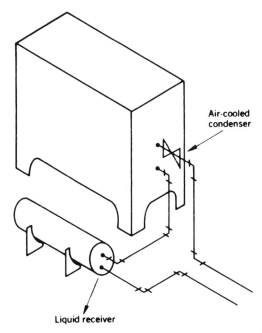

**Figure 3.9   AIR-COOLED CONDENSER—PIPING HOOKUP**

**TABLE 3.19**   Compressor Units—Workhours and Material

For remote condenser hookup, based on Refrigerant-22 for standard air-conditioning service. Includes compressor, motor, drive set, shutoff valves, holding charge, dual pressure control, and oil pressure safety switch, completely assembled on base. For capacity control, add $420 per unit.

| Nominal tons............... | 15 | 20 | 25 | 30 | 40 | 50 | 60 | 75 | 100 |
|---|---|---|---|---|---|---|---|---|---|
| Weight, lb.................. | 950 | 1,500 | 1,560 | 2,360 | 2,425 | 2,550 | 3,650 | 4,300 | 5,400 |
| Base unit, $ ............... | 4,240 | 4,760 | 5,130 | 5,710 | 8,280 | 10,840 | 11,550 | 12,630 | 15,750 |
| Unload from truck.......... | 1.05 | 1.65 | 1.70 | 2.10 | 2.20 | 2.30 | 3.30 | 3.60 | 4.50 |
| Move to within 40 ft........ | 0.76 | 1.20 | 1.50 | 2.24 | 2.35 | 2.45 | 3.45 | 4.30 | 5.00 |
| Uncrate, align, and erect .... | 1.19 | 1.65 | 1.80 | 2.86 | 2.95 | 3.05 | 3.20 | 5.10 | 6.50 |
| Total workhours.......... | 3.00 | 4.50 | 5.00 | 7.20 | 7.50 | 7.80 | 9.95 | 13.00 | 16.00 |

**TABLE 3.20**   Compressor Units—Piping Hookup

Based on piping scheme illustrated in Fig. 3.10, using type L copper pipe with brazed joints. Material cost includes 10-ft hot-gas line and three ells, plus 5-ft suction line. *Workhours* includes handling pipe and fittings from truck to equipment location within 40 ft, measuring, cutting, making up joints, and placing.

| Nominal tons........ | 15 | 20 | 25 | 30 | 40 | 50 | 60 | 75 | 100 |
|---|---|---|---|---|---|---|---|---|---|
| Total material, $..... | 43 | 54 | 65 | 76 | 76 | 76 | 111 | 111 | 158 |
| Total workhours ..... | 4.25 | 5.00 | 5.25 | 5.85 | 5.85 | 6.75 | 6.75 | 6.75 | 8.00 |

**TABLE 3.21**   Condensing Units—Workhours and Material

As in Table 3.19, but includes shell and tube condenser for water-cooled system with factory-piped hot-gas line.

| Nominal tons............... | 15 | 20 | 25 | 30 | 40 | 50 | 60 | 75 | 100 |
|---|---|---|---|---|---|---|---|---|---|
| Weight, lb.................. | 1,130 | 1,350 | 2,360 | 2,450 | 2,600 | 2,700 | 3,750 | 3,950 | 5,500 |
| Base unit, $ ................ | 4,350 | 5,460 | 5,990 | 6,470 | 8,790 | 11,260 | 14,170 | 17,760 | 24,580 |
| Unload from truck.......... | 1.02 | 1.22 | 2.10 | 2.25 | 2.35 | 2.45 | 3.40 | 3.50 | 5.00 |
| Move to within 40 ft ........ | 1.07 | 1.28 | 2.24 | 2.35 | 2.45 | 2.56 | 3.55 | 3.85 | 5.00 |
| Uncrate, align, and erect .... | 1.36 | 1.65 | 2.86 | 3.00 | 3.10 | 3.24 | 4.50 | 4.75 | 6.25 |
| Total workhours .......... | 3.45 | 4.15 | 7.20 | 7.60 | 7.90 | 8.25 | 11.45 | 12.10 | 16.25 |

**TABLE 3.22**   Condensing Units—Piping Hookup

Based on piping scheme illustrated in Fig. 3.11, using type L copper with brazed joints. Material cost includes 5-ft suction line, 5-ft liquid line, and one ell each. *Workhours* includes handling pipe and fittings from truck to equipment location within 40 ft, measuring, cutting, making up joints, and placing.

| Nominal tons........ | 15 | 20 | 25 | 30 | 40 | 50 | 60 | 75 | 100 |
|---|---|---|---|---|---|---|---|---|---|
| Total material, $..... | 43 | 54 | 63 | 35 | 35 | 110 | 110 | 110 | 155 |
| Total workhours ..... | 4.25 | 5.00 | 5.25 | 5.85 | 6.75 | 6.75 | 6.75 | 6.75 | 8.00 |

**TABLE 3.23**   Water-Cooled Condensers—Material

Water-cooled shell and tube condensers—with removable ends for punching tubes, ASME code stamped. Selection based on 105°F condensing temperature, 3 gpm water on at 85°F and water off at 95°F, average pressure drop at 7 lb. To determine pumpdown capacity of Refrigerant-22, multiply Ref.-12 capacity in column 4 by 0.9.

| Nominal tons | Dimension, nominal in. | Weight, lb | Capacity, lb Ref.-12 | Base unit, $ | Extra for saddle legs, $ |
|---|---|---|---|---|---|
| 3 | 7 × 40 | 120 | 30 | 650 | 32 |
| 5 | 7 × 40 | 130 | 39 | 735 | 32 |
| 8 | 9 × 52 | 200 | 73 | 925 | 40 |
| 10 | 9 × 52 | 215 | 70 | 1,320 | 40 |
| 16 | 9 × 52 | 240 | 60 | 1,600 | 40 |
| 21 | 10 × 53 | 370 | 100 | 3,540 | 45 |
| 27 | 10 × 53 | 400 | 95 | 2,980 | 45 |
| 32 | 12 × 54 | 450 | 150 | 3,930 | 52 |
| 43 | 12 × 54 | 500 | 140 | 4,150 | 52 |
| 54 | 12 × 54 | 650 | 127 | 4,580 | 52 |
| 64 | 16 × 54 | 675 | 236 | 4,780 | 65 |
| 80 | 16 × 54 | 750 | 216 | 5,190 | 65 |
| 107 | 18 × 56 | 940 | 258 | 6,140 | 75 |
| 134 | 16 × 102 | 1,350 | 451 | 7,350 | 75 |
| 160 | 16 × 102 | 1,450 | 432 | 7,680 | 75 |
| 187 | 18 × 104 | 1,650 | 540 | 8,750 | 75 |
| 214 | 18 × 104 | 1,800 | 516 | 10,000 | 75 |

**TABLE 3.24** Receivers—Material

Liquid receivers—ASME code includes tappings but does not include pressure-relief device, purge cock, shutoff valves, or gage glass. Based on 6 lb per ton. To determine capacity for refrigerants other than Refrigerant-12 as listed in column 2, use the following formulas:

Refrigerant-22: multiply column 2 by 0.90
Refrigerant-500: multiply column 2 by 0.88
Ammonia: multiply column 2 by 0.46

| Operating tons | Capacity, lb Ref.-12 | Dimension, nominal in. | Weight, lb | Base unit, $ | Extra for saddle legs, $ |
|---|---|---|---|---|---|
| 2 | 17 | 7 × 18 | 40 | 90 | 25 |
| 3 | 24 | 7 × 24 | 50 | 105 | 25 |
| 5 | 39 | 7 × 36 | 55 | 115 | 25 |
| 10 | 55 | 9 × 36 | 60 | 210 | 30 |
| 15 | 115 | 9 × 60 | 85 | 255 | 30 |
| 20 | 165 | 9 × 96 | 120 | 285 | 30 |
| 25 | 220 | 11 × 84 | 225 | 330 | 35 |
| 35 | 315 | 13 × 96 | 280 | 450 | 40 |
| 50 | 435 | 13 × 120 | 375 | 510 | 40 |
| 65 | 630 | 16 × 96 | 480 | 600 | 50 |

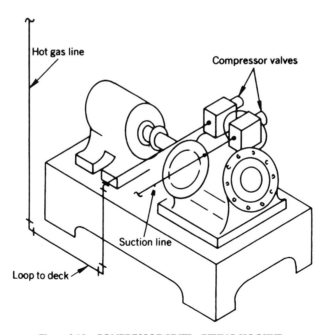

Figure 3.10   COMPRESSOR UNIT—PIPING HOOKUP

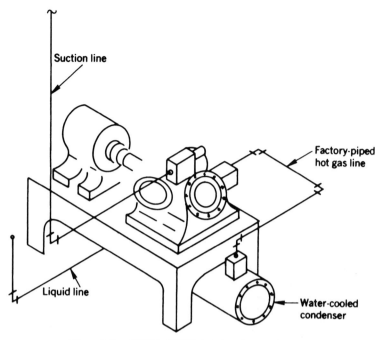

**Figure 3.11   CONDENSING UNIT—PIPING HOOKUP**

## CENTRAL STATION EVAPORATIVE CONDENSER PACKAGE UNITS

Completely self-contained factory-assembled units, shipped in one piece, are covered in Table 3.25. They are factory-piped units and require only plumbing connections for makeup water and blowdown and final connections to ductwork.

## PACKAGED WATER CHILLERS

A large variety of packaged water chillers with either reciprocating or centrifugal compressor sections are available on the market today. The packages may be shipped in either one, two, or three sections, depending on both the size of the unit and the manufacturer. Reciprocating compressor equipment is available in one-, two-, three-, or even four-compressor modules, depending on the tonnage range and the manufacturer. In most cases a good range of step control and unloader capacity is available. Centrifugal equipment is available in either one or two stages and can easily unload to meet almost any operating condition required. On a first-cost comparison basis, it may be said that the reciprocating types will cost less in the smaller sizes, and conversely, the centrifugals will cost less in the larger capacities; the crossover point is in the range of 175 to 200 tons.

### Reciprocating Compressors

The costs in Tables 3.26 and 3.27 are based on factory-assembled units shipped in one section and include compressor, motor, condenser, heat exchanger, insulated chiller, unloaders, and all valves, completely piped and assembled on steel frames.

**TABLE 3.25** Central Station Evaporative Condenser Units

**Material**

| Nominal tons | 7½ | 10 | 15 | 20 | 25 | 30 | 40 | 50 | 60 |
|---|---|---|---|---|---|---|---|---|---|
| Number of compressors | 1 | 1 | 2 | 2 | 3 | 3 | 4 | 2 | 4 |
| Weight, lb | 2,225 | 2,750 | 3,900 | 4,850 | 5,400 | 6,000 | 7,525 | 9,000 | 9,750 |
| Unit cost, $ | 6,670 | 8,210 | 8,680 | 12,500 | 14,100 | 15,100 | 19,600 | 22,800 | 25,600 |

**Erection, workhours**

| | | | | | | | | | |
|---|---|---|---|---|---|---|---|---|---|
| Unload from truck | 2.00 | 2.50 | 3.50 | 4.50 | 4.85 | 5.40 | 6.50 | 8.10 | 8.80 |
| Move within 40 ft | 2.15 | 2.60 | 3.70 | 4.70 | 5.10 | 5.70 | 7.20 | 8.50 | 9.20 |
| Uncrate, set, and align | 2.85 | 3.40 | 4.30 | 5.80 | 6.05 | 7.40 | 9.30 | 12.40 | 13.50 |
| Total workhours | 7.00 | 8.50 | 11.50 | 15.00 | 16.00 | 18.50 | 23.00 | 29.00 | 31.50 |

**TABLE 3.26** Water Chillers, Reciprocating Compressors—Material

| Nominal tons | 15 | 20 | 25 | 30 | 40 | 50 |
|---|---|---|---|---|---|---|
| Basic unit, $ | 12,210 | 14,980 | 16,810 | 19,320 | 21,900 | 25,720 |
| Extra for chiller pump piped in place, $ | 480 | 480 | 480 | 480 | 1,100 | 1,100 |
| Extra for condenser pump piped in place, $ | 490 | 490 | 580 | 650 | 650 | 740 |
| Extra for rubber in shear vibration, $ | 150 | 150 | 150 | 180 | 240 | 260 |
| Total unit cost, $ | 13,330 | 16,100 | 18,020 | 20,630 | 23,890 | 27,820 |
| Nominal tons | 60 | 75 | 100 | 125 | 150 | |
| Basic unit, $ | 29,490 | 34,970 | 44,580 | 46,660 | 53,280 | |
| Extra for chiller pump piped in place, $ | 1,100 | 1,200 | 1,300 | 1,700 | 1,700 | |
| Extra for condenser pump piped in place, $ | 850 | 850 | 1,200 | 1,700 | 1,700 | |
| Extra for rubber in shear vibration, $ | 300 | 500 | 500 | 500 | 600 | |
| Total unit cost, $ | 31,740 | 37,520 | 47,580 | 50,560 | 57,280 | |

**TABLE 3.27** Water Chillers, Reciprocating Compressors—Erection, Workhours
Does not include concrete pad, piping hookup, start and check, or extra rigging.

| Nominal tons | 15 | 20 | 25 | 30 | 40 | 50 |
|---|---|---|---|---|---|---|
| Weight, lb . . . . . . . . . | 2,300 | 2,900 | 3,400 | 3,750 | 4,175 | 4,900 |
| Unload from trailer . . . . | 2.06 | 2.71 | 3.05 | 3.42 | 3.75 | 4.40 |
| Move to 40 ft. . . . . . . . | 2.20 | 2.80 | 3.24 | 3.55 | 4.17 | 4.90 |
| Uncrate, set, and align . . | 3.54 | 4.29 | 5.21 | 5.78 | 7.13 | 8.70 |
| Total workhours . . . . | 7.80 | 9.80 | 11.50 | 12.75 | 15.05 | 18.00 |
| Nominal tons | 60 | 75 | 100 | 125 | 150 | |
| Weight, lb . . . . . . . . . | 5,400 | 5,900 | 7,800 | 8,900 | 10,300 | |
| Unload from trailer . . . . | 4.80 | 6.75 | 7.00 | 8.00 | 9.30 | |
| Move to 40 ft . . . . . . . | 5.40 | 5.90 | 7.80 | 8.90 | 10.30 | |
| Uncrate, set, and align. . . | 9.50 | 10.50 | 12.00 | 15.10 | 18.40 | |
| Total workhours . . . . | 19.70 | 23.15 | 26.80 | 32.00 | 38.00 | |

**TABLE 3.28**   Centrifugal Water Chillers

| Nominal tons | Material, $ | Ref. 11, lb | Rigging wt, lb | Additional for rigging, $ | Additional for insulation, $ |
|---|---|---|---|---|---|
| 200 | 53,000 | 625 | 12,500 | 5,500 | 2,150 |
| 400 | 73,000 | 1,600 | 26,750 | 9,000 | 3,270 |
| 1,000 | 149,000 | 2,750 | 50,000 | 13,200 | 4,220 |
| 1,300 | 181,000 | 3,750 | 68,000 | 14,300 | 5,100 |
| 1,500 | 204,500 | 5,500 | 80,000 | 15,200 | 6,300 |
| 2,000 | 324,000 | 7,500 | 90,000 | 16,300 | 6,750 |

### Centrifugal Compressors

Budget prices for hermetic units are shown in Table 3.28. The package includes compressor, motor and drive, shell-and-tube condenser, shell-and-tube evaporator, controls, and vibration eliminators. It does not include auxiliary starters, refrigerant relief piping, or vessel insulation. The manufacturer will usually provide factory supervision for dehydrating, charging, and start-up, and that is included in the price.

Figure 3.12 shows labor requirements for installation and erection of centrifugal compressors.

Table 3.29 gives workhours for start-up of large centrifugal compressors.

### Absorption Machines

The nominal capacities in Table 3.30 are based on 85°F condensing temperature and 12-psig steam. Budget prices for these hermetic units include the solution pump, evaporator pump, purge pump, solution, capacity-control valve, and isolation pads. Pumps for condenser water and chilled water, bypass valves, and starters are not included. The manufacturer will usually provide factory supervision and operation instructions. A one-week allowance for this task is included in the price. Room and board for factory supervision is not included. See Chap. 19 for a detailed discussion of rigging.

## HIGH-VELOCITY INDUCTION SYSTEMS

The basic terminal induction unit is available in over 100 different combinations of unit size, unit style, coil size, and nozzle size, and costs may range from $250 to $425 each. To this base unit price must be added all accessories, controls, secondary water connections, and primary-air connections. Figures 2.3 to 2.7 present a quick method for estimating the total system, including the primary-air side. The erection workhours given in Table 3.31 are valid for most applications.

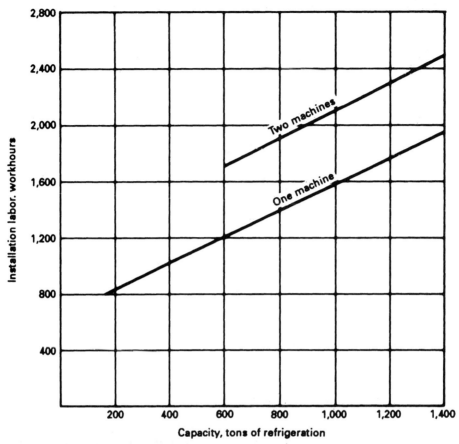

**Figure 3.12  LABOR TO INSTALL AND ERECT CENTRIFUGAL REFRIGERATION COMPRESSORS**
**Workhours to Erect, Test, and Start Up**
*Includes compressor, motor, starter, cooler, control console, speed increaser, purge unit, refrigerant, oil, thermometers, and 40 hr of supervision. Does not include hoisting to machine room, cooling towers, pumps, piping, external controls, foundation, or insulation.*

**TABLE 3.29**  Large Centrifugal Compressor Start-up

For large centrifugals, allows the following for start-up:

| Size, tons | Single machine, workhours | Each additional machine, workhours |
|---|---|---|
| 200–400 | 22 | 15 |
| 1,000–1,300 | 25 | 18 |

**TABLE 3.30**  Absorption Water Chillers

Steam or hot water, water-cooled, single stage. For two-stage, add 65% to cost of material. Labor does not include startup. Crane costs for these weights run $2,000 to $10,000. In southern Florida permit costs are currently $13/ton; a 1,000-ton absorption installation would cost $13,000 for a permit.

| Nominal tons | Material, $ | Rigging wt, lb | Labor for rigging and setting, $ | Allowance for steam piping, $ |
|---|---|---|---|---|
| 100 | 41,000 | 10,500 | 4,000 | 6,000 |
| 150 | 53,000 | 12,000 | 4,200 | 7,500 |
| 200 | 60,000 | 18,300 | 6,400 | 9,000 |
| 350 | 80,000 | 30,500 | 10,700 | 11,000 |
| 420 | 92,000 | 42,000 | 14,700 | 12,000 |
| 665 | 130,000 | 59,000 | 20,650 | 13,200 |
| 750 | 146,400 | 61,000 | 22,100 | 15,000 |
| 850 | 156,800 | 65,000 | 23,000 | 16,000 |
| 955 | 168,300 | 68,400 | 23,900 | 18,600 |
| 1,125 | 195,000 | 79,600 | 27,850 | 20,000 |
| 1,250 | 214,000 | 87,500 | 30,650 | 21,300 |
| 1,465 | 250,700 | 103,000 | 36,000 | 24,700 |
| 1,660 | 298,500 | 120,000 | 42,000 | 30,500 |

**TABLE 3.31**  Induction Units—Erection, Workhours

Based on standard vertical units for either floor or wall mounting. *Workhours* includes unloading material from truck, moving to within 40 ft and erecting in place but does not include bringing up to floors. For test and balance data, see Chap. 15. For condensate drain systems, multiply number of units by $60 for copper or by $30 for PVC, based on 400-unit project.

| Item | Task | Workhours |
|---|---|---|
| Basic unit, 115 lb . . . . . . . . | Align and erect . . . . . . . . . . . . . . | 1.0 |
| Mounting strips . . . . . . . . | Erect on wall (depends on length) . . . . . | 1.0 per each +0.05 per ft |
| Unit enclosure . . . . . . . . . | Erect . . . . . . . . . . . . . . . . . . . . | 0.75 |
| Runout enclosure . . . . . . . . | Erect . . . . . . . . . . . . . . . . . . . . | 0.50 |
| Coil . . . . . . . . . . . . . . . | Erect on base unit . . . . . . . . . . . . | 0.50 |
| Piping, final connections . . . . | Supply and return runouts to 10-ft length, piped in place . . . . . . . . . . | 3.50 |
| Piping, final connections . . . . | Pipe and bypass cluster (when not factory fabricated) . . . . . . . . . . . | 1.00 |

# THROUGH-THE-WALL UNITS

The use of the self-contained through-the-wall cooling unit (packaged terminal air conditioner) for multiroom, perimeter cooling in conjunction with central steam or hot-water heating is quite popular with engineers as well as owners.

When applied as part of a modernization program for an existing multiroom building which has been using steam or hot-water radiation, this may often be the most practical, if not the only, method of complete air conditioning.

Features are low initial cost, individual metering, individual control, four-season conditioning, and the fact that this method can be programmed for minimum disruption of building activities during installation.

Unit costs for a typical building, before overhead, taxes, or profits, are shown in the following example:

Cost per sq ft      **$2.96**
Square feet per ton     320

**Example 3.1** Typical Installation for a 65,000-sq-ft Building

| Item | 1994 cost, $ |
|---|---|
| 1½-hp self-contained cooling units, including junction box and control center, wall sleeve, outside louver, chassis, and cabinet; 200 units at $585 each | 117,000 |
| Cutting holes through 10-in. concrete wall, at 6 workhours per hole; includes all outside rigging, inside patching, and cleanup; 200 units at $165 each | 33,000 |
| Installing 200 sleeves, units, and cabinets at $40 | 8,000 |
| Steamfitting; removing existing radiators and connecting to new units; 200 units at $65 each | 13,000 |
| Pipe and fittings | 8,000 |
| Service reserve for one year at $50 per unit | 10,000 |
| Two spare chassis for changing defective units under warranty plan at $700 | 1,400 |
| Supervision | 2,100 |
| Total cost | 192,500 |

The cost of a steam or hot-water distribution system for a new building will be similar to that for a standard radiator system. Boiler requirements will be the same as those for a standard convector system. The openings for the units will, of course, be provided as the building progresses and would therefore not be included in the mechanical estimate. Table 3.32 offers a schedule of estimating labor and materials. In existing buildings the cost of preparation for holes is a critical item and may run as high as 30% of total job cost. It will be necessary to make a careful physical inspection of the structure to determine the thickness of the wall, the material of construction, and the rigging requirements. This significant phase of the job should be handled as a subcontract whenever possible.

## CONVENTIONAL WINDOW MODELS

Most manufacturers make varied models and styles with diverse features ranging from no thermostat and fixed air louvers to three-speed fan control with fresh-air exhaust controls. Air quantities and capacities have a wide range. Aside from special features, window and portable units can be purchased at about $35 to $45 per 1,000 Btu/hr (Btuh) cooling capacity. Some average costs are shown in Tables 3.33 and 3.34.

**TABLE 3.32** Estimating Labor and Materials

Labor includes uncrating, setting, and start but does not include cartage, delivery, or carrying to floors.

| Item | Description | Workhours | Material, $ |
|------|-------------|-----------|-------------|
| Convector unit..... | 8,000 Btu per hr self-contained cooling chassis only ...................... | 0.45 | 550 |
| Convector unit..... | 12,000 Btu per hr self-contained cooling chassis only....................... | 0.45 | 605 |
| Convector unit..... | 16,000 Btu per hr self-contained cooling chassis only....................... | 0.45 | 640 |
| Cabinet ........... | Decorative cabinet without cooling chassis; includes wall sleeve and out- side louver ........................ | 1.30 | 195 |
| Heating coil ....... | For steam or hot water ............... | 0.45 | 45 |
| Solenoid valve ..... | For steam or hot water ............... | 0.50 | 32 |
| Filter ............. | — | — | — |
| Complete unit ..... | Includes cooling system, heating coil, steam valve and vent, decorative cabi- net, wall sleeve, and outside louver: | | |
| | 8,000 Btu per hr................ | 2.00 | 825 |
| | 12,000 Btu per hr................ | 2.00 | 875 |
| | 16,000 Btu per hr................ | 2.00 | 910 |
| Wiring............ | New buildings, per unit (varies) ....... | 0.85 | 15 |
| Wiring............ | Existing buildings, per unit (varies) .... | 5.00 | 20 |

NOTE: The cost of preparing holes, as required, varies from $50 to $200 per unit.

**TABLE 3.33** Window Units—Base Costs

| Capacity, Btu | Horsepower | Volts | Net per unit, $ |
|---------------|------------|-------|------------------|
| Cooling only | | | |
| 8,700 | 1 | 115 | 350 |
| 9,000 | 1 | 230 | 325 |
| 10,000 | 1 | 230 | 375 |
| 13,500 | 1 | 230 | 515 |
| 16,500 | 1½ | 230 | 625 |
| 19,500 | 2 | 230 | 740 |
| 23,000 | 2½ | 230 | 825 |
| Heat pump | | | |
| 10,000 | 1 | 115 | 475 |
| 10,000 | 1 | 230 | 485 |
| 13,000 | 1 | 230 | 635 |
| 15,500 | 1½ | 230 | 275 |
| 18,500 | 2 | 230 | 910 |
| 22,250 | 2½ | 230 | 1,125 |

**TABLE 3.34**   Window Units—Installation Costs

Based on a one-at-a-time installation for average conditions. Includes all necessary cutting and patching, removing glass, and caulking, but does not include materials for cradles, brackets, etc. Dollar column gives prevailing selling price from subcontractors for this work.

| Description | Workhours | Selling price, $ |
|---|---|---|
| Correct size precast opening .... | 3 | 75 |
| Enlarge a precast opening ...... | 5 | 125 |
| Concrete block wall ............ | 8 | 185 |
| Jalousie window .............. | 5 | 150 |
| Casement window.............. | 8 | 185 |
| Awning window ............... | 7 | 175 |
| Double-hung window........... | 4 | 115 |
| Transom..................... | 6 | 150 |

## PLACING THE SYSTEM IN OPERATION

Testing the system before charging, inspecting, charging, placing system in operation, and final 72-hr check are covered in Table 3.35. This activity applies to the refrigeration side of the system and is not to be confused with air and water balancing and total system test and check. They are separate functions, covered in Chap. 15.

**TABLE 3.35**   System Start-up: Test, Evacuate, and Charge—Workhours

Based on average close-coupled hookups with reciprocating compressor, workhours include moving tools and equipment on jobsite, performing tasks as outlined in Chaps. 20 and 21 of *Trane Refrigeration Manual,* and recording all nameplate data and operating conditions on start-up sheet.
It is assumed that tasks are performed by a skilled two-person team; if one person is working alone, use multiplying factor of 1.5. Does not include balancing air or water side, leak repairing, retesting after leak repairing, or standby time during evacuation.

| Nominal tons per system | Water cooled condensing | Air-cooled condensing | Add for operating instructions to owner |
|---|---|---|---|
| 5 | 6 | 7 | 4 |
| 7½ | 6 | 7 | 4 |
| 10 | 8 | 10 | 4 |
| 15 | 8 | 10 | 4 |
| 20 | 10 | 13 | 5 |
| 25 | 10 | 13 | 6 |
| 30 | 10 | 13 | 6 |
| 35 | 12 | 15 | 6 |
| 40 | 16 | 20 | 8 |
| 50 | 16 | 20 | 8 |
| 50 Duplex | 18 | 24 | 10 |
| 80 Duplex | 19 | 24 | 10 |
| 100 Duplex | 22 | 26 | 10 |
| 150 | 24 | 30 | 12 |

*Trane Reciprocating Refrigeration Manual, The Trane Company, La Crosse, Wisconsin, 1977.

## AIR-CONDITIONER OPERATING COSTS

Figure 3.13 shows the approximate cost to operate electric air-conditioning units as a function of tonnage and power cost per kilowatt.

## REFRIGERANTS, CFCS, HCFCS, AND HFCS

The driving issues facing the HVAC industry today are the environmental concerns of ozone depletion, global warming, and energy efficiency. These issues will be the focus of much activity at ARI and ASHRAE for the foreseeable future. There is no single, more critical, more challenging issue confronting the HVAC industry than CFCs. Section 608 of the Clean Air Act has effectively ended the debate about ozone depletion and CFCs and has mandated a phase-out schedule (Table 3.36), which has motivated the industry to search for a perfect refrigerant. There is no doubt that the days—and years—ahead will witness enormous changes in the industry, the exact direction of which is not yet determinable.

The CFC ban affects the industry in many ways, not the least of which is cost. Table 3.37 compares the relative movement of prices between CFCs, HCFCs, and HFCs. As production on the two reliable workhorses, CFC-11 and CFC-12, passes through its scheduled curtailment, prices will increase. Conversely, as HCF production speeds up, prices will decrease. In addition, the Energy Policy Act of 1992 has mandated an Excise Tax on CFCs intended to drive the industry toward alternative refrigerants. Table 3.38 covers this tax from 1994 to 1999.

Whatever direction production and cost of current refrigerants will take, new refrigerants are certain to make their debut in the period ahead. A variety of binary and tertiary blends of various refrigerants is already entering the market, and with this impact comes a transition to alternative refrigerant terminology—additional to the technical vocabulary: *azeotropic mixture, NARMS, alkylbenzene, blend temperature glide,* etc. Table 3.39 provides a ready reference chart to help identify some of the replacement blends already on the market.

There is general agreement that HFC blends are the best alternatives for R-22 and R-502. HCFC-123 is the refrigerant of choice for interim conversion of R-11 centrifugals; and HFC-134a, for R-12. Meanwhile, the ASHRAE Standard 34 Committee is in the process of adding new blends to the Standard. There are 80,000 chillers in the field that must be replaced or converted from R-11, R-12, R-113, R-114, and R-500 in the next few years. They represent about 400,000 lb of alternative refrigerants. And 1996 is the cutoff date for world CFC production.

In the hot, volatile market of refrigerant recovery, recycle, reclaim, conversion, and the production of new refrigerants, the estimator is burdened with new responsibilities—and risks.

When specifications place the responsibility for refrigerant losses with the contractor, the installing contractor must be particularly wary. The refrigerant replacement clause will generally call for contractors to replace, at their own cost, any refrigerant lost during the first year of system operation. Occasionally, however, the period specified may be only 90 days. An amount equal to the cost of a complete charge should be set aside in the reserve funds for the 90-day period, and two complete charges for the one-year period. Table 3.40 gives the rule of thumb for rapid estimating of refrigerant charges for average systems. Table 3.41 gives mid-1994 market costs of refrigerants. A typical 1,000-ton centrifugal at 4 lb/ton subjected to a broken sight glass or fitting could blow a complete charge of medium pressure refrigerant costing $26,000. Two such losses would be catastrophic. The estimator must bear in mind that any refrigerant losses will have to be replaced not at current prices but at the prices in effect when the loss occurs. Table 3.37 should be of some help in that matter.

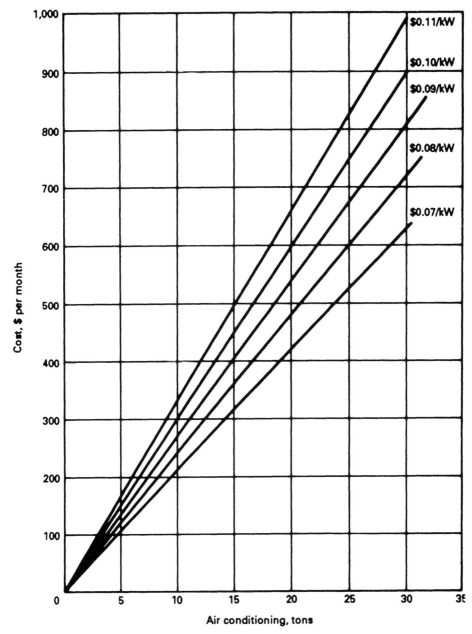

**Figure 3.13 APPROXIMATE COST TO OPERATE ELECTRIC AIR CONDITIONING**
*Based on 300 hr/month operating time.*

**TABLE 3.36** Phase-out Schedule of CFC and HCFC

(Mandated by the Clean Air Act of Nov. 15, 1990 and the Montreal Protocol.)

| Production, year | % of 1986 production |
|---|---|
| CFC | |
| 1993 | 50 |
| 1994 | 25 |
| 1995 | 25 |
| 1996 | Banned |
| HCFC | |
| 1996 | 100 |
| 2004 | 65 |
| 2010 | 35 |
| 2015 | 10 |
| 2020 | 0.5 |
| 2030 | Banned |

**TABLE 3.37** Relative Price Chart

Showing the relative costs of CFC-11 to two replacement alternatives over the time period 1991–1996. HCFC is the 1993 baseline.

| Refrigerant | 1991 | 1993 | 1996 | 1999 |
|---|---|---|---|---|
| CFC-11 | 1.0 | 1.6 | 2.9 | 7.1 |
| HCFC-123 | 1.4 | 1.0 | 0.9 | 0.7 |
| HFC-134a | 4.0 | 1.5 | 1.3 | 1.0 |

**TABLE 3.38** Excise Tax on CFCs (Energy Policy Act of 1992)

| Year | Excise tax, $/lb |
|---|---|
| 1994 | 4.35 |
| 1995 | 5.35 |
| 1996 | 5.80 |
| 1999 | 7.15 |

**TABLE 3.39** Approved Replacement Blends for CFC Refrigerants

Number designations are not generic.

| Manufacturer's no. | Base | Blend | Term | Application | Comments |
|---|---|---|---|---|---|
| AZ-50 | HFC | 125/143a azeotropic | Long | Low temp. | Will become R-507 |
| HP-62 | HFC | 125/143a/134a | Long | Low temp. | Not for retrofit |
| MP-39 | HCFC | 52/152a/124 | Short | Medium temp. | Good replacement for R-12 |
| MP-66 | HCFC | 22/152a/124 | Short | Low temp. | Good replacement for R-12 |
| MP-80 | HCFC | 22/125/290 | Short | Low temp. | Replaces R-502 |
| HP-81 | HCFC | 22/125/290 | Short | Low temp. | Replaces R-5 ice machines |
| AC-9000 | HFC | 30/125/134a | Long | Medium temp. | Replaces R-22 residential AC |

**TABLE 3.40** Rapid Estimating of Refrigerant Charge in Systems

| System | Pound of refrigerant per ton |
|---|---|
| Package units | 3–5 |
| Centrifugals | 2–6 |

**TABLE 3.41** Common Refrigerants, $/lb

| Container size, lb | Cost per lb, $ | | | | | |
|---|---|---|---|---|---|---|
| | R-11 | R-12 | R-13 | R-22 | R-113 | R-114 |
| 200 | 10.47 | | | | 10.80 | |
| 150 | | | | | | 12.67 |
| 145 | | 9.59 | | | | |
| 125 | | | | 1.79 | | |
| 100 | 10.50 | | | | 11.00 | |
| 80 | | | 37.50 | | | |
| 30 | | 9.85 | | 1.86 | | |
| | R-123 | R-124 | R-134a | R-500 | R-502 | |
| 200 | 4.76 | | | | | |
| 145 | | 8.84 | | | | |
| 125 | | | 6.26 | 10.40 | 8.48 | |
| 100 | 4.89 | | | | | |
| 50 | | | | | 8.63 | |
| 30 | | 9.19 | 6.58 | 11.00 | 8.77 | |
| | MP-39 | MP-66 | HP-80 | HP-81 | | |
| 125 | 5.29 | 5.29 | | | | |
| 110 | | | 8.21 | | | |
| 30 | 6.25 | 6.25 | | | | |
| 27 | | | 8.52 | 9.13 | | |

Ammonia, R-717, may be purchased in 150-lb containers for $0.65/lb. Most large users of ammonia—minimum order 2,000 lb—buy at $0.25 to $0.35/lb delivered by tank truck within 48 hr, pumped into buyer's receiver.

## SERVICE RESERVE

Service reserve and warranty reserve are perhaps the most often overlooked items in a mechanical estimate. When not overlooked, and actually entered into the estimate, the service reserve is invariably underestimated, if not completely misunderstood.

Many contractors feel that if they ignore service, then service will ignore them; consequently, they sweep the service reserve under the rug where no one can see it. The need for servicing mechanical equipment, however, remains a very real contingency of any installation and should be given proper consideration. Just as the manufacturer must provide for the accessibility of a compressor, valve, or motor in the design of the equipment, so must the application engineer allow for service accessibility in the design of the system. In the final analysis, then, it becomes the responsibility of the installing contractor to provide for servicing the equipment and the reserve fund for this purpose.

The service reserve should be treated as part of the job overhead and never as a direct cost. As such, it is not to be marked up. For purposes of job cost analysis and tax computation, however, the amount estimated for the service reserve should be separated from any other overhead and placed in a special fund to be drawn from as required. Of course, if service is to be subcontracted out, the estimate will reflect the selected bid and be handled accordingly.

In some instances, the specifications do not call for the installing contractor to provide for a set service period. It will be assumed that the plant engineer will take over as soon as the system is cranked up, and therefore no service will be required. Experience has shown, however, that some form of service call will be made on every job, and every job should have a service reserve. The data in Table 3.42 include monthly inspection, service labor including emergencies, parts replacement including freight, and refrigerant losses; they reflect the total annual costs to maintain large compressor systems after the one-year warranty period has expired.

When a once-through treated water system is used instead of a tower, deduct 6% from the amounts shown in Table 3.43; however, on raw-water systems from a well on site, it may be nec-

**TABLE 3.42** Service and Maintenance on Large Compressors

| Tonnage range................... | 40–80 | 90–120 | 125–175 | 180–225 | 230–260 | 270–300 |
|---|---|---|---|---|---|---|
| Centrifugal, $ per ton per year ...... | 55 | 52 | 48 | 45 | 41 | 36 |
| Reciprocating, $ per ton per year .... | 60 | 56 | 52 | 98 | 44 | 40 |

**TABLE 3.43** Service Reserve Schedule—Package Unit Systems

Based on system operation of approximately 200 hr per month under average conditions with water tower on roof. For chilled water, add 15%.

| System tons | 90 days, $ | 1 year, $ |
|---|---|---|
| 3 | 60 | 105 |
| 5 | 60 | 175 |
| 7½ | 75 | 265 |
| 10 | 90 | 350 |
| 13 | 115 | 455 |
| 15 | 130 | 525 |
| 18 | 160 | 630 |
| 20 | 175 | 700 |
| 25 | 250 | 1,000 |
| 30 | 335 | 1,350 |
| 40 | 450 | 1,800 |
| 50 | 565 | 2,250 |
| 60 | 675 | 2,700 |
| 70 | 785 | 3,150 |
| 80 | 900 | 3,600 |
| 90–125 | 10 per ton | 40 per ton |
| 150–200 | 8 per ton | 38 per ton |
| Over 200 | 6 per ton | 30 per ton |

**TABLE 3.44** Service Reserve Schedule—Small Units

Self-contained, through-the-wall units and window units.
When used in multiroom application, 1-year service guaranty
is usually required. Generally done below standard labor rates.
Use following schedule.

| Nominal size, hp | Cooling unit, $ per year | Heat pump $ per year |
|:---:|:---:|:---:|
| 1 | 30 | 46 |
| 1½ | 46 | 62 |
| 2 | 62 | 76 |
| 2½ | 76 | 92 |

essary to add 2% to take care of well and pump problems during the first 90 days. For systems using air-cooled condensers, deduct 10% from the figures shown. For small-unit service reserve schedules, see Table 3.44.

When a multiple-room convector system is used, add the following:

| | |
|---|---|
| Systems under 50 tons | $3.00/room/month |
| Systems over 50 tons | 2.25/room/month |

When multiple-package units are used in one system, add 70% of each of the smaller units to 100% of the largest one for the total figure.

When the service period includes heating, with either heat pump, gas-, or oil-fired forced air, or steam systems, and extends for the full year, add 25% to the total. Of course, this is not required for a 90-day service period. See Fig. 2.15 for budget prices on systems up to 1,000 tons.

## MOBILE AIR-CONDITIONING SYSTEMS

In recent years, instant portable air-conditioning systems have made an appearance around the country. These systems—reflecting a growing need for "loaner" air-conditioning equipment—are available on a temporary, rental basis to provide emergency service during power outages, sudden breakdowns, delays in delivery, etc. Geared mainly toward hospitals, auditoriums, schools, laboratories, computer rooms, and general commercial establishments, these rental contractors offer mobile equipment from 2 to 100 tons, including power generators, chillers, and cooling towers. Private parties under tents and pavilions, as well as public events out of doors, are also part of the growing market for these services.

Table 3.45 gives costs for cart or trailer-mounted portable systems from ½ to 880 tons. Purchase price is also listed. Table 3.46 gives rental rates for mobile generators.

**TABLE 3.45**  Mobile, Portable Air Conditioning

Cart- or trailer-mounted. Includes complete electrical system of pan lock pigtails and quick disconnects for hookup to existing electrical power supply, necessary flexible supply and return ductwork as needed, move on and off jobsite, setup and knockdown.

| Capacity, Btuh | Type of system | $/day | $/week or weekend | $/month | Purchase price, $ |
|---|---|---|---|---|---|
| 6,000 | Air-cooled | N/A | 125 | 250 | 900 |
| 10,000 | | 100 | 250 | 550 | 2,500 |
| 12,500 | | 125 | 350 | 650 | — |
| 12,500 | Water-cooled | 130 | 350 | 650 | 3,250 |
| 16,500 | | 140 | 375 | 700 | 3,550 |
| 22,000 | Air-cooled | 130 | 350 | 850 | 3,910 |
| 60,000 | | 500 | 1,250 | 2,500 | 8,600 |
| 120,000 | | 1,000 | 2,500 | 5,000 | 18,000 |
| 600,000 | | 5,000 | 12,500 | 26,000 | 84,500 |
| 720,000 | | 6,000 | 15,000 | 30,000 | 98,000 |
| 960,000 | Chiller | 6,000 | 15,000 | 30,000 | — |

**TABLE 3.46**  Rental Generators

Available with or without air-conditioning equipment to provide electrical power, these mobile generators are complete. Prices include delivery, move on and move off jobsite. Fuel cost not included. Units are diesel.

| Capacity, kVA | $/day |
|---|---|
| 43 | 500 |
| 60 | 600 |
| 85 | 850 |
| 150 | 1000 |

## AMMONIA: COLD STORAGE AND INDUSTRIAL REFRIGERATION

Ammonia may be the best alternative refrigerant in many applications. Currently applied in 80% of all large industrial food processing applications, it can be used in many more situations, including air-conditioning chillers, thermal storage, and smaller air-conditioning and refrigeration systems. With the ban of CFC production and use, ammonia (R-717)—which has long been an economical choice for industrial systems—is attracting fresh attention. Because of its superior thermodynamic properties and low cost, ammonia has always been recognized as an excellent refrigerant, but it is, unfortunately, considered toxic at low concentration levels of 35 to 50 ppm. It is also flammable as a cold liquid—a proportion of 16 to 25% by volume in air will burn rapidly in the presence of an open flame and can explode. Now, with worldwide attention focused on atmospheric ozone depletion, this environment-friendly, nonhalocarbon refrigerant, its drawbacks notwithstanding, will surely gain wider acceptance and application. Ammonia becomes a viable option for tomorrow's systems.

Safety hazards as well as service problems can be easily avoided by intelligent and well-trained personnel taking adequate precautions during design, construction, and installation. Some basic standard practices need to be followed. The estimating tables in this section are based on these practices.

## Piping Requirements

All piping should conform with ANSI/ASME *Code for Pressure Piping,* B31.5-1992, ANSI/ASHRAE 15-1989, and ANSI/IIAR 2-1984. No copper or copper bearing materials may be used in ammonia systems. Pipe materials should be as follows:

| Refrigerant lines | Pipe material |
| --- | --- |
| Liquid lines ≤1½ in. | Schedule 80 carbon steel |
| Liquid lines 2–6 in. | Schedule 40 carbon steel |
| Vapor lines ≤6 in. | Schedule 40 carbon steel |

Cleanliness is critical in ammonia systems. Pipe should be rotary wire brushed, with all foreign matter blown out as it is installed. It should be cut and beveled before welding; backup rings should be used to keep pipe free of slag and particles. Before evacuating and charging, the piping system should be blown through with compressed air or nitrogen. High-side piping should be tested to 300 psig, low-side to 150 psig.

Pipe sizes 1¼ in. or smaller may be threaded or socket-welded. Pipe sizes larger than 1¼ in. are welded. Pipe hangers should be spaced 8 to 10 ft apart and within 2 ft of a change in direction. Stop valves should have welded flanges or be welded in line. Control valves should have welding companion flanges.

Large-size cold storage plants for supermarket chains and similar applications may run about $10 million installed, with basic equipment cost going for about $4 million, and piping, fittings, controls, and labor for about $6 million. In a range of 20 to 100 tons, coolers cost about $2,800 to $3,000 per ton. Two-stage built freezers are about $4,000 per ton, including insulation costs.

## Refrigerated Warehouse Design Guide

Figure 3.14 offers a speed sheet method for quick load estimating of large-size coolers and freezers. This graph is based on the work of the nationally recognized refrigeration expert Hugo C. Smith. Smith's contribution appeared in *Air Conditioning and Refrigeration Business* during the late 1960s. The speed sheet graph is designed for heavy service at 95°F ambient, 16-hr compressor running time with an allowance for lights, people, and lift trucks on an average square-foot basis. Product temperature reduction was calculated on 30°F for coolers and 10°F for freezers. Smith calculated his design on the following insulation schedule:

| | |
| --- | --- |
| 35°F cooler | 4-in. cork or equivalent |
| 30°F cooler | 5-in. cork or equivalent |
| 0°F freezer | 6-in. cork or equivalent |
| −10°F freezer | 7-in. cork or equivalent |
| −20°F freezer | 8-in. cork or equivalent |

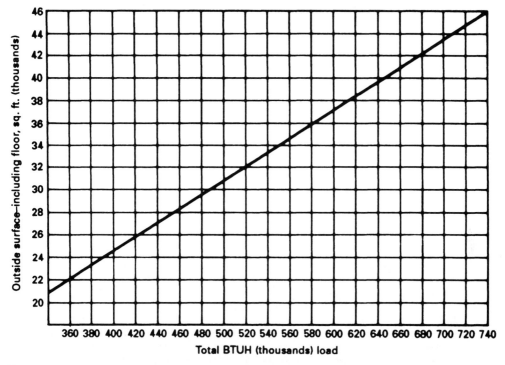

**Figure 3.14   SPEED SHEET: QUICK LOAD ESTIMATING FOR LARGE FREEZERS AND COOLERS**

Assuming the cork had a $K$ value of 0.27, this would be slightly under present-day practice. Table 3.47 gives ASHRAE-recommended $R$ values. In conjunction with the insulation, cold storage buildings *must* be thoroughly sealed with a vapor barrier system.

To use the speed sheet, enter the graph on the left ordinate at the actual total sq ft of the structure, move toward the right to the diagonal intersection, and drop down to the abscissa to read total Btuh load.

**TABLE 3.47**   Recommended Values of $R$ for Freezers and Coolers

| Application | Temperature range, °F | Floors, $R$ | Suspended ceiling and walls, $R$ | Roofs, $R$ |
|---|---|---|---|---|
| Cooler | 40–50 | Perimeter | 25 | 30–35 |
| Chiller cooler | 25–35 | 20 | 24–32 | 35–40 |
| Holding freezer | −10 to −20 | 27–32 | 35–40 | 45–50 |
| Blast freezer | −40 to −50 | 30–40 | 45–50 | 50–60 |

**Example 3.2**   Given a refrigerated warehouse 200 ft L × 50 ft W × 20 ft H.

**solution**   Enter the graph at 30,000 sq ft and move out to the diagonal intersecting line. Drop down to the bottom scale and read 482,000 Btuh total load.

When selecting compressor temperatures, they should be several degrees lower than the required process temperature, particularly if indirect cooling is used and if the coolant is pumped any distance. A good rule of thumb for assessing an industrial refrigeration system at the early stages for most refrigerants, except $CO_2$, is

| Evaporator temperature, °F | +30 | 0 | −30 |
|---|---|---|---|
| hp requirements per ton ref. | 1.2 | 2 | 4.0 |
| kW requirements per ton ref. | 0.9 | 1.5 | 3.0 |

Selection of insulating material may be made on this basis:

| Type of insulation | K factor |
|---|---|
| Polyurethane (expanded) | 0.16 |
| Polyurethane (board) | 0.18 |
| Polystyrene (extruded) | 0.20 |
| Glass fiber and polystyrene (molded beads) | 0.25 |

## Estimating

The estimating data in Tables 3.48 to 3.53 assumes that piping systems conform to code and includes the labor and material to hook up to the equipment listed. Compressors are all reciprocating ammonia compressors up to 200 tons of refrigeration (TR). A 1,000-TR plant, for example, would require a bank of five 200-ton compressor assemblies plus five evaporative condensers and piping to interconnect to the mains. Valves are part of the cost of the receiver as are stands, safeties, etc. Figures 3.15 through 3.17 give the basis for these tables.

**TABLE 3.48**   Compressors

Based on 10°F suction, 95°F. Includes compressor unit, oil separator, check valve, motor, and starter.

| Capacity | 25 | 50 | 75 | 100 | 150 | 200 |
|---|---|---|---|---|---|---|
| Cylinders | 2 | 4 | 6 | 8 | 12 | 16 |
| Price, $ | 11,400 | 16,400 | 21,800 | 27,200 | 35,300 | 43,750 |
| Weight, lb | 2,500 | 3,450 | 4,250 | 4,900 | 7,300 | 8,200 |
| Workhours | 80 | 85 | 90 | 95 | 130 | 150 |
| Materials, $ | 120 | 150 | 170 | 200 | 300 | 425 |
| Motor, hp | 40 | 75 | 125 | 150 | 250 | 300 |

**TABLE 3.49**   Condensers

Based on 10°F suction, 95 and 78°F WB. All galvanized construction with centrifugal fan.

| Capacity | 25 | 50 | 75 | 100 | 150 | 200 |
|---|---|---|---|---|---|---|
| Price, $ | 5,660 | 8,150 | 9,550 | 13,600 | 17,350 | 21,350 |
| Weight, lb | 2,650 | 5,250 | 6,200 | 8,800 | 12,700 | 14,100 |
| Workhours | 40 | 52 | 62 | 110 | 120 | 150 |
| Materials, $ | 250 | 300 | 350 | 450 | 500 | 550 |

**TABLE 3.50**  Receivers

Full to 90% capacity at 90°F. Material and weight include stands, service valves, dual relief assembly, and liquid-level indicator.

| Capacity | 25 | 50 | 75 | 100 | 150 | 200 |
|---|---|---|---|---|---|---|
| Diameter, in. | 20 | 20 | 24 | 30 | 36 | 42 |
| Length, ft | 12 | 16 | 18 | 16 | 14 | 14 |
| Cost, $ | 3,600 | 3,950 | 4,750 | 5,800 | 6,500 | 8,150 |
| Capacity, lb $NH_3$ | 868 | 1,164 | 1,732 | 2,417 | 3,039 | 4,120 |
| Workhours | 25 | 30 | 35 | 40 | 45 | 50 |
| Materials, $ | 120 | 130 | 140 | 170 | 185 | 200 |
| Weight, lb | 1,260 | 1,850 | 2,050 | 2,100 | 2,250 | 3,100 |

**TABLE 3.51**  Suction Accumulator

Based on 10°F suction, capacity calculated with 100 fpm for liquid separation. Physical height 8 ft. Priced bare.

| Capacity | 25 | 50 | 75 | 100 | 150 | 200 |
|---|---|---|---|---|---|---|
| Diameter, in. | 12 | 16 | 20 | 24 | 30 | 36 |
| Price, $ | 1,600 | 1,800 | 3,225 | 3,900 | 5,550 | 7,550 |
| Workhours | 16 | 21 | 27 | 31 | 36 | 44 |
| Materials, $ | 600 | 650 | 700 | 750 | 800 | 850 |
| Weight, lb | 450 | 750 | 950 | 1,425 | 1,600 | 2,400 |

**TABLE 3.52**  Transfer Systems

Based on 10°F suction. Includes pumper drum, valves, and controls.

| Capacity | Up to 120 tons refrigeration | 120 to 200 tons refrigeration |
|---|---|---|
| Price, $ | 3,830 | 4,000 |
| Workhours | 12 | 14 |
| Materials, $ | 130 | 160 |
| Weight, lb | 350 | 375 |

**TABLE 3.53**  Air Units

Ceiling-hung units, based on 10°F suction and 10° TD. Priced bare, with pan for hot-gas defrost and direct expansion. Materials include all valves and controls for hot-gas defrost, including timer.

| Capacity | 10 | 12.5 | 15 |
|---|---|---|---|
| Price, $ | 6,500 | 7,500 | 9,400 |
| Workhours | 65 | 80 | 95 |
| Materials, $ | 1,550 | 1,750 | 1,900 |
| Weight, lb | 2,500 | 3,000 | 4,200 |

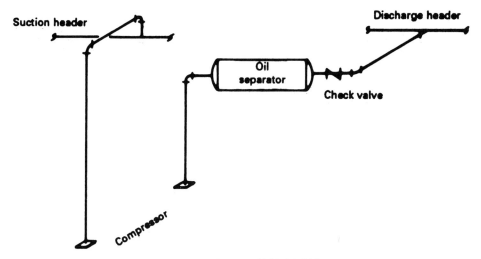

Figure 3.15    COMPRESSOR PIPING

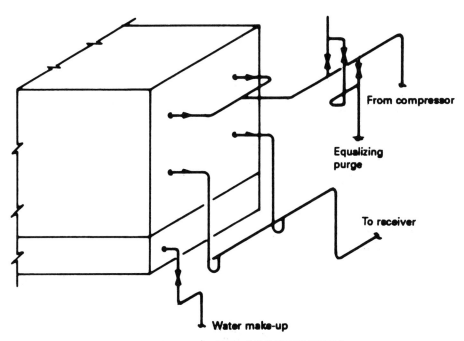

Figure 3.16    EVAPORATIVE CONDENSER PIPING

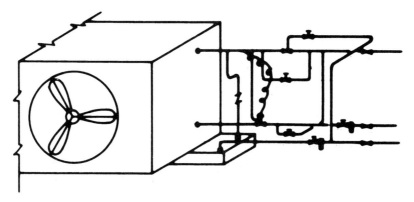

**Figure 3.17   AIR UNIT PIPING**

Tables do not include crane time, structural arrangements for the evaporative condensers, compressor bases, grouting, etc., but leveling and supervision of the grouting is included. All capacities listed are in TR.

Piping prices vary considerably depending on location, size of job, etc. Safety valves need to be changed every five years, and a covering amount should be included in the warranty period. Approximately $100 per valve covers this item. Ammonia prices appear to be steady. This refrigerant is available in 150-lb tanks at 75 cents (¢)/lb. Large users, 2,000 lb minimum, can buy at 25 to 30¢/lb delivered to the user's plant and pumped directly into the receiver.

Figure 3.18 offers a speed sheet graph for picking quick budget figures for industrial vapor compression refrigeration systems. Costs represent the complete system fully installed ready to cool the product or heat transfer media to evaporator temperature. Installed cost includes compressor, condensers, evaporator, controls, foundations, and all auxiliaries but does not include piping runs for product or coolant lines.

## ICE STORAGE SYSTEMS

Thermal ice storage banks are becoming a pertinent option as increasing numbers of corporate computer facilities are being constructed nationwide, and utilities have begun promoting the principle of selling electricity at off-peak times. To encourage this concept, most utilities have restructured their rates in such a way as to discourage use of power during the regular weekday stretch and shift more demand to night hours and weekends. A number of utilities now have thermal-energy storage (TES) incentive programs offering cash contributions toward feasibility or design studies and advance payment of up to $30/ton for installation.

In 1994 seven Florida school districts were using ice storage systems. The Florida Power and Light Company owns several such systems in its own buildings, and a number of national chains such as JC Penney have made the switch. One 1994 project for a group of buildings at the University of Miami Marine Laboratories and Schools reveals the following data.

System has a total capacity of 800 tons developed by three six-cylinder reciprocating compressors, 150 hp each, using ammonia refrigerant, producing 40°F chiller water and 120 tons of ice. Ice is stored in a set of 12-ton-hr fiber-glass tanks. The project cost pertaining to this

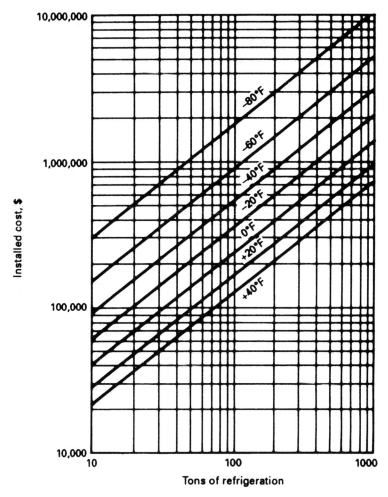

**Figure 3.18  SPEED SHEET ESTIMATING FOR INDUSTRIAL VAPOR COMPRES-SION REFRIGERATION SYSTEMS**

portion of the mechanical system was about $800,000 or $1,000 per ton. Projected air-conditioning operating cost is $532,000 per year—down 24% from the previous $700,000 per year. Payback period, 5 years.

Full-storage systems for complete load shifting with a conventionally designed chiller are usually used in retrofit applications. In new construction, a partial storage system is most practical and cost-efficient. In this load-leveling method, the chiller runs continuously, charging the ice storage at night and cooling the load directly during the day with help from stored cooling.

Typical economic analysis of a partial storage system:

Assume a 100-ton peak cooling load, 10-hr cooling day, 75% diversity factor, $8.00/month/kW demand charge, and a 12-month power ratchet.

1. Conventional chilled-water air-conditioning system
   *a.* 100-ton conventional chiller at $600/ton installed (includes cooling towers, fan coils, pumps, piping control, etc.)  = **$60,000**
   *b.* Air distribution system  =  60,000

   Total system  $120,000

2. Partial ice storage system. The true cooling load at 75% diversity factor translates into 750 ton-hr. A conventional 40-ton chiller provides 400 ton-hr, and the balance of the load, 350 ton-hr, is picked up by the ice banks:
   *a.* 40-ton chiller @ $600/ton installed  $24,000
   *b.* Stored cooling @ $60/ton-hr installed  21,000
   *c.* Air distribution system  60,000

   Total ice storage system  $105,000

3. Summary
   *a.* First-cost savings  $15,000
   *b.* Demand savings
       (60 tons × 1.5 kW/ton × 12 mo × $8.00 = $8,640)
   *c.* Equipment prices are end-user purchase.

By transferring cooling loads to off-peak hours via nighttime ice production for use during the next day's peak hours, the chiller works over a greater spread and thus reduces peak electrical loads. In buildings and facilities where occupancy occurs over a 10- or 12-hr period, ice storage systems are a viable option. In addition, ice storage systems offer the possibility of reducing the size of the mechanical components, e.g., towers, air handlers, pumps, and ductwork, and lend themselves to the ready application of heat recovery at a very slight first-cost premium. Figure 3.19 is a simplified schematic showing a typical ice storage system using the chiller priority strategy, wherein the ice storage tanks are placed downstream of the chiller. The critical discharge rate of the ice storage system is controlled by adjusting the rate of glycol flow through the storage tank by means of the three-way mixing valve shown in the diagram.

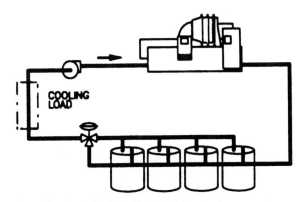

**Figure 3.19 CHILLER PRIORITY ICE STORAGE**
*Chiller and ice storage tanks in series. The ice and three-way diverter valve are downstream of the chiller. (Source: The Trane Company, La Crosse, Wisc.)*

## Case Study No. 1

Arizona Public Service Company, Peoria Avenue Service Center, Phoenix

1,500 sq ft of conditioned offices

Chiller size: two 80-ton generator-chiller units

Ice storage capacity: 4,000 ft³, 2,660 ton-hr

Cost of chiller (1986 prices): $200,000

Cost of ice storage tanks: $100,000

Total cost: $300,000 ($750/kW)

Operation savings: $49,000 per year

Payback period on ice storage system: 6 years

System shifts 400 kW of peak demand to off-peak hours. Replaces two 360-ton capacity chillers.

## Case Study No. 2

Worthington Hotel, Fort Worth, Tex.

525,000 sq ft of conditioned space; 510 guest rooms plus public space facilities

Chiller size: one 230-ton screw machine

Ice storage capacity: 14,900 ft³, 5,000 ton-hr

Cost of chillers: $100,000 material, $50,000 labor

Cost of ice storage tanks: $250,000

Typical cost: $400,000

Operation savings: $72,000 per year

Cash incentive from Texas Utility: $200,800

Net cost to Worthington Hotel: $149,200

Payback period on ice storage system: 2.1 years

Figure 3.20 depicts a load profile for a typical ice storage system. The conventional cooling load is seen to occur between 2 and 7 pm. At full storage the total load shifts to the low-demand nighttime hours and the partial load operation flattens out.

## Estimating

The entire system, less the storage tanks and their accessories, is estimated in the standard manner: chillers, piping, towers, pumps, air-handling units, and air distribution. Only the tanks need to be added. Ice storage tanks are usually made of modular polyethylene and may be installed above or below ground. Base price for ice tanks is about $38/ton-hour. Table 3.54 does not include freight or glycol solution. Modular tanks for multiple hookup are factory equipped with prepiped, preinsulated supply and return headers; only two flange connections are required. There are no moving parts; they are easily shipped and installed.

Propylene glycol may be purchased for $18.75/gal.; 55-gal. drums cost $600.

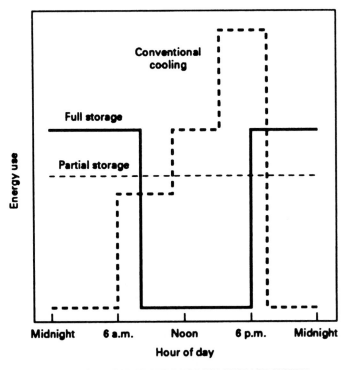

**Figure 3.20   LOAD PROFILE FOR ICE STORAGE SYSTEM**

**TABLE 3.54**   Ice Storage Tanks

| Capacity, ton-hours | 115 | 190 | 570 |
|---|---|---|---|
| Dimensions (OD × H), in. | 89 × 68 | 89 × 101 | — |
| Dimensions (W × L × H), in. | — | — | 96 × 268 × 102 |
| Weight, empty, lb | 1,060 | 1,550 | 4,850 |
| Weight, filled, lb | 9,940 | 16,750 | 50,720 |
| Floor loading, lb/sq ft | 230 | 388 | 284 |
| Volume of water/ice, gal | 980 | 1,820 | 4,860 |
| Volume of solution, gal | 90 | 108 | 475 |
| Connection to tanks, in. | 2.5 mpt | 2.5 mpt | 4 flange |
| Header pipe size, in. | 2 fpt | 2 fpt | 2 fpt |
| Tank cost, $ | 4,675 | 6,485 | 19,995 |
| Ice inventory meter, $ | 800 | 800 | 800 |
| Coolant tester, $ | 150 | 150 | 150 |
| Flexible connector, $ | 175 | 175 | 175 |
| Workhours | 12 | 12 | 16 |
| Labor, $ | 295 | 295 | 395 |
| Underground tanks require special construction: extra, $ | 400 | 500 | 1,500 |

## WALK-IN COOLERS

For hospitals, restaurants, supermarkets, and hotels, the walk-in coolers listed in Table 3.55 are based on 8-ft 5-in. overall height. Included are 2-ft 6-in. × 6-ft 6-in. door, all hardware, matched coil and condensing unit, and all labor to deliver and erect. Not included are plumbing and electrical wiring.

**TABLE 3.55** Walk-in Coolers

| Width, ft | Length, ft | Square feet | Condensing unit, hp | In-place, $ |
|---|---|---|---|---|
| 6 | 6 | 36 | ½ | 4,500 |
| 6 | 8 | 48 | ½ | 5,250 |
| 6 | 10 | 60 | ¾ | 6,125 |
| 6 | 12 | 72 | 1 | 6,750 |
| 8 | 8 | 64 | 1 | 6,000 |
| 8 | 10 | 80 | 1½ | 7,000 |
| 8 | 12 | 96 | 1½ | 7,500 |
| 8 | 14 | 112 | 1½ | 8,000 |
| 8 | 16 | 128 | 2 | 9,000 |
| 10 | 10 | 100 | 1½ | 7,750 |
| 10 | 12 | 120 | 1½ | 8,250 |
| 10 | 14 | 140 | 1½ | 8,625 |
| 10 | 16 | 160 | 2 | 9,750 |
| 10 | 18 | 180 | 2 | 10,750 |
| 10 | 20 | 200 | 2 | 11,500 |
| 12 | 12 | 144 | 1½ | 8,750 |
| 12 | 14 | 168 | 2 | 9,500 |
| 12 | 16 | 192 | 2 | 10,375 |
| 12 | 18 | 216 | 2 | 11,375 |
| 12 | 20 | 240 | 2 | 12,500 |
| 12 | 24 | 288 | 2 | 13,750 |

## WATER COOLERS

The water coolers listed in Table 3.56 are based on 80°F entering water and 50°F drinking water. They are self-contained refrigeration system drinking-water coolers with air-cooled condensers. For water-cooled condensers, increase the listed capacities by 25% and the costs by 15%. Labor includes rough-in piping and setting, but not wiring.

**TABLE 3.56** Water Coolers—Labor and Material

| Type | GPM | Cost, $ | Labor, workhours |
|---|---|---|---|
| Floor-mounted (compact) | 3 | 382 | 2 |
| Floor-mounted | 5 | 432 | 2 |
| Floor-mounted | 14.3 | 500 | 2 |
| Wall-hung (compact) | 3 | 417 | 2 |
| Wall-hung | 5 | 478 | 2 |
| Wall-hung | 14.3 | 490 | 2 |
| Wall-hung, wheelchair | 7.5 | 550 | 2 |
| Floor-mounted, hot and cold | 8.9 | 675 | 2 |

## REFRIGERATION SPECIALTIES

Workhour costs for erection of valves, specials, and flexible pipe may be found in Chaps. 9 and 13.

## RECOMMENDED READING

ANSI/ASHRAE, *Safety Code for Mechanical Refrigeration*, Standard 15-1989, American Society of Heating, Refrigerating and Air-Conditioning Engineers, Atlanta, Ga., 1989.

ANSI/ASME, *Code for Pressure Piping*, Standard B31.5-1992, American Society of Mechanical Engineers, New York, 1992.

ANSI/IIAR, *Equipment, Design, and Installation of Ammonia Mechanical Refrigeration Systems*, 2-1984, International Institute of Ammonia Refrigeration, Chicago, 1984.

ASHRAE, *Handbook: Refrigeration Systems and Application*, Chap. 4, 1990.

## ACKNOWLEDGMENT

The editors wish to acknowledge the contribution of Alvaro A. Cadenas, Filbert Corporation, Miami/Orlando for his assistance with this chapter.

# CHAPTER 4
# MECHANICAL HEATING EQUIPMENT[1]

## GENERAL DISCUSSION

Estimating considerations for several types of mechanical heating equipment are covered in this chapter. Boilers include complete packaged, cast-iron sectional, steel, and six-sectional boilers. Other mechanical heating equipment includes hot-water radiation and steam radiation. Material cost, labor workhours, and labor cost of basic heat-generating and distributing units are treated in this chapter.

The most economical heat-generating unit, from the standpoint of installed first cost, is the complete packaged boiler. A cast-iron sectional boiler costs about 15% more than a steel boiler and requires more hours to install. However, in some instances the knocked-down shipment of a boiler may be a decided cost advantage (e.g., six-sectional boiler).

The heating surface for hot-water radiation will be about 1½ times that of steam, since the heat radiation for steam is based on 240 Btu/sq ft, while that of water is based on 160 Btu/sq ft. Boiler horsepower is rated at 33,475 Btu/hr.

When the estimator is required to size the boiler for budget figures, the singular requirement is building heat loss. Regardless of the type of heat distribution system, building heat loss should be divided by 160 Btu for a water boiler or 240 Btu for a steam boiler. The 160 Btu/hr water and 240 Btu/hr steam calculations include provisions for up to two bathrooms and domestic hot-water demand of up to 75 gal./day. When the domestic hot-water demand exceeds 75 gal./day, boiler size should be increased by ½ sq ft of steam or ⅔ sq ft of water for each gallon of storage tank capacity. Conversion ratios and equivalents are given in Table 4.1.

Contractor overhead and profit are not included in any of the following tables unless otherwise noted. Budget cost figures for commercial boilers may be found in Fig. 2.13 and budget figures for chimneys, in Fig. 2.14. Table 4.2[2] compares various types of boilers to aid in their selection. Table 4.3 gives a comparison of boiler installation times.

## COMMERCIAL CAST-IRON BOILERS

Table 4.4 shows workhours and material costs for cast-iron section boilers. The listed prices are for steam or hot water and either gas or oil firing. Material price includes steel jacket, insulation, pedestal-mounted burner, draft regulator, and stack switch. It does not include stack

---

[1] By Kerry L. Kost, Project Time & Cost, Atlanta, Ga.

[2] The source of Tables 4.2, 4.3, 4.17, and 4.25 is *Means Estimating Handbook*, R. S. Means Co., Kingston, Mass., 1994.

**TABLE 4.1** Conversion Ratios and Equivalents

| Multiply | x | To obtain |
|---|---|---|
| sq ft EDR steam . . . . . . | 240 | Btu per hr |
| sq ft EDR water . . . . . . | 160 | Btu per hr |
| Boiler hp . . . . . . . . . | 33.5 | MBtu per hr |
| Boiler hp . . . . . . . . . | 140 | sq ft EDR steam |
| Boiler hp . . . . . . . . . | 223 | sq ft EDR water |
| Boiler hp . . . . . . . . . | 34.5 | lb per hr steam |
| lb per hr steam . . . . . . | 970 | Btu per hr |
| sq ft EDR steam . . . . . . | 0.247 | lb per hr steam |
| sq ft EDR water . . . . . . | 0.155 | lb per hr steam |
| **To obtain above** | **Divide by above** | **Starting with above** |

**TABLE 4.2** Boiler Selection Chart

Several types of boilers are available to meet the hot-water and heating needs of both residential and commercial buildings. Some different boiler types are shown in this table. Most hot-water boilers operate at less than 30 psig (low-pressure boilers). Low-pressure steam boilers operate at less than 15 psig. Above 30 psig high-pressure boilers must conform to stricter requirements. Water is lost to a heating system through minor leaks and evaporation; therefore, a makeup water line to feed the boiler with fresh makeup water must be provided.

| Boiler type | Output capacity range, MBh efficiency range | Fuel types | Uses |
|---|---|---|---|
| Cast-iron sectional | 80–14,500, 80–92% | Oil, gas, coal, wood and fossil | Steam and hot water |
| Steel | 1,200–18,000, 80–92% | Oil, gas, coal, wood and fossil, electric | Steam and hot water |
| Scotch marine | 3,400–24,000, 80–92% | Oil, gas | Steam and hot water |
| Pulse condensing | 40–150, 90–95% | Gas | Hot water |
| Residential/wall-hung | 15–60, 90–95% | Gas, electric | Hot water |

Efficiencies shown are averages and will vary with specific manufacturers. For existing equipment, efficiencies may be 60 to 75%.

or breeching circulators, water heaters, or special controls. Workhours include moving components 40 ft to the machine room, uncrating, installing, assembling and drawing up sections, and start-up. Steam is rarely used in heating systems today except in replacing existing boilers or in very large installations. Hot-water heating systems are more common in current construction.

Table 4.5[3] shows material and installation costs for larger cast-iron, oil-fired boilers with standard controls and a flame retention burner. Costs are the same for steam and hot-water units.

---

[3]The source of Tables 4.5, 4.7 to 4.9, 4.11, 4.14, 4.22 to 4.24, 4.26, and 4.29 is *Means Mechanical Cost Data 1994*, R. S. Means Co., Kingston, Mass.

**TABLE 4.3** Installation Time in Workhours for Boilers

| Description | | Workhours/unit |
|---|---|---|
| Electricity-fired, steel, output MBh | | |
| | 60 | 20 |
| | 500 | 36 |
| | 1,000 | 60 |
| | 2,000 | 94 |
| | 3,000 | 114 |
| | 7,000 | 178 |
| Gas-fired, cast-iron, output MBh | | |
| | 80 | 22 |
| | 500 | 53 |
| | 1,000 | 64 |
| | 2,000 | 99 |
| | 3,000 | 133 |
| | 7,000 | 400 |
| Oil-fired, cast-iron, output MBh | | |
| | 100 | 27 |
| | 500 | 64 |
| | 1,000 | 76 |
| | 2,000 | 114 |
| | 3,000 | 139 |
| | 7,000 | 400 |
| Scotch Marine packaged units, gas- or oil-fired, output MBh | | |
| | 1,300 | 80 |
| | 3,350 | 80 |
| | 4,200 | 85 |
| | 5,000 | 90 |
| | 6,700 | 90 |
| | 8,370 | 110 |
| | 10,000 | 120 |
| | 20,000 | 130 |
| | 23,400 | 140 |

**TABLE 4.4** Small Commercial Cast-Iron Boilers

For tankless-type water heaters, add 15%; for storage-type
water heaters, add 10%.

| MBh | Boiler cost, $ | Installation, workhours |
|---|---|---|
| 53 | 1,370 | 20 |
| 70 | 1,510 | 22 |
| 89 | 1,120 | 24 |
| 115 | 1,480 | 27 |
| 175 | 1,800 | 32 |
| 235 | 1,950 | 40 |
| 275 | 1,960 | 42 |
| 311 | 2,930 | 45 |
| 404 | 3,290 | 48 |
| 534 | 3,770 | 51 |
| 664 | 4,250 | 55 |
| 794 | 4,680 | 59 |
| 940 | 6,800 | 69 |
| 1,054 | 5,650 | 76 |
| 1,184 | 6,130 | 86 |
| 1,314 | 6,610 | 98 |
| 1,600 | 11,190 | 115 |
| 1,770 | 9,600 | 120 |
| 1,942 | 10,320 | 127 |
| 2,480 | 15,060 | 132 |

**TABLE 4.5** Large Commercial Cast-Iron Boilers

Oil-fired, standard controls, flame-retention burner.

| Gross output steam, MBh | Material cost, $ | Installation, workhours | Installation labor, $ | Total cost, $ |
|---|---|---|---|---|
| 2,175 | 12,300 | 114 | 3,075 | 15,375 |
| 2,480 | 14,000 | 128 | 3,450 | 17,450 |
| 3,000 | 16,200 | 139 | 3,750 | 19,950 |
| 3,550 | 18,300 | 145 | 3,925 | 22,225 |
| 3,820 | 19,200 | 168 | 4,550 | 23,750 |
| 4,360 | 21,600 | 188 | 5,075 | 26,675 |
| 4,940 | 35,400 | 213 | 5,750 | 41,150 |
| 5,520 | 40,300 | 246 | 6,650 | 46,950 |
| 6,100 | 46,400 | 266 | 7,200 | 53,600 |
| 6,390 | 48,900 | 320 | 8,650 | 57,550 |
| 6,680 | 50,500 | 355 | 9,600 | 60,100 |
| 6,970 | 52,000 | 400 | 10,800 | 62,800 |

Crew of two steamfitters, one steamfitter apprentice, and one steamfitter supervisor for a total of 32
workhours per day.

**TABLE 4.6**   Commercial Packaged Scotch Marine Boilers

Packaged Scotch marine fire tube, no. 2 oil, ASME 15 psi steam, 30 psi water. Material price includes skids and steam or hot-water trimmings, does not include condensate sets, preheaters, burners, or refractories. Labor includes jacking up, placing on dollies, moving on skids to machine room, 75 ft lining up precisely, set, level, and start-up.

| MBh | hp | Boiler cost, $ | Installation, workhours |
|---|---|---|---|
| 1,005 | 30 | 15,700 | 110 |
| 1,675 | 50 | 20,200 | 126 |
| 3,350 | 100 | 27,500 | 152 |
| 5,025 | 150 | 25,000 | 169 |
| 6,700 | 200 | 41,600 | 176 |
| 8,375 | 250 | 48,200 | 183 |
| 10,050 | 300 | 54,900 | 191 |

## PACKAGED SCOTCH-TYPE BOILERS

Data on commercial boilers of the packaged Scotch type are given in Table 4.6.

## RESIDENTIAL BOILERS

Table 4.7 gives data for packaged gas-fired steel boilers for hot water. Material prices include burner, one-zone valve, and standard controls.

**TABLE 4.7**   Residential Packaged Steel Boilers

Hot water, includes burner, one-zone valve, standard controls. Natural gas or propane.

| Gross output, MBh | Material cost, $ | Installation, workhours | Installation labor, $ | Total cost, $ |
|---|---|---|---|---|
| 51.2 | 1,425 | 12 | 315 | 1,740 |
| 72 | 1,600 | 12 | 315 | 1,915 |
| 89 | 1,650 | 13 | 335 | 1,985 |
| 105 | 1,850 | 13 | 350 | 2,200 |
| 132 | 2,100 | 14 | 375 | 2,475 |
| 155 | 2,450 | 16 | 425 | 2,875 |
| 186 | 2,950 | 17 | 455 | 3,405 |
| 227 | 3,750 | 18 | 490 | 4,240 |
| 292 | 4,225 | 20 | 530 | 4,755 |
| 400 | 5,350 | 30 | 795 | 6,145 |
| 480 | 6,100 | 34 | 905 | 7,005 |
| 640 | 7,250 | 40 | 1,050 | 8,300 |
| 800 | 8,450 | 48 | 1,275 | 9,725 |
| 960 | 10,500 | 53 | 1,400 | 11,900 |
| 1,200 | 12,900 | 60 | 1,575 | 14,475 |
| 1,440 | 14,600 | 69 | 1,800 | 16,400 |
| 1,960 | 19,400 | 80 | 2,125 | 21,525 |
| 2,400 | 23,600 | 120 | 3,175 | 26,775 |
| 3,000 | 29,200 | 160 | 4,225 | 33,425 |

Crew of two steamfitters and one apprentice, i.e., 24 workhours per day.

*Note:* For tankless water heater on smaller gas units, add 10%. For additional zone valves up to 312 MBh, add $93.

**TABLE 4.8** Pulse Boilers

Natural gas or propane. Standard controls.

| Btu per hr | Material cost, $ | Installation, workhours |
|---|---|---|
| 44,000 | 1,925 | 11 |
| 88,000 | 2,350 | 11.5 |
| 134,000 | 3,125 | 13.5 |

**TABLE 4.9** Wall-hung Boilers

Cast iron, sealed combustion, direct vent. Standard controls, natural gas or propane.

| Btu per hr | Material cost, $ | Installation, workhours |
|---|---|---|
| 45,000 | 1,150 | 18 |
| 60,800 | 1,300 | 18 |
| 77,000 | 1,425 | 18 |

## PULSE COMBUSTION BOILERS

Material cost and installation workhours for gas-fired pulse boilers with standard controls are shown in Table 4.8.

## WALL-HUNG BOILERS

Material cost and installation workhours for gas-fired wall-hung boilers with standard controls are shown in Table 4.9.

## BOILER HOOKUPS

Material cost and installation workhours for boiler hookups are shown in Table 4.10.

## OIL-BURNER UNITS

The prices listed in Table 4.11 are based on standard models and do not include the stack switch, fuel pump, limit control, thermostat, or mounting accessories.

## UNIT HEATERS FOR STEAM AND HOT-WATER SYSTEMS

Unit heater costs are shown in Tables 4.12 and 4.13. The ratings are based on 2-psi steam and 60°F entering air. Material includes fan, motor, heating coil, and casing for one-phase 115-V 60-cycle service.

## RADIATORS AND BASEBOARDS

Radiators and baseboard heating components are manufactured in a variety of tubes, heights, and tappings. The prices shown in Table 4.14 are for the base unit only and do not include accessories. Tables 4.15 and 4.16 show workhours for the typical radiator and unit heat hookups illustrated in Figs. 4.1 and 4.2. Table 4.17 shows installation time for a complete forced-hot-water heating system.

**TABLE 4.10**  Boiler Hookups

**Screwed**

Material cost includes four lin ft pipe, two gate valves, two unions, four reducing tees, four 90° ells, two therm-o-wells, two thermometers, one manual air vent, one drain valve, one pressure-relief valve of next-smaller pipe size, 8 lin ft copper pipe of next-smaller pipe size, and one copper 90° ell of next-smaller pipe size.

| Pipe size, in | 1 | 1¼ | 1½ | 2 | 2½ |
|---|---|---|---|---|---|
| Material cost, $ | 209 | 246 | 257 | 377 | 474 |
| Workhours | 11 | 12 | 13 | 15 | 19 |
| Labor cost, $ | 206 | 231 | 250 | 291 | 347 |
| Equipment cost, $ | 4 | 5 | 5 | 6 | 7 |
| Total | 419 | 482 | 512 | 674 | 828 |

**Welded**

Material cost includes 4 lin ft pipe, two gate valves, six weld neck flanges, six bolt nut and gasket sets, one reducing tee, four 90° ells, two ¾-in thread-o-lets, two therm-o-wells, two thermometers, one manual air vent, one drain valve, one 2-in pressure-relief valve, 8 lin ft of 2-in copper pipe, and one 2-in copper 90° ell.

| Pipe size, in. | 3 | 4 | 6 | 8 | 10 | 12 |
|---|---|---|---|---|---|---|
| Material cost, $ | 605 | 688 | 1,212 | 1,701 | 2,777 | 3,769 |
| Workhours | 40 | 63 | 86 | 103 | 129 | 151 |
| Labor cost, $ | 729 | 1,141 | 1,566 | 1,702 | 2,146 | 2,506 |
| Equipment cost, $ | 29 | 44 | 65 | 165 | 198 | 242 |
| Total | 1,363 | 1,873 | 2,843 | 3,568 | 5,121 | 6,517 |

**TABLE 4.11**  Oil-burner Units

Flame retention, oil-fired assembly, input.

| Capacity, gph | Unit cost | Workhours |
|---|---|---|
| 0.50 to 2.25 | $280 | 6.7 |
| 2 to 5 | $450 | 8 |
| 3 to 7 | $460 | 9 |
| 6 to 12 | $755 | 10 |

**TABLE 4.12**  Unit Heaters, Ceiling-Suspended, Horizontal Delivery

Labor includes moving equipment 40 ft to set location, uncrating, and hanging from ceiling to 12 ft high.

| Capacity, MBh | 18 | 24 | 33 | 47 | 63 | 86 | 106 |
|---|---|---|---|---|---|---|---|
| cfm | 237 | 363 | 582 | 725 | 1,025 | 1,320 | 1,842 |
| Unit cost, $ | 174 | 174 | 201 | 266 | 307 | 319 | 407 |
| Workhours | 2.2 | 2.2 | 2.7 | 3.2 | 3.5 | 3.8 | 4.0 |

| Capacity, MBh | 121 | 165 | 193 | 285 | 290 | 340 |
|---|---|---|---|---|---|---|
| cfm | 2,090 | 2,770 | 3,230 | 3,840 | 4,590 | 5,120 |
| Unit cost, $ | 425 | 546 | 581 | 714 | 888 | 1,006 |
| Workhours | 4.3 | 4.5 | 4.9 | 5.1 | 5.4 | 8.9 |

**TABLE 4.13** Unit Heaters, Ceiling-Suspended, Vertical Delivery

Labor includes moving equipment 40 ft to set location, uncrating, and hanging from ceiling to 12 ft high.

| Capacity, MBh | 42 | 59 | 78 | 95 | 139 | 161 |
|---|---|---|---|---|---|---|
| cfm | 685 | 1,040 | 1,370 | 1,715 | 2,360 | 2,900 |
| Unit cost, $ | 293 | 275 | 341 | 357 | 428 | 441 |
| Workhours | 2.7 | 3.2 | 3.8 | 4.3 | 4.9 | 5.4 |

| Capacity, MBh | 193 | 212 | 247 | 279 | 333 | |
|---|---|---|---|---|---|---|
| cfm | 3,530 | 4,250 | 4,450 | 5,200 | 5,350 | |
| Unit cost, $ | 514 | 514 | 741 | 767 | 926 | |
| Workhours | 5.9 | 6.5 | 6.9 | 7.7 | 8.0 | |

**TABLE 4.14** Radiators and Baseboard Material

| *Item* | *Installed unit cost $* |
|---|---|
| Cast-iron radiator, free-standing or wall-hung: | |
| 6-tube, 25 in. high.................................. | $27.25 per section |
| 4-tube, 25 in. high.................................. | 21.45 per section |
| 4-tube, 19 in. high.................................. | 20.25 per section |
| Cast-iron radiator, recessed without grille: | |
| 20 in. high by 5 in. deep........................... | 26.05 per section |
| Inlet grille.......................................... | 1.36 per section |
| Cast-iron baseboard ................................. | 32.85 per lin ft |
| Fin-tube, wall-hung, 14-in. slope top cover with damper: | |
| 1¼-in. copper tube, 4¼-in. aluminum fin.............. | 43.25 per lin ft |
| 1¼-in. steel tube, 4¼-in. steel fin .................... | 40.80 per lin ft |
| 2-in. steel tube, 4¼-in. steel fin ...................... | 44.25 per lin ft |
| Fin-tube, baseboard: | |
| ½-in. copper tube, 7-in. aluminum fin................. | 14.25 per lin ft |
| ¾-in. copper tube, 7-in. aluminum fin................. | 15.10 per lin ft |
| 1-in. copper tube, 8⅞-in. aluminum fin ............... | 21.75 per lin ft |
| 1¼-in. copper tube, 8⅞-in. aluminum fin.............. | 28.05 per lin ft |
| 1¼-in. IPS steel tube, steel fin ....................... | 30.35 per lin ft |

**TABLE 4.15**   Heating Piping Connections—Workhours

| Pipe size, in. | ¾ | 1 | 1¼ | 1½ | 2 | 2½ | 3 | 3½ | 4 | 5 | 6 |
|---|---|---|---|---|---|---|---|---|---|---|---|
| One-piece risers ... | 0.45 | 0.53 | 0.56 | 0.62 | 0.72 | 0.90 | 1.08 | 1.26 | 1.44 | 1.98 | 2.52 |
| Two-piece risers ... | 0.63 | 0.72 | 0.81 | 1.10 | 1.17 | 1.53 | 1.71 | 1.98 | 2.34 | 3.24 | 4.05 |
| Riser runouts ..... | 1.0 | 1.1 | 1.3 | 1.5 | 1.9 | 2.7 | 3.2 | 3.9 | 5.2 | 6.9 | 9.8 |
| Riser breaks ....... | 0.90 | 1.0 | 1.1 | 1.3 | 1.5 | 2.2 | 2.6 | 2.9 | 3.9 | 5.3 | 6.8 |

**TABLE 4.16**   Radiator and Unit Heater Branch Hookups—Workhours

This table is based on below-floor hookup. For above-floor connection, multiply listed amounts by 0.80. See Fig. 4.1 for typical illustration.

| Pipe size, in. | ½ | ¾ | 1 | 1¼ | 1½ | 2 | 2½ | 3 | 4 |
|---|---|---|---|---|---|---|---|---|---|
| Three-piece branch ... | 1.2 | 1.2 | 1.4 | 1.5 | 1.7 | 1.9 | 2.7 | 3.1 | 4.4 |
| Four-piece branch .... | 1.4 | 1.4 | 1.8 | 1.9 | 2.2 | 2.6 | 3.1 | 3.9 | 5.5 |
| Five-piece branch .... | 1.8 | 1.8 | 2.0 | 2.3 | 2.4 | 3.1 | 4.3 | 4.7 | 6.2 |

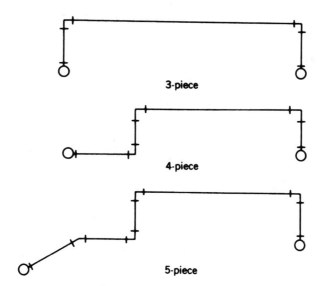

3-piece

4-piece

5-piece

Figure 4.1   **RADIATOR AND UNIT HEATER BRANCH HOOKUPS**

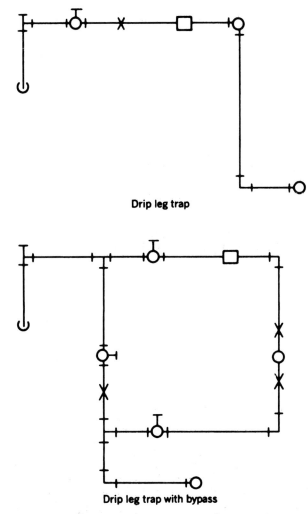

Drip leg trap

Drip leg trap with bypass

**Figure 4.2  DRIP LEG AND TRAP HOOKUPS USED FOR STEAM SYSTEMS**

| Main size, in. | 2 | 2½ | 3 | 4 | 6 | 8 |
|---|---|---|---|---|---|---|
| Length of drip leg, in. | 15 | 18 | 15 | 24 | 18 | 18 |

Diameter of leg is same as that of main.

**TABLE 4.17**  Installation Time in Workhours for Forced-Hot-Water Heating Systems

| Description | Workhours |
|---|---|
| Hot-water heating system, area to 2,400 sq ft | |
| Boiler package, oil-fired, 225 MBh | 17.143 each |
| Oil piping system | 4.584 each |
| Oil tank, 550 gal. with black steel fill pipe | 4 each |
| Supply piping, ¾-in. copper tubing | 0.182 per lin ft |
| Supply fittings, copper | 0.421 per lin ft |
| Baseboard radiation | 0.667 per lin ft |

## HEATING AND PIPING FOR STEAM AND HOT-WATER SYSTEMS

The estimated workhours for specific-size pipe installation, including final connections to units, are treated in Tables 4.15 to 4.18. These are labor costs only and are based on standard weight schedule 40 steel and wrought-iron screwed fittings. The installation labor includes moving materials and equipment on the jobsite, aligning, joining and installing, and making fittings servicetight. Setting sleeves, installing hangers and supports, cutting holes, and leak testing are not included. Risers and breaks are based on average 10-ft length per piece; runouts are based on one valve and union per each. If valves and unions are not used, a runout should be treated as a break. For schedule 80 pipe, multiply the listed amounts by 150%. For schedule 120 pipe, multiply by 275%. Material costs and other pipe installation are covered in Chap. 9.

**TABLE 4.18**  Miscellaneous Steam System Unit Hookups—Workhours

For typical drip connection, see Fig. 4.2.

| Pipe size, in. | $\frac{1}{2}$ | $\frac{3}{4}$ | 1 | $1\frac{1}{4}$ | $1\frac{1}{2}$ | 2 |
|---|---|---|---|---|---|---|
| Connecting stub from branch to valve or trap at radiator . . . . . . . . . . . . . . . . . . . . | 0.45 | 0.48 | 0.54 | 0.58 | 0.63 | 0.68 |
| Connecting stub from branch to valve or trap at unit heater . . . . . . . . . . . . . . . . . | 0.52 | 0.57 | 0.68 | 0.75 | 0.86 | 0.99 |
| Main drip and trap connection, no bypass . . . . | 1.70 | 1.80 | 2.00 | 2.20 | 2.50 | 3.50 |
| Main drip and trap connection, with bypass . . . | 2.50 | 2.80 | 3.30 | 3.70 | 4.20 | 5.20 |
| Temperature control and regulating valves, no bypass . . . . . . . . . . . . . . . . . . . . . . | 1.1 | 1.3 | 1.7 | 2.1 | 2.6 | 3.1 |
| Temperature control and regulating valves, with bypass . . . . . . . . . . . . . . . . . . . . | 1.9 | 2.2 | 2.7 | 3.0 | 3.5 | 4.2 |

## STEAM HEATING COILS

Typical piping arrangements for steam coils are shown in Figs. 4.3 and 4.4. Tables 4.19 and 4.20 are based on screwed black iron pipe, except as indicated, and include moving equipment and materials on the jobsite, measuring, joint, and fitting makeup and installing the assembly within 10 ft from floor height. Labor and material costs for steam traps are given in Table 4.21.

## WARM-AIR FURNACES AND GAS-FIRED HEATING UNITS

The warm-air furnaces listed in Tables 4.22 to 4.24 are residential models and are based on factory fabrication and shipping in one-piece units. Factory-fabricated units include a centrifugal fan with adjustable pulley motor, burner, fan limit, control, pressure regulator, and pilot safety for gas-fired or stack control for oil-fired units. They do not include any gas, oil, or flue piping. Table 4.25 gives installation time for a complete gas-fired forced-air heating system.

Workhours include moving equipment 40 ft to location, uncrating, lining up, and setting floor-mounted units, start-up, and test check.

Table 4.26 gives material costs and labor workhours for installing duct heaters. Material cost and installation workhours for gas-fired unit heaters are shown in Table 4.27.

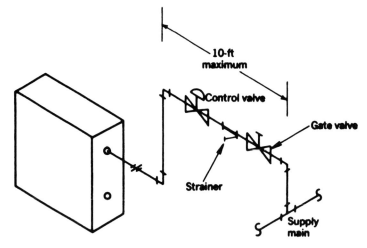

**Figure 4.3   STEAM COIL—SUPPLY HOOKUP**

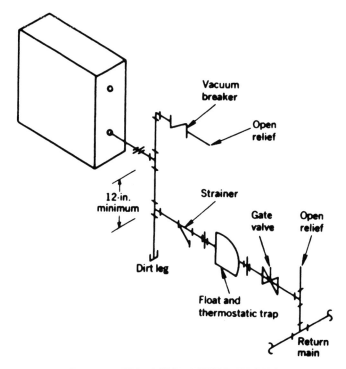

**Figure 4.4   STEAM COIL—RETURN HOOKUP**

**TABLE 4.19**   Steam Coil Supply Hookup—Workhours

|  | Screwed | | | | | | Welded | | |
|---|---|---|---|---|---|---|---|---|---|
| Pipe size, in. . . . . . . . | ¾ | 1 | 1¼ | 1½ | 2 | 2½ | 2½ | 3 | 4 |
| Installation workhours . . | 5.5 | 7.0 | 7.50 | 8.0 | 10.5 | 13.5 | 15.0 | 20.0 | 27.0 |

**TABLE 4.20**   Steam Coil Return Hookup—Workhours
Includes trap and dirt leg.

| Pipe size, in. | ¾ | 1 | 1¼ | 1½ | 2 |
|---|---|---|---|---|---|
| Installation workhours . . . . . . . . | 9.0 | 10.5 | 11.5 | 13.0 | 15.5 |

**TABLE 4.21**   Steam Traps—Labor and Material
Based on one-third continuous discharge ratings at 15 lb maximum pressure. Trap selection should be made from manufacturers' tables for actual condensate requirements.

| Size, in. | Differential pressure: lb per hr condensate | | | | | | | Installation workhours | Material, $ |
|---|---|---|---|---|---|---|---|---|---|
|  | ¼ lb | ½ lb | 1 lb | 3 lb | 5 lb | 10 lb | 15 lb | | |
| Float and thermostatic condensate traps | | | | | | | | | |
| ½ | 23 | 33 | 46 | 66 | 70 | 73 | 75 | 0.5 | 72.5 |
| ¾ | 58 | 83 | 116 | 167 | 175 | 192 | 192 | 0.53 | 110 |
| 1 | 142 | 200 | 283 | 400 | 420 | 460 | 460 | 0.62 | 135 |
| 1¼ | 283 | 400 | 565 | 800 | 840 | 920 | 920 | 0.89 | 195 |
| 2 | 591 | 833 | 1,186 | 1,666 | 1,750 | 1,916 | 1,916 | 1.33 | 355 |

| Size, in. | Differential pressure: lb per hr condensate | | | | Installation workhours | Material, $ |
|---|---|---|---|---|---|---|
|  | 2 lb | 5 lb | 10 lb | 15 lb | | |
| Inverted-bucket-type condensate traps | | | | | | |
| ½ | 238 | 278 | 320 | 347 | 0.67 | 73.5 |
| ¾ | 640 | 790 | 933 | 1,073 | 0.8 | 126 |
| 1 | 777 | 973 | 1,197 | 1,300 | 0.89 | 194 |
| 1¼ | 1,363 | 1,660 | 1,997 | 2,187 | 1.00 | 295 |
| 2 | 4,033 | 4,900 | 5,933 | 6,667 | 1.33 | 490 |

**TABLE 4.22**   Electric Warm-Air Furnace on Slab or Platform
Electric, UL (Underwriters Laboratories) listed, heat staging, 240 V, standard controls.

| MBh output | 10.2 | 17.1 | 27.3 | 34.1 | 51.6 | 68.3 | 85.3 |
|---|---|---|---|---|---|---|---|
| Material, $ | 286 | 300 | 345 | 370 | 460 | 555 | 605 |
| Installation, workhours | 4 | 4.2 | 4.3 | 4.5 | 4.8 | 5 | 5.3 |

**TABLE 4.23**   Gas-Fired Warm-Air Furnace on Slab or Platform

Gas, AGA-certified, direct drive models, standard controls. Not including piping.

| MBh output | 45 | 60 | 75 | 100 | 125 |
|---|---|---|---|---|---|
| Material, $ | 305 | 345 | 370 | 405 | 430 |
| Installation, workhours | 4 | 4.2 | 4.4 | 5 | 5.3 |
| MBh output | 150 | 200 | 300 | 400 | |
| Material, $ | 575 | 1575 | 1975 | 2,350 | |
| Installation, workhours | 5.7 | 6.2 | 7 | 8 | |

**TABLE 4.24**   Oil-Fired Warm-Air Furnace on Slab

Oil, UL-listed, atomizing-gun-type burner, standard controls. Not including piping.

| MBh output | 56 | 84 | 95 | 134 | 151 | 200 | 300 | 400 |
|---|---|---|---|---|---|---|---|---|
| Material, $ | 745 | 765 | 795 | 1,075 | 1,100 | 1,900 | 2,275 | 2,600 |
| Installation, workhours | 4.4 | 4.6 | 4.7 | 5 | 5.3 | 6.2 | 7 | 8 |

**TABLE 4.25**   Installation Time in Workhours for Forced-Air Heating Systems

| Description | Workhours | Unit |
|---|---|---|
| Heating only, gas-fired hot air, one zone, 1200-sq. ft building | | |
| Furnace, gas, upward flow | 4.71 | Each |
| Intermittent pilot | 4.71 | Each |
| Supply duct, rigid fiberglass | 0.007 | lin ft |
| Return duct, sheet metal, galvanized | 0.102 | lb |
| Lateral ducts, 6-in. flexible fiberglass | 0.062 | lin ft |
| Register, elbows | 0.267 | Each |
| Floor registers, enameled steel | 0.25 | Each |
| Floor grille, return air | 0.364 | Each |
| Thermostat | 1 | Each |
| Plenum | 1 | Each |
| Ductwork: fabricated rectangular, includes fittings, joists, supports, allowance for flexible connections, no insulation. | | |
| Aluminum alloy 3003-H14 | | |
| <300 lb | 0.320 | lb |
| 300–500 lb | 0.300 | lb |
| 500–1,000 lb | 0.253 | lb |
| 1,000–2,000 lb | 0.200 | lb |
| 2,000–10,000 lb | 0.185 | lb |
| >10,000 lb | 0.166 | lb |
| Galvanized steel, <400 lb | | |
| 400–1,000 lb | 0.094 | lb |
| 1,000–2,000 lb | 0.091 | lb |
| 2,000–5,000 lb | 0.087 | lb |
| 5,000–10,000 lb | 0.084 | lb |
| >10,000 lb | 0.080 | lb |

**TABLE 4.26** Electric Duct Heaters

440 V, three-phase. Installation crew based on one sheet-metal worker, one sheet-metal apprentice, ½ electrician (20 workhours/day).

| Kilowatts | Size, in. | Material cost, $ | Workhours |
|---|---|---|---|
| 4.0 | 8 × 6 | 440 | 1.25 |
| 8.0 | 8 × 12 | 675 | 1.33 |
| 12.0 | 8 × 18 | 990 | 1.4 |
| 16.0 | 8 × 24 | 1,275 | 1.5 |
| 20.0 | 8 × 30 | 1,550 | 1.7 |
| 6.7 | 12 × 6 | 455 | 1.33 |
| 13.3 | 12 × 12 | 730 | 1.4 |
| 20.0 | 12 × 18 | 1,025 | 1.5 |
| 26.7 | 12 × 24 | 1,325 | 1.7 |
| 33.3 | 12 × 30 | 1,600 | 1.8 |
| 13.3 | 18 × 6 | 485 | 1.4 |
| 26.7 | 18 × 12 | 835 | 1.5 |
| 40.0 | 18 × 18 | 1,100 | 1.7 |
| 53.3 | 18 × 24 | 1,475 | 1.8 |
| 66.7 | 18 × 30 | 1,850 | 2 |
| 17.8 | 24 × 6 | 545 | 1.5 |
| 35.6 | 24 × 12 | 905 | 1.7 |
| 53.3 | 24 × 18 | 1,275 | 1.8 |
| 71.1 | 24 × 24 | 1,650 | 2 |
| 88.9 | 24 × 30 | 2,000 | 2.2 |
| 22.2 | 30 × 6 | 565 | 1.7 |
| 44.4 | 30 × 12 | 955 | 1.8 |
| 66.7 | 30 × 18 | 1,350 | 2 |
| 88.9 | 30 × 24 | 1,725 | 2.2 |
| 111.0 | 30 × 30 | 2,125 | 2.5 |

**TABLE 4.27** Gas-Fired Unit Heaters

For use with natural, mixed, or manufactured liquefied petroleum gas (LPG). Includes propeller-type fan, 115/24 V transformer, solenoid, high/low limit switch, safety pilot, and pressure regulator. Labor includes uncrating, suspending from average ceiling, and start-up. For powered venter and adaptor, add $219 material.

| MBh output | Heater cost, $ | Workhours |
|---|---|---|
| 20 | 380 | 1.9 |
| 40 | 420 | 2.1 |
| 60 | 470 | 2.3 |
| 80 | 525 | 2.7 |
| 100 | 620 | 2.9 |
| 130 | 695 | 3.2 |
| 140 | 745 | 3.6 |
| 160 | 775 | 4.0 |
| 180 | 845 | 4.6 |
| 200 | 900 | 5.3 |
| 240 | 1,075 | 5.9 |
| 280 | 1,250 | 6.9 |
| 320 | 1,425 | 8.0 |

## *CHIMNEYS AND STACKS*

Chimney sizes should be carefully computed and taken off. When the size of the stack has not yet been determined, Fig. 4.5 may be used for quick budget sizing in relation to the MBtu/hr steam rating. In larger-size chimneys, concrete is generally lowest in first cost, then steel and brick, respectively. Table 4.28 provides costs for prefabricated commercial smokestacks. Smokestack sections come in 4-ft lengths. However, the labor workhours are per foot installed in place. For boiler breeching, see Chap. 10. For data on prefabricated vent chimneys for residential and small commercial applications, see Table 4.29.

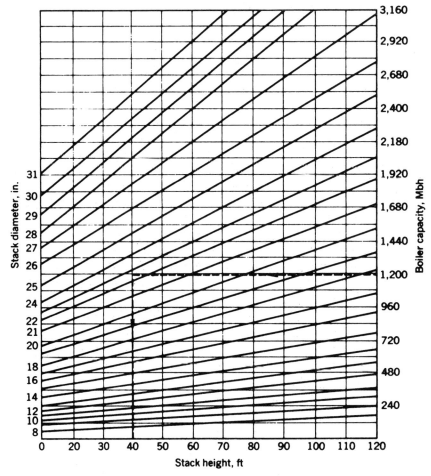

Where the Mbh is known, enter the scale at the right where this line intersects the desired diameter, drop down to find the required height.

**Figure 4.5  BUDGET SIZING FOR STACKS**

**TABLE 4.28**  Smokestacks, Steel Jacket, Refractory Lining

| Inside diameter, in. | Outside diameter, in. | 26-gage, cost/ft, $ | 11-gage, cost/ft, $ | Workhours per foot |
|---|---|---|---|---|
| 10 | 14 | 154 | 290 | 1.8 |
| 12 | 16 | 166 | 325 | 2.1 |
| 18 | 23 | 236 | 412 | 3.2 |
| 24 | 30 | 341 | 681 | 5.2 |
| 30 | 37 | 437 | 724 | 6.5 |
| 36 | 44 | 554 | 892 | 9.0 |

*Note:* Steel wall/refractory lined straight sections only. Tees, end caps, supports, etc. are not included. Use the above prices per foot and add for contractors' labor and markup.

**TABLE 4.29**  Prefabricated Vent Chimney, Gas

Double wall, galvanized steel, UL-approved.

| Flue size, in. | Workhours per foot | Material cost, $/ft | Item installed costs, $ | | | | | |
|---|---|---|---|---|---|---|---|---|
| | | | 45° ell | 90° ell | Flash-ing | Tee | Tee cap | Top |
| 3 | 0.22 | 2.83 | 17.95 | 23.60 | 15.79 | 31.80 | 10.12 | 14.95 |
| 4 | 0.24 | 3.46 | 19.85 | 25.85 | 18.35 | 33.10 | 11.06 | 15.75 |
| 5 | 0.25 | 4.08 | 22.00 | 28.75 | 19.65 | 34.60 | 11.67 | 18.65 |
| 6 | 0.27 | 4.79 | 24.65 | 33.00 | 23.50 | 37.40 | 12.76 | 21.70 |
| 7 | 0.29 | 7.05 | 30.85 | 45.55 | 27.10 | 45.65 | 14.73 | 28.10 |
| 8 | 0.31 | 7.85 | 34.50 | 48.65 | 29.35 | 49.90 | 15.66 | 33.95 |

## RESIDENTIAL AND COMMERCIAL WATER HEATERS

Tables 4.30 and 4.31 provide estimating data for gas-fired and electric residential water heaters. These tables are based on standard models with glass-lined tanks, insulating jackets, and standard controls. Labor includes moving material and equipment 40 ft, uncrating, setting, and finishing. Data on commercial gas-fired and electric water heaters are given in Table 4.32.

**TABLE 4.30**  Automatic Gas-Fired Water Heaters—Residential

| Capacity, gal. | 30 | 40 | 52 | 66 | 82 |
|---|---|---|---|---|---|
| Material, $ | 182.70 | 189.00 | 239.40 | 484.40 | 515.20 |
| Installation, workhours | 1.5 | 1.5 | 2 | 2 | 3 |

**TABLE 4.31**    Automatic Electric Water Heaters—Residential

| Capacity, gal. | 30 | 40 | 52 | 66 | 82 |
|---|---|---|---|---|---|
| Material, $ | 174.20 | 175.70 | 177.10 | 297.50 | 337.75 |
| Installation, workhours | 1.5 | 1.5 | 2 | 2 | 3 |

**TABLE 4.32**    Automatic Water Heaters—Commercial

| Energy-efficient, heavy-duty, natural gas: | | | |
|---|---|---|---|
| Capacity, gal. | Heavy-duty 72 | Standard 72 | Standard 92 |
| Recovery, gph, 100°F rise | 327 | 327 | 216 |
| Weight, lb | 402 | 480 | 453 |
| Material, $ | 2,600 | 1,900 | 1,500 |
| Erection, workhours | 4 | 4 | 4 |

| Energy-efficient, electric: | | | | |
|---|---|---|---|---|
| Capacity, gal. | 85 | 120 | 120 | 120 |
| Total wattage | 36,000 | 18,000 | 36,000 | 36,000 |
| Voltage | 240 | 240 | 240 | 480 |
| Weight, lb | 297 | 359 | 384 | 384 |
| Material, $ | 1,500 | 1,300 | 1,600 | 1,700 |

# CHAPTER 5
# FANS AND BLOWERS

*GENERAL DISCUSSION*

Fans and blowers, as treated in this chapter, cover the normal range of ventilation systems as encountered in comfort air conditioning. Except for industrial ventilation, restaurants, and other exhaust jobs, the mechanical ventilation on the average job will run between 1 and 3% of the total job cost. Centrifugal utility sets of economy construction will average $14 per 100 cfm and those of better-quality heavy-duty blowers, about $25 per 100 cfm. Power roof exhausters will average about $24 per 100 cfm and propeller-blade wall fans about $14 per 100 cfm. For toilet exhausting large office buildings of over 25,000 cfm, allow $140 per 100 cfm.

The material prices for the package unit sets are for complete basic units including motor and drive. Optional accessories such as vibration bases, guards, and louvers are not included. All other material prices are for bare equipment only. Starters are not included unless specifically noted.

Workhours are based on factory-assembled shipped-in-one-piece fans requiring no special arrangements. Rigging to a roof, cutting openings, curb caps, and flashings are not included.

Fans used for commercial, industrial, and agricultural ventilation will have waterproof motors and polypropylene blades. They will vary in size from 8 to 24 in. Fans used in greenhouses will be heavy-gauge galvanized steel.

Industrial-grade fans are also designed for use in corrosive atmospheres found in chemical plants and in poultry and swine confinement areas. Fiber-glass shutters and fiber-glass-reinforced polypropylene fan blades are used to resist fumes from ammonia, carbon dioxide, hydrogen sulfide, and methane. Industrial-grade fans use stainless-steel pivots and hardware. Epoxy-coated wire guards comply with U.S. Occupational Safety and Health Administration (OSHA) regulations. Blades are also found to be made of aluminum and plastic.

Exhaust fans handle many atmospheres containing flammable, explosive vapors, or gases. These fans have spark-resistant cast aluminum blades with totally enclosed motors.

Figure 5.1 illustrates Air Movement and Control Association (AMCA) standards for drive arrangements for centrifugal fans. Figure 5.2 gives AMCA designations for rotation and discharge of centrifugal fans. For flexible connections from fan to apparatus, see Chap. 10. [For further information on AMCA standards, contact AMCA, 30 West University Drive, Arlington Heights, IL 60004-1843; phone (708) 344-0150; fax (708) 253-0088.]

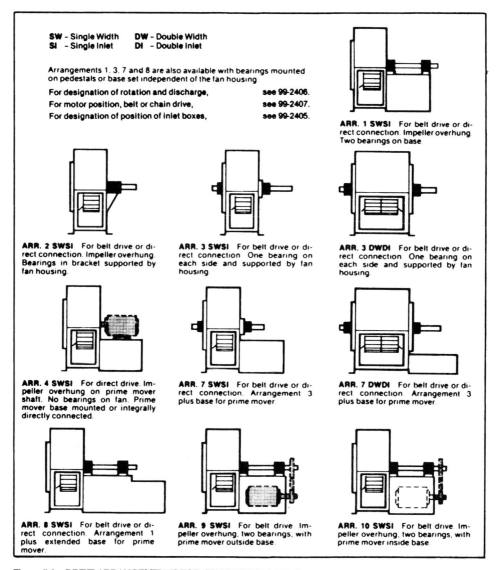

SW – Single Width    DW – Double Width
SI – Single Inlet    DI – Double Inlet

Arrangements 1, 3, 7 and 8 are also available with bearings mounted on pedestals or base set independent of the fan housing.

For designation of rotation and discharge,        see 99-2406.
For motor position, belt or chain drive,          see 99-2407.
For designation of position of inlet boxes,       see 99-2405.

**ARR. 1 SWSI** For belt drive or direct connection. Impeller overhung. Two bearings on base.

**ARR. 2 SWSI** For belt drive or direct connection. Impeller overhung. Bearings in bracket supported by fan housing.

**ARR. 3 SWSI** For belt drive or direct connection. One bearing on each side and supported by fan housing.

**ARR. 3 DWDI** For belt drive or direct connection. One bearing on each side and supported by fan housing.

**ARR. 4 SWSI** For direct drive. Impeller overhung on prime mover shaft. No bearings on fan. Prime mover base mounted or integrally directly connected.

**ARR. 7 SWSI** For belt drive or direct connection. Arrangement 3 plus base for prime mover.

**ARR. 7 DWDI** For belt drive or direct connection. Arrangement 3 plus base for prime mover.

**ARR. 8 SWSI** For belt drive or direct connection. Arrangement 1 plus extended base for prime mover.

**ARR. 9 SWSI** For belt drive. Impeller overhung, two bearings, with prime mover outside base.

**ARR. 10 SWSI** For belt drive. Impeller overhung, two bearings, with prime mover inside base.

**Figure 5.1   DRIVE ARRANGEMENTS FOR CENTRIFUGAL FANS**
*(Reprinted from AMCA Standard 99-2404-78 with written permission of the Air Movement and Control Association, Inc.)*

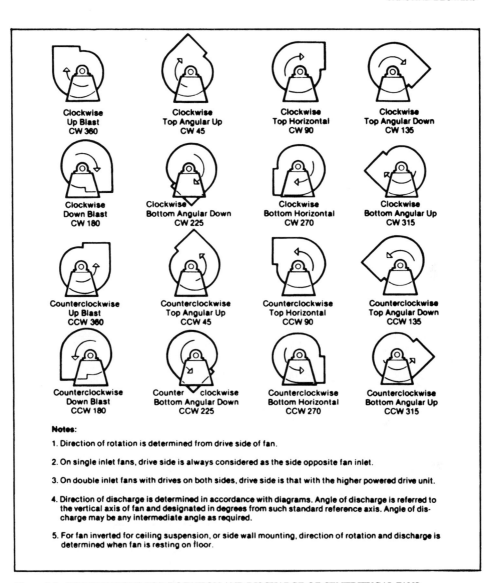

**Notes:**

1. Direction of rotation is determined from drive side of fan.

2. On single inlet fans, drive side is always considered as the side opposite fan inlet.

3. On double inlet fans with drives on both sides, drive side is that with the higher powered drive unit.

4. Direction of discharge is determined in accordance with diagrams. Angle of discharge is referred to the vertical axis of fan and designated in degrees from such standard reference axis. Angle of discharge may be any intermediate angle as required.

5. For fan inverted for ceiling suspension, or side wall mounting, direction of rotation and discharge is determined when fan is resting on floor.

**Figure 5.2  DESIGNATIONS FOR ROTATION AND DISCHARGE OF CENTRIFUGAL FANS**
*(Reprinted from AMCA Standard 99-2406-83 with written permission of the Air Movement and Control Association, Inc.)*

## ESTIMATING

Tables 5.1 through 5.8 provide estimating data and installation labor requirements for blowers, fans, and exhaust ventilators. Table 5.9 provides data on fan finishes and coatings.

Table 5.10 gives workhour requirements for installation of vane axial fans.

Table 5.11 gives material costs and labor requirements for installation of gravity relief vents.

Table 5.12 gives material costs and labor requirements for kitchen and bath ventilators for residences.

Tables 5.13 to 5.15 give installation labor requirements for V-belt drives, fan motors, and roof ventilators. Figure 5.3 illustrates the various types of roof ventilators shown in Table 5.13.

**TABLE 5.1**   Shaded Pole Blowers

Provide economic air delivery for heat, ventilating, exhausting, or cooling components.

| Diameter, in. | cfm | Revolutions per minute (rpm) | Material, $ | Erection, workhours |
|---|---|---|---|---|
| 2 | 12 | 3,300 | 34 | 1 |
| 3 | 76 | 2,880 | 62 | 1 |
| 5¼ | 134 | 1,500 | 70 | 1 |
| 7⅛ | 200 | 1,400 | 115 | 1 |

**TABLE 5.2**   Plastic Centrifugal In-Line Duct Fan

For use in commercial and residential applications where moisture is a problem, e.g., spa and hot-tub venting to help prevent radon leakage.

| Diameter in. | Horsepower | Material, $ | Erection, workhours |
|---|---|---|---|
| 4 | ⅟₆₀ | 260 | 1 |
| 6 | ⅟₂₀ | 275 | 1 |
| 8 | ⅟₁₀ | 450 | 1 |
| 10 | ⅛ | 540 | 1 |

**TABLE 5.3**   Belt-Driven Tube Axial Fans

Fans with aluminum spark-resistant blade used as exhausters in paint-spray booths, cleaning tanks, and sizing rooms. Also used in industrial ventilating systems handling temperatures up to 200°F.

| Blade diameter, in. | cfm at ¼-in. static | Fan rpm | Horsepower | Totally enclosed fan, $ | Hazardous location, $ | Erection, workhours |
|---|---|---|---|---|---|---|
| 12 | 990 | 1,670 | 0.25 | 325 | 390 | 4 |
|  | 1,280 | 1,946 | 0.33 | 340 | 410 | 4 |
|  | 1,560 | 2,253 | 0.50 | 370 | 425 | 4 |
|  | 2,095 | 2,877 | 0.75 | 400 | 460 | 4 |
| 16 | 1,190 | 1,366 | 0.33 | 375 | 440 | 5 |
|  | 2,350 | 1,800 | 0.50 | 410 | 460 | 5 |
|  | 3,090 | 2,221 | 0.75 | 440 | 490 | 5 |
|  | 3,630 | 2,547 | 1 | 450 | 510 | 5 |
| 18 | 2,195 | 1,213 | 0.33 | 410 | 480 | 6 |
|  | 3,000 | 1,487 | 0.50 | 440 | 490 | 6 |
|  | 3,625 | 1,719 | 0.75 | 470 | 525 | 6 |
|  | 4,320 | 1,988 | 1 | 480 | 540 | 6 |
|  | 5,000 | 2,255 | 1.5 | 540 | 560 | 6 |
| 24 | 6,370 | 1,312 | 1 | 600 | 660 | 8 |
|  | 7,285 | 1,466 | 1.5 | 650 | 680 | 8 |
|  | 8,590 | 1,688 | 2 | 670 | 700 | 8 |
|  | 9,850 | 1,910 | 3 | 690 | 720 | 8 |
| 30 | 9,815 | 1,030 | 1.5 | 720 | 840 | 10 |
|  | 11,180 | 1,146 | 2 | 740 | 870 | 10 |
|  | 13,180 | 1,320 | 3 | 770 | 900 | 10 |
|  | 15,785 | 1,551 | 5 | 790 | 960 | 10 |
| 34 | 13,020 | 936 | 2 | 810 | 940 | 10 |
|  | 15,350 | 1,074 | 3 | 840 | 980 | 10 |
|  | 18,280 | 1,251 | 5 | 880 | 1,050 | 10 |
| 36 | 13,570 | 837 | 2 | 840 | 970 | 12 |
|  | 16,135 | 964 | 3 | 870 | 1,000 | 12 |
|  | 19,460 | 1,133 | 5 | 900 | 1,070 | 12 |
| 42 | 19,275 | 746 | 3 | 1,110 | 1,250 | 16 |
|  | 23,505 | 880 | 5 | 1,150 | 1,320 | 16 |
|  | 27,610 | 1,013 | 7.5 | 1,210 | 1,425 | 16 |
|  | 31,670 | 1,147 | 10 | 1,270 | 1,465 | 16 |
| 48 | 28,745 | 731 | 5 | 1,380 | 1,550 | 20 |
|  | 33,185 | 827 | 7.5 | 1,450 | 1,650 | 20 |
|  | 36,105 | 891 | 10 | 1,500 | 1,710 | 20 |

**TABLE 5.4**   Centrifugal In-Line Duct Fans

Fans for installation within horizontal or vertical duct systems where space is limited. Used as a primary fan to exhaust foul air or supply fresh air in duct system.

| Blade diameter, in. | cfm at ¼-in. static | Fan rpm | Horsepower | 115/230-V material, $ | 230/460-V material, $ | Erection, workhours* |
|---|---|---|---|---|---|---|
| 13½ | 1,265 | 1,350 | 0.25 | 950 | 995 | 2 |
| | 1,425 | 1,477 | 0.25 | 960 | 1,000 | 2 |
| | 1,605 | 1,620 | 0.33 | 990 | 1,000 | 2 |
| | 1,900 | 1,862 | 0.50 | 1,030 | 1,020 | 2 |
| 15 | 2,110 | 1,333 | 0.50 | 1,030 | 1,020 | 2 |
| | 2,475 | 1,520 | 0.75 | 1,100 | 1,070 | 2 |
| | 2,775 | 1,678 | 1 | 1,130 | 1,080 | 2 |
| 16¾ | 2,840 | 1,318 | 0.75 | 1,350 | 1,310 | 2.5 |
| | 3,200 | 1,450 | 1 | 1,370 | 1,320 | 2.5 |
| | 3,725 | 1,661 | 1.5 | 1,480 | 1,350 | 2.5 |
| 20 | 4,355 | 888 | 0.75 | 1,600 | 1,560 | 2.5 |
| | 4,890 | 977 | 1 | 1,630 | 1,580 | 2.5 |
| | 5,720 | 1,119 | 1.5 | 1,740 | 1,600 | 2.5 |
| | 6,375 | 1,232 | 2 | 1,820 | 1,640 | 2.5 |
| 24½ | 6,440 | 905 | 1.5 | — | 2,100 | 3 |
| | 7,190 | 996 | 2 | 2,240 | 2,120 | 3 |
| | 8,335 | 1,135 | 3 | 2,300 | 2,210 | 3 |
| | 10,050 | 1,352 | 5 | — | 2,260 | 3 |
| 30 | 9,635 | 695 | 2 | 2,860 | 2,670 | 4 |
| | 11,315 | 795 | 3 | — | 2,790 | 4 |
| | 13,725 | 942 | 5 | — | 2,800 | 4 |
| | 15,930 | 1,078 | 7.5 | — | 3,000 | 4 |
| 36½ | 15,960 | 628 | 5 | — | 3,500 | 6 |
| | 18,405 | 718 | 7.5 | — | 3,690 | 6 |
| | 20,410 | 792 | 10 | — | 3,870 | 6 |

*Crew = two sheet-metal workers and one electrician.

**TABLE 5.5** Direct-Drive Exhaust Ventilators

Aluminum housing and base, built-in bird screen, backdraft damper, safety disconnect switch, and curb.

| Blade diameter, in. | cfm at ¼-in. static | Motor hp | rpm | 115/230-V material, $ | Curb | Erection, workhours* |
|---|---|---|---|---|---|---|
| 10 | 310 | 1/30 | 1,470 | 185 | 100 | 2.0 |
| 12 | 590 | 1/10 | 1,450 | 250 | 100 | 2.0 |
| 14 | 1,050 | ⅙ | 1,130 | 385 | 100 | 2.0 |
| 18 | 2,170 | ⅓ | 1,100 | 475 | 100 | 2.0 |

Belt drive; axial roof exhausters, aluminum housing and base built-in bird screen and back-draft, and curb.

| Blade diameter, in. | cfm at ¼-in. static | Motor hp | rpm | 115/230-V material, $ | Curb | Erection, workhours* |
|---|---|---|---|---|---|---|
| 24 | 2,420 | ⅓ | 1,725 | 700 | 135 | 3.0 |
| | 3,025 | ½ | 1,725 | 710 | 135 | 3.0 |
| | 3,575 | ¾ | 1,725 | 715 | 135 | 3.0 |
| | 4,125 | ¾ | 1,725 | 720 | 135 | 3.0 |
| | 4,850 | 1 | 1,725 | 770 | 135 | 3.0 |
| 30 | 4,560 | 1 | 1,725 | 1,035 | 135 | 3.0 |
| | 5,295 | 1 | 1,725 | 1,040 | 135 | 3.0 |
| | 6,415 | 1½ | 1,725 | 1,070 | 135 | 3.0 |
| | 7,130 | 2 | 1,725 | 1,150 | 135 | 3.0 |

*Crew = 2 sheet-metal workers and 0.5 electrician.

**TABLE 5.6** Ventilators for Exhaust or Supply

Roof-mounted ventilators with heavy-duty, belt-driven fans; motor, drive, and roof hood—galvanized steel.

| Blade diameter, in. | cfm at ¼-in. static | Fan rpm | Horsepower | 115/230-V material, $ | 208–220/440-V material, $ | Erection, workhours* |
|---|---|---|---|---|---|---|
| 24 | 2,350 | 650 | ¼ | 645 | 705 | 3 |
| | 3,250 | 710 | ⅓ | 655 | 710 | 3 |
| | 5,350 | 835 | ½ | 665 | 725 | 3 |
| | 6,650 | 945 | ¾ | 715 | 745 | 3 |
| 30 | 2,700 | 500 | ⅓ | 720 | 775 | 4 |
| | 5,100 | 585 | ½ | 730 | 790 | 4 |
| | 7,400 | 670 | ¾ | 780 | 810 | 4 |
| | 8,500 | 720 | 1 | 835 | 820 | 4 |
| 36 | 5,000 | 485 | ½ | 880 | 940 | 4 |
| | 8,350 | 540 | ¾ | 900 | 935 | 4 |
| | 11,200 | 605 | 1 | 950 | 940 | 4 |
| | 12,900 | 660 | 1½ | 980 | 960 | 4 |
| 42 | 7,150 | 430 | ¾ | 1,100 | 1,130 | 5 |
| | 10,900 | 460 | 1 | 1,750 | 1,120 | 5 |
| | 15,100 | 520 | 1½ | 1,150 | 1,140 | 5 |
| 48 | 7,550 | 370 | ¾ | 1,270 | 1,300 | 5 |
| | 11,350 | 400 | 1 | 1,320 | 1,320 | 5 |
| | 18,400 | 450 | 1½ | 1,410 | 1,380 | 5 |
| | 21,350 | 490 | 2 | 1,480 | 1,400 | 5 |

*Crew = 2 sheet-metal workers and 0.5 electrician.

**TABLE 5.7**  Standard-Duty Heavy-Gauge Centrifugal Fans—Cost Comparison by Class and Arrangement

Based on Class I, single-inlet single-width backward-curved-airfoil type, with all-welded-steel construction, and statically and dynamically balanced wheels, shipped assembled in either arrangement. All data shown are nominal. Weights are less motors. Prices based on arrangement 3.

For quick estimating of arrangements other than 3:

| Arrangement | % cost |
|---|---|
| 1 | 120 |
| 2 | 100 |
| 3 | 100 |
| 4 | 122 |
| 9 | 125 |

For quick estimating of fans other than Class I:

| Class | % cost |
|---|---|
| I | 100 |
| II | 110 |
| III | 130 |
| IV | 145 |
| V | 155 |

Double-inlet, double-width pans, add 10%; inlet vane controls, add 10%; split centrifugal housing, add 40%.

Erection workhours and costs. Workhours includes unloading from truck, moving within 40 ft, setting and aligning, and adjusting bearings; erection is at floor level. Erection of motor and drives, inlet vane control, and outlet dampers not included; select motor and drive erection from separate tables.

| Wheel diameter, in. | Maximum cfm range | Weight, lb | Material, $ | Erection, workhours |
|---|---|---|---|---|
| 12¼ | 2,100 | 140 | 850 | 7 |
| 13½ | 2,700 | 165 | 920 | 8 |
| 15 | 2,900 | 185 | 990 | 9 |
| 16½ | 3,500 | 195 | 1,030 | 9 |
| 18¼ | 5,000 | 235 | 1,230 | 10 |
| 20 | 6,500 | 300 | 1,420 | 10 |
| 22¼ | 8,000 | 330 | 1,620 | 10 |
| 24½ | 9,100 | 425 | 2,080 | 11 |
| 27½ | 12,000 | 626 | 2,270 | 11 |
| 30 | 14,750 | 640 | 2,680 | 11 |
| 33 | 18,000 | 775 | 3,070 | 11 |
| 36½ | 25,000 | 940 | 3,580 | 13 |
| 40¼ | 30,000 | 1,575 | 4,420 | 15 |
| 44½ | 37,000 | 1,870 | 5,360 | 17 |
| 49 | 45,000 | 2,225 | 6,320 | 21 |
| 54¼ | 55,000 | 2,750 | 7,390 | 27 |
| 60 | 67,000 | 3,050 | 8,800 | 35 |
| 66 | 81,000 | 3,900 | 13,600 | 51 |
| 73 | 99,000 | 5,325 | 18,200 | 63 |
| 80¾ | 122,000 | 6,850 | 22,600 | 79 |
| 89 | 148,000 | 8,800 | 27,400 | 92 |

**TABLE 5.8**  Propeller-Blade Wall Exhausters

Includes automatic backdraft shutter, rpm range 1,500 to 1,750. Labor includes unloading from truck, moving within 40 ft, setting and aligning, checking shutter linkage, and shaft movement. Based on properly sized existing wall opening to 8 ft height.

| cfm at ¼-in. static | Drive | Blade size, in. | Material, $ | Erection, workhours |
|---|---|---|---|---|
| 200 | Direct | 8 | 130 | 1.5 |
| 325 | Direct | 8 | 145 | 1.5 |
| 360 | Direct | 10 | 168 | 1.5 |
| 530 | Direct | 10 | 182 | 1.5 |
| 875 | Direct | 12 | 230 | 2 |
| 1,480 | Direct | 14 | 252 | 2 |
| 1,950 | Direct | 16 | 320 | 2 |
| 3,080 | Direct | 18 | 370 | 2 |
| 3,500 | Direct | 20 | 416 | 2 |
| 4,000 | Direct | 24 | 550 | 3 |
| 6,800 | Belt | 24 | 607 | 3 |
| 20,000 | Belt | 36 | 1,300 | 6 |
| 31,000 | Belt | 42 | 1,600 | 6 |
| 36,000 | Belt | 48 | 1,920 | 8 |

**TABLE 5.9**  Special Finishes and Coatings for Fans

Average cost, $, for special finishes, but wide variation between manufacturers. Fan size is wheel or propeller size.

| Fan size, in. | Primed for field painting | Bitumastic coating | Polyvinyl coating | Acrylic enamel | Anodized | Caustic etch |
|---|---|---|---|---|---|---|
| 5–10 | 29 | 39 | 99 | 45 | 176 | 84 |
| 11–15 | 36 | 78 | 111 | 59 | 239 | 101 |
| 16–25 | 58 | 117 | 210 | 88 | 315 | 118 |
| 26–35 | 88 | 143 | 304 | 118 | 378 | 134 |
| 36–48 | 118 | 196 | 372 | 134 | 462 | 168 |
| 54–60 | 134 | 235 | 582 | 164 | 567 | 210 |
| 61–80 | 168 | 286 | 1,120 | 189 | 680 | 252 |

**TABLE 5.10** Vane Axial Fans

Based on all-welded-steel construction, belt-driven Class I fans, arrangement 3. Erection workhours includes unloading from truck, moving within 40 ft, setting and aligning at floor working height. Erection of motor and drives, screens, and motor guards not included. Diameters and weights are nominal.

| Wheel diameter, in. | Weight, lb | Erection, workhours | Erect inlet-outlet tapered cone, workhours | Erect stream-lined inlet, workhours |
|---|---|---|---|---|
| 15 | 100 | 5.50 | 1.25 | 0.75 |
| 18¼ | 150 | 5.70 | 1.30 | 1.00 |
| 20 | 180 | 6.10 | 1.30 | 1.00 |
| 24½ | 270 | 7.25 | 1.30 | 1.00 |
| 27 | 330 | 8.20 | 1.30 | 1.00 |
| 30 | 400 | 8.25 | 1.50 | 1.00 |
| 33 | 490 | 8.55 | 1.50 | 1.50 |
| 36½ | 600 | 8.75 | 1.80 | 1.50 |
| 40¼ | 730 | 9.15 | 1.80 | 1.50 |
| 44½ | 890 | 10.25 | 1.90 | 1.75 |
| 49 | 1,080 | 11.25 | 2.20 | 1.75 |
| 54¼ | 1,350 | 12.40 | 2.25 | 1.85 |

**TABLE 5.11** Gravity Relief Vents

For infiltration or exfiltration, aluminum housing low contour, includes backdraft damper and bird screen.

| cfm @ ⅛ in. static | Roof opening, in. | Erection, workhours | Material, $ |
|---|---|---|---|
| 500 | 12 × 16 | 2.0 | 450 |
| 750 | 12 × 20 | 2.2 | 495 |
| 1,000 | 12 × 24 | 2.4 | 535 |
| 1,500 | 12 × 36 | 2.8 | 645 |
| 3,000 | 20 × 42 | 4.0 | 920 |
| 6,000 | 20 × 84 | 6.2 | 1,400 |
| 8,000 | 24 × 96 | 7.0 | 1,600 |

SOURCE: *Means Mechanical Cost Data,* R.S. Means Co., Kingston, Mass., 1994.

**TABLE 5.12**  Kitchen and Bath Ventilators for Residences

Includes housing, motor wheel assembly, and remote wall switch.

| cfm @ ¼ in. static | Watts | Wheel diameter, in. | Material, $ | Erection, workhours |
|---|---|---|---|---|
| 100 | 50 | 4 | 48 | 0.8 |
| 300 | 105 | 6 | 72 | 0.8 |
| 425 | 130 | 2 × 4 | 102 | 0.9 |
| 520 | 200 | 10 | 145 | 1.10 |

**TABLE 5.13**  Erecting V-Belt Drives

| Motor hp | Erection, workhours |
|---|---|
| 3 | 0.50 |
| 5 | 0.75 |
| 7½ | 1.00 |
| 10 | 1.10 |
| 15 | 1.20 |
| 20 | 1.30 |
| 25 | 1.50 |
| 30 | 2.25 |
| 40 | 2.40 |
| 50 | 3.00 |
| 60 | 3.70 |
| 75 | 4.50 |

**TABLE 5.14**  Mounting Fan Motors

Erection workhours includes unloading from truck, moving within 40 ft, uncrating, mounting on base, and adjusting drive alignment. Motor weights are nominal.

| Motor hp | Uncrated weight, lb | Maximum fan size | Erection, workhours |
|---|---|---|---|
| 3 | 85 | — | 1.55 |
| 5 | 95 | — | 2.00 |
| 7½ | 125 | To 36 in. | 2.45 |
| 10 | 175 | — | 3.00 |
| 15 | 230 | — | 3.80 |
| 20 | 350 | — | 4.50 |
| 25 | 465 | To 40 in. | 5.20 |
| 30 | 510 | — | 6.00 |
| 40 | 600 | — | 6.50 |
| 50 | 670 | To 49 in. | 7.25 |
| 60 | 745 | — | 8.15 |
| 75 | 820 | — | 10.00 |
| 100 | 875 | To 73 in. | 14.00 |

**TABLE 5.15** Erection Time in Workhours for Roof Ventilators

| Description | Workhours per unit |
|---|---|
| Rotary syphons, spinner ventilators, stationary gravity syphons, and rotating chimney caps* | |
| 3 in. diameter | 0.67 |
| 4 in. diameter | 0.80 |
| 5 in. diameter | 0.89 |
| 6 in. diameter | 1.00 |
| 7 in. diameter | 1.07 |
| 8 in. diameter | 1.14 |
| 10 in. diameter | 1.33 |
| 12 in. diameter | 1.60 |
| 14 in. diameter | 1.60 |
| 16 in. diameter | 1.78 |
| 18 in. diameter | 1.78 |
| 20 in. diameter | 2.00 |
| 24 in. diameter | 2.00 |
| 30 in. diameter | 2.29 |
| 36 in. diameter | 2.67 |
| 42 in. diameter | 4.00 |
| Relief hoods, intake/exhaust | |
| 500 cfm 12 × 16 in. | 2.00 |
| 750 cfm 12 × 20 in. | 2.22 |
| 1,000 cfm 12 × 24 in. | 2.42 |
| 1,500 cfm 12 × 36 in. | 2.76 |
| 3,000 cfm 20 × 42 in. | 4.00 |
| 6,000 cfm 20 × 84 in. | 6.15 |
| 8,000 cfm 24 × 96 in. | 6.96 |
| 10,000 cfm 48 × 60 in. | 8.89 |
| 12,500 cfm 48 × 72 in. | 10.00 |
| 15,000 cfm 48 × 96 in. | 12.31 |
| 20,000 cfm 48 × 120 in. | 13.33 |
| 25,000 cfm 60 × 120 in. | 17.78 |
| 30,000 cfm 72 × 120 in. | 22.86 |
| 40,000 cfm 96 × 120 in. | 26.67 |
| 50,000 cfm 96 × 144 in. | 32.00 |

*See Fig. 5.3 for illustrations of each type of ventilator. Size ranges for this table are rotary syphons, 6 to 42 in.; spinner ventilators, 4 to 36 in.; stationary gravity syphons, 3 to 42 in.; rotating chimney caps, 4 to 10 in.

The computer disk provided with this book lists the cfm capacity of each size and type of ventilator.

SOURCE: *Means Estimating Handbook,* R. S. Means Co., Kingston, Mass., 1990.

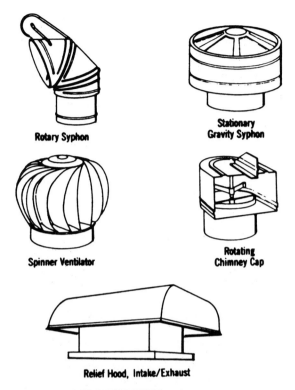

**Rotary Syphon**

**Stationary Gravity Syphon**

**Spinner Ventilator**

**Rotating Chimney Cap**

**Relief Hood, Intake/Exhaust**

**Figure 5.3   ROOF VENTILATORS**
*(SOURCE: Means Estimating Handbook, R. S. Means Co., Kingston, Mass., 1990.)*

Table 5.16 summarizes fan and air laws that may be used to predict the performance of any air-moving system for a given fan after changes or adjustments to the system have been made. The fan and air laws may also be used to calculate the required adjustments necessary to meet a new design or altered conditions. Table 5.16 is not included on the computer disk provided with this book.

**TABLE 5.16**   Fan and Air Laws

| Application | Formula |
|---|---|
| *Fan performance* | |
| Airflow, cfm, varies in direct proportion to fan speed, rpm | $cfm_2 = cfm_1 \times \dfrac{rpm_2}{rpm_1}$ |
| Static pressure, Sp, varies as the square of the rpm | $Sp_2 = Sp_1 \times \left(\dfrac{rpm_2}{rpm_1}\right)^2$ |

*(Continued)*

**TABLE 5.16** Fan and Air Laws (*Continued*)

| Application | Formula |
|---|---|
| Fan performance (*Cont.*) | |
| Horsepower, hp, varies as the cube of the rpm | $hp_2 = hp_1 \times \left(\dfrac{rpm_2}{rpm_1}\right)^3$ |
| Amperage varies as the cube of the cfm | $amps_2 = amps_1 \times \left(\dfrac{cfm_2}{cfm_1}\right)^3$ |
| Cfm and rpm vary as the square root of the pressure ratio | $cfm_2 = cfm_1 \times \sqrt{\dfrac{Sp_2}{Sp_1}}$ |
| | $rpm_2 = rpm_1 \times \sqrt{\dfrac{Sp_2}{Sp_1}}$ |
| Hp varies as the square root of the pressure ratio cubed | $hp_2 = hp_1 \times \sqrt{\left[\dfrac{Sp_2}{Sp_1}\right]^3}$ |
| Cfm varies as the square of the fan size ratio (at given Sp and rating) | $cfm_2 = cfm_1 \times \left(\dfrac{size_2}{size_1}\right)^2$ |
| Ducted airflow | |
| Total pressure, Tp | $Tp = Sp + Vp$ <br> where Tp = total pressure <br> Sp = static pressure <br> Vp = velocity pressure |
| Duct capacity, cfm | $cfm = fpm \times duct\ area$ <br> where fpm = duct velocity |
| Cfm varies in direct proportion to duct air velocity, fpm | $cfm_2 = cfm_1 \times \dfrac{fpm_2}{fpm_1}$ |
| Sp varies as the square of the duct cfm and of fpm | $Sp_2 = Sp_1 \times \left(\dfrac{cfm_2}{cfm_1}\right)^2$ |
| | $Sp_2 = Sp_1 \times \left(\dfrac{fpm_2}{fpm_1}\right)^2$ |

# CHAPTER 6
# COOLING TOWERS

## GENERAL DISCUSSION

The *ASHRAE Handbook* states that

> Towers are typically classified as either factory-assembled when the entire tower or a few larger components are factory-assembled and shipped to the site or installation, or field-erected where the tower is completely erected on site.
>
> Most factory-assembled towers are of metal construction, usually galvanized steel. Other constructions include treated wood, stainless steel, and plastic towers or components. Field-erected towers are predominantly framed of preservative treated redwood or treated fir with fiber-glass-reinforced plastic used for special components and the casing. Coated metals, primarily steel, are used for complete towers or components. Concrete or ceramic materials are usually restricted to the largest sizes.

Chimney towers (hyperbolic) have been used primarily for large power installations. Materials used on chimney construction have been primarily steel-reinforced concrete. Elevations are typically 350 to 500 ft above grade.

Mechanical draft towers can have fans on the inlet-air side (forced-draft) or exit-air side (induced-draft).

Selecting the proper water-cooling equipment for a specific application requires consideration of many interrelated factors that should be evaluated individually. The optimum choice should be made after an economic evaluation. Commonly used techniques are described in the American Society of Testing and Materials (ASTM) *Standards on Building Economics*.

For cost analysis comparisons, the following must be considered:

1. Erected cost of equipment
2. Cost of
    *a.* basic grillage
    *b.* pumps and prime movers
    *c.* electrical wiring
    *d.* piping, valves, and ladders

Operation and maintenance costs, e.g., system energy costs, must be considered along with expected equipment life and cost of money.

Although the 1994 first cost of an atmospheric tower will average about $40 per ton in larger sizes (100-ton) versus $65 per ton for the mechanical-draft type, there are many economic

**TABLE 6.1**    Vital Ratios for Cooling Towers

Based on standard built-up towers of 1,000-ton cooling capacity.

| Item of comparison | Mechanical draft | Natural draft |
|---|---|---|
| Cubic area . . . . . . . . . . . . . . . | 1 | 4.10 |
| Basin area. . . . . . . . . . . . . . . | 1 | 2.00 |
| Foundation concrete . . . . . . . . . | 1 | 3.50 |
| Dry weight . . . . . . . . . . . . . . | 1 | 2.75 |
| Pumping head . . . . . . . . . . . . | 1 | 2.00 |
| Drift loss . . . . . . . . . . . . . . | 1 | 10.00 |
| Makeup water . . . . . . . . . . . | 1 | 10.00 |

advantages in favor of the latter. Table 6.1 illustrates some of these advantages as ratios. For example, a natural-draft tower has 10 times as much draft loss as a mechanical draft; consequently, the makeup water costs are tenfold.

## ESTIMATING

Although the control of pH for cooling-tower water is widely recognized as an inhibitor of corrosive action to metal towers, a misconception persists concerning the need for such control with the use of the all-wood tower. A low pH would hasten acid attack against the metal tower; however, if the pH is too high in a wood tower, the delignification damage to the wood will be serious. For this reason cooling-tower water should be kept slightly above neutral, say, pH 7.3. (See Table 7.3 for pH scale.)

The estimator should consider the cost of chemical treatment for algae control in addition to the cost of a blowdown drain for mitigating the concentration of dissolved solids in the system. The first cost of such chemical treatment may be estimated at approximately $4 to $5 per ton.

Towers above 20 tons are not normally stocked at local points and are usually shipped from the factory direct to the jobsite. The job coordinator will then have a crane meet the truck and set the tower members at the erection site. If the tower must be moved from local stocking points, loaded and unloaded, moved and shifted, and vertically lifted, see Chap. 19.

Tables 6.2 to 6.4 are based on standard rooftop installation with sleepers properly sized to distribute 29 lb/sq ft, properly flashed pitch pans, and steel guys to withstand 120-mile-per-hour (mph) wind velocity. Tower capacities are nominal and are based on 4 gpm/ton at 95, 87½, and 80°F and 250 Btu/min per ton. For a comparison of costs of absorption and centrifugal systems, see Fig. 6.1.

These costs do not include crane service, special rigging, water makeup and drain, wiring, pumps and starters, piping and controls, or steel grillage. For a more detailed discussion on sleepers, timbers, steel grillage, and foundations, see Chap. 17.

Wiring for pump motors, fan motors, etc., for cooling-tower erection may be estimated at $150/hp.

To estimate structural steel supports such as angles, channels, and I-beams for larger towers, allow $75/cwt, set in place. Quick budget figures for estimating rigging costs for towers on high roofs are given in Fig. 6.2.

When quick budget figures are required for cooling-tower supports for systems over 100 tons, use the following:

| | |
|---|---|
| Existing buildings | $75 per system ton |
| New buildings | $30 per system ton |

**TABLE 6.2** Atmospheric Natural-Draft Cooling Towers

Redwood or fir, factory-packaged, field-assembled. *Workhours* is based on erecting posts, slats, and nozzles with header. Last line is an allowance for moving sections 40 physical feet horizontally before erection.

| Capacity, tons | 10 | 15 | 20 | 25 |
|---|---|---|---|---|
| Dry weight, lb | 625 | 850 | 1,250 | 1,350 |
| Wet weight, lb | 1,350 | 1,600 | 2,800 | 3,350 |
| Base area, sq ft | 25 | 30 | 45 | 50 |
| Tower cost, $ | 620 | 800 | 1,150 | 1,280 |
| Workhours, assemble | 8 | 8 | 12 | 12 |
| Sleeper material, $ | 90 | 90 | 125 | 125 |
| Workhours, sleepers | 4 | 4 | 4 | 4 |
| Workhours, move 40 ft | 1 | 1 | 2 | 2 |

| Capacity, tons | 30 | 40 | 50 | 60 |
|---|---|---|---|---|
| Dry weight, lb | 1,600 | 2,200 | 2,500 | 2,900 |
| Wet weight, lb | 3,850 | 5,100 | 6,200 | 6,650 |
| Base area, sq ft | 70 | 90 | 115 | 130 |
| Tower cost, $ | 1,620 | 2,050 | 2,250 | 2,400 |
| Workhours, assemble | 12 | 16 | 16 | 20 |
| Sleeper material, $ | 125 | 210 | 210 | 210 |
| Workhours, sleepers | 4 | 8 | 8 | 8 |
| Workhours, move 40 ft | 2 | 2 | 2 | 2 |

| Capacity, tons | 70 | 80 | 100 | 115 |
|---|---|---|---|---|
| Dry weight, lb | 3,300 | 3,500 | 4,000 | 5,200 |
| Wet weight, lb | 6,150 | 8,800 | 10,500 | 12,000 |
| Base area, sq ft | 160 | 170 | 210 | 225 |
| Tower cost, $ | 3,000 | 3,250 | 3,900 | 4,500 |
| Workhours, assemble | 24 | 24 | 24 | 24 |
| Sleeper material, $ | 300 | 300 | 300 | 350 |
| Workhours, sleepers | 8 | 8 | 8 | 8 |
| Workhours, move 40 ft | 2 | 2 | 2 | 2 |

The required bleedoff, or blowndown for cooling towers, is usually based on ppm (parts per million) of solids in the circulating water and should be determined in actual operation by chemical analysis. As the tower water evaporates, the solids concentration in the remaining water increases. High concentrations of solids will cause scale formation and corrosion in the heat exchanger. For purposes of estimating water makeup requirements for cooling towers, Table 6.5 gives a simple method of approximating the bleedoff rate based on tower range. To calculate the total makeup water for the tower, both drift loss and evaporation must be added to the bleedoff. Under normal conditions a tower will evaporate about 1% for each 10°F of range and will have a drift loss of about 0.2% for mechanical towers and 0.3% for natural draft towers.

**TABLE 6.3** Induced-Draft Cooling Towers—Galvanized

Hot-dipped galvanized, factory-shipped completely assembled. No field assembly time allowed; workhours are for alignment and anchoring and erecting the accessories normally shipped with this type of tower.

| Capacity, tons | 10 | 15 | 20 | 25 | 30 | 40 | 50 |
|---|---|---|---|---|---|---|---|
| Shipping weight, lb | 770 | 950 | 1,000 | 1,050 | 1,250 | 1,350 | 1,900 |
| Operating weight, lb | 1,275 | 1,875 | 2,400 | 3,400 | 3,650 | 4,550 | 4,800 |
| Base area, sq ft | 12 | 18 | 24 | 32 | 36 | 48 | 56 |
| Tower cost, $ | 1,150 | 1,500 | 1,750 | 2,300 | 2,400 | 3,100 | 3,800 |
| Workhours, erecting | 2 | 2 | 2.5 | 3 | 4 | 4 | 4 |
| Crane, hoist to roof | 2 | 2 | 2 | 2 | 2 | 2 | 2 |

| Capacity, tons | 60 | 80 | 100 | 125 | 170 | 200 | 300 |
|---|---|---|---|---|---|---|---|
| Shipping weight, lb | 2,200 | 3,400 | 4,850 | 5,125 | 6,400 | 7,500 | 9,500 |
| Operating weight, lb | 5,650 | 9,000 | 9,500 | 11,000 | 12,500 | 13,850 | 15,000 |
| Base area, sq ft | 56 | 92 | 112 | 112 | 120 | 125 | 140 |
| Tower cost, $ | 4,500 | 5,600 | 6,500 | 7,800 | 10,000 | 15,000 | 20,000 |
| Workhours, erecting | 6 | 10 | 10 | 10 | 10 | 12 | 12 |
| Crane, hoist to roof | 2 | 2 | 3 | 3 | 3 | 4 | 4 |

| Capacity, tons | 400 | 500 | 600 | 700 | 800 | 900 | 1,000 |
|---|---|---|---|---|---|---|---|
| Shipping weight, lb | 15,000 | 17,500 | 22,000 | 26,000 | 28,400 | 34,000 | 35,000 |
| Operating weight, lb | 21,000 | 26,500 | 31,800 | 37,100 | 42,400 | 48,000 | 53,000 |
| Base area, sq ft | 160 | 200 | 220 | 300 | 400 | 450 | 500 |
| Tower cost, $ | 25,000 | 30,000 | 36,000 | 43,000 | 42,000 | 52,000 | 60,000 |
| Workhours, erecting | 12 | 12 | 14 | 14 | 16 | 20 | 20 |
| Crane, hoist to roof | 4 | 4 | 4 | 4 | 4 | 4 | 4 |

**TABLE 6.4** Induced-Draft Cooling Towers—Redwood

Redwood construction frames with PVC fill and eliminators, shipped knocked down ready for field assembly. Workhours includes erecting, aligning, and anchoring.

| Capacity, tons | 20 | 25 | 30 | 40 | 50 |
|---|---|---|---|---|---|
| Shipping weight, lb | 2,000 | 2,150 | 2,225 | 2,400 | 2,600 |
| Wet weight, lb | 4,000 | 4,300 | 4,300 | 4,800 | 5,200 |
| Base area, sq ft | 40 | 45 | 50 | 55 | 60 |
| Fan hp | 0.75 | 1 | 1.5 | 1.5 | 2 |
| Tower cost, $ | 2,000 | 2,350 | 2,550 | 3,100 | 3,400 |
| Workhours, erecting | 25.3 | 30.2 | 35.0 | 44.6 | 50.6 |

| Capacity, tons | 55 | 65 | 85 | 110 | 130 |
|---|---|---|---|---|---|
| Shipping weight, lb | 2,800 | 3,000 | 4,000 | 4,500 | 5,500 |
| Wet weight, lb | 6,000 | 6,500 | 8,800 | 9,000 | 11,250 |
| Base area, sq ft | 65 | 70 | 88 | 98 | 112 |
| Fan hp | 2 | 3 | 3 | 5 | 5 |
| Tower cost, $ | 3,900 | 4,500 | 5,900 | 6,000 | 7,000 |
| Workhours, erecting | 60.2 | 65.0 | 84.4 | 108.5 | 130.0 |

| Capacity, tons | 170 | 220 | 260 | 320 | 380 |
|---|---|---|---|---|---|
| Shipping weight, lb | 8,750 | 9,750 | 12,300 | 14,500 | 18,500 |
| Wet weight, lb | 18,000 | 20,000 | 24,250 | 30,000 | 37,250 |
| Base area, sq ft | 200 | 230 | 270 | 360 | 400 |
| Fan hp | 7.5 | 7.5 | 10 | 15 | 15 |
| Tower cost, $ | 8,500 | 10,500 | 11,900 | 12,800 | 14,800 |
| Workhours, erecting | 169 | 222 | 260 | 300 | 374 |

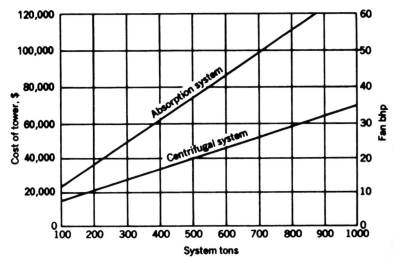

**Figure 6.1    COOLING-TOWER COST COMPARISON**
*Quick-estimating budget figures show the relation of fan horsepower and costs to system tons for cooling towers with absorption vs. centrifugal systems. Based on a 7° approach. Does not include rigging.*

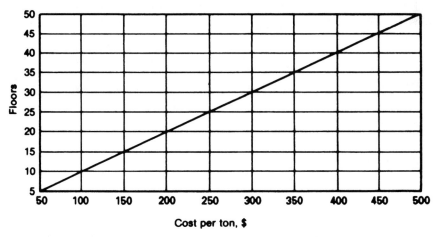

**Figure 6.2    COOLING-TOWER RIGGING**
*Quick budget figures for estimating rigging costs for towers on high roofs.*

**TABLE 6.5** Blowdown Requirements at Varying Conditions

| Cooling range, °F | Blow-down factor* |
|:---:|:---:|
| 6 | 0.0015 |
| 7½ | 0.0020 |
| 10 | 0.0033 |
| 15 | 0.0054 |
| 20 | 0.0075 |

*The blow-down factor is a percent of the total water circulated through the system. For a 300-gpm tower with a cooling range of 10°F the blow-down rate will be approximately one gpm.

## CHEMICAL TREATMENT

Chemical treatment costs for cooling towers vary widely with the quality and acidity of the makeup water, quality of ambient air, type of chemical system used, degree of sophistication (i.e., automatic controls), etc. Table 6.6 gives a range of costs for three typical systems using automatic sampling, automatic feeding of inhibitors, and automatic bleed systems. System A is minimal; it is applied to fairly soft water and is used on towers from 50 to 150 tons. It includes inhibitor feed. System B is for larger towers with tolerably soft water not requiring acid feed but including two biocides feed. System C is similar to B but includes chemical pumps with locked enclosures, sample stream piping, shutoff safety switches for the chemical drums, alarms, and liquid level switch. Dollar costs include installation labor. Makeup water pipe size indicates tower size.

**TABLE 6.6** Chemical Treatment

| System | Supply water pipe size, in. | Cost, $ |
|:---:|:---:|:---:|
| A | ¾ | 1,000–1,800 |
| B | ¾–1 | 4,500–6,500 |
|  | 1¼–1½ | 4,800–7,200 |
| C | ¾–1 | 6,000–8,500 |
|  | 1¼–1½ | 6,500–9,000 |

## FREEZE PROTECTION

Table 6.7 gives some average costs for cooling tower freeze protection when tower piping and tower basins need to be fitted with heating systems. Heating systems consist of heat tracer lines or heat tape covered with insulation and waterproof jacket for exterior application and automatic temperature-controlled pipe and basin draining. Dollar costs include heat tape, insulation, piping, fittings and specialties, thermostats, control switches and low-voltage controls, and wiring on the low side of the control box. The interlock control sequence brings the basin heater on until the basin is drained and the makeup water valve closes and drain valves open.

**TABLE 6.7**  Freeze Protection

| Supply water pipe size, in. | Drain pipe size, in. | Condenser water pipe size, in. | Piping, $ | Basin heater, $ | Total, $ |
|---|---|---|---|---|---|
| ¾ | 2 | 4 | 2,700 | 1,150 | 3,850 |
| 1¼ | 2 | 6 | 300 | 1,200 | 4,200 |
| 1½ | 4 | 8 | 4,750 | 1,300 | 6,050 |

## MOBILE RENTAL COOLING TOWERS

Trailer-mounted cooling towers are in demand when a breakdown occurs or when plants need to be kept running during scheduled maintenance. They are also being used to augment existing systems when unusual environmental circumstances or peak load demands require temporarily increasing the tower capacity. Mobile cooling towers are available in a range of capacities up to 1,500 tons of cooling. They are quickly set up at the jobsite (in 2 to 3 hr) and hooked into the existing electrical connections and tapped into the existing hot-water return line. Discharge water can be gravity fed via a fiber-glass chute into the existing cold-water basin or connected to the existing tower pump from the lower sump in the rental tower. The estimator should be aware that large trailer-mounted cooling towers, when transported across highways, require special permits; nighttime and weekend travel are usually restricted. Table 6.8 shows costs for mobile rental cooling towers by day, week, month, quarter year, or year. Dollar costs include delivery, moving onto jobsite, start-up, breakdown, and move-off.

**TABLE 6.8**  Mobile Cooling Towers

Rental costs for mobile towers. Tower ratings are based on 95°F on, 85°F off, and 78°F WB for HVAC; 100°F on, 85°F off, and 78°F WB for industrial Btuh standard.

| Capacity, industrial MBtuh | Capacity, HVAC tons | L × W × H, ft | Weight, lb | $ per week | $ per month | $ per quarter | $ per year |
|---|---|---|---|---|---|---|---|
| | 50 | | | 1,000 | 3,250 | | |
| | 167 | | | 2,000 | 5,000 | | |
| | 200 | | | 2,000 | 6,500 | | |
| 9.23 | 500 | 30 × 9 × 15 | 12,000 | 2,750 | 8,000 | 21,200 | 80,600 |
| 13.84 | 750 | 37 × 9 × 15 | 19,000 | 3,500 | 12,000 | 32,400 | 115,200 |
| 23.10 | 1,250 | 53 × 9 × 15 | 35,000 | 7,500 | 25,000 | 67,000 | 240,000 |
| 27.68 | 1,500 | 61 × 9 × 15 | 38,000 | 9,000 | 30,000 | 81,000 | 288,000 |

**TABLE 6.9**   Portable Cooling Tower Pumps

Rental costs based on Class 1 explosionproof electrical equipment to withstand tough process cooling requirements; gpm = Btuh/500 × t.

| gpm | hp | Suction × discharge, in. | psi | Weight, lb | Week, $ | Month, $ | Quarter, $ | Year, $ |
|-----|-----|-----|-----|-----|-----|-----|-----|-----|
| 2,200 | 75 | 8 × 6 | 43 | 4,000 | 1,000 | 3,000 | 8,100 | 28,800 |
| 3,200 | 125 | 10 × 8 | 32 | 4,000 | 1,200 | 3,600 | 9,720 | 34,560 |
| 3,200 | 150 | 10 × 8 | 60 | 4,800 | 1,500 | 6,000 | 12,150 | 43,200 |
| 4,000 | 125 | 12 × 10 | 40 | 4,000 | 2,000 | 4,500 | 16,200 | 57,600 |
| 5,000 | 200 | 12 × 10 | 52 | 6,000 | 2,500 | 7,500 | 20,250 | 72,000 |
| 6,000 | 200 | 12 × 12 | 43 | 6,000 | 2,500 | 7,500 | 20,250 | 72,000 |

In those cases where existing tower pumps and/or hot taps on the hot-water return are not available, portable pumps may be used. Table 6.9 gives costs for portable pumps.

For estimating cooling tower certification testing, see Chap. 15. [For further information regarding cooling tower and pump rentals, call Mobile Auxiliary Cooling Towers (800) 486-9377.]

# CHAPTER 7
# PUMPS

## GENERAL DISCUSSION

Many types of pumps are available for conducting and raising fluids as applied to comfort and industrial cooling and heating, and the final selection is often made by the estimator. It is necessary for the estimator to understand the basic hydraulics and the services of pumping machinery. Table 7.1[1] shows services of and applications for various pumps.

Centrifugal pumps are built with open, semiclosed, and enclosed impellers, end suction, double suction, and multistage for specific duties. The number of pump configurations is almost infinite, and many older units are not standardized. For that reason and to facilitate future replacements, only pumps complying with American National Standards Institute

---

[1]Tables 7.1 through 7.6 do not appear on the computer disk provided with this book.

**TABLE 7.1**   Services and Applications of Various Pumps

| Type | Application | Service |
|------|-------------|---------|
| Reciprocating . . . . | General service, hot and cold water, small boiler feeding, condensate return, light oil pumping | Efficient at small capacities and high heads, self-priming, positive displacement |
| Rotary . . . . . . . . | Lubricating and fuel-oil pumps, syrups, paints, varnish, thick liquids | Best on self-lubricating liquids, small capacity with medium heads but high suction lift. Self-priming, positive displacement |
| Centrifugal . . . . . . | General water services, condensers, evaporators, brine, hot- and cold-water circulation on wells or cooling towers, high-pressure spray, sprinkler, and boiler feed. Pipe line and transfer work, process and chemical work, sump, bilge, and unwatering | Non-positive acting, low-suction lifts, efficient at high capacities, low heads. Handles liquid with foreign matter |

Pumps: General-purpose centrifugal
(single and two-stage, single-suction)

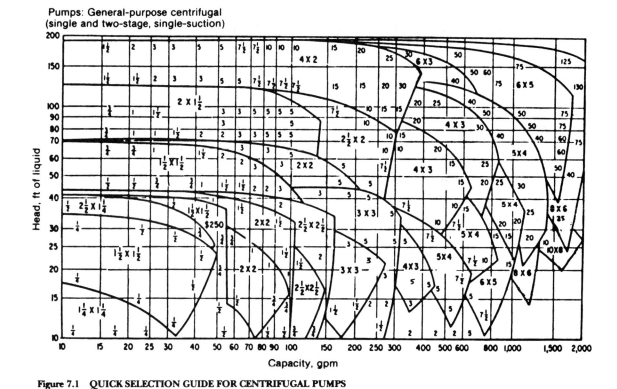

**Figure 7.1   QUICK SELECTION GUIDE FOR CENTRIFUGAL PUMPS**
*Small numbers within the selection blocks indicate approximate horsepower.*

(ANSI) standard B73.1 should be chosen. This standard is also known as the American Voluntary Standard (AVS).

The pressure developed by a centrifugal pump is always specified as head in feet of liquid. For reciprocating pumps, pounds per square inch is always used. Because of the universality of the centrifugal pump for air-conditioning applications, this discussion will embrace only centrifugals, and pressures will be considered as feet of head. Figure 7.1 and Table 7.2 offer a quick selection guide for centrifugal pumps.

**TABLE 7.2**   Quick Selection Guide for Centrifugal-Pump Duties

| Type | Duty | Max. head | gpm range | Max. °F | hp range |
|---|---|---|---|---|---|
| Fractional hp . . . | Light, air conditioning | 120 ft | Up to 150 | 200 | ¼–1½ |
| Close-coupled . . . | General, air conditioning | 500 ft | 10–2,000 | 250 | 1–100 |
| Frame-mounted . . | Any drive, air conditioning | 500 ft | 10–3,000 | 500 | 1–125 |
| Self-priming . . . . | Wells, air conditioning | 130 ft | Up to 120 | 200 | ½–5 |
| Double suction. . . | Extra heavy, industrial | 1,000 ft | 50–200,000 | 250 | 2–3,000 |
| Multistage. . . . . . | Hot water, boiler feed | 3,000 psi | 10–3,000 | 650 | 15–3,000 |
| Nonclogging . . . . | Sewage | 125 ft | 100–10,000 | 250 | 5–200 |

It may be said of centrifugal pumps that *capacity* varies in direct proportion to speed, *horsepower* varies in proportion to the cube of the speed, and *head in feet* varies in proportion to the square of the speed; when the impeller diameter is constant.

It may be stated further that, with the speed constant, the *capacity* varies directly with the impeller diameter, *horsepower* varies in proportion to the cube of the impeller diameter, and *head in feet* varies in proportion to the square of the impeller diameter (for relatively small changes in impeller size only).

**Example 7.1**  With the above laws of affinity, a pump is rated at 200 gpm, 50-ft head, 5 hp, and 3,500 rpm. What will the capacity, head, and horsepower at 1,750 rpm be?

**solution**

$$\text{Capacity} = \frac{1,750}{3,500} \times 200 = 100 \text{ gpm}$$

$$\text{Head} = \left(\frac{1,750}{3,500}\right)^2 \times 50 = 12.5 \text{ ft}$$

$$\text{hp} = \left(\frac{1,750}{3,500}\right)^3 \times 5 = 0.625 \text{ hp}$$

It is axiomatic that, whenever the engineer selects a 1,750-rpm pump for reasons of sound attenuation, the cost will be greater than that of a 3,500-rpm pump.

The *specific gravity* (sp gr) of a liquid will affect the pump horsepower when the head is constant. When the horsepower is fixed, the head will be affected. This is true because specific gravity enters the function of horsepower.

The formula to obtain brake horsepower is

$$\text{bhp} = \frac{\text{gpm} \times \text{head feet} \times \text{specific gravity}}{3,960 \times \text{efficiency}}$$

$$\text{where } 3,960 = \frac{33,000}{8.33} \text{ a constant}$$

$$\text{where } 33,000 = \text{ft-lb per hp}$$
$$8.33 = \text{lb per gal } H_2O$$

**Example 7.2**  Against a total head of 100 ft at 80% pump efficiency, 100 gpm of liquid is desired. What will be the required horsepower for water? For brine? For gasoline?

**solution**

$$\text{Water (sp gr 1)hp} = \frac{100 \times 100 \times 1.0}{3,960 \times 0.80} = 3.16$$

$$\text{Brine (sp gr 1.2)hp} = \frac{100 \times 100 \times 1.2}{3,960 \times 0.80} = 3.78$$

$$\text{Gasoline (sp gr 0.70)hp} = \frac{100 \times 100 \times 0.70}{3,960 \times 0.80} = 2.21$$

Many problems are encountered in the analysis of the corrosive qualities of a solution. For the recommended pump construction for handling such a solution, Table 7.3 offers a quick selection guide when the pH is known.

**TABLE 7.3** Material of Construction Selection on Pumps Where pH of Solution to Be Handled Is Known

| Value of pH | Hydrogen-Hydroxide | Pump construction |
|---|---|---|
| 0–4 | Acid increase | Alloy steels |
| 4–6 | ↑ | All bronze |
| 7 | Neutral | Standard |
| 6–8 | | Bronze or standard fitted |
| 8–10 | ↓ | All iron |
| 10–14 | Alkaline increases | Alloys |

## Specific Gravity

When a liquid is thick or viscous, it increases the internal pump losses, which, in turn, reduces capacity and head and increases the power. Each liquid has its own specific gravity. The specific gravity of fresh water at 60°F is 1, unity. For this reason, formulas for pumping water may be simplified by omitting the specific gravity. Table 7.4 gives specific gravity of selected liquids. Two rules about the effect of specific gravity on pump performance:

1. For a given head in feet, horsepower will vary according to the specific gravity of the liquid.
2. For a given pressure in pounds per square inch, the head will vary according to the specific gravity and the horsepower remains constant.

**TABLE 7.4** Specific Gravity for Selected Liquids

| Liquid | Specific gravity | Liquid | Specific gravity | Liquid | Specific gravity |
|---|---|---|---|---|---|
| Acetic acid | 1.06 | Gasoline | 0.70 | Petroleum oil | 0.82 |
| Alcohol, commercial | 0.83 | Kerosene | 0.80 | Phosphoric acid | 1.78 |
| Alcohol, pure | 0.79 | Linseed oil | 0.94 | Rape oil | 0.92 |
| Ammonia | 0.89 | Mineral oil | 0.92 | Sulfuric acid | 1.84 |
| Benzine | 0.69 | Muriatic acid | 1.20 | Tar | 1.00 |
| Bromine | 2.97 | Naphtha | 0.76 | Turpentine oil | 0.87 |
| Carbolic acid | 0.96 | Nitric acid | 1.22 | Vinegar | 1.08 |
| Carbon disulfide | 1.26 | Olive oil | 0.92 | Water | 1.00 |
| Cottonseed oil | 0.93 | Palm oil | 0.97 | Water, sea | 1.03 |
| Ether, sulfuric | 0.72 | | | | |

**Example 7.3**    Assume 200 gpm at a total head of 100 ft and a pump efficiency of 70%.

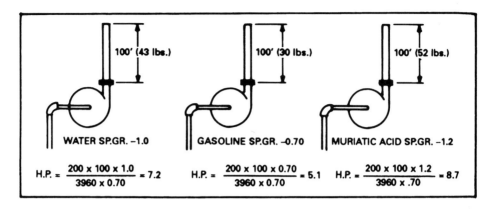

**Example 7.4**    Assume 200 gpm required at a pressure of 43 lb and a pump efficiency of 70%.

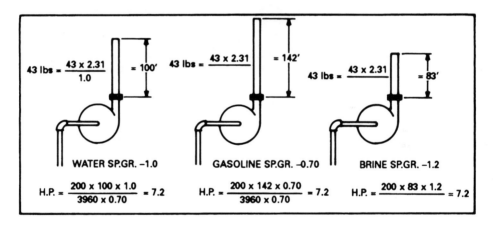

(*Note:* Centrifugal pumps handle feet of liquid. When applying a pump for a given pressure, convert pounds pressure into equivalent feet head and select pump accordingly.)

## Making the Pump Connections

When piping the pump, make the suction pipe one size larger than the pump inlet and use an eccentric reducer—flat on top—at the suction nozzle to prevent air pockets. Make the suction pipe as short and direct as possible. Figure 7.2 shows the right and wrong ways to make the pump suction connections. To prevent vibration transmission, pumps need to rest on a proper base. Figure 7.3 illustrates some typical foundation designs for a centrifugal pump. For speeds below 2,000 rpm, cork is not the preferred isolation material. In critical areas

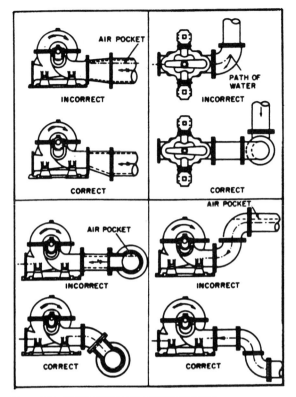

**Figure 7.2  PUMP SUCTION CONNECTIONS**

where the pump is located on a floor above occupied space such as libraries, executive offices, and hospitals, steel spring isolation is recommended. The concrete pad for the pump should be twice the weight of the machinery.

No valves or restrictions of any kind should be placed between the pump outlet or inlet and the pressure gage. Figure 7.4 illustrates a typical gage hookup. For multiple pump piping arrangement, see Fig. 7.5.

## Calculating the Water Quantity, gpm

Water quantities for air-conditioning systems can be calculated from the following equation:

$$gpm = \frac{Btuh}{500} \times \Delta t$$

where $500 = 8.33$ lb/gal $\times$ 60 min, $\Delta t$ = difference in water temperature "off" and "on" the condenser or chiller.

For most cooling-tower applications, the quantity may be taken at 3 gpm *per ton* of cooling. Table 7.5 gives guidelines for approximate condenser water rates.

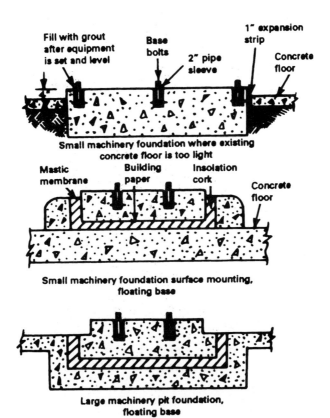

Figure 7.3  PUMP FOUNDATIONS

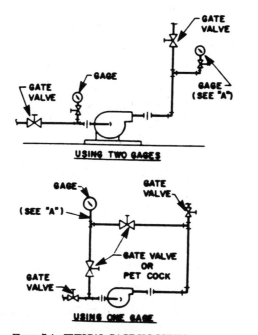

Figure 7.4  TYPICAL GAGE HOOKUPS

151

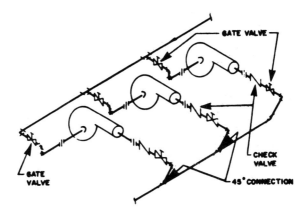

**Figure 7.5  MULTIPLE PUMP HOOKUPS**

**TABLE 7.5**  Approximate Condenser Water Rates for Various Systems

| System description | Water rates in gpm per ton refrigeration |
|---|---|
| Refrigerant-12, city water | 1½ |
| Refrigerant-22, city water | 1½–2 |
| Refrigerant-12, cooling tower | 3–4 |
| Refrigerant-22, cooling tower | 3–4 |
| Ammonia, city water | 3 |
| Ammonia, cooling tower | 4–6 |
| Lithium bromide, cooling tower | 3–4 |

## Calculating the System Resistance, Total Head

Three resistances may be observed in a water system:

1. Static head
2. Pressure head
3. Friction losses

The most frequently encountered head is the *static head*. It is the height to which the liquid is raised.

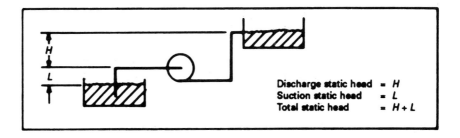

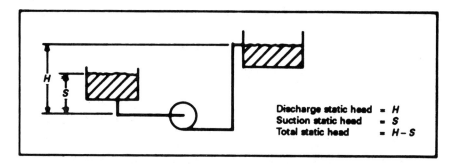

Discharge static head  =  *H*
Suction static head    =  *S*
Total static head      =  *H – S*

In the two preceding illustrations, pressure head, friction, and entrance and exit head losses have been purposely disregarded. The *pressure head* applies to closed receivers.

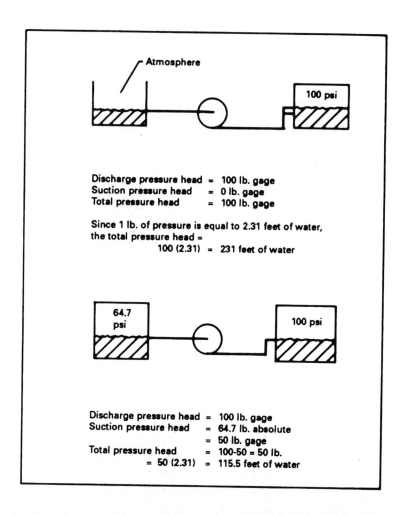

Discharge pressure head  =  100 lb. gage
Suction pressure head    =  0 lb. gage
Total pressure head      =  100 lb. gage

Since 1 lb. of pressure is equal to 2.31 feet of water, the total pressure head =
        100 (2.31)   =  231 feet of water

Discharge pressure head  =  100 lb. gage
Suction pressure head    =  64.7 lb. absolute
                         =  50 lb. gage
Total pressure head      =  100-50 = 50 lb.
        = 50 (2.31)      =  115.5 feet of water

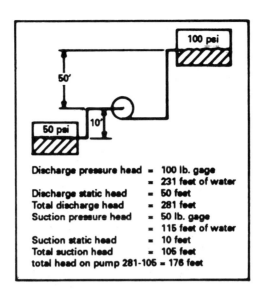

Discharge pressure head = 100 lb. gage
= 231 feet of water
Discharge static head = 50 feet
Total discharge head = 281 feet
Suction pressure head = 50 lb. gage
= 115 feet of water
Suction static head = 10 feet
Total suction head = 105 feet
total head on pump 281-105 = 176 feet

In these two preceding illustrations, friction, entrance and exit head losses have been purposely disregarded. *Friction head losses* are caused by velocity of flow in the suction and discharge piping system. The friction losses include the skin friction between the piping and the moving liquid (rough pipe creates greater friction than smooth pipe) and other head losses arising from valves, fittings, and bends in the piping system.

The actual selection of pipe sizes for water service is based on friction loss, but the concern for noise will place limits on the velocity, which is also a criterion. Water pipe sizes for heating and cooling systems are usually selected for friction losses of about 4 psi per 100 ft of equivalent length up to a velocity of 7 to 8 ft per second. In large air-conditioning applications a friction loss of 10 ft of water per 100 ft of equivalent-length pipe may be taken. Table 7.6 gives recommended velocities.

**TABLE 7.6** Recommended Maximum Pipe Velocities

| Service | Velocity, fps |
| --- | --- |
| Hot water | 6 |
| Cold water to 4-in. pipe | 8 |
| Cold water over 4-in. pipe | 12 |
| Pump suction—no static head | 4 |
| Drain lines | 4 |

## *ESTIMATING*

Tables 7.7 to 7.14 reflect the labor required to unload from truck to ground, haul 100 level feet to foundation, uncrate, set, and align. The *foundation pad* row is based on a concrete pad weighing 2½ times the listed weight of the pump and includes the labor and material for forming, setting rods and bolt sleeves, and floating the concrete. Material is bare pump price only. See other chapters for starters, vibration absorbers, and electric wiring. A quick labor-estimating guide to centrifugal pump installation is given in Fig. 7.6. Table 7.15 shows the effect of material of construction on pump cost. For conversion ratios and equivalents for water and pressure, see Table 7.16.

**TABLE 7.7**  Centrifugal Pumps, General-Purpose, 3,500-rpm, Three-Phase 208/220/440-V

Cast-iron, bronze-fitted, close-coupled with mechanical seal and screwed or flanged connections. For all-bronze pump, add 35% to *material* row.

| Horsepower | ½ | ¾ | 1 | 1½ | 2 | 3 | 5 | 7½ | 10 |
|---|---|---|---|---|---|---|---|---|---|
| Gallons per minute | 15 | 20 | 30 | 60 | 80 | 125 | 150 | 200 | 300 |
| Head, ft | 40 | 40 | 40 | 40 | 80 | 80 | 80 | 80 | 80 |
| Weight, lb | 60 | 65 | 60 | 80 | 85 | 220 | 255 | 275 | 280 |
| Material, $ | 365 | 420 | 450 | 500 | 600 | 940 | 1,100 | 1,300 | 1,760 |
| Workhours to erect | 1.5 | 1.5 | 2.0 | 2.0 | 2.5 | 3.0 | 3.5 | 4.5 | 5.0 |
| Foundation pad, $ | 60 | 60 | 60 | 80 | 80 | 200 | 200 | 200 | 200 |
| Horsepower | 15 | 20 | 25 | 30 | 40 | 50 | 60 | 75 | |
| Gallons per minute | 400 | 500 | 600 | 400 | 550 | 650 | 700 | 825 | |
| Head, ft | 100 | 100 | 100 | 200 | 200 | 200 | 250 | 250 | |
| Weight, lb | 490 | 520 | 550 | 750 | 1,135 | 1,200 | 1,450 | 1,600 | |
| Material, $ | 2,400 | 2,850 | 3,300 | 3,800 | 4,800 | 6,000 | 6,500 | 7,600 | |
| Workhours to erect | 7.5 | 8 | 8 | 10 | 15 | 16 | 19 | 21 | |
| Foundation pad, $ | 300 | 400 | 500 | 700 | 800 | 900 | 1,000 | 1,000 | |

**TABLE 7.8**  Centrifugal Pumps, General-Purpose, 3,500-rpm, One-Phase, 115/230-V

Cast-iron, bronze-fitted, close-coupled with mechanical seal, and screwed or flanged connections. For all-bronze pump, add 35% to *material* row.

| Horsepower | ½ | ¾ | 1 | 1½ | 2 | 3 | 5 | 7½ |
|---|---|---|---|---|---|---|---|---|
| Gallons per minute | 15 | 20 | 40 | 20 | 25 | 80 | 90 | 120 |
| Head, ft | 30 | 40 | 80 | 60 | 80 | 80 | 80 | 80 |
| Weight, lb | 60 | 65 | 80 | 85 | 90 | 220 | 225 | 275 |
| Material, $ | 350 | 375 | 360 | 500 | 700 | 1,350 | 2,000 | 3,000 |
| Workhours to erect | 2 | 2 | 2 | 2 | 3 | 3 | 4 | 5 |
| Foundation pad, $ | 60 | 60 | 60 | 80 | 80 | 200 | 200 | 200 |

**TABLE 7.9** Centrifugal Pumps, General-Purpose, 1,750-rpm, Three-Phase, 208/220/440-V

Cast-iron, bronze-fitted, close-coupled with mechanical seal, and screwed or flanged connections. For all-bronze pump, add 35% to *material* row.

| Horsepower | ½ | ¾ | 1 | 1½ | 2 | 3 | 5 | 7½ | 10 |
|---|---|---|---|---|---|---|---|---|---|
| Gallons per minute | 20 | 30 | 30 | 40 | 60 | 70 | 100 | 200 | 300 |
| Head, ft | 40 | 40 | 60 | 60 | 60 | 80 | 80 | 80 | 80 |
| Weight, lb. | 75 | 80 | 215 | 220 | 230 | 255 | 275 | 300 | 550 |
| Material, $ | 370 | 440 | 850 | 950 | 980 | 1,100 | 1,350 | 1,900 | 2,100 |
| Workhours to erect | 1.5 | 2.0 | 3.0 | 3.0 | 3.0 | 3.25 | 4.5 | 5.25 | 8.0 |
| Foundation pad, $ | 60 | 60 | 60 | 60 | 80 | 200 | 200 | 200 | 200 |

| Horsepower | 15 | 20 | 25 | 30 | 40 | 50 | 60 | 75 |
|---|---|---|---|---|---|---|---|---|
| Gallons per minute | 400 | 500 | 600 | 800 | 500 | 650 | 700 | 800 |
| Head, ft | 80 | 100 | 100 | 100 | 200 | 200 | 250 | 250 |
| Weight, lb. | 775 | 800 | 900 | 1,000 | 1,200 | 1,550 | 1,700 | 1,850 |
| Material, $ | 2,650 | 3,050 | 3,400 | 4,100 | 4,600 | 6,000 | 6,800 | 8,000 |
| Workhours to erect | 10.0 | 11.0 | 12.0 | 14.0 | 16.0 | 20.0 | 22.0 | 24.0 |
| Foundation pad, $ | 300 | 400 | 500 | 700 | 800 | 900 | 1,000 | 1,000 |

**TABLE 7.10** Centrifugal Pumps, Multistage, 3,500-rpm, Three-Phase, 208/220/440-V

High-pressure boiler feed, etc. Cast-iron, bronze-fitted.

| Horsepower | 7½ | 10 | 15 | 20 | 25 | 30 | 40 | 50 |
|---|---|---|---|---|---|---|---|---|
| Gallons per minute | 30 | 50 | 75 | 80 | 80 | 80 | 100 | 100 |
| Head, ft | 250 | 300 | 350 | 400 | 500 | 600 | 600 | 700 |
| Weight, lb. | 620 | 690 | 780 | 850 | 890 | 970 | 1,100 | 1,260 |
| Material, $ | 2,850 | 3,100 | 3,500 | 4,250 | 4,700 | 4,900 | 5,300 | 5,900 |
| Workhours to erect | 9.0 | 10.0 | 11.0 | 12.0 | 12.0 | 14.0 | 16.0 | 18.0 |
| Foundation pad, $ | 200 | 200 | 300 | 400 | 500 | 500 | 700 | 800 |

**TABLE 7.11** Centrifugal Booster Pumps

Low-head pumps. Forced-hot-water systems, etc. Cast-iron, flanged connections; for domestic water, all-bronze, add 35% to *material* row.

| Horsepower | 1/12 | 1/12 | 1/12 | 1/12 | ⅙ | ¼ |
|---|---|---|---|---|---|---|
| Pipe size, in. | ¾ | 1 | 1¼ | 1½ | 2 | 2½ |
| Material, $ | 150 | 150 | 150 | 175 | 220 | 285 |
| Workhours to erect | 1 | 1 | 1 | 1.5 | 1.65 | 1.9 |

Multistage pressure booster pumps; 12 to 16 stages, 3,450-rpm motor, cast-iron, stainless-steel shaft, and pump heads. Multistage booster pumps increase water pressure from city mains or private water systems. They are especially important for proper operation of water softeners and filtration equipment. Stainless-steel models can handle saltwater and contaminated water in reverse osmosis filters and in other aggressive water applications.

| Horsepower | ½ | ¾ | 1 | 1½ |
|---|---|---|---|---|
| Gallons per minute, 20 ft head | 582 | 813 | 990 | 996 |
| Weight, lb | 22 | 22 | 24 | 26 |
| Material, $ | 355 | 360 | 390 | 400 |

**TABLE 7.12**  Condensate Lift Pumps

Fractional horsepower for removing condensate in tight air-handler areas where obstructions limit gravity flow. *Material* includes sump tank and float assembly. *Labor* includes setting and final connections and wiring.

| Maximum vertical lift, ft.... | 9 | 18 | 25 | 25 |
|---|---|---|---|---|
| Gallons per hour .......... | 50 | 60 | 45 | 125 |
| Pounds per square inch .... | 5 | 8½ | 11 | 12½ |
| Material, $ ................ | 115 | 140 | 150 | 175 |
| Labor, $ .................. | 90 | 90 | 115 | 115 |

**TABLE 7.13**  Chilled-Water and Condenser Water Pumps

| Horsepower | 5 | 10 | 15 | 15 | 20 |
|---|---|---|---|---|---|
| Gallons per minute | 100 | 200 | 300 | 400 | 500 |
| Head, ft | 100 | 100 | 100 | 100 | 100 |
| Weight, lb | 475 | 500 | 600 | 600 | 600 |
| Pipe discharge size, in. | 1½ | 2 | 2 | 3 | 3 |
| Pump, motor, base $ | 1,700 | 2,400 | 3,000 | 3,250 | 3,400 |
| Workhours | 6 | 6 | 8 | 8 | 8 |
| Horsepower | 30 | 40 | 50 | 60 | 100 |
| Gallons per minute | 750 | 1,000 | 1,500 | 2,000 | 3,000 |
| Head, ft | 100 | 100 | 100 | 100 | 100 |
| Weight, lb | 900 | 1,000 | 1,100 | 1,900 | 2,000 |
| Pipe discharge size, in. | 4 | 4 | 5 | 6 | 8 |
| Pump, motor, base $ | 4,000 | 4,300 | 5,000 | 6,500 | 8,500 |
| Workhours | 8 | 8 | 8 | 12 | 12 |

**TABLE 7.14**  Straight Centrifugal Chemical-Resistant Pumps (Stainless Steel)

Single-phase motors, 115/230-V, 3,450-rpm, NEMA 565 frame with base.

| Horsepower | ½ | ¾ | 1 | 1½ | |
|---|---|---|---|---|---|
| Gallons per minute | 23 | 59 | 95 | 117 | |
| Weight, lb | 21 | 25 | 28 | 32 | |
| Material cost, $ | 585 | 685 | 715 | 730 | |
| Workhours to erect | 1.5 | 2 | 3 | 3 | |
| Foundation pad, $ | 25 | 25 | 60 | 60 | |

Three-phase motors, 208 to 220/440-V, NEMA 565 frame with base

| Horsepower | ¾ | 1 | 1½ | 2 | 3 |
|---|---|---|---|---|---|
| Gallons per minute | 59 | 89 | 110 | 118 | 131 |
| Weight, lb | 28 | 28 | 34 | 38 | 43 |
| Material cost, $ | 685 | 715 | 730 | 850 | 875 |
| Workhours to erect | 2 | 3 | 3 | 3.5 | 3.5 |
| Foundation pad, $ | 30 | 60 | 60 | 60 | 70 |

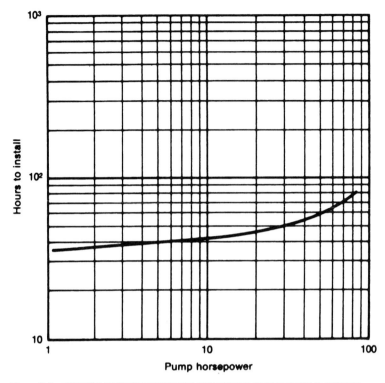

**Figure 7.6** **QUICK LABOR-ESTIMATING GUIDE FOR CENTRIFUGAL PUMPS**
*Gives approximate workhours to install pump and motor.*

**TABLE 7.15**  Effect of Material of Construction on Cost of Centrifugal Pumps

Centrifugal pump cost, $ = base cost $\times F_m \times F_o$. The adjustment factors are as follows:

| Material | $F_m$ |
|---|---|
| Cast iron (May be bronze-fitted) ................ | 1.00 |
| Bronze ...................................... | 1.35 |
| Cast steel ................................... | 1.41 |
| Stainless steel (316) .......................... | 1.94 |
| Alloy 20 .................................... | 2.27 |
| Monel ...................................... | 3.31 |
| Nickel ...................................... | 3.47 |
| Hastelloy C ................................. | 3.78 |
| Hastelloy B ................................. | 3.93 |
| Titanium ................................... | 5.71 |

| Operating Limits | $F_o$ |
|---|---|
| Suction pressure: | |
|    Below 275 psig at 100°F..................... | 1.0 |
|    Below 350 psig at 100°F..................... | 1.5 |
| System temperature: | |
|    0 to 500°F (at ANSI allowable pressures)....... | 1.0 |
|    Above 500°F (at ANSI allowable pressures) .... | 1.5 |

SOURCE: J. Matley (ed.), *Modern Cost Engineering: Methods and Data*, Vol. 2, McGraw-Hill, New York, 1984, p. 133.

**TABLE 7.16**  Conversion Ratios and Equivalents for Water and Pressure

| Multiply | By | To obtain |
|---|---|---|
| U.S. gallons | 0.8327 | Imperial gallons |
| U.S. gallons | 231.0 | Cubic inches |
| U.S. gallons | 0.13368 | Cubic feet |
| U.S. gallons | 8.337 | Pounds of water |
| U.S. gallons | 42.0 | Barrels of oil |
| U.S. gallons | 0.00418 | Tons of water |
| U.S. gallons | 3.785 | Liters |
| U.S. gallons | 0.00378 | Cubic meters |
| Meters | 3.28 | Feet of water |
| Pounds per square inch | 2.307 | Feet of water |
| Inches of water | 0.073483 | Inches of mercury |
| Inches of mercury | 0.4912 | Pounds per square inch |
| Feet of water | 0.4335 | Pounds per square inch |
| Cubic feet per second | 448.8 | Gallons per minute |
| To obtain above | Divide by above | Starting with above |

*Note:* To cover 1 acre to a depth of 1 in., 27,152 gal of water will be required. One acre-inch pumped for 12 hr will require approximately 38 gpm.

## *ACKNOWLEDGMENTS*

Portions of the text of this chapter were excerpted by permission from *Moving Water through Pumps and Pipes for HPAC* by John Gladstone, Engineers Press, Coral Gables, Florida, 1992.

Figures 7.1 and 7.6 were originally published in *Chemical Engineering* magazine, March 16, 1984 and are used by permission.

Illustrations used in Examples 7.3 and 7.4 are courtesy of Gould's Pump.

Figures 7.2, 7.3, 7.4, and 7.5 are copyrighted by the Carrier Corporation and are used by permission.

The illustrations of static head and pressure head are courtesy of Ingersoll-Rand.

The editors express their appreciation to these firms for these materials.

# CHAPTER 8
# TANKS

## GENERAL DISCUSSION

The cost of tanks may show considerable variation by geography, owing to the high freight cost in relation to the total cost of the vessel. If local fabricating facilities are available, the cost for these tanks will usually be less than that for shipped-in tanks. Increasingly, particularly for underground installations, fiber-glass is replacing steel in tank construction. Virtually without exception, tanks that operate at elevated pressures and temperatures are required by local building codes to meet the requirements of the American Society of Mechanical Engineers (ASME) codes for pressure vessels. These tanks must be inspected to ensure compliance with the ASME code and must bear a nameplate so indicating. Cost figures given in this chapter for ASME-related tanks include the cost of inspection and labeling.

New underground storage tanks which will be used to contain petroleum products such as fuel oil must meet Environmental Protection Agency (EPA) installation requirements. The installation must meet the following conditions:

1. The tank and piping must be properly designed and constructed. The underground portion which routinely contains the product must be protected against corrosion.
2. The new tank must be equipped with spill and overfill prevention equipment. The overfill prevention equipment must automatically shut off the flow into the tank when the tank is 95% full. Alternately, an alarm to alert the operator delivering the product may be used if the alarm is triggered when the tank is 90% full.
3. The installing contractor must notify the local regulatory agency, on the owner's behalf, that the tank has been properly installed within 90 days after completion. The tank owner or operator can meet the installation certification requirement by the following methods:
   a. Mandatory: The tank installer has been certified by the tank and piping manufacturer.
   b. If required by state or local regulations:
      (1) The installer has been certified or licensed by the local regulatory agency.
      (2) The installation has been inspected and certified by a registered professional engineer.
      (3) The installation has been inspected and approved by the local regulatory agency.
   c. All work must be completed in accordance with the manufacturer's installation procedures, and their checklists must be completed by a certified installer.
4. The new underground storage tank system must have a leak detection device.

## ESTIMATING

Table 8.1 gives an analysis of the costs of underground storage tanks. Costs of commercial fuel-oil storage tanks are given in Table 8.2.

**TABLE 8.1** Underground Storage Tank Cost-Value Analysis

Approximate price index of tanks fob (free-on-board) jobsite.
Price index basis equals 100 for steel tank with asphaltum coating.

| Capacity, gal | Steel with asphaltum coating only | Steel with "Triple-Protection" cathodic anodes | Plastic* |
|---|---|---|---|
| 550 | 100 | 243 | 460 |
| 1,000 | 100 | 236 | 376 |
| 1,500 | 100 | 198 | 258 |
| 4,000 | 100 | 155 | 242 |
| 5,000 | 100 | 145 | N.A. |
| 6,000 | 100 | 142 | 205 |
| 8,000 | 100 | 140 | 209 |
| 10,000 | 100 | 141 | 217 |
| 12,000 | 100 | 141 | 228 |
| 15,000 | 100 | 128 | 200 |
| 20,000 | 100 | 133 | 219 |
| 25,000 | 100 | 134 | 224 |
| 30,000 | 100 | 134 | 222 |

*Varies greatly.
SOURCE: Steel Tank Institute.

**TABLE 8.2** Commercial Fuel-Oil Storage Tanks

All data are nominal for standard commercial sizes of black steel tanks finished in red oxide primer for aboveground, or black asphalt coating for underground service. Standard screwed openings; does not include piping or swing joints. *Workhours* includes unloading from open carrier, moving 40 ft and setting on prefabricated legs or into preexcavated pit.

| Capacity, gal | Diameter, in. | Length, ft | Weight, lb | Thickness, in. | Cost, $ | Erection, workhours |
|---|---|---|---|---|---|---|
| 550 | 48 | 6 | 800 | 3/16 | 1,525 | 4.0 |
| 1,000 | 48 | 10½ | 1,300 | 3/16 | 2,050 | 5.0 |
| 1,100 | 48 | 12 | 1,400 | 3/16 | 2,250 | 5.0 |
| 1,500 | 48 | 15½ | 1,625 | 3/16 | 3,100 | 6.0 |
| 2,000 | 65 | 11½ | 2,000 | 3/16 | 3,500 | 8.0 |
| 2,500 | 65 | 15 | 2,300 | 3/16 | 3,800 | 9.0 |
| 3,000 | 65 | 17½ | 3,000 | 3/16 | 4,100 | 12.0 |
| 4,000 | 65 | 23½ | 3,600 | 3/16 | 4,375 | 14.0 |
| 5,000 | 72 | 24 | 5,875 | ¼ | 5,100 | 23.0 |
| 7,500 | 96 | 19½ | 6,400 | ¼ | 5,875 | 25.0 |
| 8,500 | 108 | 18 | 7,500 | ¼ | 6,650 | 30.0 |
| 10,000 | 96 | 26½ | 8,500 | ¼ | 7,850 | 34.0 |
| 12,000 | 120 | 21 | 9,500 | ¼ | 9,400 | 42.0 |
| 15,000 | 120 | 25½ | 12,000 | 5/16 | 12,500 | 48.0 |
| 20,000 | 120 | 34½ | 15,500 | 5/16 | 16,000 | 62.0 |
| 25,000 | 120 | 42½ | 22,500 | 3/8 | 18,000 | 90.0 |
| 30,000 | 120 | 51 | 28,000 | 3/8 | 21,000 | 112.0 |
| 50,000 | 144 | 60 | 40,000 | 3/8 | 26,600 | 160.0 |

Table 8.3[1] will aid in determining areas for excavating and surface covering; costs for excavating, insulating, painting, pipe legs, and grillage may be found in the respective appropriate chapters. Workhours shown in Tables 8.1 and 8.2 do not include rigging aloft, excavating, grouting, foundations, antiflotation slabs, insulation, trim, and thermometers.

---

[1] Table 8.3 does not appear on the computer disk included with this book.

**TABLE 8.3** Capacities and Areas of Cylindrical Tanks

*Note:* Read square feet of surface in bold type; read gallons in light type. Formula to find capacity, in gallons, of cylindrical tank:

$$D^2 \times \text{length} \times 5.9 = \text{U.S. gal.}$$

Formula to find the surface area of cylindrical tank:

$$(\pi R^2 \times 2) + (\pi D \times \text{length}) = \text{sq ft of surface area}$$

| Diameter, ft | Length, ft | | | | | | | | | | | | | | | |
|---|---|---|---|---|---|---|---|---|---|---|---|---|---|---|---|---|
| | 1 | 2 | 3 | 4 | 5 | 6 | 7 | 8 | 9 | 10 | 11 | 12 | 13 | 14 | 15 | 16 |
| 1 | **6** | **12** | **18** | **24** | **30** | **36** | **42** | **48** | **54** | **60** | **66** | **72** | **78** | **84** | **90** | **96** |
| | 6 | 9 | 13 | 16 | 19 | 22 | 25 | 28 | 31 | 35 | 38 | 41 | 44 | 47 | 50 | 53 |
| 1½ | **13** | **26** | **39** | **52** | **65** | **78** | **91** | **104** | **117** | **130** | **143** | **156** | **169** | **182** | **195** | **208** |
| | 8 | 11 | 18 | 22 | 27 | 32 | 37 | 41 | 46 | 51 | 55 | 60 | 65 | 69 | 74 | 79 |
| 2 | **24** | **48** | **72** | **96** | **120** | **144** | **168** | **192** | **216** | **240** | **264** | **288** | **312** | **336** | **360** | **384** |
| | 13 | 19 | 25 | 32 | 38 | 44 | 50 | 57 | 63 | 69 | 75 | 82 | 88 | 94 | 100 | 107 |
| 2½ | **37** | **74** | **111** | **148** | **185** | **222** | **259** | **296** | **333** | **370** | **407** | **444** | **481** | **518** | **555** | **592** |
| | 18 | 26 | 33 | 41 | 49 | 57 | 65 | 73 | 80 | 88 | 96 | 104 | 112 | 120 | 128 | 135 |
| 3 | **53** | **106** | **159** | **212** | **265** | **318** | **371** | **424** | **477** | **530** | **583** | **636** | **689** | **742** | **795** | **848** |
| | 24 | 33 | 42 | 52 | 61 | 71 | 80 | 89 | 99 | 108 | 118 | 127 | 137 | 146 | 155 | 165 |
| 3½ | **72** | **144** | **216** | **288** | **360** | **432** | **504** | **576** | **648** | **720** | **792** | **864** | **936** | **1,008** | **1,080** | **1,152** |
| | 30 | 41 | 52 | 63 | 74 | 85 | 96 | 107 | 118 | 129 | 140 | 151 | 162 | 173 | 184 | 195 |
| 4 | **94** | **188** | **282** | **376** | **470** | **564** | **658** | **752** | **846** | **940** | **1,034** | **1,128** | **1,222** | **1,316** | **1,410** | **1,504** |
| | 38 | 50 | 63 | 75 | 88 | 100 | 113 | 126 | 138 | 151 | 163 | 176 | 188 | 201 | 214 | 226 |
| 4½ | **120** | **240** | **360** | **480** | **600** | **720** | **840** | **960** | **1,080** | **1,200** | **1,320** | **1,440** | **1,560** | **1,680** | **1,800** | **1,920** |
| | 46 | 60 | 74 | 88 | 102 | 117 | 131 | 145 | 159 | 173 | 187 | 201 | 215 | 230 | 244 | 258 |
| 5 | **145** | **290** | **435** | **580** | **725** | **870** | **1,015** | **1,170** | **1,305** | **1,450** | **1,595** | **1,740** | **1,885** | **2,030** | **2,175** | **2,320** |
| | 55 | 71 | 86 | 102 | 118 | 133 | 149 | 165 | 181 | 196 | 212 | 228 | 243 | 259 | 275 | 290 |
| 5½ | **180** | **360** | **540** | **720** | **900** | **1,080** | **1,260** | **1,440** | **1,620** | **1,800** | **1,980** | **2,160** | **2,340** | **2,520** | **2,700** | **2,880** |
| | 65 | 82 | 99 | 117 | 134 | 151 | 168 | 186 | 203 | 220 | 237 | 255 | 272 | 289 | 307 | 324 |
| 6 | **210** | **420** | **630** | **840** | **1,050** | **1,260** | **1,470** | **1,680** | **1,890** | **2,100** | **2,310** | **2,520** | **2,730** | **2,940** | **3,150** | **3,360** |
| | 75 | 94 | 113 | 132 | 151 | 170 | 188 | 207 | 226 | 245 | 264 | 283 | 301 | 320 | 339 | 358 |
| 6½ | **250** | **500** | **750** | **1,000** | **1,250** | **1,500** | **1,750** | **2,000** | **2,250** | **2,500** | **2,750** | **3,000** | **3,250** | **3,500** | **3,750** | **4,000** |
| | 87 | 107 | 128 | 148 | 168 | 189 | 209 | 230 | 250 | 270 | 291 | 311 | 332 | 352 | 373 | 393 |
| 7 | **290** | **580** | **870** | **1,160** | **1,450** | **1,740** | **2,030** | **2,320** | **2,610** | **2,900** | **3,190** | **3,480** | **3,770** | **4,060** | **4,350** | **4,640** |
| | 49 | 121 | 142 | 165 | 187 | 209 | 231 | 253 | 275 | 297 | 319 | 341 | 363 | 385 | 407 | 429 |
| 7½ | **330** | **660** | **990** | **1,320** | **1,650** | **1,980** | **2,310** | **2,640** | **2,970** | **3,300** | **3,630** | **3,960** | **4,290** | **4,620** | **4,950** | **5,280** |
| | 112 | 135 | 159 | 183 | 206 | 230 | 253 | 277 | 300 | 324 | 347 | 371 | 394 | 418 | 442 | 465 |
| 8 | **375** | **750** | **1,125** | **1,500** | **1,875** | **2,250** | **2,625** | **3,000** | **3,315** | **3,750** | **4,125** | **4,500** | **4,875** | **5,250** | **5,625** | **6,000** |
| | 126 | 151 | 176 | 201 | 226 | 251 | 276 | 301 | 327 | 352 | 377 | 402 | 427 | 452 | 477 | 502 |
| 8½ | **425** | **850** | **1,275** | **1,700** | **2,125** | **2,550** | **2,975** | **3,400** | **3,825** | **4,250** | **4,675** | **5,100** | **5,525** | **5,950** | **6,375** | **6,800** |
| | 140 | 167 | 194 | 220 | 247 | 274 | 300 | 327 | 354 | 380 | 407 | 434 | 460 | 487 | 514 | 541 |
| 9 | **475** | **950** | **1,425** | **1,900** | **2,375** | **2,850** | **3,325** | **3,800** | **4,275** | **4,750** | **5,225** | **5,700** | **6,175** | **6,650** | **7,125** | **7,600** |
| | 155 | 184 | 212 | 240 | 269 | 297 | 325 | 353 | 381 | 410 | 438 | 466 | 495 | 523 | 551 | 579 |

## *UNDERGROUND STORAGE TANKS*

Fiber-glass and other plastic-type tanks for underground service have an obvious advantage over steel tanks because of their corrosion-resistant properties. Although the cost penalties are usually high (Table 8.4), fiber-glass tanks are taking an increasingly larger share of the market. But in many cases steel tanks could be made reasonably defensive against corrosion by means of cathodic protection at an in-place cost that is still well under the cost of a plastic tank of equal capacity (see Table 8.1).

When tanks are used to store corrosive liquids, they must be fabricated of materials that are compatible with the liquids stored. For *mildly* corrosive liquids, appropriate interior lining may suffice. For normal underground service, steel tanks are susceptible to corrosion from the outside environment or battery-like reaction between dissimilar metals or dissimilar areas of a similar metal on the tank itself. Usually the action is set up by the mixing of different soils or simply by the flow of dc current from the steel of the tank into the moist backfill—even when the surrounding soil has been kept clean and free of the smallest amount of foreign matter.

Some steel tank manufacturers offer a special "triple protection": corrosion-prevention system with a limited 20-year warranty. This triple protection consists of the following: (1) *electrical isolation*—dielectric nylon reducing bushings or isolators used in each opening to interrupt stray currents that would otherwise enter the tank through the piping connections; (2) *electrically insulating exterior protective coating*—heavy-duty, amine-cured, coal-tar epoxy after proper blast cleaning and surface preparation; (3) *cathodic protection*—factory-installed and factory-connected sacrificial magnesium anodes to reverse the current flow. The economics of this kind of cathodic protection can be examined in Table 8.1.

The estimator should be familiar with ANSI B137.1 as well as the installation procedures contained in NFPA 30. All labor tasks required for excavating, backfilling, and handling need to be considered; labor costs for fiber-glass tanks are usually higher than those for steel tanks. According to NFPA 30, tanks subject to vehicular traffic shall be covered with a minimum of either 3 ft of earth or 18 in. of earth plus 6 in. of reinforced concrete. In addition, prevailing local codes must usually be observed. For associated concrete costs, see Chap. 17.

**TABLE 8.4**  Fiber-Glass Underground Storage Tanks

UL-listed tanks including accessway, fittings, and holddown. Workhours includes installation in preexcavated pit.

| Capacity, gal | Crew required | Installation, workhours | Material cost, $ |
|---|---|---|---|
| 550 | 2 steamfitters, 1 apprentice | 8 | 4,100 |
| 1,000 | 2 steamfitters, 1 apprentice | 12 | 5,600 |
| 2,000 | 2 steamfitters, 1 apprentice, 1 supervisor | 16 | 3,500 |
| 4,000 | 2 steamfitters, 1 apprentice, 1 supervisor | 25 | 10,100 |
| 6,000 | 2 steamfitters, 1 apprentice, 1 supervisor | 32 | 11,400 |
| 8,000 | 2 steamfitters, 1 apprentice, 1 supervisor | 40 | 12,400 |
| 10,000 | 2 steamfitters, 1 apprentice, 1 supervisor | 53 | 14,700 |
| 12,000 | 2 steamfitters, 1 apprentice, 1 supervisor | 64 | 17,600 |
| 15,000 | 2 steamfitters, 1 apprentice, 1 supervisor | 80 | 21,800 |
| 20,000 | 2 steamfitters, 1 apprentice, 1 supervisor | 107 | 29,000 |
| 25,000 | 2 steamfitters, 1 apprentice, 1 supervisor | 160 | 44,100 |
| 30,000 | 2 steamfitters, 1 apprentice, 1 supervisor | 160 | 53,200 |
| 40,000 | 2 steamfitters, 1 apprentice, 1 supervisor | 320 | 63,000 |
| 48,000 | 2 steamfitters, 1 apprentice, 1 supervisor | 320 | 75,000 |

## ANTIFLOTATION ANCHORAGE

To figure the required amount of concrete to hold a tank down in groundwater conditions, it is necessary to first find the effective weight of the concrete. If a tank is buoyed up by the weight of the displaced groundwater, the actual tie-down weight of the tank will be equal to the tank capacity in gallons × 8.3 (pounds of water per gallon).

The weight of concrete in air may be assumed to be between 110 and 160 lb/cu ft. When the concrete is immersed in water, its actual *effective weight* is the difference between 150 and 62.5 (weight of 1 cu ft of water), or 87.5 lb.

If the weight of the displaced water minus the weight of the tank is divided by the *effective weight of the concrete* (87.5 lb), the answer will be the cubic feet of concrete required for the tie-down slab.

**Example 8.1** An empty 4,000-gal. fuel-oil tank weighs 3,600 lb. What is the required amount of concrete, in cubic feet, for the antiflotation slab?

**solution**

$$4,000 \text{ gal.} \times 8.3 \text{ lb/gal.} \qquad 33,200 \text{ lb displaced water}$$

Weight of tank

$$-3,600 \text{ lb}$$

Net weight of displaced water 29,600 lb

$$\frac{29,600 \text{ lb (weight of displaced water)}}{87.5 \text{ lb (effective weight of concrete per cu ft)}} = 338 \text{ cu ft concrete}$$

## EXPANSION TANKS

The most common compression or expansion tank is the *open tank* set at least 4 ft above the highest point in the system to ensure proper venting. Additional head may be required if the system pump is so located as to reduce pressure between the tank and the pump suction. It is sometimes possible to achieve economies in tank size by carefully rechecking the designer's tank selection. If compressed air is available, the size of a closed-type tank may be reduced by injecting air under pressure into the tank. In such a case, however, one should not overlook the additional requirements of an air-fill valve, pressure gauge, and water column. The higher the location of the expansion tank, the lower the initial fill pressure at the tank; consequently, the smaller the tank requirement. Tables 8.5 and 8.6 provide expansion tank capacities for gravity and forced-hot-water systems. Table 8.7 lists dimensional data for expansion tanks up to 40-gal. capacity. Typical expansion tank piping details are shown in Fig. 8.1. For expansion tank costs, see Table 8.8.

The ASME formula for sizing closed-type expansion tanks with operating temperatures between 160 and 280°F is

$$V_t = \frac{(0.00041t - 0.0466)\,V_s}{(P_a/P_f) - (P_a/P_o)}$$

where $V_t$ = minimum volume of expansion tank, gal.
$V_s$ = system volume, gal.
$P_a$ = atmospheric pressure, ft of water absolute
$P_f$ = initial fill or minimum pressure at tank required to hold water at highest point of system, ft of water absolute
$P_o$ = maximum operating pressure, ft of water absolute
$t$ = average operating temperature, °F

If compressed air is injected into the tank to economize on tank size, the value of $P_a$ in the preceding formula should include the addition of the air pressure. For example, if 7½-psig air is used, the new $P_a$ will be 1 atmosphere (atm) + (7.5 psig × 2.31) = 2.31 × 7.5 + 34 = 51.325 ft $H_2O$ absolute.

Water heater storage tank data are given in Table 8.9.

**TABLE 8.5** Expansion Tank Capacities for Gravity Hot-Water Systems

Based on two-pipe system, 170°F water temperature, cast-iron radiation heat emission, 150 Btuh/ft² EDR.

| Sq ft EDR | Tank capacity, gal. |
|---|---|
| ≤350 | 18 |
| 351–450 | 21 |
| 451–650 | 24 |
| 651–900 | 30 |
| 901–1,100 | 35 |
| 1,101–1,400 | 40 |
| 1,401–1,600 | 2 × 30 |
| 1,601–1,800 | 2 × 30 |
| 1,801–2,000 | 2 × 35 |
| 2,001–2,400 | 2 × 40 |

**TABLE 8.6** Expansion Tank Capacities for Forced-Hot-Water Systems

Based on 195°F water temperature, 12-psi fill pressure, and 30-psig maximum operating temperature.

| System volume, gal. | Tank capacity, gal. |
|---|---|
| 100 | 15 |
| 200 | 30 |
| 300 | 45 |
| 400 | 60 |
| 500 | 75 |
| 1,000 | 150 |
| 2,000 | 300 |

**TABLE 8.7** Dimension of Expansion Tanks

30-psi maximum working pressure; 14-gage shell thickness.

| Inside diameter of tank, in. | Length of shell,* in. | Nominal capacity, gal. | Tappings Number | Tappings Pipe size, in. | Finish | Type |
|---|---|---|---|---|---|---|
| 12 | 20 | 10 | 3 | 1 | Galvanized | Vertical |
| 12 | 30 | 15 | 3 | 1 | Galvanized | Vertical |
| 14 | 30 | 20 | 3 | 1 | Galvanized | Vertical |
| 12 | 30 | 15 | 2 | ½ & ¾ | Painted | Horizontal |
| 12 | 36 | 18 | 2 | ½ & ¾ | Painted | Horizontal |
| 12 | 48 | 24 | 2 | ½ & ¾ | Painted | Horizontal |
| 12 | 60 | 30 | 2 | ½ & ¾ | Painted | Horizontal |
| 14 | 60 | 40 | 2 | ½ & ¾ | Painted | Horizontal |

*Length of sheet, not overall length of tank.

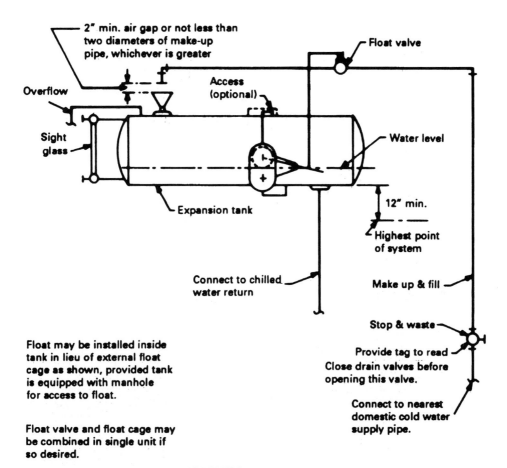

**2" min. air gap or not less than two diameters of make-up pipe, whichever is greater**

**Overflow**

**Sight glass**

**Access (optional)**

**Float valve**

**Water level**

**Expansion tank**

**12" min.**

**Highest point of system**

**Connect to chilled water return**

**Make up & fill**

**Stop & waste**

**Provide tag to read Close drain valves before opening this valve.**

**Connect to nearest domestic cold water supply pipe.**

Float may be installed inside tank in lieu of external float cage as shown, provided tank is equipped with manhole for access to float.

Float valve and float cage may be combined in single unit if so desired.

**Figure 8.1   EXPANSION TANK PIPING DETAILS**

**TABLE 8.8**   Expansion Tanks

Galvanized-steel construction includes standard tappings. Does not include piping or accessories. *Workhours* includes unloading, moving 40 ft, and setting in place.

| Capacity, gal. | Galvanized 30 psi, $ | ASME 125 psi, $ | Erection, workhours |
|---|---|---|---|
| 15 | 450 | 480 | 2 |
| 24 | 500 | 525 | 2 |
| 30 | 575 | 600 | 2 |
| 40 | 675 | 700 | 2 |
| 60 | — | 800 | 3 |
| 80 | — | 900 | 4 |
| 100 | — | 1,100 | 4 |
| 120 | — | 1,300 | 4 |
| 180 | — | 1,600 | 4 |
| 400 | — | 3,300 | 6 |

**TABLE 8.9** Water Heater Storage Tanks, 125 psi ASME

| Capacity, gal | Diameter, in. | Overall length, in. | Installation, workhours | Cost, $ |
|---|---|---|---|---|
| Copper-lined | | | | |
| 190 | 30 | 66 | 2 | 3,100 |
| 225 | 30 | 78 | 2.7 | 3,600 |
| 325 | 36 | 81 | 4 | 4,500 |
| 460 | 42 | 84 | 5.3 | 6,200 |
| 605 | 48 | 87 | 6.4 | 7,100 |
| 740 | 54 | 91 | 8 | 8,400 |
| 940 | 60 | 93 | 10.7 | 9,800 |
| 1,505 | 66 | 119 | 16 | 12,500 |
| 1,615 | 72 | 110 | 16 | 14,200 |
| 2,275 | 84 | 116 | 24 | 20,000 |
| 3,815 | 96 | 145 | 24 | 25,200 |
| Galvanized steel | | | | |
| 18 | 12 | 39 | 0.7 | 450 |
| 30 | 14 | 40 | 0.7 | 575 |
| 75 | 18 | 72 | 0.9 | 750 |
| 140 | 24 | 75 | 1.3 | 1,200 |
| 225 | 30 | 78 | 2 | 1,750 |
| 325 | 36 | 81 | 2.7 | 2,200 |
| 460 | 36 | 117 | 4 | 2,800 |
| 605 | 48 | 87 | 5.3 | 4,000 |
| Glass-lined porcelain-enameled | | | | |
| 80 | 20 | 60 | 0.9 | 1,200 |
| 140 | 24 | 80 | 1.3 | 1,900 |
| 225 | 30 | 78 | 2 | 2,300 |
| 325 | 36 | 81 | 2.7 | 3,000 |
| 460 | 42 | 84 | 4 | 3,700 |
| 605 | 48 | 87 | 5.3 | 5,100 |
| 740 | 54 | 91 | 5.3 | 6,100 |
| 940 | 60 | 93 | 6.4 | 7,100 |
| 1,330 | 66 | 107 | 8 | 10,000 |
| 1,615 | 72 | 110 | 10.7 | 11,000 |
| 2,275 | 84 | 116 | 16 | 15,000 |
| 3,815 | 96 | 145 | 16 | 21,000 |

## RECOMMENDED READING

NFPA 30, *Flammable and Combustible Liquids Code.*

NFPA 329, *Underground Leakage of Flammable and Combustible Liquids.*

*Installation of Underground Petroleum Storage Systems,* API Publication 1615, American Petroleum Institute, Washington, D.C.

*Underground Spill Clean Up Manual,* American Petroleum Institute, Washington, D.C.

Public Law 98-616, United States of America.

Young, A. D., *Underground Storage Tank Management,* Rockville, Md., 1986.

# CHAPTER 9
# PIPING

## GENERAL DISCUSSION

A correct cost comparison of piping systems (e.g., copper vs. plastic vs. steel) must be made on a basis of *cost-effectiveness*, i.e., the optimization of the owner's ultimate owning and operating cost for transporting a particular fluid. Given a required quantity, velocity, and temperature of a particular fluid, the following cost-affecting factors come into play:

1. The inner wall diameter (together with smoothness) affects
    a. Pumping head
2. The outer wall diameter affects
    a. Space availability
    b. Size of insulation
    c. Size of hangers
3. Type of joint affects
    a. Erection time
    b. Leak-testing and leak-repairing time
    c. Cost of owning, using, and transporting pipe-joining equipment
4. Type of material affects
    a. Electrolytic action
    b. Lifetime of system
    c. Ease of installation

In addition, security of joints, extent of trench excavation, heat exchange of the fluid, and other cost factors must be entered before a fair comparison can be made. Too many contractors—and engineers—decide on a piping system out of old habit.

## CONDENSATE DRAINS

Because condensate moves by gravity, the minimum size waste and drain line should be ¾-in. pipe or ⅞-in. tubing. Some codes require 1¼-in. for systems totaling over 10 tons of refrigeration capacity.

Line should be pitched ½ in. per 10 ft of horizontal run. Table 9.1 lists sewer capacities for condensate.

*All* condensate drain lines shall have a trap seal of at least 2 in. as shown in Fig. 9.1. Systems over 3 tons shall have a minimum 3-in. trap seal and a union installed on the pan side.

Condensate may be discharged into a French drain. A *French drain* consists of a pit not less than 24 in. in diameter, 24 in. deep, or a 24-in.-long pipe 10 in. in diameter. Either shall be

**TABLE 9.1**   Sewer Capacities for Condensate

| Sewer diameter, in. | Capacity, gpm | |
|---|---|---|
| | ⅛-in./ft pitch | ¼in./ft pitch |
| 1½ | 5.8 | 8.2 |
| 2 | 12.6 | 17.6 |
| 3 | 36.0 | 51.0 |
| 4 | 77.0 | 110.0 |
| 5 | 139.0 | 197.0 |
| 6 | 221.0 | 313.0 |
| 7 | 329.0 | 466.0 |
| 8 | 463.0 | 656.0 |

SOURCE:   U.S. Bureau of Standards, Publication BH 13.

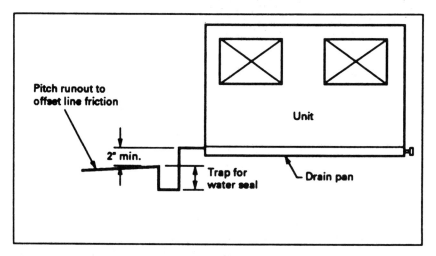

**Figure 9.1   CORRECT PIPING FOR DRAIN PANS**

filled with ¾ in. of crushed rock or gravel. The drain pipe should extend at least 6 in. below grade and be securely anchored.

When pipe is installed in a concrete slab, it must be enclosed in a sleeve, casing, or conduit at least ¾ in. greater than the outer diameter (OD) of the tubing or pipe and protected against corrosion, and be at least 1¼ in. in diameter.

When an evaporator coil or unit is located in attic spaces, suspended ceilings, or furred spaces, it should have an auxiliary drain pan. Such auxiliary drain pan should have a minimum depth of 1½ in. and extend at least 3 in. beyond the dimensions of the unit dimensions. The pan must be made of no less than 24-gage galvanized sheet metal and have a separate drain line to some conspicuous location that would alarm the owner to an emergency overflow. All interior horizontal piping in unconditioned spaces should be insulated. No live steam pipe should connect directly to any part of a drainage or plumbing system.

Local codes prevail, and they may vary. Local codes should be checked.

**TABLE 9.2** Equivalent of Pipe-Carrying Capacity: Approximate Number of Smaller Pipes to Equal One Larger Pipe

| Pipe size, in. | 1 | 1¼ | 1½ | 2 | 2½ | 3 | 3½ | 4 | 5 | 6 | 8 | 10 | 12 |
|---|---|---|---|---|---|---|---|---|---|---|---|---|---|
| 1 | | 2 | 3 | 5.5 | 8.5 | 15 | 21 | 29 | 51 | 80 | 160 | 282 | 434 |
| 1¼ | 2 | | 1.5 | 3 | 4.5 | 7.5 | 11 | 15 | 26 | 40 | 80 | 142 | 223 |
| 1½ | 3 | 1.5 | | 2 | 3 | 5 | 7.5 | 10 | 17 | 28 | 55 | 97 | 152 |
| 2 | 6 | 3 | 2 | | 2 | 3 | 4 | 5.5 | 9.5 | 15 | 29 | 52 | 81 |
| 2½ | 9 | 4.5 | 3 | 1.5 | | 2 | 2.5 | 3.5 | 6 | 9.5 | 19 | 33 | 52 |
| 3 | 16 | 8 | 5 | 3 | 2 | | 1.5 | 2 | 3.5 | 5.5 | 11 | 19 | 30 |
| 3½ | 23 | 11 | 7.5 | 4 | 2.5 | 1.5 | | 1.5 | 2.5 | 4 | 7.5 | 13 | 21 |
| 4 | 32 | 16 | 10 | 5.5 | 3.5 | 2 | 1.5 | | 2 | 3 | 5.5 | 10 | 15 |
| 5 | 57 | 28 | 18 | 10 | 6 | 3.5 | 2.5 | 2 | | 1.5 | 3 | 5.5 | 9 |
| 6 | 89 | 43 | 29 | 15 | 10 | 6 | 4 | 3 | 2 | | 2 | 3.5 | 5.5 |
| 8 | 179 | 87 | 59 | 31 | 20 | 11 | 8 | 6 | 3 | 2 | | 2 | 3 |
| 10 | 331 | 161 | 108 | 57 | 36 | 21 | 14 | 10 | 6 | 4 | 2 | | 1.5 |
| 12 | 528 | 256 | 172 | 90 | 58 | 33 | 23 | 17 | 10 | 6 | 3 | 1.5 | |

*Note:* The figures shown in italics are for extraheavy wall pipe; the bold figures are for standard wall pipe.

## PIPE-CARRYING CAPACITY

The volume of water delivered by two pipes of different sizes is proportional to the squares of their diameters at the same velocity. However, with the same head, the velocity is less in the small pipe and the delivered volume varies as the square root of the fifth power.

Table 9.2 gives the approximate carrying capacities for relative numbers of pipe to equal one larger pipe at the same head.[1]

**Example 9.1** One 12-in. pipe has a water-carrying capacity equal to that of fifteen 4-in. pipes.

**Example 9.2** One 8-in. pipe equals five and one-half 4-in. pipes.

## REFRIGERATION PIPING

Piping systems for refrigeration are code-referenced by ASME B31.5, *Refrigeration Piping*, and ASHRAE Standard 15, *Safety Code for Mechanical Refrigeration*. Extensive discussion on refrigeration piping may be found in the *Carrier Handbook of Air Conditioning Systems Design*, the *Trane Reciprocating Refrigeration Manual*, and the *Handbook of Air Conditioning, Heating and Ventilation* by Clifford Strock and Richard Koral, Industrial Press.

For refrigerants R-12, R-22, and R-500, hard copper tubing type L, or steel pipe with wrought copper or brass fittings may be used. Aluminum, zinc, or magnesium shall not be used in a refrigerating system with methyl chloride. Magnesium alloy shall not be used in any system with any halogenated refrigerant. Copper and its alloys shall not be used in contact with ammonia.

Table 9.3 offers a suggested pipe and fitting schedule for various air-conditioning and refrigeration applications. The selection of refrigerant piping should be based on economics

[1] Tables 9.2, 9.3, and 9.8 do not appear on the computer disk included with this book.

**TABLE 9.3**  Suggested Pipe and Fitting Schedule for Various Air-Conditioning and Refrigeration Applications

| Service | Pipe | Fittings |
|---|---|---|
| Steam | Black steel | 125-lb cast iron |
| Hot water | Black steel | 125-lb cast iron |
| Condenser water | Hard copper, type M, galvanized steel, PVC (≤50 psi, 100°F) | Cast brass, wrought brass, copper, cast iron, galvanized, welding solvent, or threaded |
| Chilled water | Black steel, galvanized, hard copper, type M | Cast iron, galvanized, welding cast brass, wrought brass, copper |
| Condensate drains, etc. | PVC, type M copper, galvanized steel | Solvent or threaded, copper |
| Refrigerants (1,2) | Hard copper, type L (3,4) | Wrought copper or brass |

*Notes:*

1. Butt-welded carbon steel, butt-welded wrought iron, and cast iron shall not be used.
2. Group A2, A3, B1, B2 systems shall be brazed.
3. When steel pipe is used for refrigerant lines, the following shall be observed:
   a. For group A2, A3, B1, and B2 liquid lines ≤1½ in., use no less than schedule 80 pipe
   b. For liquid lines >1½ in., use no less than schedule 40 pipe, lap-welded or seamless
   c. For liquid lines ≤6 in., use no less than schedule 40 pipe
   d. For vapor lines ≤6 in., use no less than schedule 40 pipe
   e. For steel piping systems, use 150-lb welding or threaded malleable iron for suction lines, but 300-lb welding or threaded malleable iron for hot gas or liquid lines
4. For copper pipe applications the following rules should be observed:
   a. DWV drainage type: nonpressure
   b. Type M: light-duty
   c. Type L: ≤250 psi
   d. Type K: ≤400 psi

and sound engineering judgment. Although steel pipe and fittings have lower material cost in larger sizes, copper pipe is better because it is entirely free of scale and is not corroded by Refrigerant R-12 or R-22 even when mixed with moisture. Safe working pressures always need to be observed.

When selecting general service valves, one should consider bonnet and body connection.

## Bonnet and Body Connection

*Threaded:* for light-duty, low-pressure systems.

*Union bonnet:* general-purpose duty for pipe to 2 in.

*Bolted bonnet:* for duty >2 in.; must have suitable pressure seals on higher-pressure systems.

*Valve stem operation:* condenser water and general service; should have rising stem valves. Nonrising stems should be used only where required because of space restrictions. Inaccessible overhead valves should be provided with chain-operated hand wheels.

*Gate valves:* should only be used for fully open or fully closed positioning, not for throttling service, and shall be solid wedge type.

*Globe valves:* used for throttling service; should have a regrinding seat ring and plug. Where low-pressure drop is a prerequisite, use Y valve or angle valve.

*Plug cocks:* used for balancing systems not subject to frequent changes in flow.

*Check valves:* Swing check valves should be used for horizontal and vertical pipelines where reversal of flow is not desired. Water valves should have a regrinding seat with renewable composition disk. Steam and condensate valves should have a regrinding seat and disk. A silent, spring-loaded check valve should be provided on the discharge of each pump.

TABLE 9.4 Refrigerant Piping Operating Charge, Pounds per 100 ft of Pipe

| Pipe OD, in. | Refrigerant-12 | | | Refrigerant-22 | | |
|---|---|---|---|---|---|---|
| | Suction | Discharge | Liquid | Suction | Discharge | Liquid |
| ½ | 0.1 | 0.30 | 8.1 | 0.2 | 0.36 | 7.3 |
| ⅝ | 0.2 | 0.48 | 13.0 | 0.3 | 0.57 | 11.8 |
| ¾ | 0.3 | 0.72 | 19.4 | 0.4 | 0.85 | 17.6 |
| ⅞ | 0.4 | 1.0 | 27.0 | 0.5 | 1.2 | 24.4 |
| 1⅛ | 0.7 | 1.7 | 46.0 | 0.9 | 2.0 | 41.7 |
| 1⅜ | 1.1 | 2.6 | 70.0 | 1.3 | 3.1 | 63.5 |
| 1⅝ | 1.6 | 3.7 | 99.0 | 1.9 | 4.4 | 89.8 |
| 2⅛ | 2.8 | 6.4 | 172.2 | 3.3 | 7.6 | 156.2 |
| 2⅝ | 4.3 | 9.9 | 265.5 | 5.0 | 11.7 | 249.0 |
| 3⅛ | 6.1 | 14.1 | 379.1 | 7.2 | 16.7 | 344.0 |
| 3⅝ | 8.3 | 19.1 | 512.7 | 9.7 | 22.6 | 465.2 |
| 4⅛ | 10.8 | 24.9 | 667.6 | 12.7 | 29.4 | 605.7 |
| 5⅛ | 16.8 | 39.8 | — | 19.8 | 45.9 | — |
| 6⅛ | 24.0 | 55.6 | — | 28.3 | 65.7 | — |

Based on 105°F condensing, 40°F suction, 15°F subcooling, 90°F liquid, 50°F superheat.

SOURCE: Reproduced by permission of the Trane Company, LaCrosse, Wis.

Designing and erecting piping systems requires reliable data on weights of pipe, both full and empty. Table 9.4 gives the approximate operating charge directly in pounds per 100 ft for refrigerant piping. Tables 9.5 and 9.6 give the physical properties of type L and K copper pipe for refrigeration and general service.

TABLE 9.5 Dimensions and Weights of Type L Copper Tube

Operating pressure ≤250 lb.

| OD size, in. | Nominal size, in. | OD, in. | Wall thickness, in. | Inside diameter (ID), in. | Transverse area of bore, sq. in. | Surface area per foot of length, sq ft | | Weight, lb/ft | Lineal feet per cubic foot of volume |
|---|---|---|---|---|---|---|---|---|---|
| | | | | | | External | Internal | | |
| ¼ | ⅛ | 0.250 | 0.025 | 0.200 | — | — | — | 0.0685 | 4,580 |
| ⅜ | ¼ | 0.375 | 0.030 | 0.315 | 0.0779 | 0.0982 | 0.0825 | 0.126 | 1,840 |
| ½ | ⅜ | 0.500 | 0.035 | 0.430 | 0.145 | 0.131 | 0.113 | 0.198 | 990 |
| ⅝ | ½ | 0.625 | 0.040 | 0.545 | 0.233 | 0.164 | 0.142 | 0.285 | 617 |
| ¾ | ⅝ | 0.750 | 0.042 | 0.666 | 0.348 | 0.196 | 0.174 | 0.365 | 412 |
| ⅞ | ¾ | 0.875 | 0.045 | 0.785 | 0.484 | 0.229 | 0.206 | 0.455 | 297 |
| 1⅛ | 1 | 1.125 | 0.050 | 1.025 | 0.625 | 0.295 | 0.268 | 0.655 | 174 |
| 1⅜ | 1¼ | 1.375 | 0.055 | 1.265 | 1.267 | 0.360 | 0.331 | 0.884 | 114 |
| 1⅝ | 1½ | 1.625 | 0.060 | 1.505 | 1.78 | 0.425 | 0.394 | 1.14 | 80.8 |
| 2⅛ | 2 | 2.125 | 0.070 | 1.985 | 2.10 | 0.556 | 0.520 | 1.75 | 46.4 |
| 2⅝ | 2½ | 2.625 | 0.080 | 2.465 | 4.77 | 0.687 | 0.645 | 2.48 | 30.1 |
| 3⅛ | 3 | 3.125 | 0.090 | 2.945 | 6.81 | 0.818 | 0.771 | 3.33 | 21.1 |
| 3⅝ | 3½ | 3.625 | 0.100 | 3.425 | 9.21 | 0.949 | 0.897 | 4.29 | 15.6 |
| 4⅛ | 4 | 4.125 | 0.110 | 3.905 | 12.0 | 1.08 | 1.02 | 5.38 | 12.0 |
| 5⅛ | 5 | 5.125 | 0.125 | 4.875 | 18.7 | 1.34 | 1.28 | 7.61 | 7.69 |
| 6⅛ | 6 | 6.125 | 0.140 | 5.845 | 26.8 | 1.60 | 1.53 | 10.2 | 5.37 |

**TABLE 9.6** Dimensions and Weights of Type K Copper Tube

Operating pressure ≤400 lb.

| OD size, in. | Nominal size, in. | OD, in. | Wall thickness, in. | ID, in. | Transverse area of bore, sq in. | Surface area per foot of length, sq ft | | Weight, lb/ft | Lineal feet per cubic foot of volume |
|---|---|---|---|---|---|---|---|---|---|
| | | | | | | External | Internal | | |
| ¼ | ⅛ | 0.250 | 0.032 | 0.186 | — | — | — | 0.085 | 5,300 |
| ⅜ | ¼ | 0.375 | 0.032 | 0.311 | 0.0760 | 0.0982 | 0.0814 | 0.133 | 1,890 |
| ½ | ⅜ | 0.500 | 0.049 | 0.402 | 0.127 | 0.131 | 0.105 | 0.269 | 1,130 |
| ⅝ | ½ | 0.625 | 0.049 | 0.527 | 0.218 | 0.164 | 0.138 | 0.344 | 660 |
| ¾ | ⅝ | 0.750 | 0.049 | 0.652 | 0.334 | 0.196 | 0.171 | 0.418 | 431 |
| ⅞ | ¾ | 0.875 | 0.065 | 0.745 | 0.436 | 0.229 | 0.195 | 0.641 | 331 |
| 1⅛ | 1 | 1.125 | 0.065 | 0.995 | 0.778 | 0.295 | 0.261 | 0.839 | 184 |
| 1⅜ | 1¼ | 1.375 | 0.065 | 1.245 | 1.22 | 0.360 | 0.326 | 1.04 | 118 |
| 1⅝ | 1½ | 1.625 | 0.072 | 1.481 | 1.72 | 0.425 | 0.388 | 1.36 | 83.2 |
| 2⅛ | 2 | 2.125 | 0.083 | 1.959 | 3.01 | 0.556 | 0.513 | 2.06 | 47.8 |
| 2⅝ | 2½ | 2.625 | 0.095 | 2.435 | 4.66 | 0.687 | 0.638 | 2.92 | 30.9 |
| 3⅛ | 3 | 3.125 | 0.109 | 2.907 | 6.64 | 0.818 | 0.761 | 4.00 | 21.7 |
| 3⅝ | 3½ | 3.625 | 0.120 | 3.385 | 9.00 | 0.949 | 0.886 | 5.12 | 15.9 |
| 4⅛ | 4 | 4.125 | 0.134 | 3.857 | 11.7 | 1.0800 | 1.01 | 6.51 | 12.3 |
| 5⅛ | 5 | 5.125 | 0.160 | 4.805 | 18.1 | 1.3400 | 1.26 | 9.67 | 7.91 |
| 6⅛ | 6 | 6.125 | 0.192 | 5.741 | 25.9 | 1.6000 | 1.99 | 13.87 | 5.55 |

## GENERAL SERVICE PIPING

The applicable codes for general building service piping are the ASME B31.9, *Building Service Piping*, and ASME B31.1, *Power Piping Code*. ASME B31.9 covers air conditioning, heating (external boiler piping ≤15-psig steam and 160-psig, 250°F hot water), compressed air, vacuum, steam and other condensate, and nontoxic liquids.

### Piping Costs—General

Piping costs vary greatly for different materials, and close attention must be paid to the economics of the *complete* piping system installed, including insulation. Figure 9.2 gives approximate cost comparisons for various pipes. These are in-place costs per foot, including material (pipe, fittings, valves) and labor to handle and erect for average piping runs based on a cost of $28.57/hr per pipefitter, including fringes.

Table 9.7 gives weight data for PVC pipe. Table 9.8 gives the physical characteristics of commercial wrought steel pipe and may be used to estimate weights, dimensions, and wall thickness.

Table 9.9 gives the suggested maximum spacing for pipe hangers when not dictated by local or national codes, and Fig. 9.3 illustrates the recommended procedures for hanger systems.

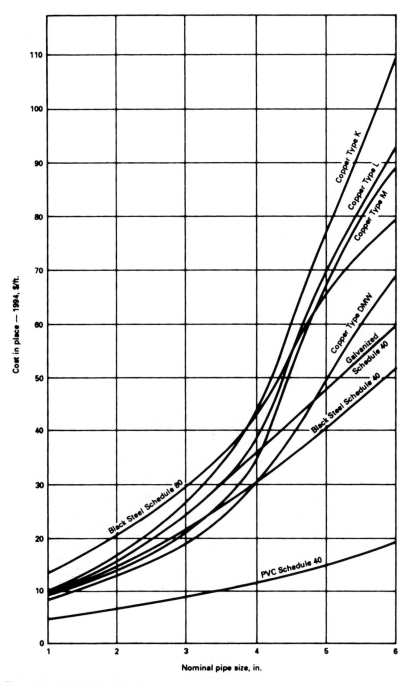

**Figure 9.2    COST COMPARISON OF COMMON PIPE MATERIALS**

**TABLE 9.7**   Dimensions and Weights of PVC Pipe

| Nominal pipe size, in. | OD, in. | lb per ft | | | |
|---|---|---|---|---|---|
| | | Schedule 40 | | Schedule 80 | |
| | | Empty pipe | With water | Empty pipe | With water |
| ½ | 0.84 | 0.15 | 0.27 | 0.19 | 0.28 |
| ¾ | 1.05 | 0.20 | 0.43 | 0.26 | 0.45 |
| 1 | 1.31 | 0.30 | 0.69 | 0.38 | 0.73 |
| 1¼ | 1.66 | 0.41 | 1.00 | 0.55 | 1.10 |
| 1½ | 1.90 | 0.49 | 1.35 | 0.65 | 1.90 |
| 2 | 2.37 | 0.64 | 2.10 | 0.91 | 2.25 |
| 2½ | 2.87 | 1.10 | 3.25 | 1.50 | 3.55 |
| 3 | 3.50 | 1.35 | 4.40 | 2.00 | 4.90 |
| 4 | 4.50 | 1.95 | 7.25 | 3.00 | 8.15 |
| 6 | 6.25 | 3.50 | 15.50 | 5.85 | 17.25 |
| 8 | 8.25 | 5.75 | 26.75 | 8.00 | 28.00 |
| 10 | 10.25 | 8.00 | 40.86 | 10.75 | 41.00 |
| 12 | 12.25 | 10.00 | 57.00 | 13.25 | 57.50 |

## Estimating Piping Costs

Much has been published on the subject of estimating piping costs. Engineers involved in the design, installation, and replacement of piping systems have developed data for the assignment of labor time units for almost every possible function in the erection of such systems and including every kind of material from synthetic plastics to exotic metals. The variations of the published data, however, accentuate the practical difficulties of making realistic piping estimates. Obviously we cannot, in this brief chapter, cover more than some of the basic simple systems encountered by the average mechanical contractor.

Whatever source of workhour information is applied by the estimator, some judgment will always be required to meet the particular conditions of each phase of mechanical construction. An intelligent approach to the adjustments on a per-foot basis will result in the same degree of accuracy as the per-joint method. Final connections at apparatuses, intricate piping schemes, valves, and specialties must, of course, be viewed with refinement; in these cases it is necessary to determine the time required for each joint, fitting, and piece of pipe.

Unless otherwise stated, all the tables in this chapter are expressed in per-foot ($ft^{-1}$) units; they are based on 20-ft lengths of pipe with five fittings (10 joints) per every 100 ft of pipe. The fittings are an average mix of coupling connections, ells, etc., but they do not include unions or flanges.

**TABLE 9.8**   Physical Properties of Steel Pipe

| Nominal Pipe Size (D) Inches | Outside Diameter (D) Inches | Schedule No. See Note 1 | Wall Thickness (t) Inches | Inside Diameter (d) Inches | Area of Metal (a) Square Inches | Transverse Internal Area Square Inches | Transverse Internal Area Square Feet See Note 2 | Moment of Inertia (I) Inches to 4th Power | Weight of Pipe Pounds per foot | Weight of Water Pounds per foot | External Surface Sq. Ft. per foot of pipe | Section Modulus $\left(2\frac{I}{D}\right)$ |
|---|---|---|---|---|---|---|---|---|---|---|---|---|
| 1/8 | 0.405 | 40s | .068 | .269 | .0720 | .0568 | .00040 | .00106 | .244 | .025 | .106 | .00523 |
|  |  | 80x | .095 | .215 | .0925 | .0364 | .00025 | .00122 | .314 | .016 | .106 | .00602 |
| 1/4 | 0.540 | 40s | .088 | .364 | .1250 | .1041 | .00072 | .00331 | .424 | .045 | .141 | .01227 |
|  |  | 80x | .119 | .302 | .1574 | .0716 | .00050 | .00377 | .535 | .031 | .141 | .01395 |
| 3/8 | 0.675 | 40s | .091 | .493 | .1670 | .1910 | .00133 | .00729 | .567 | .083 | .178 | .02160 |
|  |  | 80x | .126 | .423 | .2173 | .1405 | .00098 | .00862 | .738 | .061 | .178 | .02554 |
| 1/2 | 0.840 | 40s | .109 | .622 | .2503 | .3040 | .00211 | .01709 | .850 | .132 | .220 | .04069 |
|  |  | 80x | .147 | .546 | .3200 | .2340 | .00163 | .02008 | 1.087 | .102 | .220 | .04780 |
|  |  | 160 | .187 | .466 | .3836 | .1706 | .00118 | .02212 | 1.300 | .074 | .220 | .05267 |
|  |  | ...xx | .294 | .252 | .5043 | .050 | .00035 | .02424 | 1.714 | .022 | .220 | .05772 |
| 3/4 | 1.050 | 40s | .113 | .824 | .3326 | .5330 | .00371 | .03704 | 1.130 | .231 | .275 | .07055 |
|  |  | 80x | .154 | .742 | .4335 | .4330 | .00300 | .04479 | 1.473 | .188 | .275 | .08531 |
|  |  | 160 | .218 | .614 | .5698 | .2961 | .00206 | .05269 | 1.940 | .128 | .275 | .10036 |
|  |  | ...xx | .308 | .434 | .7180 | .148 | .00103 | .05792 | 2.440 | .064 | .275 | .11032 |
| 1 | 1.315 | 40s | .133 | 1.049 | .4939 | .8640 | .00600 | .08734 | 1.678 | .375 | .344 | .1328 |
|  |  | 80x | .179 | .957 | .6388 | .7190 | .00499 | .1056 | 2.171 | .312 | .344 | .1606 |
|  |  | 160 | .250 | .815 | .8365 | .5217 | .00362 | .1251 | 2.840 | .230 | .344 | .1903 |
|  |  | ...xx | .358 | .599 | 1.0760 | .282 | .00196 | .1405 | 3.659 | .122 | .344 | .2136 |
| 1 1/4 | 1.660 | 40s | .140 | 1.380 | .6685 | 1.495 | .01040 | .1947 | 2.272 | .649 | .435 | .2346 |
|  |  | 80x | .191 | 1.278 | .8815 | 1.283 | .00891 | .2418 | 2.996 | .555 | .435 | .2913 |
|  |  | 160 | .250 | 1.160 | 1.1070 | 1.057 | .00734 | .2839 | 3.764 | .458 | .435 | .3421 |
|  |  | ...xx | .382 | .896 | 1.534 | .630 | .00438 | .3411 | 5.214 | .273 | .435 | .4110 |
| 1 1/2 | 1.900 | 40s | .145 | 1.610 | .7995 | 2.036 | .01414 | .3099 | 2.717 | .882 | .497 | .3262 |
|  |  | 80x | .200 | 1.500 | 1.068 | 1.767 | .01225 | .3912 | 3.631 | .765 | .497 | .4118 |
|  |  | 160 | .281 | 1.338 | 1.429 | 1.406 | .00976 | .4824 | 4.862 | .608 | .497 | .5078 |
|  |  | ...xx | .400 | 1.100 | 1.885 | .950 | .00660 | .5678 | 6.408 | .42 | .497 | .5977 |
| 2 | 2.375 | 40s | .154 | 2.067 | 1.075 | 3.355 | .02330 | .6657 | 3.652 | 1.45 | .622 | .5606 |
|  |  | 80x | .218 | 1.939 | 1.477 | 2.953 | .02050 | .8679 | 5.022 | 1.28 | .622 | .7309 |
|  |  | 160 | .343 | 1.689 | 2.190 | 2.241 | .01556 | 1.162 | 7.440 | .97 | .622 | .979 |
|  |  | ...xx | .436 | 1.503 | 2.656 | 1.774 | .01232 | 1.311 | 9.029 | .77 | .622 | 1.104 |
| 2 1/2 | 2.875 | 40s | .203 | 2.469 | 1.704 | 4.788 | .03322 | 1.530 | 5.79 | 2.07 | .753 | 1.064 |
|  |  | 80x | .276 | 2.323 | 2.254 | 4.238 | .02942 | 1.924 | 7.66 | 1.87 | .753 | 1.339 |
|  |  | 160 | .375 | 2.125 | 2.945 | 3.546 | .02463 | 2.353 | 10.01 | 1.54 | .753 | 1.638 |
|  |  | ...xx | .552 | 1.771 | 4.028 | 2.464 | .01710 | 2.871 | 13.70 | 1.07 | .753 | 1.997 |
| 3 | 3.500 | 40s | .216 | 3.068 | 2.228 | 7.393 | .05130 | 3.017 | 7.58 | 3.20 | .916 | 1.724 |
|  |  | 80x | .300 | 2.900 | 3.016 | 6.605 | .04587 | 3.894 | 10.25 | 2.86 | .916 | 2.225 |
|  |  | 160 | .438 | 2.624 | 4.205 | 5.408 | .03755 | 5.032 | 14.32 | 2.35 | .916 | 2.876 |
|  |  | ...xx | .600 | 2.300 | 5.466 | 4.155 | .02885 | 5.993 | 18.58 | 1.80 | .916 | 3.424 |
| 3 1/2 | 4.000 | 40s | .226 | 3.548 | 2.680 | 9.886 | .06870 | 4.788 | 9.11 | 4.29 | 1.047 | 2.394 |
|  |  | 80x | .318 | 3.364 | 3.678 | 8.888 | .06170 | 6.280 | 12.51 | 3.84 | 1.047 | 3.140 |
| 4 | 4.500 | 40s | .237 | 4.026 | 3.174 | 12.73 | .08840 | 7.233 | 10.79 | 5.50 | 1.178 | 3.214 |
|  |  | 80x | .337 | 3.826 | 4.407 | 11.50 | .07986 | 9.610 | 14.98 | 4.98 | 1.178 | 4.271 |
|  |  | 120 | .438 | 3.624 | 5.595 | 10.31 | .0716 | 11.65 | 19.00 | 4.47 | 1.178 | 5.178 |
|  |  | 160 | .531 | 3.438 | 6.621 | 9.28 | .0645 | 13.27 | 22.51 | 4.02 | 1.178 | 5.898 |
|  |  | ...xx | .674 | 3.152 | 8.101 | 7.80 | .0542 | 15.28 | 27.54 | 3.38 | 1.178 | 6.791 |
| 5 | 5.563 | 40s | .258 | 5.047 | 4.300 | 20.01 | .1390 | 15.16 | 14.62 | 8.67 | 1.456 | 5.451 |
|  |  | 80x | .375 | 4.813 | 6.112 | 18.19 | .1263 | 20.67 | 20.78 | 7.88 | 1.456 | 7.431 |
|  |  | 120 | .500 | 4.563 | 7.953 | 16.35 | .1136 | 25.73 | 27.10 | 7.09 | 1.456 | 9.250 |
|  |  | 160 | .625 | 4.313 | 9.696 | 14.61 | .1015 | 30.03 | 32.96 | 6.33 | 1.456 | 10.796 |
|  |  | ...xx | .750 | 4.063 | 11.340 | 12.97 | .0901 | 33.63 | 38.55 | 5.61 | 1.456 | 12.090 |
| 6 | 6.625 | 40s | .280 | 6.065 | 5.581 | 28.89 | .2006 | 28.14 | 18.97 | 12.51 | 1.734 | 8.50 |
|  |  | 80x | .432 | 5.761 | 8.405 | 26.07 | .1810 | 40.49 | 28.57 | 11.29 | 1.734 | 12.22 |
|  |  | 120 | .562 | 5.501 | 10.70 | 23.77 | .1650 | 49.61 | 36.40 | 10.30 | 1.734 | 14.98 |
|  |  | 160 | .718 | 5.189 | 13.32 | 21.15 | .1469 | 58.97 | 45.30 | 9.16 | 1.734 | 17.81 |
|  |  | ...xx | .864 | 4.897 | 15.64 | 18.84 | .1308 | 66.33 | 53.16 | 8.16 | 1.734 | 20.02 |
| 8 | 8.625 | 20 | .250 | 8.125 | 6.57 | 51.85 | .3601 | 57.72 | 22.36 | 22.47 | 2.258 | 13.39 |
|  |  | 30 | .277 | 8.071 | 7.26 | 51.16 | .3553 | 63.35 | 24.70 | 22.17 | 2.258 | 14.69 |
|  |  | 40s | .322 | 7.981 | 8.40 | 50.03 | .3474 | 72.49 | 28.55 | 21.70 | 2.258 | 16.81 |
|  |  | 60 | .406 | 7.813 | 10.48 | 47.94 | .3329 | 88.73 | 35.64 | 20.77 | 2.258 | 20.58 |
|  |  | 80x | .500 | 7.625 | 12.76 | 45.66 | .3171 | 105.7 | 43.39 | 19.78 | 2.258 | 24.51 |
|  |  | 100 | .593 | 7.439 | 14.96 | 43.46 | .3018 | 121.3 | 50.87 | 18.83 | 2.258 | 28.14 |
|  |  | 120 | .718 | 7.189 | 17.84 | 40.59 | .2819 | 140.5 | 60.63 | 17.59 | 2.258 | 32.58 |
|  |  | 140 | .812 | 7.001 | 19.93 | 38.50 | .2673 | 153.7 | 67.76 | 16.68 | 2.258 | 35.65 |
|  |  | ...xx | .875 | 6.875 | 21.30 | 37.12 | .2578 | 162.0 | 72.42 | 16.10 | 2.258 | 37.56 |
|  |  | 160 | .906 | 6.813 | 21.97 | 36.46 | .2532 | 165.9 | 74.69 | 15.80 | 2.258 | 38.48 |

*Notes:*

1. The letters "s," "x," and "xx" in column 3 (Schedule No.) indicate standard, extrastrong, and double extrastrong pipe, respectively.
2. The values shown in square feet for the transverse internal area (column 8) also represent the volume in cubic feet per foot of pipe length.

SOURCE:   Reproduced by permission of the Trane Co., LaCrosse, Wis.

(*Continued*)

**TABLE 9.8**  Physical Properties of Steel Pipe  (*Continued*)

| Nominal Pipe Size (Inches) | Outside Diameter (D) (Inches) | Schedule No. See Note 1 | Wall Thickness (t) (Inches) | Inside Diameter (d) (Inches) | Area of Metal (a) (Square Inches) | Transverse Internal Area | | Moment of Inertia (I) (Inches to 4th Power) | Weight of Pipe (Pounds per foot) | Weight of Water (Pounds per foot of pipe) | External Surface (Sq. Ft. per foot of pipe) | Section Modulus $\left(\frac{2I}{D}\right)$ |
|---|---|---|---|---|---|---|---|---|---|---|---|---|
| | | | | | | Square Inches | See Note 2 Square Feet | | | | | |
| 10 | 10.750 | 20 | .250 | 10.250 | 8.24 | 82.52 | .5731 | 113.7 | 28.04 | 35.76 | 2.814 | 21.15 |
| | | 30 | .307 | 10.136 | 10.07 | 80.69 | .5603 | 137.4 | 34.24 | 34.96 | 2.814 | 25.57 |
| | | 40x | .365 | 10.020 | 11.90 | 78.86 | .5475 | 160.7 | 40.48 | 34.20 | 2.814 | 29.90 |
| | | 60x | .500 | 9.750 | 16.10 | 74.66 | .5185 | 212.0 | 54.74 | 32.35 | 2.814 | 39.43 |
| | | 80 | .593 | 9.564 | 18.92 | 71.84 | .4989 | 244.8 | 64.33 | 31.13 | 2.814 | 45.54 |
| | | 100 | .718 | 9.314 | 22.63 | 68.13 | .4732 | 286.1 | 76.93 | 29.53 | 2.814 | 53.22 |
| | | 120 | .843 | 9.064 | 26.24 | 64.53 | .4481 | 324.2 | 89.20 | 27.96 | 2.814 | 60.32 |
| | | 140 | 1.000 | 8.750 | 30.63 | 60.13 | .4176 | 367.8 | 104.13 | 26.06 | 2.814 | 68.43 |
| | | 160 | 1.125 | 8.500 | 34.02 | 56.75 | .3941 | 399.3 | 115.65 | 24.59 | 2.814 | 74.29 |
| 12 | 12.75 | 20 | .250 | 12.250 | 9.82 | 117.86 | .8185 | 191.8 | 33.38 | 51.07 | 3.338 | 30.2 |
| | | 30 | .330 | 12.090 | 12.87 | 114.80 | .7972 | 248.4 | 43.77 | 49.74 | 3.338 | 39.0 |
| | | ..s | .375 | 12.000 | 14.58 | 113.10 | .7854 | 279.3 | 49.56 | 49.00 | 3.338 | 43.8 |
| | | 40 | .406 | 11.938 | 15.77 | 111.93 | .7773 | 300.3 | 53.53 | 48.50 | 3.338 | 47.1 |
| | | ..x | .500 | 11.750 | 19.24 | 108.43 | .7528 | 361.5 | 65.42 | 46.92 | 3.338 | 56.7 |
| | | 60 | .562 | 11.626 | 21.52 | 106.16 | .7372 | 400.4 | 73.16 | 46.00 | 3.338 | 62.8 |
| | | 80 | .687 | 11.376 | 26.03 | 101.64 | .7058 | 475.1 | 88.51 | 44.04 | 3.338 | 74.6 |
| | | 100 | .843 | 11.064 | 31.53 | 96.14 | .6677 | 561.6 | 107.20 | 41.66 | 3.338 | 88.1 |
| | | 120 | 1.000 | 10.750 | 36.91 | 90.76 | .6303 | 641.6 | 125.49 | 39.33 | 3.338 | 100.7 |
| | | 140 | 1.125 | 10.500 | 41.08 | 86.59 | .6013 | 700.5 | 133.68 | 37.52 | 3.338 | 109.9 |
| | | 160 | 1.312 | 10.126 | 47.14 | 80.53 | .5592 | 781.1 | 160.27 | 34.89 | 3.338 | 122.6 |
| 14 | 14.00 | 10 | .250 | 13.500 | 10.80 | 143.14 | .9940 | 255.3 | 36.71 | 62.03 | 3.665 | 36.6 |
| | | 20 | .312 | 13.376 | 13.42 | 140.52 | .9758 | 314.4 | 45.68 | 60.89 | 3.665 | 45.0 |
| | | 30s | .375 | 13.250 | 16.05 | 137.88 | .9575 | 372.8 | 54.57 | 59.75 | 3.665 | 53.2 |
| | | 40 | .438 | 13.124 | 18.66 | 135.28 | .9394 | 429.1 | 63.37 | 58.64 | 3.665 | 61.3 |
| | | ..x | .500 | 13.000 | 21.21 | 132.73 | .9217 | 483.8 | 72.09 | 57.46 | 3.665 | 69.1 |
| | | 60 | .593 | 12.814 | 24.98 | 128.96 | .8956 | 562.3 | 84.91 | 55.86 | 3.665 | 80.3 |
| | | 80 | .750 | 12.500 | 31.22 | 122.72 | .8522 | 687.3 | 106.13 | 53.18 | 3.665 | 98.2 |
| | | 100 | .937 | 12.126 | 38.45 | 115.49 | .8020 | 824.4 | 130.73 | 50.04 | 3.665 | 117.8 |
| | | 120 | 1.093 | 11.814 | 44.32 | 109.62 | .7612 | 929.6 | 150.67 | 47.45 | 3.665 | 132.8 |
| | | 140 | 1.250 | 11.500 | 50.07 | 103.87 | .7213 | 1027.0 | 170.22 | 45.01 | 3.665 | 146.8 |
| | | 160 | 1.406 | 11.188 | 55.63 | 98.31 | .6827 | 1117.0 | 189.12 | 42.60 | 3.665 | 159.6 |
| 16 | 16.00 | 10 | .250 | 15.500 | 12.37 | 188.69 | 1.3103 | 383.7 | 42.05 | 81.74 | 4.189 | 48.0 |
| | | 20 | .312 | 15.376 | 15.38 | 185.69 | 1.2895 | 473.2 | 52.36 | 80.50 | 4.189 | 59.2 |
| | | 30s | .375 | 15.250 | 18.41 | 182.65 | 1.2684 | 562.1 | 62.58 | 79.12 | 4.189 | 70.3 |
| | | 40x | .500 | 15.000 | 24.35 | 176.72 | 1.2272 | 731.9 | 82.77 | 76.58 | 4.189 | 91.5 |
| | | 60 | .656 | 14.688 | 31.62 | 169.44 | 1.1766 | 932.4 | 107.50 | 73.42 | 4.189 | 116.6 |
| | | 80 | .843 | 14.314 | 40.14 | 160.92 | 1.1175 | 1155.8 | 136.46 | 69.73 | 4.189 | 144.5 |
| | | 100 | 1.031 | 13.938 | 48.48 | 152.58 | 1.0596 | 1364.5 | 164.83 | 66.12 | 4.189 | 170.5 |
| | | 120 | 1.218 | 13.564 | 56.56 | 144.50 | 1.0035 | 1555.8 | 192.29 | 62.62 | 4.189 | 194.5 |
| | | 140 | 1.438 | 13.124 | 65.78 | 135.28 | .9394 | 1760.3 | 223.64 | 58.64 | 4.189 | 220.0 |
| | | 160 | 1.593 | 12.814 | 72.10 | 128.96 | .8956 | 1893.5 | 245.11 | 55.83 | 4.189 | 236.7 |
| 18 | 18.00 | 10 | .250 | 17.500 | 13.94 | 240.53 | 1.6703 | 549.1 | 47.39 | 104.21 | 4.712 | 61.1 |
| | | 20 | .312 | 17.376 | 17.34 | 237.13 | 1.6467 | 678.2 | 59.03 | 102.77 | 4.712 | 75.5 |
| | | ..s | .375 | 17.250 | 20.76 | 233.71 | 1.6230 | 806.7 | 70.59 | 101.18 | 4.712 | 89.6 |
| | | 30 | .438 | 17.124 | 24.17 | 230.30 | 1.5990 | 930.3 | 82.06 | 99.84 | 4.712 | 103.4 |
| | | ..x | .500 | 17.000 | 27.49 | 226.98 | 1.5763 | 1053.2 | 93.45 | 98.27 | 4.712 | 117.0 |
| | | 40 | .562 | 16.876 | 30.79 | 223.68 | 1.5533 | 1171.5 | 104.75 | 96.93 | 4.712 | 130.1 |
| | | 60 | .750 | 16.500 | 40.64 | 213.83 | 1.4849 | 1514.7 | 138.17 | 92.57 | 4.712 | 168.3 |
| | | 80 | .937 | 16.126 | 50.23 | 204.24 | 1.4183 | 1833.0 | 170.75 | 88.50 | 4.712 | 203.8 |
| | | 100 | 1.156 | 15.688 | 61.17 | 193.30 | 1.3423 | 2180.0 | 207.96 | 83.76 | 4.712 | 242.3 |
| | | 120 | 1.375 | 15.250 | 71.81 | 182.66 | 1.2684 | 2498.1 | 244.14 | 79.07 | 4.712 | 277.6 |
| | | 140 | 1.562 | 14.876 | 80.66 | 173.80 | 1.2070 | 2749.0 | 274.23 | 75.32 | 4.712 | 305.5 |
| | | 160 | 1.781 | 14.438 | 90.75 | 163.72 | 1.1369 | 3020.0 | 308.51 | 70.88 | 4.712 | 335.6 |
| 20 | 20.00 | 10 | .250 | 19.500 | 15.51 | 298.65 | 2.0740 | 756.4 | 52.73 | 129.42 | 5.236 | 75.6 |
| | | 20s | .375 | 19.250 | 23.12 | 290.04 | 2.0142 | 1113.0 | 78.60 | 125.67 | 5.236 | 111.3 |
| | | 30x | .500 | 19.000 | 30.63 | 283.53 | 1.9690 | 1457.0 | 104.13 | 122.87 | 5.236 | 145.7 |
| | | 40 | .593 | 18.814 | 36.15 | 278.00 | 1.9305 | 1703.0 | 122.91 | 120.46 | 5.236 | 170.4 |
| | | 60 | .812 | 18.376 | 48.95 | 265.21 | 1.8417 | 2257.0 | 166.40 | 114.92 | 5.236 | 225.7 |
| | | 80 | 1.031 | 17.938 | 61.44 | 252.72 | 1.7550 | 2772.0 | 208.87 | 109.51 | 5.236 | 277.1 |
| | | 100 | 1.281 | 17.438 | 75.33 | 238.83 | 1.6585 | 3315.2 | 256.10 | 103.39 | 5.236 | 331.5 |
| | | 120 | 1.500 | 17.000 | 87.18 | 226.98 | 1.5762 | 3754.0 | 296.37 | 98.35 | 5.236 | 375.5 |
| | | 140 | 1.750 | 16.500 | 100.33 | 213.82 | 1.4849 | 4216.0 | 341.10 | 92.66 | 5.236 | 421.7 |
| | | 160 | 1.968 | 16.064 | 111.49 | 202.67 | 1.4074 | 4585.5 | 379.01 | 87.74 | 5.236 | 458.5 |
| 24 | 24.00 | 10 | .250 | 23.500 | 18.65 | 433.74 | 3.0121 | 1315.4 | 63.41 | 187.95 | 6.283 | 109.6 |
| | | 20s | .375 | 23.250 | 27.83 | 424.56 | 2.9483 | 1942.0 | 94.62 | 183.95 | 6.283 | 161.9 |
| | | ..x | .500 | 23.000 | 36.91 | 415.48 | 2.8853 | 2549.5 | 125.49 | 179.87 | 6.283 | 212.5 |
| | | 30 | .562 | 22.876 | 41.39 | 411.00 | 2.8542 | 2843.0 | 140.80 | 178.09 | 6.283 | 237.0 |
| | | 40 | .687 | 22.626 | 50.31 | 402.07 | 2.7921 | 3421.3 | 171.17 | 174.23 | 6.283 | 285.1 |
| | | 60 | .968 | 22.064 | 70.04 | 382.35 | 2.6552 | 4652.8 | 238.11 | 165.52 | 6.283 | 387.7 |
| | | 80 | 1.218 | 21.564 | 87.17 | 365.22 | 2.5362 | 5672.0 | 296.36 | 158.26 | 6.283 | 472.8 |
| | | 100 | 1.531 | 20.938 | 108.07 | 344.32 | 2.3911 | 6849.9 | 367.40 | 149.06 | 6.283 | 570.8 |
| | | 120 | 1.812 | 20.376 | 126.31 | 326.08 | 2.2645 | 7825.0 | 429.39 | 141.17 | 6.283 | 652.1 |
| | | 140 | 2.062 | 19.876 | 142.11 | 310.28 | 2.1547 | 8625.0 | 483.13 | 134.45 | 6.283 | 718.9 |
| | | 160 | 2.343 | 19.314 | 159.41 | 292.98 | 2.0346 | 9455.9 | 541.94 | 126.84 | 6.283 | 787.9 |

*Notes:*

1. The letters "s," "x," and "xx" in column 3 (Schedule No.) indicate standard, extrastrong, and double extrastrong pipe, respectively.

2. The values shown in square feet for the transverse internal area (column 8) also represent the volume in cubic feet per foot of pipe length.

SOURCE:  Reproduced by permission of the Trane Co., LaCrosse, Wis.

**TABLE 9.9**  Pipe Hangers

Suggested maximum spacing of pipe hangers and
minimum diameter hanger rod for standard
weight pipe filled with water.

| Nominal pipe size, in. | Maximum span, ft | Minimum rod size, in. |
|:---:|:---:|:---:|
| 1 | 7 | ⅜ |
| 1½ | 10 | ⅜ |
| 2 | 10 | ⅜ |
| 2½ | 12 | ½ |
| 3 | 12 | ½ |
| 3½ | 13 | ½ |
| 4 | 14 | ⅝ |
| 5 | 16 | ⅝ |
| 6 | 18 | ¾ |
| 8 | 19 | ⅞ |
| 10 | 21 | ⅞ |
| 12 | 22 | ⅞ |
| 14 | 25 | 1 |
| 16 | 27 | 1 |
| 18 | 28 | 1 |

Table 9.10 lists the weights and rigging workhour requirements for setting up the basic field shop. Correction factors for varying job conditions are discussed in Chap. 1. These factors should be carefully examined by the estimator and adjusted to the peculiarities of each job or phase during the quantity survey. All weights and dimensions listed are nominal and are intended as a convenience to the estimator to calculate rigging, handling, fabricating, and erecting cost; they are not intended for purposes of design. Power tools are assumed throughout.

## ESTIMATING

For testing and repairing leaks for piping systems, allow 5% of the total workhours for each system. If the piping contract is figured separately from other work, allow 2.5% of the total workhours for cleanup; if it is part of a larger mechanical job, cleanup should be covered in the final estimate. Water balancing, cooling system hookups, cooling tower hookups, heating system hookups, fastenings, and supports are discussed in detail in other chapters.

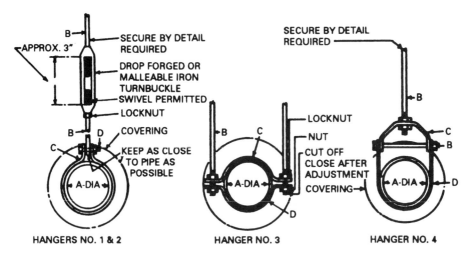

HANGERS NO. 1 & 2          HANGER NO. 3          HANGER NO. 4

HANGER NO. 1: FOR ALL PIPE CARRYING STEAM OVER 15 POUNDS PRESSURE
HANGER NO. 2: FOR ALL LOW PRESSURE STEAM, RETURN, WATER, AIR, GAS, SOIL, WASTE, VENT PIPES, ETC., EXCEPT WHERE HANGER NO. 3 IS REQUIRED.

FOR USE WHERE SPACE WILL NOT PERMIT INSTALLATION OF HANGERS NO. 1, 2, & 4

FOR ALL STEAM RETURN, WATER, AIR, GAS, WASTE, VENT PIPE, ETC., AND FOR ELECTRICAL CONDUITS, EXCEPT WHERE HANGER NO. 3 IS REQUIRED.

NOTE: ALL BOLTS TO HAVE SQUARE OR HEXAGONAL HEADS. ALL NUTS TO BE SQUARE OR HEXAGONAL. STOVE BOLTS ARE NOT ACCEPTABLE.

| HANGER NO. 1 | | | | HANGER NO. 2 | | | | HANGER NO. 3 | | | | HANGER NO. 4 | | | |
|---|---|---|---|---|---|---|---|---|---|---|---|---|---|---|---|
| A | B | C | D | A | B | C | D | A | B | C | D | A | B | C | D |
| $1/2$ | $3/8$ | $3/4 \times 1/8$ | $3/8$ | $1/2$ | $3/8$ | $3/4 \times 1/8$ | $3/8$ | $1/2$ | $1/4$ | $3/4 \times 1/8$ | $3/4 \times 1/4$ | $1/2$ | $3/8$ | $1 1/8 \times 10GA$ | $1 1/8 \times 10GA$ |
| $3/4$ | $3/8$ | $1 \times 1/8$ | $3/8$ | $3/4$ | $3/8$ | $3/4 \times 1/8$ | $3/8$ | $3/4$ | $1/4$ | $3/4 \times 1/8$ | $3/4 \times 1/4$ | $3/4$ | $3/8$ | $1 1/8 \times 10GA$ | $1 1/8 \times 10GA$ |
| 1 | $3/8$ | $1 \times 1/8$ | $3/8$ | 1 | $3/8$ | $3/4 \times 1/8$ | $3/8$ | 1 | $1/4$ | $3/4 \times 1/8$ | $3/4 \times 1/4$ | 1 | $3/8$ | $1 1/8 \times 10GA$ | $1/8 \times 10GA$ |
| $1 1/4$ | $3/8$ | $1 \times 1/8$ | $3/8$ | $1 1/4$ | $3/8$ | $1 \times 1/8$ | $3/8$ | $1 1/4$ | $1/4$ | $1 \times 1/8$ | $1 \times 1/4$ | $1 1/4$ | $3/8$ | $1 1/4 \times 1/8$ | $1 1/4 \times 1/8$ |
| $1 1/2$ | $3/8$ | $1 1/4 \times 3/16$ | $3/8$ | $1 1/2$ | $3/8$ | $1 \times 1/8$ | $3/8$ | $1 1/2$ | $1/4$ | $1 \times 1/8$ | $1 \times 1/4$ | $1 1/2$ | $3/8$ | $1 1/4 \times 1/8$ | $1 1/4 \times 1/8$ |
| 2 | $3/8$ | $1 1/4 \times 3/16$ | $3/8$ | 2 | $3/8$ | $1 \times 1/8$ | $3/8$ | 2 | $1/4$ | $1 \times 1/8$ | $1 \times 1/4$ | 2 | $3/8$ | $1 1/4 \times 3/16$ | $1 1/4 \times 1/8$ |
| $2 1/2$ | $1/2$ | $1 1/4 \times 1/4$ | $1/2$ | $2 1/2$ | $1/2$ | $1 \times 1/8$ | $3/8$ | $2 1/2$ | $1/4$ | $1 \times 1/8$ | $1 \times 1/4$ | $2 1/2$ | $1/2$ | $1 1/4 \times 3/16$ | $1 1/4 \times 1/8$ |
| 3 | $1/2$ | $1 1/4 \times 1/4$ | $1/2$ | 3 | $1/2$ | $1 1/4 \times 1/8$ | $1/2$ | 3 | $3/8$ | $1 1/4 \times 1/8$ | $1 1/4 \times 5/16$ | 3 | $1/2$ | $1 1/2 \times 3/16$ | $1 1/2 \times 3/16$ |
| $3 1/2$ | $1/2$ | $1 1/4 \times 1/4$ | $1/2$ | $3 1/2$ | $1/2$ | $1 1/4 \times 1/8$ | $1/2$ | $3 1/2$ | $3/8$ | $1 1/4 \times 1/8$ | $1 1/4 \times 5/16$ | $3 1/2$ | $1/2$ | $1 1/2 \times 3/16$ | $1 1/2 \times 3/16$ |
| 4 | $5/8$ | $1 1/4 \times 5/16$ | $5/8$ | 4 | $1/2$ | $1 1/4 \times 1/8$ | $1/2$ | 4 | $3/8$ | $1 1/4 \times 1/8$ | $1 1/4 \times 5/16$ | 4 | $1/2$ | $1 1/2 \times 1/4$ | $1 1/2 \times 3/16$ |
| 5 | $5/8$ | $1 1/2 \times 5/16$ | $5/8$ | 5 | $1/2$ | $1 1/4 \times 1/8$ | $1/2$ | 5 | $3/8$ | $1 1/4 \times 1/8$ | $1 1/4 \times 3/8$ | 5 | $1/2$ | $1 1/2 \times 1/4$ | $1 1/2 \times 3/16$ |
| 6 | $3/4$ | $2 \times 5/16$ | $3/4$ | 6 | $5/8$ | $1 1/4 \times 3/16$ | $5/8$ | 6 | $1/2$ | $1 1/2 \times 1/8$ | $1 1/2 \times 3/8$ | 6 | $5/8$ | $1 1/2 \times 3/8$ | $1 1/2 \times 1/4$ |
| 8 | $7/8$ | $2 \times 3/8$ | $7/8$ | 8 | $5/8$ | $1 1/4 \times 3/16$ | $5/8$ | 8 | $1/2$ | $1 1/2 \times 1/8$ | $1 1/2 \times 1/2$ | 8 | $5/8$ | $2 \times 3/8$ | $2 \times 1/4$ |
| 10 | 1 | $2 \times 1/2$ | 1 | 10 | $3/4$ | $1 1/2 \times 1/4$ | $3/4$ | 10 | $5/8$ | $2 \times 1/4$ | $2 \times 1/2$ | 10 | $3/4$ | $2 \times 1/2$ | $2 \times 5/16$ |
| 12 | 1 | $2 \times 1/2$ | 1 | 12 | $3/4$ | $1 1/2 \times 1/4$ | $3/4$ | 12 | $5/8$ | $2 \times 1/4$ | $2 \times 1/2$ | 12 | $3/4$ | $2 \times 1/2$ | $2 \times 5/16$ |

FILE NO.

# PIPE HANGERS

PUBLIC BUILDINGS SERVICE GENERAL SERVICES ADMINISTRATION

SCALE    NONE
DWG. NO.    10-1-1A
STANDARD DETAIL

Figure 9.3   PIPE HANGERS

**TABLE 9.10** Basic Field Workshop

The weights shown are average for standard equipment to guide the estimator in figuring rigging and trucking costs from warehouse to jobsite. *Workhours* are based on loading, unloading, moving into place, and rough leveling. Traveling time for truck is not included.

| Item | Description | Weight, lb | Workhours | Electrical requirements |
|---|---|---|---|---|
| Welding machine | 200 amperes (A) | 400 | 0.5 | — |
| Welding machine | 500 A | 400 | 0.5 | — |
| Pipe threader | Light duty, to 2 in. | 450 | 2.3 | ½ hp, 110 V |
| Pipe machine | Heavy duty, to 4 in. | 1,850 | 9.5 | 3 hp, 220 V |
| Copper finisher | Six-spindle, to 4 in. | 225 | 1.4 | ⅛ hp, 110 V |
| Chain hoist | Four at 250 lb | 1,000 | 3.0 | — |
| Box of hand tools | Two at 250 lb | 500 | 1.7 | — |

## PIPE HANGERS, BRACKETS, AND SLEEVES

Maximum spacings of pipe hangers and minimum diameters of hanger rods are given in Tables 9.11 and 9.12, respectively. See Table 9.13 for pipe-hanger assemblies, Table 9.14 for pipe-hanger brackets, and Table 9.15 for riser clamp assemblies. Data on sleeves and pipe-covering shields are given in Tables 9.16 and 9.17, respectively. See Chaps. 16 and 17 for a detailed discussion of fastenings, inserts, hole drilling, and miscellaneous supports.

**TABLE 9.11** Maximum Spacing of Hanger Rod

| Nominal pipe size, in. | 1 | 1½ | 2 | 3 | 4 | 6 | 8 | 10 | 12 | 14 | 16 | 18 | 20 | 24 | 30 |
|---|---|---|---|---|---|---|---|---|---|---|---|---|---|---|---|
| Hanger spacing, ft | 7 | 10 | 10 | 12 | 14 | 17 | 19 | 22 | 23 | 25 | 27 | 28 | 30 | 32 | 33 |

**TABLE 9.12** Minimum Diameter of Hanger Rod

| Nominal pipe size, in. | 1½ | 2 | 3 | 4 | 6 | 8 | 10 | 12 | 14 | 16 | 18 | 20 | 24 |
|---|---|---|---|---|---|---|---|---|---|---|---|---|---|
| Rod diameter, in. | ⅜ | ⅜ | ½ | ⅝ | ¾ | ⅞ | ⅞ | 1 | 1 | 1 | 1 | 1¼ | 1¼ |

**TABLE 9.13** Pipe-Hanger Assembly

Based on standard rod suspension design in overhead position and includes moving of ladders into position in area of average congestion. *One-rod hanger assembly* includes beam clamp, hanger rod, and split ring or clevis. *Two-rod hanger assembly* includes two rods fitted with crossbar and roller for use with saddle for insulated pipe.

| Pipe size, in.......... | 1 | 1¼ | 1½ | 2 | 2½ | 3 | 3½ | 4 | 5 | 6 | 8 |
|---|---|---|---|---|---|---|---|---|---|---|---|
| One-rod split ring |||||||||||
| Labor, workhours .... | 0.32 | 0.32 | 0.32 | 0.32 | 0.39 | 0.39 | 0.39 | 0.46 | 0.46 | 0.58 | 0.75 |
| Material, $ .......... | 5.75 | 6.00 | 6.20 | 6.50 | 7.00 | 7.60 | 7.90 | 10.30 | 15.00 | 20.00 | 26.00 |
| Two-rod roller |||||||||||
| Labor, workhours .... | 0.41 | 0.41 | 0.41 | 0.41 | 0.49 | 0.49 | 0.49 | 0.62 | 0.62 | 0.76 | 1.17 |
| Material, $ .......... | 15.10 | 15.20 | 15.30 | 15.70 | 16.50 | 17.00 | 18.80 | 23.60 | 25.20 | 29.70 | 41.00 |

**TABLE 9.14** Pipe-Hanger Bracket

Based on heavyweight carbon-steel prefabricated brackets with three bolt holes, 3,000-lb capacity for bare pipe. *Workhours* include aligning, drilling holes with expansion shield in concrete wall, and erecting bracket. Backplate thickness, $\frac{1}{2}$ in.

| Top protrusion from wall, in...... | 12 | 18 | 24 | 30 | 36 | 42 |
|---|---|---|---|---|---|---|
| Bracket weight, lb............... | 25 | 50 | 65 | 83 | 140 | 167.5 |
| Hole diameter, in............... | $^{13}/_{16}$ | $^{13}/_{16}$ | $1^{1}/_{16}$ | $1^{1}/_{16}$ | $1^{1}/_{16}$ | $1^{1}/_{16}$ |
| Material, $....................... | 140 | 195 | 230 | 265 | 405 | 450 |
| Workhours ..................... | 1.88 | 1.93 | 2.04 | 2.04 | 2.25 | 2.25 |

**TABLE 9.15** Riser Clamp Assembly

Based on heavy carbon-steel prefabricated two-bolt sets. *Workhours* includes erecting, aligning, and tightening up bolt fastenings.

| Pipe size, in......... | 2 | $2\frac{1}{2}$ | 3 | $3\frac{1}{2}$ | 4 | 5 | 6 | 8 | 10 | 12 |
|---|---|---|---|---|---|---|---|---|---|---|
| Max. load, lb ........ | 250 | 375 | 525 | 650 | 800 | 1,150 | 1,550 | 2,500 | 2,600 | 2,700 |
| Clamp weight, lb .... | 2.15 | 2.3 | 2.5 | 3.25 | 3.5 | 5.0 | 5.3 | 10.0 | 11.0 | 16.0 |
| Material, $ .......... | 4.45 | 4.70 | 5.20 | 6.20 | 6.30 | 8.60 | 10.00 | 17.80 | 22.20 | 26.50 |
| Workhours .......... | 0.21 | 0.22 | 0.23 | 0.24 | 0.28 | 0.29 | 0.30 | 0.35 | 0.35 | 0.38 |

**TABLE 9.16** Setting Sleeves

Based on 8-in. cut lengths of carbon-steel pipe in flat decks; for wall sleeve add 20%; for 12-in. sleeve, add 25%. *Workhours* includes laying out, setting and fastening sleeve in position, and capping sleeve to keep clean of concrete.

| Sleeve size, in. | 2 | 3 | 4 | 6 | 8 | 10 | 12 | 14 | 16 | 18 | 20 |
|---|---|---|---|---|---|---|---|---|---|---|---|
| Workhours ... | 0.40 | 0.45 | 0.49 | 0.56 | 0.64 | 0.80 | 0.96 | 1.29 | 1.77 | 2.05 | 2.20 |

**TABLE 9.17** Minimum Requirements for Pipe-Covering and Tubing-Covering Shields

Shields rolled to 180° arc for protection of insulation covering.

| Pipe-covering shields | | | | | | | | | | | |
|---|---|---|---|---|---|---|---|---|---|---|---|
| Pipe size, in. | $1\frac{1}{2}$ | 2 | 3 | 4 | 6 | 8 | 10 | 12 | 14 | 16 | 18 | 24 |
| Shield length | 12 | 12 | 12 | 12 | 24 | 24 | 24 | 24 | 24 | 24 | 24 | 24 |
| Gage | 18 | 18 | 18 | 16 | 16 | 14 | 14 | 14 | 14 | 12 | 12 | 12 |

| Copper-tubing-covering shields | | | | | | | | |
|---|---|---|---|---|---|---|---|---|
| Pipe size, in. | $\frac{1}{4}$ | $\frac{3}{4}$ | 1 | $1\frac{1}{4}$ | $1\frac{1}{2}$ | 2 | $2\frac{1}{2}$ | 3 |
| Shield length | 12 | 12 | 12 | 12 | 12 | 12 | 12 | 12 |
| Gage | 18 | 18 | 18 | 18 | 18 | 18 | 18 | 18 |

## COPPER PIPE AND TUBING

Tables 9.18 and 9.19 provide recommended sizes of connecting tubing for heating and cooling systems. Figure 9.4 is a speed sheet for selecting water pipe sizes for air-conditioning applications.

Tables 9.20 to 9.23 provide tubing costs for per-foot units based on hard-drawn seamless copper tube shipped in standard 20-ft lengths and with an average number of horizontal and

**TABLE 9.18**   Sizing Connecting Tubing for Heating

| Heating load, Btu/hr | gpm circulated, 20° ΔT | Recommended connecting tubing size (type M) for various heating loads and connecting tubing lengths (figures based on 10,000 Btu per gpm, or on temperature drop of 20°F through the circuit) | | | | |
|---|---|---|---|---|---|---|
| | | Total length, ft, connecting tubing | | | | |
| | | 0–50 | 50–100 | 100–150 | 150–200 | 200–300 |
| | | Tubing, nominal OD, in., type M | | | | |
| 5,000 | 0.5 | ⅜ | ⅜ | ½ | ½ | ½ |
| 10,000 | 1.0 | ⅜ | ⅜ | ½ | ½ | ½ |
| 15,000 | 1.5 | ½ | ½ | ½ | ½ | ¾ |
| 20,000 | 2.0 | ½ | ½ | ½ | ¾ | ¾ |
| 30,000 | 3.0 | ½ | ½ | ¾ | ¾ | ¾ |
| 40,000 | 4.0 | ½ | ¾ | ¾ | ¾ | ¾ |
| 50,000 | 5.0 | ¾ | ¾ | ¾ | 1 | 1 |
| 60,000 | 6.0 | ¾ | ¾ | 1 | 1 | 1 |
| 75,000 | 7.5 | ¾ | 1 | 1 | 1 | 1 |
| 100,000 | 10.0 | 1 | 1 | 1 | 1¼ | 1¼ |
| 125,000 | 12.5 | 1 | 1 | 1¼ | 1¼ | 1¼ |
| 150,000 | 15.0 | 1 | 1¼ | 1¼ | 1¼ | 1½ |
| 200,000 | 20.0 | 1¼ | 1¼ | 1½ | 1½ | 1½ |
| 250,000 | 25.0 | 1¼ | 1½ | 1½ | 2 | 2 |
| 300,000 | 30.0 | 1½ | 1½ | 2 | 2 | 2 |
| 400,000 | 40.0 | 2 | 2 | 2 | 2 | 2 |
| 500,000 | 50.0 | 2 | 2 | 2 | 2½ | 2½ |
| 600,000 | 60.0 | 2 | 2 | 2½ | 2½ | 2½ |
| 800,000 | 80.0 | 2½ | 2½ | 2½ | 2½ | 3 |
| 1,000,000 | 100.0 | 2½ | 2½ | 3 | 3 | 3 |
| 1,250,000 | 125.0 | 2½ | 3 | 3 | 3 | 3½ |
| 1,500,000 | 150.0 | 3 | 3 | 3 | 3½ | 3½ |
| 2,000,000 | 200.0 | 3 | 3½ | 3½ | 4 | 4 |
| 2,500,000 | 250.0 | 3½ | 3½ | 4 | 4 | 5 |
| 3,000,000 | 300.0 | 3½ | 4 | 4 | 4 | 5 |
| 4,000,000 | 400.0 | 4 | 4 | 5 | 5 | 5 |
| 5,000,000 | 500.0 | 5 | 5 | 5 | 6 | 6 |
| 6,000,000 | 600.0 | 5 | 6 | 6 | 6 | 8 |
| 8,000,000 | 800.0 | 8 | 6 | 8 | 8 | 8 |
| 10,000,000 | 1,000.0 | 8 | 8 | 8 | 8 | 10 |

SOURCE: *Means Estimating Handbook*, R. S. Means, Kingston, Mass., 1990.

**TABLE 9.19** Sizing Connecting Tubing for Cooling

| Cooling load, Btu/hr | Cooling load, tons | gpm circulated, 3 gpm/ton, 8°F rise | Recommended connecting tubing (type M) for various cooling loads and connecting tubing lengths (figures based on 3 gpm/ton, or on temperature rise of 8°F through the circuit) | | | | |
|---|---|---|---|---|---|---|---|
| | | | Total length connecting tubing, ft | | | | |
| | | | 0–50 | 50–100 | 100–150 | 150–200 | 200–300 |
| | | | Tubing, nominal OD, in., type M | | | | |
| 6,000 | 0.5 | 1.5 | ½ | ½ | ½ | ½ | ¾ |
| 9,000 | 0.75 | 2.25 | ½ | ½ | ½ | ¾ | ¾ |
| 12,000 | 1.0 | 3.0 | ½ | ½ | ¾ | ¾ | ¾ |
| 18,000 | 1.5 | 4.5 | ¾ | ¾ | ¾ | 1 | 1 |
| 24,000 | 2.0 | 6.0 | ¾ | ¾ | 1 | 1 | 1 |
| 30,000 | 2.5 | 7.5 | ¾ | 1 | 1 | 1 | 1 |
| 36,000 | 3.0 | 9.0 | 1 | 1 | 1 | 1¼ | 1¼ |
| 48,000 | 4.0 | 12.0 | 1 | 1 | 1¼ | 1¼ | 1¼ |
| 60,000 | 5.0 | 15.0 | 1 | 1¼ | 1¼ | 1¼ | 1½ |
| 72,000 | 6.0 | 18.0 | 1¼ | 1¼ | 1½ | 1½ | 1½ |
| 96,000 | 8.0 | 24.0 | 1¼ | 1½ | 1½ | 2 | 2 |
| 120,000 | 10.0 | 30.0 | 1½ | 1½ | 2 | 2 | 2 |
| 144,000 | 12.0 | 36.0 | 1½ | 2 | 2 | 2 | 2 |
| 180,000 | 15.0 | 45.0 | 2 | 2 | 2 | 2 | 2½ |
| 240,000 | 20.0 | 60.0 | 2 | 2 | 2½ | 2½ | 2½ |
| 300,000 | 25.0 | 75.0 | 2½ | 2½ | 2½ | 2½ | 3 |
| 360,000 | 30.0 | 90.0 | 2½ | 2½ | 2½ | 3 | 3 |
| 480,000 | 40.0 | 120.0 | 2½ | 3 | 3 | 3 | 3½ |
| 600,000 | 50.0 | 150.0 | 3 | 3 | 3 | 3½ | 3½ |
| 720,000 | 60.0 | 180.0 | 3 | 3½ | 3½ | 4 | 4 |
| 900,000 | 75.0 | 225.0 | 3½ | 3½ | 4 | 4 | 5 |
| 1,200,000 | 100.0 | 300.0 | 3½ | 4 | 4 | 4 | 5 |
| 1,500,000 | 125.0 | 375.0 | 4 | 4 | 5 | 5 | 5 |
| 1,800,000 | 150.0 | 450.0 | 4 | 5 | 5 | 5 | 6 |
| 2,400,000 | 200.0 | 600.0 | 5 | 5 | 6 | 6 | 6 |
| 3,000,000 | 250.0 | 750.0 | 5 | 6 | 6 | 6 | 8 |
| 3,600,000 | 300.0 | 900.0 | 6 | 6 | 8 | 8 | 8 |
| 4,800,000 | 400.0 | 1,200.0 | 8 | 8 | 8 | 8 | 10 |
| 6,000,000 | 500.0 | 1,500.0 | 8 | 8 | 10 | 10 | 10 |
| 7,200,000 | 600.0 | 1,800.0 | 10 | 10 | 10 | 10 | 12 |

SOURCE:  *Means Estimating Handbook*, R. S. Means, Kingston, Mass., 1990.

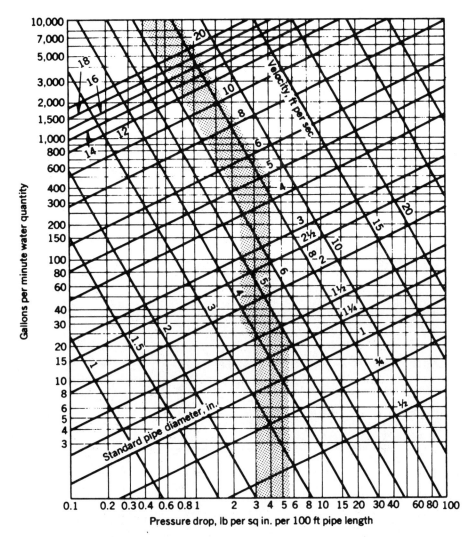

**Figure 9.4   WATER PIPE SIZE SELECTOR—SPEED SHEET**
*For rapid estimating of water pipe sizes for average air-conditioning applications. The shaded area indicates acceptable design range. Enter the required gpm at the left and follow horizontally to the shaded area. At the first diagonal line to intersect the gpm, read the pipe size for acceptable velocity for most air-conditioning pumping jobs. Where the gpm does not intersect a pipeline within the shaded area, use the diagonal immediately above. (Reproduced by permission of Engineers Press, Coral Gables, Fla.)*

**TABLE 9.20** Copper DWV Drainage Tube, Nonpressure

| Nominal pipe size, in. | 1¼ | 1½ | 2 | 3 | 4 | 5 | 6 |
|---|---|---|---|---|---|---|---|
| Pipe, per ft, $ | 2.20 | 2.70 | 3.50 | 6.10 | 10.85 | 23.10 | 32.75 |
| Fitting allowance, $ | 0.63 | 0.78 | 1.15 | 1.95 | 3.25 | 6.90 | 9.75 |
| Total material, $ | 2.83 | 3.48 | 4.65 | 8.05 | 14.10 | 30.00 | 42.50 |
| Total workhours | 0.26 | 0.27 | 0.29 | 0.36 | 0.52 | 0.66 | 0.89 |

**TABLE 9.21** Copper Type M Tube, Light-Duty

| Nominal pipe size, in. | ⅜ | ½ | ¾ | 1 | 1¼ | 1½ | 2 |
|---|---|---|---|---|---|---|---|
| Pipe, per ft, $ | 0.62 | 0.69 | 0.94 | 1.26 | 2.17 | 2.88 | 4.33 |
| Fitting allowance, $ | 0.52 | 0.52 | 0.47 | 0.52 | 0.75 | 0.92 | 1.32 |
| Total material, $ | 1.14 | 1.21 | 1.41 | 1.78 | 2.92 | 3.80 | 5.65 |
| Total workhours | 0.20 | 0.24 | 0.25 | 0.26 | 0.27 | 0.28 | 0.29 |

| Nominal pipe size, in. | 2½ | 3 | 3½ | 4 | 5 | 6 | |
|---|---|---|---|---|---|---|---|
| Pipe, per ft, $ | 6.12 | 7.85 | 11.50 | 14.95 | 37.00 | 47.00 | |
| Fitting allowance, $ | 1.47 | 2.10 | 3.75 | 3.75 | 11.15 | 15.70 | |
| Total material, $ | 7.59 | 9.95 | 15.25 | 18.70 | 48.15 | 62.70 | |
| Total workhours | 0.31 | 0.36 | 0.42 | 0.53 | 0.66 | 0.89 | |

**TABLE 9.22** Copper Type L Tube, ≤250 lb Working Pressure

| Nominal pipe size, in. | ⅜ | ½ | ¾ | 1 | 1¼ | 1½ | 2 |
|---|---|---|---|---|---|---|---|
| Pipe, per ft, $ | 0.71 | 0.83 | 1.20 | 1.60 | 2.96 | 3.66 | 5.41 |
| Fitting allowance, $ | 0.46 | 0.46 | 0.44 | 0.47 | 0.77 | 0.94 | 1.24 |
| Total material, $ | 1.17 | 1.29 | 1.64 | 2.07 | 3.73 | 4.60 | 6.65 |
| Total workhours | 0.20 | 0.25 | 0.26 | 0.27 | 0.28 | 0.29 | 0.31 |

| Nominal pipe size, in. | 2½ | 3 | 3½ | 4 | 5 | 6 | |
|---|---|---|---|---|---|---|---|
| Pipe, per ft, $ | 7.57 | 10.15 | 13.50 | 16.95 | 38.70 | 48.40 | |
| Fitting allowance, $ | 1.47 | 2.15 | 3.50 | 3.50 | 10.35 | 14.70 | |
| Total material, $ | 9.04 | 12.30 | 17.00 | 20.45 | 49.05 | 63.10 | |
| Total workhours | 0.35 | 0.39 | 0.47 | 0.57 | 0.73 | 0.97 | |

**TABLE 9.23** Copper Type K Tube, ≤400 lb Working Pressure

| Nominal pipe size, in. | ⅜ | ½ | ¾ | 1 | 1¼ | 1½ | 2 |
|---|---|---|---|---|---|---|---|
| Pipe, per ft, $ | 0.98 | 1.07 | 1.72 | 2.15 | 3.19 | 4.00 | 5.95 |
| Fitting allowance, $ | 0.50 | 0.50 | 0.55 | 0.60 | 0.75 | 0.90 | 1.25 |
| Total material, $ | 1.48 | 1.57 | 2.27 | 2.75 | 3.94 | 4.90 | 7.20 |
| Total workhours | 0.22 | 0.25 | 0.26 | 0.28 | 0.29 | 0.31 | 0.34 |

| Nominal pipe size, in. | 2½ | 3 | 3½ | 4 | 5 | 6 | |
|---|---|---|---|---|---|---|---|
| Pipe, per ft, $ | 8.70 | 11.90 | 16.30 | 20.70 | 43.20 | 63.00 | |
| Fitting allowance, $ | 1.50 | 2.20 | 3.75 | 3.75 | 10.10 | 14.55 | |
| Total material, $ | 10.20 | 14.10 | 20.05 | 24.45 | 53.30 | 77.55 | |
| Total workhours | 0.37 | 0.43 | 0.50 | 0.61 | 0.81 | 1.07 | |

vertical runs and directional changes. Workhours include moving equipment and materials on the jobsite, brazing joints and fittings, and erecting pipe within 10 ft from floor height. They do not include pipe hangers, supports, valves, expansion joints, or specialties. Costs for coiled refrigeration tube and flexible vibration eliminators are shown in Tables 9.24 and 9.25. Handling weights are given in Table 9.26. Table 9.27 provides labor factors for ceiling heights above 15 ft.

**TABLE 9.24**   Soft Copper Refrigeration Tube

Dehydrated seamless with sealed ends, shipped in 50-ft coils.

| OD, in. . . . . . . . . . . | 3/16 | 1/4 | 5/16 | 3/8 | 1/2 | 5/8 | 3/4 | 7/8 | 1 1/8 | 1 3/8 |
|---|---|---|---|---|---|---|---|---|---|---|
| Tube, per ft, $ . . . | 0.26 | 0.32 | 0.40 | 0.47 | 0.60 | 0.80 | 0.94 | 1.40 | 1.99 | 2.78 |

**TABLE 9.25**   Vibration Eliminators, Bronze-Braided, Flexible

| To copper nominal pipe size, in. | Overall length, in. | Dollars per each | Erection, workhours |
|---|---|---|---|
| 3/8 | 12 | 20 | 0.27 |
| 1/2 | 12 | 26 | 0.28 |
| 5/8 | 12 | 31 | 0.29 |
| 3/4 | 12 | 36 | 0.32 |
| 1 | 18 | 53 | 0.41 |
| 1 1/4 | 18 | 64 | 0.80 |
| 1 1/2 | 18 | 76 | 0.90 |
| 2 | 18 | 124 | 1.15 |
| 2 1/2 | 24 | 155 | 1.25 |
| 3 | 24 | 195 | 1.85 |
| 3 1/2 | 24 | 250 | 2.00 |
| 4 | 24 | 285 | 2.30 |

**TABLE 9.26**  Weights of Copper Tubing

| Nominal pipe size, in. | OD, in. | lb per ft | | | | | |
|---|---|---|---|---|---|---|---|
| | | Type M | | Type L | | Type K | |
| | | Empty pipe | With water | Empty pipe | With water | Empty pipe | With water |
| ¼ | 0.375 | 0.11 | 0.15 | 0.13 | 0.16 | 0.14 | 0.17 |
| ⅜ | 0.500 | 0.15 | 0.21 | 0.20 | 0.26 | 0.27 | 0.32 |
| ½ | 0.625 | 0.20 | 0.31 | 0.28 | 0.39 | 0.34 | 0.44 |
| ⅝ | 0.750 | 0.26 | 0.40 | 0.36 | 0.51 | 0.42 | 0.56 |
| ¾ | 0.875 | 0.33 | 0.55 | 0.45 | 0.67 | 0.64 | 0.84 |
| 1 | 1.125 | 0.46 | 0.85 | 0.65 | 1.01 | 0.84 | 1.18 |
| 1¼ | 1.375 | 0.68 | 1.25 | 0.88 | 1.43 | 1.04 | 1.57 |
| 1½ | 1.625 | 0.94 | 1.77 | 1.14 | 1.90 | 1.36 | 2.58 |
| 2 | 2.125 | 1.46 | 2.82 | 1.75 | 3.10 | 2.06 | 3.37 |
| 2½ | 2.625 | 2.03 | 4.15 | 2.49 | 4.55 | 2.93 | 4.95 |
| 3 | 3.125 | 2.68 | 5.72 | 3.33 | 6.30 | 4.00 | 6.90 |
| 3½ | 3.625 | 3.58 | 7.65 | 4.30 | 8.30 | 5.12 | 9.05 |
| 4 | 4.125 | 4.66 | 9.90 | 5.38 | 10.60 | 6.51 | 11.60 |
| 5 | 5.125 | 6.66 | 14.85 | 7.61 | 15.70 | 9.67 | 17.55 |
| 6 | 6.125 | 8.92 | 20.70 | 10.20 | 21.80 | 13.90 | 25.10 |
| 8 | 8.125 | 16.50 | 37.25 | 19.30 | 39.50 | 25.90 | 45.50 |
| 10 | 10.130 | 25.60 | 57.80 | 30.10 | 61.75 | 40.30 | 71.00 |

**TABLE 9.27**  Piping Labor Factors Due to
Elevated Installations

For installations higher than an average of 15 ft,
labor costs may be increased by the following
suggested percentages.

| Ceiling height, ft | Labor increases, % |
|---|---|
| 15–20 | 10 |
| 20–25 | 20 |
| 25–30 | 30 |
| 30–35 | 40 |
| 35–40 | 50 |
| >40 | 60 |

SOURCE: *Means Estimating Handbook,* R. S. Means,
Kingston, Mass., 1990.

## BRAZING AND SOLDERING

Tables 9.28 to 9.31 list necessary estimating data for brazing and soldering copper tube.

## PVC PIPE

Tables 9.32 to 9.35 provide estimating information for per-foot units based on plain-end rigid plastic, shipped in standard 20-ft lengths, and with an average number of horizontal and vertical runs and directional changes. *Workhours* includes moving equipment and materials on the jobsite, cementing joints and fittings, and erecting pipe within 10 ft from floor height. Not included are pipe hangers, supports, valves, or specialties.

**TABLE 9.28**  Consumption of Brazing Alloys, in Linear Inches of Wire per Joint

| Pipe size, in. | Torch-tip size | Acetylene, cu ft/hr | $\frac{1}{16}$-in. alloy wire | $\frac{3}{32}$-in. alloy wire | 0.050 × $\frac{1}{8}$-in. strip |
|---|---|---|---|---|---|
| $\frac{1}{4}$ | 54 | 15.9 | $\frac{3}{4}$ | – | $\frac{3}{4}$ |
| $\frac{3}{8}$ | 54 | 15.9 | 1 | – | 1 |
| $\frac{1}{2}$ | 51 | 24.8 | $1\frac{1}{2}$ | $\frac{3}{4}$ | $1\frac{1}{4}$ |
| $\frac{3}{4}$ | 51 | 24.8 | 2 | 1 | 2 |
| 1 | 48 | 31.6 | 3 | $1\frac{1}{2}$ | $3\frac{1}{2}$ |
| $1\frac{1}{4}$ | 48 | 31.6 | 4 | 2 | 4 |
| $1\frac{1}{2}$ | 44 | 38.7 | – | $2\frac{1}{2}$ | $4\frac{1}{2}$ |
| 2 | 40 | 60.0 | – | $3\frac{3}{4}$ | 6 |
| $2\frac{1}{2}$ | 40 | 60.0 | – | 6 | 8 |
| 3 | 35 | 70.0 | – | 10 | 12 |
| $3\frac{1}{2}$ | 35 | 70.0 | – | 12 | 16 |
| 4 | 30 | 88.5 | – | 14 | 20 |
| Linear inches of alloy per lb | | | 1,068 | 475 | 524 |

**TABLE 9.29**  Brazing Alloys and Solders

| Item | Cost per lb, $ |
|---|---|
| 50–50 wire (avoir.*).................. | 5.50 |
| 95–5 wire (avoir.) .................... | 8 |
| Silver alloy, 5% (avoir.)............... | 19 |
| Silver alloy, 15% (avoir.) ............. | 42 |
| Silver alloy, 35% (troy)............... | 73 |
| Silver alloy, 45% (troy)............... | 87 |
| Silver alloy, 50% (troy)............... | 94 |
| Flux (avoir.)......................... | 6 |

*Avoirdupois weight.

**TABLE 9.30** Safe Strength of Soldered Joints

| Solder | Service temp., °F | Maximum pressure, psi | | |
|---|---|---|---|---|
| | | ¼ to 1 in. | 1¼ to 2 in. | 2½ to 4 in. |
| 50–50 tin lead* . . . . . . . . . . | 100 | 200 | 175 | 150 |
| | 150 | 150 | 125 | 100 |
| | 200 | 100 | 90 | 75 |
| | 250 | 85 | 75 | 50 |
| 95–5 tin antimony . . . . . . . . | 100 | 500 | 400 | 300 |
| | 150 | 400 | 350 | 275 |
| | 200 | 300 | 250 | 200 |
| | 250 | 200 | 175 | 150 |
| Brazing filler . . . . . . . . . . . . | 250 | 300 | 210 | 170 |
| Metal at 1,000°F melt or over . . . | 350 | 270 | 190 | 155 |

\* **Lead-containing solder may not be used for potable-water systems**

**TABLE 9.31** Estimated Quantity of Soft Solder Required to Make 100 Joints

| Size, in. | Quantity in pounds |
|---|---|
| ⅜ | 0.5 |
| ½ | 0.75 |
| ¾ | 1.0 |
| 1 | 1.5 |
| 1¼ | 1.75 |
| 1½ | 2.0 |
| 2 | 2.5 |
| 2½ | 3.4 |
| 3 | 4.0 |
| 3½ | 4.8 |
| 4 | 6.8 |
| 5 | 8.0 |
| 6 | 15.0 |
| 8 | 32.0 |
| 10 | 42.0 |

*Notes:*
1. The quantity of hard solder used is dependent on the skill of the operator, but for estimating purposes 75% of the above figures may be used.
2. Two ounces of solder flux will be required for each pound of solder.
3. Includes an allowance for waste.
4. Drainage fittings consume 20% less.

**TABLE 9.32** PVC Pipe, Rigid Schedule 40 Plain End

| Pipe size, in. | ½ | ¾ | 1 | 1¼ | 1½ | 2 |
|---|---|---|---|---|---|---|
| Pipe, per ft, $ | 0.51 | 0.57 | 0.66 | 0.72 | 1.10 | 1.25 |
| Fitting allowance, $ | 0.14 | 0.15 | 0.28 | 0.36 | 0.42 | 0.62 |
| Total material, $ | 0.65 | 0.72 | 0.94 | 1.08 | 1.52 | 1.87 |
| Total workhours | 0.12 | 0.13 | 0.13 | 0.14 | 0.15 | 0.16 |
| Pipe size, in. | 2½ | 3 | 4 | 6 | 8 | 10 |
| Pipe, per ft, $ | 1.73 | 2.06 | 2.70 | 4.56 | 6.50 | 18.90 |
| Fitting allowance, $ | 1.13 | 1.25 | 1.76 | 2.37 | 4.65 | 14.85 |
| Total material, $ | 2.86 | 3.31 | 4.46 | 6.93 | 11.15 | 33.75 |
| Total workhours | 0.18 | 0.21 | 0.28 | 0.40 | 0.50 | 0.64 |

**TABLE 9.33** PVC Pipe, Rigid Schedule 80 Plain End

| Pipe size, in. | ½ | ¾ | 1 | 1¼ | 1½ | 2 |
|---|---|---|---|---|---|---|
| Pipe, per ft, $ | 0.59 | 0.69 | 0.79 | 0.91 | 1.39 | 1.58 |
| Fitting allowance, $ | 0.35 | 0.45 | 0.53 | 0.64 | 0.70 | 0.75 |
| Total material, $ | 0.94 | 1.14 | 1.32 | 1.55 | 2.09 | 2.33 |
| Total workhours | 0.12 | 0.13 | 0.13 | 0.14 | 0.15 | 0.16 |
| Pipe size, in. | 2½ | 3 | 4 | 6 | 8 | 10 |
| Pipe, per ft, $ | 2.05 | 2.75 | 3.60 | 6.30 | 11.25 | 15.85 |
| Fitting allowance, $ | 1.70 | 1.85 | 2.50 | 3.95 | 7.10 | 12.30 |
| Total material, $ | 3.75 | 4.60 | 6.10 | 10.25 | 18.35 | 28.15 |
| Total workhours | 0.18 | 0.21 | 0.28 | 0.40 | 0.50 | 0.64 |

**TABLE 9.34** Weights of PVC Pipe

| Nominal pipe size, in. | OD, in. | lb per ft | | | |
|---|---|---|---|---|---|
| | | Schedule 40 | | Schedule 80 | |
| | | Empty pipe | With water | Empty pipe | With water |
| ½ | 0.84 | 0.15 | 0.27 | 0.19 | 0.28 |
| ¾ | 1.05 | 0.20 | 0.43 | 0.26 | 0.45 |
| 1 | 1.31 | 0.30 | 0.69 | 0.38 | 0.73 |
| 1¼ | 1.66 | 0.41 | 1.00 | 0.55 | 1.10 |
| 1½ | 1.90 | 0.49 | 1.35 | 0.65 | 1.90 |
| 2 | 2.37 | 0.64 | 2.10 | 0.91 | 2.25 |
| 2½ | 2.87 | 1.10 | 3.25 | 1.50 | 3.55 |
| 3 | 3.50 | 1.35 | 4.40 | 2.00 | 4.90 |
| 4 | 4.50 | 1.95 | 7.25 | 3.00 | 8.15 |
| 6 | 6.25 | 3.50 | 15.50 | 5.85 | 17.25 |
| 8 | 8.25 | 5.75 | 26.75 | 8.00 | 28.00 |
| 10 | 10.25 | 8.00 | 40.86 | 10.75 | 41.00 |
| 12 | 12.25 | 10.00 | 57.00 | 13.25 | 57.50 |

**TABLE 9.35** Consumption of Solvent for PVC Pipe

| Pipe size, in. | Joints per gal | ft pipe per gal |
|---|---|---|
| ½ | 1,950 | 19,500 |
| ¾ | 1,175 | 11,750 |
| 1 | 780 | 7,800 |
| 1¼ | 690 | 6,900 |
| 1½ | 505 | 5,050 |
| 2 | 270 | 2,700 |
| 3 | 225 | 2,250 |
| 4 | 165 | 1,650 |
| 6 | 110 | 1,100 |
| 8 | 70 | 700 |

Solvent cost: $22 per gal.

## SCREWED PIPE

Tables 9.36 to 9.41 give estimating data for per-foot units based on plain-end pipe cut and threaded and erected in place with an average number of horizontal and vertical runs and directional changes. *Workhours* includes moving equipment and materials on the jobsite, makeup joints and fittings, and erecting pipe within 10 ft from floor height. Not included are pipe hangers, supports, valves, expansion joints, or specialties. Handling weights are given in Table 9.8.

**TABLE 9.36**  Black Steel Schedule 40 Screwed Pipe

| Pipe size, in. | ¾ | 1 | 1¼ | 1½ | 2 | 2½ |
|---|---|---|---|---|---|---|
| Pipe, per ft, $ | 1.08 | 1.67 | 2.03 | 2.34 | 3.11 | 5.12 |
| Fitting allowance, $ | 0.20 | 0.25 | 0.37 | 0.45 | 0.79 | 1.23 |
| Total material, $ | 1.28 | 1.92 | 2.40 | 2.79 | 3.90 | 6.35 |
| Total workhours | 0.26 | 0.27 | 0.29 | 0.35 | 0.37 | 0.40 |

| Pipe size, in. | 3 | 3½ | 4 | 5 | 6 | |
|---|---|---|---|---|---|---|
| Pipe, per ft, $ | 6.55 | 9.25 | 10.40 | 13.95 | 19.75 | |
| Fitting allowance, $ | 1.85 | 3.45 | 3.65 | 4.75 | 5.80 | |
| Total material, $ | 8.40 | 12.70 | 14.05 | 18.70 | 25.55 | |
| Total workhours | 0.45 | 0.49 | 0.57 | 0.76 | 0.89 | |

**TABLE 9.37**  Black Steel Schedule 80 Screwed Pipe

| Pipe size, in. | ¾ | 1 | 1¼ | 1½ | 2 | 2½ |
|---|---|---|---|---|---|---|
| Pipe, per ft, $ | 1.36 | 1.79 | 2.28 | 2.66 | 3.89 | 6.12 |
| Fitting allowance, $ | 0.49 | 0.60 | 0.77 | 0.97 | 1.35 | 2.27 |
| Total material, $ | 1.85 | 2.39 | 3.05 | 3.63 | 5.24 | 8.39 |
| Total workhours | 0.37 | 0.39 | 0.43 | 0.49 | 0.55 | 0.60 |

| Pipe size, in. | 3 | 3½ | 4 | 5 | 6 | |
|---|---|---|---|---|---|---|
| Pipe, per ft, $ | 8.00 | 10.30 | 12.00 | 23.25 | 28.25 | |
| Fitting allowance, $ | 3.35 | 5.70 | 6.60 | 10.25 | 13.10 | |
| Total material, $ | 11.35 | 16.00 | 18.60 | 33.50 | 41.35 | |
| Total workhours | 0.66 | 0.73 | 0.82 | 1.17 | 1.32 | |

**TABLE 9.38**  Galvanized Steel Schedule 40 Screwed Pipe

| Pipe size, in. | ¾ | 1 | 1¼ | 1½ | 2 | 2½ |
|---|---|---|---|---|---|---|
| Pipe, per ft, $ | 1.31 | 2.11 | 2.53 | 2.90 | 3.85 | 6.50 |
| Fitting allowance, $ | 0.28 | 0.35 | 0.56 | 0.68 | 0.88 | 1.92 |
| Total material, $ | 1.59 | 2.46 | 3.09 | 3.58 | 4.73 | 8.42 |
| Total workhours | 0.26 | 0.27 | 0.29 | 0.35 | 0.37 | 0.40 |

| Pipe size, in. | 3 | 3½ | 4 | 5 | 6 | |
|---|---|---|---|---|---|---|
| Pipe, per ft, $ | 8.50 | 12.05 | 13.50 | 19.35 | 24.50 | |
| Fitting allowance, $ | 2.90 | 5.60 | 6.05 | 6.75 | 9.05 | |
| Total material, $ | 11.40 | 17.65 | 19.55 | 26.10 | 33.55 | |
| Total workhours | 0.45 | 0.49 | 0.57 | 0.76 | 0.89 | |

**TABLE 9.39**   Galvanized Steel Schedule 80 Screwed Pipe

| Pipe size, in. | ¾ | 1 | 1¼ | 1½ | 2 | 2½ |
|---|---|---|---|---|---|---|
| Pipe, per ft, $ | 1.81 | 1.90 | 3.08 | 3.64 | 5.37 | 8.33 |
| Fitting allowance, $ | 0.52 | 0.55 | 0.84 | 1.06 | 1.52 | 2.50 |
| Total material, $ | 2.33 | 2.45 | 3.92 | 4.70 | 6.89 | 10.83 |
| Total workhours | 0.37 | 0.39 | 0.43 | 0.49 | 0.55 | 0.60 |

| Pipe size, in. | 3 | 3½ | 4 | 5 | 6 |
|---|---|---|---|---|---|
| Pipe, per ft, $ | 11.00 | 13.95 | 16.20 | 30.30 | 36.95 |
| Fitting allowance, $ | 3.70 | 6.30 | 7.20 | 11.00 | 13.75 |
| Total material, $ | 14.70 | 20.25 | 23.40 | 41.30 | 50.70 |
| Total workhours | 0.66 | 0.73 | 0.82 | 1.17 | 1.3 |

**TABLE 9.40**   Stainless-Steel Type 304 Schedule 40 Screwed Pipe

| Pipe size, in. | ¾ | 1 | 1¼ | 1½ | 2 | 2½ | 3 | 3½ |
|---|---|---|---|---|---|---|---|---|
| Pipe, per ft, $ | 3.89 | 4.80 | 6.00 | 7.00 | 9.15 | 11.85 | 15.20 | 21.15 |
| Fitting allowance, $ | 0.82 | 0.95 | 1.35 | 1.90 | 2.95 | 6.35 | 8.60 | 13.30 |
| Total material, $ | 4.71 | 5.75 | 7.35 | 8.90 | 12.10 | 18.20 | 23.80 | 34.45 |
| Total workhours | 0.30 | 0.31 | 0.33 | 0.40 | 0.43 | 0.46 | 0.52 | 0.65 |

**TABLE 9.41**   Stainless-Steel Type 304 Schedule 80 Screwed Pipe

| Pipe size, in. | ¾ | 1 | 1¼ | 1½ | 2 |
|---|---|---|---|---|---|
| Pipe, per ft, $ | 5.85 | 7.60 | 10.50 | 12.00 | 15.25 |
| Fitting allowance, $ | 1.00 | 1.35 | 2.15 | 2.95 | 4.85 |
| Total material, $ | 6.85 | 8.95 | 12.65 | 14.95 | 20.10 |
| Total workhours | 0.42 | 0.45 | 0.49 | 0.56 | 0.63 |

# WELDED PIPE

Tables 9.42 and 9.43 give estimating data for per-foot units based on straight-run butt welds for black steel pipe erected in place. *Workhours* includes moving equipment and materials on the jobsite, measuring, cutting, clamping, tacking, and welding. Not included are pipe hangers, supports, valves, expansion joints, fittings, or specialties. Tables 9.44 and 9.45 give check figures for welding equipment and materials.

**TABLE 9.42**   Black Steel Schedule 40 Welded Pipe

| Pipe size, in. | ¾ | 1 | 1¼ | 1½ | 2 | 2½ |
|---|---|---|---|---|---|---|
| Pipe, per ft, $ | 0.97 | 1.52 | 1.85 | 2.09 | 2.82 | 4.48 |
| Total workhours | 0.29 | 0.30 | 0.33 | 0.35 | 0.37 | 0.38 |

| Pipe size, in. | 3 | 4 | 6 | 8 | 10 | 12 |
|---|---|---|---|---|---|---|
| Pipe, per ft, $ | 5.85 | 8.87 | 17.45 | 24.50 | 38.75 | 48.70 |
| Total workhours | 0.40 | 0.50 | 0.69 | 0.90 | 1.15 | 1.40 |

**TABLE 9.43**   Black Steel Schedule 80 Welded Pipe

| Pipe size, in. | ¾ | 1 | 1¼ | 1½ | 2 | 2½ |
|---|---|---|---|---|---|---|
| Pipe, per ft, $ | 1.08 | 1.48 | 1.88 | 2.20 | 3.20 | 5.13 |
| Total workhours | 0.39 | 0.42 | 0.42 | 0.44 | 0.46 | 0.50 |
| Pipe size, in. | 3 | 4 | 6 | 8 | 10 | 12 |
| Pipe, per ft, $ | 6.70 | 10.00 | 24.30 | 43.20 | 56.40 | 58.90 |
| Total workhours | 0.60 | 0.75 | 0.97 | 1.15 | 1.43 | 1.75 |

**TABLE 9.44**   Welding Equipment Rental Cost

| Item | $ per day | $ per week | $ per month |
|---|---|---|---|
| Gas welder, to 300 amp........ | 64 | 190 | 570 |
| Electric welder, to 300 amp .... | 60 | 180 | 540 |
| Oxyacetylene ................. | 20 | 60 | 180 |

**TABLE 9.45**   Consumption of Welding Materials per Joint

| Pipe size, in. | 2 | 2½ | 3 | 3½ | 4 | 6 | 8 | 10 | 12 | 14 |
|---|---|---|---|---|---|---|---|---|---|---|
| Acetylene, cu ft ...... | 2 | 3 | 4 | 6 | 7 | 13 | 20 | 35 | 45 | 50 |
| Oxygen, cu ft ...... | 2 | 3 | 4 | 6 | 7 | 13 | 20 | 35 | 45 | 50 |
| Welding rod, lb ..... | 0.20 | 0.25 | 0.30 | 0.35 | 0.45 | 0.85 | 1.15 | 1.80 | 2.15 | 2.50 |

## VALVES AND SPECIALTIES

Tables 9.46 to 9.52 provide estimating data for valves and specialties based on standard materials. Flanged bolt-ups include inserting gasket, inserting bolts, and making up the joint. Erection includes moving material, erecting, and aligning.

## RECOMMENDED READING

McKetta, John J., ed., *Piping Design Handbook,* Marcel Dekker, New York, 1992.

Mendel, O., *Practical Piping Handbook,* PennWell Publishing Co., Tulsa, Okla., 1981.

Page, J. S., *Estimator's Piping Man-hour Manual,* 4th ed., Gulf Publishing Co., Houston, Tex., 1987.

Peles, C. J., "Controlling Shop-Fabricated Pipe Costs," *1978 Transactions of the American Association of Cost Engineers,* Morgantown, W. Va., 1978.

## ACKNOWLEDGMENT

Portions of the text of this chapter are excerpted by permission from *Moving Water through Pumps and Pipes for HPAC* by John Gladstone, Engineer's Press, Coral Gables, Fla., 1993.

**TABLE 9.46** Flanged Valves and Specialties—Workhours

For making up joint and erecting, per piece.

| Pipe size, in. | 2 | 2½ | 3 | 3½ | 4 | 5 |
|---|---|---|---|---|---|---|
| Erect valve . . . . . . . . | 0.62 | 0.80 | 0.97 | 1.34 | 1.75 | 2.19 |
| Bolt up valve . . . . . . . . | 0.40 | 0.40 | 0.40 | 0.81 | 0.98 | 1.10 |
| Total workhours. . . . . | 1.02 | 1.20 | 1.37 | 2.15 | 2.73 | 3.29 |
| Pipe size, in. | 6 | 8 | 10 | 12 | 14 | 16 |
| Erect valve . . . . . . . . | 2.53 | 3.24 | 3.95 | 4.50 | 5.60 | 7.75 |
| Bolt up valve . . . . . . . . | 1.50 | 1.50 | 2.19 | 2.19 | 2.80 | 3.44 |
| Total workhours. . . . . | 4.03 | 4.74 | 6.14 | 6.69 | 8.40 | 11.19 |
| Pipe size, in. | 2 | 2½ | 3 | 3½ | 4 | 5 |
| Erect special . . . . . . . . | 0.30 | 0.56 | 0.67 | 0.93 | 1.24 | 1.52 |
| Bolt up special . . . . . . . | 0.40 | 0.40 | 0.40 | 0.81 | 0.98 | 1.10 |
| Total workhours. . . . . | 0.70 | 0.96 | 1.07 | 1.74 | 2.22 | 2.62 |
| Pipe size, in. | 6 | 8 | 10 | 12 | 14 | 16 |
| Erect special . . . . . . . . | 1.77 | 2.29 | 2.80 | 3.16 | 3.90 | 4.95 |
| Bolt up special . . . . . . . | 1.50 | 1.50 | 2.19 | 2.19 | 2.80 | 3.44 |
| Total workhours. . . . . | 3.27 | 3.79 | 4.99 | 5.35 | 6.70 | 8.39 |

**TABLE 9.47** Screwed Valves and Specialties—Workhours

For making up joint and erecting, per piece.

| Pipe size, in. | ¼ | ⅜ | ½ | ¾ | 1 | 1½ | 2 |
|---|---|---|---|---|---|---|---|
| Workhours per special . . . . | 0.55 | 0.60 | 0.65 | 0.75 | 0.90 | 1.0 | 1.3 |
| Workhours per valve . . . . . | 0.60 | 0.65 | 0.70 | 0.80 | 0.95 | 1.1 | 1.5 |
| Pipe size, in. | 2½ | 3 | 3½ | 4 | 5 | 6 | |
| Workhours per special. . . . | 1.8 | 3.2 | 3.5 | 3.7 | 4.5 | 5.5 | |
| Workhours per valve. . . . . | 2.0 | 3.5 | 3.8 | 4.0 | 4.8 | 5.9 | |

**TABLE 9.48** Sweat Connection Valves and Specialties—Workhours

For making up joint and erecting, per piece.

| Pipe size, in. | ⅜ | ½ | ⅝ | ¾ | ⅞ | 1⅛ | 1⅜ | 1⅝ |
|---|---|---|---|---|---|---|---|---|
| Workhours per special . . . . | 0.85 | 0.85 | 0.90 | 0.95 | 1.0 | 1.25 | 1.40 | 1.50 |
| Workhours per valve . . . . . | 0.90 | 1.0 | 1.15 | 1.20 | 1.25 | 1.40 | 1.60 | 1.75 |
| Pipe size, in. | 2⅛ | 2⅝ | 3⅛ | 3⅝ | 4⅛ | 5⅛ | 6⅛ | |
| Workhours per special . . . . | 1.90 | 2.25 | 2.50 | 3.0 | 3.5 | 4.7 | 6.0 | |
| Workhours per valve . . . . . | 2.10 | 2.40 | 2.75 | 3.3 | 3.8 | 5.1 | 6.7 | |

**TABLE 9.49** Flanged Valves and Specialties—Material Cost

Based on standard construction and working pressure to 125 lb of steam and 200 lb of cold water, gas, or oil. Does not include bypass or gear accessories for larger-size valves. Dollars per each.

| Pipe size, in. | 2 | 2½ | 3 | 4 | 5 | 6 | 8 | 10 | 12 |
|---|---|---|---|---|---|---|---|---|---|
| Gate, nonrising steam (iron) | 206 | 213 | 239 | 345 | 580 | 580 | 1,025 | 1,800 | 2,450 |
| Globe or angle (iron) | 235 | 250 | 295 | 420 | 750 | 750 | 1,500 | — | — |
| Butterfly, water type (iron) | 65 | 67 | 75 | 98 | 135 | 157 | 212 | 290 | 435 |
| Swing check (iron) | 98 | 125 | 137 | 217 | — | 370 | 700 | 1,200 | 1,850 |
| Plug (semisteel) | 126 | 175 | 207 | 277 | — | 605 | 965 | 1,600 | 2,450 |
| Flange, threaded, iron | 12.90 | 15.10 | 19.40 | 26 | 37 | 42 | 66 | 109 | 175 |
| Gasket and bolt set | 4.73 | 5.00 | 5.25 | 9.50 | 14.10 | 14.80 | 15.80 | 33 | 35 |

**TABLE 9.50** Screwed Joint Valves and Specialties—Material Cost

Based on standard construction and working pressure to 125 lb of steam and 200 lb of cold water, gas, or oil. Dollars per each.

| Pipe size, in. | ½ | ¾ | 1 | 1¼ | 1½ | 2 | 2½ | 3 |
|---|---|---|---|---|---|---|---|---|
| Bronze gate, nonrising steam | 14.70 | 17.50 | 23 | 31 | 38 | 53 | 122 | 171 |
| Bronze globe | 22 | 29 | 46 | 73 | 86 | 131 | 263 | 375 |
| Bronze angle | 36 | 49 | 71 | 92 | 123 | 193 | — | — |
| Bronze ball | 5.85 | 9.70 | 12.20 | 20.50 | 26 | 33 | — | — |
| Bronze swing check | 16.60 | 19.80 | 27.50 | 38 | 45 | 66 | 158 | 235 |
| Brass cock | 5.10 | 6.70 | 10.10 | 17.05 | 24 | 41 | — | — |

**TABLE 9.51** Miscellaneous Items

| Items | $ | Workhours |
|---|---|---|
| Gage cock | 5.35 | 0.45 |
| Dial gage, 2½ in. | 9.40 | 0.20 |
| Thermometer, dial type, 3½ in. | 95.00 | 0.20 |

**TABLE 9.52** Pipe Markers—Valve Tags and Nameplates

| Description | Material, 1994 $ |
|---|---|
| Blank brass tags, 1⁷⁄₁₆-in. diameter with ⁷⁄₁₆-in. hole | 10.75/10 |
| 2-in. diameter with ⁷⁄₁₆-in. hole | 13.00/10 |
| 2-in. square with ⁷⁄₁₆-in. hole | 14.40/10 |
| Prenumbered brass tags, 1¾-in. diameter with ⅛-in. hole | 38.70/25 |
| Brass tag chain, 4¼ in. | 18.40/100 |
| Copper wire lead seals, 10 in. | 27.00/100 |
| Write-on plastic tags (color-coded), 3-in. diameter | 1.45 ea |
| 2½ in. × 2 in. | 1.45 ea |
| 5¾ in. × 3⅜ in. | 1.72 ea |
| Pipe banding tape (color-coded), 1 in. × 180 ft | 11.25/roll |
| 1½ in. × 180 ft | 18.25/roll |
| 2 in. × 180 ft | 23.00/roll |
| 2½ in. × 180 ft | 29.90/roll |
| 3 in. × 180 ft | 34.50/roll |
| Arrow banding tape (color-coded), 2 in. × 18 yd | 23.30/roll |
| 4 in. × 18 yd | 42.00/roll |
| Self-adhesive markers, for pipe or panelboard: | |
| Standard wording, in stock (216 markers, 1 in. × 9 in.) | 62.25 |
| (216 markers, 2 in. × 9 in.) | 69.50 |
| Custom wording, on order (216 markers, 1 in. × 9 in.) | 76.00 |
| (6 roll minimum order) | 83.15 |

# CHAPTER 10
# DUCTWORK

## GENERAL DISCUSSION

The duct system in any air-conditioning installation deserves especially close attention on the part of the estimator, as well as the design engineer, because of its high cost in proportion to the total job.

The initial economics of a duct system are determined by the design engineer, who, working within the prescribed and often severe limitations of structural space, sound attenuation, moisture penetration, and thermal losses, drafts the final design. Average jobs will reflect approximately 30% of the total job cost against the ductwork, erected and insulated. Restaurant and apartment kitchens, toilets, boiler rooms, etc., require exhaust ductwork, which adds considerably to this 30%.

As an air conveyance, a duct can be constructed of almost any material. Certain standards as set by the American Society of Heating, Refrigerating and Air Conditioning Engineers, the National Board of Fire Underwriters, National Warm Air Heating and Air Conditioning Association, and local codes must be followed. Duct materials must be fireproof, free of odors, not subject to disintegration from vapor penetration or air velocity, and moldproof. In recent years a number of new materials with varying degrees of insulating properties have been brought to market.

Some materials used for ducts are

Glass fiber, aluminum board

Glass fiber, prefabricated rectangular sections

Glass fiber, prefabricated round sections

PVC plastic

Fiber-glass-reinforced plastic (FRP)

Vitreous pipe

Cement pipe

Stainless steel

Monel metal

Lead

Lead-coated steel

Copper

Aluminum

Galvanized steel

Aside from some small residential work and special applications requiring handling of corrosive fumes, probably 70% of all duct installations are job-fabricated from galvanized steel or aluminum sheets. About 30% are job-fabricated fibrous glass duct. It may be expected that as the code regulations become less restrictive, the percent of fibrous glass duct systems will increase.

Although the differences in labor and material costs between aluminum and galvanized ducts are significant, one cancels out the other quite evenly. Approximately three times as many pounds of aluminum can be fabricated and erected as pounds of steel can be, but this is offset by the higher cost for aluminum sheets. One may, therefore, use the same method of estimating for either material and make allowances for freight differences due to proximity of fabricating plant.

Prices for sheet-metal ducting trades in 1994 showed the following average skidweight costs in dollars:

| | | | |
|---|---|---|---|
| Galvanized | $80 per cwt | Copper | $968 per cwt |
| Aluminum | $180 per cwt | Stainless steel | $200 per cwt |

Sheet bundles, 4 × 8 ft, have the following average costs, in dollars per hundredweight:

| U.S. gage | Galvanized | Stainless steel | Aluminum |
|---|---|---|---|
| 16 | 80 | 200 | 180 |
| 18 | 80 | 205 | 176 |
| 20 | 81 | 215 | 176 |
| 22 | 81 | 215 | 175 |
| 24 | 83 | 225 | 175 |
| 26 | 84 | 230 | 175 |
| 28 | 86 | — | — |

When the distance between fabricating plant and jobsite is great, it is usual to set up a sheet-metal field shop at the site. Most contractors use the field shop for job-measured pieces only; others prefer to fabricate the entire system in the field. Tables 10.1 and 10.2 list the weights and rigging workhour requirements for setting up the field shop.

**TABLE 10.1** Basic Sheet-Metal Field Shop

Weights shown are average for standard equipment to guide estimator in figuring rigging and trucking costs from warehouse to jobsite. *Workhours* is based on loading, unloading, skidding in place, and leveling. Traveling time for truck is not included.

| Item | Description | Weight, lb | Workhours | Electrical requirements |
|---|---|---|---|---|
| Lock former . . . . . . . | 20 ga capacity | 350 | 1.80 | ¼ hp, 110/220 volts |
| Brake . . . . . . . . . . | 4 ft capacity | 650 | 3.30 | — |
| Easy edger . . . . . . . . | 20 ga capacity | 25 | 0.12 | — |
| Set of rolls . . . . . . . . | 36 in. capacity | 175 | 0.93 | — |
| Hanger maker . . . . . . | — | 150 | 0.80 | — |
| Box of hand tools . . . . | Two—@ 250 lb | 500 | 1.40 | — |
| Total . . . . . . . . . . | — | 1,850 | 8.35 | — |

**TABLE 10.2**  Accessory Sheet-Metal Field Shop

Rigging workhours and electrical requirements for miscellaneous equipment occasionally required for on-job field shop.

| Item | Description | Weight, lb | Workhours | Electrical requirements |
|---|---|---|---|---|
| Lock former | 18 ga capacity | 600 | 4.10 | 2 hp, 220/440 volts |
| Brake | 8 ft capacity | 1,500 | 8.45 | – |
| Jump shear | 4 ft capacity | 1,200 | 6.75 | – |
| Cleat machine | 22 ga capacity | 500 | 2.70 | 1½ hp, 220/440 volts |
| Snap lock machine | 20 ga capacity | 575 | 3.40 | 3 hp, 220/440 volts |
| Band saw | – | 400 | 2.25 | ¾ hp, 110/220 volts |
| Notching machine | – | 1,000 | 5.60 | 3 hp, 220/440 volts |
| Welding machine | 200 amp | 4,000 | 1.64 | – |

Correction factors for varying job conditions are given in Chap. 1; they should be examined carefully by the estimator and adjusted to the peculiarities of each job or phase during the quantity survey.

## ESTIMATING WEIGHTS OF MATERIALS

Because all ductwork estimating is based on weight of material for handling, fabricating, erecting, and hauling, it is necessary to know the weights of all materials used. Tables 10.3 to 10.8 list the weights of materials encountered on most jobs; only a few exotic materials are omitted. The weights and diameters shown are nominal in all cases and may sometimes vary slightly with the manufacturer. When tolerances are critical, the figures should be checked with the manufacturer's submittal data. Figure 10.1 presents a nomograph for quick comparisons of various materials of sheet-metal ductwork in straight runs.

## WEIGHTS AND AREAS OF RECTANGULAR GALVANIZED DUCTS

Table 10.9 is based on commonly used standards, and it includes a 20% allowance for bracing, hangers, waste, and seams. Column 1 gives the total dimensions of the duct rectangle; e.g., 20 in. wide by 19 in. deep equals 39 in. Columns 2 to 6 give the weight of galvanized-iron ducts in pounds per linear foot. Column 8 gives the square feet of surface per linear foot, and it may be used for estimating insulation.

Table 10.10 gives weights and areas of galvanized round ducts.

**TABLE 10.3**  Weights of Steel Sheet Duct Material

| U.S. gage | Decimal | lb per sq ft | lb per sheet 36 x 96 | lb per sheet 48 x 96 | lb per sheet 48 x 120 |
|---|---|---|---|---|---|
| | | | **lb per sheet** | | |
| | | | 36 x 96 | 48 x 96 | 48 x 120 |
| *Galvanized steel* | | | | | |
| 28 | 0.020 | 0.781 | 18.75 | — | — |
| 26 | 0.022 | 0.906 | 21.75 | 29.0 | 36.2 |
| 24 | 0.028 | 1.156 | 27.75 | 37.0 | 46.2 |
| 22 | 0.034 | 1.406 | 33.75 | 45.0 | 56.2 |
| 20 | 0.040 | 1.656 | 39.75 | 53.0 | 66.2 |
| 18 | 0.052 | 2.156 | 51.75 | 70.0 | 86.2 |
| 16 | 0.064 | 2.656 | 63.75 | 85.0 | 102.2 |
| 14 | 0.080 | 3.281 | 78.75 | 105.0 | 131.2 |
| 12 | 0.112 | 4.531 | 108.75 | 145.0 | 181.2 |
| 10 | 0.142 | 5.781 | 138.75 | 185.0 | 231.2 |
| *Hot-rolled steel* | | | | | |
| 26 | 0.018 | 0.750 | 18.0 | 24.0 | 30.0 |
| 24 | 0.024 | 1.000 | 24.0 | 32.0 | 40.0 |
| 22 | 0.030 | 1.250 | 30.0 | 40.0 | 50.0 |
| 20 | 0.036 | 1.500 | 36.0 | 48.0 | 60.0 |
| 18 | 0.048 | 2.000 | 48.0 | 64.0 | 80.0 |
| 16 | 0.057 | 2.500 | 60.0 | 80.0 | 100.0 |
| 14 | 0.075 | 3.125 | 75.0 | 100.0 | 125.0 |
| 12 | 0.108 | 4.250 | 102.0 | 138.0 | 170.0 |
| 10 | 0.135 | 5.625 | 137.0 | 180.0 | 225.0 |
| *Stainless steel* | | | | | |
| 28 | 0.016 | 0.66 | 15.8 | 21.1 | 26.4 |
| 26 | 0.019 | 0.79 | 18.9 | 25.2 | 31.6 |
| 24 | 0.025 | 1.05 | 25.2 | 33.6 | 42.0 |
| 22 | 0.031 | 1.31 | 31.5 | 42.0 | 52.5 |
| 20 | 0.038 | 1.58 | 37.8 | 50.4 | 63.0 |
| 18 | 0.050 | 2.10 | 50.4 | 61.2 | 84.0 |
| 16 | 0.063 | 2.63 | 63.0 | 84.0 | 105.0 |
| 14 | 0.078 | 3.28 | 78.7 | 104.9 | 131.2 |
| 12 | 0.109 | 4.60 | 110.0 | 147.0 | 183.8 |

**TABLE 10.4**   Weights of Nonferrous Sheet Duct Material

| B & S gage | Decimal | lb per sq ft | lb per sheet | | |
|---|---|---|---|---|---|
| | | | 36 x 96 | 48 x 96 | 48 x 120 |
| Aluminum 3003 | | | | | |
| 26 | 0.016 | 0.226 | 5.4 | 7.2 | 9.0 |
| 24 | 0.020 | 0.282 | 6.8 | 9.0 | 11.3 |
| 22 | 0.025 | 0.357 | 8.6 | 11.4 | 14.3 |
| 20 | 0.032 | 0.450 | 10.8 | 14.4 | 18.0 |
| 18 | 0.040 | 0.568 | 13.6 | 18.7 | 22.7 |
| 16 | 0.051 | 0.716 | 17.2 | 22.9 | 28.6 |
| 14 | 0.064 | 0.903 | 21.7 | 28.9 | 36.1 |
| 12 | 0.071 | 1.000 | 24.0 | 32.0 | 40.0 |
| 10 | 0.080 | 1.130 | 27.1 | 36.2 | 45.2 |

| B & S gage | Decimal | oz per sq ft | lb per sheet | | |
|---|---|---|---|---|---|
| | | | 36 x 96 | 48 x 96 | 48 x 120 |
| Cold-rolled copper | | | | | |
| 24 | 0.021 | 16 | 24 | 32 | 40 |
| 23 | 0.024 | 18 | 30 | 40 | 50 |
| 20 | 0.032 | 24 | 36 | 48 | 64 |
| 18 | 0.040 | 30 | 48 | 64 | 80 |
| 16 | 0.051 | 38 | 54 | 72 | 90 |
| 15 | 0.053 | 40 | 60 | 80 | 100 |

**TABLE 10.5**   Weights of Galvanized-Steel Bands

| Band size, in. | lb per lin ft |
|---|---|
| $\frac{1}{8}$ x 1 | 0.425 |
| $\frac{1}{8}$ x $1\frac{1}{4}$ | 0.531 |
| $\frac{1}{8}$ x $1\frac{1}{2}$ | 0.638 |
| $\frac{1}{8}$ x 2 | 0.850 |
| $\frac{3}{16}$ x 1 | 0.670 |
| $\frac{3}{16}$ x $1\frac{1}{4}$ | 0.837 |
| $\frac{3}{16}$ x $1\frac{1}{2}$ | 1.00 |
| $\frac{3}{16}$ x 2 | 1.34 |
| $\frac{1}{4}$ x 1 | 0.90 |
| $\frac{1}{4}$ x $1\frac{1}{2}$ | 1.35 |
| $\frac{1}{4}$ x 2 | 1.78 |

**TABLE 10.6** Weights of Metal Angles, Equal Legs, lb/lin ft

| Size, in. | Galvanized steel | Hot-rolled steel | Aluminum |
|---|---|---|---|
| $\frac{1}{8}$ x 1 | 0.84 | 0.80 | 0.28 |
| $\frac{1}{8}$ x $1\frac{1}{4}$ | 1.06 | 1.01 | 0.36 |
| $\frac{1}{8}$ x $1\frac{1}{2}$ | 1.29 | 1.23 | 0.44 |
| $\frac{1}{8}$ x $1\frac{3}{4}$ | 1.51 | 1.44 | 0.51 |
| $\frac{1}{8}$ x 2 | 1.73 | 1.65 | 0.59 |
| $\frac{3}{16}$ x 1 | 1.22 | 1.16 | 0.41 |
| $\frac{3}{16}$ x $1\frac{1}{4}$ | 1.55 | 1.48 | 0.53 |
| $\frac{3}{16}$ x $1\frac{1}{2}$ | 1.89 | 1.80 | 0.64 |
| $\frac{3}{16}$ x $1\frac{3}{4}$ | 2.23 | 2.12 | 0.75 |
| $\frac{3}{16}$ x 2 | 2.56 | 2.44 | 0.87 |
| $\frac{1}{4}$ x $1\frac{1}{2}$ | 2.46 | 2.34 | 0.83 |
| $\frac{1}{4}$ x $1\frac{3}{4}$ | 2.91 | 2.77 | 0.98 |
| $\frac{1}{4}$ x 2 | 3.35 | 3.19 | 1.14 |
| $\frac{1}{4}$ x $2\frac{1}{2}$ | 4.26 | 4.10 | 1.45 |
| $\frac{1}{4}$ x 3 | 5.15 | 4.90 | 1.70 |
| $\frac{3}{8}$ x 2 | 4.93 | 4.70 | 1.65 |
| $\frac{3}{8}$ x $2\frac{1}{2}$ | 6.20 | 5.90 | 2.11 |
| $\frac{3}{8}$ x 3 | 7.55 | 7.20 | 2.55 |

**TABLE 10.7** Weights of Floor Plates, Skid-Resistant, Raised Pattern

| Thickness, in. | $\frac{1}{8}$ | $\frac{3}{16}$ | $\frac{1}{4}$ | $\frac{5}{16}$ | $\frac{3}{8}$ | $\frac{7}{16}$ | $\frac{1}{2}$ | $\frac{5}{8}$ | $\frac{3}{4}$ | $\frac{7}{8}$ | 1 |
|---|---|---|---|---|---|---|---|---|---|---|---|
| lb per sq ft . . . | 6.15 | 8.70 | 11.25 | 13.80 | 16.35 | 18.90 | 21.45 | 26.55 | 31.65 | 36.75 | 41.85 |

**TABLE 10.8** Weights of Round Hanger Rod, Threaded Ends

| Diameter, in. | lb per lin ft | | |
|---|---|---|---|
| | Steel | Aluminum | Brass |
| $\frac{1}{4}$ | 0.167 | 0.06 | 0.181 |
| $\frac{5}{16}$ | 0.261 | 0.09 | 0.283 |
| $\frac{3}{8}$ | 0.376 | 0.13 | 0.407 |
| $\frac{7}{16}$ | 0.511 | 0.18 | 0.554 |
| $\frac{1}{2}$ | 0.668 | 0.24 | 0.723 |
| $\frac{5}{8}$ | 1.043 | 0.37 | 1.130 |
| $\frac{3}{4}$ | 1.502 | 0.54 | 1.163 |
| $\frac{7}{8}$ | 2.044 | 0.73 | 2.220 |
| 1 | 2.670 | 0.96 | 2.900 |
| $1\frac{1}{4}$ | 4.172 | 1.50 | 4.520 |

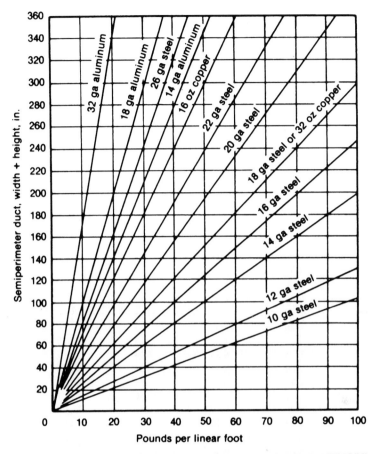

**Figure 10.1  WEIGHTS OF ALUMINUM, STEEL, AND COPPER DUCTWORK FOR STRAIGHT RUNS, IN POUNDS PER LINEAR FOOT**
*No allowances included. Add 20% allowance to each item for bracing and waste. For fittings, add the following:*

| | |
|---|---|
| *90° elbow* | *3 ft* |
| *45° elbow* | *2.5 ft* |
| *Offset* | *4 ft* |
| *Transition offset* | *6 ft* |
| *Square-to-round transition* | *4 ft* |
| *Reducing elbow* | *5 ft* |

**TABLE 10.9** Weights and Areas of Rectangular Galvanized Ducts

| Width + depth, total in. | 26-gage, largest dimension through 12 in. | 24-gage, largest dimension through 30 in. | 22-gage, largest dimension through 54 in. | 20-gage, largest dimension through 84 in. | 18-gage, largest dimension over 84 in. | 16-gage, largest dimension over 84 in. | sq ft/ lin ft |
|---|---|---|---|---|---|---|---|
| 10 | 1.89 | 2.42 | 2.95 | — | — | — | 1.67 |
| 11 | 2.09 | 2.65 | 3.23 | — | — | — | 1.83 |
| 12 | 2.28 | 2.90 | 3.54 | — | — | — | 2.00 |
| 13 | 2.47 | 3.14 | 3.83 | — | — | — | 2.17 |
| 14 | 2.65 | 3.39 | 4.13 | — | — | — | 2.34 |
| 15 | 2.85 | 3.62 | 4.42 | — | — | — | 2.50 |
| 16 | 3.04 | 3.83 | 4.72 | — | — | — | 2.67 |
| 17 | 3.22 | 4.10 | 5.00 | — | — | — | 2.83 |
| 18 | 3.42 | 4.35 | 5.30 | — | — | — | 3.00 |
| 19 | 3.61 | 4.58 | 5.59 | — | — | — | 3.17 |
| 20 | 3.80 | 4.84 | 5.88 | — | — | — | 3.34 |
| 21 | 4.00 | 5.06 | 6.18 | — | — | — | 3.50 |
| 22 | 4.18 | 5.30 | 6.47 | — | — | — | 3.67 |
| 23 | 4.36 | 5.55 | 6.77 | — | — | — | 3.83 |
| 24 | 4.56 | 5.80 | 7.06 | — | — | — | 4.00 |
| 25 | 4.76 | 6.02 | 7.35 | — | — | — | 4.17 |
| 26 | 4.95 | 6.28 | 7.65 | — | — | — | 4.34 |
| 27 | — | 6.52 | 7.95 | 8.70 | 12.10 | — | 4.50 |
| 28 | — | 6.75 | 8.24 | 9.04 | 12.55 | — | 4.67 |
| 29 | — | 7.00 | 8.54 | 9.35 | 13.00 | — | 4.83 |
| 30 | — | 7.24 | 8.82 | 9.80 | 13.65 | — | 5.00 |
| 31 | — | 7.47 | 9.12 | 10.30 | 14.05 | — | 5.17 |
| 32 | — | 7.72 | 9.42 | 10.40 | 14.50 | — | 5.34 |
| 33 | — | 7.95 | 9.79 | 10.75 | 14.95 | — | 5.50 |
| 34 | — | 8.20 | 10.00 | 11.00 | 15.35 | — | 5.67 |
| 35 | — | 8.45 | 10.30 | 11.30 | 15.80 | — | 5.83 |
| 36 | — | 8.67 | 10.60 | 11.70 | 16.25 | — | 6.00 |
| 37 | — | 8.95 | 10.90 | 12.00 | 16.66 | — | 6.17 |
| 38 | — | 9.18 | 11.20 | 12.30 | 17.05 | — | 6.34 |
| 39 | — | 9.40 | 11.50 | 12.60 | 17.50 | — | 6.50 |
| 40 | — | 9.65 | 11.80 | 12.90 | 17.96 | — | 6.67 |
| 41 | — | 9.90 | 12.10 | 13.24 | 18.38 | — | 6.83 |
| 42 | — | 10.15 | 12.35 | 13.56 | 18.85 | — | 7.00 |
| 43 | — | 10.40 | 12.65 | 13.80 | 19.25 | — | 7.17 |
| 44 | — | 10.60 | 13.00 | 14.20 | 19.84 | — | 7.34 |
| 45 | — | 10.85 | 13.25 | 14.65 | 20.25 | — | 7.50 |
| 46 | — | 11.10 | 13.50 | 14.90 | 20.75 | — | 7.67 |
| 47 | — | 11.35 | 13.80 | 15.25 | 21.20 | — | 7.83 |
| 48 | — | 11.60 | 14.10 | 15.50 | 21.60 | 26.55 | 8.00 |
| 49 | — | 11.80 | 14.40 | 15.90 | 22.00 | 27.10 | 8.17 |
| 50 | — | 12.10 | 14.70 | 16.20 | 22.55 | 27.61 | 8.34 |
| 51 | — | 12.30 | 15.00 | 16.50 | 22.95 | 28.15 | 8.50 |
| 52 | — | 12.55 | 15.30 | 16.80 | 23.45 | 28.67 | 8.67 |
| 53 | — | 12.80 | 15.60 | 17.15 | 23.90 | 29.20 | 8.83 |
| 54 | — | 13.00 | 15.90 | 17.50 | 24.30 | 29.74 | 9.00 |
| 55 | — | 13.25 | 16.20 | 17.80 | 24.85 | 30.27 | 9.17 |

**TABLE 10.9**  Weights and Areas of Rectangular Galvanized Ducts   (*Continued*)

| Width + depth, total in. | 26-gage, largest dimension through 12 in. | 24-gage, largest dimension through 30 in. | 22-gage, largest dimension through 54 in. | 20-gage, largest dimension through 84 in. | 18-gage, largest dimension over 84 in. | 16-gage, largest dimension over 84 in. | sq ft/ lin ft |
|---|---|---|---|---|---|---|---|
| 56 | — | 13.50 | 16.50 | 18.10 | 25.15 | 30.80 | 9.34 |
| 57 | — | 13.75 | 16.80 | 18.40 | 25.55 | 31.30 | 9.50 |
| 58 | — | 14.00 | 17.10 | 18.70 | 26.00 | 31.85 | 9.67 |
| 59 | — | 14.25 | 17.40 | 19.00 | 26.55 | 32.40 | 9.83 |
| 60 | — | 14.50 | 17.70 | 19.50 | 26.90 | 33.19 | 10.00 |
| 61 | — | — | 18.00 | 19.80 | 27.45 | 33.75 | 10.17 |
| 62 | — | — | 18.30 | 20.10 | 27.75 | 34.25 | 10.34 |
| 63 | — | — | 18.50 | 20.40 | 28.15 | 34.78 | 10.50 |
| 64 | — | — | 18.80 | 20.75 | 28.65 | 35.32 | 10.67 |
| 65 | — | — | 19.10 | 21.00 | 29.10 | 35.85 | 10.83 |
| 66 | — | — | 19.40 | 21.35 | 29.55 | 36.38 | 11.00 |
| 67 | — | — | 19.70 | 21.65 | 30.00 | 36.90 | 11.17 |
| 68 | — | — | 20.00 | 22.20 | 30.45 | 37.44 | 11.34 |
| 69 | — | — | 20.30 | 22.50 | 30.90 | 38.00 | 11.50 |
| 70 | — | — | 20.50 | 23.00 | 31.30 | 38.50 | 11.67 |
| 71 | — | — | 20.80 | 23.20 | 31.70 | 39.00 | 11.83 |
| 72 | — | — | 21.10 | 23.50 | 32.15 | 39.55 | 12.00 |
| 73 | — | — | 21.40 | 24.00 | 32.55 | 40.00 | 12.17 |
| 74 | — | — | 21.80 | 24.20 | 32.90 | 40.62 | 12.34 |
| 75 | — | — | 22.00 | 24.50 | 33.20 | 41.42 | 12.50 |
| 76 | — | — | 22.30 | 24.85 | 33.75 | 42.00 | 12.67 |
| 77 | — | — | 22.60 | 25.10 | 34.15 | 42.48 | 12.83 |
| 78 | — | — | 22.90 | 25.50 | 34.65 | 43.00 | 13.00 |
| 79 | — | — | 23.20 | 25.80 | 35.10 | 43.54 | 13.17 |
| 80 | — | — | 23.50 | 26.04 | 35.55 | 44.00 | 13.34 |
| 81 | — | — | 23.80 | 26.52 | 36.00 | 44.60 | 13.50 |
| 82 | — | — | 24.10 | 26.90 | 36.45 | 45.10 | 13.67 |
| 83 | — | — | 24.40 | 27.10 | 36.90 | 45.65 | 13.83 |
| 84 | — | — | 24.70 | 27.60 | 37.30 | 46.20 | 14.00 |
| 85 | — | — | 25.00 | 27.90 | 37.70 | 46.70 | 14.17 |
| 86 | — | — | 25.30 | 28.10 | 38.15 | 47.25 | 14.34 |
| 87 | — | — | 25.60 | 28.50 | 38.65 | 47.80 | 14.50 |
| 88 | — | — | 25.80 | 28.83 | 39.00 | 48.30 | 14.67 |
| 89 | — | — | 26.10 | 29.06 | 39.50 | 48.85 | 14.83 |
| 90 | — | — | 26.40 | 29.42 | 39.90 | 49.60 | 15.00 |
| 91 | — | — | 26.70 | 30.10 | 41.00 | 50.20 | 15.17 |
| 92 | — | — | 26.80 | 31.00 | 41.20 | 50.70 | 15.34 |
| 93 | — | — | 27.40 | 31.20 | 41.90 | 51.25 | 15.50 |
| 94 | — | — | 27.60 | 31.50 | 42.00 | 51.75 | 15.67 |
| 95 | — | — | 27.90 | 31.90 | 42.85 | 52.30 | 15.83 |
| 96 | — | — | 28.20 | 32.00 | 43.10 | 52.85 | 16.00 |
| 97 | — | — | 28.50 | 32.40 | 43.50 | 53.35 | 16.17 |
| 98 | — | — | 28.80 | 32.70 | 44.00 | 53.90 | 16.34 |
| 99 | — | — | 29.10 | 33.00 | 44.50 | 54.45 | 16.50 |
| 100 | — | — | 29.30 | 33.25 | 45.00 | 55.00 | 16.67 |
| 101 | — | — | 29.60 | 34.00 | 45.60 | 55.55 | 16.83 |

(*Continued*)

**TABLE 10.9** Weights and Areas of Rectangular Galvanized Ducts   (*Continued*)

| Width + depth, total in. | 26-gage, largest dimension through 12 in. | 24-gage, largest dimension through 30 in. | 22-gage, largest dimension through 54 in. | 20-gage, largest dimension through 84 in. | 18-gage, largest dimension over 84 in. | 16-gage, largest dimension over 84 in. | sq ft/ lin ft |
|---|---|---|---|---|---|---|---|
| 102 | — | — | 29.85 | 34.40 | 45.90 | 56.00 | 17.00 |
| 103 | — | — | 30.02 | 34.80 | 46.10 | 56.55 | 17.17 |
| 104 | — | — | 30.08 | 34.95 | 46.50 | 57.00 | 17.34 |
| 105 | — | — | 30.15 | 35.10 | 47.00 | 57.85 | 17.50 |
| 106 | — | — | 30.30 | 35.30 | 47.75 | 58.40 | 17.67 |
| 107 | — | — | 30.50 | 35.50 | 48.00 | 58.94 | 17.83 |
| 108 | — | — | 30.70 | 35.85 | 48.20 | 59.45 | 18.00 |
| 109 | — | — | 31.08 | 36.20 | 49.00 | 60.00 | 18.17 |
| 110 | — | — | 31.55 | 36.60 | 49.50 | 60.55 | 18.34 |
| 111 | — | — | 31.87 | 36.96 | 49.90 | 61.00 | 18.50 |
| 112 | — | — | 32.06 | 37.10 | 50.18 | 61.60 | 18.67 |
| 113 | — | — | 32.25 | 37.38 | 50.40 | 62.10 | 18.83 |
| 114 | — | — | 32.46 | 37.80 | 50.90 | 62.65 | 19.00 |
| 115 | — | — | 33.00 | 38.04 | 51.22 | 63.20 | 19.17 |
| 116 | — | — | 33.37 | 38.50 | 52.03 | 63.75 | 19.34 |
| 117 | — | — | 33.70 | 38.86 | 52.50 | 64.25 | 19.50 |
| 118 | — | — | 33.88 | 39.00 | 52.86 | 64.80 | 19.67 |
| 119 | — | — | 34.03 | 39.34 | 53.00 | 65.30 | 19.83 |
| 120 | — | — | 34.75 | 40.00 | 53.80 | 66.15 | 20.00 |

## WEIGHTS AND AREAS OF RECTANGULAR ALUMINUM DUCTS

Table 10.11, which is based on commonly used standards, includes a 20% allowance for bracing, hangers, waste, and seams. Column 1 gives the total dimensions of the duct rectangle; e.g., 20 in. wide by 19 in. deep equals 39 in. Columns 2 to 4 give the weight of aluminum in pounds per linear foot. Column 5 gives the square feet per linear foot, and it may be used for estimating insulation.

Tables 10.12 and 10.13 give the weights and costs of prefabricated high-velocity spiral and round ducts, respectively, and Table 10.14 gives cost data on flexible spiral ducts.

**TABLE 10.10**  Weights and Areas of Galvanized Round Ducts

Based on commonly used standards; includes allowance for waste and seams.

| Diameter, in. | sq ft per lin ft | Gage | | | | |
|---|---|---|---|---|---|---|
| | | 26 | 24 | 22 | 20 | 18 |
| | | lb per lin ft | | | | |
| 4 | 1.05 | 1.13 | 1.47 | 1.69 | 1.97 | 2.56 |
| 5 | 1.31 | 1.39 | 1.80 | 2.08 | 2.43 | 3.19 |
| 6 | 1.57 | 1.65 | 2.14 | 2.47 | 2.89 | 3.76 |
| 7 | 1.83 | 1.91 | 2.48 | 2.86 | 3.34 | 4.39 |
| 8 | 2.09 | 2.18 | 2.83 | 3.27 | 3.81 | 5.01 |
| 9 | 2.36 | 2.44 | 3.17 | 3.66 | 4.27 | 5.61 |
| 10 | 2.62 | 2.79 | 3.51 | 4.05 | 4.72 | 6.21 |
| 11 | 2.88 | 2.96 | 3.85 | 4.41 | 5.18 | 6.80 |
| 12 | 3.15 | 3.22 | 4.18 | 4.83 | 5.63 | 7.40 |
| 13 | 3.40 | 3.48 | 4.52 | 5.22 | 6.09 | 8.00 |
| 14 | 3.67 | 3.74 | 4.86 | 5.61 | 6.54 | 8.60 |
| 15 | 3.93 | 4.01 | 5.21 | 6.01 | 7.01 | 9.22 |
| 16 | 4.19 | 4.27 | 5.55 | 6.40 | 7.47 | 9.82 |
| 17 | 4.45 | 4.53 | 5.85 | 6.79 | 7.92 | 10.42 |
| 18 | 4.72 | 4.87 | 6.33 | 7.30 | 8.51 | 11.18 |
| 19 | 4.98 | 5.14 | 6.68 | 7.71 | 9.00 | 11.80 |
| 20 | 5.24 | 5.40 | 7.02 | 8.10 | 9.45 | 12.42 |
| 21 | 5.50 | 5.59 | 7.10 | 8.39 | 9.78 | 12.85 |
| 22 | 5.76 | 5.92 | 7.26 | 8.88 | 10.35 | 13.60 |
| 23 | 6.02 | 6.18 | 8.04 | 9.21 | 10.81 | 14.40 |
| 24 | 6.28 | 6.45 | 8.38 | 9.61 | 11.30 | 14.84 |
| 25 | 6.54 | 6.71 | 8.70 | 10.06 | 11.74 | 15.41 |
| 26 | 6.80 | 6.97 | 9.05 | 10.45 | 12.20 | 16.00 |
| 27 | 7.07 | 7.33 | 9.40 | 10.85 | 12.61 | 16.62 |
| 28 | 7.33 | 7.50 | 9.75 | 11.21 | 13.13 | 17.26 |
| 29 | 7.59 | 7.75 | 10.00 | 11.63 | 13.58 | 17.81 |
| 30 | 7.85 | 8.10 | 10.54 | 12.17 | 14.20 | 18.62 |
| 31 | 8.11 | 8.36 | 10.81 | 12.54 | 14.63 | 19.20 |
| 32 | 8.38 | 8.62 | 11.20 | 12.93 | 15.10 | 19.84 |
| 33 | 8.65 | 8.88 | 11.56 | 13.34 | 15.56 | 20.42 |
| 34 | 8.91 | 9.15 | 11.90 | 13.73 | 16.00 | 21.08 |
| 35 | 9.17 | 9.41 | 12.23 | 14.10 | 16.49 | 21.65 |
| 36 | 9.43 | 9.67 | 12.57 | 14.50 | 16.91 | 22.22 |
| 37 | 9.69 | 9.93 | 12.91 | 14.90 | 17.40 | 22.84 |
| 38 | 9.95 | 10.19 | 13.25 | 15.29 | 17.81 | 23.40 |
| 39 | 10.21 | 10.46 | 13.60 | 15.60 | 18.31 | 24.02 |
| 40 | 10.47 | 10.72 | 13.95 | 16.08 | 18.76 | 24.68 |

**TABLE 10.11**  Weights and Areas of Rectangular Aluminum Ducts

| (1)<br><br>Width + depth,<br>total in. | (2)<br>22 ga,<br>largest dimension<br>to 30 in. | (3)<br>20 ga,<br>largest dimension<br>through 54 in. | (4)<br>18 ga,<br>largest dimension<br>through 84 in. | (5)<br>Square ft<br>per<br>lin ft |
|---|---|---|---|---|
| 22 | 1.75 | 2.40 | — | 3.67 |
| 23 | 1.81 | 2.50 | — | 3.83 |
| 24 | 1.90 | 2.60 | — | 4.00 |
| 25 | 1.96 | 2.70 | — | 4.17 |
| 26 | 2.02 | 2.80 | — | 4.34 |
| 27 | 2.10 | 2.90 | — | 4.50 |
| 28 | 2.18 | 3.00 | — | 4.67 |
| 29 | 2.26 | 3.10 | — | 4.83 |
| 30 | 2.32 | 3.20 | — | 5.00 |
| 31 | 2.38 | 3.30 | — | 5.17 |
| 32 | 2.46 | 3.40 | — | 5.34 |
| 33 | 2.53 | 3.50 | — | 5.50 |
| 34 | 2.61 | 3.60 | — | 5.67 |
| 35 | 2.69 | 3.70 | — | 5.83 |
| 36 | 2.75 | 3.80 | — | 6.00 |
| 37 | 2.82 | 3.90 | — | 6.17 |
| 38 | 2.90 | 4.00 | — | 6.34 |
| 39 | 2.99 | 4.12 | — | 6.50 |
| 40 | 3.08 | 4.25 | 5.60 | 6.67 |
| 41 | 3.18 | 4.37 | 5.70 | 6.83 |
| 42 | 3.26 | 4.50 | 5.80 | 7.00 |
| 43 | 3.34 | 4.60 | 5.95 | 7.17 |
| 44 | 3.41 | 4.70 | 6.10 | 7.34 |
| 45 | 3.48 | 4.80 | 6.25 | 7.50 |
| 46 | 3.55 | 4.90 | 6.40 | 7.67 |
| 47 | 3.62 | 5.00 | 6.55 | 7.83 |
| 48 | 3.66 | 5.10 | 6.65 | 8.00 |
| 49 | 3.75 | 5.22 | 6.82 | 8.17 |
| 50 | 3.84 | 5.35 | 6.90 | 8.34 |
| 51 | 3.91 | 5.42 | 7.05 | 8.50 |
| 52 | 3.98 | 5.50 | 7.20 | 8.67 |
| 53 | 4.10 | 5.65 | 7.37 | 8.83 |

**TABLE 10.11**  Weights and Areas of Rectangular Aluminum Ducts  (*Continued*)

| (1)<br>Width + depth,<br>total in. | (2)<br>22 ga,<br>largest dimension<br>to 30 in. | (3)<br>20 ga,<br>largest dimension<br>through 54 in. | (4)<br>18 ga,<br>largest dimension<br>through 84 in. | (5)<br>Square ft<br>per<br>lin ft |
|---|---|---|---|---|
| 54 | 4.20 | 5.80 | 7.55 | 9.00 |
| 55 | 4.29 | 5.90 | 7.65 | 9.17 |
| 56 | 4.35 | 6.00 | 7.75 | 9.34 |
| 57 | 4.43 | 6.10 | 7.87 | 9.50 |
| 58 | 4.50 | 6.20 | 8.00 | 9.67 |
| 59 | 4.58 | 6.30 | 8.15 | 9.83 |
| 60 | 4.64 | 6.40 | 8.30 | 10.00 |

| (1)<br>Width + depth,<br>total in. | (2)<br>20 ga,<br>largest dimension<br>to 54 in. | (3)<br>18 ga,<br>largest dimension<br>through 84 in. | (4)<br>16 ga,<br>largest dimension<br>over 84 in. | (5)<br>Square ft<br>per<br>lin ft |
|---|---|---|---|---|
| 61 | 6.50 | 8.42 | — | 10.17 |
| 62 | 6.60 | 8.55 | — | 10.34 |
| 63 | 6.70 | 8.70 | — | 10.50 |
| 64 | 6.80 | 8.85 | — | 10.67 |
| 65 | 6.90 | 8.92 | — | 10.83 |
| 66 | 7.01 | 9.10 | — | 11.00 |
| 67 | 7.11 | 9.25 | — | 11.17 |
| 68 | 7.24 | 9.40 | — | 11.34 |
| 69 | 7.32 | 9.52 | — | 11.50 |
| 70 | 7.44 | 9.65 | — | 11.67 |
| 71 | 7.53 | 9.77 | — | 11.83 |
| 72 | 7.65 | 9.90 | 12.25 | 12.00 |
| 73 | 7.75 | 10.05 | 12.42 | 12.17 |
| 74 | 7.88 | 10.22 | 12.60 | 12.34 |
| 75 | 7.95 | 10.35 | 12.80 | 12.50 |
| 76 | 8.10 | 10.50 | 13.00 | 12.67 |
| 77 | 8.20 | 10.62 | 13.10 | 12.83 |
| 78 | 8.30 | 10.75 | 13.20 | 13.00 |
| 79 | 8.40 | 10.87 | 13.40 | 13.17 |
| 80 | 8.49 | 11.00 | 13.60 | 13.34 |
| 81 | 8.61 | 11.20 | 13.75 | 13.50 |
| 82 | 8.73 | 11.40 | 13.90 | 13.67 |
| 83 | 8.86 | 11.50 | 14.10 | 13.83 |
| 84 | 8.94 | 11.60 | 14.30 | 14.00 |
| 85 | 9.00 | 11.70 | 14.47 | 14.17 |
| 86 | 9.10 | 11.80 | 14.65 | 14.34 |
| 87 | 9.16 | 11.90 | 14.82 | 14.50 |
| 88 | 9.25 | 12.00 | 15.00 | 14.67 |
| 89 | 9.38 | 12.20 | 15.20 | 14.83 |
| 90 | 9.55 | 12.40 | 15.40 | 15.00 |
| 91 | 9.68 | 12.57 | 15.50 | 15.17 |
| 92 | 9.80 | 12.75 | 15.60 | 15.34 |
| 93 | 9.91 | 12.87 | 15.80 | 15.50 |
| 94 | 10.00 | 13.00 | 16.00 | 15.67 |
| 95 | 10.09 | 13.15 | 16.23 | 15.83 |

(*Continued*)

**TABLE 10.11**   Weights and Areas of Rectangular Aluminum Ducts   (*Continued*)

| (1) Width + depth, total in. | (2) 20 ga, largest dimension to 54 in. | (3) 18 ga, largest dimension through 84 in. | (4) 16 ga, largest dimension over 84 in. | (5) Square ft per lin ft |
|---|---|---|---|---|
| 96 | 10.19 | 13.22 | 16.45 | 16.00 |
| 97 | 10.28 | 13.30 | 16.62 | 16.17 |
| 98 | 10.39 | 13.55 | 16.80 | 16.34 |
| 99 | 10.53 | 13.75 | 17.00 | 16.50 |
| 100 | 10.65 | 14.00 | 17.20 | 16.67 |
| 101 | 10.78 | 14.10 | 17.35 | 16.83 |
| 102 | 10.90 | 14.20 | 17.50 | 17.00 |
| 103 | 11.00 | 14.30 | 17.65 | 17.17 |
| 104 | 11.10 | 14.40 | 17.80 | 17.34 |
| 105 | 11.20 | 14.52 | 18.00 | 17.50 |
| 106 | 11.30 | 14.65 | 18.20 | 17.67 |
| 107 | 11.40 | 14.82 | 18.35 | 17.83 |
| 108 | 11.50 | 15.00 | 18.50 | 18.00 |
| 109 | 11.60 | 15.13 | 18.65 | 18.17 |
| 110 | 11.70 | 15.25 | 18.80 | 18.34 |
| 111 | 11.81 | 15.37 | 18.95 | 18.50 |
| 112 | 11.91 | 15.50 | 19.10 | 18.67 |
| 113 | 12.02 | 15.67 | 19.22 | 18.83 |
| 114 | 12.12 | 15.75 | 19.35 | 19.00 |

| (1) Width + depth, total in. | (2) 18 ga, largest dimension through 84 in. | (3) 16 ga, largest dimension over 84 in. | (4) Square ft per lin ft |
|---|---|---|---|
| 115 | 15.92 | 19.60 | 19.17 |
| 116 | 16.10 | 19.80 | 19.34 |
| 117 | 16.20 | 19.95 | 19.50 |
| 118 | 16.30 | 20.10 | 19.67 |
| 119 | 16.45 | 20.25 | 19.83 |
| 120 | 16.60 | 20.45 | 20.00 |
| 122 | 16.75 | 20.80 | 20.33 |
| 124 | 16.92 | 21.10 | 20.66 |
| 126 | 17.15 | 21.40 | 21.00 |
| 128 | 17.50 | 21.80 | 21.33 |
| 130 | 17.80 | 22.20 | 21.66 |
| 132 | 18.10 | 22.60 | 22.00 |
| 134 | 18.30 | 22.80 | 22.33 |
| 136 | 18.65 | 23.16 | 22.66 |
| 138 | 18.86 | 23.50 | 23.00 |
| 140 | 19.10 | 23.88 | 23.33 |
| 142 | 19.50 | 24.20 | 23.66 |
| 144 | 19.75 | 24.60 | 24.00 |
| 146 | 20.00 | 25.00 | 24.33 |
| 148 | 20.24 | 25.40 | 24.66 |
| 150 | 20.60 | 25.75 | 25.00 |
| 152 | 20.80 | 25.98 | 25.33 |

**TABLE 10.11** Weights and Areas of Rectangular Aluminum Ducts (*Continued*)

| (1)<br>Width + depth,<br>total in. | (2)<br>18 ga,<br>largest dimension<br>through 84 in. | (3)<br>16 ga,<br>largest dimension<br>over 84 in. | (4)<br>Square ft<br>per<br>lin ft |
|---|---|---|---|
| 154 | 21.10 | 26.23 | 25.66 |
| 156 | 21.37 | 26.60 | 26.00 |
| 158 | 21.62 | 27.00 | 26.33 |
| 160 | 21.95 | 27.40 | 26.66 |
| 162 | 22.16 | 27.60 | 27.00 |
| 164 | 22.30 | 28.00 | 27.33 |
| 166 | 22.60 | 28.25 | 27.66 |
| 168 | 22.95 | 28.65 | 28.00 |
| 170 | 23.19 | 28.92 | 28.33 |
| 172 | 23.42 | 29.30 | 28.66 |
| 174 | 23.78 | 29.65 | 29.00 |
| 176 | 24.04 | 30.00 | 29.33 |
| 178 | 24.26 | 30.38 | 29.66 |
| 180 | 24.60 | 30.65 | 30.00 |

**TABLE 10.12** Weight and Cost of Prefabricated High-Velocity Spiral Ducts

Based on rigid airtight, zinc-coated coil sheet-metal construction for high-velocity systems, in standard sizes of 10, 12, or 20 ft. Column marked *insulated* is for double-wall type, with perforated inner wall and 1-in. fiber-glass sandwich center.

| Diameter,<br>in. | Standard<br>gage | lb per lin<br>ft | Standard,<br>$ per ft | Insulated,<br>$ per ft |
|---|---|---|---|---|
| 3 | 26 | 0.83 | 2.00 | 5.40 |
| 4 | 26 | 1.09 | 2.60 | 6.00 |
| 5 | 26 | 1.37 | 3.25 | 6.60 |
| 6 | 26 | 1.55 | 3.70 | 8.00 |
| 7 | 26 | 1.80 | 4.30 | 9.00 |
| 8 | 26 | 2.08 | 5.00 | 10.00 |
| 9 | 24 | 2.95 | 7.00 | 12.00 |
| 10 | 24 | 3.25 | 7.75 | 13.00 |
| 11 | 24 | 3.59 | 8.50 | 14.50 |
| 12 | 24 | 3.85 | 9.20 | 16.00 |
| 14 | 24 | 4.47 | 10.50 | 17.00 |
| 16 | 24 | 5.15 | 12.25 | 18.75 |
| 18 | 24 | 5.75 | 13.75 | 21.00 |
| 20 | 24 | 6.40 | 15.25 | 23.50 |
| 22 | 24 | 7.00 | 16.75 | 26.50 |
| 24 | 22 | 9.50 | 22.75 | 34.00 |
| 26 | 22 | 10.25 | 24.50 | 37.00 |
| 28 | 22 | 11.07 | 26.50 | 40.50 |
| 30 | 22 | 11.85 | 28.25 | 43.00 |
| 32 | 22 | 12.65 | 30.25 | 46.50 |
| 34 | 22 | 13.45 | 32.00 | 50.00 |
| 36 | 22 | 14.25 | 34.00 | 54.50 |
| 38 | 20 | 17.45 | 41.50 | 61.00 |
| 40 | 20 | 18.50 | 44.00 | 65.00 |
| 42 | 20 | 19.22 | 45.75 | 68.00 |
| 44 | 20 | 20.05 | 47.75 | 71.00 |
| 46 | 20 | 21.00 | 50.00 | 74.00 |
| 48 | 20 | 21.90 | 52.25 | 77.00 |

**TABLE 10.13** Weight and Cost of High-Velocity Round Ducts

Based on galvanized-steel sheet construction in standard 4-ft lengths, fabricated with longitudinal lock-type seams as per SMACNA (Sheet Metal and Air Conditioning Contractors' National Assoc.) standards for high-velocity ducts, and 4-in. welded seams on ends for coupling connections.

| Diameter, in. | Standard gage | lb per lin ft | $ per lin ft |
|---|---|---|---|
| 22 | 20 | 11 | 8.90 |
| 24 | 20 | 12 | 9.75 |
| 26 | 20 | 13 | 10.55 |
| 28 | 20 | 14 | 11.35 |
| 30 | 20 | 15 | 12.25 |
| 32 | 20 | 16 | 13.00 |
| 34 | 20 | 17 | 14.00 |
| 36 | 20 | 18 | 14.50 |
| 40 | 18 | 25 | 20.00 |
| 44 | 18 | 28 | 22.50 |
| 48 | 18 | 30 | 24.00 |
| 52 | 18 | 32 | 26.00 |
| 56 | 18 | 36 | 29.00 |
| 60 | 18 | 38 | 30.50 |

**TABLE 10.14** Flexible Spiral Duct

Based on standard 12-ft lengths, NBFU (National Board of Fire Underwriters)-approved construction with galvanized spring steel helix, 1-in. fiber-glass blanket with neoprene fiber-glass liner, and aluminum/fiber-glass/kraft-laminated outer cover.

| Diameter, in. | 4 | 5 | 6 | 7 | 8 | 9 | 10 | 12 | 14 | 16 |
|---|---|---|---|---|---|---|---|---|---|---|
| $ per ft | 4.50 | 4.75 | 4.90 | 5.00 | 5.50 | 6.00 | 6.20 | 7.00 | 8.00 | 9.00 |
| lb per ft | 0.48 | 0.64 | 0.84 | 0.99 | 1.15 | 1.32 | 1.50 | 1.84 | 2.08 | 2.36 |

## RECOMMENDED GAGES

The recommended gages shown in Table 10.15 are based on the 1985 *SMACNA HVAC Duct Construction Standards Metal and Flexible,* which establishes industrywide standards for HVAC ductwork. The standards are based on pressure criteria and reinforcement spacing; the closer the spacing intervals for reinforcement, the lighter the gage of the metal. Ducts without reinforcement require heavier-gage construction. For complete tables of standards, the fabricator must refer to the 1985 SMACNA manual. In almost all cases the plan and specifications will refer to a local code or national standard as the criterion or will specify the gage to be used. Table 10.15 is suggested as an aid to the estimator when gages are not specified.[1] Since ductwork estimates are universally made on a weight unit basis, the gages selected are critical to the cost. For descriptions of classifications for reinforcements see *HVAC Duct Construction Standards Metal and Flexible,* SMACNA, 1985 (SMACNA, 4201 Lafayette Center Drive, Chantilly, VA 22021).

---

[1] Table 10.15 does not appear on the computer disk provided with this book.

**TABLE 10.15**  Recommended Gages for Various Duct Systems

For residential work, consult NFPA 90B.

For residential work, consult NFPA 90B.

*A.*  Rectangular ductwork, ½-in. wg static pressure, positive or negative, up to 2,000 fpm, based on proper reinforcements spaced at 10-ft intervals.

| Largest dimension, in. | Galvanized steel gage | Aluminum,* B&S gage | Copper,* B&S gage |
|---|---|---|---|
| Through 26 | 26 | 24 | 24 |
| 27–30 | 24 | 22 | 20 |
| 31–36 | 22 | 20 | 18 |
| 37–48 | 20 | 18 | 18 |
| 49–60 | 18 | 16 | 14 |
| 61–72 | 16 | 14 | 12 |
| 73–84 | 16 | But 8-ft reinforcement spacing required | |
| 85–96 | 16 | But 8-ft reinforcement spacing required | |
| Over 96 | 18 | But 5-ft Class H spacing | |

*B.*  Rectangular ductwork, 1-in. wg static pressure, positive or negative, up to 2,500 fpm, based on proper reinforcements spaced at 10-ft intervals.

| Largest dimension, in. | Galvanized steel gage | Aluminum,* B&S gage | Copper,* B&S gage |
|---|---|---|---|
| Through 14 | 26 | 24 | 24 |
| 15–24 | 24 | 22 | 20 |
| 25–30 | 22 | 20 | 18 |
| 31–36 | 20 | 18 | 18 |
| 37–42 | 18 | 16 | 14 |
| 43–54 | 16 | 14 | 12 |
| 55–60 | 18 | But 8-ft reinforcement spacing required | |
| 61–84 | 18 | But 5-ft reinforcement spacing required | |
| 85–96 | 16 | But 5-ft reinforcement spacing required | |
| Over 96 | 18 | But 2½-ft class H spacing | |

*C.*  Rectangular ductwork, 2-in. static pressure positive or negative, up to 2,500 fpm.

| Largest dimension, in. | Galvanized steel gage | Reinforcement spacing intervals, ft |
|---|---|---|
| Through 18 | 22 | 10 |
| 19–26 | 20 | 10 |
| 27–30 | 18 | 10 |
| 31–36 | 16 | 10 |
| 37–48 | 16 | 8 |
| 49–60 | 18 | 5 |
| 61–72 | 16 | 5 |
| 73–84 | 18 | 4, class J |
| 85–96 | 16 | 4, class K |
| Over 96 | 18 | 2½, class H |

*(Continued)*

**TABLE 10.15**   Recommended Gages for Various Duct Systems   (*Continued*)

For residential work, consult NFPA 90B.

*D.*   Rectangular ductwork, 3-in. wg static pressure positive or negative, up to 4,000 fpm.

| Largest dimension, in. | Galvanized steel gage | Reinforcement spacing intervals, ft |
|---|---|---|
| Through 28 | 18 | 10 |
| 29–30 | 16 | 10 |
| 31–36 | 16 | 8 |
| 37–42 | 20 | 5 |
| 43–54 | 18 | 5 |
| 55–60 | 16 | 5, class H |
| 61–72 | 16 | 4, class I |
| 73–84 | 18 | 3, class J |
| 85–96 | 16 | 3, class L |
| Over 96 | 18 | 2½, class H |

*E.*   Rectangular ductwork, 4-in. wg static pressure positive, up to 4,000 fpm.

| Largest dimension, in. | Galvanized steel gage | Reinforcement spacing intervals, ft |
|---|---|---|
| Through 12 | 22 | 10 |
| 13–16 | 20 | 10 |
| 17–26 | 18 | 10 |
| 27–30 | 16 | 10 |
| 31–36 | 20 | 5 |
| 37–48 | 18 | 5 |
| 49–54 | 16 | 5, class H |
| 55–60 | 16 | 5, class I |
| 61–72 | 18 | 3, class I |
| 73–84 | 16 | 3, class K |
| 85–96 | 16 | 2½, class L |
| Over 96 | 18 | 2½, class H with tie rod |

*F.*   Rectangular ductwork, 6-in. wg static pressure positive, velocities determined by designer.

| Largest dimension, in. | Galvanized steel gage | Reinforcement spacing intervals, ft |
|---|---|---|
| Through 14 | 20 | 10 |
| 15–18 | 18 | 10 |
| 19–22 | 16 | 10 |
| 23–24 | 18 | 8 |
| 25–28 | 16 | 8 |
| 29–36 | 18 | 5 |
| 37–42 | 16 | 5 |
| 43–48 | 18 | 4 |
| 49–54 | 16 | 4 |
| 55–60 | 18 | 3 |
| 61–72 | 16 | 3 |
| 73–84 | 16 | 2½ |
| 85–96 | 18 | 2, class L |
| Over 96 | 18 | 2, class H with tie rod |

**TABLE 10.15**   Recommended Gages for Various Duct Systems   (*Continued*)

For residential work, consult NFPA 90B.

*G.*   Rectangular ductwork, 10-in. wg static pressure positive, velocities determined by designer.

| Largest dimension, in. | Galvanized steel gage | Reinforcement spacing intervals, ft |
|---|---|---|
| Through 14 | 18 | 8 |
| 15–20 | 16 | 8 |
| 21–28 | 18 | 5 |
| 29–36 | 16 | 5 |
| 37–42 | 16 | 4 |
| 43–48 | 18 | 3, class H |
| 49–54 | 16 | 3, class I |
| 55–60 | 16 | 3, class J |
| 61–72 | 16 | 2½, class K |
| 73–84 | 16 | 2 |
| Over 85 | 16 | 2, class H with tie rod |

*H.*   Round ductwork, galvanized steel, gage selection.

| Duct diameter, in. | Maximum 2-in. wg static positive | | Maximum 10-in wg static positive | | Maximum 2-in. wg static negative | |
|---|---|---|---|---|---|---|
| | Spiral seam gage, in. | Longitudinal seam gage, in. | Spiral seam gage, in. | Longitudinal seam gage, in. | Spiral seam gage, in. | Longitudinal seam gage, in. |
| 3–8 | 28 | 28 | 26 | 24 | 28 | 24 |
| 9–14 | 28 | 26 | 26 | 24 | 26 | 24 |
| 15–26 | 26 | 24 | 24 | 22 | 24 | 22 |
| 27–36 | 24 | 22 | 22 | 20 | 22 | 20 |
| 37–50 | 22 | 20 | 20 | 20 | 20 | 18 |
| 51–60 | 20 | 18 | 18 | 18 | 18 | 16 |
| 61–84 | 18 | 16 | 18 | 16 | 16 | 14 |

*I.*   Round ductwork, aluminum, gage selection.

| Duct diameter, in. | Maximum 2-in. wg static positive | | Maximum 10-in. wg static positive | |
|---|---|---|---|---|
| | Spiral seam gage, in. | Longitudinal seam gage, in. | Spiral seam gage, in. | Longitudinal seam gage, in. |
| 3–8 | 0.025 | 0.032 | 0.025 | 0.040 |
| 9–14 | 0.025 | 0.032 | 0.032 | 0.040 |
| 15–26 | 0.032 | 0.040 | 0.040 | 0.050 |
| 27–36 | 0.040 | 0.050 | 0.050 | 0.063 |
| 37–50 | 0.050 | 0.063 | 0.063 | 0.071 |
| 51–60 | 0.063 | 0.071 | N.A. | 0.090 |
| 61–84 | N.A. | 0.090 | N.A. | N.A. |

(*Continued*)

**TABLE 10.15**    Recommended Gages for Various Duct Systems (*Continued*)

For residential work, consult NFPA 90B.

*J.*  Industrial ventilation.

| Largest dimension, in. | Standard gage |
|---|---|
| Up to 8 | 24 |
| 9–15 | 22 |
| 16–22 | 20 |
| 23–30 | 18 |
| Over 30 | 16 |

*K.*  Boiler breeching—hot-rolled steel, welded seams.

| Largest dimension, in. | Standard gage |
|---|---|
| Up to 12 | 18 |
| 13–24 | 16 |
| 25–36 | 14 |
| 37–60 | 12 |
| Over 60 | 10 |

## ROUND DUCTS VS. RECTANGULAR DUCTS[2]

Round ductwork is generally less expensive to install than rectangular ductwork. Round ducts use up to 27% less material than do rectangular ducts. Round ductwork is also a more efficient configuration for ductwork design. Higher duct velocities can be used without noise problems because pulsations that occur with rectangular ducts are avoided.

On the negative side, round duct mains require more space above ceilings for installation as compared to rectangular ducts. A 42-in. round duct for a 15,000-cfm system, for example, requires 18 in. more space than does a 60 × 24-in. rectangular duct. In some cases, therefore, the most economical choice is to install a rectangular main duct and round branch ducts.

Round ducts are also less prone to leakage than are rectangular ducts. Duct leakage can be a major air-distribution problem. With unsealed ductwork, as much as 40% of the air entering a supply duct is lost before reaching its intended destination. With either type of duct, duct sealing should be specified and practiced and duct pressures should be kept as low as practical.

## ESTIMATING COSTS

Although ductwork may be estimated by the per-piece or square-foot method, the installed cost per-pound basis is most commonly used. Labor productivity rates vary widely with the type of duct system (high- or low-pressure, commercial or industrial service, etc.), material of

[2]Adapted from Cohen, H. R., *HVAC Systems Evaluation*, R. S. Means Co., Kingston, Mass., 1990, pp. 158–159.

construction, weight of gages, sizes of sheets, and specific job conditions, as well as with the specific duct configurations and number of fittings and the quality of available labor and efficacy of the crew concept. Prices used in this discussion—unless otherwise stated—are based on $0.80/lb cost of galvanized metal and a crew average direct wage cost, including fringe benefits, of $27.35/hr before overhead and profit. *Means Building Construction Cost Data* (1994) shows this to be the average 1994 wage rate for sheet metal workers.

Other variables affecting costs are geography, time of year, and scope of work. The professional estimator will, of course, be informed of the general local conditions affecting these costs. The specific job conditions which will affect the cost may be considered to be as follows:

*Size of job:* Larger jobs have lower unit costs.

*Number of fittings, transitions, elbows, dampers, etc.:* The greater the number of fittings, the higher the unit cost.

*Number of miscellaneous duct items:* The greater the number of such items, the higher the job cost. Tables 10.18 to 10.24 may be used to estimate the cost of miscellaneous items.

*Ceiling height, number of floors, and special structural and other conditions requiring scaffolding and rigging:* Although not directly affecting the unit cost per pound, such features will, of course, increase the erection cost.

The baseline index in the sheet-metal industry is *unlined low-pressure galvanized ductwork,* based on 24-gage average, 25% fittings by weight, and standard conditions without workhour correction factors.

Table 10.16 shows the cost-in-place index for various systems with appropriate multipliers. To estimate other than bare low-pressure galvanized ductwork, make the takeoff as if it were for

**TABLE 10.16** Cost-in-Place Index for Ductwork Systems—Labor and Material

Based on average duct configurations and number of fittings for typical applications and using the common low-pressure galvanized duct system as the baseline. For budget estimating make the takeoff in square feet and/or pounds, establish the selling price of galvanized, low-pressure bare ductwork, and apply the appropriate multiplying factor for the equivalent price.

| *Type of ductwork* | *Factor* |
| --- | --- |
| Low-pressure galvanized; *baseline* ................... | 1.00 |
| Aluminum, light gages ........................... | 1.25 |
| Automatic duct coil ............................. | 0.80 |
| Fiber-glass-reinforced plastic ....................... | 2.85 |
| Fiber glass ductboard............................ | 0.95 |
| High-pressure galvanized........................... | 1.38 |
| Low-pressure galvanized lined with 1-in. fiber glass .... | 1.35 |
| Low-pressure galvanized with 1½-in. insulation ........ | 1.40 |
| Medium-pressure galvanized....................... | 1.28 |
| Medium-pressure galvanized with 1½-in. insulation .... | 1.65 |
| PVC plastic...................................... | 2.45 |
| PVC plastic-coated galvanized ....................... | 1.63 |
| Spiral high-pressure............................... | 0.82 |
| Spiral low-pressure................................ | 0.70 |
| Stainless-steel, light gages .......................... | 2.05 |
| Taping seams and connections ....................... | 1.10 |

bare low-pressure galvanized, estimate the price, and apply the proper factor from Table 10.16. For example, if the selling price—including labor, material, overhead, and profit—totals $15,000 for a low-pressure galvanized system, the selling price for a high-pressure system will be $15,000 × 1.38, or $20,700. For workhour correction factors, see appropriate tables in Chap. 1.

Figure 10.2 shows a cost-in-place graph, in dollars per linear foot, for four different gages of low-pressure galvanized ductwork. Table 10.17 offers some typical cost-in-place figures for galvanized, aluminum, or stainless-steel ductwork.

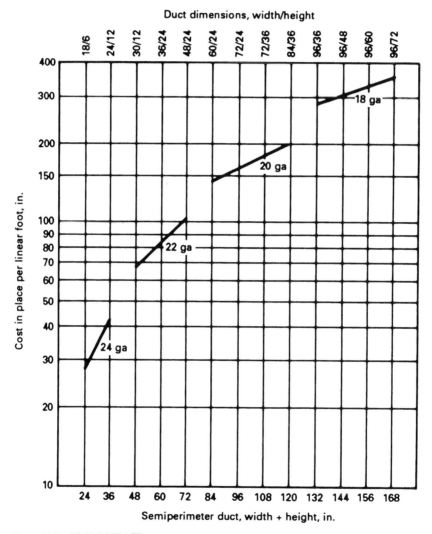

**Figure 10.2   COST IN PLACE**
**Galvanized Ductwork, $/lin ft**
*Based on average number of fittings, new construction, rolling scaffold; includes labor, material, and profit.*

**TABLE 10.17**  Typical Selling Prices for Ductwork in Place, $

Based on low-pressure, average job with 25% fittings, mostly straight runs. For medium pressure multiply by factor 1.28; for high pressure, multiply by factor 1.38. Includes labor, fabrication and erection, material, overhead, and profit.

| Compensated weight, lb* | Galvanized steel, $ per lb | Aluminum 3003 equivalent, $ | Stainless type 304 equivalent, $† |
|---|---|---|---|
| Under 500 | 5.00 | 13.00 | 8.00 |
| 500–1,000 | 4.75 | 11.00 | 7.50 |
| 1,000–2,000 | 4.20 | 10.00 | 7.00 |
| 2,000–5,000 | 4.00 | 9.00 | 6.50 |
| 5,000–7,500 | 3.75 | 8.00 | 6.25 |
| 7,500–10,000 | 3.50 | 7.75 | 6.00 |
| Over 10,000 | 3.25 | 7.50 | 6.00 |

\* Includes fittings, joints, and supports—no insulation.
† Stainless-steel figures are for 24 gage with clear connections.

To estimate the weight of the ductwork, make a takeoff from the scale drawing on a suitable estimating form. A typical form which is used for both design work and cost estimating is shown in Fig. 10.3. After the gage, dimensions, and linear footages are carefully noted on the estimate form, the height and width dimensions of each section are totaled. Table 10.9 may then be referred to for conversion to pounds per foot. The pounds per foot multiplied by the linear feet will give the weight of each section. The sum of the weights of each section equals the total weight in pounds for the job.

It is general practice to make the insulating takeoff in total square feet at the same time that the ducts are being weighed. For details on duct insulation, see Chap. 12. The final step remains to take off all miscellaneous items and multiply the number of units by the cost per unit.

Computers are extensively used for both design and cost estimating. See Chap. 26 for a discussion of computer-aided estimating. If manual estimating techniques are preferred, the DUCTOGRAPH II, a sheet-metal estimating rule designed by John Gladstone (Gladstone, 1985), is a handy tool for making takeoffs and estimating costs of duct systems.

## METHODS OF DUCT MEASUREMENT

The methods of measuring ducts for estimating purposes and for determining friction are different. The method shown here is recommended for cost estimating only. In making the takeoff, each fitting should be measured as part of the duct having the largest single dimension. A radius elbow should be viewed as though it were a square elbow. In the case of a 90° elbow, the length of each leg of the 90° run should be figured to the heel of the ell. This will overlap the metal as shown in Fig. 10.4. This method of measurement will increase the theoretical weight of the job and thus compensate for the additional labor required to fabricate fittings and elbows. On a per-pound in-place cost estimate this is an acceptable takeoff. It follows that the method cannot be used when a quantity takeoff is called for; here every fitting and elbow would have to be classified and figured separately.

| ESTIMATE SHEET METAL & DUCT INSULATION | | | | | | | | | | |
|---|---|---|---|---|---|---|---|---|---|---|
| PROJECT | | | | | | | | JOB NO. | | |
| ADDRESS | | | | | | | | SHEET OF SHEETS | | |
| DATE IN   DATE DUE   ESTIMATOR | | | | | | | | CHECKED BY | | |

| SHEET METAL | | | | | | | INSULATION | | |
|---|---|---|---|---|---|---|---|---|---|
| CFM | GA | DIMENSIONS | HEIGHT PLUS WIDTH | LBS. PER FT. | LINEAL FT. | TOTAL LBS. | LINEAL FT. | SQ. FT. PER LINEAR FT. | TOTAL SQ. FT. |

ENTER TOTALS HERE — CFM — LBS — SQ. FT.

Figure 10.3   SHEET-METAL AND DUCT INSULATION ESTIMATING FORM

CARRY FORWARD, FROM PAGE 1; TOTAL POUNDS OF SHEET METAL INCLUDING:
ALL SUPPLY, RETURN, OUTSIDE AIR, EXHAUST CONNECTIONS, COLLARS, ETC. & ENTER AS ITEM A.

ITEM A TOTAL LBS. _____ X $ _____ PER LB. = $ _____

| ITEM B MISCELLANEOUS SHEET METAL ITEMS | QUANTITY | UNIT COST | TOTAL |
|---|---|---|---|
| MOUNTING SIDE OUTLETS | | | |
| MOUNTING CEILING GRILLES | | | |
| CUTTING HOLES FOR GRILLE COLLARS | | | |
| ERECTING GRILLE COLLARS | | | |
| ERECTING RELIEF GRILLES IN DOOR | | | |
| MOUNTING REMOTE WALL CONTROLLER | | | |
| REMOTE BUTTERFLY DAMPER | | | |
| SPLITTER DAMPER, HAND OPERATED | | | |
| QUADRANT DAMPER, HAND OPERATED | | | |
| FUSIBLE LINK FIRE DAMPER | | | |
| ACCESS DOOR | | | |
| STRAIGHTENING VANES, STATIONERY | | | |
| STRAIGHTENING VANES, ADJUSTABLE | | | |
| WATERPROOF MOTOR COVER | | | |
| CONDENSATE PAN | | | |
| PUMP DRAIN PAN | | | |
| CANVAS CONNECTION | | | |
| COPPER SCREENED LOUVER | | | |
| GOOSENECK WITH BIRD SCREEN | | | |
| MOUNTING FAN | | | |
| CUTTING HOLE IN ROOF | | | |
| PITCH PAN | | | |
| FLASHING | | | |
| FILTER RACK | | | |
| MOUNTING COIL | | | |
| MOUNTING SOUND TRAP | | | |
| | | | |
| | | | |
| | | | |
| | | | |
| | | | |
| | | | |
| | | | |
| | ENTER HERE TOTAL MISCELLANEOUS ITEM B ◆ | | |
| | ENTER HERE TOTAL SHEET METAL COST ITEM A ◆ | | |
| | ENTER HERE TOTAL ALL SHEET METAL WORK ◆ | | |

| TYPE OF INSULATION | TOTAL SQ. FT. | X | 115% WASTE | COST PER SQ. FT. | TOTAL INSULATION |
|---|---|---|---|---|---|
| | | | | | |
| | | | | | |
| | | | | | |
| | | | | | |
| | | | | TOTAL ◆ | |

Figure 10.3  (*Continued*)  **SHEET-METAL AND DUCT INSULATION ESTIMATING FORM**

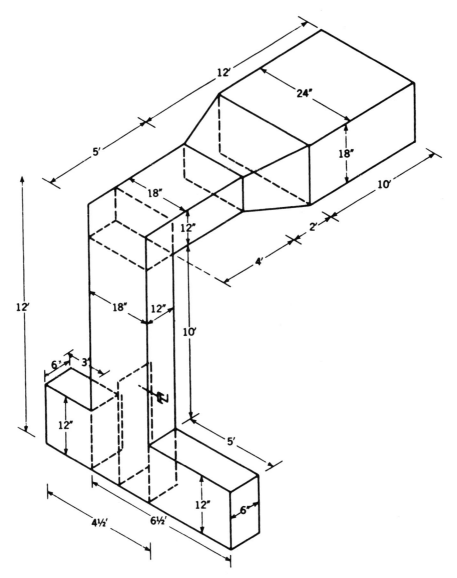

**Figure 10.4  METHOD OF DUCT MEASUREMENT FOR COST ESTIMATING ON THE PER-POUND IN-PLACE METHOD**

**TABLE 10.18**  Comparison of Weights of Measured Ducts

| Duct size | Length, ft | Pounds per ft | Pounds |
|---|---|---|---|
| *Actual weight* | | | |
| 24/18 | 10 | 10.15 | 102 |
| 18/12 | 14 | 7.24 | 101 |
| 12/6 | 9½ | 3.42 | 32 |
| 1 reducer 24/18 to 18/12 | 2 | 8.69 | 17 |
| Total | | | 252 |
| *Compensated weight* | | | |
| 24/18 | 12 | 10.15 | 122 |
| 18/12 | 17 | 7.24 | 123 |
| 12/16 | 11 | 3.42 | 38 |
| Total | | | 283 |

Table 10.18 offers a comparison of weights using the standard of measurement illustrated in Fig. 10.4 versus straight measurement.[3] The difference of 31 lb at, say, $5.00 per lb will compensate for the additional fabricating labor. For offsets, both elbows should be overlapped and the inside dimension should be added to the straight run. A transformer with no change in area should be viewed as an elbow and overlapped.

---

[3] Table 10.18 does not appear on the computer disk provided with this book.

**TABLE 10.19**  Total Job Workhour Production Rates

Guide for estimating workhour production rates for average jobs in various classifications. These figures are for ideal working conditions.

| Category | Total weight range, lb | lb per workhour | |
|---|---|---|---|
| | | Sketch and prepare | Fabricate and erect |
| Industrial job, straight duct runs with few fittings............... | Over 50,000 | 150 | 35 |
| Industrial job, 50% straight runs, 50% branch and fittings ........... | Over 50,000 | 125 | 30 |
| Comfort cooling, straight runs, few fittings ................. | Over 50,000 | 110 | 25 |
| Comfort cooling, 50% straight runs, 50% branch and fittings ........ | Over 50,000 | 95 | 21 |
| Comfort cooling, straight runs, few fittings ................. | 20,000–40,000 | 95 | 21 |
| Comfort cooling, 50% straight runs, 50% branch and fittings ........ | 20,000–40,000 | 80 | 18 |
| Comfort cooling, straight runs, few fittings ................. | 5,000–17,000 | 85 | 20 |
| Comfort cooling, 50% straight runs, 50% branch and fittings ........ | 5,000–17,000 | 72 | 17 |
| Comfort cooling.............. | Under 5,000 | 65 | 15 |

Workhour production rates for average jobs in various classifications are given in Table 10.19. Tables 10.20 and 10.21 list production data for erecting dampers and access doors, respectively. Material and workhours for erecting flexible fan connections are listed in Tables 10.22 and 10.23. Production data for belt guards are given in Table 10.24, and those for miscellaneous items are given in Tables 10.25 and 10.26.

**TABLE 10.20**   Erecting Dampers—Workhours

Includes all the following operations as required for respective dampers: placing damper in position and anchoring in place; connecting sections; trimming flange; mounting fusible link; mounting quadrant, adjusting trunnions, linkages, and quadrants; and checking for free movement. Does not include cutting, patching, or mounting of damper motors. Based on SMACNA construction standards for steel gages.

| Damper type | Description | Workhours per sq ft of damper | | | | | |
|---|---|---|---|---|---|---|---|
| | | 1 sq ft | 4 sq ft | 6 sq ft | 10 sq ft | 16 sq ft | 30 sq ft |
| Relief . . . . . . . | Fixed louvers | 0.35 | 0.50 | 0.75 | 1.25 | 1.50 | 2.10 |
| Automatic . . . . | Multi blade | 0.39 | 0.55 | 0.92 | 1.38 | 1.65 | 2.35 |
| Fire . . . . . . . . | Pivot type | 0.75 | 1.00 | 2.50 | 4.00 | — | — |
| Fire . . . . . . . . | Multi blade | 0.75 | 1.35 | 2.35 | 3.25 | 4.00 | 5.10 |
| Quadrant . . . . . | Single blade | 0.65 | 0.80 | 1.00 | 1.50 | — | — |
| Splitter . . . . . . | Rod adjustment | 0.75 | 1.00 | 1.20 | 1.75 | 2.00 | — |
| Splitter . . . . . . | Rack adjustment | 1.25 | 1.60 | — | — | — | — |

**TABLE 10.21**   Erecting Access Doors—Workhours

Includes laying out opening, cutting opening, setting and adjusting door. Based on SMACNA construction standards using 24-gage steel or 22-gage aluminum, double-panel construction with 1-in. rigid insulation, hinged mounting frame, and sash lock closure tight against gasket; 22 × 46 in. and larger are double-acting walk-through.

| Size, in. | Workhours per each |
|---|---|
| 12 x 12 | 0.65 |
| 12 x 16 | 0.70 |
| 16 x 16 | 0.75 |
| 16 x 24 | 1.00 |
| 18 x 36 | 1.20 |
| 22 x 36 | 1.35 |
| 22 x 46 | 1.55 |
| 22 x 58 | 1.68 |

**TABLE 10.22** Flexible Fan Connections—Material

Prefabricated flexible connectors to meet NFPA standards.
Based on 3 in. of metal double-locked to fabric on both sides,
constructed of 24-gage galvanized steel.

| | Cost per 100-ft roll, $ | |
|---|---|---|
| Description | 3-in. fabric | 6-in. fabric |
| 20-oz canvas .......... | 125 | 180 |
| 28-oz neoprene........ | 180 | 200 |
| 24-oz duralon ........ | 180 | 200 |
| 10-oz fiber glass ....... | 150 | — |

NOTE: For average fan connections some contractors allow
$25 to $30 material plus 2 workhours, or a unit cost of approximately $120 per connection.

**TABLE 10.23** Erecting Flexible Fan Connections—Workhours

Based on SMACNA construction standards for flexible connections between
fan and metal ducts or casings.

| Inlet diameter, in. | Erection, workhours |
|---|---|
| Through 23 | 1.0 |
| 24–36 | 1.5 |
| 37–44 | 2.2 |
| 45–54 | 3.0 |
| 55–64 | 3.8 |
| 65–96 | 4.7 |

**TABLE 10.24** Belt Guards—Workhours

Based on two-piece construction, 18-gage galvanized form, with 1-in. hem
and expanded metal flat tack welded to form, and tachometer flap at driver
and driven shaft. Erection includes fitting on, bolting together with ¼-in.
stove bolts, and fastening to base angle.

| Nominal wheel diameter, in. | Approximate weight, lb | Shop, workhours | Erection, workhours |
|---|---|---|---|
| 12 | 23 | 2.00 | 0.50 |
| 15 | 25 | 2.00 | 0.50 |
| 16 | 26 | 2.00 | 0.50 |
| 18 | 27 | 2.15 | 0.65 |
| 20 | 28 | 2.30 | 0.75 |
| 22 | 29 | 2.45 | 0.75 |
| 24 | 30 | 2.60 | 0.90 |
| 28 | 31 | 2.75 | 1.00 |
| 30 | 32 | 2.90 | 1.00 |
| 34 | 33 | 3.05 | 1.00 |
| 36 | 34 | 3.20 | 1.15 |
| 40 | 35 | 3.75 | 1.40 |
| 44 | 38 | 4.30 | 1.65 |
| 48 | 45 | 4.90 | 2.00 |
| 54 | 52 | 5.50 | 2.30 |
| 60 | 61 | 6.00 | 2.65 |
| 66 | 70 | 6.50 | 3.00 |
| 72 | 84 | 7.00 | 3.50 |
| 80 | 100 | 8.00 | 4.00 |

**TABLE 10.25**    Miscellaneous Items—Erection Workhours

| Operation | Erection, workhours | Material, $ |
|---|---|---|
| Mounting side outlets, average size........................... | 0.36 | — |
| Mounting ceiling grilles, average size........................ | 0.95 | — |
| Cuting holes for grille collar................................ | 0.60 | — |
| Erecting grille collar........................................ | 0.60 | — |
| Erecting relief grille in wood door—12 × 8 in................. | 1.85 | 20 |
| Erecting sight-tite grille in wood door—12 × 8 in............. | 1.85 | 45 |
| Erecting sight-tite grille in wood door—18 × 18 in............ | 1.90 | 60 |
| Erecting remote wall controller, including OB* damper behind grille............................................... | 1.43 | 150 |
| Erecting remote butterfly damper for duct relief or bypass....... | 2.89 | — |
| Erecting stationary straightening vanes—average size............ | 1.13 | — |
| Erecting adjustable extractors—average size .................... | 0.48 | — |
| Cover an opening with blank—average size.................... | 0.30 | — |
| Cutting hole in roof, flash and cap—average construction up to 2½ sq feet ............................................... | 5.50 | — |
| Mounting fan on roof—set, flash, and counterflash but not including rigging or hole cutting—average construction ....... | 5.00 | — |

* Opposed-blade.

**TABLE 10.26**    Miscellaneous Items—Fabrication Workhours

| Operation | Fabrication, workhours | Erection, workhours |
|---|---|---|
| Waterproof motor cover, 22-ga with Pittsburgh seam— 12 x 12 x 24 in. ...................... | 1.10 | 0.10 |
| Motor guard, 4 ft long x 18 in. diameter—single hem on all edges ............................ | 0.60 | 0.14 |
| Drip pan, 72 in. long x 16 in. wide x 2 in. deep—double-hem edges, rivet and solder corners .............. | 1.22 | — |
| Condensate drip pan, insulated and coated ........... | 2.24 | — |
| Venting hood, 24-ga galvanized—24 x 26 in. standard type with Pittsburgh seams—to 6 x 6 in. exhaust duct ...... | 3.00 | 1.00 |
| Venting hood, as above but 30 x 30 in. with 6-in. round exhaust duct off center..................... | 4.25 | 1.00 |
| Fabricate 100 "S" slip joints, 24-ga . . . . . . . . . . . . . . | 4.00 | — |
| Fabricate 500 rectangular duct hangers, 11-ga bar stock . . . | 6.00 | — |
| Fabricate 250 round duct hangers, 11-ga bar stock ...... | 7.80 | — |
| Fabricate 300 drive locks for rectangular duct, 24-ga . . . . . | 10.00 | — |

## *BOILER BREECHING*

To estimate boiler breechings, oven exhausts, etc., figure the total weight of the metal (usually 14- or 12-gage black iron, welded construction), add 30% as a scrap allowance for fabrication production, and allow 30 lb per workhour. For field erection, allow 40 lb per workhour but do not add scrap allowance.

**Example 10.1**  Given 2,000 lb of 14-gage galvanized steel.

**fabrication**

| | | |
|---|---|---|
| Material | 2,000 lb × 1.30 = 2,600 lb | |
| | 2,600 × $0.80/lb = | $2,080 |
| Labor | $\dfrac{2,600 \text{ lb}}{30} \times \$42.65/\text{workhour} =$ | $3,700 |

**erection**

| | | |
|---|---|---|
| Labor | $\dfrac{2,000}{40} \times \$42.65/\text{workhour} =$ | $2,130 |
| | Total | $7,910 |

The $7,910 total represents approximately $3.96 per lb installed. Where 16-gage is permissible, the cost of labor will be about 10% less than 14-gage; for 12-gage the labor cost will be about 15% more, and for 10-gage it will be about 30% more. See Table 10.15*K* for recommended gages, also *Accepted Industry Practice for Industrial Duct Construction,* SMACNA, 1975; and *Guide for Steel Stack Design and Construction,* SMACNA, 1983. For insulation of breeching, see Chap. 12, and for data on duct dampers and fire dampers, see Tables 10.27 and 10.28, respectively.

**TABLE 10.27**  Duct Dampers, Multiblade—Material **$**

For automatic control, OB, includes frames.

| Size | Automatic control, $ | Manual set, $ |
|---|---|---|
| 10 × 6 | 53 | 40 |
| 12 × 6 | 57 | 45 |
| 12 × 12 | 62 | 48 |
| 18 × 12 | 66 | 50 |
| 18 × 18 | 75 | 55 |
| 24 × 12 | 70 | 56 |
| 24 × 24 | 130 | 83 |
| 30 × 12 | 79 | 65 |
| 30 × 18 | 100 | 81 |
| 30 × 24 | 115 | 92 |
| 36 × 18 | 108 | 87 |
| 36 × 36 | 119 | 92 |
| 42 × 42 | 135 | 104 |
| 48 × 24 | 149 | 118 |
| 48 × 48 | 275 | 246 |

**TABLE 10.28**   Fire Dampers—Material

If cap for blades is out of air stream, add 25%. For 22-gage UL sleeve, add 35%; for 22-gage UL sleeve 100% free area, add 60%.

| Size | Vertical UL curtain type, $ | Multiblade, UL louver type, $ |
|---|---|---|
| 10 × 6 | 30 | 110 |
| 12 × 6 | 35 | 115 |
| 12 × 12 | 38 | 120 |
| 18 × 12 | 42 | 135 |
| 18 × 18 | 50 | 145 |
| 24 × 12 | 55 | 150 |
| 24 × 24 | 90 | 175 |
| 30 × 12 | 60 | 155 |
| 30 × 18 | 98 | 180 |
| 30 × 24 | 100 | 195 |
| 36 × 18 | 75 | 190 |
| 36 × 36 | 115 | 215 |
| 42 × 42 | 110 | 250 |
| 48 × 24 | 105 | 265 |
| 48 × 48 | 175 | 525 |

## APPARATUS CASINGS

The estimating procedure presented here is based on SMACNA-approved construction and is suggested only for average casings. When equipment casings constitute a substantial portion of the total construction, the takeoff must be fastidious and analytical on a panel-by-panel basis. All the auxiliaries and correction factors must be extended for each panel.

1. Take off the square footage of the casing and add 35% for scrap and seams.
2. Allow 0.20 lin ft of reinforcing angle for each square foot of galvanized sheet in step 1. Data on casing angles are given in Table 10.29.
3. Total the weight of sheets and angle in steps 1 and 2. Allow 60 lb per workhour for shop fabrication and 15 lb per workhour for field erection. Where caulking cement is required, add 15% to the erection estimate to cover material and added labor. For welded seams add 35% to the erection labor.

**Example 10.2**   Assume an apparatus casing 8 ft high, 5 ft long, and 9 ft wide with welded seams.

### fabrication

| | |
|---|---|
| Material, square footage | |
| Two sides (8 × 5 ft) | 80 sq ft |
| One top (8 × 9 ft) | 72 sq ft |
| Subtotal | 152 sq ft |

| | |
|---|---|
| Seam and scrap allowance, 152 × 1.35 | 205 sq ft |
| Convert to pounds (18-gage galvanized, Table 10.3), 205 × 2.156 | 442 lb |
| Add angle weight (Table 10.6), 152 × 0.20 × 1.23 | 37 lb |
| Material cost of casing, 442 lb × $0.80 | $354 |
| Material cost of angle, 37 lb × $1.30 | $48 |
| Shop labor: (442 lb + 37) = 60 × $42.65/workhour | $340 |

**erection**

| | |
|---|---|
| (442 + 37)/15 × $42.65/workhour | $1,362 |
| Welded seams, 35% of erection: (442 + 37)/15 × 0.35 | 11 workhours |
| 11 workhours × $42.65/workhour | $469 |
| Fabrication, material and labor | $742 |
| Erection, labor | $1,831 |
| Grand total | $2,573 |

This example is based on $0.80/lb of galvanized sheet, $1.30 per pound of 1½ × 1½ × ⅛-in. hot-rolled-steel angle, and $42.65 per workhour for both field and shop labor. Prevailing rates must, of course, be applied. For casings less than 12 ft long, 1½ × 1½ × ⅛-in. reinforcing angles may be used; for casings more than 12 ft long, figure 1¾ × 1¾ × ³⁄₁₆-in. angles for reinforcing and diagonal bracing.

**TABLE 10.29**  Apparatus Casing Angles

This table is a guide for estimating the weight and cost of angles for casings of either steel or aluminum construction.

| Inside reinforcing angles* | | | Diagonal braces | |
|---|---|---|---|---|
| Height of side walls or width of roof, ft | Number of angles required | Spacing of angles | Length of casing | Pairs of braces |
| Up to 6 | None | — | N.A. | None |
| 6–8 | 1 | At center | N.A. | None |
| 8–12 | 2 | At ⅓ points or above door | N.A. | None |
| Over 12 | x | 4 ft o.c. | 3 or 4 panels | 1 |
| | | | 5 or 6 panels | 2 |
| | | | 7 or 8 panels | 3 |

*For casings up to 12 ft use 1½ × 1½ × ⅛ in. angles; for casings over 12 ft use 1¾ × 1¾ × ³⁄₁₆ in. angles. Reinforcing and diagonal bracing angles same size.

Erection labor does not include moving materials and equipment from sidewalk of erection site, installation of flexible connections, or installing access doors. For access doors and flexible connections, see Tables 10.21 and 10.22. Also not included in erection labor are measuring, cutting, forming, punching, fastening angles to casing, bolting up equipment, closing seams, gasketing, and anchoring to floor or wall.

## HIGH-VELOCITY SYSTEMS

Wherever possible, high-velocity systems are designed for streamlined round or spiral ducts; Tables 10.12 to 10.14 cover weights and material costs for these types. The method of estimating low-velocity systems, described earlier, may also be used for high-velocity ones.

However, the prevailing rate per pound must be increased an additional 15% to cover the treatment of seams; with static pressures of ≤6 in. of water, all seams must be well sealed against air loss. Locked seams are either soldered or caulked with a sealing compound and taped with fiber-glass. Cost of erecting the high-pressure diffusers will depend on the type used.

For high-velocity induction-unit connections, allow the following:

1. For flexible runouts, floor-mounted units, estimate 0.35 workhour.

2. For flexible runouts, ceiling-mounted units, estimate 0.90 workhour.

3. When estimating material cost for flexible spiral duct, add $9 per end joint for adhesive and clamps.

For check-data figures covering primary-air risers and headers, as well as the return-air side, see Figs. 2.4 to 2.8.

## COMMERCIAL KITCHEN VENTILATION

Standard commercial kitchen exhaust hoods may be factory-made on a production line or "tailor made" by a sheet-metal contractor. *Tailor-made* exhaust hoods may be either island type or shed type. The *shed type* is a wall-hung canopy; the *island type* is a center-hung canopy. These hoods are generally 24 in. high and constructed in stainless steel. However, there are many variations in height, design, and material construction. The minimum design gage for galvanized-iron hoods is 18 gage; for stainless-steel hoods, it is 20 gage. All seams and joints must have a liquidtight continuous external weld. The exhaust duct system minimum design gage for galvanized iron is 16 gage; for stainless steel, it is 18 gage. The ducts, too, must have a liquidtight continuous external weld. Aluminum will scratch easily because of its softness and is used infrequently; black iron may be used, but it is obviously unsightly and difficult to keep clean.

Table 10.30 gives costs for both galvanized-iron and stainless-steel hoods, based on the standard as illustrated in Fig. 10.5. The prices shown start at 4-ft minimum length with add-on figures in 1-ft increments and are based on sloped design as shown. For rolled design, add 3% to the price. The listed prices include the labor and material for fabricating, heliarc welding and polishing joints, and hanging the hood with accessories. Hanger chains, ductwork connections, exhaust fans, and electric wiring are not included.

Material cost for 16-gage galvanized averages $0.80/lb bare cost and sells at about $5.00/lb installed. For insulation of commercial kitchen exhaust ducts, see Chap. 12. Standard-mesh grease filters 24 × 24 × 2 in. may cost between $30 and $40 each. Better-quality baffle-type filters offer more fire protection, ease of laundering, and longer life; they cost between $55 and $100 each, but they are well worth the difference in fire protection. Table 10.31 gives per piece data for typical kitchen exhaust ductwork. See Chap. 22 for detailed grease filter costs.

Factory-built, push-pull commercial kitchen hoods, although high in first cost compared to conventional hoods, could save considerable money in operating costs by lowering heating and cooling tempering cost of makeup air and also improving grease capturability. The *push-pull principle* is a compound supply-exhaust design in which makeup air is introduced in a raw state without pretempering. Factory prices vary widely depending on the design and quality of the hood as well as the manufacturer. High-technology (hi-tech) stainless-steel hoods including automatic washdown, piped-in dry fire extinguishment, and illumination may range between $1,100 and $2,400 per lin ft delivered. Erection costs average 5 workhours per lin ft, or about 5% of the factory price of the hood.

**TABLE 10.30** Commercial Kitchen Hoods—Cost, in Dollars

| Erected shed-type canopy | Galvanized | | | | Stainless steel | | |
|---|---|---|---|---|---|---|---|
| | 40 in. wide | 48 in. wide | 54 in. wide | | 40 in. wide | 48 in. wide | 54 in. wide |
| First 4-ft length | 420 | 460 | 500 | | 1,300 | 1,400 | 1,500 |
| Each additional ft | 80 | 85 | 90 | | 245 | 270 | 280 |
| Sloped ends | 45 | 50 | 60 | | 90 | 90 | 105 |

| Erected island canopy | Galvanized | | Stainless steel | |
|---|---|---|---|---|
| | 72 in. wide | 96 in. wide | 72 in. wide | 96 in. wide |
| First 4-ft length | 780 | 1,000 | 2,300 | 2,800 |
| Each additional ft | 125 | 225 | 420 | 480 |
| Sloped ends | 85 | 95 | 160 | 210 |

| Accessories | Galvanized | Stainless steel |
|---|---|---|
| Filter-holding frame, single bank for shed, per ft | 20 | 50 |
| Filter-holding frame, double V for island, per ft | 35 | 90 |
| Grease filter, per each | 30 | 100 |
| Vapor lights, per each UL-listed, incandescent | 150 | 150 |
| Duct connecting collars, per each | 100 | 100 |
| Top plenum chamber, 12 in. high, per ft | 75 | 200 |

| Stainless-steel backsplash panels— quilted, fluted, or plain | First 3 ft | Additional ft |
|---|---|---|
| 30 in. high | 250 | 80 |
| 36 in. high | 275 | 90 |
| 42 in. high | 310 | 100 |
| 48 in. high | 350 | 110 |

## FIBER-GLASS DUCTWORK

Comparatively, fiber-glass ductwork costs approximately 12 to 15% less than bare galvanized-steel fabricated ductwork, about 45% less than insulated sheet metal, and about 50% less than lined sheet metal. Because of its light weight, excellent acoustical and thermal insulating properties, ease of fabricating, and reduced shop costs, fiber-glass duct is deservedly popular among contractors and owners. Its primary use is for low-pressure systems tested at 1.5 times the recommended static pressure. It is not recommended for use with air temperatures over 250°F. The decibel attenuation, airborne equipment noise, and crosstalk reduction are greater than can be achieved with standard duct liners. Boards are shipped with male and female shiplaps on the 48-in. dimension with foil overlap and are available in flat cartons of six 4 × 10-ft sheets per box. Prices run about $95 per box for R6, 1½ in. thickness.

Metal ductwork may be estimated either by the piece method or by the pound-weight method; fiber-glass ductwork may be estimated by the piece method or by the square-foot-unit method. The latter is by far the most commonly used. Unlike the method used for sheet

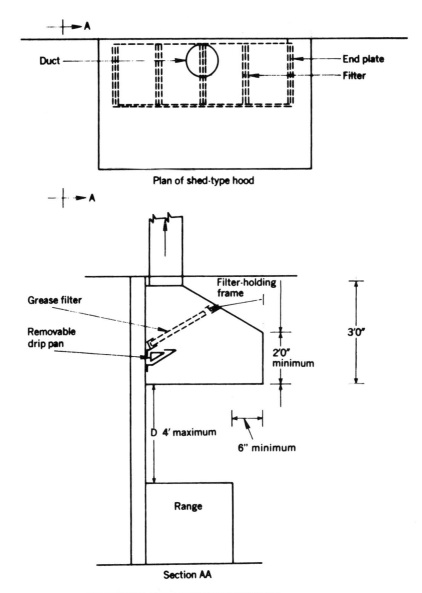

Plan of shed-type hood

Section AA

**Figure 10.5 COMMERCIAL KITCHEN EXHAUST HOOD**
*For long hoods, branch takeoffs on 6-ft centers. Ducts sized at 1,700 fpm. (Note: No gutter around perimeter; use removable drip trough under filter-holding frame.)*

**TABLE 10.31** Kitchen Exhaust Ductwork

Based on per-piece costs as shown for fabrication and field assembly with externally welded seams and joints using 16-gage hot-rolled steel and including waste allowance.

| Duct dimensions, in. | lb per lin ft | sq ft per lin ft | Erection workhours per 4-ft section |
|---|---|---|---|
| 12 × 12 | 13.00 | 4.00 | 3.5 |
| 18 × 12 | 16.00 | 5.00 | 4.0 |
| 24 × 12 | 19.75 | 6.00 | 4.6 |
| 30 × 12 | 23.10 | 7.00 | 5.5 |
| 36 × 12 | 26.55 | 8.00 | 6.0 |
| 36 × 18 | 28.07 | 8.67 | 6.5 |
| 42 × 18 | 33.20 | 10.00 | 7.0 |
| 48 × 18 | 36.38 | 11.00 | 8.0 |
| 54 × 18 | 39.55 | 12.00 | 8.5 |
| 60 × 18 | 43.00 | 13.00 | 9.0 |
| 66 × 18 | 46.20 | 14.00 | 10.0 |
| 72 × 18 | 49.60 | 15.00 | 11.0 |
| 72 × 24 | 43.10 | 16.00 | 12.0 |
| 78 × 24 | 45.90 | 17.00 | 13.0 |

metal, cost estimating of fiber-glass is not greatly influenced by the duct size or aspect ratio owing to gage changes. Table 10.32 gives the stretchout feet of various sizes of ducts. Depending on the particular job requirements, geographic area, shop facilities, and *know-how*, the installed cost may vary between $2.50 and $4.00 per sq ft. The budget cost per square foot may approximate 95% of bare metal for the same job. That is, if a takeoff is estimated at $4.00 per sq ft for bare galvanized duct (about $3.10 per lb), the material may be transposed to a fibrous glass duct system for $3.80 per sq ft. Average selling prices in 1994 were $2.80/sq ft installed fiber-glass duct with nonunion labor. Union shops averaged about $3.50. Boards of 3-lb density cost $0.80 to $1.00/sq ft; 5-lb board ranged from $1.00 to $1.30. Standard boards are 1 in. thick and are rated by their flexural rigidity (E1) in three classes: 475, 800, or 1,400 lb/sq in.

Fiber-glass ducts should be sized approximately 1.15 times the galvanized semiperimeter to achieve equal static. For accurate sizing, proceed in the same manner as for galvanized and then refer to the current edition of the SMACNA *Fibrous Glass Duct Construction Standards Manual* for the air friction correction factor.

**Example 10.3** A metal duct system is designed to distribute 6,000 cfm of standard air at an equivalent friction loss of 0.10 wg. Find the duct size and actual friction loss for a fibrous duct system.

**solution**

1. From the standard friction chart for 6,000 cfm at 0.10 friction, find the velocity. It equals 1,500 fpm, and the duct size reads 25 × 25.
2. From the SMACNA correction chart select correction factor 1.37. Then, 0.10 ÷ 1.37 = 0.07 new friction loss required.
3. From the standard friction chart locate 6,000 cfm at 0.07 friction and select the final duct size, 25 × 29 for a fibrous glass system.

**TABLE 10.32**    Fibrous Glass Duct Stretchout Areas

Method of estimating amount of material required for rectangular ducts fabricated from 1-in.-thick fibrous glass board; includes allowance for overlap and 8-in. grooving.

| Width + depth, total in. | Square feet per lin ft | Width + depth, total in. | Square feet per lin ft | Width + depth, total in. | Square feet per lin ft |
|---|---|---|---|---|---|
| 10 | 2.33 | 41 | 7.50 | 71 | 12.50 |
| 11 | 2.50 | 42 | 7.67 | 72 | 12.67 |
| 12 | 2.67 | 43 | 7.83 | 73 | 12.83 |
| 13 | 2.83 | 44 | 8.00 | 74 | 13.00 |
| 14 | 3.00 | 45 | 8.17 | 75 | 13.17 |
| 15 | 3.17 | 46 | 8.33 | 76 | 13.33 |
| 16 | 3.33 | 47 | 8.50 | 77 | 13.50 |
| 17 | 3.50 | 48 | 8.67 | 78 | 13.67 |
| 18 | 3.67 | 49 | 8.83 | 79 | 13.83 |
| 19 | 3.83 | 50 | 9.00 | 80 | 14.00 |
| 20 | 4.00 | 51 | 9.17 | 81 | 14.17 |
| 21 | 4.17 | 52 | 9.33 | 82 | 14.33 |
| 22 | 4.33 | 53 | 9.50 | 83 | 14.50 |
| 23 | 4.50 | 54 | 9.67 | 84 | 14.67 |
| 24 | 4.67 | 55 | 9.83 | 85 | 14.83 |
| 25 | 4.83 | 56 | 10.00 | 86 | 15.00 |
| 26 | 5.00 | 57 | 10.17 | 87 | 15.17 |
| 27 | 5.17 | 58 | 10.33 | 88 | 15.33 |
| 28 | 5.33 | 59 | 10.55 | 89 | 15.50 |
| 29 | 5.50 | 60 | 10.67 | 90 | 15.67 |
| 30 | 5.67 | 61 | 10.83 | 91 | 15.83 |
| 31 | 5.83 | 62 | 11.00 | 92 | 16.00 |
| 32 | 6.00 | 63 | 11.17 | 93 | 16.17 |
| 33 | 6.17 | 64 | 11.33 | 94 | 16.33 |
| 34 | 6.33 | 65 | 11.55 | 95 | 16.50 |
| 35 | 6.50 | 66 | 11.67 | 96 | 16.67 |
| 36 | 6.67 | 67 | 11.83 | 97 | 16.83 |
| 37 | 6.83 | 68 | 12.00 | 98 | 17.00 |
| 38 | 7.00 | 69 | 12.17 | 99 | 17.17 |
| 39 | 7.17 | 70 | 12.33 | 100 | 17.33 |
| 40 | 7.33 | | | | |

**TABLE 10.33**   Sheet-Metal Accessories

Unit costs for sheet-metal accessories, fabrication, and erection for
fiber-glass duct systems based on average jobs with sizes ranging from
12 × 6 in. to 60 × 40 in.

| Item | Average Workhours | |
|---|---|---|
| | Machine | Manual |
| Fabricate straight duct section......... | 0.12 | 0.28 |
| Fabricate U-duct section.............. | 0.23 | 0.37 |
| Fabricate 4-piece fitting .............. | 0.68 | 0.85 |
| Fabricate transition piece ............. | 0.30 | 0.35 |
| Fabricate cap....................... | 0.10 | 0.13 |
| Fabricate miter ..................... | — | 0.17 |
| Join duct sections.................... | — | 0.25 |
| Hang and assemble two duct lengths .. | — | 1.00 |
| Attach to air handler................. | — | 3.00 |
| Attach grille collars ................. | — | 0.18 |
| Erect grille (includes cutting hole)..... | — | 0.85 |
| Insert splitter or extractor ........... | — | 0.25 |
| Reinforce metal component.......... | — | 0.30 |

| Item | Size, in. | Direct cost labor and materials, $ |
|---|---|---|
| Electric coil sleeves.................. | 12 × 12 | 50 |
| | 24 × 12 | 75 |
| | 36 × 12 | 100 |
| | 48 × 12 | 140 |
| Fire damper sleeves.................. | 12 × 12 | 75 |
| | 24 × 12 | 100 |
| | 36 × 12 | 130 |
| | 48 × 12 | 175 |
| Access doors ........................ | 12 × 12 | 50 |
| | 24 × 12 | 65 |

# OTHER

Table 10.33 gives unit labor costs for estimating typical metal accessories for fiber-glass duct systems.

Figure 10.6 shows approximate costs of toilet ductwork for multistory apartment buildings.

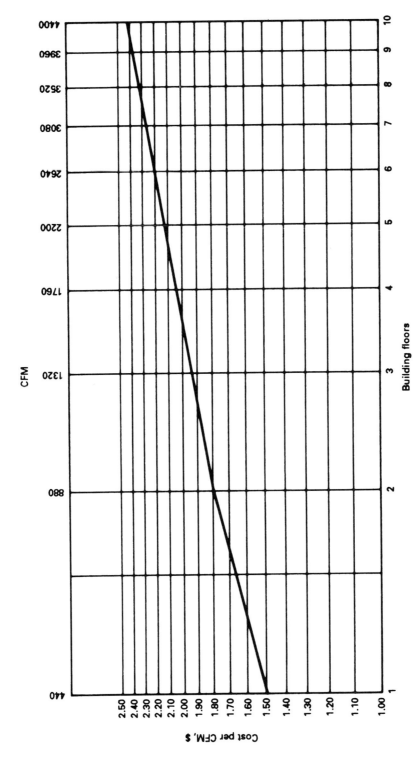

CFM

Cost per CFM, $

Building floors

Figure 10.6   TOILET EXHAUST DUCTWORK FOR MULTILEVEL APARTMENT COMPLEXES

## RECOMMENDED READING

Cohen, H. R., *HVAC Systems Evaluation,* R. S. Means Co., Kingston, Mass., 1990.

*Duct Manual Fibrous Glass Construction for Ventilating and Air Conditioning Systems,* Sheet Metal and Air Conditioning Contractors National Association (SMACNA), Chantilly, Va., current edition.

Gladstone, J., *DUCTOGRAPH II—Sheet Metal Calculator,* Engineer's Press, Coral Gables, Fla., 1985.

*HVAC Duct Construction Standards Metal and Flexible,* SMACNA, 1985.

"Special Report—Fibrous Glass Ducts," *Air Conditioning, Heating and Ventilating,* February 1968, pp. 39–60.

*Means Mechanical Estimating Standards and Procedures,* R. S. Means Co., Kingston, Mass., 1992.

Rowe, W. H., *HVAC Design Criteria, Options, Selection,* 2d ed., R. S. Means Co., Kingston, Mass., 1994.

*Sheet Metal Estimating,* Wendes Engineering and Air Conditioning Services, Elk Grove Village, Ill., 1985.

Stamper, E., and R. E. Koral (eds.), "Estimating Weight of Metal in Ducts," in *Handbook of Air Conditioning, Heating and Ventilating,* 3d ed., Industrial Press, New York, 1979.

Wendes, H. C., *Sheet Metal Estimating Handbook,* Van Nostrand Reinhold, New York, 1982.

# CHAPTER 11
# AIR DISTRIBUTION

## GENERAL DISCUSSION

On most jobs the estimator will be working with a large variety of styles of outlets, shapes, sizes, and damper devices and will frequently find several manufacturers specified on one job. The air distribution for a conventional system falls into three categories: ceiling diffusers, sidewall grilles, and return and relief grilles.

Most jobs 40 tons and over will average approximately $15.00 per 100 cfm of total air. The cost will generally fall at about 6% of the entire job. High-velocity systems will run well above that figure, and residential air-distribution systems at the competitive project level will average about $6 per 100 cfm.

The tables in this chapter are constructed in dollars for the material cost only. Labor for grille erection is normally included in the sheet-metal estimate and is handled as part of the sheet-metal contract. Outlets are manufactured items and are rarely included in the sheet-metal bid. For erection costs and other workhour factors, see Chap. 10. Whether air balancing is performed by the sheet-metal contractor, the mechanical contractor, or an independent test-and-balance agency, it must be considered as a separate function and so entered into the estimate; see Chap. 15.

## ESTIMATING

When making the quantity takeoff, the estimator must use a suitable takeoff sheet or be subject to serious errors and omissions. Figure 11.1 shows such a takeoff sheet, which may also serve as a design sheet. Tables 11.1 to 11.8 offer some average costs for popular-size air-distribution devices.

Tables 11.9 to 11.11 show prices for high-pressure distribution boxes for use in high-velocity systems. Data for stormproof louvers, ceiling diffusers, and ceiling return grilles are given in Tables 11.12, 11.13, and 11.14, respectively.

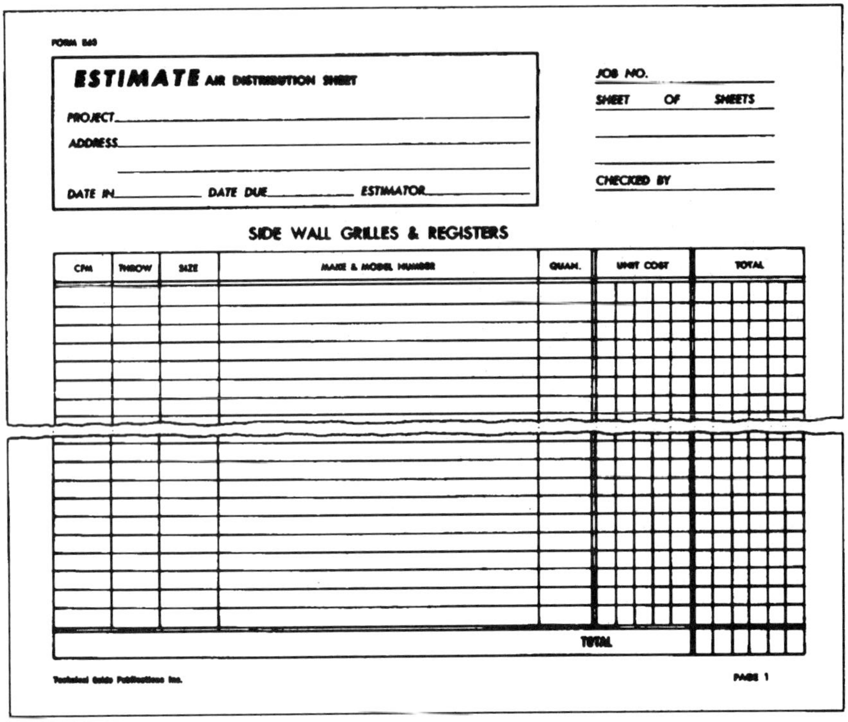
ESTIMATE AIR DISTRIBUTION SHEET

PROJECT

ADDRESS

DATE IN DATE DUE ESTIMATOR

JOB NO.

SHEET OF SHEETS

CHECKED BY

SIDE WALL GRILLES & REGISTERS

| CFM | THROW | SIZE | MAKE & MODEL NUMBER | QUAN. | UNIT COST | TOTAL |
|---|---|---|---|---|---|---|
| | | | | | | |
| | | | | TOTAL | | |

Technical Guide Publications Inc.

PAGE 1

Figure 11.1 ESTIMATE FORM—AIR DISTRIBUTION

**TABLE 11.1** Ceiling Diffusers, Round Shapes, Steel Construction, with Opposed-Blade Dampers

| Size, in. | Nominal cfm (43 db) | Flush mount, fixed, $ | Step-down, adjustable, $ |
|---|---|---|---|
| 6 | 225 | 20 | 45 |
| 8 | 400 | 25 | 58 |
| 10 | 600 | 27 | 69 |
| 12 | 750 | 36 | 79 |
| 14 | 1,100 | 42 | 98 |
| 16 | 1,250 | 48 | 132 |
| 18 | 1,550 | 60 | 168 |
| 20 | 2,100 | 90 | 220 |
| 24 | 2,500 | 120 | 235 |
| 30 | 3,400 | 190 | 285 |
| 38 | 5,000 | 235 | 355 |

**TABLE 11.2**   Ceiling Diffusers, Square Shapes, Steel Construction

| Size, in. | Nominal cfm (43 db) | Flush mount, $ | With equalizing grid and damper, $ |
|---|---|---|---|
| 6 | 250 | 30 | 39 |
| 8 | 400 | 31 | 41 |
| 10 | 600 | 43 | 58 |
| 12 | 750 | 56 | 73 |
| 15 | 1,100 | 67 | 93 |
| 18 | 1,550 | 93 | 124 |

**TABLE 11.3**   Accessories for Ceiling Diffusers

| Size, in. | Equalizing grid, $ | Volume extractor, $ | Volume damper, $ |
|---|---|---|---|
| 6 | 11.00 | 22.00 | 17.00 |
| 8 | 11.50 | 26.00 | 18.00 |
| 10 | 12.00 | 27.00 | 20.00 |
| 12 | 19.00 | 31.00 | 22.00 |
| 14 | 20.00 | 35.00 | 23.00 |
| 15 | 22.00 | 37.00 | 26.00 |
| 16 | 26.00 | 41.00 | 27.00 |
| 18 | 30.00 | 43.00 | 33.00 |
| 20 | 24.00 | 54.00 | 36.00 |
| 24 | 38.00 | 69.00 | 45.00 |
| 30 | 44.00 | — | 60.00 |
| 38 | 52.00 | — | 75.00 |

**TABLE 11.4**   Ceiling Grilles, Rectangular Shapes with Adjustable Curved Blades, Aluminum Construction

| Grille size, in. | Nominal cfm @ 600 fpm | One-way throw, $ | One-way throw with multi-shutter, $ | Two-way throw, $ |
|---|---|---|---|---|
| 6 × 4 | 50 | 22.00 | 16.75 | 22.00 |
| 8 × 4 | 75 | 24.00 | 16.75 | 24.00 |
| 8 × 8 | 125 | 33.00 | 26.25 | 33.00 |
| 10 × 4 | 90 | 25.50 | 18.75 | 26.00 |
| 10 × 6 | 120 | 26.00 | 18.75 | 26.00 |
| 10 × 10 | 215 | 30.50 | 31.00 | 40.00 |
| 12 × 4 | 100 | 28.00 | 27.50 | 30.00 |
| 12 × 6 | 150 | 30.00 | 56.00 | 31.00 |
| 12 × 8 | 200 | 40.75 | 27.00 | 41.00 |
| 12 × 12 | 300 | 48.00 | 76.00 | 48.00 |
| 14 × 6 | 180 | 34.00 | 25.50 | 41.00 |
| 14 × 8 | 250 | 43.00 | 34.50 | 44.00 |
| 14 × 14 | 400 | 58.00 | 45.75 | 60.00 |

**TABLE 11.5** Sidewall Supply Grilles, Aluminum or Prime-Coat

| Grille size, in. | Nominal cfm @ 1000 fpm | Single-deflection, multi-shutter damper control, $ | Double-deflection, no damper control, $ | Double-deflection, opposed-blade damper control, $ |
|---|---|---|---|---|
| 8 × 4 | 125 | 10.00 | 10.90 | 16.27 |
| 10 × 4 | 175 | 11.25 | 12.26 | 18.30 |
| 10 × 6 | 225 | 12.50 | 13.63 | 20.34 |
| 12 × 4 | 200 | 12.50 | 13.63 | 20.34 |
| 12 × 6 | 300 | 13.25 | 14.44 | 21.56 |
| 12 × 8 | 375 | 15.00 | 16.35 | 24.41 |
| 14 × 4 | 225 | 13.40 | 14.61 | 21.80 |
| 14 × 5 | 300 | 14.25 | 15.53 | 23.80 |
| 14 × 6 | 325 | 14.90 | 16.24 | 24.24 |
| 14 × 8 | 500 | 15.80 | 17.22 | 25.71 |
| 16 × 5 | 300 | 15.90 | 17.33 | 25.87 |
| 16 × 6 | 400 | 16.00 | 17.44 | 26.03 |
| 16 × 8 | 550 | 17.50 | 19.08 | 28.47 |
| 18 × 6 | 450 | 17.00 | 18.53 | 27.66 |
| 20 × 5 | 400 | 17.00 | 18.53 | 27.66 |
| 20 × 6 | 500 | 18.00 | 19.62 | 29.29 |
| 20 × 8 | 630 | 19.50 | 21.26 | 31.73 |
| 24 × 5 | 500 | 20.25 | 22.07 | 32.95 |
| 24 × 6 | 700 | 21.00 | 22.89 | 34.17 |
| 24 × 8 | 900 | 23.25 | 25.34 | 37.83 |
| 24 × 10 | 1,200 | 25.25 | 27.52 | 41.08 |
| 24 × 12 | 1,300 | 28.00 | 30.52 | 45.56 |
| 30 × 6 | 800 | 26.75 | 29.16 | 43.52 |
| 30 × 8 | 1,250 | 30.50 | 33.25 | 49.62 |
| 30 × 10 | 1,350 | 32.50 | 35.10 | 52.39 |
| 30 × 12 | 1,600 | 36.00 | 39.24 | 58.57 |
| 36 × 6 | 1,000 | 32.75 | 35.66 | 53.24 |
| 36 × 8 | 1,325 | 36.00 | 39.24 | 58.57 |
| 36 × 10 | 1,600 | 27.75 | 30.25 | 45.15 |
| 36 × 12 | 1,800 | 44.75 | 48.78 | 72.81 |
| 40 × 8 | 1,800 | 49.50 | 53.96 | 80.54 |
| 40 × 12 | 2,400 | 61.25 | 66.76 | 99.65 |
| 48 × 6 | 1,300 | 52.50 | 57.23 | 85.42 |
| 48 × 8 | 1,700 | 57.75 | 62.95 | 96.96 |

**TABLE 11.6** Return-Air Grilles, Aluminum Construction

| Grille size, in. | Nominal cfm @ 600 fpm | Standard wall single face bars, $ | Hinged with filter back, $ | Standard door, sight-tite with frame, $ | Register with OB damper, $ |
|---|---|---|---|---|---|
| 10 × 6 | 170 | 10.00 | — | — | 18.00 |
| 10 × 8 | 240 | 12.25 | — | — | 22.00 |
| 12 × 6 | 200 | 11.00 | — | — | 20.00 |
| 12 × 8 | 290 | 15.00 | — | 17.00 | 22.00 |
| 12 × 12 | 455 | 18.00 | — | 20.00 | 23.00 |
| 14 × 6 | 300 | 14.25 | — | 16.00 | 22.00 |
| 14 × 8 | 390 | 19.00 | — | 21.50 | 28.00 |
| 14 × 10 | 490 | 23.50 | — | 26.50 | 30.00 |
| 18 × 6 | 325 | 20.00 | — | 22.50 | 27.00 |
| 18 × 12 | 660 | 26.50 | 37.00 | 30.00 | 35.50 |
| 18 × 18 | 785 | 27.50 | 41.00 | 31.00 | 41.00 |
| 24 × 10 | 850 | 20.50 | 29.60 | 23.00 | 31.00 |
| 24 × 12 | 900 | 23.50 | 36.00 | 26.50 | 34.50 |
| 24 × 18 | 1,400 | 34.75 | 53.00 | 39.25 | 51.50 |
| 24 × 24 | 1,925 | 47.75 | 67.00 | 54.00 | 70.00 |
| 30 × 10 | 1,000 | 25.00 | 41.00 | — | 38.25 |
| 30 × 12 | 1,200 | 30.25 | 46.00 | — | 45.00 |
| 30 × 18 | 1,770 | 56.50 | 78.00 | — | 77.50 |
| 30 × 24 | 2,450 | 59.00 | 82.00 | — | 87.00 |
| 36 × 12 | 1,525 | 32.25 | 48.00 | — | 52.00 |
| 36 × 18 | 2,180 | 53.00 | 82.00 | — | 80.00 |
| 36 × 24 | 3,000 | 75.00 | 128.00 | — | 112.00 |
| 36 × 30 | 3,700 | 106.00 | 146.00 | — | 155.00 |
| 48 × 24 | 3,950 | 114.00 | — | — | 161.00 |
| 48 × 30 | 5,000 | 145.00 | — | — | 205.00 |
| 48 × 36 | 6,025 | 180.00 | — | — | 255.00 |

**TABLE 11.7** Volume-Control Dampers, for Installation in Ducts behind Grilles; Key-Operated, Opposed-Blade

| Duct size, in. | Prime-coat finish, $ | Duct size, in. | Prime-coat finish, $ |
|---|---|---|---|
| 10 × 6 | 19.00 | 24 × 10 | 40.50 |
| 10 × 8 | 21.50 | 24 × 12 | 43.00 |
| 12 × 6 | 21.50 | 24 × 18 | 50.00 |
| 12 × 8 | 24.00 | 24 × 24 | 58.00 |
| 12 × 12 | 29.00 | 30 × 10 | 48.00 |
| 14 × 6 | 24.00 | 30 × 12 | 50.00 |
| 14 × 8 | 26.00 | 30 × 18 | 58.00 |
| 14 × 10 | 29.00 | 30 × 24 | 65.00 |
| 18 × 6 | 33.50 | 36 × 12 | 50.00 |
| 18 × 8 | 38.50 | 36 × 18 | 65.00 |
| 18 × 18 | 55.00 | 36 × 24 | 72.00 |

Remote controllers for above dampers, cadmium-plated-finish faceplates with open and closed position, and standard 8-ft-length cable with tubing, $50.00 each. For extra cable with tubing, add $1.50 per ft. Where automatic fire dropout is required with above dampers, springtight, fusible links are available [150°F melting point (mp)] at $2.00 each.

**TABLE 11.8**   Linear Ceiling Diffusers, Slim Line

| Diffuser, in. | $3\frac{1}{2} \times 36$ | $3\frac{1}{2} \times 48$ | $3\frac{1}{2} \times 60$ | $3\frac{1}{2} \times 72$ |
|---|---|---|---|---|
| Nominal cfm (43 db) | 250 | 320 | 400 | 500 |
| One-way throw, $ | 49.00 | 60.00 | 70.00 | 80.00 |
| Two-way throw, $ | 84.00 | 109.00 | 116.00 | 133.00 |
| Extra for OB damper, $ | 27.00 | 35.00 | 45.00 | 55.00 |
| Erection labor, $ | 30.00 | 40.00 | 50.00 | 60.00 |

**TABLE 11.9**   High-Velocity Box with Center Discharge

| Nominal cfm @ $2\frac{1}{4}$-in. sp | 125 | 250 | 350 | 450 | 600 |
|---|---|---|---|---|---|
| Neck opening, in. | 4 | 6 | 10 | 12 | 15 |
| Single-duct system, $ | 400 | 450 | 500 | 525 | 550 |
| Double-duct system, $ | 450 | 500 | 550 | 600 | 625 |

**TABLE 11.10**   High-Velocity Box with Quadruplex Discharge

| Nominal cfm @ $2\frac{1}{4}$-in. sp | 350 | 450 | 600 | 750 |
|---|---|---|---|---|
| Outlet sizes, four each | 4 | 5 | 6 | 8 |
| Single-duct system, $ | 600 | 625 | 650 | 675 |
| Double-duct system, $ | 650 | 700 | 725 | 800 |

**TABLE 11.11**   Floor-Standing Box (Under-Window Application), Hot/Cold Induction System

| Nominal cfm @ $2\frac{1}{4}$-in. sp | 80 | 150 | 200 | 300 |
|---|---|---|---|---|
| Diffuser length, in. | 16 | 24 | 36 | 48 |
| Double-duct system, $ | 325 | 375 | 400 | 450 |

**TABLE 11.12**   Extruded Aluminum Stormproof Louvers

For fresh-air intakes, relief of exhaust. Includes $\frac{1}{2}$-in.-mesh galvanized bird screen. Free area is approximately 50% of total opening.

| Height, in. | Width, in. | Net cost, $ |
|---|---|---|
| 24 | 12 | 32.50 |
| 36 | 24 | 65 |
| 48 | 36 | 100 |
| 60 | 48 | 120 |
| 48 | 24 | 100 |
| 60 | 36 | 130 |
| 72 | 48 | 200 |
| 72 | 36 | 240 |
| 84 | 48 | 300 |
| 96 | 48 | 400 |
| 108 | 48 | 500 |
| 120 | 48 | 600 |
| 144 | 72 | 900 |
| 120 | 36 | 550 |
| 168 | 84 | 980 |
| 144 | 48 | 800 |
| 152 | 56 | 900 |

**TABLE 11.13**   Perforated Ceiling Diffusers, Aluminum Frame and Grid, Flat Surface Mounting

| Neck size, in. | 6 × 6 | 8 × 8 | 10 × 10 | 12 × 12 |
|---|---|---|---|---|
| Nominal hole size, in. | 12 × 12 | 14 × 14 | 16 × 16 | 18 × 18 |
| Nominal cfm @ 1 in. sp | 175 | 300 | 500 | 750 |
| Nonadjustable, $ | 32 | 36 | 40 | 46 |
| Adjustable, $ | 38 | 42 | 48 | 56 |
| OB damper—extra, $ | 10.50 | 13.00 | 15.00 | 18.00 |

**TABLE 11.14**   Perforated Ceiling Return Grilles, Aluminum Frame and Grid, Flat Surface Mounting or Lay-in

| Neck size, in. | 10 × 10 | 14 × 14 | 18 × 18 | 22 × 10 | 22 × 22 |
|---|---|---|---|---|---|
| Nominal hole size, in. | 12 × 12 | 16 × 16 | 20 × 20 | 24 × 12 | 24 × 24 |
| Nominal cfm @ 0.075 in. sp | 300 | 675 | 1,125 | 760 | 1,675 |
| Less damper, $ | 31 | 35 | 37 | 43 | 56 |
| OB damper—extra, $ | 14.00 | 19.50 | 24.00 | 24.75 | 35.00 |

## VARIABLE-AIR-VOLUME DISTRIBUTION

Variable-air-volume (VAV) has achieved widespread popularity in recent years because of its energy conservation features. In addition, the benefits of VAV evolution have spilled over into the area of building pressurization. When used with an accurate static pressure regulator, good building pressurization control can be achieved for about $1,200 per pressurization loop. VAV terminals may be used conjunctively with cooling, heating, chilled-water air handlers, rooftops, penthouse, or self-contained packages. System installed costs range from $4 to $9/sq ft. See Tables 11.15 and 11.16 for VAV terminal units.

**TABLE 11.15**   Variable-Air-Volume Boxes—Material Costs, $

Pressure-independent with pneumatic control and pneumatic volume regulator, less thermostat.*

| Nominal cfm | 200 | 400 | 800 | 1,200 | 2,000 | 3,000 | 4,000 | 6,000 |
|---|---|---|---|---|---|---|---|---|
| Cooling only, $ | 350 | 365 | 425 | 460 | 650 | 900 | 925 | 1,000 |

Pressure-dependent, with electric actuator and thermostat.

| Nominal cfm | 200 | 400 | 800 | 1,200 | 2,000 |
|---|---|---|---|---|---|
| Cooling only, $ | 425 | 430 | 490 | 525 | 725 |

Fan-powered with pneumatic volume regulator, less thermostat.

| Nominal cfm | 400 | 800 | 1,200 | 2,000 | 4,000 |
|---|---|---|---|---|---|
| Cooling only, $ | 550 | 580 | 600 | 800 | 1,000 |

Fan-powered with electric actuator and thermostat.

| Nominal cfm | 400 | 800 | 1,200 | 2,000 |
|---|---|---|---|---|
| Cooling only, $ | 675 | 700 | 725 | 900 |

*For reheat coil, multiply above by 1.44.

**TABLE 11.16**   Variable-Air-Volume Boxes—Hookups

Does not include control hookup.

| Nominal cfm | 200 | 400 | 800 | 1,200 | 2,000 | 3,000 | 4,000 | 6,000 |
|---|---|---|---|---|---|---|---|---|
| Erection workhours | 2 | 2 | 3 | 3 | 4 | 5 | 5 | 5 |

## MISCELLANEOUS AIR-DISTRIBUTION DEVICES

Material costs for VAV boxes in popular sizes are given in Table 11.15. Table 11.16 gives the workhour labor time to erect VAV boxes. Table 11.17 gives material costs for a variety of flow-measuring stations for air balancing.

## RESIDENTIAL AIR-DISTRIBUTION DEVICES

Data on a few of the more popular residential air-distribution devices are given in Tables 11.18 to 11.22.

**TABLE 11.17**   Air Balance Flow-Measuring Stations

| Size | Material, $ |
|---|---|
| 16 × 16 | 130 |
| 18 × 12 | 115 |
| 24 × 12 | 140 |
| 24 × 24 | 240 |
| 36 × 24 | 315 |
| 36 × 36 | 430 |
| 48 × 24 | 400 |
| 48 × 36 | 510 |
| 60 × 24 | 450 |
| 60 × 36 | 625 |
| 72 × 36 | 725 |
| 72 × 42 | 825 |

**TABLE 11.18**   Round Diffusers, Flush-Mounted, Butterfly Damper, Aluminum

| Size, in. | 6 | 8 | 10 | 12 | 14 | 18 | 22 |
|---|---|---|---|---|---|---|---|
| Material, $ | 14 | 18 | 21 | 24 | 30 | 57 | 75 |

**TABLE 11.19**   Square Diffusers, Flush-Mounted, Steel, with Opposed-Blade Damper

| Size, in. | 6 × 6 | 8 × 8 | 10 × 10 | 12 × 12 |
|---|---|---|---|---|
| Fixed, $ | 28 | 32 | 39 | 50 |

**TABLE 11.20** Floor Diffusers, Steel

| Size, in. | 10 × 4 | 12 × 4 | 12 × 6 | 14 × 4 | 14 × 6 |
|---|---|---|---|---|---|
| Including dampers, $ | 5.00 | 7.00 | 8.50 | 9.00 | 11.25 |

**TABLE 11.21** Heating Registers, Steel

| Size, in. | 8 × 6 | 10 × 6 | 10 × 8 | 12 × 6 | 12 × 8 | 14 × 6 | 14 × 8 | 16 × 6 | 16 × 8 | 24 × 6 | 24 × 8 |
|---|---|---|---|---|---|---|---|---|---|---|---|
| Including scoop valve, $ | 10.00 | 10.50 | 10.75 | 11.00 | 11.50 | 11.50 | 12.00 | 13.00 | 13.25 | 14.50 | 16.50 |

**TABLE 11.22** Return-Air Grilles, Flush-Mounted

| Size, in. | Material, $ |
|---|---|
| 16 × 8 | 9 |
| 12 × 12 | 10 |
| 24 × 12 | 15 |
| 30 × 12 | 18 |
| 14 × 14 | 11 |
| 16 × 16 | 13 |
| 18 × 18 | 16 |
| 24 × 18 | 20 |
| 36 × 18 | 32 |
| 24 × 24 | 25 |
| 36 × 24 | 36 |
| 48 × 24 | 61 |
| 48 × 30 | 80 |
| 36 × 36 | 63 |
| 48 × 36 | 90 |

# CHAPTER 12
# INSULATION

## GENERAL DISCUSSION

The application of industrial insulations has become an indispensable part of every mechanical construction. Each year new insulations appear; some remain, while others quietly disappear. Some old-timers continue to design, specify, and recommend materials that are now economically and practically obsolete. This practice often stems from habit or distrust of new materials. Nomenclature, too, is often archaic and should be reappraised in the light of new materials and new techniques of manufacture and application. It is necessary for the estimator to have a working knowledge of these materials and techniques and an understanding of the various services to which the materials may be applied.

The economic thickness of insulation is that thickness which results in the minimum total life-cycle cost when considering both the initial cost and the cost of energy.

It is beyond the scope of this book to provide a detailed explanation of methods for calculating the economic thickness of insulation. For information on the subject, refer to Turner and Malloy's (1980) *Handbook of Thermal Insulation Design Economics for Pipes and Equipment,* which explains the required calculations in detail and provides numerous tables and charts for determining economic thickness under a wide range of conditions and cost considerations.

With the sharp increases in energy costs occurring in the mid-1970s, in part as an outgrowth of the oil embargo and governmental actions to reduce dependence on imported oil, efforts to improve insulation in structures have dramatically increased. The efforts were spurred on by tax credits for improving energy efficiency of existing structures and by government grants to help pay the cost of insulating low-income housing. This situation has resulted in greater consumer awareness of the benefits of thermal insulation and has accelerated the development of new forms of insulation and improved insulating techniques.

One product, urea formaldehyde, which rapidly gained prominence in the late 1970s and early 1980s, suffered declining use because of health problems reportedly caused by formaldehyde fumes. As a result of those problems, the U.S. Consumer Product Safety Commission banned the use of urea formaldehyde for residential or school use as of August 10, 1982. Its use is still permitted in commercial and industrial buildings, but it is declining.

Another product that is rapidly being phased out of use is asbestos. Once a primary insulating material, asbestos has been virtually abandoned because of concerns about its carcinogenic effects. Lawsuits from persons claiming to have developed cancer from asbestos exposure have been so numerous as to force several major manufacturers of insulating materials into bankruptcy. The previous edition of this book listed many insulation manufacturers by name, some of which are no longer in existence because of the asbestos problem.

Existing asbestos insulation often must be removed from ducts and pipes, particularly if it is in public buildings such as schools or if a building is being offered for sale. Table 12.1 gives some typical costs of asbestos removal. These costs should be considered to be very approxi-

**TABLE 12.1**  Bulk Asbestos Removal Costs

Includes disposable tools and four suits and respirators per day per worker. Does not include overhead or profit.

| | | | 1994 Costs, $ | | |
|---|---|---|---|---|---|
| Item | Workhours per unit* | Unit | Labor | Material and equipment | Total† |
| Boiler insulation (add 50% with metal lath) | 0.133 | sq ft | 3.59 | 0.44 | 4.03 |
| Boiler breeching or flue insulation (add 100% for active boiler) | 0.123 | sq ft | 3.32 | 0.41 | 3.73 |
| Duct or AHU insulation | 0.089 | sq ft | 2.40 | 0.29 | 2.69 |
| Duct vibration isolation joints: | | | | | |
| ≤24-sq-in. duct | 1.143 | ea | 31.00 | 3.77 | 34.77 |
| 25–48-sq-in. duct | 1.333 | ea | 36.00 | 4.40 | 40.40 |
| 49–76-sq-in. duct | 1.600 | ea | 43.00 | 5.30 | 48.30 |
| Pipe insulation: | | | | | |
| ≤4-in.-diameter pipe | 0.071 | lin ft | 1.92 | 0.23 | 2.15 |
| 4–8-in.-diameter pipe | 0.080 | lin ft | 2.16 | 0.26 | 2.42 |
| 10–12-in.-diameter pipe | 0.091 | lin ft | 2.46 | 0.30 | 2.76 |
| 14–16-in.-diameter pipe | 0.116 | lin ft | 3.14 | 0.38 | 3.52 |
| >16-in.-diameter pipe | 0.098 | sq ft | 2.65 | 0.32 | 2.97 |
| With glove bag, ≤3-in.-diameter pipe | 0.640 | lin ft | 17.25 | 8.11 | 25.36 |
| Pipefitting insulation: | | | | | |
| ≤4-in.-diameter pipe | 0.200 | ea | 5.40 | 0.66 | 6.06 |
| 6–8-in.-diameter pipe | 0.211 | ea | 5.70 | 0.69 | 6.39 |
| 10–12-in.-diameter pipe | 0.333 | ea | 9.00 | 1.10 | 10.10 |
| 14–16-in.-diameter pipe | 0.500 | ea | 13.50 | 1.65 | 15.15 |
| >16-in.-diameter pipe | 0.364 | sq ft | 9.80 | 1.20 | 11.00 |
| With glove bag, ≤8-in.-diameter pipe | 1.600 | ca | 43.00 | 11.55 | 54.55 |
| Scrape foam fireproofing | | | | | |
| From flat surfaces | 0.027 | sq ft | 0.72 | 0.09 | 0.81 |
| From irregular surfaces | 0.053 | sq ft | 1.44 | 0.18 | 1.62 |
| Remove cementitious material | | | | | |
| From flat surfaces | 0.080 | sq ft | 2.16 | 0.26 | 2.42 |
| From irregular surfaces | 0.160 | sq ft | 4.31 | 0.53 | 4.84 |
| Radiator backing, not including radiator removal | 0.053 | sq ft | 1.44 | 0.18 | 1.62 |

*Crew consists of seven asbestos workers and one supervisor. Equipment items required are four airless sprayers and three HEPA vacuums, 16 gal.

†Add 10% for type C (supplied air) respirator equipment

SOURCE:  *Means Mechanical Cost Data*, R. S. Means Co., Kingston, Mass., 1994.

mate as costs of asbestos removal vary widely from location to location and subcontractor to subcontractor.

Cellulose, perlite, and vermiculite are heavily used as blow-in or loose-fill insulation in hollow-wall construction. Rapid growth in insulation demand and the problems with urea formaldehyde caused heavy use of cellulose as a low-cost alternative. This, in turn, created problems with flammability and structural fires. Since 1987, therefore, federal law has required all cellulose-based insulation materials to meet minimum requirements for flame resistance.

Thermal insulation is used in three major instances: (1) to retard the heat flow (in either direction) through a pipe, duct, vessel, or structure; (2) to prevent condensation; and (3) to control the surface temperature of a vessel structure. Materials are available in a wide variety of forms from loose fills and granules to preformed rigid materials in standard shapes and lengths. Often, the specification will be for a general name or product name which is unfamiliar to the estimator.

**TABLE 12.2** Common Thermal Insulations

| Type | K factor | |
|---|---|---|
| | At 75°F | At 200°F |
| Expanded plastics, −300 to +180/220°F | | |
|     Polystyrene | 0.24 | |
|     Polyvinyl chloride | 0.17 | |
|     Urethane | 0.14 | |
|     Neoprene | 0.26 | |
| Mineral wool, −300 to +350°F (fibrous glass) | 0.24 | 0.34 |
| Cellular glass, −450 to +800°F | 0.39 | |
| Calcium silicate, +200 to +1,200°F | | 0.35 |

Table 12.2 lists some of the common types of insulation and the application temperatures. This table is offered only as a general source of identification of materials and is not intended as a guide for specifications for materials. No attempt is made here to list manufacturers of insulating materials. Many of the insulations noted in a particular temperature range may overlap and have application elsewhere. The product form also may vary, and a particular material may be available in several different forms.

All pipe coverings except cellular glass are standard 36-in. lengths regardless of thickness. Cellular glass may be supplied in either 18- or 24-in. lengths.

Where temperature ranges are indicated in this chapter, they are not meant as design criteria. The temperature ranges are indicated only as a convenience for the estimator to use when the thickness has not been specified, such as budget figures and cost projections.

The estimator should examine the specifications carefully to determine a departure from standard finishes. Special finishes are shown in this text as a separate item; otherwise, it is assumed that the finish is standard. It is not uncommon for a specifier merely to copy off an existing specification without fully understanding the application specified. Although bands are often specified, they serve little purpose in pipe insulation other than decoration. Most manufacturers include bands with some types of pipe covering for sizes of ≤20 in. In cases where bands are necessary to the pipe-covering application, the estimator will have to estimate this separately. Bands are not included in the material prices shown in the following tables unless they are standard with the insulation material.

The workhours used in this chapter are based on average conditions for a typical commercial structure and the work being performed at heights of ≤10 ft. It is assumed that working temperatures are below 90°F and that all materials are stocked at the site. When materials are remotely stored, add 15%. When a worker is working in a supine position in a small area, add 60% to the affected portion of the labor figure. For conditions other than stated, various correction tables may be found in Chap. 1.

Unless otherwise indicated, the labor figures in this chapter are based on *feet per worker per day*. Overhead and profit are not included.

## METHOD OF MEASUREMENT OF APPLIED INSULATION

When selection is left to the discretion of the estimating engineer, the following fundamental rules should be observed:

When pipe is installed underground, the use of fibrous glass should be avoided because of the product's lack of strength and tendency to deteriorate when wetted.

The old 90% efficiency method of selecting heat insulation should be discontinued. The thickness should be based on the economic analysis method.

All low-temperature insulations should have vapor-barrier jackets with a minimum value of 0.1 perm (indicating degree of permeability) along with the adhesives and sealants.

Equal insulation protection should be provided for fittings, valves, and flanges for both hot and cold pipes, and the same vapor-barrier protection should be afforded.

In selecting synthetic insulation materials for low-temperature application, extreme caution should be used to avoid any substandard manufacture, since the chemical, thermal, and physical characteristics of the foamed plastics of unidentified manufacture have been observed to vary greatly.

Saddle brackets are normally handled in the piping contractor's specifications, painting under the painting section of the specifications, and internal duct liner under the sheet-metal specifications, since the insulation contractor is not normally equipped to handle this type of work.

## EQUIPMENT

Equipment measurements shall be exact, and areas should be computed to the nearest square foot.

The area of a cylindrical surface is computed from the length of the cylinder multiplied by the circumference. The circumference should be measured outside the finished insulation for external application and inside the cylinder wall for internal insulation.

The area of standard dish and flathead vessels is estimated as the square of the outside diameter of the insulation on the shell body. The actual insulation area should be calculated for other shapes of equipment and/or heads.

There should be no deductions in area for accessways, nozzles, hand holes, etc. All projections should be measured separately as piping.

Flat surfaces should be measured over the outside of the insulation.

## PIPING

All straight pipe should be measured from origin to terminus points of junctures. Measurement should be made through all insulated or uninsulated fittings in insulated lines, except that measurement through valves applies only if the valve is insulated. The length of bent piping should be measured separately along the outside radius of insulation between tangent points.

Fittings include tees, reducers, all valve bodies regardless of type, steam traps, ells with radius of $\leq 1\frac{1}{2}$ the pipe diameter, miters, stub-in connections, and caps.

Valve bodies include the bonnet, but not the inlet and outlet flanges. Bonnet flanges shall be counted as one pair of flanges when insulated.

Each flange on fittings shall be counted as a flange and not as part of the fittings.

All fittings which connect two different sizes of pipe shall be counted as one fitting of the largest size involved and shall be omitted from the count of the smaller size. Bosses shall be considered fittings and shall be priced at twice ($2\times$) the unit price for the size of boss.

All branches where a smaller size of pipe is joined to a larger size, by welding, will be counted as one fitting of the smaller size of pipe, except that fitting of a $\leq 2$-in. branch into a $\geq 4$-in. line shall not be counted as a fitting of either size. If only one of the lines—either the larger or the smaller—is insulated, the fitting will not be counted and no factor of unit prices will be considered.

Insulation of steam-traced lines will be paid for on a basis of the actual insulation size required to cover both line and tracer, except that if "heat transfer cement" is used between the main line and the tracer line, the line shall have a separate price.

Couplings shall be considered as straight pipe.

*Bent pipe* shall be defined as any bent pipe of a radius greater than 1½ times the pipe diameter.

Pipe, flanges, fittings, and bends will be paid for on a basis of their equivalent of the value of a foot of straight-pipe insulation of corresponding thickness and size in accordance with the following straight-pipe-insulation equivalents:

| Item | Equivalent factor |
|---|---|
| Pipe bends >1½-in. diameter | 2× length |
| Flanges (pair) | 3-ft straight pipe |
| Fittings | 2-ft straight pipe |

Unit price per linear foot for each size and thickness of pipe insulation shall include beveling and fitting at supports, hangers, pipe shoes, angles, clips, and termination points.

Figure 12.1 shows a sample of the method of field measurement.

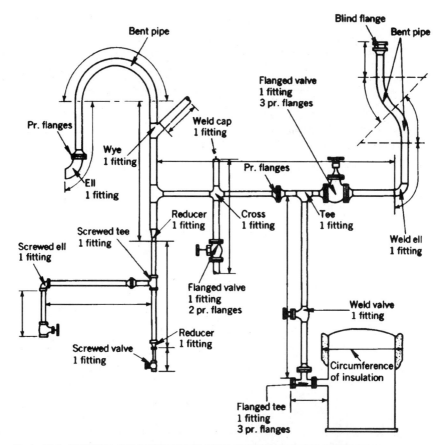

**Figure 12.1  METHOD OF MEASUREMENT FOR COST-ESTIMATING INSULATION**

## ESTIMATING

Tables 12.3 to 12.6 are based on aboveground installation. When estimating underground installation—in an accessible trench—reduce pipe-covering labor by 25%. When making the takeoff, add 4 ft of equivalent pipe for each screwed fitting and 10 ft for each flanged fitting. For equipment-room work, add 25% to the labor time shown. Powerhouse work is not covered in this discussion.

**TABLE 12.3** Applying Roof Jackets, Feet per Worker per Day

| Diameter, in. | 1½ | 2 | 3 | 4 | 6 | 8 | 10 | 12 | 14 | 16 | 18 | 20 |
|---|---|---|---|---|---|---|---|---|---|---|---|---|
| ft per workday . . . . | 185 | 175 | 175 | 140 | 140 | 125 | 75 | 50 | 40 | 40 | 30 | 30 |

**TABLE 12.4** Square Feet of Roofing Jacket per Linear Foot of Pipe

Roof jacket is based on 2-in. circumferential lap and 1-in. end lap. For lap cement, allow ½ gal. per 100 sq ft of roofing jacket for pipe ≤4 in. and ¼ gal. per 100 sq ft for pipe >4 in.

| Pipe size, in. | 2 | 3 | 4 | 6 | 8 | 10 | 12 |
|---|---|---|---|---|---|---|---|
| 1 in. thick. . . . | 1.42 | 1.74 | 2.02 | 2.63 | 3.19 | 3.80 | 4.36 |
| 2 in. thick . . . | 1.99 | 2.31 | 2.59 | 3.19 | 3.76 | 4.36 | 4.93 |
| 3 in. thick. . . . | 2.56 | 2.87 | 3.16 | 3.76 | 4.33 | 4.93 | 5.50 |

**TABLE 12.5** Square Feet of Surface per Linear Foot of Insulated Pipe

Based on total diameter of pipe and 85% magnesia covering. This table may be used to compute areas for painting, canvas covering, or roofing felt. For canvas or weatherproof felt, total square feet in takeoff should be multiplied by 120% to allow for lapping, folding, and waste.

| Pipe size, in. | 1½ | 2 | 3 | 4 | 6 | 8 |
|---|---|---|---|---|---|---|
| 1-in. insulation . . . . . . | 0.96 | 1.12 | 1.47 | 1.80 | 2.35 | 2.95 |
| 1½-in. insulation. . . . . . | 1.30 | 1.40 | 1.70 | 2.00 | 2.55 | 3.08 |
| 2-in. insulation. . . . . . . | 1.55 | 1.87 | 1.98 | 2.24 | 2.82 | 3.34 |
| 2½-in. insulation. . . . . . | 1.82 | 1.95 | 2.25 | 2.50 | 3.07 | 3.60 |
| Pipe size, in. | 10 | 12 | 14 | 16 | 18 | 20 |
| 1-in. insulation. . . . . . | 3.55 | 4.16 | 4.55 | 4.97 | 5.40 | 6.05 |
| 1½-in. insulation. . . . . | 3.64 | 4.16 | 4.55 | 4.97 | 5.40 | 6.05 |
| 2-in. insulation. . . . . . | 3.90 | 4.42 | 4.83 | 5.24 | 5.72 | 6.30 |
| 2½-in. insulation. . . . . | 4.16 | 4.68 | 5.10 | 5.50 | 5.93 | 6.55 |

**TABLE 12.6**  Covering Capacity of Coatings

| Material | Coverage |
|---|---|
| Hot asphalt | 35 lb per 100 sq ft |
| Asphalt paint | 100 sq ft per gal |
| Asphalt varnish | 150 sq ft per gal |
| Asphalt emulsion | 70 sq ft per gal |
| Aluminum | 150 sq ft per gal |
| Cold water, 5 lb per gal | 100 sq ft per gal |
| Glue sizing, 2 lb per gal | 200 sq ft per gal |
| Lap cement | 50 sq ft per gal |
| Lead and oil | 200 sq ft per gal |
| Primer | 150 sq ft per gal |

## PIPE COVERING

Data for hot-pipe insulation are given in Tables 12.7 and 12.8; for polyethylene tubing flexible closed-cell foam insulation, in Table 12.9; and for rubber tube flexible closed-cell foam, in Table 12.10. Table 12.11 gives recommended thicknesses of fiber-glass and mineral wool insulation on pipes and ducts.

**TABLE 12.7**  Hot-Pipe Insulation—Range to 1,200°F

Calcium silicate, sectional pipe insulation with manufacturer's standard canvas jacket, side and end flaps of jacket pasted down with cold-water paste, and banded. For 6-oz canvas, add 8% to material; for 8-oz canvas, add 10%. Material cost is for indoor application. For outdoor application with 45-lb felt jacket, 3-in. laps, and cold seal adhesive at all laps, add 15%. For outdoor application, increase labor productivity 25%.

| Iron pipe size, in. | ¾ | 1 | 1¼ | 1½ | 2 | 2½ | 3 | 4 | 6 | 8 | 10 | 12 |
|---|---|---|---|---|---|---|---|---|---|---|---|---|
| | 1-in. thickness | | | | | | | | | 1½-in. thickness | | |
| Material, $ per ft | 2.25 | 2.25 | 2.25 | 2.25 | 2.70 | 2.90 | 3.00 | 3.50 | 4.25 | 6.70 | 8.90 | 10.50 |
| Labor, ft/worker per day | 150 | 150 | 150 | 150 | 150 | 140 | 135 | 130 | 100 | 70 | 60 | 50 |
| | 1½-in. thickness | | | | | | | | | 2-in. thickness | | |
| Material, $ per ft | 2.50 | 2.75 | 3.00 | 3.15 | 3.40 | 3.75 | 3.90 | 4.60 | 5.30 | 13.00 | 16.00 | 18.00 |
| Labor, ft/worker per day | 135 | 135 | 135 | 135 | 135 | 125 | 120 | 115 | 85 | 50 | 40 | 30 |
| | 2-in. thickness | | | | | | | | | 2½-in. thickness | | |
| Material, $ per ft | 4.05 | 4.25 | 4.60 | 4.85 | 5.10 | 6.08 | 5.85 | 6.85 | 8.75 | 14.50 | 18.50 | 19.50 |
| Labor, ft/worker per day | 120 | 120 | 120 | 120 | 120 | 100 | 100 | 95 | 75 | 40 | 30 | 20 |

**TABLE 12.8**    Hot-Pipe Insulation—Range to 900°F

Glass fibers with all-service jacket. For standard canvas jacket, deduct 5%.

| Iron pipe size, in. | ½ | ¾ | 1 | 1¼ | 1½ | 2 | 2½ | 3 | 4 | 5 | 6 |
|---|---|---|---|---|---|---|---|---|---|---|---|
| | | | | | ½-in. thickness | | | | | | |
| Material, $ per ft | 1.00 | 1.10 | 1.15 | 1.25 | 1.40 | 1.50 | 1.70 | 1.90 | 2.40 | 2.75 | 2.90 |
| Labor, ft per worker per day | 175 | 175 | 175 | 175 | 175 | 175 | 175 | 150 | 150 | 140 | 100 |
| | | | | | 1-in. thickness | | | | | | |
| Material, $ per ft | 1.15 | 1.35 | 1.90 | 1.50 | 1.70 | 1.80 | 2.00 | 2.25 | 2.90 | 3.40 | 3.50 |
| Labor, ft per worker per day | 185 | 185 | 185 | 185 | 185 | 185 | 185 | 160 | 160 | 150 | 105 |

**TABLE 12.9**    Polyethylene Tubing Flexible Closed-Cell Foam, Hot or Cold Lines, −90 to +212°F UV-Resistant

| Iron pipe size, in. | ½ | ¾ | 1 | 1¼ | 1½ | 2 | 2½ | 3 | 4 |
|---|---|---|---|---|---|---|---|---|---|
| | | | | ¾-in. thickness | | | | | |
| Material, $ per ft | 0.38 | 0.42 | 0.56 | 0.74 | 0.82 | 1.19 | 1.42 | 1.66 | 2.14 |
| Labor, ft/worker per day | 106 | 104 | 102 | 100 | 100 | 98 | 96 | 94 | 90 |
| | | | | 1-in. thickness | | | | | |
| Material, $ per ft | 0.61 | 0.65 | 0.94 | 1.05 | 1.09 | 1.40 | 1.58 | 1.76 | |
| Labor, ft/worker per day | 96 | 94 | 92 | 90 | 90 | 88 | 86 | 84 | |

SOURCE:    *Means Mechanical Cost Data*, R. S. Means Co., Kingston, Mass., 1994.

**TABLE 12.10**    Flexible Closed-Cell Foam, Cold Pipes

Slide-on sections in rubber tube 6-ft lengths for indoor application, butted ends with rubber tape.

| Iron pipe size, in. | ¼ | ⅜ | ½ | ¾ | 1 | 1¼ | 1½ |
|---|---|---|---|---|---|---|---|
| | | | | ⅜-in thickness | | | |
| Material, $ per ft | 0.32 | 0.37 | 0.41 | 0.46 | 0.53 | 0.67 | 0.78 |
| Labor, ft/worker per day | 120 | 120 | 115 | 115 | 110 | 110 | 110 |
| | | | | ½-in. thickness | | | |
| Iron pipe size, in. | ¼ | ⅜ | ½ | ¾ | 1 | 1¼ | 1½ |
| Material, $ per ft | 0.49 | 0.55 | 0.61 | 0.67 | 0.75 | 0.87 | 1.04 |
| Labor, ft/worker per day | 90 | 90 | 89 | 89 | 88 | 87 | 87 |
| Iron pipe size, in. | 2 | 2½ | 3 | 3½ | 4 | 5 | |
| Material, $ per ft | 1.28 | 1.69 | 2.35 | 2.45 | 2.63 | 3.89 | |
| Labor, ft/worker per day | 86 | 86 | 85 | 85 | 80 | 80 | |

SOURCE:    *Means Mechanical Cost Data*, R. S. Means Co., Kingston, Mass., 1994.

**TABLE 12.11**  Recommended Thickness of Insulation for Fiber-Glass and Mineral Wool on Piping and Ductwork

| Nominal pipe size, in. | | Process temperature | | | | | | | | | |
|---|---|---|---|---|---|---|---|---|---|---|---|
| | | 150°F | 250°F | 350°F | 450°F | 550°F | 650°F | 750°F | 850°F | 950°F | 1,050°F |
| ½ | Thickness | 1 | 1½ | 2 | 2½ | 3 | 3½ | 4 | 4 | 4½ | 5½ |
| | Heat loss | 8 | 16 | 24 | 33 | 43 | 54 | 66 | 84 | 100 | 114 |
| | Surf. temp. | 72 | 75 | 76 | 78 | 79 | 81 | 82 | 86 | 87 | 87 |
| 1 | Thickness | 1 | 1½ | 2 | 2½ | 3½ | 4 | 4 | 4½ | 5 | 5½ |
| | Heat loss | 11 | 21 | 30 | 41 | 49 | 61 | 79 | 96 | 114 | 135 |
| | Surf. temp. | 73 | 76 | 78 | 80 | 79 | 81 | 84 | 86 | 88 | 89 |
| 1½ | Thickness | 1 | 2 | 2½ | 3 | 4 | 4 | 4 | 5½ | 5½ | 6 |
| | Heat loss | 14 | 22 | 33 | 45 | 54 | 73 | 94 | 103 | 128 | 152 |
| | Surf. temp. | 73 | 74 | 77 | 79 | 79 | 82 | 86 | 84 | 88 | 90 |
| 2 | Thickness | 1½ | 2 | 3 | 3½ | 4 | 4 | 4 | 5½ | 6 | 6 |
| | Heat loss | 13 | 25 | 24 | 47 | 61 | 81 | 105 | 114 | 137 | 168 |
| | Surf. temp. | 71 | 75 | 75 | 77 | 79 | 83 | 87 | 85 | 87 | 91 |
| 3 | Thickness | 1½ | 2½ | 3½ | 4 | 4 | 4½ | 4½ | 6 | 6½ | 7 |
| | Heat loss | 16 | 28 | 39 | 54 | 75 | 94 | 122 | 133 | 154 | 184 |
| | Surf. temp. | 72 | 74 | 75 | 77 | 81 | 83 | 87 | 86 | 87 | 90 |
| 4 | Thickness | 1½ | 3 | 4 | 4 | 4 | 5 | 5½ | 6 | 7 | 7½ |
| | Heat loss | 19 | 29 | 42 | 63 | 88 | 102 | 126 | 152 | 174 | 206 |
| | Surf. temp. | 72 | 73 | 74 | 78 | 82 | 86 | 85 | 87 | 88 | 90 |
| 6 | Thickness | 2 | 3 | 4 | 4 | 4½ | 5 | 5½ | 6½ | 7½ | 8 |
| | Heat loss | 21 | 38 | 54 | 81 | 104 | 130 | 159 | 181 | 208 | 246 |
| | Surf. temp. | 71 | 74 | 75 | 79 | 82 | 84 | 87 | 88 | 89 | 91 |
| 8 | Thickness | 2 | 3½ | 4 | 4 | 5 | 5 | 5½ | 7 | 8 | 8½ |
| | Heat loss | 26 | 42 | 65 | 97 | 116 | 155 | 189 | 204 | 234 | 277 |
| | Surf. temp. | 71 | 73 | 76 | 80 | 81 | 86 | 89 | 88 | 89 | 92 |
| 10 | Thickness | 2 | 3½ | 4 | 4 | 5 | 5½ | 5½ | 7½ | 8½ | 9 |
| | Heat loss | 32 | 50 | 77 | 115 | 136 | 170 | 220 | 226 | 259 | 307 |
| | Surf. temp. | 72 | 74 | 77 | 81 | 82 | 85 | 90 | 87 | 89 | 91 |
| 12 | Thickness | 2 | 3½ | 4 | 4 | 5 | 5½ | 5½ | 7½ | 8½ | 9½ |
| | Heat loss | 36 | 57 | 87 | 131 | 154 | 192 | 249 | 253 | 290 | 331 |
| | Surf. temp. | 72 | 74 | 77 | 82 | 82 | 86 | 91 | 88 | 89 | 91 |
| 14 | Thickness | 2 | 3½ | 4 | 4 | 5 | 5½ | 6½ | 7½ | 9 | 9½ |
| | Heat loss | 40 | 61 | 94 | 141 | 165 | 206 | 236 | 271 | 297 | 352 |
| | Surf. temp. | 72 | 74 | 77 | 82 | 83 | 86 | 87 | 89 | 89 | 91 |
| 16 | Thickness | 2½ | 3½ | 4 | 4 | 5½ | 5½ | 7 | 8 | 9 | 10 |
| | Heat loss | 37 | 68 | 105 | 157 | 171 | 228 | 247 | 284 | 326 | 372 |
| | Surf. temp. | 71 | 74 | 78 | 83 | 82 | 87 | 86 | 88 | 89 | 91 |
| 18 | Thickness | 2½ | 3½ | 4 | 4 | 5½ | 5½ | 7 | 8 | 9 | 10 |
| | Heat loss | 41 | 75 | 115 | 173 | 187 | 250 | 270 | 310 | 354 | 404 |
| | Surf. temp. | 71 | 74 | 78 | 83 | 83 | 87 | 87 | 88 | 90 | 91 |
| 20 | Thickness | 2½ | 3½ | 4 | 4 | 5½ | 5½ | 7 | 8 | 9 | 10 |
| | Heat loss | 45 | 82 | 126 | 189 | 204 | 272 | 292 | 335 | 383 | 436 |
| | Surf. temp. | 71 | 75 | 78 | 83 | 83 | 87 | 87 | 89 | 90 | 92 |
| 24 | Thickness | 2½ | 4 | 4 | 4 | 5½ | 6 | 7½ | 8 | 9 | 10 |
| | Heat loss | 53 | 86 | 147 | 221 | 237 | 295 | 320 | 386 | 439 | 498 |
| | Surf. temp. | 71 | 74 | 78 | 83 | 83 | 86 | 86 | 89 | 91 | 93 |

(*Continued*)

**TABLE 12.11** Recommended Thickness of Insulation for Fiber-Glass and Mineral Wool on Piping and Ductwork (*Continued*)

| Nominal pipe size, in. | | Process temperature | | | | | | | | | |
|---|---|---|---|---|---|---|---|---|---|---|---|
| | | 150°F | 250°F | 350°F | 450°F | 550°F | 650°F | 750°F | 850°F | 950°F | 1,050°F |
| 30 | Thickness | 2½ | 4 | 4 | 4 | 5½ | 6½ | 7½ | 8½ | 10 | 10 |
| | Heat loss | 65 | 105 | 179 | 268 | 286 | 332 | 383 | 439 | 481 | 591 |
| | Surf. temp. | 71 | 74 | 79 | 84 | 84 | 85 | 87 | 89 | 89 | 94 |
| 36 | Thickness | 2½ | 4 | 4 | 4 | 5½ | 7 | 8 | 9 | 10 | 10 |
| | Heat loss | 77 | 123 | 211 | 316 | 335 | 364 | 422 | 486 | 556 | 683 |
| | Surf. temp. | 71 | 74 | 79 | 84 | 84 | 84 | 86 | 88 | 90 | 94 |
| Flat | Thickness | 2 | 3½ | 4 | 4½ | 5½ | 8½ | 9½ | 10 | 10 | 10 |
| | Heat loss | 10 | 14 | 20 | 27 | 31 | 27 | 31 | 38 | 47 | 58 |
| | Surf. temp. | 72 | 74 | 77 | 80 | 82 | 80 | 82 | 85 | 89 | 93 |

Thickness = inches; heat loss = Btu/ft per hour; based on 65°F ambient temperature. Users are advised to consult manufacturer's literature for specific product temperature limitations.

SOURCE: *Means Estimating Handbook,* R. S. Means Co., Kingston, Mass., 1990.

## EQUIPMENT INSULATION IN BLOCK OR SHEET FORM

The application of equipment insulation and finishes is too varied and broad in scope to be discussed in detail in this text. Data for some of the commonly used materials and labor production rates are given in Tables 12.12 to 12.14. Labor is shown in square feet per worker per day. For rapid estimating of surface areas of tanks, see Chap. 8.

**TABLE 12.12** Equipment Insulation—Blocks and Sheets

| | Material, $ per sq ft | Labor, sq ft per worker per day |
|---|---|---|
| Calcium silicate block, 200 to 12,000°F: | | |
| 1-in. | 4.00 | 15 |
| 1½-in. | 4.35 | 12.5 |
| 2-in. | 5.50 | 11 |
| 3-in. | 8.75 | 9 |
| Boiler insulation: | | |
| 1½-in. calcium silicate, 1½-in. cement finish | 5.00 | 25 |
| 2-in. fiber-glass | 3.50 | 40 |
| Breeching: 2-in. calcium silicate, ½-in. cement finish no lath: | | |
| Rectangular | 7.00 | 25 |
| Round | 7.85 | 20 |
| Domestic water heater wrap kit: | | |
| 1½-in. with vinyl jacket, 20 to 60 gal. | 18/unit | 1 hr/unit |

**TABLE 12.13** Finishes

| Finish | Material, $ per sq ft | Labor, sq ft per worker per day |
|---|---|---|
| ½-in. cement over 1-in. wire mesh, including corner bead | 1.55 | 58 |
| Canvas, 8 oz, pasted on | 2.60 | 123 |
| Weatherproof, nonmetallic, 2 lb per sq ft | 3.85 | 50 |

**TABLE 12.14** Miscellaneous Labor Costs

| Item | Labor |
|---|---|
| Cement finishing applied at ½-in. thickness | 50 sq ft/worker per day |
| Applying 2-in. wire mesh | 200 sq ft/worker per day |
| Cold-water paint, one coat | 400 sq ft/worker per day |
| Applying rosin paper and 8-oz canvas | Double the labor shown in pipe-covering tables |

## DUCT INSULATION

Many materials for insulating warm- and cold-air ducts are in use today for both concealed and exposed application. Only the commonly used mineral wool and fibrous glass blanket and board types are treated here. Blanket rolls are shipped 4 ft wide × 100 ft long, 400 sq ft per roll; they are available in ½-, 1-, 1½-, and 2-in. thicknesses and densities of 1½, 2, and 3 lb. Rigid-board liner is available in either 2 × 4-ft or 3 × 6-ft sheets in 1- and 2-in. thickness and densities of 3, 4, 5, or 6 lb. Subcontractor to prime contractor prices in 1994 showed averages of $2.65/sq ft installed duct lining and $2.20 for duct wrap based on 1½-in.-thick fiber-glass with vapor barrier. Rigid-board fiber-glass insulation of 3-lb density with FRK vapor barrier in 1-in. thickness averaged $5.35/sq ft, and 2-in. thickness averaged $6.95/sq ft. Exterior duct insulation, 2 in. thick and of 4-lb density, with two layers of black mastic over glass mesh averaged about $6.50/sq ft.

The data in Tables 12.15 to 12.20 are based on commercial rates for jobs of ≥2,000 sq ft with ducts hung free and clear and worked from rolling scaffolding on new construction. For existing buildings, add 50% to labor *after* inspection. For new residential work, add 40% if over 1,000 sq ft and 60% if under 1,000 sq ft. Material prices do not include accessories or waste. Accessories usually run an additional 50% above the cost of the duct covering. Allowance should be made for full-thickness overlaps and 15% waste. Figure 12.2 gives costs in place per linear foot for typical runs of duct insulation.

**TABLE 12.15** Fibrous Glass Blanket, Hot-Air Ducts, Range to 250°F

| Temperature difference, °F | Thickness, in. | Density, lb per cu ft | Facing | Material, $ per sq ft | Labor, sq ft per workhours |
|---|---|---|---|---|---|
| 50 | 1 | ¾ | None | 0.37 | 50 |
| 50 | 1 | 1 | None | 0.35 | 50 |
| 50 | 1½ | ¾ | None | 0.50 | 45 |
| 100 | 1½ | 1 | None | 0.55 | 45 |
| 100 | 2 | ¾ | None | 0.60 | 40 |
| 150 | 2 | 1 | None | 0.70 | 40 |

**TABLE 12.16** Fiber-Glass Blanket, Cold-Air Ducts, Range from +35°F

| Temperature difference, °F | Thickness, in. | Density, lb per cu ft | Facing | Material, $ per sq ft | Labor, sq ft per workhour |
|---|---|---|---|---|---|
| 30 | 1 | ¾ | Foil-reinforced kraft | 0.35 | 50 |
| 30 | 1½ | ¾ | Foil-reinforced kraft | 0.48 | 45 |
| 40 | 2 | ¾ | Foil-reinforced kraft | 0.58 | 43 |
| 50 | 3 | ¾ | Foil-reinforced kraft | 0.88 | 43 |
| 20 | ½ | 2 | Kraft/asphalt | 0.53 | 54 |
| 30 | 1 | 1½ | Kraft/asphalt | 0.71 | 50 |
| 40 | 1½ | 1½ | Kraft/asphalt | 0.88 | 45 |
| 40 | 2 | 1½ | Kraft/asphalt | 1.20 | 43 |

NOTE: Vinyl jacket is same as foil-reinforced kraft.

**TABLE 12.17** Rigid-Board Fiber-Glass, Cold-Air Ducts, Range from +35°F

| Temperature difference, °F | Thickness, in. | Density, lb per cu ft | Facing | Material, $ per sq ft | Labor, sq ft per workhour |
|---|---|---|---|---|---|
| 20 | 1 | 3 | Kraft/asphalt | 1.80 | 14 |
| 30 | 1 | 3 | Reinforced foil | 1.50 | 14 |
| 40 | 1½ | 3 | Kraft/asphalt | 2.00 | 11 |
| 40 | 1½ | 3 | Reinforced foil | 1.85 | 11 |
| 40 | 2 | 3 | Kraft/asphalt | 2.55 | 10 |
| 40 | 2 | 3 | Reinforced foil | 2.15 | 10 |

**TABLE 12.18** Weather-Exposed Ductwork

| Item | Material, $ per sq ft | Labor, sq ft per worker per day |
|---|---|---|
| Mineral wool, rigid board, 1-in. thick, with white slate jacket, 55 lb | 1.75 | 7.50 |
| Mineral wool, rigid board, 2-in. thick, with white slate jacket, 35 lb | 2.25 | 6.25 |
| Foamed cellular glass block, 1½-in. thick, with white coat finish | 2.00 | 6.25 |
| Flexible foam plastic sheet, ¾-in. thick, with white coat finish | 2.40 | 12.00 |
| Flexible foam plastic sheet, 1-in. thick, with white coat finish | 3.00 | 12.00 |

**TABLE 12.19** Sound-Absorbing Fibrous Glass Duct Liner

Based on black vinyl-coated liner fabricated with ductwork; insulation is applied to flat sheet metal with adhesive and formed with metal through brake. Sheet-metal clips are used in addition to adhesive, and all exposed edges and joints are caulked with fire-retardant mastic.

| Thickness, in. | Density, lb per cu ft | Material, $ per sq ft | Workhours per 100 sq ft |
|---|---|---|---|
| ½ | 1½ | 0.35 | 3.0 |
| ½ | 2 | 0.40 | 3.0 |
| ½ | 3 | 0.52 | 3.0 |
| 1 | 1½ | 0.70 | 3.2 |
| 1 | 2 | 0.80 | 3.2 |
| 1 | 3 | 0.90 | 3.6 |
| 1½ | 1½ | 0.85 | 3.9 |
| 1½ | 2 | 1.00 | 3.9 |

NOTE: Silencers or acoustical traps are often used for noise control in ducts. As a rule of thumb, these may be estimated at $36 per MCFM of air flow for material.

**TABLE 12.20**  Top Deck, Ceiling, and Attic Insulation for Structures

Cost figures shown include labor, material, and markup as reflected in prices quoted by subcontractors to mechanical contractor or general contractor.

| R value | Thickness, in. | Type | $ per sq ft |
|---------|---------------|------|-------------|
| | | **Ceiling or attic** | |
| 11 | 4 | Blown mineral wool | 0.70 |
| 13 | 6 | Blown mineral wool | 1.00 |
| 19 | 9 | Blown mineral wool | 1.60 |
| 11 | 3½ | Blown cellular | 0.50 |
| 19 | 5⁵⁄₁₆ | Blown cellular | 0.80 |
| 22 | 6½ | Blown cellular | 1.20 |
| 26 | 8¹¹⁄₁₆ | Blown cellular | 1.25 |
| 38 | 10⅞ | Blown cellular | 1.65 |
| 11 | 5 | Blown fiber glass | 0.70 |
| 13 | 6 | Blown fiber glass | 0.90 |
| 19 | 8½ | Blown fiber glass | 1.15 |
| 22 | 10 | Blown fiber glass | 1.50 |
| 26 | 12 | Blown fiber glass | 1.80 |
| 11 | 3½ | Fiber glass batts, foil-faced, 15-in. | 0.50 |
| 19 | 6 | Fiber glass batts, foil-faced, 15-in. | 0.65 |
| 30 | 9 | Fiber glass batts, foil-faced, 15-in. | 0.90 |
| 11 | 3½ | Fiber glass batts, unfaced, 15-in. | 0.50 |
| 19 | 6 | Fiber glass batts, unfaced, 15-in. | 0.70 |
| 30 | 9 | Fiber glass batts, unfaced, 15-in. | 0.95 |
| 30 | 12 | Fiber glass batts, unfaced, 15-in. | 1.25 |
| | | **Roof deck** | |
| 2.78 | 1 | Mineral wool board | 1.00 |
| 4 | 1½ | Mineral wool board | 1.25 |
| 5.26 | 2 | Mineral wool board | 1.50 |
| 5.26 | 2 | Foamed cellular glass | 3.75 |
| 5.26 | 1 | Polystyrene | 1.15 |
| 10 | 2 | Polystyrene | 1.80 |
| | | **Perimeter** | |
| 4 | 1 | Polystyrene, molded bead board | 1.10 |
| 8 | 2 | Polystyrene, molded bead board | 1.15 |
| 1.12 | 1 | Asphalt-impregnated cork | 1.40 |
| 2.24 | 2 | Asphalt-impregnated cork | 3.80 |

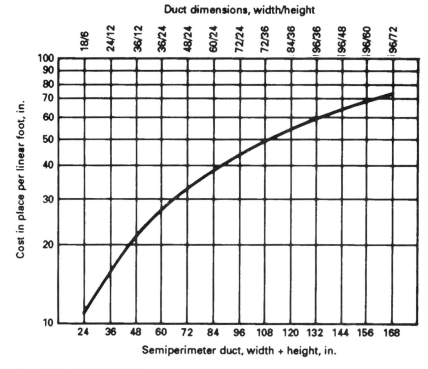

**Figure 12.2    COST IN PLACE**
**Fiber-Glass Duct Insulation, $/lin ft**
*Based on 1½-in.-thick, ¾-lb-density fiber-glass blanket with vapor barrier skin, rolling scaffold, new construction. Includes labor, material, and profit.*

## RECOMMENDED READING

Constance, J. D., "Controlling Duct Condensation," *Plant Engineering,* Oct. 25, 1984.

*Econ-I: How to Determine Economic Thickness of Thermal Insulation,* Thermal Manufacturers Association, Mt. Kisco, N.Y., 1973.

*Economic Thickness for Industrial Insulation,* Fairmont Press, Atlanta, Ga., 1983.

Hardenbrook, II., *Walker's Insulation Techniques and Estimating Handbook,* Frank R. Walker Co., Chicago, Ill., 1983.

Turner, W. C., and J. F. Malloy, *Handbook of Thermal Insulation Design Economics for Pipes and Equipment,* Robert E. Krieger Publishing Co., Huntington, N.Y., and McGraw-Hill Book Co., New York, 1980.

# CHAPTER 13
# INSTRUMENTATION AND CONTROLS

## GENERAL DISCUSSION

With the great forward strides in semiconductor and computer development in recent years, instrumentation techniques have undergone major change, and the costs of instrumentation and controls have changed significantly, in many cases for the better. A more sophisticated approach to environmental control in comfort cooling design, as well as a demand for more qualitative function in process work, has stimulated the further development of the control industry. As in every dynamic technology, the technology itself generally precedes the literature; and as the literature emerges, it is already made obsolete by new fundamental developments in technology.

Field instruments are discussed in the last part of the chapter, where Table 13.23 offers a listing of average costs for the more common portable field instruments used for testing, measuring, checking, balancing, and verifying a job—before, during, and after construction.

*Instrumentation and controls,* as viewed here, includes the recording and indicating instruments mounted on the panel, pressure gages, thermostats and thermocouples, control valves, transmitters, relief valves, and liquid-level meters. The emphasis is on the mechanical services and embraces the pneumatic, electronic, and electrical types. Although the pneumatic controller once offered a better proportioning system, the electrical controllers remain popular and electronic components are becoming increasingly common.

The instrumentation portion of a project is generally let as a subcontract. This is usually referred to as *system controls* or a *control package.* In the case of some terminal units for multiple installation, the controls may be made up at the equipment manufacturer's plant and shipped in with the units, or the mechanical contractor may purchase the control components and install them alone or in conjunction with the electrical contractor.

It is extremely difficult—and risky—to attempt to estimate instrumentation controls on a per-ton or even per-cfm basis, since the design will always determine the cost of controls. As a design varies, the relative proportions of, say, the ductwork vs. the controls may vary as much as 100% for the same tonnage.

The variation in the costs of controls in relation to tonnage or cfm is most dramatic in the application of multiroom, peripheral, year-round air conditioning. The engineer may select an induction-unit system or a fan-coil system; the fan-coil units may be all hydronic or split water and air. They may be two-pipe, reverse-return, three-pipe, or two-coil four-pipe. For a typical 500-ton building, the cost of controls could easily vary between $25,000 and $400,000, depending on the type of multiunit selection.

In attempting a unit-cost method for controls, it becomes necessary first to determine the overall design. If the project is multiroom fan-coil units, the unit cost should be per room, since the cost of controls would be identical for each room. Although the fan-coil units might vary in cfm capacity throughout the building—say, 200, 300, 400, and 500 cfm—the control cost per unit would be the same. If large air handlers are being considered, a square foot or cfm unit cost could be developed, depending on the type of control used. The number of coil circuits, face and bypass, steam, hot water or electric reheat modulation, preheat, etc., is a determining factor in cost of controls per cfm.

Typically the cost of instrumentation for the average modern structure may represent approximately 15% of the mechanical contract, which in turn may represent about 10% of the total contract for the building. This pegs the instrumentation-control cost at approximately 1.5% of the building dollar. The more stringent the temperature and humidity requirements of a system, the greater the ratio of instrumentation cost. Consequently, a hospital operating room, with an individual air unit operating off a central chilled-water plant, may reflect an instrumentation-control cost of 30% of the mechanical equipment. As applied to process plants, such as chemical or pulp, the instrumentation may be estimated to require about 10 to 15% of the plant's HVAC construction cost.

## BUDGET FIGURES

For quick budget figures the following costs of controls may be used with *only* a reasonable degree of accuracy:

| Item | Cost, $ |
| --- | --- |
| Fan-coil unit, electric control | 95 each |
| Fan-coil unit, pneumatic control | 150 each |
| Air handler, single-circuit, 1,200 cfm with face and bypass and three-way valve, electric or pneumatic | 600 each |
| Fan-coil unit with hot-water or steam humidity control, add | 950 each |
| Air handler, 1,200 cfm, with hot-water or steam humidity control, add | 180 each |
| Air handler, 8,000 cfm, with hot-water or steam humidity control, add | 300 each |
| For central control system | 350 per unit |
| For data logging center | 15,000–20,000 |

## ESTIMATING

The data in this chapter are based on bare material cost and actual field workhours. When the control package is to be sublet, a realistic allowance must be made for the subcontractor's overhead and profit.

Average working conditions are assumed, and *workhours* includes moving equipment and materials on the worksite to 40 ft, unpacking controls, and erecting within 10-ft working heights. Additional piping and flange boltup data may be found in Chap. 9, and data on electric wiring and conduit costs may be found in Chap. 14.

## PNEUMATIC SYSTEMS

For pneumatic instrumentation systems when all the controls, valves, and instruments are specified on the plans, it is common practice to make a takeoff of the instruments and find the total cost of basic material. Having found the cost of basic material, add 15% for accessory installation material and 60% for labor. Both percentage factors are added to the basic material cost. The labor figure allows for time to move the controls from the construction site to the working area, unpacking, mounting, and hooking up.

For instrument piping using copper tube or plastic tube with compression fittings up to ½-in. diameter, the following labor costs may be applied:

| | Labor per 100 ft, workhours |
|---|---|
| Single tube running wild (no support) | 13 |
| Double runs laid in channel support | 19 |
| Multiple runs laid in channel support | 10 per run |

Material costs are given in Table 13.1. Data on orifice plates, the control valve section, and the panel instrumentation section are given in Tables 13.2, 13.3, and 13.4, respectively. Labor and material costs of miscellaneous items are given in Table 13.5.

**TABLE 13.1** Material Cost for Instrument Piping

| Description | No. of tubes | Tube size, in. | Cost per 100 ft, $ | Hangers, fittings, $ | Total, $ |
|---|---|---|---|---|---|
| Single polyethylene tube | 1 | ¼ | 10 | 12 | 22 |
| | 1 | ⅜ | 22 | 15 | 37 |
| Multiple polyethylene tube | 4 | ¼ | 35 | 23 | 58 |
| | 8 | ¼ | 70 | 26 | 96 |
| | 10 | ¼ | 90 | 60 | 150 |
| | 12 | ¼ | 107 | 73 | 180 |
| | 4 | ⅜ | 85 | 65 | 150 |
| | 8 | ⅜ | 160 | 42 | 202 |
| | 10 | ⅜ | 210 | 55 | 265 |
| | 12 | ⅜ | 250 | 65 | 315 |
| Multiple copper tube | 2 | ¼ | 78 | 35 | 110 |
| | 4 | ¼ | 155 | 65 | 220 |
| | 6 | ¼ | 230 | 100 | 330 |
| | 8 | ¼ | 300 | 125 | 425 |
| | 10 | ¼ | 390 | 160 | 550 |
| | 12 | ¼ | 450 | 200 | 650 |

**TABLE 13.2** Sensing Section—Orifice Plates

Based on flange-tap-type fixture. *Workhours* includes erecting and boltup in existing flanges.

| Size, in. | 2 | 3 | 4 | 6 | 8 | 10 | 12 | 14 | 16 |
|---|---|---|---|---|---|---|---|---|---|
| Material, $ | 90 | 100 | 130 | 180 | 250 | 300 | 500 | 550 | 600 |
| Workhours | 1 | 2 | 3 | 4 | 4 | 6 | 6 | 8 | 8 |

**TABLE 13.3** Control Valve Section

Based on carbon-steel body, pneumatic diaphragm mounted on valve top at factory.

| Pipe size, in. | 2½ | 3 | 4 | 6 | | |
|---|---|---|---|---|---|---|
| Iron body, two-way, flanged | | | | | | |
| Material, $ | 490 | 530 | 960 | 1,500 | | |
| Workhours* | 2 | 2 | 3 | 5 | | |
| Iron body, three-way, flanged | | | | | | |
| Material, $ | 875 | 960 | 2,000 | 2,200 | | |
| Workhours* | 3 | 3 | 4 | 4 | | |
| Pipe size, in. | ½ | ¾ | 1 | 1¼ | 1½ | 2 |
| Brass, two-way screwed | | | | | | |
| Material, $ | 150 | 165 | 200 | 275 | 360 | 525 |
| Workhours* | 0.5 | 0.5 | 0.5 | 0.8 | 1.0 | 1.0 |
| Brass, three-way screwed | | | | | | |
| Material, $ | 225 | 230 | 285 | 420 | 450 | 560 |
| Workhours* | 1.0 | 1.0 | 1.0 | 1.0 | 1.5 | 1.5 |

*Workhours includes erecting, boltup, and adjusting.

**TABLE 13.4** Panel Instrument Section

Remote recorder controllers, to 2,000 psi. *Workhours* includes laying out on existing board, aligning, erecting, and adjusting.

| Instrument | Material, $ | Workhours |
|---|---|---|
| Flow | 900 | 10 |
| Pressure | 350 | 10 |
| Liquid level | 850 | 8 |
| Temperature | 1,300 | 10 |

**TABLE 13.5** Miscellaneous

| Instrument | Material, $ | Workhours |
|---|---|---|
| Control board, to 15 ft long ..... | 4,500 | 20.0 |
| Differential pressure cell ........ | 375 | 6.0 |
| Air filter...................... | 20 | 0.75 |
| Air regulator.................. | 10 | 0.50 |
| Multipoint recorder receiver..... | 1,500 | 16.0 |

## HIGH-SIDE CONTROL

The high-side control assembly is invariably furnished with the high-side equipment, and the price is inclusive. The kind of unloading and safety control required will, of course, be determined by the compressor design. High-low safety cutout, crankcase heaters, high-discharge gas temperature cutout, and time delays are normally furnished as part of the standard equipment. Starters, solenoid stop valves, oil pressure gages, gage boards, etc., may or may not be furnished as part of the standard equipment. Some high-side control packages are listed in Chap. 3, along with respective high-side equipment. Data on starters may be found in Chap. 14.

## SWITCHING, METERING, CONTROLLING, AND INDICATING INSTRUMENTATION

Data on instrumentation for refrigerant service are given in Table 13.6 and for water service, in Table 13.7. Material and labor costs of thermostats, valves and actuators, gage glasses, venturi balancing devices, and miscellaneous devices are given in Tables 13.8 to 13.12. *Workhours* includes unpacking, erecting to an existing apparatus or mounting to an existing panel, and final connections at the capillary and/or electrical terminal of the device. Checking out circuitry and linkage action is also included, but *not* conduit, connection boxes, or pulling conductors.

**TABLE 13.6** Refrigerant Service

| Sweat connections, in. | 5/8 × 7/8 | 7/8 × 1 1/8 | 7/8 × 1 1/8 | 1 1/8 × 1 1/8 | 1 1/8 × 1 1/8 | 1 1/8 × 1 1/8 | 1 1/8 × 1 1/8 |
|---|---|---|---|---|---|---|---|
| **Thermostatic expansion valve** | | | | | | | |
| Nominal tons | 10 | 17 | 25 | 32 | 40 | 50 | 75 |
| Material, $ | 40 | 70 | 90 | 110 | 110 | 135 | 165 |
| Erection, workhours | 1.15 | 1.25 | 1.25 | 1.40 | 1.50 | 1.50 | 1.50 |

| Sweat connections, in. | 7/8 | 1 1/8 | 1 1/8 | 1 5/8 | 2 1/8 | 2 5/8 | 3 1/8 | 3 5/8 |
|---|---|---|---|---|---|---|---|---|
| **Evaporator back-pressure valve** | | | | | | | | |
| Nominal tons | 3.4 | 6.2 | 9.3 | 13.9 | 26.2 | 41.0 | 69.7 | 92.5 |
| Material, $ | 65 | 100 | 140 | 180 | 230 | 270 | 300 | 350 |
| Erection, workhours | 1.0 | 1.25 | 1.25 | 1.75 | 1.90 | 2.25 | 2.50 | 3.00 |

| Connections, in. | 5/8 sweat | 1/2 sweat | 1/2 fpt | 3/4 fpt |
|---|---|---|---|---|
| **Solenoid valve—liquid line** | | | | |
| Nominal tons | 3 | 7.5 | 10 | 20 |
| Material, $ | 55 | 97 | 98 | 150 |
| Erection, workhours | 0.85 | 0.90 | 0.85 | 1.0 |

| Connections, in. | 1 1/4 fpt | 1 3/8 sweat | 2 fpt |
|---|---|---|---|
| **Solenoid valve—liquid line** | | | |
| Nominal tons | 50 | 62 | 150 |
| Material, $ | 110 | 115 | 120 |
| Erection, workhours | 1.25 | 1.50 | 1.8 |

**TABLE 13.7**  Water Service

| Solenoid Valve—Fan Coil, etc. | | | |
|---|---|---|---|
| Connections, in. . . . . . . . | ¾ fpt | ⅝ sweat | 1 fpt |
| Style. . . . . . . . . . . . . . . . . | 2-way | 3-way | 2-way |
| Material, $ . . . . . . . . . . . | 75 | 80 | 95 |
| Erection, workhours . . . . | 1.0 | 1.50 | 1.25 |

| Automatic Regulating Valve—Condenser Water, etc. | | | | | |
|---|---|---|---|---|---|
| Connections, in. . . . . . . . | ⅜ fpt | ½ sweat | ¾ fpt | 1 fpt | 1¼ fpt |
| Nominal tons . . . . . . . . . | 5 | 7.5 | 10 | 15 | 20 |
| Material, $ . . . . . . . . . . . | 39 | 53 | 70 | 100 | 125 |
| Erection, workhours . . . . | 1.0 | 1.10 | 1.25 | 1.50 | 1.75 |

**TABLE 13.8**  Thermostats

| Item | Description | Material, $ | Workhours |
|---|---|---|---|
| Heavy duty, line voltage | | | |
| Heating only . . . . . . . . . . . . . . . . . . . . . . . . . | Bellows-operated micro switch | 45 | 1.0 |
| Cooling only . . . . . . . . . . . . . . . . . . . . . . . . . | Bellows-operated micro switch | 45 | 1.0 |
| Two-stage. . . . . . . . . . . . . . . . . . . . . . . . . . . | Bellows-operated mercury bulb | 70 | 1.5 |
| Three-stage . . . . . . . . . . . . . . . . . . . . . . . . | Bellows-operated mercury bulb | 150 | 1.5 |
| Proportional, motor-controlled. . . . . . . . . . . | 60 to 87°F | 90 | 2.0 |
| High or low limit, motor controller (single-stage) . . . . . . . . . . . . . . . . . . . . . . . . | — | 80 | 2.0 |
| Corrosion-resistant, greenhouse, etc.. . . . . . | — | 115 | 1.0 |
| Remote-bulb, low-temperature . . . . . . . . . . . | −20 to +50°F | 60 | 2.0 |
| Remote-bulb, changeover, damper actuator. . . . . . . . . . . . . . . . . . . . . . . . . . . . | — | 70 | 2.5 |
| Explosion-proof . . . . . . . . . . . . . . . . . . . . . . | — | 115 | 1.5 |
| Light duty, low voltage only | | | |
| Heating, residential . . . . . . . . . . . . . . . . . . . . | Coiled bimetal | 30 | 1.0 |
| Cooling, residential . . . . . . . . . . . . . . . . . . . . | Coiled bimetal | 35 | 1.0 |
| Cooling and heating, residential. . . . . . . . . . | Coiled bimetal | 50 | 1.0 |
| Multistage, 1 heat + 1 cool with clock . . . . . | Coiled bimetal | 140 | 1.0 |
| Multistage, 1 heat + 2 cool with clock . . . . . | Coiled bimetal | 160 | 1.5 |
| Multistage, 2 heat + 1 cool with clock . . . . . | Coiled bimetal | 160 | 2.0 |
| Multistage, 2 heat + 2 cool with clock . . . . . | Coiled bimetal | 175 | 2.0 |
| Humidistat. . . . . . . . . . . . . . . . . . . . . . . . . . . | Relative humidity range 20 to 80% (make or break) | 35 | 1.0 |

**TABLE 13.9** Motorized Valves and Actuators

For estimator's convenience, double columns are presented for both material and workhours. Basic material includes globe valve only; basic workhours includes erecting and making up joint. Package$_1$ includes matched components, i.e., actuator motor, linkage assembly, and transformer; this should be added to basic material for costing entire assembly. Package$_2$ is estimated workhours for mounting actuator motor, and linkage and transformer, making all adjustments, making final wiring connection, and checking operation. Add package$_2$ to workhours for estimating complete assembly.

| Connection | Body size, in. | Capacity, $C_v$ | Basic material, $ | Package$_1$, $ | Basic workhours | Package$_2$ workhours |
|---|---|---|---|---|---|---|
| | | | Modulating valve, steam or liquid | | | |
| Screwed | ½ | 4.0 | 65 | 200 | 1.0 | 8.0 |
|  | ¾ | 6.3 | 76 | 200 | 1.0 | 8.0 |
|  | 1 | 10.0 | 120 | 225 | 1.5 | 8.0 |
|  | 1¼ | 16.0 | 160 | 225 | 1.5 | 8.0 |
|  | 1½ | 25.0 | 250 | 225 | 1.5 | 8.0 |
|  | 2 | 40.0 | 350 | 250 | 1.5 | 8.0 |
|  | 2½ | 100.0 | 425 | 250 | 2.0 | 8.0 |
| Flanged | 3 | 100.0 | 550 | 250 | 3.0 | 8.0 |
|  | 3 | 100.0 | 640 | 275 | 3.0 | 8.0 |
|  | 4 | 160.0 | 785 | 275 | 3.0 | 8.0 |
| | | | Three-way mixing valve, steam or liquid | | | |
| Screwed | ½ | 4.0 | 95 | 220 | 1.5 | 8.0 |
|  | ¾ | 6.3 | 300 | 220 | 2.0 | 8.0 |
|  | 1 | 10.0 | 430 | 250 | 2.0 | 8.0 |
|  | 1¼ | 16.0 | 150 | 250 | 2.5 | 8.0 |
|  | 1½ | 25.0 | 162 | 250 | 2.5 | 8.0 |
|  | 2 | 40.0 | 203 | 275 | 3.0 | 8.0 |
| Flanged | 2½ | 65.0 | 495 | 300 | 4.0 | 8.0 |
|  | 3 | 100.0 | 680 | 300 | 4.0 | 8.0 |
|  | 4 | 160.0 | 815 | 300 | 4.0 | 8.0 |

| Modulating actuator motor, 115 volts AC | Material, $ | Erection, workhours | Wiring adjustment, & checkout, workhours |
|---|---|---|---|
| Two-position | 100 | 2.0 | 2.0 |
| Spring return | 160 | 2.0 | 2.0 |
| Full modulation | 200 | 2.0 | 2.0 |
| Heavy-duty, 40-lb torque | 180 | 2.0 | 2.0 |
| Damper actuator | 215 | 2.0 | 2.0 |
| Auxiliary devices | | | |
| End switch | 27 | 0.25 | 0.50 |
| Step controller, 10-cam, mercury switches | 230 | 1.0 | 4.00 |
| Master potentiometer, 5-slave motor | 27 | 1.0 | 2.00 |
| Valve linkage | 25 | 1.0 | 2.25 |
| Transformer | 23 | 0.25 | 0.25 |

**TABLE 13.10**   Level Gage Glasses

Transparent type with gage valve, carbon-steel body screwed assembly, to 2,000 psi at 150°F.

| Nominal visible length, in. | Material, $ | Erection, valves & glass, workhours |
|:---:|:---:|:---:|
| 8 | 820 | 3.0 |
| 10 | 950 | 3.0 |
| 12 | 1,100 | 3.0 |

**TABLE 13.11**   Flow Venturi Balancing Devices

Based on line installation on venturi for measuring and balancing hydronic systems using a master flowmeter. Venturis are complete with valves, quick-disconnect connections, and metal identification tag. Working pressure to 275 psi at 100°F; sizes $\frac{1}{2}$ to 12 in. are brass with screwed joints; $2\frac{1}{2}$ to 12 in. are cast-iron or carbon-steel flanged 150-lb weldneck. Portable master flowmeters are available at $800. The gpm range is approximate at 10 in. of water differential pressure.

| Pipe size, in. | gpm range | Material, $ | Erection, workhours |
|:---:|:---:|:---:|:---:|
| $\frac{1}{2}$ | 0.2–4 | 85 | 1.0 |
| $\frac{3}{4}$ | 0.5–6 | 85 | 1.0 |
| 1 | 2–15 | 95 | 1.0 |
| $1\frac{1}{4}$ | 4–23 | 105 | 1.0 |
| $1\frac{1}{2}$ | 6–30 | 115 | 1.5 |
| 2 | 8–70 | 140 | 1.5 |
| $2\frac{1}{2}$ | 12–70 | 185 | 1.5 |
| 3 | 20–100 | 235 | 2.0 |
| 4 | 30–180 | 295 | 3.0 |
| 6 | 70–400 | 450 | 4.0 |
| 8 | 150–700 | 650 | 5.0 |
| 10 | 200–1,000 | 1,650 | 6.0 |

**TABLE 13.12**   Miscellaneous

| Item | Material, $ | Erection, workhours |
|:---|:---:|:---:|
| Aquastat control, bimetal, range 80 to 240°F.......... | 35 | 1.5 |
| Aquastat, immersion, high-low limit and circulator .... | 45 | 2.0 |
| Modulating pressure controller, to 15 lb steam........ | 60 | 2.0 |
| Modulating pressure controller, to 150 lb steam....... | 75 | 2.0 |
| Modulating pressure controller, to 300 lb steam....... | 85 | 2.0 |
| Auto-time controller, plain dial, spdt................ | 100 | 2.0 |
| Auto-time controller, skip day, spdt................. | 230 | 2.0 |
| Auto-time controller, 7-day, spdt ................... | 235 | 2.0 |
| Combination warm-air control....................... | 50 | 2.0 |
| Fan safety, firestat, to 165°F....................... | 50 | 1.0 |
| Fan safety, warm-air stat, to 250°F ................. | 60 | 1.0 |
| Three-position switch, 4pdt ........................ | 25 | 1.0 |
| Two-position switch, dpdt.......................... | 15 | 1.0 |

## FAN-COIL-UNIT CONTROL

Most manufacturers of fan-coil equipment offer a variety of control systems as part of the factory-installed standard equipment. Since the field erection of solenoids, stop valves, bypass clusters, and pipe connections is more costly than factory installation, the mechanical contractor will invariably order the complete package from the coil manufacturer. The package may be electric, pneumatic, or a combination of both, such as an electric stop solenoid plus a pneumatic two-way valve.

The total wiring cost, along with costs of the control components and pneumatic piping, must be factored into any cost projection of an electric versus a pneumatic package. The economic advantage can be determined only by the overall design and *total system cost.* In this regard, it may be mentioned that most fan-coil room units are generally supplied with shaded-pole motors. For a slight additional cost, most manufacturers will provide a permanent split-capacitor motor. A psc motor may allow additional units to be installed on the fused circuit and thereby reduce the overall wiring cost—as well as provide effective operating cost savings.

Table 13.13 lists some typical control assemblies for vertical floor-standing cabinet-type models. With substitution of remote thermostats and fan switches, most of these control packages can be used for ceiling-hung hideaway units as well. The in-place cost reflects material, labor, and internal unit wiring for the items shown. This is the factory-assembled package, and the only field labor would be connecting up the two stop valves and two 115-V wires into the control panel to energize the three-speed fan motor. When remote items are listed, neither field erection nor wiring is included.

Figure 13.1 shows some of the typical arrangements on which these costs are based. The numbers correspond to those in Table 13.13.

## LOW-SIDE CONTROL

Possible control combinations for air-conditioning systems are indeed countless; a few typical combinations are treated here from the estimator's view, and little attention is given to the advantages of one over the other.

For convenience and for simplicity in reading the diagrams, all control circuits are shown in line voltage. It is assumed that the necessary corrections will be made in the field; the circuitry is not affected, and the estimator need only add the cost of a transformer to the accompanying table. Thermostats shown in the return-air stream are meant to sense the room temperature and may be designated as space stats. It is assumed that the system is close-coupled and does not have any exceptionally long runs of refrigerant piping or control wiring. The designs are general, and the use of single- or three-phase current is only illustrative. Any of the components shown may be taken out and used in combination with any other. The cost is derived by referring to the particular components in the estimating tables.

Labor figures include moving the controls onto the jobsite, unpacking, mounting (including the switch box), connecting circuit wire to solderless terminals, ringing out the circuit, and adjusting the damper motor. Pulling conductors, erecting conduit, and wiring motor starters are not included.

Although high-side control is usually necessary in conjunction with the low-side control, the cost of the high-side control combinations is not included here. It is assumed that the high-side control cost will be added into the total bill of controls.

**TABLE 13.13**  Fan-Coil-Unit Control

| Control | Description | In-place cost, $ |
|---------|-------------|------------------|
| *Electric:* | | |
| 1. | Basic control: manual motor controller, off-high-medium-low and auto air vent................. | 25 |
| 2. | Pair of stop valves with unions.................... | 40 |
| 3. | Controls 1 and 2 plus manual throttling valve with temperature indicator ......................... | 100 |
| 4. | Controls 1 and 2 plus automatic season changeover control and *remote* spdt thermostat ............. | 140 |
| 5. | Controls 1 and 2 plus three-way manual valve and bypass cluster; full bypass control.............. | 200 |
| 6. | Control 4 plus a two-way auto solenoid with ⅛-in. bypass cluster; independent fan selection; solenoid deenergized with fan in off position .... | 240 |
| 7. | Control 6, but two-way valve is replaced with three-way solenoid and full water bypass ........ | 300 |
| *Self-contained* | | |
| | Totally self-contained thermostatic selector valve with three-valve manifold for flushing and by-pass cluster; requires no wiring other than fan motor...................................... | 225 |
| *Pneumatic:* | | |
| 8. | Basic control: manual motor controller, off-high-medium-low and auto air vent................. | 20 |
| 9. | Pair of stop valves with union .................... | 40 |
| 10. | Controls 1 and 2 plus two-way pneumatic valve and summer-winter self-contained thermostat........ | 400 |
| 11. | Control 3, but three-way pneumatic valve with automatic bypass ............................. | 575 |

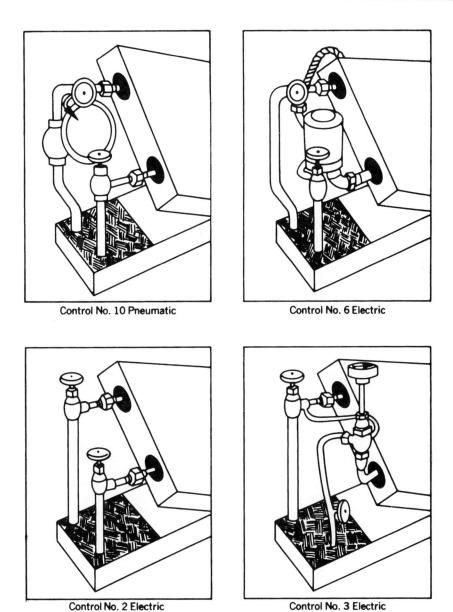

Control No. 10 Pneumatic

Control No. 6 Electric

Control No. 2 Electric

Control No. 3 Electric

**Figure 13.1  FAN-COIL-UNIT CONTROL ASSEMBLIES**

## BASIC ON/OFF CONTROL

In this basic control system, described in Table 13.14, the dry-bulb temperature is controlled by a room thermostat which energizes the liquid-line solenoid valve and opens it on temperature rise. On temperature drop, the thermostat contacts break, and the normally closed solenoid shuts off the flow of liquid refrigerant to the coil. The pressure stat will then shut off the compressor, which is operated on pumpdown control. By placing the auto-fan switch in the fan position, the fan will operate without the compressor. See Fig. 13.2.

**TABLE 13.14**    Basic On-Off Control

| Nominal cfm | 8,000 | 10,000 | 12,000 | 16,000 | 20,000 |
|---|---|---|---|---|---|
| Liquid solenoid $V_1 m$, \$ | 70 | 75 | 75 | 190 | 190 |
| Auto-fan switch, $S_1$, \$ | 10 | 10 | 10 | 10 | 10 |
| Room thermostat, $T_1$, \$ | 30 | 30 | 30 | 30 | 30 |
| Total material, \$ | 110 | 115 | 115 | 230 | 230 |
| Erection, workhours | 3 | 3 | 3 | 3 | 3 |

## FACE AND BYPASS CONTROL

The face and bypass control system will achieve improved temperature control and a good degree of humidity control. The cycle of operation is as follows. With the thermostat calling for cooling, the damper motor will close the bypass damper and open the face; the end switch will energize the solenoid and open it to permit flow of liquid. As the temperature falls, the modulating thermostat will open the bypass and close the face dampers proportionately. A further drop in temperature will move the dampers further, and the end switch will close the solenoid valve. A rise in temperature will reverse the procedure. See Fig. 13.3 and Table 13.15. *Workhours* includes erection of dampers by a sheet-metal contractor.

## COOLING WITH AUTOMATIC INTERMEDIATE-SEASON CONTROL

The basic on/off control is used here for summer cooling with $S_2$—the summer/winter switch—in the summer position. When intermediate-season operation is desired, $S_2$ is placed in the winter position; the solenoid valve will close and shut off the compressor. At the same time, the damper motor $D_1$ will be placed under the command of the modulating thermostat $T_3$. On temperature rise in the room, the return-air damper will close and the outside-air damper will open to provide space cooling. The low-limiting thermostat in the discharge air will close the outside-air damper if the discharge-air temperature becomes objectionably low. When the fan is off, the outside-air damper will close on the spring return. See Fig. 13.4 and Table 13.16. *Workhours* includes erection of dampers by a sheet-metal contractor.

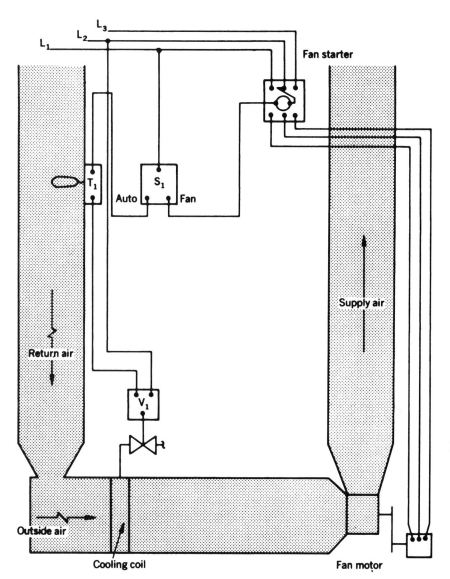

**Figure 13.2   BASIC ON-OFF CONTROL**
(See Table 13.14)

$S_1$ = auto-off fan switch

$T_1$ = space thermostat for return air

$V_1$ = solenoid valve in liquid line

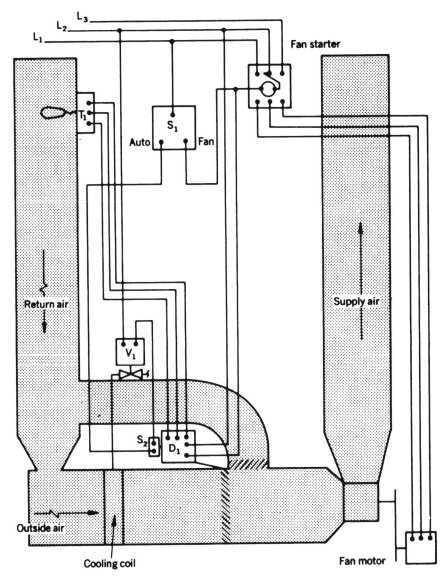

**Figure 13.3 FACE AND BYPASS CONTROL**
**(See Table 13.15)**

$S_1$ = auto-off fan switch                     $D_1$ = damper motor
$V_1$ = solenoid valve in liquid line           $T_1$ = modulating thermostat
$S_2$ = end switch

**TABLE 13.15**   Face and Bypass Control

Per zone or system.

| Nominal cfm | 8,000 | 10,000 | 12,000 | 16,000 | 20,000 |
|---|---|---|---|---|---|
| Liquid solenoid, $ | 70 | 75 | 75 | 190 | 190 |
| Auto-fan switch, $ | 10 | 10 | 10 | 10 | 10 |
| Modulating thermostat, $ | 90 | 90 | 90 | 90 | 90 |
| Damper motor, $ | 200 | 200 | 200 | 200 | 200 |
| End switch, $ | 27 | 27 | 27 | 27 | 27 |
| Transformer, $ | 25 | 25 | 25 | 25 | 25 |
| Face and bypass damper, $ | 240 | 260 | 290 | 360 | 400 |
| Total material, $ | 662 | 687 | 717 | 902 | 942 |
| Erection, workhours | 16 | 17 | 18 | 20 | 22 |

## ALL-SEASON CONTROL

The all-season control is essentially the same as the cooling with intermediate-season control shown in Fig. 13.4, but here a heating coil with modulating steam valve has been added to arrange for winter heating.

### Cycle of Operation

The summer- and intermediate-season cycles are identical with those of Table 13.16. On a further drop in room temperature, $T_3$ will allow the outside-air damper to run to its minimum position, and then the second potentiometer will take over and open the steam valve to the heating coil. When the fan is off, both the outside-air-damper motor and the steam-valve motor will automatically close on spring return. Costs shown in Table 13.17 do not include steam traps, shutoff valves, or piping away from the steam coil. See Fig. 13.5. *Workhours* includes erecting dampers but not a steam coil.

## ALL-SEASON CONTROL WITH FACE AND BYPASS DAMPERING

The all-season control with face and bypass dampering is a more refined version of the all-season control detailed in Table 13.17. The face and bypass dampers offer closer dry-bulb and humidity control during partial load conditions.

### Control Sequence

The auto switch energizes the fan and control circuit simultaneously; the outside-air damper will open to minimum. $S_2$ is a 4pdt summer/winter switch and will bring in the summer control circuit when set in summer position. When the cooling stat calls for cooling, the bypass damper will be closed and the face damper will be open; the end switch on $D_2$ will open the solenoid valve. As the room temperature drops, the bypass damper will open in opposition to

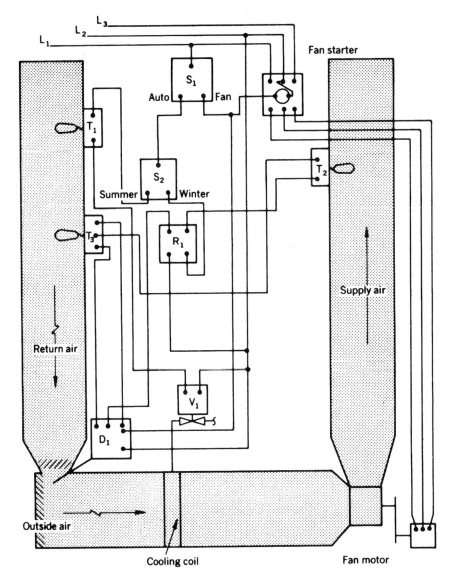

**Figure 13.4  COOLING WITH AUTOMATIC INTERMEDIATE-SEASON CONTROL (NO WINTER HEATING)**
(See Table 13.16)

$S_1$ = auto-off fan switch            $T_1$ = summer thermostat in space

$S_2$ = summer/winter switch          $T_2$ = low-limiting thermostat

$R_1$ = spdt relay                    $T_3$ = modulating space thermostat

$V_1$ = solenoid valve in liquid line  $D_1$ = spring-return damper motor

**TABLE 13.16**    Cooling with Automatic Intermediate-Season Control

Per zone or system.

| Nominal cfm | 8,000 | 10,000 | 12,000 | 16,000 | 20,000 |
|---|---|---|---|---|---|
| Liquid solenoid, $ | 70 | 75 | 75 | 190 | 190 |
| Auto-fan switch, $ | 10 | 10 | 10 | 10 | 10 |
| Summer-winter switch, $ | 20 | 20 | 20 | 20 | 20 |
| Space thermostat, $ | 30 | 30 | 30 | 30 | 30 |
| Low-limit thermostat, $ | 65 | 65 | 65 | 65 | 65 |
| Modulating thermostat, $ | 90 | 90 | 90 | 90 | 90 |
| spdt relay, $ | 30 | 30 | 30 | 30 | 30 |
| Return damper motor, $ | 200 | 200 | 200 | 200 | 200 |
| Combination damper, $ | 290 | 315 | 360 | 400 | 450 |
| Total material, $ | 805 | 835 | 880 | 1,035 | 1,085 |
| Erection, workhours | 20 | 20 | 20 | 22 | 22 |

the face, and the end switch will drop out the liquid solenoid, cutting off the flow of liquid to the cooling coil. For intermediate-season operation, $S_2$ is placed in the winter position. This will break the circuit to the liquid solenoid and shut down the compressor via the pressure stat; it will also close the bypass damper. When the thermostat calls for cooling, the outside-air damper will open in opposition to the return-air damper. If the discharge air becomes too cold, $T_2$ will bring in the modulating steam valve and temper the outside air.

During winter operation when the room air drops further, the outside-air damper will close and $T_1$ will bring in the steam-heating valve. As the room temperature rises, the sequence is reversed. See Fig. 13.6 and Table 13.18.

**TABLE 13.17**    All-Season Control

| Nominal cfm | 8,000 | 10,000 | 12,000 | 16,000 | 20,000 |
|---|---|---|---|---|---|
| Liquid solenoid, $ | 70 | 75 | 75 | 190 | 190 |
| Auto-fan switch, $ | 10 | 10 | 10 | 10 | 10 |
| Summer-winter switch, $ | 20 | 20 | 20 | 20 | 20 |
| Summer thermostat, $ | 30 | 30 | 30 | 30 | 30 |
| Low-limit thermostat, $ | 65 | 65 | 65 | 65 | 65 |
| Dual modulating stat, $ | 90 | 90 | 90 | 90 | 90 |
| spdt relay, $ | 30 | 30 | 30 | 30 | 30 |
| Return air damper motor, $ | 200 | 200 | 200 | 200 | 200 |
| Modulating steam valve, $ | 260 | 280 | 280 | 300 | 350 |
| Combination damper, $ | 290 | 315 | 360 | 400 | 450 |
| Total material, $ | 1,065 | 1,115 | 1,160 | 1,335 | 1,435 |
| Erection, workhours | 24 | 24 | 24 | 32 | 32 |

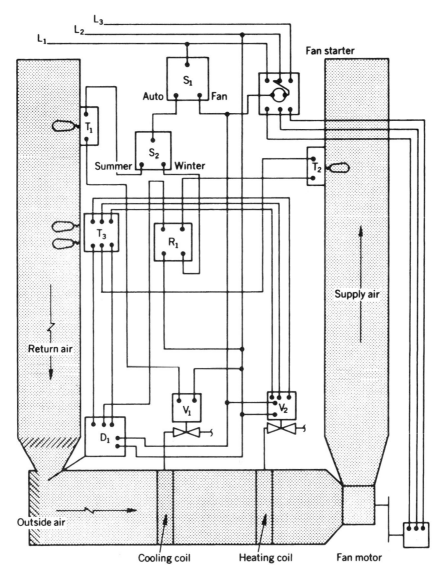

**Figure 13.5 ALL-SEASON CONTROL**
**(See Table 13.17)**

$T_1$ = summer thermostat

$T_2$ = low-limiting thermostat

$T_3$ = dual modulating thermostat

$D_1$ = damper motor, spring-return

$S_1$ = auto-off fan switch

$S_2$ = summer/winter switch

$R_1$ = relay

$V_1$ = solenoid valve in liquid line

$V_2$ = modulating steam valve, spring-return

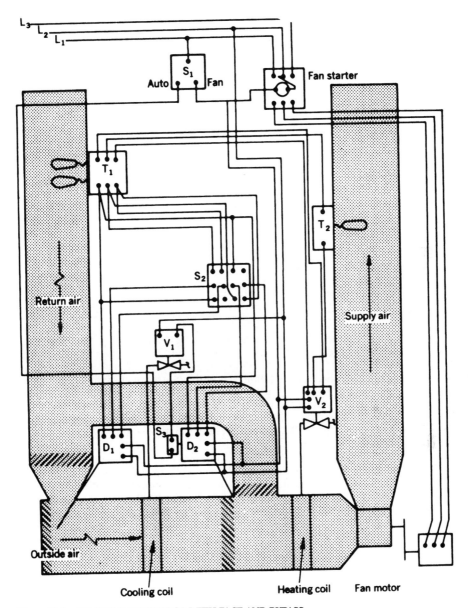

**Figure 13.6  ALL-SEASON CONTROL WITH FACE AND BYPASS**
(See Table 13.18)

$S_1$ = auto-off fan switch

$S_2$ = 4pdt summer/winter switch

$S_3$ = end switch

$T_1$ = dual potentiometer thermostat

$T_2$ = low-limiting thermostat

$V_1$ = liquid-line solenoid valve

$V_2$ = modulating steam valve

$D_1$ = O/A damper motor

$D_2$ = F/B damper motor

**TABLE 13.18** All-Season Control with Face and Bypass

| Nominal cfm | 8,000 | 10,000 | 12,000 | 16,000 | 20,000 |
|---|---|---|---|---|---|
| Liquid solenoid, $ | 70 | 75 | 100 | 190 | 190 |
| Auto-fan switch, $ | 10 | 10 | 10 | 10 | 10 |
| 4pdt summer-winter switch, $ | 150 | 150 | 150 | 150 | 150 |
| End switch, $ | 27 | 27 | 27 | 27 | 27 |
| Dual modulating stat, $ | 90 | 90 | 90 | 90 | 90 |
| Low-limit thermostat, $ | 65 | 65 | 65 | 65 | 65 |
| O/A damper motor, $ | 225 | 225 | 225 | 225 | 225 |
| F/B damper motor, $ | 200 | 200 | 200 | 200 | 200 |
| Modulating steam valve, $ | 260 | 280 | 290 | 300 | 350 |
| Total material, $ | 1,097 | 1,122 | 1,157 | 1,257 | 1,307 |
| Erection, workhours | 16 | 16 | 16 | 16 | 16 |

## SUMMER/WINTER CONTROL WITH STEAM REHEAT HUMIDITY CONTROL

Figure 13.7 illustrates a typical schematic using an additional three-position switch and humidistat to provide reheat for an existing summer/winter system that does not have humidity control.

With the exception of the humidistat and extra three-position switch, all other components have been discussed in connection with the preceding figures and may be cost-estimated from the preceding tables. The humidistat is about $35 plus another switch, bringing the total additional material to about $45. Erection workhours are 1.7. This is indeed a small additional first cost for providing a reheat system where the basic heating and cooling system already exists.

With the summer/winter switches $S_2$ and $S_3$ in the summer position, the cooling thermostat will open the liquid-line solenoid on temperature rise and close the solenoid when the room dry bulb is satisfied. If, however, the relative humidity is above the design point, the overriding humidistat will keep the liquid feeding into the coil, thereby dehumidifying. As the dry-bulb temperature drops below the design point, the modulating thermostat $T_2$ will open the steam valve and reheat the dehumidified air to its design point. When both $S_2$ and $S_3$ are placed in the winter position, the solenoid is in a normally closed position and the modulating steam valve will provide heat as determined by $T_2$. Switch $S_1$ may be placed in the fan position for intermediate-season ventilation.

## ELECTRICAL RESISTANCE DUCT HEATERS

Electrical resistance duct heaters are available in a wide variety of styles and prices. Whereas years ago the contractor would purchase the individual strips and components and assemble them into a field-fabricated holding frame, they are now offered in all sizes as a factory-assembled package in either slip-in or flanged arrangement. Costs may vary with the quality of the heater device, gage of the holding frame, quality of components, etc. In the following tables we have based the material costs and workhours for erection and wiring on line-voltage sys-

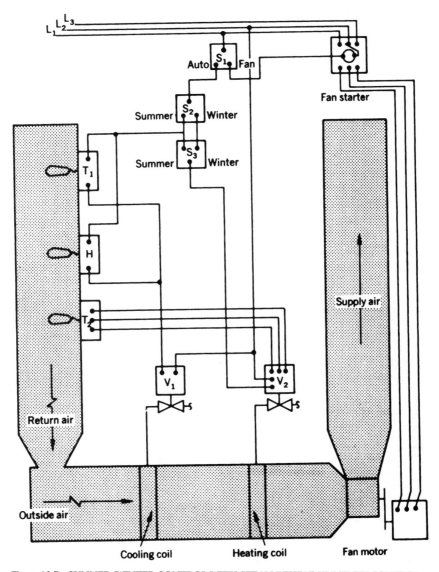

**Figure 13.7   SUMMER/WINTER CONTROL WITH STEAM REHEAT HUMIDITY CONTROL**

| | |
|---|---|
| $S_1$ = auto-off fan switch | $H$ = overriding humidistat |
| $S_2$ = summer/winter switch | $T_2$ = modulating heating thermostat |
| $S_3$ = summer/winter switch | $V_1$ = solenoid valve in liquid line |
| $T_1$ = cooling thermostat | $V_2$ = modulating steam valve |

tems using good-grade controls and components. This is simply a matter of using a convenient standard. Considerable savings may be realized when the heater package is preassembled with a 24-V contactor and more economical low-voltage controls and safety devices.

Electrical resistance duct heaters—blast heaters, strip heaters, coil heaters, and fin heaters—may be used in the duct of a standard air-conditioning system as a prime heat source for winter heating or as an auxiliary heat source for individual suites when the central heating plant is down. They are also commonly used for supplementing heat pumps, as well as tempering outside air during intermediate-season operation. As a means of zone-control reheating and general humidity control for partial-load operating conditions, they are unquestionably the most economical and efficient method.

There are, of course, other ways to wire controls than those shown in the accompanying figures; they are offered only to help understand the tables. When necessary, the estimator may make the required substitutions by referring to other tables and pricing data; some of the switches and thermostats shown may already exist in the cooling system and should not be duplicated.

## SUMMER COOLING WITH ELECTRICAL REHEAT HUMIDITY CONTROL

The application of fin-strip heaters for control of humidity on standard package units is common practice in many areas. Figure 13.8 shows a schematic for a typical setup, and data are given in Table 13.19. Switch $S_1$ is the fan firestat, which would drop out the entire circuit in the event of excessively high temperature at the bonnet; this safety feature is a must for strip-heat applications. With the $S_2$ selector switch in the auto position, the cooling thermostat $T_1$ brings the compressor in on a temperature rise in the space. If the room humidity remains too high after the dry-bulb temperature has been satisfied, the overriding humidistat will keep the compressor running to complete the necessary dehumidification. As the temperature drops below the design point, the heating thermostat $T_2$ will energize the contactor for the strip heaters.

## CONTROL FOR SUMMER COOLING AND ELECTRIC FIN-STRIP HEATING

The electric fin-strip duct heating system is arranged for supplementary heating by utilizing the available connected electrical load when the summer-cooling refrigeration system is locked out and only the fan runs. In order to increase the kilowatt load for additional Btu of heating, one would, of course, require heavier service than normally used for only the compressor horsepower. To estimate the extra conduit and conductors for additional kilowatt load, see Chap. 14. Figure 13.9 shows the diagram on which Table 13.20 is based. The cycle of operation is as follows. The fire safety switch is set at 140°F cutoff and drops the fan and heater contactors out. The bonnet control switch is set at 75°F low and 125°F high to cycle the fan. With the fan-auto-off switch in the fan position, the fan will run and provide intermediate-season ventilation. With the switch in the auto position, either the cooling or the heating room stat will be mastered by the summer/winter switch. All design figures are nominal and are used only as a basis for cost estimating.

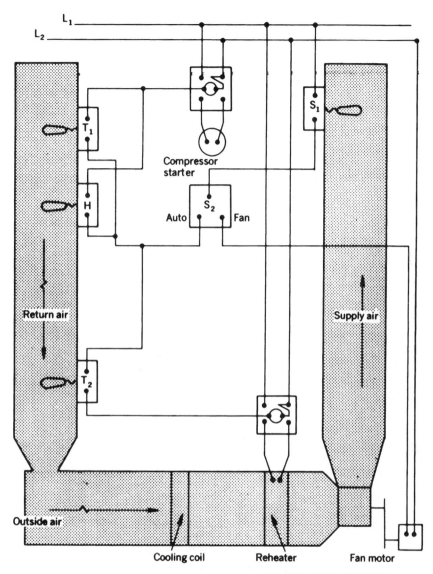

**Figure 13.8   SUMMER COOLING WITH ELECTRIC REHEAT HUMIDITY CONTROL**
**(See Table 13.19)**

$S_1$ = firestat                          $T_2$ = reheater thermostat

$S_2$ = auto-off fan switch       $H$ = overriding humidistat

$T_1$ = cooling thermostat

**TABLE 13.19** Summer Cooling with Electric Reheat Humidity Control

| Reheat load, Btu | 23,000 | 33,000 | 41,000 | 61,000 |
|---|---|---|---|---|
| Watts | 6,750 | 9,000 | 13,500 | 18,000 |
| Amperes | 39 | 24 × 2 | 34 × 2 | 40 × 2 |
| Heater package, $ | 520 | 660 | 690 | 1,040 |
| Auto-fan switch, $ | 10 | 10 | 10 | 10 |
| Cooling thermostat, $ | 45 | 45 | 45 | 45 |
| Heating thermostat, $ | 45 | 45 | 45 | 45 |
| Humidistat, $ | 175 | 175 | 175 | 175 |
| Total material, $ | 795 | 935 | 965 | 1,315 |
| Erection, workhours | 5 | 5 | 6 | 8 |

## SUMMER/WINTER CONDITIONING WITH ELECTRIC FIN-STRIP HUMIDITY CONTROL

Figure 13.10 illustrates the application of electric fin-strip heaters for humidity control during summer cooling and space heating during winter. It is a combination of Figs. 13.8 and 13.9; comparison of Tables 13.19 and 13.20 shows the relatively low costs of adding humidity control to primary heat, or vice versa. Details of the system shown in Fig. 13.10 are given in Table 13.21.

The cycle of operation is as follows: $S_1$ is a combination control; it acts as a firestat safety switch and a fan-cycling control to maintain bonnet temperature. For summer operation, $S_2$ is in the auto position and both $S_3$ and $S_4$ are in the summer position. On temperature rise in the space, the cooling thermostat $T_1$ will energize the compressor. If the relative humidity in the space remains high after the dry-bulb temperature is satisfied, the overriding humidistat will keep the compressor running for further dehumidification. As the temperature in the space falls below the design point, the heating thermostat $T_2$ will energize the strip heaters to raise the temperature. For winter operation, both $S_3$ and $S_4$ are placed in the winter position. This locks out the cooling circuit and places the heating thermostat in control of the strip-heater contactors. With $S_2$ in the fan position, the fan will run constantly for intermediate-season ventilation.

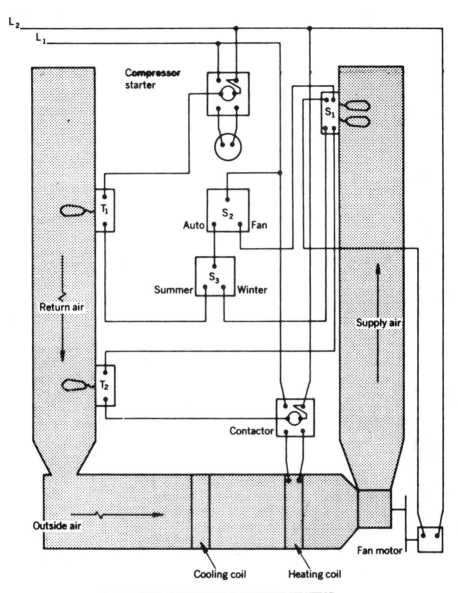

**Figure 13.9   SUMMER COOLING AND ELECTRIC FIN-STRIP HEATING**
**(See Table 13.20)**

$S_1$ = combination fan-limit switch        $T_1$ = cooling thermostat
$S_2$ = fan-off-automatic switch             $T_2$ = heating thermostat
$S_3$ = summer/winter switch

**TABLE 13.20**   Summer Cooling and Electric Strip Heating

| Compressor hp | 3 | 3 | 5 | 5 | 7½ | 10 | 15 | 20 |
|---|---|---|---|---|---|---|---|---|
| Phase | 1 | 3 | 1 | 3 | 3 | 3 | 3 | 3 |
| Heating load, Btu | 12,750 | 10,200 | 21,000 | 13,200 | 23,000 | 33,000 | 46,000 | 61,000 |
| Watts | 1,275 | 3,000 | 6,150 | 4,500 | 6,750 | 9,000 | 13,500 | 18,000 |
| Disconnect size amp | 30 | 30 | 30 | 30 | 30 | 30 | 30 | 30 |
| Heater package, $ | 275 | 300 | 350 | 400 | 525 | 660 | 960 | 1,040 |
| Combination fan-limit switch, $ | 50 | 50 | 50 | 50 | 50 | 50 | 50 | 50 |
| Auto-fan switch, $ | 10 | 10 | 10 | 10 | 10 | 10 | 10 | 10 |
| Summer-winter switch, 4pdt, $ | 150 | 150 | 150 | 150 | 150 | 150 | 150 | 150 |
| Cooling thermostat, $ | 45 | 45 | 45 | 45 | 45 | 45 | 45 | 45 |
| Heating thermostat, $ | 45 | 45 | 45 | 45 | 45 | 45 | 45 | 45 |
| Total material, $ | 575 | 600 | 650 | 700 | 825 | 960 | 1,260 | 1,340 |
| Erection, workhours | 5 | 5 | 5 | 5 | 5 | 6 | 6 | 8 |

## HOSPITAL OPERATING-ROOM CONTROL

The control shown in Fig. 13.11 and detailed in Table 13.22 is based on 100% outside air, steam or hot-water reheat, spray humidification using city water, and remote-bulb thermostats with only the bulb in the room to prevent an explosion hazard. The cycle of operation is as follows. When the fan is energized, both space thermostats become operative and control the reheating and humidifying devices. At the same time the spring-return damper motor will open the outside-air damper. With the selector switch in the summer position, the cooling thermostat brings in the compressor for cooling. The modulating steam valve controlled by the roomstat $T_2$ will maintain the room temperature either with the compressor running for summer cooling or with only cold outside air for winter heating. When the room wet-bulb temperature drops, the solenoid valve on the water spray line opens. The backpressure regulating valve is not shown in Fig. 13.11, but it must be included in this system.

Table 13.22 is based on the application of a standard 5-ton package unit with direct expansion coil. A chilled-water unit would have fundamentally the same control system. For larger

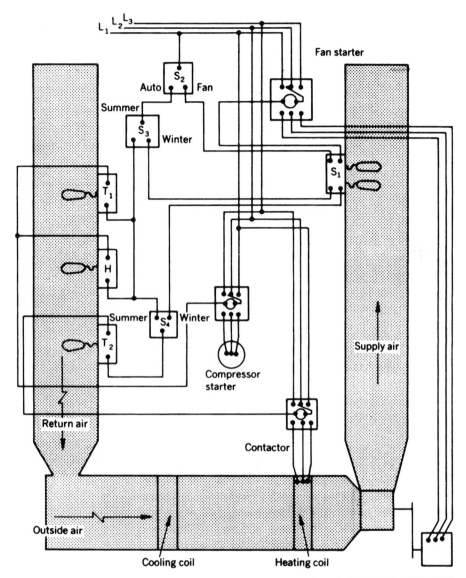

**Figure 13.10  SUMMER/WINTER CONDITIONING WITH ELECTRIC FIN-STRIP HUMIDITY CONTROL**
(See Table 13.21)

$S_1$ = combination fan-limit switch        $T_1$ = cooling thermostat
$S_2$ = fan-off-automatic switch            $T_2$ = heating thermostat
$S_3$ = summer/winter switch                $H$ = overriding humidistat
$S_4$ = summer/winter switch

**TABLE 13.21**    Summer-Winter Conditioning with Electric Fin-Strip Humidity Control

| Compressor hp | 3 | 3 | 5 | 5 | 7½ | 10 | 15 | 20 |
|---|---|---|---|---|---|---|---|---|
| Phase | 1 | 3 | 1 | 3 | 3 | 3 | 3 | 3 |
| cfm | 1,000 | 1,000 | 1,800 | 1,800 | 2,500 | 3,000 | 5,000 | 6,000 |
| Watts | 3,740 | 3,000 | 6,150 | 4,500 | 6,750 | 9,000 | 13,000 | 18,000 |
| Heater package, $ | 275 | 300 | 350 | 400 | 525 | 660 | 690 | 1,040 |
| Combination fan-limit switch, $ | 50 | 50 | 50 | 50 | 50 | 50 | 50 | 50 |
| Auto-fan switch, $ | 10 | 10 | 10 | 10 | 10 | 10 | 10 | 10 |
| Summer-winter switch, (2), $ | 300 | 300 | 300 | 300 | 300 | 300 | 300 | 300 |
| Cooling thermostat, $ | 45 | 45 | 45 | 45 | 45 | 45 | 45 | 45 |
| Heating thermostat, $ | 45 | 45 | 45 | 45 | 45 | 45 | 45 | 45 |
| Humidistat, $ | 175 | 175 | 175 | 175 | 175 | 175 | 175 | 175 |
| Total material, $ | 900 | 925 | 975 | 1,025 | 1,150 | 1,285 | 1,315 | 1,665 |
| Erection, workhours | 6 | 6 | 6 | 6 | 6 | 6 | 8 | 8 |

systems, select the components from other tables in this chapter. Water, steam, and drain lines are assumed to be at the equipment and to require only final connections. Steam condensate pump, traps, etc., are not included. Similar control systems using pneumatic and/or electric devices on an existing 15-lb air line will average about 25% higher.

## FIELD INSTRUMENTS

Some of the most frequently used field instruments for checking, measuring, and balancing are listed in Table 13.23 for quick reference. The ranges shown are inclusive for each particular instrument line and will often determine the price of the instrument. Where the price range is too wide to list separately, the indicated price range is median.

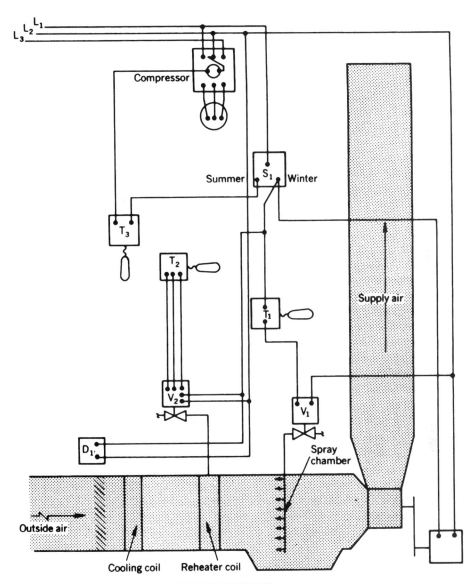

**Figure 13.11   HOSPITAL OPERATING-ROOM CONTROL**
**(See Table 13.22)**

$S_1$ = summer/winter switch

$V_1$ = solenoid valve to control water sprays

$V_2$ = modulating steam valve

$D_1$ = damper motor, spring-return

$T_1$ = remote wet-bulb thermostat

$T_2$ = remote modulating thermostat

$T_3$ = cooling thermostat

**TABLE 13.22**   Hospital Operating-Room Control

| | |
|---|---:|
| Steam coil, $ | 750 |
| Spray humidifier, $ | 900 |
| Summer-winter switch, $S_1$, $ | 150 |
| Solenoid on city water $V_1$, $ | 135 |
| Modulating steam valve $V_2$, $ | 260 |
| Wet-bulb thermostat, with water bottle and tank $T_1$, $ | 250 |
| Modulating thermostat $T_2$, $ | 90 |
| Cooling thermostat $T_3$, $ | 45 |
| Spring-return damper motor $D_1$, $ | 240 |
| Outside-air damper, $ | 250 |
| Evaporator pressure regulator, $ | 100 |
| Total material, $ | 3,170 |
| Erection and connection, workhours | 32 |

**TABLE 13.23**    Field Instruments

| Item | Description | Range or accuracy | Cost, $ |
|---|---|---|---|
| Air, gas, and pressure measurement | | | |
| Air sampler | Clean room | 1/100 micron | 240-460 |
| Air-velocity meter | Direct reading | 0–3,000 fpm | 450 |
| Anemometer | Standard | 75–10,000 fpm | 450-624 |
| $CO_2$ indicator | 0–500 ppm | — | 230 |
| Combustion test kit | Complete outfit | — | 200 |
| Draft gage | — | 0.20–0–2.0 in. | 75-120 |
| Magnehelic gage | — | 0–50 in. | 30-45 |
| Manometer | — | 18–0–18 in. | 15-40 |
| Micromanometer | — | 0.001-in. divisions | 280-400 |
| Oxygen indicator | — | 1% | 700 |
| Pitot tube | Stainless steel | Precision | 15-100 |
| Pressure recorder | — | 30–10,000 psi | 300-400 |
| Velometer | Set includes all jets | — | 350 |
| Smoke gun | Chemical, air contact | — | 30 |
| Smoke candle | Chemical, ignition | — | 0.50-1.50 |
| Radiation detection meter | — | 0–50 R per hr | 180 |
| Radiation recorder | — | 0–100 MR per hr | 400-600 |
| Refrigerant detector | Electronic-type leak checker | — | 250 |
| Temperature and air indicator | — | Hot-wire instrument | 300 |
| Vacuum gage | Zimmerli precision | 0–100 in. | 75 |
| Electrical measurement | | | |
| Ammeter-voltmeter, digital clamp-on | Light duty | — | 50 |
| Ammeter-voltmeter, digital clamp-on | Medium duty | — | 100 |
| Ammeter-voltmeter, digital clamp-on | Heavy duty | — | 250 |
| Ammeter-voltmeter, digital clamp-on | Extra-heavy, all-purpose | — | 290 |
| Continuity tester | — | — | 50 |
| Master circuit tester | — | — | 300 |
| Operation recorder | Off-on, any current | — | 250 |
| Voltage recorder | 1 volt to 2,000 mV range | — | 1,500 |
| Temperature and humidity measurement | | | |
| Indicating thermometers: | | | |
|    Dial, pocket type | Standard | −50 to +240°F | 25 |
|    Dial, pocket type | High temperature | To 1,000°F | 130 |
|    Dial, pocket bulb | 5-ft cap tube, 4-in. dial | — | 90 |
|    Glass, pocket type | Mercury | −20 to +120°F | 15 |
|    Mercury in glass | Precision test, 16 in. | — | 15-35 |
| Hygrometer | Open space | 30 to 230°F | 90-140 |
| Pyrometer | — | 0 to 2,300°F | 430 |
| Sling psychrometer | — | −20 to 120°F | 35 |
| Recording thermometers: | | | |
|    Temperature recorder | Self-contained | −30 to 120°F | 360 |
|    Temperature–operation recorder | Self-contained | −30 to 120°F | 500 |
|    Temperature–relative humidity recorder | Self-contained | −30 to 120°F | 600-750 |
|    Relative humidity recorder | Self-contained | −30 to 120°F | 350 |
| Rotation measurement | | | |
| Tachometer | Light-duty | To 4,000 rpm | 65 |
| Tachometer | With stop button | To 50,000 rpm | 475 |
| Tachometer | Recording | — | 700 |
| Photo-tach | Battery-operated | To 2,400 rpm | 370 |
| Photo-tach | Battery-operated | To 12,000 rpm | 525 |

# CHAPTER 14
# ELECTRICAL WIRING

## GENERAL DISCUSSION

Although electrical estimating is a specialty seldom ventured by the mechanical estimator, it is often necessary to include some portion of the electrical hookup in the mechanical estimate. The data presented in this chapter are a guide for electrical estimating as it may relate to heating, air-conditioning, and ventilating systems.

In almost every instance the physical wiring will be performed as an independent contract; we therefore constructed the following estimating tables in total dollars rather than a work-hour plus material unit. These labor-dollar units are based on an electrician's rate of $32 per hour.

## ESTIMATING

All final connections shown in Tables 14.1 and 14.2 are based on adequate service in proximity to the apparatus. For cooling-tower pump and fan-motor wiring—systems over 25 tons—allow $190 per horsepower. Allow $185/hp for centrifugal machinery up to 300 hp and $135/hp for machinery over 300 hp. For wiring absorption machines—all motors—allow $240/hp.

## MOTOR-STARTER HOOKUPS

Tables 14.3 to 14.5 cover labor and material for standard AC 1,800-rpm 60-cycle motors and general-purpose starters. Labor includes hauling, unloading, handling, and mounting the starter on wood panelboard; connecting line, load, and control, as well as aligning the motor and base; installing the heater; checking rotation; connecting from the end of the conduit with 3 ft of flex to the motor connection box; and connecting leads with solderless lugs. Pulling wire and conduit are not included. For weathertight starters, add 50%; for dustproof starters, add 20% to listed prices.

Tables 14.6 and 14.7 give average full-load currents for AC motors. Table 14.8 lists AC motor power factors and efficiencies. For data on disconnect safety switches, see Table 14.9. Table 14.10 provides current-capacity information for insulated copper conductors. For the costs of erecting conduit and drawing wire through conduits, see Tables 14.11 and 14.12.

**TABLE 14.1** Final Connections for Self-Contained Package Units

Consider necessary disconnect existing within 6 ft of unit. Switch sizes shown are based on use of Fusetrons and are indicated only for reference. Switches, disconnects, thermostats, cooling-tower motors, and separate starters are not included. Total installed price reflects labor and wire only, and listed horsepower is per compressor; for more than one compressor, use total horsepower.

| Horsepower | Phase | Wire size | Fusetron size | Switch size, amp | Total installed cost, $ | Addition per ft over 6 ft, $ |
|---|---|---|---|---|---|---|
| 1 | 1 | Two #12 | 8 | 30 | 190 | 13 |
| 1 | 3 | Three #12 | 3 | 30 | 200 | 18 |
| 2 | 1 | Two #12 | 15 | 30 | 190 | 13 |
| 2 | 3 | Three #12 | 7 | 30 | 200 | 18 |
| 3 | 1 | Two #10 | 17 | 30 | 275 | 20 |
| 3 | 3 | Three #12 | 12 | 30 | 200 | 18 |
| 5 | 1 | Two #6 | 35 | 60 | 350 | 44 |
| 5 | 3 | Three #10 | 25 | 30 | 280 | 30 |
| 7½ | 3 | Three #8 | 35 | 60 | 350 | 55 |
| 10 | 3 | Three #8 | 40 | 60 | 350 | 55 |
| 15 | 3 | Three #6 | 45 | 60 | 390 | 66 |
| 20 | 3 | Three #4 | 80 | 100 | 620 | 35 |
| 25 | 3 | Three #4 | 100 | 100 | 620 | 25 |
| 30 | 3 | Three #2 | 125 | 200 | 915 | 150 |
| 40 | 3 | Six #8 | 175 | 200 | 670 | 55 |
| 50 | 3 | Six #6 | 200 | 200 | 800 | 132 |
| 60 | 3 | Six #2 | 225 | 400 | 1,800 | 160 |
| 75 | 3 | Six #1 | 300 | 400 | 2,400 | 225 |

**TABLE 14.2** Remote Thermostat Hookups

Based on thermostat location within 10 ft of equipment. *Wiring per each* includes conduit and wire, and labor for handling, mounting, and wiring stat on switch box in wall or on panel.

| Thermostat | Thermostat cost, $ | Wiring per each, $ | Total erected, $ | Addition per ft beyond 10 ft, $ |
|---|---|---|---|---|
| Cooling only | 60 | 70 | 130 | 6 |
| Heating only | 60 | 70 | 130 | 6 |
| Cooling and heating | 110 | 120 | 230 | 6 |
| Three-stage | 210 | 135 | 345 | 6 |
| Two-stage | 110 | 140 | 250 | 10 |
| Humidistat | 115 | 70 | 210 | 3 |

**TABLE 14.3** 208/220 Standard Hookup, Three-Phase Circuit

| Motor hp | ¼ | ⅓ | ½ | ¾ | 1 | 1½ | 2 | 3 |
|---|---|---|---|---|---|---|---|---|
| Magnetic line starter | 00 | 00 | 00 | 00 | 00 | 00 | 0 | 0 |
| Motor cost, $ | 100 | 110 | 120 | 140 | 300 | 310 | 320 | 395 |
| Starter cost, $ | 150 | 150 | 150 | 150 | 150 | 150 | 180 | 180 |
| Labor, set motor, $ | 36 | 36 | 36 | 36 | 46 | 46 | 75 | 80 |
| Labor, set starter, $ | 60 | 60 | 60 | 60 | 60 | 60 | 75 | 75 |
| Total in place, $ | 346 | 356 | 366 | 386 | 556 | 566 | 650 | 730 |
| Motor hp | 5 | 7½ | 10 | 15 | 20 | 25 | 30 | |
| Magnetic line starter | 1 | 1 | 2 | 2 | 2 | 3 | 3 | |
| Motor cost, $ | 500 | 500 | 650 | 700 | 840 | 1,000 | 1,200 | |
| Starter cost, $ | 215 | 215 | 410 | 410 | 410 | 670 | 670 | |
| Labor, set motor, $ | 108 | 136 | 150 | 210 | 240 | 300 | 360 | |
| Labor, set starter, $ | 90 | 90 | 130 | 130 | 190 | 190 | 190 | |
| Total in place, $ | 913 | 941 | 1,340 | 1,450 | 1,680 | 2,160 | 2,420 | |
| Motor hp | 40 | 50 | 60 | 75 | 100 | 125 | 150 | 200 |
| Magnetic line starter | 4 | 4 | 4 | 4 | 4 | 5 | 5 | 5 |
| Motor cost, $ | 2,500 | 2,600 | 3,000 | 3,500 | 4,000 | 4,500 | 6,500 | 9,000 |
| Starter cost, $ | 1,550 | 1,420 | 2,050 | 2,450 | 2,205 | 5,400 | 5,400 | 5,400 |
| Labor, set motor, $ | 420 | 450 | 540 | 720 | 780 | 810 | 990 | 990 |
| Labor, set starter, $ | 190 | 230 | 270 | 270 | 400 | 525 | 525 | 800 |
| Total in place, $ | 4,660 | 4,700 | 5,860 | 6,940 | 7,385 | 11,235 | 13,415 | 16,190 |

**TABLE 14.4** 230-V Standard Hookup, One-Phase Circuit

| Motor hp | ¼ | ⅓ | ½ | ¾ | 1 | 1½ | 2 | 3 | 5 |
|---|---|---|---|---|---|---|---|---|---|
| Magnetic line starter | 00 | 00 | 00 | 00 | 00 | 0 | 0 | 1 | 1½ |
| Motor cost, $ | 100 | 110 | 120 | 140 | 300 | 310 | 320 | 395 | 500 |
| Starter cost, $ | 140 | 140 | 140 | 140 | 140 | 170 | 170 | 200 | 330 |
| Labor, set motor, $ | 36 | 36 | 36 | 36 | 50 | 65 | 85 | 100 | 120 |
| Labor, set starter, $ | 60 | 60 | 60 | 60 | 60 | 60 | 70 | 70 | 70 |
| Total in place, $ | 336 | 346 | 356 | 376 | 550 | 605 | 645 | 765 | 1,020 |

**TABLE 14.5** Manual Starter Hookup, One-Pole, One-Phase Circuit

| Motor hp | ¼ | ⅓ | ½ | ¾ | 1 |
|---|---|---|---|---|---|
| Motor cost, $ | 70 | 90 | 105 | 130 | 160 |
| Starter cost, $ | 35 | 35 | 35 | 35 | 35 |
| Labor, set motor, $ | 45 | 45 | 45 | 60 | 60 |
| Labor, set starter, $ | 15 | 15 | 15 | 15 | 15 |
| Total in place, $ | 165 | 185 | 200 | 240 | 270 |

**TABLE 14.6** Average Full-Load Currents for Three-Phase AC Motors

| hp | Squirrel-cage and wound-rotor induction type | | | | | Synchronous unity-power-factor type | | | |
|---|---|---|---|---|---|---|---|---|---|
| | 110 V | 220 V | 440 V | 550 V | 2,300 V | 220 V | 240 V | 550 V | 2,300 V |
| ½ | 4 | 2 | 1 | 0.8 | | | | | |
| ¾ | 5.6 | 2.8 | 1.4 | 1.1 | | | | | |
| 1 | 7 | 3.5 | 1.8 | 1.4 | | | | | |
| 1½ | 10 | 5 | 2.5 | 2 | | | | | |
| 2 | 13 | 6.5 | 3.3 | 2.6 | | | | | |
| 3 | | 9 | 4.5 | 4 | | | | | |
| 5 | | 15 | 7.5 | 6 | | | | | |
| 7½ | | 22 | 11 | 9 | | | | | |
| 10 | | 27 | 14 | 11 | | | | | |
| 15 | | 40 | 20 | 16 | | | | | |
| 20 | | 52 | 26 | 21 | | | | | |
| 25 | | 64 | 32 | 26 | 7 | 54 | 27 | 22 | 5.4 |
| 30 | | 78 | 39 | 31 | 8.5 | 65 | 33 | 26 | 6.5 |
| 40 | | 104 | 52 | 41 | 10.5 | 86 | 43 | 35 | 8 |
| 50 | | 125 | 63 | 50 | 13 | 108 | 54 | 44 | 10 |
| 60 | | 150 | 75 | 60 | 15 | 128 | 64 | 51 | 12 |
| 75 | | 185 | 93 | 74 | 19 | 161 | 81 | 65 | 15 |
| 100 | | 246 | 123 | 98 | 25 | 211 | 106 | 85 | 20 |

**TABLE 14.7** Average Full-Load Currents for Single-Phase Motors

| hp | 100 V | 200 V | hp | 115 V | 230 V |
|---|---|---|---|---|---|
| ⅙ | 4.4 | 2.2 | 1½ | 20 | 9.5 |
| ¼ | 5.8 | 2.9 | 2 | 24 | 12 |
| ½ | 9.8 | 4.9 | 3 | 34 | 17 |
| ¾ | 13.8 | 6.9 | 5 | 56 | 28 |
| 1 | 16 | 8 | 7½ | 80 | 40 |
| | | | 10 | 100 | 50 |

The current required for any alternating current motor can be obtained from the following equations:

*Single-phase:*

$$\text{Current} = \frac{\text{horsepower} \times 74{,}600}{\text{voltage} \times \text{power factor} \times \text{efficiency}}$$

*Two-phase, four-wire supply:*

$$\text{Current} = \frac{\text{horsepower} \times 74{,}600}{2 \times \text{voltage} \times \text{power factor} \times \text{efficiency}}$$

*Two-phase, three-wire supply:*

$$\text{Current} = \text{in outers, as above}$$
$$= \text{in common, } 1.414 \times \text{outer value}$$

*Three-phase:*

$$\text{Current} = \frac{\text{horsepower} \times 74{,}600}{1.732 \times \text{power factor} \times \text{efficiency}}$$

**TABLE 14.8** Approximate Power Factors and Efficiency of AC Motors
Based on four-pole motors at 1,500 rpm.

| | Power factor, % | | | Efficiency, % | | |
|---|---|---|---|---|---|---|
| hp | Split 1-phase | Capacitor 1-phase | 3-phase | Split 1-phase | Capacitor 1-phase | 3-phase |
| 1 | 73 | 92 | 81 | 66 | 72 | 74 |
| 1½ | 77 | 93 | 81 | 69 | 73 | 76 |
| 2 | 79 | 93 | 83 | 71 | 75 | 76 |
| 3 | 81 | 93 | 84 | 72 | 75 | 78 |
| 5 | 83 | 93 | 85 | 75 | 78 | 80 |
| 7½ | | | 86 | | | 82 |
| 10 | | | 88 | | | 84 |
| 15 | | | 88 | | | 85 |
| 20 | | | 88 | | | 86 |
| 30 | | | 89 | | | 88 |
| 40 | | | 89 | | | 89 |
| 50 | | | 89 | | | 90 |
| 75 | | | 90 | | | 91 |
| 100 | | | 91 | | | 92 |

**TABLE 14.9** Disconnect Safety Switches

Fused, 240-V, three-pole, general-purpose, solderless. Includes hauling, handling, mounting on wood
panelboard, connecting, and fusing. Does not include fuses. For 600-V switches, add 10%.

| hp | Size RH wire | Dual-element fuse size | Switch size, A | Material, $ | Labor, $ | Total in place, $ |
|---|---|---|---|---|---|---|
| 1 | 14 | 3.5 | 30 | 58 | 85 | 143 |
| 1½ | 14 | 5.6 | 30 | 58 | 85 | 143 |
| 2 | 14 | 7 | 30 | 60 | 85 | 145 |
| 3 | 14 | 10 | 30 | 60 | 85 | 145 |
| 5 | 12 | 20 | 30 | 60 | 85 | 145 |
| 7½ | 10 | 30 | 60 | 100 | 120 | 220 |
| 10 | 10 | 35 | 60 | 100 | 120 | 220 |
| 15 | 6 | 45 | 60 | 100 | 120 | 220 |
| 20 | 6 | 60 | 100 | 175 | 145 | 320 |
| 25 | 4 | 70 | 100 | 175 | 145 | 320 |
| 30 | 2 | 110 | 200 | 350 | 215 | 565 |
| 40 | 1 | 125 | 200 | 350 | 215 | 565 |
| 50 | 2/0 | 150 | 200 | 350 | 215 | 565 |
| 60 | 3/0 | 225 | 400 | 900 | 300 | 1,200 |
| 75 | 4/0 | 225 | 400 | 900 | 300 | 1,200 |
| 100 | 350 | 300 | 400 | 900 | 300 | 1,200 |

**TABLE 14.10** Current-Carrying Capacities of Insulated Copper Conductors

Based on room temperatures of 80°F, not more than three conductors in conduit.

| Size AWG MCM | Rubber, types R, RW; plastic, types T, TW | Rubber, type RH, R4-RW |
|:---:|:---:|:---:|
| | Amperes | |
| 14 | 15 | 15 |
| 12 | 20 | 20 |
| 10 | 30 | 30 |
| 8 | 40 | 45 |
| 6 | 55 | 65 |
| 4 | 70 | 85 |
| 3 | 80 | 100 |
| 2 | 90 | 115 |
| 1 | 110 | 130 |
| 0 | 125 | 150 |
| 00 | 145 | 175 |
| 000 | 165 | 200 |
| 0000 | 195 | 230 |
| 250 | 215 | 255 |
| 300 | 240 | 285 |

**TABLE 14.11** Erecting Conduit—Installed Costs

Based on runs to 15 ft high with four fittings per 100 ft. Includes laying out, handling, and fastening of tubing and fittings with average number of offsets for short runs, but does not include conductors, overhead, or profit.

| Conduit size, in. | ½ | ¾ | 1 | 1½ | 2 | 2½ | 3 | 3½ | 4 |
|---|---|---|---|---|---|---|---|---|---|
| Rigid galvanized steel, $ per lin ft | 6.25 | 7.25 | 9.00 | 11.50 | 15.00 | 21.00 | 29.00 | 34.00 | 38.00 |
| Aluminum, $ per lin ft | 5.65 | 6.25 | 8.00 | 10.75 | 12.00 | 16.50 | 20.00 | 24.00 | 27.50 |

**TABLE 14.12** Wires Drawn through Conduit—Installed Costs

| Wires per conduit $ per lin ft | Three #14 2.20 | Three #12 2.50 | Three #10 2.90 | Three #8 3.70 | Three #6 4.50 | Three #4 5.50 |
|---|---|---|---|---|---|---|
| Wires per conduit $ per lin ft | Three #2 7.60 | Three #1 10.30 | Three #0 10.60 | Three #2/0 13.00 | Three #3/0 14.30 | Three #4/0 17.30 |

## RECOMMENDED READING

Mahoney, E., *Electricity for Air Conditioning and Refrigeration Technicians*, 2d ed., Prentice-Hall, Englewood Cliffs, N.J., 1986.

*Manual of Labor Units*, National Electrical Contractors Association.

*Means Electrical Cost Data*, R. S. Means Co., Kingston, Mass. (Published annually.)

Page, J. S., *Estimator's Electrical Man-Hour Manual*, 2d ed., Gulf Publishing Co., Houston, Tex., 1979.

Tyler, E. J., *Estimating Electrical Construction*, Craftsman Book Co., Carlsbad, Calif., 1983.

Tyler, E. J., *Electrical Construction Estimator*, Craftsman Book Co., Carlsbad, Calif. (Published annually.)

# CHAPTER 15
# SYSTEM TESTING, ADJUSTING, AND BALANCING (TAB)

## GENERAL DISCUSSION

The *ASHRAE Handbook: Applications, 1991* defines *system testing, adjusting,* and *balancing* as the

> process of checking and adjusting all the building environmental systems to produce the design objectives. It includes (1) balancing air and water distribution, (2) adjustment of total system to provide design quantities, (3) electrical measurement, (4) verification and performance of all equipment and automatic controls, and (5) sound and vibration measurement. These are accomplished by (1) checking installations for conformity to design, (2) measurement and establishment of the fluid quantities of the system as required to meet specifications, and (3) recording and reporting the results.

Proper testing, adjusting, and balancing can be performed only by a well-trained, experienced, and qualified staff. This chapter does not suggest which groups or individuals are best qualified, but one single group must be responsible for testing, adjusting, and balancing all systems on each project.

The TAB function is still a relatively recent development in the industry, and few contractors have developed the combined knowledge, experience, instrumentation, personnel, and organization to perform it. The Associated Air Balance Council subscribes to the principle of *independent* test and balance and certifies its member agencies on the basis of proven experience, successful performance, and financial responsibility. The National Environment Balancing Bureau also has stringent qualifications and testing procedures before accepting individual members but does not follow the notion of "independent testing and balancing agencies." Both of these organizations have contributed much to the state of the art of TAB. With the growth of TAB many nonaffiliated agencies and companies have sprung up across the country, and many of the larger mechanical contractors have added qualified test and balance supervisory personnel to their staffs. The basic instrumentation required to perform the test-and-balance function costs $12,000 to $15,000, and annual repair calibration and replacement costs could run between $5,000 and $10,000.

Part of the responsibility of the TAB group is checking the performance data of all equipment under field conditions to ensure compliance and produce repeatable results that meet the intent of the designer and accurately reflect the requirements of the owner. All tasks, including organization, calibrated instrumentation, and execution of the actual work, must be carefully scheduled. Air-side and water-side work must be coordinated to meet seasonal temperature performance.

The workhour units and cost data in the following tables are based on standard procedures as set forth by *ASHRAE Handbook: HVAC Applications, 1991* (Chap. 34); ANSI/ASHRAE Standard 111-1988, *Practices for Measurement, Testing, Adjusting and Balancing of Building Heating, Ventilation, Air Conditioning and Refrigeration Systems*; ANSI/ASHRAE Standard 110-1985, *Method of Testing Performance of Laboratory Fume Hoods; AABC National Standards for Total System Balance,* 4th ed., 1984, Associated Air Balance Council; *CTI Standard Specifications for Thermal Testing of Wet/Dry Cooling Towers,* ATC-105-82, Cooling Tower Institute; and *NEBB Procedural Standards for Testing, Balancing and Adjusting of Environmental Systems,* 4th ed., 1983, National Environmental Balancing Bureau.

## ESTIMATING

The importance of well-designed forms for the purpose of identifying the apparatuses and equipment and recording field readings cannot be overstressed. Some contractors use their own forms. Most TAB engineers and technicians use the standard forms published by the Associated Air Balance Council (AABC), Washington, D.C.; or National Environmental Balancing Bureau (NEBB), Rockville, Md. Forms are available for air-distribution devices, induction units, mixing boxes, chillers, pumps, boilers, cooling towers, hoods, fans, etc., as well as a variety of computation forms and certifications test report forms.

For accurate estimating, a quantity takeoff form will be required. All apparatuses and devices that come within the scope of the work should be listed and a workhour value applied

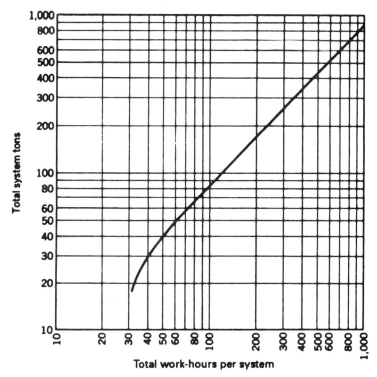

**Figure 15.1  SPEED-SHEET ESTIMATING—SYSTEM TESTING AND BALANCING, WORKHOURS PER SYSTEM**

against each. If testing and balancing is performed by an independent subcontractor, a charge of $45 per workhour (mid-1993 costs) may be used for estimating purposes. This figure includes the subcontractor's overhead and profit.

For rapid estimating and check data, the speed sheet shown in Fig. 15.1 may be used; it offers the average correlation between tons and workhours. Check data for the selling price of system test and balance may be found in Chap. 2.

The operations listed in Tables 15.1 to 15.11 are not in order of importance or procedure, nor are they necessarily grouped by sequence; they are arranged for tabular convenience only and should be abstracted to suit the particular need of the skilled estimator.

**TABLE 15.1**  Cooling-Tower Testing

As per Cooling Tower Institute (CTI) specifications.

| Item | Workhours |
|---|---|
| Towers ≤ 750 tons | |
| Setup | 26 |
| Test(s) | 16 |
| Removal or breakdown | 3 |
| Report | 6 |
| Total workhours | 51 |
| Towers ≥ 750 tons | |
| Setup | 36 |
| Test(s) | 20 |
| Removal or breakdown | 6 |
| Report | 10 |
| Total workhours | 72 |

Regardless of tower size, add $225 for materials and $960 for welding.

**TABLE 15.2**  Pumps

As per Hydraulics Institute's Centrifugal Pump Test Code.

| Item | Workhours |
|---|---|
| 5–75 hp | |
| Setup | 4 |
| Test(s) | 1.5 |
| Removal or breakdown | 1 |
| Report | 1.5 |
| Total workhours | 8 |
| 75–150 hp | |
| Setup | 6 |
| Test(s) | 2.5 |
| Removal or breakdown | 1 |
| Report | 1.5 |
| Total workhours | 11 |

Regardless of pump size, add $70 for materials and $430 for welding.

**TABLE 15.3**  Air Handlers

| Item | Chilled-water workhours | DX workhours |
|---|---|---|
| Inspection | 3.5 | 3.5 |
| Fan performance | 8.5 | 8.5 |
| Heat rejection | 2.5 | 2.5 |
| Check heating | 1.5 | 1.5 |
| Report | 1.5 | 1.5 |
| Water balance | 2 | — |
| Heat rejection | 1 | — |
| Condensing unit | — | 4.5 |
| Total workhours | 20.5 | 22 |

**TABLE 15.4**  VAV Terminals

| Item | Workhours |
|---|---|
| Pneumatic, pressure-independent, 200–1,500 cfm per box | |
| Set min/max | 2.5 |
| Calibrate stat | 0.5 |
| With heat | 0.5 |
| Total workhours | 3.5 |
| With DDC controls 200–1,500 cfm per box | |
| Set min/max | 3 |
| Calibration | 0.5 |
| With heat | 0.5 |
| Total workhours | 4 |
| Fan-powered induction VAV terminals 200–1,500-cfm units | |
| Set min/max | 2.25 |
| Check induction unit | 0.75 |
| Calibration | 0.5 |
| Total workhours without heat | 3.5 |
| Heat | 0.5 |
| Total workhours with heat | 4 |

**TABLE 15.5**  Air Distribution

Low-pressure constant volume. Based on 0.8 to 1.1 cfm per square foot of floor space.

Allow $0.10–$0.28/sq ft
Allow $5.25/exhaust grille (toilets) or return air
Allow $25/supply air diffusers, slots, etc.

**TABLE 15.6**  Fan-Coil Units—Horizontal

| Item | Workhours |
|---|---|
| Inspection | 0.25 |
| Check performance and calibration | 1.5 |
| Heat rejection | 0.5 |
| With heat | 0.5 |
| Total workhours | 2.75 |

**TABLE 15.7**  Restaurant Kitchen Ventilation

| Item | Workhours |
|---|---|
| 1 range exhaust hood | 4.5 |
| 1 supply air makeup | 3 |
| 1 dishwasher | 2.5 |
| Mechanical inspection | 2.75 |
| Total workhours | 12.75 |

**TABLE 15.8**   Ventilation Systems

| Item | Workhours |
|---|---|
| ¼–2-hp-powered roof exhausters | |
| Mechanical checkout | 1.75 |
| Set total air, fan rpm, etc. | 3.00 |
| Total workhours | 4.75 |
| ½–10-hp utility vent sets | |
| Mechanical checkout | 2.50 |
| Set total air, fan rpm, etc. | 3.50 |
| Total workhours | 6.00 |

**TABLE 15.9**   Hoods: Laboratory, etc.

| Item | Workhours: hood only | Workhours: ventilation system |
|---|---|---|
| Fume hoods | 2.75 | 1.50 |
| Snorkel exhaust | 1.50 | 1.50 |
| Chemical storage cabinets | 3.00 | 1.50 |
| Canopy hoods | 3.00 | 2.70 |
| Isotope hoods | 4.25 | 2.70 |
| Check controls (various) | 1.00 | — |
| Class II biohazard cabinets | 4.25 | 2.70 |

**TABLE 15.10**   Reports

Bound reports, total job—not including analysis or job profile.

| Item | Cost, $ |
|---|---|
| Small job | 700 |
| Average job | 1,120 |
| Large job | 1,600 |

For indoor-air-quality (IAQ) testing, see Chap. 22.

**TABLE 15.11**   Chiller Apparatus

| Item | Workhours |
|---|---|
| Setup | 1.5 |
| Test and adjust to design | 3.0 |
| Removal or breakdown | 1.0 |
| Total workhours | 5.5 |

Example 15.1 illustrates a common approach to estimating air distribution and compares the square foot or cfm method with the diffuser quantification method for estimating low-pressure, constant volume systems as well as VAV. The cost values shown for VAV using direct digital controls (DDCs) are based on laptop computers being used for this task, but the costs for the computer and program are not included. A few prominent test-and-balance agencies are using the laptop computer in the field at the point of production and writing their own programs for VAV DDC balancing where the laptop plays a particularly significant role. An allowance for engineering and field supervision should be made for each job; it should include jobsite survey and orientation, making a takeoff of the apparatuses and devices, setting up all the forms and necessary preliminary office work, coordinating at the job, making entries on summation forms, and submitting reports and miscellaneous engineering calculations. Such an allowance may be figured at approximately 8 workhours per 10,000 cfm for average jobs. See also Table 15.5.

**Example 15.1**  Assume a typical 7,000-sq-ft office space with

1. 6,750 cfm of total air
2. ±27 supply-air diffusers
3. ±18 return-air grilles
4. 10 VAV terminals

**solution**

1. $0.10 × 7,000 sq ft = $700.00
2. 27 diffusers × $25 = $675.00
3. 18 return-air grilles × $5.25 = $94.50
4. 10 VAV terminals at 3.5 hr × $35/hr = $1,225.00

**summary**

| Item | Per-sq-ft method | Per-grille method |
|------|------------------|-------------------|
| Air balance only | $ 700.00 | $ 769.50 |
| VAV terminals | 1,225.00 | 1,225.00 |
| Total | $1,925.00 | $1,994.00 |

$1,925/7,000 sq ft = $0.275/sq ft for total air balance, VAVs, and air-distribution constant volume.

## RECOMMENDED READING

*AABC 1984, National Standards for Total System Balance,* 4th ed., Associated Air Balance Council, Washington, D.C.

*AMCA 1987, Fan Application Manual,* Air Movement and Control Association, Arlington Heights, Ill., 1987.

*ASHRAE Handbook, Applications, 1991,* American Society of Heating, Refrigerating and Air Conditioning Engineers, Inc., Atlanta, Ga., 1991, Chap. 34.

ANSI/ASHRAE Standard 111-1988, *Practices for Measurement, Testing, Adjusting, and Balancing of Building Heating, Ventilation, Air Conditioning and Refrigeration Systems.*

ANSI/ASHRAE Standard 110-1985, *Method of Testing Performance of Laboratory Fume Hoods.*

*ASHRAE Technical Data Bulletin, Developments in Kitchen Ventilation Technology,* Vol. 8, No. 4, 1992.

*CTI Standard Specification ATC-105-82 for Thermal Testing of Wet/Dry Cooling Towers,* Cooling Tower Institute, Houston, Tex.

Gladstone, J., *Air Conditioning Testing/Adjusting/Balancing: A Field Practice Manual,* 2d ed., Engineer's Press, Coral Gables, Fla., 1981.

Gladstone, J., "Beyond NFPA 96: Practical Design for Restaurant Fire Protection," *Heating/Piping/Air Conditioning,* January 1985, pp. 97–105.

*NEBB 1983 Procedural Standards for Testing, Balancing and Adjusting of Environmental Systems,* 4th ed., National Environmental Balancing Bureau, Vienna, Va.

Sauer, H. J., and R. H. Howell, "Airflow Measurements at Coil Faces with Vane Anemometers: Statistical Correction and Recommended Field Measurement Procedure," *Transactions, ASHRAE,* Vol. 96, No. i, 1990, pp. 502–511.

SMACNA, *HVAC Systems—Testing, Adjusting and Balancing,* Sheet Metal and Air Conditioning Contractors National Association, Chantilly, Va., 1993.

## ACKNOWLEDGMENT

The editors wish to acknowledge the contribution of Earl Hagood, of Earl Hagood Inc., Miami, Fla., for his assistance with this chapter.

# CHAPTER 16
# FASTENING

Developments in fastening products and tools have caused many contractors, both large and small, to depart from traditional approaches in hanging fixtures and pipes and anchoring heavy apparatus. On a large mechanical job—with everything else equal—the choice of fastenings can easily determine the successful bid. The difference in an estimate can amount to many thousands of dollars.

Since no fastener is universal, the cost-conscious contractor will sometimes choose several fastening methods for a particular job. Plans and specifications rarely spell out the types of fasteners and almost never specify the tools to be used in an application. Therefore, an estimator must select the devices and specify the fastening method when preparing the job estimate.

Before proceeding with a cost estimate of a job, three important technical items have to be answered:

1. To what type of masonry material will the apparatus be fastened?
2. What is the effective weight of the apparatus?
3. What operating conditions are encountered?

With conditions of heavy vibration, most lead anchors have a tendency to "creep" loose. Plastic anchors undergo weakening physical change when exposed to temperature extremes, and jute-fiber plugs react to chemical exposure and wetting.

The accepted holding power of a masonry anchor in concrete is rated at a 4:1 safety ratio to the average pull-out strength of that anchor when tested in 3,500-psi concrete under ideal conditions. Some manufacturers of fasteners, anchors, stud guns, and drilling devices rate their products by pull-out strength only. An expansion shield that is rated at 1,000-lb pull-out strength could have a safe holding power of only 250 lb. Generally, these ratings are offered for concrete usage. When the masonry material is cinder block, the same shield would have only a 125-lb holding power.

Table 16.1[1] provides the approximate pull-out strength of various masonry materials for guidance in selecting the most suitable anchoring devices.

---

[1] Tables 16.1 to 16.4 do not appear on the computer disk provided with this book.

**TABLE 16.1**   Pull-out Strength of Common Anchors in Various Masonry Materials Compared with Concrete

Symbol x indicates anchor can be used in this material.

| Masonry material | Pull-out strength, % | Jute fiber | Lead plug | Lag shield | Punch-drive expansion | Wing toggle | Self-drilling | Stud gun | Plastic plug |
|---|---|---|---|---|---|---|---|---|---|
| Brick | 50 | x | x | x | x | | x | | x |
| Concrete | 100 | x | x | x | x | | x | x | x |
| Concrete block | 90 | x | x | | | x | | | x |
| Cinder block | 50 | x | x | | | x | | | x |
| Marble | 90 | x | x | | x | | | | x |
| Plaster | 25 | x | | | | x | | | x |
| Stone | 100 | x | x | x | x | | x | | x |
| Stucco | 25 | x | x | | | | | | x |
| Terrazzo | 90 | x | x | x | x | | x | | x |
| Tile | 75 | x | x | | | x | | | x |

## STUD-GUN LIMITATIONS

The powder-actuated stud gun is probably the most popular of all fastening methods in current use. This is because of its application speed, time savings, and consequent job cost reductions. However, it has some definite limitations. Certain states and municipalities have regulated the use of stud guns following numerous accidents caused by ricochet, shoot-through, and explosive spall. Contractors successfully using stud guns have had to provide extensive on-job training to every operator before a tool is assigned. Some of the disadvantages of the powder-actuated stud gun are

1. Costs for training operators are substantial.
2. Charge and stud requirements vary with the masonry aggregate, making it difficult and more costly to select the proper charge and stud.
3. Powder cartridges must be protected from dampness.
4. Some guns have limited holding-power range and cannot handle heavy weight.
5. Guns cannot be used in tight spots and close corners.
6. Guns cannot be used near masonry edges.
7. Guns have a tendency to spall high-strength concrete.
8. Concrete must be of good quality, with a smooth surface.

An alternative method is the drill and insert combination. The drill first creates a void, and the insert is then compacted into it—similar to a dentist filling a tooth. A stud gun simply forces a stud or pin into the concrete. Concrete that is displaced by stud intrusion is forced against the surrounding mass, thus weakening the concrete and forming fissures. Under a vibrating load, there is always a danger of stud pull-out. This is a serious objection to using the powder-actuated stud gun.

*Screw-in concrete fasteners,* which have become increasingly popular in recent years, are essentially large self-tapping screws that are driven into predrilled holes and that cut threads into the concrete in much the same manner as a sheet-metal screw threads into metal. Screw-in fasteners overcome some of the problems of stud guns and avoid the use of soft low-strength inserts, such as lead or plastic.

Table 16.2 identifies some common anchors and fasteners. Figure 16.1 shows a few of these. No attempt was made to list all the manufacturers or available products. Additional fastening devices available to the estimator for industrial applications are listed in Table 16.3.

The rotary hammer or impact drill is now widely used for fastening and core drilling. With this tool, one can drill a perfect hole to a measured depth in one-fourth the time needed for a standard carbide drill. Heavy-impact blows of the hammer limit this tool to use on heavy masonry having lateral support. The rotary hammer should not be used near masonry edges. The impact drill is further limited to larger-diameter holes. It is most efficient for drop-in-type anchors.

## COST ANALYSIS

After determining the weight of the apparatus and identifying the masonry material, the estimator should make a cost analysis to determine which fastener will be most economical. Table 16.4 gives five hypothetical examples of a method of determining the total cost for setting 500 fasteners when the holding power required per fastener is 135, 225, 500, 900, and 2,150 lb, respectively. The masonry material used throughout these examples is good-quality

**TABLE 16.2**  Identification of Common Anchors and Fasteners*

| Product | Trade name | Manufacturer |
|---------|-----------|--------------|
| Self-drilling anchor (for use with power hammer) | Self-drilling anchor<br>Self-drilling shield<br>Red Head<br>Saber-tooth | Ackerman Johnson<br>Arro<br>Phillips<br>Rawlplug |
| Lag expansion | Lag expansion shield<br>Lag expansion shield<br>Lag screw shield<br>Lag-shield | Ackerman Johnson<br>Arro<br>Ramset<br>Rawlplug |
| Jute fiber | Jiff-E-Plug Fibre<br>Jute plug<br>Rawlplug | Ackerman Johnson<br>Arro<br>Rawlplug |
| Plastic fiber | Plastic plug<br>Plastic screw anchor<br>Hi-Red<br>Tap-it nylon<br>Plastic screw anchor<br>Bantam plug | Ackerman Johnson<br>Arro<br>Holub<br>Partridge<br>Ramset<br>Rawlplug |
| Screw-in concrete fasteners | Scru 'n' tap<br>Tapcon | Star<br>Drill Drive |
| Powder fasteners | Pow-R-Set<br>Drive Pins | Ramset<br>Speed Fastener |

*(Continued)*

**TABLE 16.2** Identification of Common Anchors and Fasteners*   (*Continued*)

| Product | Trade name | Manufacturer |
|---|---|---|
| Lead screw plug | Jiff-E-Plug Lead | Ackerman Johnson |
| | Lead screw anchor | Arro |
| | Lead anchor | Ramset |
| | Scru-lead | Rawlplug |
| | Snapins | Star |
| Toggle wing bolt | Spring-wing toggle | Ackerman Johnson |
| | Toggle bolt | Arro |
| | Spring-wing toggle | Ramset |
| | Rawl spring wings | Rawlplug |
| | Snapins | Star |
| Nail drive | Nail anchor | Arro |
| | Shure-drive | Ramset |
| | Nailin | Rawlplug |
| | Pin Grip | Star |
| Punch-drive expansive screw anchor (used with setting tool) | Expansive screw anchor | Ackerman Johnson |
| | Expansive anchor | Arro |
| | Di-ex | Diamond |
| | Calk-in | Rawlplug |
| Drop-in machine bolt shields, single or multiple type (no setting tool required) | Drop-in | Ackerman Johnson |
| | Hold-it | Arro |
| | Di-ex | Diamond |
| | Rawl double | Rawlplug |
| | Drop-grip | Star |
| Hollow wall anchor (light duty) | Hollow wall anchor | Ackerman Johnson |
| | Dazy | Arro |
| | Molly anchor | Molly |
| | Hollow wall anchor | Ramset |
| | Rawly | Rawlplug |
| | Wallgrip | Star |
| One-piece slim-line expansion anchor | Dynabolt | Ramset |
| | Taper-tite | Remington |
| | Thunderbolt | Universal |
| | Rawl-drive | Rawlplug |

*Popular trade names and manufacturer identities are used for reader guidance. Omission of other equivalent available products is unintentional.

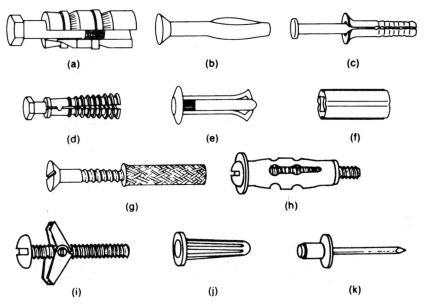

**Figure 16.1  FASTENER TYPES**
*(a) Multiple-type drop-in machine bolt, (b) one-piece slim-line expansion anchor, (c) lead screw plug, (d) lag expansion, (e) nail drive, (f) plastic tubular, (g) jute-fiber plug, (h) hollow-wall anchor, (i) toggle-wing bolt, (j) plastic conical, (k) blind rivet.*

**TABLE 16.3**  Typical Applications for Masonry Anchors

Symbol x indicates suitability.

| Application | Jute fiber plug | Self-drilling anchor | Punch-drive expansive anchor, caulking type | Punch-drive expansive anchor, single section | One-piece slim-line expansive anchor | Punch-drive noncaulking type | Lead screw plug | Lag expansion bolt | Toggle wing bolt | Nail drive | Hollow wall anchor |
|---|---|---|---|---|---|---|---|---|---|---|---|
| Acoustical ceilings | x | x | | x | x | x | | | x | | |
| Awnings | x | x | | x | x | x | x | x | x | x | x |
| Bathroom fixtures | x | x | | | | x | x | x | x | | |
| Benches, gym | x | x | x | x | x | x | x | x | | | x |
| Blowers | x | x | x | x | x | x | x | x | x | x | x |
| Brackets | x | x | | x | x | x | x | x | x | x | |
| Burglar alarms | x | x | x | x | x | x | x | x | x | x | |
| Cabinets | x | x | x | x | x | x | x | x | x | x | |
| Carpet tacking | x | | | | | | | | | | |
| Conveyor equipment | x | x | x | x | x | x | x | x | x | x | x |
| Conduit clamps | x | x | | x | x | x | x | | x | | x |
| Curtain fixtures | x | x | | x | x | x | x | | x | | |
| Door bucks | x | x | | x | x | x | | | | | |
| Doors, folding | x | | | x | | x | x | x | x | | x |
| Drapery hardware | x | | | x | x | x | x | | x | | x |
| Electric meters | x | x | x | x | x | x | x | x | x | | |
| Elevator equipment | x | x | x | x | x | x | | x | x | x | |
| Fixtures, office | x | x | | x | x | x | | x | | | |
| Furring strips | x | x | x | x | x | x | | | x | x | |
| Lockers | x | x | x | x | x | x | x | x | x | | |
| Machinery | x | x | x | x | x | x | x | x | | | |
| Metal lath | x | x | | | | | | | | | |
| Office machines | x | x | x | | x | | x | x | | | |
| Ornamental iron | x | x | | x | x | x | x | x | x | | x |
| Outlet boxes | x | x | | x | x | x | x | | x | x | x |

314

| Use | | | | | | | | | | | |
|---|---|---|---|---|---|---|---|---|---|---|---|
| Partitions ............ | X | | | | X | X | | | | X | |
| Pipe strap ........... | X | X | | | X | X | X | | X | X | |
| Pipe railings ......... | X | X | X | | X | X | | | | | |
| Plaster ends ......... | X | X | X | | X | | | | | | |
| Plumbing fixtures .... | X | X | | X | X | X | X | X | X | X | X |
| Radiators ........... | X | X | | X | X | X | X | X | X | X | X |
| Saddles, door ........ | X | X | | X | | X | X | | | | |
| Seating ............. | X | X | X | X | X | | | | | | |
| Sheet metal ducts .... | X | X | | | X | X | | | | | |
| Signs ............... | X | X | X | | X | X | X | | X | X | |
| Stair treads ......... | X | X | | | | | | | | | |
| Stairs, iron ......... | X | | X | | | | | | | | |
| Store fronts ......... | X | X | X | X | X | X | X | X | X | X | |
| Towel cabinets ...... | X | X | | X | X | X | | | X | X | X |
| Vending machines .... | X | X | | X | X | X | X | | X | X | X |
| Venetian blinds ...... | X | | | X | X | | X | | X | X | X |

Reproduced by permission of the Rawlplug Co.; products from several manufacturers are available in various forms and sizes for these and other special uses.

315

**TABLE 16.4** Hypothetical Example of Cost Comparisons for Installing 500 Fasteners at Various Pull-out Loads

This table illustrates the calculation method only. Figures in this table should not be used in preparing estimates.

| Load requirement | Operation | Jute fiber plug | Lead plug | Machine-screw expansion shield | Self-drilling anchor | Multi-machine bolt | Stud gun | |
|---|---|---|---|---|---|---|---|---|
| Pull-out at 540 lb | Cost of anchors | $40 | $60 | $120 | $225 | | Charge | $60 |
| (safe holding at 135 lb) | Cost of drills | 55 | 55 | 55 | — | | Studs | 120 |
| | Cost of fasteners | 5 | 10 | 5 | 5 | | Labor | 690 |
| | Labor to drill holes | 695 | 850 | 1,650 | 2,450 | | | |
| | Labor to screw in | 160 | 160 | 265 | 265 | | | |
| | Total charges | $955 | $1,135 | $2,095 | $2,945 | | | $870 |
| Pull-out at 900 lb | Cost of anchors | $40 | $80 | $120 | | | Charge | $60 |
| (safe holding at 225 lb) | Cost of drills | 55 | 55 | 55 | | | Studs | 120 |
| | Cost of fasteners | 10 | 15 | 5 | | | Labor | 690 |
| | Labor to drill holes | 960 | 1,920 | 1,920 | | | | |
| | Labor to screw in | 265 | 265 | 425 | | | | |
| | Total charges | $1,330 | $2,335 | $2,525 | | | | $870 |
| Pull-out at 2,000 lb | Cost of anchors | $95 | $120 | $240 | | | Charge | $60 |
| (safe holding at 500 lb) | Cost of drills | 55 | 75 | 80 | | | Studs | 160 |
| | Cost of fasteners | 30 | 30 | 10 | | | Labor | 690 |
| | Labor to drill holes | 2,620 | 3,300 | 3,040 | | | | |
| | Labor to screw in | 530 | 850 | 850 | | | | |
| | Total charges | $3,330 | $4,375 | $4,220 | | | | $910 |
| Pull-out at 3,600 lb | Cost of anchors | $225 | $480 | $440 | $260 | | Charge | $60 |
| (safe holding at 900 lb) | Cost of drills | 75 | 150 | 175 | — | | Studs | 185 |
| | Cost of fasteners | 45 | 55 | 30 | 10 | | Labor | 690 |
| | Labor to drill holes | 3,420 | 8,430 | 3,740 | 2,450 | | | |
| | Labor to screw in | 960 | 1,650 | 1,120 | 850 | | | |
| | Total charges | $4,725 | $10,765 | $5,505 | $3,570 | | | $895 |
| Pull-out at 8,600 lb | Cost of anchors | $375 | | $1,600 | $500 | $500 | | |
| (safe holding at 2,150 lb) | Cost of drills | 75 | | 350 | — | 225 | | |
| | Cost of fasteners | 65 | | 100 | 65 | 65 | | |
| | Labor to drill holes | 6,080 | | 9,070 | 4,000 | 4,540 | | |
| | Labor to screw in | 1,230 | | 1,810 | 160 | 1,500 | | |
| | Total charges | $7,825 | | $12,930 | $4,725 | $6,830 | | |

concrete. Total costing involves combining the following five factors: cost of anchors, cost of carbide drill bits (allowing 50 holes per bit), cost of fasteners, labor to drill holes (assuming $26.95/hr base), and labor to set and screw up the fastener (same hourly base rate).

In each example, the hole-drilling operation employs a standard type of drill with carbide bit. If an application permits the use of a rotary hammer or impact drill, the labor cost of drilling holes will be reduced by 75%.

Each operation includes moving in, setting up, and laying out holes in groups of four, then moving along, and repeating the sequence. Specific steps for different types of fasteners include

*Jute-fiber plug:* Drill hole, flare end with screw, insert and screw in three turns, back out screw, and screw in after fixture is set. Flaring the end of the plug is necessary for sheetrock applications and other hollow materials. For solid masonry, drill hole, insert anchor, and screw in with fixture in place. This would cut the workhours required in column 3 (see Table 16.4).

*Lead plug:* Drill hole, insert plug, insert screw after fixture is set, and screw in.

*Lag expansion shield:* Drill hole, insert plug, insert screw after fixture is set, and screw in.

*Machine-screw expansion shield.* Drill hole, insert anchor, punch-drive down, insert screw after fixture is set, and screw in.

*Machine-bolt expansion shield:* Drill hole, insert anchor, punch-drive down, insert bolt after fixture is set, and bolt up.

*Self-drilling anchor:* Insert anchor in chuck head, drill masonry, remove drill, clean hole, insert expander plug in drill, drill in expander, snap off taper, insert screw after fixture is set, and screw in.

*Stud gun:* Load stud pins, load charges, fix cylinder, fire stud pin, and eject shell.

The last example of Table 16.4 does not have a column for stud-gun fastening, since the safe holding load is beyond the range of the stud guns examined. The data in Table 16.4 are illustrative only and are not intended for use in actual estimates. The data do, however, depict the wide range of costs that can be entailed in using different types of fasteners. The large differences in drill costs and in labor costs to drill holes reflect the varying hole sizes required for the different types of anchors.

## ESTIMATING LABOR

In Tables 16.5 through 16.11, workhours allowed for hole drilling assume use of a standard drill with carbide bit. If a rotary hammer or impact drill is applicable, multiply the workhours by 0.25. For powder-actuated stud guns, allow 0.05 workhour per shot.

For longest life and most effective hole drilling, standard rotary carbide bits should be used only in slow-speed drills: 350 to 750 rpm. Contrary to common practice, this holds true for the smaller ¼-in. drill as well as the larger sizes.

Rotary hammer bits cost from 50 to 500% more than standard carbide drills. But in addition to considerable savings in workhours drilling time, they have a much longer life span as measured in hole inches.

**TABLE 16.5** Workhours Required to Drill Anchor Holes in Concrete or Brick for Drop-in Expansion Shields

Operation includes tooling up, laying out and drilling hole, and inserting shield but does not include inserting or screwing in fastener.

| Shield size, in. | Hole diameter, in. | Hole depth, in. | Workhours per wall hole | Workhours per ceiling hole |
|---|---|---|---|---|
| ³⁄₁₆ | ⁷⁄₁₆ | ⅞ | 0.18 | 0.27 |
| ¼ | ½ | ⅞ | 0.22 | 0.33 |
| ⁵⁄₁₆ | ⅝ | 1 | 0.27 | 0.40 |
| ⅜ | ¾ | 1¼ | 0.31 | 0.46 |
| ½ | ⅞ | 1½ | 0.42 | 0.63 |
| ⅝ | 1 | 2 | 0.58 | 0.87 |
| ¾ | 1¼ | 2¼ | 0.67 | 1.00 |

**TABLE 16.6** Workhours Required to Drill Anchor Holes in Concrete or Brick for Jute Fiber, Plastic, or Lead Plugs

Operation includes tooling up, laying out and drilling hole, and inserting plug but does not include inserting or screwing in fastener.

| Anchor size | Screw size | Hole diameter, in. | Workhours per wall hole | Workhours per ceiling hole |
|---|---|---|---|---|
| 6 x $\frac{3}{4}$ | 6 x 1 | $\frac{5}{32}$ | 0.05 | 0.08 |
| 6 x 1 | 6 x $1\frac{1}{4}$ | $\frac{5}{32}$ | 0.06 | 0.09 |
| 8 x $\frac{3}{4}$ | 8 x 1 | $\frac{11}{64}$ | 0.07 | 0.11 |
| 8 x 1 | 8 x $1\frac{1}{4}$ | $\frac{11}{64}$ | 0.08 | 0.12 |
| 8 x $1\frac{1}{2}$ | 8 x 2 | $\frac{11}{64}$ | 0.10 | 0.15 |
| 10 x $\frac{3}{4}$ | 10 x 1 | $\frac{3}{16}$ | 0.09 | 0.14 |
| 10 x 1 | 10 x $1\frac{1}{4}$ | $\frac{3}{16}$ | 0.10 | 0.15 |
| 10 x $1\frac{1}{2}$ | 10 x 2 | $\frac{3}{16}$ | 0.12 | 0.18 |
| 12 x $\frac{3}{4}$ | 12 x 1 | $\frac{1}{4}$ | 0.11 | 0.16 |
| 12 x 1 | 12 x $1\frac{1}{4}$ | $\frac{1}{4}$ | 0.12 | 0.18 |
| 12 x $1\frac{1}{2}$ | 12 x 2 | $\frac{1}{4}$ | 0.14 | 0.21 |
| 14 x 1 | 14 x $1\frac{1}{4}$ | $\frac{9}{32}$ | 0.13 | 0.19 |
| 14 x $1\frac{1}{2}$ | 14 x 2 | $\frac{9}{32}$ | 0.15 | 0.22 |
| 14 x 2 | 14 x $2\frac{1}{2}$ | $\frac{9}{32}$ | 0.18 | 0.27 |
| 16 x 1 | 16 x $1\frac{1}{4}$ | $\frac{5}{16}$ | 0.17 | 0.25 |
| 16 x $1\frac{1}{2}$ | 16 x 2 | $\frac{5}{16}$ | 0.19 | 0.29 |
| 16 x 2 | 16 x $2\frac{1}{2}$ | $\frac{5}{16}$ | 0.22 | 0.33 |
| 18 x 2 | 18 x $2\frac{1}{2}$ | $\frac{3}{8}$ | 0.24 | 0.36 |
| 20 x 2 | 20 x $2\frac{1}{2}$ | $\frac{3}{8}$ | 0.24 | 0.36 |

**TABLE 16.7** Workhours Required to Drill Holes in Hollow Walls or Ceilings for Wing-Toggle Bolts

Operation includes laying out and drilling hole, inserting fastener, and screwing in after fixture is set, using manually driven tool.

| Bolt size, in. | Wing spread, in. | Hole diameter, in. | Workhours per wall hole | Workhours per ceiling hole |
|---|---|---|---|---|
| $\frac{1}{8}$ x 4 | $1\frac{7}{16}$ | $\frac{3}{8}$ | 0.125 | 0.19 |
| $\frac{5}{32}$ x 4 | $1\frac{7}{8}$ | $\frac{1}{2}$ | 0.190 | 0.29 |
| $\frac{3}{16}$ x 4 | $1\frac{7}{8}$ | $\frac{1}{2}$ | 0.190 | 0.29 |
| $\frac{1}{4}$ x 6 | $2\frac{1}{16}$ | $\frac{11}{16}$ | 0.220 | 0.33 |
| $\frac{5}{16}$ x 6 | $2\frac{7}{8}$ | 1 | 0.250 | 0.38 |
| $\frac{3}{8}$ x 8 | $2\frac{7}{8}$ | 1 | 0.250 | 0.38 |
| $\frac{1}{2}$ x 8 | $3\frac{3}{8}$ | $1\frac{1}{4}$ | 0.330 | 0.49 |

**TABLE 16.8** Workhours Required for Screwing in Wood and Lag Screw Fasteners

Operation includes inserting fastener into anchor and screwing up tight after fixture is set, using manually driven tool.

| Fastener size | Jute fiber plug | Lead plug | Expansion shield |
|---|---|---|---|
| **Wood screws:** | | | |
| No. 6, 1 in. | 0.01 | 0.01 | — |
| No. 8, $1\frac{1}{2}$ in. | 0.02 | 0.01 | — |
| No. 10, $1\frac{1}{2}$ in. | 0.02 | 0.01 | — |
| No. 12, 2 in. | 0.03 | 0.02 | — |
| No. 14, 2 in. | 0.04 | 0.02 | — |
| **Lag screws:** | | | |
| $\frac{1}{4}$ x 2 in. | 0.05 | 0.04 | 0.045 |
| $\frac{5}{16}$ x $2\frac{1}{2}$ in. | 0.07 | 0.06 | 0.054 |
| $\frac{3}{8}$ x $2\frac{1}{2}$ in. | 0.07 | 0.06 | 0.063 |
| $\frac{1}{2}$ x 3 in. | 0.09 | 0.08 | 0.082 |
| $\frac{3}{4}$ x 3 in. | 0.10 | 0.10 | 0.095 |

**TABLE 16.9** Workhours Required to Manually Punch-Drive and Screw in One Expansion Anchor-Type Fastener

Operation includes punch-driving anchor with setting punch, inserting fastener, and screwing up tight after fixture is set.

| Fastener size<br>Hole depth, in. | No. 8<br>$\frac{1}{2}$ | No. 10<br>$\frac{5}{8}$ | $\frac{1}{4}$ in.<br>$\frac{7}{8}$ | $\frac{5}{16}$ in.<br>1 | $\frac{3}{8}$ in.<br>$1\frac{1}{4}$ | $\frac{1}{2}$ in.<br>$1\frac{3}{4}$ | $\frac{5}{8}$ in.<br>2 | $\frac{3}{4}$ in.<br>3 |
|---|---|---|---|---|---|---|---|---|
| Machine screw . . . . . | 0.03 | 0.03 | 0.04 | 0.06 | 0.08 | 0.10 | 0.12 | 0.14 |
| Machine bolt . . . . . . | 0.03 | 0.03 | 0.04 | 0.05 | 0.07 | 0.09 | 0.11 | 0.13 |
| Two-piece anchor . . . | — | — | — | — | 0.09 | 0.11 | 0.13 | 0.15 |

**TABLE 16.10** Workhours Required for Bolting up Fasteners (Metal-to-Metal through Two Drilled Holes)

Operation includes inserting bolt through the holes, placing washer, placing nut, bolting up until servicetight, and following up on bolt after apparatus is in service.

| Bolt diameter, in. | Workhours per each |
|:---:|:---:|
| 3/16 | 0.03 |
| 1/4 | 0.03 |
| 5/16 | 0.03 |
| 3/8 | 0.04 |
| 7/16 | 0.05 |
| 1/2 | 0.05 |
| 5/8 | 0.06 |
| 3/4 | 0.07 |
| 7/8 | 0.09 |
| 1 | 0.11 |
| 1 1/8 | 0.13 |
| 1 1/4 | 0.16 |
| 1 1/2 | 0.20 |
| 1 5/8 | 0.25 |

**TABLE 16.11** Workhours Required to Install Pipe-Hanger Assemblies

Operation includes field measuring, cutting, threading in, and aligning for pipe. Overhead working conditions are assumed, involving moving ladders into position in average congestion.

| Pipe diameter, in. | Rod diameter, in. | One-rod split ring* | Two-rod split ring† |
|:---:|:---:|:---:|:---:|
| 1 | 3/8 | 0.32 | 0.41 |
| 1 1/4 | 3/8 | 0.32 | 0.41 |
| 1 1/2 | 3/8 | 0.32 | 0.41 |
| 2 | 3/8 | 0.32 | 0.41 |
| 2 1/2 | 1/2 | 0.39 | 0.49 |
| 3 | 1/2 | 0.39 | 0.49 |
| 3 1/2 | 1/2 | 0.39 | 0.49 |
| 4 | 5/8 | 0.46 | 0.62 |
| 5 | 5/8 | 0.46 | 0.62 |
| 6 | 3/4 | 0.58 | 0.76 |
| 8 | 7/8 | 0.75 | 1.17 |
| 10 | 7/8 | 0.75 | 1.17 |
| 12 | 7/8 | 0.75 | 1.17 |
| 14 | 1 | 0.93 | 1.30 |
| 16 | 1 | 0.93 | 1.30 |

*One-rod split ring type includes beam clamp, hanger rod, and split ring or clevis hanger.

†Two-rod type includes two rods fitted with crossbar and roller for use with saddle for insulated pipe.

Tables 16.12 through 16.17 give material costs of various fasteners. The cost data in these tables are taken from mid-1993 price lists of several fastener and anchor manufacturers and suppliers.

Several manufacturers market preformed clamps and clips that are quickly erected with a minimum of tools. They are designed to wedge or clip on bar joists, I-beams, cell decks, bulb tees, etc. Although these fasteners are occasionally used to erect light ductwork, small copper water lines, and instrument tubing bundles, they are primarily used by electricians for lightweight static loads and are impractical for the mechanical contractor.

Where a manufacturer does not publish adequate load-limit or pull-out-strength data for its products, such fasteners should be considered unacceptable even though they may *appear* to be similar to another manufacturer's fastener for which for the pull-out strength is known.

**TABLE 16.12**  Cost of Commonly Used Anchor Fasteners—Dollars per 100 Pieces

| Fastener type | Size | Cost per 100, $ |
|---|---|---|
| Blind rivets (steel or aluminum) | $\frac{1}{8}$-in. diameter, $\frac{1}{8}$-in. grip | 3.90 |
| | $\frac{1}{8}$-in. diameter, $\frac{1}{4}$-in. grip | 5.30 |
| | $\frac{1}{8}$-in. diameter, $\frac{1}{2}$-in. grip | 6.90 |
| | $\frac{5}{32}$-in. diameter, $\frac{1}{8}$-in. grip | 5.50 |
| | $\frac{5}{32}$-in. diameter, $\frac{1}{4}$-in. grip | 5.70 |
| | $\frac{5}{32}$-in. diameter, $\frac{1}{2}$-in. grip | 7.45 |
| | $\frac{5}{16}$-in. diameter, $\frac{1}{8}$-in. grip | 8.80 |
| | $\frac{5}{16}$-in. diameter, $\frac{1}{4}$-in. grip | 9.30 |
| | $\frac{5}{16}$-in. diameter, $\frac{1}{2}$-in. grip | 9.90 |
| Machine screw expansion anchor bolts | $\frac{1}{4} \times 1\frac{1}{2}$ in. | 95 |
| | $\frac{1}{4} \times 2\frac{1}{2}$ in. | 97 |
| | $\frac{1}{4} \times 3$ in. | 99 |
| | $\frac{5}{16} \times 2$ in. | 140 |
| | $\frac{3}{8} \times 2$ in. | 168 |
| | $\frac{3}{8} \times 2\frac{1}{2}$ in. | 171 |
| Plastic wall anchors, tubular | 6/7/8 screw $\times \frac{3}{4}$ in. | 6.50 |
| | 9/10/11 screw $\times$ 1 in. | 9.75 |
| | 10/11/12 screw $\times 1\frac{1}{2}$ in. | 13.00 |
| | 13/14/15 screw $\times 1\frac{1}{2}$ in. | 15.60 |
| Plastic wall anchors, conical | 4/6/8 screw $\times \frac{3}{4}$ in. | 3.20 |
| | 6/8/10 screw $\times \frac{7}{8}$ in. | 3.50 |
| | 10/12 screw $\times$ 1 in. | 3.90 |
| | 14/16 screw $\times 1\frac{1}{2}$ in. | 7.20 |
| Nail drive anchors | $\frac{1}{4} \times 1$ in. | 15 |
| | $\frac{1}{4} \times 1\frac{1}{2}$ in. | 20 |
| | $\frac{1}{4} \times 2$ in. | 27 |
| Hollow-wall anchors | 6-32 screw to $\frac{1}{4}$-in. wall | 20 |
| | 6-32 screw to $\frac{1}{2}$-in. wall | 20 |
| | 6-32 screw to 1-in. wall | 21 |
| | 10-24 screw to $\frac{5}{8}$-in. wall | 27 |
| | 10-24 screw to $1\frac{1}{4}$-in. wall | 28 |
| Lead screw plug | $\frac{1}{8} \times \frac{3}{4}$ in. (no. 8 screw) | 16.50 |
| | $\frac{3}{16} \times 1$ in. (no. 10 screw) | 22.50 |
| Lag expansion shields | 1 in. for $\frac{1}{4}$-in. screw | 37 |
| | $1\frac{1}{2}$ in. for $\frac{1}{4}$-in. screw | 42 |
| | $1\frac{3}{4}$ in. for $\frac{3}{8}$-in. screw | 72 |

*(Continued)*

**TABLE 16.12**  Cost of Commonly Used Anchor Fasteners—Dollars per 100 Pieces  (*Continued*)

| Fastener type | Size | Cost per 100, $ |
|---|---|---|
| Toggle-wing bolts | $\frac{1}{8}$-in. wing; 6-32 × 3-in. bolt | 23 |
| | $\frac{3}{16}$-in. wing; 10-24 × 3-in. bolt | 24 |
| | $\frac{1}{4}$-in. wing; $\frac{1}{4}$-20 × 4-in. bolt | 35 |
| Self-drilling screws (hexagonal), washer head—slotted | 8-18 screw × $\frac{1}{2}$ in. | 8.70 |
| | 8-18 screw × $\frac{3}{4}$ in. | 9.60 |
| | 8-18 screw × 1 in. | 10.50 |
| | $\frac{1}{4}$ × $\frac{3}{4}$ in. | 9.90 |
| Drywall screws, coarse thread | 6 screw × 1$\frac{5}{8}$ in. | 1.15 |
| | 7 screw × 2$\frac{1}{2}$ in. | 1.15 |
| | 8 screw × 3 in. | 4.35 |
| Drywall screws, fine thread | 6 screw × 1 in. | 0.80 |
| | 6 screw × 1$\frac{5}{8}$ in. | 1.15 |
| | 8 screw × 3 in. | 4.35 |
| Screw-in concrete fasteners, hex head | $\frac{3}{16}$ × 1$\frac{1}{4}$ in. | 23 |
| | $\frac{3}{16}$ × 1$\frac{3}{4}$ in. | 26 |
| | $\frac{3}{16}$ × 2$\frac{1}{4}$ in. | 28 |
| | $\frac{3}{16}$ × 2$\frac{3}{4}$ in. | 32 |
| | $\frac{3}{16}$ × 3$\frac{1}{4}$ in. | 42 |
| | $\frac{3}{16}$ × 4 in. | 54 |
| | $\frac{1}{4}$ × 1$\frac{1}{4}$ in. | 31 |
| | $\frac{1}{4}$ × 1$\frac{3}{4}$ in. | 35 |
| | $\frac{1}{4}$ × 2$\frac{1}{4}$ in. | 38 |
| | $\frac{1}{4}$ × 2$\frac{3}{4}$ in. | 45 |
| | $\frac{1}{4}$ × 3$\frac{1}{4}$ in. | 54 |
| | $\frac{1}{4}$ × 4 in. | 67 |
| Powder fasteners | 0.300 × 1-in. fastener | 4.04 |
| | 0.300 × 1$\frac{1}{2}$-in. fastener | 6.08 |
| | 0.300 × 2-in. fastener | 6.75 |
| | 22 caliber powder load | 5.90 |
| | 27 caliber powder load | 9.38 |

**TABLE 16.13**  Cost of Wood Screw Fasteners, Round-Head Steel Type—Dollars per Hundred

| Screw no. | Screw length, in. | | | |
|---|---|---|---|---|
| | 1 | 1$\frac{1}{2}$ | 2 | 2$\frac{1}{2}$ |
| 6 | 2.30 | 3.00 | 6.10 | 13.60 |
| 8 | 2.80 | 3.30 | 4.50 | 5.80 |
| 10 | 3.20 | 4.40 | 5.40 | 6.70 |
| 12 | 4.10 | 5.80 | 6.90 | 8.80 |
| 14 | 7.70 | 9.10 | 11.20 | 12.00 |

**TABLE 16.14** Cost of Sheet Metal Screw Fasteners, Pan Head, Type A—Dollars per Hundred

| Screw No. | Screw length, in. | | | |
|:---:|:---:|:---:|:---:|:---:|
| | 1 | $1\frac{1}{2}$ | 2 | $2\frac{1}{2}$ |
| 6 | 2.20 | 3.10 | — | — |
| 8 | 2.60 | 3.60 | 5.30 | 8.50 |
| 10 | 3.10 | 4.20 | 5.60 | 7.80 |
| 12 | 4.30 | 5.10 | 7.70 | 11.50 |
| 14 | 6.20 | 7.50 | 9.50 | 16.90 |

**TABLE 16.15** Cost of Lag Bolt Fasteners with Plated Finish—Dollars per Hundred

| Bolt length, in. | Bolt diameter, in. | | | |
|:---:|:---:|:---:|:---:|:---:|
| | $\frac{1}{4}$ | $\frac{5}{16}$ | $\frac{3}{8}$ | $\frac{1}{2}$ |
| 1 | 4.25 | 6.85 | 10.50 | — |
| $1\frac{1}{2}$ | 5.75 | 9.35 | 13.50 | 29.00 |
| 2 | 6.75 | 11.50 | 15.95 | 33.90 |
| $2\frac{1}{2}$ | 8.70 | 13.50 | 18.80 | 41.00 |
| 3 | 9.05 | 15.95 | 21.00 | 41.90 |

**TABLE 16.16** Labor and Material Costs for Setting Hooked-type Foundation Bolts in Concrete

Based on 23-in. standard finish bolts with hex nuts and washers in sets of four, using templates in the accepted manner. For galvanized bolts, add 40% to base cost; for 22-ga galvanized pans, allow $4.50.

| Cost item | Bolt diameter, in. | | | | |
|:---|:---:|:---:|:---:|:---:|:---:|
| | $\frac{1}{2}$ | $\frac{5}{8}$ | $\frac{3}{4}$ | $\frac{7}{8}$ | 1 |
| Material, per set, $ | 2.00 | 5.50 | 8.00 | 12.00 | 15.00 |
| Workhours per set | 1.45 | 1.65 | 1.80 | 2.05 | 2.25 |

**TABLE 16.17**    Hardware Sundries—Materials

| Item | Size, in. | Unit | $ per unit |
|---|---|---|---|
| Machine bolts, zinc plated*..... | 2 × ¼ | 100 | 8 |
| (including hex nuts) | 2 × ⅜ | 100 | 17 |
| | 2 × ½ | 100 | 30 |
| | 3 × ¼ | 100 | 10 |
| | 3 × ⅜ | 100 | 23 |
| | 3 × ½ | 100 | 39 |
| | 4 × ¼ | 100 | 13 |
| | 4 × ⅜ | 100 | 30 |
| | 4 × ½ | 100 | 52 |
| Eye bolts ..................... | 2 × ¼ | Each | 0.29 |
| | 3 × ⅜ | Each | 0.75 |
| | 4 × ½ | Each | 1.95 |
| Eye lags ..................... | 3¾ × ¼ | Each | 0.45 |
| | 4½ × ⅜ | Each | 0.99 |
| | 5¼ × ⁷⁄₁₆ | Each | 1.59 |
| Turnbuckles ................. | ¼ × 7½ | Each | 1.35 |
| | ⅜ × 11 | Each | 2.25 |
| | ½ × 17 | Each | 9.19 |
| U bolt clamps................ | ¼ × 1⅛ × 2¼ | Each | 0.95 |
| | ⁵⁄₁₆ × 2½ × 5 | Each | 1.65 |
| Wire rope, galvanized ......... | ¼ | Foot | 0.53 |
| | ⅜ | Foot | 0.67 |
| | ½ | Foot | 0.95 |
| Threaded rod ............... | ¼ | 100 ft | 35 |
| | ⅜ | 100 ft | 51 |
| | ½ | 100 ft | 90 |
| Hex nuts .................... | ¼ NC | 100 | 2 |
| | ⅜ NC | 100 | 4 |
| | ½ NC | 100 | 8 |
| | ¼ NF | 100 | 3 |
| | ⅜ NF | 100 | 4 |
| | ½ NF | 100 | 11 |

## AIR-POWERED PNEUMATIC NAILERS

Occasionally the HVAC contractor needs to do nailing and stapling. If sufficient work of this nature is required, it will usually be cost-efficient to use an air nailer. Costs of pneumatic nailers and staplers range from $300 to $500. Table 16.18 gives costs for portable air compressors used in conjunction with nailers and staplers. Table 16.19 gives costs of nail and staple cartridges.

## EPOXY INJECTION SYSTEMS

Epoxy fastening, as illustrated in Fig. 16.2, is capable of great holding power and excellent performance for vibrating loads in solid concrete, hollow wall and brick, but it is a relatively slow process. After drilling, the proper-size hole must be dusted out with a blowout bulb or

**TABLE 16.18**  Portable Air Compressors

| hp | Capacity, gal. | cfm at 100 psi | Cost, $ |
|----|----------------|----------------|---------|
| 1  | 12             | 2.2            | 300     |
| 2  | 20             | 6.2            | 425     |
| 3  | 30             | 7.6            | 475     |
| 5  | 30             | 9.5            | 550     |

**TABLE 16.19**  Nail and Staple Cartridges

| Size | Type of nail | Length, in. | Quantity per package | Cost, $ |
|------|--------------|-------------|----------------------|---------|
| 6d | Common | 2 | 6,700 | 75 |
| 8d | Common | $2\frac{3}{8}$ | 5,000 | 62 |
| 10d | Common | 3 | 3,200 | 40 |
| 8d | Galvanized | $2\frac{3}{8}$ | 5,000 | 100 |
| 10d | Galvanized | 3 | 3,000 | 62 |
| $\frac{7}{16}$-in. crown | Galvanized staples | $1\frac{1}{2}$ | 10,000 | 50 |
| $\frac{7}{16}$-in. crown | Galvanized staples | $1\frac{3}{4}$ | 10,000 | 58 |
| $\frac{7}{16}$-in. crown | Galvanized staples | 2 | 10,000 | 62 |

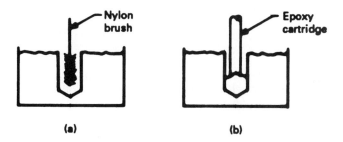

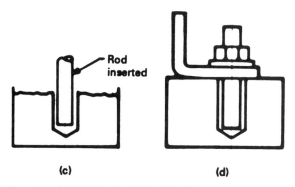

**Figure 16.2  EPOXY FASTENING SYSTEM**
*(a) Using nylon brush, (b) inserting epoxy, (c) inserting rod, (d) fixture anchored.*

**TABLE 16.20**  Epoxy Injection Systems

| Item | Cost, $ |
|------|---------|
| Derringer dispensing tool | 50.00 |
| 1.7-oz ceramic epoxy cartridge | 6.00 |
| High-flow nozzle (package 24) | 17.50 |
| Rods, in. | |
| $\frac{1}{2} \times 5\frac{1}{2}$ | 1.00 |
| $\frac{5}{8} \times 12$ | 3.50 |
| $\frac{3}{4} \times 16$ | 7.00 |
| $1 \times 17$ | 20.00 |

air compressor and cleaned with a nylon brush—*not a wire brush* (see Fig. 16.2*a*). The epoxy must then be evenly blended to a light gray color and injected to a depth of one-half of the hole (see Fig. 16.2*b*). The precut rod is then inserted and slowly twisted into place by hand; no tool is required (see Fig. 16.2*c*). The fixture may be installed and tightened after about one hour of curing time (see Fig. 16.2*d*). A complete *epoxy injection system* starter set, including Derringer dispensing tool, six ceramic epoxy cartridges, screens, rods, and washers, costs about $145. Table 16.20 gives costs for individual items.

## ACKNOWLEDGMENTS

The editors express their appreciation to the staff of the Baton Hardware Company, Lenoir, N.C. and Brinkley Lumber Company, Inc., Rutherford College, N.C. for their assistance in compiling the information provided in this chapter.

# CHAPTER 17
# FOUNDATIONS
# AND SUPPORTS

## GENERAL DISCUSSION

Every mechanical construction requires structural pieces of steel, aluminum, and wood for brackets, braces, grillage, hangers, and racks to support pipe, pumps, towers, tanks, and blowers. Concrete pads are required for compressors, chillers, and pumps for the purpose of vibration dampening as well as structural loading. Proper isolation and fastening of moving machinery can ensure reasonable sound attenuation; improper fastening and isolation may amplify the noise.

For speedy estimating, Tables 17.1 through 17.4[1] give weights and load limits for common materials and conditions, and they may be used with a good degree of accuracy for cost estimating. *They are not, however, intended for use in design.*

---

[1] Table 17.4 does not appear on the computer disk supplied with this book.

**TABLE 17.1**  Quick Selection—Maximum Safe Load for Standard Beams

Allowable load per beam for spanning parapets and sumps for heavy equipment such as pumps, blowers, and condensers, where load is concentrated. Based on $f = 20,000$ psi and loads concentrated toward center of span. All weights are in pounds; weight per foot is for the steel beam itself and is not included in allowable load per beam. Loads shown are for laterally unsupported beams. (*Note:* This table is for rapid estimating of costs and is not intended for use in design.)

| Size, in. | 3 | 4 | 5 | 6 | 7 | 8 | 10 | 12 |
|---|---|---|---|---|---|---|---|---|
| Weight per ft | 5.7 | 7.7 | 10.0 | 12.5 | 15.3 | 18.4 | 25.4 | 31.8 |
| **Span, ft:** | | | | | | | | |
| 4 | 2,120 | 3,750 | 6,000 | 9,700 | 13,000 | 17,400 | 27,800 | 38,000 |
| 5 | 1,680 | 3,000 | 4,850 | 7,350 | 10,400 | 14,200 | 24,600 | 36,000 |
| 6 | 1,405 | 2,510 | 4,040 | 6,100 | 8,660 | 11,815 | 20,120 | 30,000 |
| 7 | — | 2,160 | 3,450 | 5,230 | 7,420 | 10,200 | 17,350 | 25,600 |
| 8 | — | 1,875 | 3,000 | 4,570 | 6,500 | 8,900 | 15,300 | 24,700 |
| 9 | — | 1,650 | 2,660 | 4,060 | 5,800 | 7,800 | 13,500 | 20,000 |
| 10 | — | — | 2,410 | 3,550 | 5,200 | 7,060 | 12,800 | 19,800 |
| 11 | — | — | — | 3,320 | 4,740 | 6,425 | 11,200 | 16,500 |
| 12 | — | — | — | — | 4,350 | 5,900 | 10,200 | 15,000 |
| 13 | — | — | — | — | — | — | 930 | 13,850 |
| 14 | — | — | — | — | — | — | 865 | 12,700 |
| 15 | — | — | — | — | — | — | 825 | 12,000 |
| 16 | — | — | — | — | — | — | 750 | 11,300 |
| 17 | — | — | — | — | — | — | — | 10,500 |

**TABLE 17.2** Quick Selection—Maximum Safe Load for Steel Floor Plate

Total allowable load for steel floor plate platforms for setting air handlers, blowers, etc. Based on $f$ = 20,000 psi, ¼-in. steel plate supported on all four sides, and a uniform live load. Boldface figures give total square feet of plate for span; lightface figures give allowable load in pounds. (*Note:* This table is for rapid estimating of costs and is not intended for use in design.) Weight per square foot of plate is approximately 11¼ lb.

| Long side span, ft | Short side span, ft | | | | | | | |
|---|---|---|---|---|---|---|---|---|
| | 2.5 | 3 | 3.5 | 4 | 4.5 | 5 | 5.5 | 6 |
| 2.5 | 6.25 | — | — | — | — | — | — | — |
| | 4,100 | — | — | — | — | — | — | — |
| 3.0 | 7.5 | 9.0 | — | — | — | — | — | — |
| | 3,850 | 4,050 | — | — | — | — | — | — |
| 3.5 | 8.75 | 10.5 | 12.25 | — | — | — | — | — |
| | 3,860 | 3,850 | 4,050 | — | — | — | — | — |
| 4.0 | 10.0 | 12.0 | 14.0 | 16.0 | — | — | — | — |
| | 3,850 | 3,800 | 3,840 | 4,030 | — | — | — | — |
| 4.5 | 11.25 | 13.5 | 15.75 | 18.0 | 20.25 | — | — | — |
| | 4,100 | 3,525 | 3,775 | 3,785 | 4,000 | — | — | — |
| 5.0 | 12.5 | 15.0 | 17.0 | 20.0 | 22.5 | 25.0 | — | — |
| | 4,400 | 3,925 | 3,800 | 3,700 | 3,750 | 3,900 | — | — |
| 5.5 | 13.75 | 16.5 | 19.25 | 22.0 | 24.75 | 27.5 | 30.25 | — |
| | 4,650 | 4,050 | 3,715 | 3,700 | 3,685 | 3,700 | 3,800 | — |
| 6.0 | 15.00 | 18.0 | 21.0 | 24.0 | 27.0 | 30.0 | 33.0 | 36.0 |
| | 4,935 | 4,325 | 3,900 | 3,700 | 3,600 | 3,590 | 3,650 | 3,750 |
| 6.5 | — | — | 22.75 | 26.0 | 29.25 | 32.5 | 35.75 | 39.0 |
| | — | — | 4,000 | 3,725 | 3,550 | 3,520 | 3,350 | 3,525 |
| 7.0 | — | — | 24.5 | 28.0 | 31.5 | 35.0 | 38.5 | 42.0 |
| | — | — | 4,250 | 3,750 | 3,600 | 3,550 | 3,500 | 3,200 |
| 7.5 | — | — | 26.25 | 30.0 | 33.75 | 37.5 | 41.25 | 45.0 |
| | — | — | 4,500 | 4,000 | 3,750 | 3,550 | 3,450 | 3,350 |
| 8.0 | — | — | — | — | 36.0 | 40.0 | 44.0 | 48.0 |
| | — | — | — | — | 3,815 | 3,600 | 3,400 | 3,400 |
| 8.5 | — | — | — | — | 38.25 | 42.5 | 46.75 | 51.0 |
| | — | — | — | — | 3,800 | 3,700 | 3,500 | 3,400 |
| 9.0 | — | — | — | — | — | — | 49.5 | 54.0 |
| | — | — | — | — | — | — | 3,500 | 3,400 |

**TABLE 17.3**  Quick Selection—Maximum Safe Load for Timbers

Allowable load per beam for spanning parapets and sumps, as grillage for small cooling towers, pumps, motors, condensers, etc., where load is concentrated. Based on $f = 1,000$ psi and loads concentrated toward center of span. All weights are in pounds; weight per foot is for timber itself and is not included in allowable load per beam. (*Note:* This table is for rapid estimating of costs and is not intended for use in design.)

| Nominal in. | 2 x 4 | 2 x 6 | 2 x 8 | 2 x 10 | 4 x 4 | 4 x 6 | 4 x 8 | 6 x 6 | 6 x 8 |
|---|---|---|---|---|---|---|---|---|---|
| Weight per ft | 1.64 | 2.54 | 3.39 | 4.29 | 3.65 | 5.66 | 7.55 | 8.40 | 11.4 |
| Span in feet: | | | | | | | | | |
| 4 | 225 | 535 | 960 | 1,540 | 505 | 1,510 | 2,150 | 1,750 | 3,240 |
| 5 | 178 | 430 | 768 | 1,270 | 400 | 1,040 | 1,725 | 1,390 | 2,960 |
| 6 | 150 | 360 | 640 | 1,025 | 300 | 810 | 1,440 | 1,180 | 2,130 |
| 7 | 128 | 307 | 545 | 875 | 285 | 685 | 1,230 | 965 | 1,850 |
| 8 | 114 | 269 | 480 | 790 | 250 | 600 | 1,070 | 870 | 1,620 |
| 9 | – | 239 | 450 | 680 | 220 | 535 | 950 | 760 | 1,445 |
| 10 | – | 215 | 385 | 615 | 200 | 495 | 860 | 690 | 1,270 |

In quantity, aluminum and steel are purchased by the pound; timber, by the board foot. Average cost of steel shapes—angles, channels, beams—is about $55/cwt; hole drilling, as required, will cost an additional $20/cwt, or about $5 per hole. For shearing, stamping, and cutting, generally required by the mechanical contractor, add $20/cwt. For galvanizing, add $18/cwt.

To find the board feet of lumber, calculate

$$BF = \frac{\text{in. thickness} \times \text{in. width} \times \text{ft length}}{12}$$

## ESTIMATING

Tables 17.5 to 17.7 give material costs for common structural pieces. Workhours for platform erection and miscellaneous fabrication are shown in Tables 17.8 and 17.9. Table 17.10 gives costs for vibration isolators.

To estimate field welding of structural-steel pieces, figure $10 per cwt of steel. This includes labor, weld rod, and equipment cost, but not rigging. Lally columns, concrete-filled, 3-in. diameter by 8 ft long, $120 per each. Steel plate, 1/4 in. sheared to specification, $6/sq ft.

**TABLE 17.4**   Concrete Volume and Weight Computer

| Thickness, in. | Length, ft | Width, ft | Approx. cu yd | Weight, lb | Thickness, in. | Length, ft | Width, ft | Approx. cu yd | Weight, lb |
|---|---|---|---|---|---|---|---|---|---|
| 4 | 6 | 8 | 0.50 | 2,000 | 14 | 6 | 10 | 2.60 | 10,400 |
| 4 | 6 | 10 | 0.75 | 3,000 | 14 | 6 | 12 | 3.10 | 12,400 |
| 4 | 6 | 12 | 0.85 | 3,400 | 14 | 6 | 14 | 3.60 | 14,400 |
| 4 | 6 | 14 | 1.10 | 4,400 | 14 | 8 | 8 | 2.75 | 11,000 |
| 4 | 8 | 8 | 0.75 | 3,000 | 14 | 8 | 10 | 3.50 | 14,000 |
| 4 | 8 | 10 | 1.00 | 4,000 | 14 | 8 | 12 | 4.10 | 16,400 |
| 4 | 8 | 12 | 1.20 | 4,800 | 14 | 10 | 8 | 3.50 | 14,000 |
| 4 | 10 | 12 | 1.50 | 6,000 | 14 | 10 | 10 | 4.30 | 17,200 |
| 4 | 10 | 14 | 1.75 | 7,000 | 14 | 10 | 12 | 5.20 | 21,000 |
| 4 | 10 | 16 | 2.00 | 8,000 | 14 | 10 | 14 | 6.00 | 24,000 |
| 6 | 6 | 8 | 0.85 | 3,400 | 16 | 6 | 8 | 2.30 | 9,200 |
| 6 | 6 | 10 | 1.13 | 4,500 | 16 | 6 | 10 | 3.00 | 12,000 |
| 6 | 6 | 12 | 1.30 | 5,200 | 16 | 6 | 12 | 3.50 | 14,000 |
| 6 | 6 | 14 | 1.60 | 6,400 | 16 | 8 | 8 | 3.15 | 12,600 |
| 6 | 8 | 8 | 1.20 | 4,800 | 16 | 8 | 10 | 4.00 | 16,000 |
| 6 | 8 | 10 | 1.50 | 6,000 | 16 | 8 | 12 | 4.75 | 19,000 |
| 6 | 8 | 12 | 1.80 | 7,200 | 16 | 10 | 8 | 4.00 | 16,000 |
| 6 | 10 | 8 | 1.50 | 6,000 | 16 | 10 | 10 | 5.00 | 20,000 |
| 6 | 10 | 10 | 1.85 | 7,400 | 18 | 6 | 8 | 2.65 | 10,600 |
| 6 | 10 | 12 | 2.25 | 9,000 | 18 | 6 | 10 | 3.30 | 13,100 |
| 8 | 6 | 8 | 1.20 | 4,800 | 18 | 6 | 12 | 4.00 | 16,000 |
| 8 | 6 | 10 | 1.50 | 6,000 | 18 | 8 | 8 | 3.50 | 14,000 |
| 8 | 6 | 12 | 1.75 | 7,000 | 18 | 8 | 10 | 4.50 | 18,000 |
| 8 | 6 | 14 | 2.10 | 8,400 | 18 | 8 | 12 | 4.30 | 17,200 |
| 8 | 8 | 8 | 1.60 | 6,400 | 18 | 10 | 8 | 4.50 | 18,000 |
| 8 | 8 | 10 | 2.00 | 8,000 | 18 | 10 | 10 | 5.50 | 22,000 |
| 8 | 8 | 12 | 2.30 | 9,200 | 18 | 10 | 12 | 6.70 | 26,800 |
| 8 | 10 | 8 | 2.00 | 8,000 | 20 | 6 | 8 | 3.00 | 12,000 |
| 8 | 10 | 10 | 2.50 | 10,000 | 20 | 6 | 10 | 3.75 | 15,000 |
| 8 | 10 | 12 | 3.00 | 12,000 | 20 | 6 | 12 | 4.50 | 18,000 |
| 10 | 6 | 8 | 1.50 | 6,000 | 20 | 8 | 8 | 4.00 | 16,000 |
| 10 | 6 | 10 | 1.80 | 7,200 | 20 | 8 | 10 | 5.00 | 20,000 |
| 10 | 6 | 12 | 2.25 | 9,000 | 20 | 8 | 12 | 6.00 | 24,000 |
| 10 | 6 | 14 | 2.60 | 10,400 | 20 | 10 | 8 | 5.00 | 20,000 |
| 10 | 8 | 8 | 2.00 | 8,000 | 20 | 10 | 10 | 6.15 | 24,500 |
| 10 | 8 | 10 | 2.50 | 10,000 | 20 | 10 | 12 | 7.40 | 29,500 |
| 10 | 8 | 12 | 3.00 | 12,000 | 24 | 6 | 8 | 3.50 | 14,000 |
| 10 | 10 | 8 | 2.50 | 10,000 | 24 | 6 | 10 | 4.50 | 18,000 |
| 10 | 10 | 10 | 3.10 | 12,400 | 24 | 8 | 8 | 4.75 | 19,000 |
| 10 | 10 | 12 | 3.75 | 15,000 | 24 | 8 | 10 | 6.00 | 24,000 |
| 12 | 6 | 8 | 1.75 | 7,000 | 24 | 8 | 12 | 7.00 | 28,000 |
| 12 | 6 | 10 | 2.25 | 9,000 | 24 | 10 | 8 | 6.00 | 24,000 |
| 12 | 6 | 12 | 2.70 | 10,800 | 24 | 10 | 10 | 7.50 | 30,000 |
| 12 | 8 | 8 | 2.35 | 9,400 | 24 | 10 | 12 | 8.75 | 35,000 |
| 12 | 8 | 10 | 3.00 | 12,000 | 30 | 6 | 8 | 4.50 | 18,000 |
| 12 | 8 | 12 | 3.60 | 14,400 | 30 | 6 | 10 | 5.50 | 22,000 |
| 12 | 10 | 8 | 3.00 | 12,000 | 30 | 6 | 12 | 6.50 | 26,000 |
| 12 | 10 | 10 | 3.75 | 15,000 | 30 | 8 | 8 | 6.00 | 24,000 |
| 12 | 10 | 12 | 4.50 | 18,000 | 30 | 8 | 10 | 7.50 | 30,000 |
| 12 | 12 | 8 | 3.60 | 14,400 | 30 | 8 | 12 | 8.75 | 35,000 |
| 12 | 12 | 10 | 4.50 | 18,000 | 30 | 10 | 8 | 7.50 | 30,000 |
| 12 | 12 | 12 | 5.35 | 21,000 | 30 | 10 | 10 | 9.25 | 37,000 |
| 14 | 6 | 8 | 2.10 | 8,400 | 30 | 10 | 12 | 10.50 | 42,000 |

**TABLE 17.5**   Steel Pieces—Cost per Foot

Based on 20-ft lengths, 5-ton lots.

| Shape | Size, in. | | | | | Pounds per ft | Cost per ft, plain, $ | Cost per ft, galv., $ |
|---|---|---|---|---|---|---|---|---|
| Strap ....... | 1 | × ⅛ | | | | 0.425 | 0.50 | 0.65 |
| Angle....... | 1 | × 1 | × ⅛ | | | 0.800 | 0.90 | 1.15 |
| Angle....... | 1¼ | × 1¼ | × ¼ | | | 1.920 | 2.00 | 2.75 |
| Angle....... | 2 | × 2 | × ¼ | | | 3.19 | 3.25 | 4.60 |
| Angle....... | 2½ | × 2½ | × ¼ | | | 4.10 | 4.25 | 6.00 |
| Channel .... | 3 | × 1½ | × ¼ | | | 5.0 | 5.50 | 7.25 |
| Channel .... | 4 | × 1⅝ | × 5⁄16 | | | 5.4 | 6.00 | 7.25 |
| Channel .... | 5 | × 1¾ | × 5⁄16 | | | 6.7 | 7.50 | 9.90 |
| Channel .... | 6 | × 2 | × ⅜ | | | 10.5 | 11.50 | 15.00 |
| Channel .... | 7 | × 2¼ | × ⅜ | | | 12.25 | 13.50 | 17.50 |
| I beam...... | 4 | × 2⅝ | × 5⁄16 | | | 7.7 | 8.50 | 11.00 |
| I beam...... | 5 | × 3 | × 5⁄16 | | | 10.0 | 11.25 | 14.50 |
| I beam...... | 6 | × 3⅝ | × ⅜ | | | 17.25 | 19.00 | 25.00 |
| I beam...... | 7 | × 3⅞ | × ⅜ | | | 20.0 | 22.50 | 29.00 |
| I beam...... | 8 | × 4⅛ | × 7⁄16 | | | 23.0 | 25.00 | 33.00 |

**TABLE 17.6**   Aluminum Pieces—Cost per Foot

Based on 25-ft lengths, 5-ton lots.

| Shape | Size, in. | | | Pounds per ft | Cost per lin ft, $ |
|---|---|---|---|---|---|
| Strap ....... | 1 | × ⅛ | | 0.150 | 0.85 |
| Angle....... | 1 | × 1 | × ⅛ | 0.283 | 1.60 |
| Angle....... | 1¼ | × 1¼ | × 3⁄16 | 0.530 | 3.00 |
| Channel .... | 2 | × 1¼ | × ⅛ | 0.637 | 3.50 |
| Channel .... | 3 | × 1 | × ⅛ | 0.713 | 4.00 |
| Channel .... | 4 | × 1¼ | × ½ | 3.284 | 18.00 |
| I beam...... | 3 | × 2 | × ⅛ | 1.013 | 6.00 |

**TABLE 17.7**   Framing Timber Pieces—Cost per Foot

Based on 12-ft lengths, fir, carload lots.

| Size, in. | Length, ft | Board ft measure | Cost per lin ft, $ |
|---|---|---|---|
| 2 × 4 | 12 | 8 | 0.48 |
| 2 × 6 | 12 | 12 | 0.72 |
| 2 × 8 | 12 | 16 | 0.96 |
| 2 × 10 | 12 | 20 | 1.00 |
| 2 × 12 | 12 | 24 | 1.20 |
| 4 × 4 | 12 | 16 | 1.12 |
| 4 × 6 | 12 | 24 | 1.68 |
| 4 × 8 | 12 | 32 | 2.25 |
| 4 × 10 | 12 | 40 | 2.80 |
| 4 × 12 | 12 | 48 | 4.80 |
| 6 × 6 | 12 | 36 | 3.60 |
| 6 × 8 | 12 | 48 | 4.80 |

**TABLE 17.8** Steel Platforms—Workhours to Fabricate and Erect

Based on welded construction of structural-steel supports with gussets as required and ¼-in. steel plate deck. *Island type* is floor-supported on four sides with steel uprights to 8 ft high and across bracing as required. *Suspended type* is ceiling-hung from structural-steel members. *Canopy type* is bracketed and supported from perpendicular surface with two steel angle brackets. Minimum of 2.5 workhours should be allowed for any platform construction. For wood platforms, to support motors and blowers, figure 0.25 workhour per sq ft of platform with minimum of 2 hr. For laying 1 × 4 white pine planking, allow 0.05 workhour per sq ft.

| Platform surface, sq ft | Island type, workhours per sq ft | Suspended type, workhours per sq ft | Canopy type, workhours per sq ft |
|---|---|---|---|
| 6–10 | 0.40 | 0.80 | 0.30 |
| 11–20 | 0.38 | 0.75 | — |
| 21–54 | 0.34 | 0.69 | — |

**TABLE 17.9** Miscellaneous Fabricating—Workhours

Based on arc welding, steel construction.

| Operation | Workhours |
|---|---|
| Fabricate four angle-iron support brackets, 1½ x 1½ x ³⁄₁₆ in. with four holes punched per each. | 1.00 |
| Fabricate "three section" 1½-in. pipe, double guard rail with four stanchions and anchor plates. | 2.85 |
| Fabricate 4 x 4 ft steel platform, 3 ft high with ¼-in. plate top and four 2 x 2 x ¼ in. angle-iron legs. | 4.50 |
| Fabricate two pipe support frames 4 x 4 x ½ in. angles with 3 x 3 x ⅜ in. cross arms and a ¾-in. baseplate. | 12.0 |
| Fabricate six brackets 12 x 12 in. from 2 x ¼ in. bar stock with ¼-in gussets. | 1.5 |
| Fabricate double LP gas cylinder rack by bending two 1½ x ¼ in. bars to half circle and welding to 3 x ¼ in. crossbar, and punching four holes for chain. | 0.5 |
| Shear and fabricate four 6 x 6 x ¼ in. gussets. | 0.4 |

**TABLE 17.10**   Vibration Isolators—Load Selection and Material Cost

| Isolator | Load range, lb | Material, $ |
|---|---|---|
| Neoprene-in-shear hangers . . . . . . . . . . . . . . . . . . . . . . . . . . . | 10–120 | 8.50 |
|  | 75–550 | 11 |
|  | 250–1,100 | 20 |
|  | 1,000–4,000 | 60 |
| Spring-type hangers . . . . . . . . . . . . . . . . . . . . . . . . . . . | 60–450 | 15 |
|  | 85–450 | 25 |
|  | 600–900 | 30 |
|  | 1,100–1,300 | 35 |
| Neoprene-in-shear floor mountings, neoprene nonskid pad bottom . . . . . . . . . . . . . . . . . . . . . . . . . . . | 135–380 | 8.50 |
|  | 250–1,100 | 20 |
|  | 1,000–4,000 | 45 |
| Spring-type floor mountings, neoprene nonskid pad bottom. . . . . . . . . . . . . . . . . . . . . . . . . . . . . | 60–450 | 17 |
|  | 85–900 | 25 |
|  | 1,100–4,000 | 30 |
|  | 900–1,800 | 43 |
|  | 2,200–2,600 | 47 |
|  | 1,800–3,600 | 71 |
|  | 4,400–5,200 | 78 |
|  | 3,150–6,300 | 100 |
|  | 5,400–10,800 | 200 |
|  | 9,600–14,400 | 350 |
|  | 12,000–18,000 | 500 |
| Mounting pads, cross-ribbed neoprene ⅜ in. thick; max. loading, 50 psi, 18 × 18 in. sheet, per each . . . . . . . . . . | — | 40 |
| Cork sandwich, ½-in. cork center with ⅜-in. neoprene both sides; max. loading, 50 psi, 18 × 18 in. sheet, per each . . . . . . . . . . . . . . . . . . . . . . . . . . . . . . . . . . . . . . . . | — | 70 |

## ROOF LOADING

In erecting small towers, condensing units, blowers, etc. in new construction, accepted practice is for the mechanical contractor to lay out the location of sleepers and supply the general contractor with the pitch pans. For loading on an existing building, directly on a built-up tar and gravel roof, the erection crew must skin back all gravel before setting the pitch pans. Such skinning operations will usually require 3 workhours for every 10 ft of sleeper (assuming a 4-in. flange around a 6-in. pocket). Old, dry roofs will skin in about half the time. If a roofer with hot pitch is not readily available, the erection crew must trowel in cold liquid asphalt; this will require about 10 gal. per each 10 ft of sleeper at a cost of about $15.00 per gal.

Assuming a 3-in.-high × 6-in.-wide pitch pan with 4-in. flange and fabricated from 24-gage galvanized steel with spot weld, the cost of a 10-ft pitch pan may be estimated at $60. This brings the cost for a 10-ft sleeper, set in pitch with pitch pan (not including skinning), at about $240.

## CONCRETE

Recommended practice calls for the use, wherever possible, of a floating concrete pan or slab as foundation for moving machinery such as pumps, motors, compressors, and condensing units. For lighterweight, smaller units a surface foundation slab is generally formed directly on the concrete floor with a cork or treated Celotex separation membrane. For the larger compressors and pumps, a pit foundation is generally used, with the floating slab countersunk in the pit.

The physical dimensions of the machinery will always determine the outside dimensions of the pad; however, the weight of the machinery will determine the amount of concrete to be used. The minimum acceptable amount of concrete for any pad is 2½ times the weight of the machinery. Hence, a 50-hp pump weighing 1,550 lb would require a foundation pad of 4,000 lb or 1 cu yd (approximate).

In most cases ready-mix will be available, and the delivered price will average $85/yd. Another $20 should be allowed for form material plus $65 for labor, bringing the estimated cost to $170/yd, in place.

Where ready-mix is not available, or for small pads, field mix may be used: 1 part cement, 2 parts smooth aggregate, 3 parts coarse aggregate, using 6½ gal. of water for each sack of cement. A one-sack batch using these proportions will have a weight of 665 lb and a volume of 4½ cu ft.

One cubic foot of concrete weighs about 150 lb. One cubic yard of concrete weighs about 4,000 lb. To estimate the cost of any concrete pad, calculate cost of pad = 2½ × weight of machine × 17¢. This includes the mix, forms, steel, bolts, and sleeves and labor to place. A ratio of 2½ times the weight of machinery is assumed; where other ratios are to be used, substitute the necessary factor.

**Example 17.1**   A rotating machine weighs 700 lb. What should the estimated cost of the concrete foundation be?

**solution**   2½ × 700 lb × 17¢ = $297.50.

Figure 17.1 illustrates three typical standards for estimating the erection of concrete pads. The following labor and material costs may be applied to the figure:

| | |
|---|---|
| Setting forms | $6.82/sq ft |
| Reinforcing steel | $13.50/sq yd |
| Placing concrete | $21.00/cu yd |
| Grouting | $35.00/sq yd surface |
| Setting bolts and sleeves | $7.45/each |

When ordering ready-mix, 1.1 cu yd should be figured for each actual yard required, to allow for waste. Table 16.16 gives costs for hooked-type bolts.

For residential and small commercial jobs where a pad is required for an outdoor condensing unit or pump, prefabricated pads are generally available from a local precast contractor. These may be purchased delivered to the jobsite (within a 2-mile radius for most cities) at the prices shown in Table 17.11.

For fastenings, anchoring, and hardware sundries, see Chap. 16; for concrete drilling, see Chap. 21.

## RECOMMENDED READING

Siddens, R. S. (ed.), *Walker's Building Estimator's Reference Book*, 24th ed., Frank R. Walker Co., Lisle, Ill., 1992.

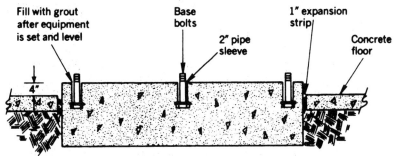

Small machinery foundation where existing concrete floor is too light

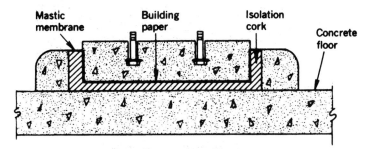

Small machinery foundation
surface mounting, floating base

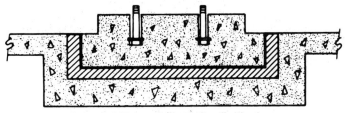

Large machinery pit foundation, floating base

**Figure 17.1   CONCRETE PADS AND FOUNDATIONS**
*Cost of pad = $2\frac{1}{2}$ × weight of machine (lb) × $8\frac{1}{2}$¢.*

**TABLE 17.11**   Prefabricated Pads—Cost

| Slab size, in. | Cost, $ | Slab size, in. | Cost, $ | Slab size, in. | Cost, $ |
|---|---|---|---|---|---|
| 39 × 29 | 21 | 44 × 34 | 30 | 54 × 42 | 39 |
| 48 × 26 | 24 | 54 × 36 | 33 | 76 × 36 | 42 |
| 51 × 26 | 27 | 64 × 32 | 36 | 64 × 46 | 45 |

# CHAPTER 18
# EXCAVATING
# AND TRENCHING

## GENERAL DISCUSSION

When the installation of underground pipe, tanks, and drainage structures is required, the estimator must be apprised of the soil conditions in order to estimate earthwork costs accurately. Excavating, trenching, and backfill are often treated too lightly, and they frequently have determined the difference between profit and loss in a large job involving a good portion of earthwork.

Soil may be classified into four general categories for practical purposes:

*Sandy or light:* easily shoveled, requiring no loosening.

*Medium light or ordinary:* earth easily loosened by pick or jabbing shovel. When power equipment is considered, no preliminary loosening is required.

*Heavy, hard, or clay:* requires heavy pick work to loosen, or may be dug with heavy power shovel without preliminary loosening.

*Hardpan:* requires light blasting and heavy excavating machinery.

Soils not classified here, such as rock, must be carefully considered and should be handled under separate agreement.

The unit used to compute quantity takeoffs is generally the cubic yard, but the cubic foot and the linear foot are sometimes used. Each type of soil should be listed separately and the method of excavating determined. It should be noted whether bracing will be required; whether the excavated material must be disposed of and, if so, how far it must be hauled; whether pumping will be required; what the probable weather will be; and how many laborers will be required.

The average depth, in feet, of the two ends of the trench, multiplied by the length and width and divided by 27, will give the total cubic yards. In figuring hand excavating, it must be remembered that the deeper the trench, the lower the efficiency of the laborer. All the estimating costs shown in this chapter are based on a depth of 5 ft as being 100%. Figure 18.1 may be used to determine the efficiency factor for trenches from 6 to 12 ft deep.

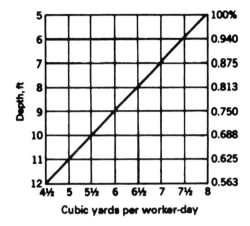

**Figure 18.1 PRODUCTION SCALE FOR HAND EXCAVATING**

## ESTIMATING

Tables 18.1 to 18.3 supply cost data for hand trenching, backhoe excavating, and bulldozer backfilling. Table 18.4 gives minimum widths for pipe trenching.

Table 18.5 gives production hours for pipe trenching with a backhoe to depths of 5 ft. For deeper cuts, OSHA requirements call for a sloped angle of repose, shoring, or bracing. Backhoe rental cost with an operator may range between $60 and $70 per hour (1994 costs). An additional one-time charge of $20 to $30 for move-on is usually added. A move-off charge of the same amount is also added to the job. One worker will hand-tamp 1 to 1.25 cu yd per hour.

Table 18.6 gives volumes of trench excavation in cu yd per 100 lin ft of trench.

To estimate hauling off, it is necessary to know distances, traffic conditions, and truck capacities. When these variables cannot be determined, an average of $3/cu yd for the first mile, plus 90¢ for each additional mile, may be used.

Shallow trenches (to 12 in.) for small pipe (to 3 in. ID) may be estimated at approximately 60¢/lin ft.

Large-pipe trench costs for 1994 averaged about $3/cu yd.

**TABLE 18.1** Hand Trenching—Workhours per Cubic Yard

| Soil classification | Excavating labor | Backfilling labor | Tamping labor |
|---|---|---|---|
| Sandy . . . . . . . . . . . . | 1.55 | 0.40 | 0.75 |
| Medium . . . . . . . . . . . | 2.15 | 0.50 | 1.00 |
| Heavy . . . . . . . . . . . . | 3.50 | 0.60 | 1.30 |
| Hard . . . . . . . . . . . . | 4.25 | 0.70 | 1.40 |

**TABLE 18.2** Excavating with 1-cu-yd Backhoe—Subcontract Costs, Dollars per Cubic Yard

| Soil classification | Cost, 1994 $ |
|---|---|
| Sandy | 2.10 |
| Medium | 2.45 |
| Heavy | 3.15 |
| Hardpan | 3.80 |

**TABLE 18.3** Backfill by Bulldozer—Subcontract Costs, Dollars per Cubic Yard

| Labor, equipment operator, and laborer | Bulldozer rental and operating cost | Total cost, 1994 $ |
|---|---|---|
| 0.35 | 1.10 | 1.45 |

**TABLE 18.4** Minimum Width for Pipe Trenches

| Pipe diameter, in. | Trench width, in. |
|---|---|
| To 2 | 12 |
| 2¼–4 | 18 |
| 4¼–8 | 22 |
| 8½–12 | 30 |
| 12½–15 | 34 |
| 15½–18 | 36 |
| 18½–24 | 42 |
| 24½–30 | 51 |
| 30½–36 | 66 |

**TABLE 18.5** Trenching by Backhoe—Production Hours per Linear Foot

Based on a straight 90° wall in average soil, including trenching, backfilling, and compacting. Does not include watering in, stone removal, etc.

| Depth of trench, ft | Trench width, ft | | | |
|---|---|---|---|---|
| | 1 | 2 | 3 | 4 |
| 2 | 2.5 | 4.9 | 7.4 | 9.8 |
| 3 | 3.6 | 7.3 | 11.0 | 14.5 |
| 4 | 4.9 | 9.8 | 14.7 | 19.5 |
| 5 | 6.0 | 12.0 | 18.2 | 24.2 |

**TABLE 18.6**   Volume of Trench Excavation, Cubic Yards per 100 Linear Feet

| Depth of trench, ft | Trench width, ft | | | |
|---|---|---|---|---|
| | 1 | 2 | 3 | 4 |
| 1 | 3.7 | 7.4 | 11.1 | 14.8 |
| 2 | 7.4 | 14.8 | 22.2 | 29.6 |
| 3 | 11.1 | 22.2 | 33.3 | 44.5 |
| 4 | 14.8 | 29.6 | 44.5 | 59.2 |
| 5 | 18.6 | 37.0 | 55.5 | 74.1 |

## RECOMMENDED READING

*Means Site Work & Landscape Cost Data*, R. S. Means Co., Kingston, Mass. (Published annually.)

Scullin, M. C., *Excavation and Grading Code Administration, Inspection, and Enforcement*, Prentice-Hall, Englewood Cliffs, N.J., 1983.

Siddens, R. S. (ed.), "Site Work," in *Walker's Building Estimator's Reference Book*, 24th ed., Frank R. Walker, Lisle, Ill., 1992, pp. 2.1–2.116.

# CHAPTER 19
# RIGGING

## GENERAL DISCUSSION

Because rigging is a highly specialized field demanding clearly defined safety procedures, riggers are often licensed in metropolitan areas, making it mandatory to subcontract the handling of heavy equipment from dock to erection location. But even when it is not mandatory, rigging is generally sublet to a specialty contractor for reasons of economy. Whenever practical, the estimator should have a firm bid from a rigging contractor to prepare an estimate.

Often, it is not possible for the estimator to procure a firm rigging bid, and a detailed rigging estimate must be prepared. A firm bid from a rigging contractor would require very detailed advance information, and it would still be contingent on delays caused by late delivery, bad weather, accidents, and breakdowns. Consequently, the rigging contractor generally submits a rough estimate based on dollars per hour or per ton. In any case, the estimator must know whether the delivery is fob factory; how many pieces there are in the shipment; whether the shipment is arriving via steamship, railway, or motor freight; and every pertinent detail of weight, size, and type of crate. The estimator must also be aware of insurance and demurrage responsibilities as well as where the responsibilities of each freight agency begin and end.

A rigging job may run between $2,000 and $4,000 per day. When delays of 5 days (not uncommon) can cost over $20,000, the need for careful estimating, scheduling, and coordinating is obvious.

## EQUIPMENT CLASSIFICATION

The estimating tables in this chapter are based on simplified general groupings of mechanical equipment into five categories:

*Category I:* Weight range 200 to 1,000 lb/piece—compact and easily handled apparatus, such as small pumps, compressors, motors, and high-pressure blowers.

*Category II:* Weight range 1,000 lb to 2 tons/piece—compact and easily handled apparatus, such as boilers, ventilators, tanks, heat exchangers, and smokestack sections.

*Category III:* Weight range 1,000 lb to 4 tons/piece—bulky and awkwardly handled apparatus, such as blowers, ventilators, tanks, heat exchangers, and smokestack sections.

*Category IV:* Weight range 2 to 10 tons/piece—compact and easily handled apparatus, such as boilers, compressors, motors, and engines.

*Category V:* Weight range 10 to 50 tons/piece—compact and easily handled apparatus, such as boilers, large central station equipment, engines, and heavy machinery.

## ESTIMATING

Rigging crews vary with the size of the job and the type of equipment required and may consist of anywhere from 4 to 10 workers. It is not uncommon to consider the total crew cost as a dollars-per-day unit and to estimate the job on the basis of the number of crewdays required. A crew that reports for work that is canceled by bad weather is generally paid a minimum of one half-day. The estimator should always allow a minimum of one crewday for any job.

Table 19.1 is based on average 1994 costs. This is the typical 5-person crew most frequently used, and it is the basis of crewhours in the following tables. When rigging equipment costs are required, see Chap. 21.

Table 19.2 covers the loading, unloading, moving, and setting up of equipment in the categories discussed above. Guying, riveting, and welding are not included. The listed workhours are calculated per ton weight of the equipment to be moved and are average figures subject to adjustment to particular job conditions, type of equipment, and kind of rigging gear available.

Tables 19.3 and 19.4 supply data on vertical lifts and miscellaneous estimating, respectively.

**TABLE 19.1** Typical Rigging Crew Cost

| | |
|---|---:|
| Winch truck and driver . . . . . . . . . . . . . . . . . . . . . | $ 90 |
| Supervisor . . . . . . . . . . . . . . . . . . . . . . . . . . . . . . . | 28 |
| Four-man crew @ $25.50 . . . . . . . . . . . . . . . . . . | 102 |
| Total per crewhour . . . . . . . . . . . . . . . . . . . | $ 220 |
| Crewhour per 8-hr day . . . . . . . . . . . . . . . . . . . . . | $1,760 |
| Overhead, profit, and insurance . . . . . . . . . . . . | 840 |
| Total rigging crew cost per day . . . . . . . . . . . | $2,600 |

**TABLE 19.2** Loading, Unloading, and Moving Machinery—Workers/Ton

| Operation | Category | | | | |
|---|---|---|---|---|---|
| | I | II | III | IV | V |
| Unload from railway flatcar with gin pole or derrick . . . . | 2.50 | 2.24 | 3.50 | 2.03 | 1.75 |
| Unload from trailer to ground . . . . . . . . . . . . . . . . | 2.00 | 1.80 | 2.80 | 1.65 | 1.40 |
| Jack up and insert skids under load . . . . . . . . . . . . . | 0.85 | 0.95 | 1.40 | 1.15 | 1.00 |
| Jack up and down and place or remove dolly . . . . . . . . | 1.00 | 1.10 | 1.65 | 1.40 | 1.16 |
| Move on skids and rollers, per 100 ft . . . . . . . . . . . . | 0.75 | 1.10 | 1.30 | 1.00 | 0.85 |
| Jack up and place cribbing, per ft height . . . . . . . . . . | 0.85 | 0.70 | 1.00 | 0.60 | 0.48 |
| Bull, shove, and turn, per 10 ft . . . . . . . . . . . . . . . | 1.50 | 1.75 | 2.00 | 1.20 | 1.10 |
| Line up, rough . . . . . . . . . . . . . . . . . . . . . . . . . . | 0.95 | 1.10 | 1.45 | 1.30 | 1.50 |
| Line up, precise . . . . . . . . . . . . . . . . . . . . . . . . . | 1.10 | 1.40 | 3.80 | 3.50 | 4.00 |
| Set, level, and plumb . . . . . . . . . . . . . . . . . . . . . | 1.00 | 1.30 | 1.60 | 2.00 | 3.00 |
| Erect uprights and stacks with gin pole or derrick . . . . . | — | — | 5.80 | — | — |

**TABLE 19.3**   Vertical Lifts

| Operation | Crewhours |
|---|---|
| Vertical lift, minimum per piece . . . . . . . . . . | 2 |
| Vertical lift, average per piece . . . . . . . . . . . | 4 |
| Vertical lift, tight maneuver . . . . . . . . . . . . | 6–8 |
| Set up and take down rig, average job . . . . . . . | 12 |
| Set up and take down rig, complicated . . . . . . | 32 |

*Note:* If rig must be moved to spot the load, duplicate last item for each move.

**TABLE 19.4**   Miscellaneous Estimating

| Operation | Crewdays per each |
|---|---|
| Pick up and haul to jobsite, 25 tons . . . . . . . . . . . . . . . . . . . . . . . . | 1.0 |
| Move one 25-ton piece horizontally 100 ft . . . . . . . . . . . . . . . . . . . . | 1.5 |
| Unload, set up, erect, and remove hand derrick, 5 tons capacity . . . . . . . . | 1.0 |
| Unload, set up, erect, and remove gin pole, 15 tons capacity . . . . . . . . . . | 1.25 |
| Unload, set up, erect, and remove gin pole, 30 tons capacity . . . . . . . . . . | 2.5 |
| Unload, set up, erect and remove stiffleg derrick, 30 tons capacity . . . . . . . | 4.0 |

As an illustration of preparing a rigging estimate by using Tables 19.1 to 19.4, assume that a 900-ton packaged centrifugal chilling machine is to be picked up from a flatcar, delivered to the jobsite, moved into position, lowered down to a deep subbasement through a shaft, moved into the machine room, and lined up rough.

**Example 19.1**   From the manufacturer's specifications the following is known:

| | |
|---|---|
| Shipping weight | 56,700 lb (e.g., 28 tons) |
| Dimensions | 23 ft long × 15 ft wide × 12 ft high |
| Refrigerant | 2,450 lb |
| Miscellaneous parts | 5,000 lb |

Equipment classification is *Category V.*

| Operation | Table reference | Crewhours |
|---|---|---|
| Unload from railway flatcar to trailer | 19.2 | 8.15 |
| Haul 4 miles, approximately 1 hr | 19.4 | 1.00 |
| Unload from trailer to ground | 19.2 | 6.50 |
| Skid and roll 40 ft to shaft and 60 ft to machine room | 19.2 | 4.00 |
| Bull, shove, and turn 10 ft | 19.2 | 5.15 |
| Set up and take down rig | 19.3 | 20.00 |
| Lower through shaft to subbasement | 19.3 | 4.00 |
| Line up, rough | 19.2 | 7.00 |
| Allowance for handling refrigerant and miscellaneous parts | — | 8.00 |
| Total crewhours | | 63.80 = 8 crewdays |

**solution**   From Table 19.1, crew cost per day is $2,600. Therefore, $2,600 × 8 = $20,800 estimated rigging cost.

## HELICOPTER RIGGING

In many installations the fastest, simplest, and most cost-efficient means of placing rooftop equipment is by helicopter airlifting. On existing construction and retrofit jobs it may, in cases where a crane cannot reach all areas, be the only way to set the equipment without the risk of damaging the roof. In general, helicopter airlifting should be considered whenever a rigging job appears to be labor-intensive. The advantages of helicopter airlifting become apparent where construction-site obstacles, building configuration, or surrounding terrain impose limitations on a crane or where the equipment needs to be raised to great height. Helicopters work with amazing speed and are able to keep the work spread within a short time frame. With 6 to 8 persons in the mechanical contractor's rigging crew, saving labor time for a given task could justify the cost of a helicopter.

Helicopter operators specializing in construction usually bid a contract price based on the known conditions, and the estimator will treat this bid like any other subcontract. But it is essential for the estimator, as well as the job superintendent, to have a thorough understanding of the crew concept for this particular task. The helicopter operator's bid is based on a pilot plus two signalers, one at the pickup point on the ground and the other at the delivery point on the roof. On heavier lifts using big equipment, a copilot is required. The mechanical contractor must schedule two workers on the ground to hook the equipment to the spreader bar under the helicopter and, depending on the load, four to six workers on the roof to set the equipment in place and unshackle it from the sling. The special sling and spreader bar are standard equipment with the copter.

A helicopter may churn up winds from 30 to 75 mph. Before the arrival of the copter, the contractor must secure the roof, i.e., remove or secure all debris, loose insulation boards, loose lumber, roofing materials, etc. and also clear the ground around the pickup point. Furthermore, the mechanical contractor's rigging crew will probably be on overtime pay; helicopter lifts are usually made at daybreak or Sunday morning, at a time of least vehicular and pedestrian traffic, and when the other trades are not working. Crew safety requires hard hats, goggles, and rubber gloves.

In most cities, police coordination is required. The department of public safety—or in smaller towns, the police—must grant permission for the lift, and the area of operation must be cordoned off by public safety officers.

Most rooftop work is done using Sikorsky helicopters; the twin-engine S-58T and S-61 units are the most popular. The larger S-61 helicopter can lift up to 10,000 lb, while the S-58T is generally used for loads under 5,000 lb. No generalization can be made about the cost of helicopter lifts because of widely varying job conditions, weather, and altitude. However, particularly when multiple lifts must be made, use of helicopters can result in significant cost savings as compared to use of cranes.

Carson Helicopters of Perkasie, Pa., a major provider of helicopter services for construction, had one job in which an S-61 helicopter was used to lift 27 sections of nine air-conditioning units to the roof of a one-story South Carolina fibers plant in less than 2 hr of flying time. By comparison, it would have taken 2 days to complete the job using a crane.

On another job, 119 HVAC sections weighing up to 9,700 lb were airlifted and set on curbs in a single day at an average rate of 4.5 min per lift.

On another job in Wisconsin, two helicopters, an S-58T and an S-61, working in tandem erected the entire superstructure for a building, setting 14 columns, seven beams, and hundreds of structural members over a single weekend at one-third the cost and one-third the time required with a crane.

Another advantage of helicopters is that rain, snow, and low temperatures do not generally impede the helicopters from working. In fact, a helicopter actually operates more efficiently on cold days because air is more dense and the rotor blades get a better "bite" when operating in cold air. Obviously, however, high winds will create problems and, consequently, higher costs.

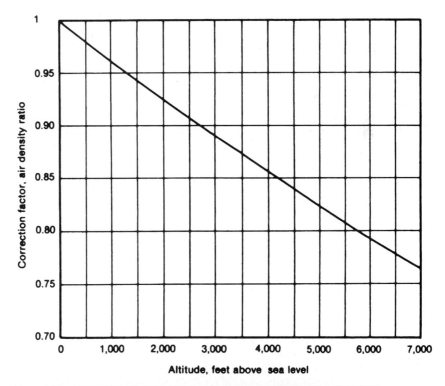

**Figure 19.1    ALTITUDE CORRECTIONS FOR HELICOPTER LIFTING CAPACITY**
*To find the effective helicopter load capacity at altitudes other than sea level, find the correction factor (air-density ratio) on the left ordinate and divide into the rated load capacity.*

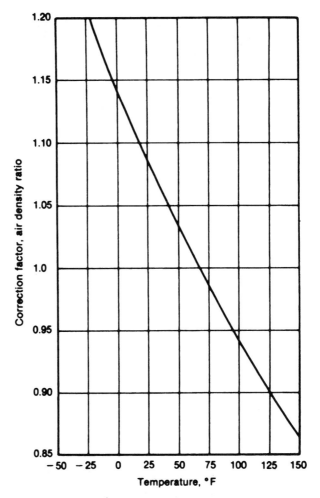

**Figure 19.2  TEMPERATURE CORRECTIONS FOR HELICOPTER LIFTING CAPACITY**
*To find the effective helicopter load capacity at temperatures other than 70°F, find the correction factor (air-density ratio) on the left ordinate and divide into the rated load capacity.*

Temperature, humidity, and precipitation are other factors impacting costs, but the most important factor is altitude. Rated lifting capacity is based on lifts at sea level and air temperature of 70°F—the higher the temperature and/or altitude, the lower the lifting capacity and the lower the temperature and/or altitude, the greater the air density and resultant lifting capacity. As a consequence, helicopter lifting ability maximizes at sea level and very cold weather as indicated earlier. Figures 19.1 and 19.2 respectively give altitude and temperature graphs for calculating loads under conditions other than sea level and 70°F.

Helicopter rigging bids should be procured and treated as a subcontract item. But the estimator must not underestimate the labor costs for preparing the jobsite, as well as ground and roof rigging crew costs, before the helicopter arrives.

# CHAPTER 20
# PAINTING

## GENERAL DISCUSSION

The painting estimate is usually based on units of 1 sq ft, and the cost will be determined by the material to be covered and its surface texture, the kind of paint and number of coats specified, and the required surface preparation. The importance of proper surface preparation before applying a protective coating on any type of surface should not be underestimated.

Takeoff units for the most commonly encountered items in a mechanical construction are as follows:

| | |
|---|---|
| Radiators | sq ft of radiation |
| Pipe | lin ft of length |
| Ductwork | sq ft of surface |
| Tanks | sq ft of surface |
| Walls | sq ft of surface |
| Structural steel | tons or sq ft |
| Machinery | sq ft of surface |

## STRUCTURAL STEEL

All surface rust and loose mill scale should be completely removed by a power-driven rotary wire brush or hand scraping and a wire brush. For large areas, sandblasting should be used. Preferably, structural steel should be acid-pickled or mechanically blasted to a near-white finish and primed before erection. If cleaning and priming are not performed until after erection, costs are increased significantly. The following rules of thumb graphically illustrate the cost savings possible if cleaning and priming are done before erection[1,2]:

| | |
|---|---|
| Acid pickling to a millscale-free surface | $0.13 to $0.25/sq ft |
| Mechanical blasting to a near-white finish | $0.20 to $0.30/sq ft |
| Sandblasting to a near-white finish on the ground | $0.75 to $0.95/sq ft |
| Sandblasting bare steel to a near-white finish in the air | $1.00 to $1.50/sq ft |
| Sandblasting previously painted and corroded steel in the air[2] | $1.60 to $5.00/sq ft |

---

[1] Quoted from B. Wood, "Painting Costs," *AACE Bulletin,* vol. 12, no. 5, 1970, p. 139, but adjusted to 1994 costs.

[2] Depending on the type of previous coating and condition of the steel.

Primers for steel must be a proper combination of rust-inhibitive pigments and a vehicle which will ensure the formation of a stabilized dried coating that will withstand normal exposure. Allow 36 hr of drying time between the intermediate primer and the following coat. Allow 1 week's drying time for the finish coat before placing it into service.

The most common rust-inhibitive pigments are zinc oxide and zinc chromate. Raw linseed oil, which has a slow setting characteristic, has excellent surface wetting and adhesion properties and is generally the best vehicle. Fish-oil vehicles are also considered excellent rust inhibitors and are widely used on steel surfaces.

It should be carefully noted, however, that lead-containing paints and primers are no longer permitted because of the toxic effects of prolonged exposure to lead. Zinc oxide, zinc chromate, or other lead-free coatings should be used. Newer types of coatings that have rapidly gained in popularity in recent years are various epoxy, vinyl, and latex materials. Table 20.1 lists costs for common coating materials.

One workerday should be estimated for cleaning and painting 1,200 sq ft or 5.75 tons of steel. One gallon of prepared primer will cover approximately 500 sq ft. For areas of steel of various shapes and thicknesses, see Tables 20.2 and 20.3. For areas not covered by the tables, see Fig. 20.1.

## LEAD-BASED COATINGS

Lead-based primers and paints were once widely used both in residential and industrial applications but are no longer used because of environmental and health problems associated with lead. Use in residential applications was ended some years ago. Until the 1970s, red lead primer was widely used on steel structures and still finds application on many projects, particularly military and marine applications.

The previous widespread use of lead primers presents a major problem during removal of existing coatings because the primer contains "leachable lead" in sufficiently high concentrations (5 parts per million or higher) to be classified as a hazardous material by the U.S. Environmental Protection Agency.

The primer can be removed using conventional techniques (hand scraping and brushing, abrasive cleaning, etc.), but all resulting materials must be collected and disposed of as hazardous wastes. Air monitoring, respirators, protective clothing, etc. are also required to limit worker exposure. Workers must be fully protected from inhaling, ingesting, or otherwise contacting the debris no matter what technique is used to remove the lead-containing coating materials.

Regulatory requirements for removal of the coatings, worker protection, collection of waste material, onsite temporary storage, and transportation and disposal of the wastes are stringent and costly. While no general guidelines can be given about the attendant costs, they can be expected to exceed the cost of removal of nonhazardous coatings by 50 to 100% and more. In addition, disposal costs for the resultant hazardous debris are substantial. Taylor[3] cited average costs of $250 per barrel in the Albuquerque, N.M. area. The Taylor article is highly recommended for those desiring more information on this critical subject.

---

[3] T. D. Taylor, "Recoating Existing Structures—the Lead Primer Issue," *1993 AACE Transactions,* paper no. B.5.

**TABLE 20.1**    Cost of Paint and Coating Materials

| Coating material | Cost per gal. in 5-gal. lots, 1994 $* |
|---|---|
| Exterior, alkyd (oil base) | |
| Flat | $18.75 |
| Gloss | 18.00 |
| Primer | 16.75 |
| Exterior, latex (water base) | |
| Gloss | 21.85 |
| Flat | 15.25 |
| Primer | 16.00 |
| Semigloss | 16.30 |
| Interior, alkyd (oil base) | |
| Flat | 12.80 |
| Gloss | 19.65 |
| Primer-sealer | 17.75 |
| Semigloss | 18.75 |
| Interior, latex (water base) | |
| Flat | 11.50 |
| Gloss | 23.80 |
| Primer-sealer | 13.00 |
| Semigloss | 16.25 |
| Metal coatings | |
| Galvanized | 19.65 |
| High-heat | 25.75 |
| Machinery enamel, alkyd | 17.50 |
| Normal-heat | 17.50 |
| Rust inhibitor (ferrous metal) | 18.50 |
| Zinc chromate | 16.50 |
| Heavy-duty coatings | |
| Acrylic urethane | 47.50 |
| Metal pretreatment (polyvinyl butyral) | 20.00 |
| Polyamide epoxy finish | 27.40 |
| Polyamide epoxy primer | 25.25 |
| Silicone alkyd | 27.50 |
| Two-component solvent-based acrylic epoxy | 28.75 |
| Two-component solvent-based polyester epoxy | 35.00 |
| Vinyl | 22.50 |
| Zinc-rich primer | 42.00 |
| Miscellaneous | |
| Aluminum | 15.80 |
| Fire retardant, intumescent agent | 30.35 |
| Linseed oil | 7.75 |
| Turpentine | 9.25 |

*For 100-gal. lots, deduct 10%.

SOURCE:    *Means Building Construction Cost Data,* R. S. Means Co., Kingston, Mass., 1994.

**TABLE 20.2** Square Feet per Ton of Steel of Various Shapes

| Shape | sq ft per ton |
|---|---|
| Standard I beams . . . . . . . . . . . . . . . . | 200 |
| H columns . . . . . . . . . . . . . . . . . . . | 200 |
| Standard channels . . . . . . . . . . . . . . . | 325 |
| 3- to 8-in. L's . . . . . . . . . . . . . . . . | 300 |
| WF beams . . . . . . . . . . . . . . . . . . . | 225 |

**TABLE 20.3** Square Feet per Ton of Steel of Various Thicknesses

| Thickness, in. | $\frac{1}{8}$ | $\frac{3}{16}$ | $\frac{1}{4}$ | $\frac{5}{16}$ | $\frac{3}{8}$ | $\frac{1}{2}$ | $\frac{5}{8}$ | $\frac{3}{4}$ | $\frac{7}{8}$ | 1 | $1\frac{1}{2}$ | 2 |
|---|---|---|---|---|---|---|---|---|---|---|---|---|
| sq ft per ton | 800 | 530 | 400 | 325 | 265 | 200 | 160 | 135 | 115 | 100 | 67 | 50 |

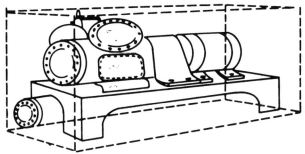

To find the area of an odd-shaped piece of machinery: Assume the machinery enclosed in a snug crate; take off the total square feet of surface of the crate.

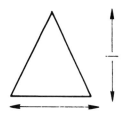

To find the area of a triangle: ½ the altitude × the base

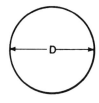

To find the area of a sphere: Diameter squared × 3.1416

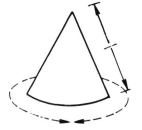

To find the area of a cone: (3.1416 × base radius squared) + (base circumference × ½ the slant height).

**Figure 20.1  DETERMINING AREAS FOR ESTIMATING PAINTING**
*(To find areas of tanks, see Chap. 8.)*

# PIPE

Color should be used to identify the characteristic hazards of the contents of piping. Safety colors, in order to be of value, should be restricted in their use to the identification of safety hazards and pipe contents and not be applied to equipment unrelated to the safety program. American National Standards Institute (ANSI) Standard A13.1-1981 specifies that color should be "displayed on, or contiguous to, the piping by any physical means, but its use shall be in combination with legend. Color may be used in continuous, total length coverage or in intermittent displays." Table 20.4 summarizes the color classification system specified in ANSI A13.1-1981.[4]

Prior to adoption of ANSI 13.1-1981, another piping color-code scheme was recommended by the American Society of Mechanical Engineers. It remains in use in many areas today and therefore is summarized in Table 20.5.

With these systems, the entire length of piping is painted in the designated color or, alternately, color bands are conspicuously painted or applied with adhesive tape along the length of the pipe. It suggested that the name of the pipe contents be stenciled on the color bands. Such identification should be adjacent to valves and fittings for easy recognition, especially during emergencies or repairs and maintenance.

*Dangerous materials* include combustible gases and oils, hot water, and steam above atmospheric pressure. *Safe materials* include compressed air, cold water, and steam under vacuum.

A parallel color-code system is applicable to other industrial facilities and is summarized at the end of this chapter.

---

[4] Tables 20.4 and 20.5 do not appear on the computer disk provided with this book.

**TABLE 20.4**   Piping Color Classification System*

| Material | Pipe color | Color of legend |
|---|---|---|
| Fire-protection materials | Red | White |
| Inherently hazardous materials | Yellow | Black |
| Materials presenting a low hazard level | | |
| Liquids | Green | White |
| Gases | Blue | White |

*Colors should be as recommended in ANSI Z53.1 latest revision, Safety Color Code for Marking Physical Hazards.

**TABLE 20.5**   Safety Color-Code System

| Classification | Code | Color |
|---|---|---|
| Fire protection | F | Red |
| Dangerous materials | D | Yellow or orange |
| Safe materials | S | Green, white, black, gray, or aluminum |
| Protective materials | P | Bright blue |
| Extravaluable materials | V | Deep purple |

## GALVANIZED SHEET METAL

New galvanized surfaces offer very poor adhesion because of lubricants used in the galvanizing process, and they must be thoroughly scrubbed with a solvent cleaner or detergent before painting. A solution of 5 oz of copper acetate in 1 gal. of water is an accepted etching solution. After washing the metal, rinse with clean water and allow to dry thoroughly before applying the primer coat. A good-quality galvanized-iron primer should be laid on before the final color coating with a good oil-base paint. Allow 24 hr of drying time between the primer and finish coats.

One gallon of prepared primer will cover approximately 650 sq ft of smooth galvanized surface including straps, hangers, and joints. To arrive at the square feet of surface when making the takeoff, see Chap. 10.

To convert linear feet of pipe to square feet of surface, use the data in Table 20.6. Brush covering capacities per workhour are given in Table 20.7. Average surface preparation costs for pipe are given in Table 20.8.

**TABLE 20.6**   Conversion of Linear Feet of Pipe to 400 sq ft of Surface

This table converts linear feet of pipe to 400 sq ft equivalent to simplify estimating paint quantities. One gallon of prepared primer will cover approximately 400 sq ft of pipe surface in one coat.

| Nominal pipe size, in. | ½ | ¾ | 1 | 1¼ | 1½ | 2 | 2½ | 3 | 4 |
|---|---|---|---|---|---|---|---|---|---|
| lin ft per 400 sq ft | 1,820 | 1,450 | 1,160 | 920 | 800 | 645 | 550 | 435 | 340 |
| Nominal pipe size, in. | 6 | 8 | 10 | 12 | 14 | 16 | 18 | 20 | 24 |
| lin ft per 400 sq ft | 230 | 175 | 140 | 117 | 108 | 95 | 84 | 75 | 63 |

**TABLE 20.7**   Brush Covering Capacities per Workhour

For estimating labor this table may be used as a guide to figure surface area one painter may cover in 1 hr based on average conditions, using brush to cover one coat on clean surfaces. When a painting contract is to be let to a subcontractor, the estimator should add approximately 43% to labor to cover insurance, overhead, and profit. Brushes and drop cloths may be figured at approximately $60 per painter.

| Surface | Area per workhour |
|---|---|
| ½- to 1-in. pipe . . . . . . . . . . . . . . . | 60 lin ft |
| 1¼- to 2-in. pipe . . . . . . . . . . . . . . | 58 lin ft |
| 2½- to 3-in. pipe . . . . . . . . . . . . . . | 55 lin ft |
| 4-in. pipe . . . . . . . . . . . . . . . . . . | 50 lin ft |
| 6-in. pipe . . . . . . . . . . . . . . . . . . | 45 lin ft |
| 8-in. pipe . . . . . . . . . . . . . . . . . . | 25 lin ft |
| 10-in. pipe . . . . . . . . . . . . . . . . . | 18 lin ft |
| 12-in. pipe . . . . . . . . . . . . . . . . . | 15 lin ft |
| 14-in. pipe . . . . . . . . . . . . . . . . . | 14 lin ft |
| 16-in. pipe . . . . . . . . . . . . . . . . . | 12 lin ft |
| 18-in. pipe . . . . . . . . . . . . . . . . . | 10 lin ft |
| 20-in. pipe . . . . . . . . . . . . . . . . . | 9 lin ft |
| 24-in. pipe . . . . . . . . . . . . . . . . . | 8 lin ft |
| Flat areas, small . . . . . . . . . . . . . . | 50 sq ft |
| Flat areas, large . . . . . . . . . . . . . . | 75 sq ft |
| Machinery . . . . . . . . . . . . . . . . . . | 25 sq ft |

**TABLE 20.8**   Average Surface Preparation Costs for (≤14-in.-diameter) Pipe

| Cleaning method | Average cost per sq ft, 1994 $ |
| --- | --- |
| Hand wire brushing | 0.85 |
| Air-powered wire brushing | 0.60 |
| Brushoff blast cleaning | 1.25 |
| Commercial blast cleaning | 1.70 |
| Near-white blast cleaning | 3.50 |
| White metal blast cleaning | 4.60 |

SOURCE:   Siddens, R. S. (ed.), *Walker's Building Estimator's Reference Book,* 24th ed., F.R. Walker Co., Lisle, Ill., 1992. (Prices have been adjusted to 1994 costs.)

## *SAFETY COLOR CODE AND IDENTIFICATIONS IN COMMON USE*

| | |
| --- | --- |
| Red | Fire-alarm boxes |
| | Fire hose locations |
| | Fire hydrants |
| | Fire pumps |
| | Indicator valves for sprinkler system |
| | Emergency stop buttons on electrical switches |
| Orange | Safety starting buttons |
| | Guards for gears, pulleys, chain drives, and transmissions |
| Yellow | Vertical edges of sliding fire doors |
| | Pillars or posts that constitute a physical hazard |
| | Low beams and pipes, dangerous projections |
| Green | First-aid equipment |
| | Gas masks |
| | Safety areas |
| Blue | Any equipment under repair to be cautioned against moving |
| | Scaffolding |
| | Ladders |
| | Elevators |
| Purple | Radioactive areas |
| | Containers for the storage or disposal of radioactive materials |

## *RECOMMENDED READING*

Adams, L., "Comparative Costs of Painting Steel," *1974 AACE Transactions,* American Association of Cost Engineers, Morgantown, W.Va., 1974, pp. 191–196.

Baumeister, T. (ed.), *Mark's Standard Handbook for Mechanical Engineers,* current edition, McGraw-Hill, New York.

Siddens, R. S. (ed.), *Walker's Building Estimator's Reference Book,* 24th ed., F.R. Walker Co., Lisle, Ill., 1992, pp. 9.122–9.149.

*Standard Scheme for Identification of Piping Systems* (ANSI A13.1-1981), American Society of Mechanical Engineers, New York, 1981.

Taylor, T. D., "Recoating Existing Structures—The Lead Primer Issue," *1993 AACE Transactions,* AACE International, Morgantown, W.Va., 1993, pp. B.5.1–B.5.4.

Wood, B., "Painting Costs," *AACE Bulletin,* Vol. 21, No. 5, 1970, pp. 138–141.

# CHAPTER 21
# TOOLS AND
# SPECIAL EQUIPMENT

## GENERAL DISCUSSION

The estimator must have the "value engineering" approach to every job: creative open-end thinking and a continuous flow-through of new product information and application techniques. As the technological advancement of the craft increases, mechanization becomes an ever-greater factor in production costs.

Along with purchase and rental costs of tools and equipment, the estimator must know the weights and capacities of each piece and must also be thoroughly familiar with rigging practices and understand the use, application, and load limitations of the common fiber and wire ropes, booms and derricks, scaffolding, hauling capacities of various motorized equipment, etc.

Tools and equipment may be purchased outright or rented by the job, which may be an hourly, daily, weekly, or monthly requirement. In any case, it should show as a job cost.

## RENTAL

The rental rates given in the following tables are approximate only and should be applied with particular discretion in the case of heavy equipment and long rental periods. The rates are based on an 8-hr day, 40-hr week, or consecutive 30-day month of 176 hr. The costs of operator, fuel, oil, lubricants, repairs, and maintenance should be added to the rental rate. Sometimes, however, the rate may include an operator, and in the case of trucks, an initial tank of gas. Traveling time is always considered the burden of the lessee, and the estimator should compute the rental fee beginning and ending at the lessor's warehouse or yard. An allowance must also be made for insurance, sales taxes, and sometimes license fees.

## PURCHASE

The correct allocation of equipment costs to job costs is more complicated when the equipment is owned outright than when it is rented. Given the purchase price of the equipment, it is possible to determine the *workhour owning cost* and apply this to the number of working hours per project. A schedule of workhour owning and operating costs should be made available by the accounting department to the estimating department, and it should include *all* company equipment.

The *workhour owning cost* is a function of the capital investment, average useful life, total depreciation, total repair, and total interest, insurance, taxes, and storage for the particular equipment. *Workhour operating costs* are derived from the fuel, power, and supplies required. Table 21.1 shows some average workhour owning and operating costs based on available data; it may be used for arriving at approximate values.

**TABLE 21.1**   Owning and Operating Workhour Costs

| Equipment | Description | Workhour owning cost, $ | Workhour operating cost, $ | Total workhour cost, $ |
|---|---|---|---|---|
| Automobiles | | 2.50 | 12.50 | 15.00 |
| Cranes, 5-ton | Crawler, gas-powered | 2.25 | 15.00 | 17.25 |
| Derricks, no power | Steel, stiffleg, to 20 tons | 1.00 | 8.00 | 9.00 |
| Electric generators | Jobsite, power to 50 kW | 6.25 | 6.00 | 12.50 |
| Gasoline engines | To 25 hp | 2.00 | 2.00 | 6.60 |
| Jacks | To 50 tons | 1.80 | 4.60 | 1.80 |
| Hand tools | Electric power | 0.50 | 0.50 | 1.00 |
| Trenching machines | Rubber-tired, gas | 5.75 | 21.00 | 26.75 |
| Trucks | Light-duty | 2.50 | 12.50 | 15.00 |
| Trucks | Medium-duty | 2.75 | 15.50 | 18.25 |
| Trucks | Heavy-duty | 3.50 | 20.50 | 24.00 |
| Welding machines | Acetylene torch, average | 0.85 | 7.75 | 8.60 |
| Welding machines | ac arc to 400 amp | 2.00 | 5.50 | 7.50 |
| Welding machines | dc arc to 600 amp | 2.85 | 4.00 | 13.85 |

## BUY/RENT DECISIONS

Equipment rental rates often are a significant percentage of the cost of purchasing the equipment outright. Because of this many persons assume that equipment ownership is preferable to renting. This is not necessarily the case because ownership cost considerations go far beyond first cost and operating costs. Ownership represents funds which are tied up in capital investment and which thus are not available for other business purposes.

The question of whether to rent (or lease) or purchase a particular piece of equipment is directly related to the length of time the equipment will be needed, availability of a rental unit, and other factors such as storage, future jobs, initial cost, and maintenance requirements. Local rental rates vary widely, and the data herein are intended only as a guide and not for bid preparation. When long-term requirements are obvious, purchasing may be justified.

The proper buy/rent decision depends on the anticipated level of usage of the equipment item and its present value life-cycle ownership cost versus the present value cost of rentals. Life-cycle cost is discussed in some detail in Chap. 27.

Some things to be considered in buy/rent (or buy/lease) decisions are

1. The effect of adding new assets on the tax structure of the company and the bookkeeping effort required for depreciation calculations, etc.
2. Keeping records on usage and maintenance of the various equipment items so that they are maintained and replaced as necessary and so that necessary funds are set aside for maintenance and periodic replacement.

3. Availability of parts and maintenance facilities for the equipment and storage when not in use.

4. Frequency of equipment use during the year, mobility of equipment, its potential use on other projects, and distribution of charges for use to various jobs.

5. Security of the equipment, including spare parts and tools. Ownership creates a permanent requirement for security.

6. Move-in and move-out costs of rented or leased equipment versus expense of bringing owned equipment to the jobsite.

There is no single best choice. The buy/rent decision depends on the individual contractor's costs and economic considerations.

## CONCRETE DRILLING AND SAWING

In drilling holes through concrete for pipe chases, etc., diamond bits powered by water-cooled industrial drills may save as much as 60% of the cost of former methods using a standard carbide bit. Although each drilling job is different, the following rule of thumb may be used to estimate the cutting time through an average reinforced-concrete wall or floor: 2 min per inch depth per inch diameter, assuming an onsite industrial diamond drill, with power and water hooked up. Thus, a 4-in. hole through an 8-in. reinforced-concrete floor would require approximately 64 min.

The costs of concrete drills and diamond bits are given in Table 21.2 and those of concrete sawing machines and blades, in Table 21.3. Labor costs of sawing concrete are listed in Table 21.4. See Tables 21.5 and 21.6 for subcontractor rates for concrete core drilling and sawing. The costs of power-operated hand-held portable tools are given in Table 21.7.

**TABLE 21.2**   Concrete Drills and Diamond Bits

| Industrial core drill, electric-powered with water swivel and hose | | | | | | $7,000 | | | | | |
|---|---|---|---|---|---|---|---|---|---|---|---|
| Industrial drill, air-powered with water swivel and hose | | | | | | $5,000 | | | | | |

Diamond drill bits listed in nominal inches OD

| Size | 1 | $1\frac{1}{2}$ | 2 | 3 | 4 | $4\frac{1}{2}$ | 5 | 6 | 7 | 8 | 9 | 10 |
|---|---|---|---|---|---|---|---|---|---|---|---|---|
| Cost, $ | 152 | 180 | 260 | 340 | 400 | 500 | 535 | 650 | 900 | 975 | 1,200 | 1,400 |

**TABLE 21.3**   Concrete—Sawing Machines

| Gasoline engine, light-duty, 8 hp, 5-in. cut | $5,000 |
|---|---|
| Gasoline engine, medium-duty, 14 hp | $6,000 |
| Self-propelled gasoline engine, medium-duty, 14 hp | $7,000 |
| Self-propelled gasoline engine, heavy-duty, 30 hp | $9,000 |

| Blade type | Cost of blades, $, of following sizes, in. | | | |
|---|---|---|---|---|
| | 12 | 14 | 16 | 18 |
| Standard abrasive | 10 | 12 | 20 | 25 |
| Concrete abrasive | 12 | 15 | 25 | 30 |
| Diamond | 700 | 750 | 900 | 1,100 |

**TABLE 21.4**  Sawing Concrete—Workhours

Average workhours for sawing cured concrete using equipment given in Table 21.3.

| Depth of cut, in.......... | 1 | 1½ | 2 | 2½ | 3 | 3½ | 4 | 5 |
|---|---|---|---|---|---|---|---|---|
| Workhours per 100 ft .... | 2.5 | 3.0 | 3.5 | 4.0 | 4.4 | 5.2 | 5.8 | 6.9 |

**TABLE 21.5**  Subcontractor Rates for Concrete Core Drilling

Based on current subcontractor's selling prices for drilling average reinforced-concrete decks to 6 and 10 in. thickness. It is assumed that holes are laid out, water and electricity are available, and area is readily accessible. Standby time will be charged at a rate of $40.00/hr per worker and drill.

| Core diameter, in....... | 1 | 2 | 3 | 4 | 6 | 8 | 10 | 12 | 14 | 18 |
|---|---|---|---|---|---|---|---|---|---|---|
| $ per hole to 6 in....... | 50 | 50 | 65 | 90 | 95 | 100 | 150 | 300 | 350 | 400 |
| $ per hole to 10 in...... | 60 | 70 | 85 | 95 | 125 | 150 | 250 | 425 | 500 | 550 |

**TABLE 21.6**  1994 Subcontractor Rates for Sawing Reinforced-Concrete Slabs

| Depth of cut, in.......... | 1 | 1½ | 2 | 3 | 4 | 5 | 6 |
|---|---|---|---|---|---|---|---|
| Mesh-reinforced: | | | | | | | |
|   Minimum charge, $..... | 250 | 250 | 250 | 250 | 350 | 400 | 500 |
|   Cost per lin ft, $........ | 0.80 | 1.20 | 1.60 | 2.50 | 3.25 | 4.00 | 5.00 |
| Rod-reinforced: | | | | | | | |
|   Cost per lin ft, $........ | 2.00 | 3.00 | 6.50 | 10.00 | 13.50 | 17.00 | 20.00 |

## PIPE CUTTING, THREADING, AND FINISH MACHINES

Threading and cutting machines and mobile shops are available in a variety of sizes, ranges, and duties. Purchasing costs vary between $400 and $12,000; rentals vary from $45 to $1,400 per week. Purchase prices and rental rates of various pipe machines are given in Table 21.8.

## SHEET-METAL MACHINES

Lock formers, brakes, and shears for field shop use are available on rental as well as purchase (Table 21.9). Smaller machines and tools are not included.

## MOVING AND LIFTING

Purchase prices and rental rates for vertical moving and lifting devices are listed in Table 21.10.

**TABLE 21.7** Power-Operated Hand-Held Portable Tools

| Item | Description | Purchase price, $ | Rental rate, $ | | |
|---|---|---|---|---|---|
| | | | Day | Week | Month |
| Drill | ¼–⅜-in., heavy-duty | 150 | 10 | 30 | 90 |
| | ½-in., heavy-duty | 170 | 10 | 30 | 90 |
| | ¾-in., heavy-duty | 350 | 25 | 45 | 135 |
| | Rotary hammer, to ¾-in. | 625 | 25 | 75 | 225 |
| | Rotary hammer, to ½-in. | 1,100 | 45 | 130 | 375 |
| | Core drill, electric, 2½ hp | — | 60 | 180 | 500 |
| Grinder | Disk, all sizes | 325 | 15 | 40 | 100 |
| Saw | Circular, 7¼-in., elec. | 250 | 10 | 30 | 85 |
| | Circular, 8-in., gas | — | 35 | 100 | 280 |
| | Cutoff, 14-in., elec. | 700 | 30 | 90 | 250 |
| | Concrete, 12-in. | — | 45 | 115 | 300 |
| Stud driver | Low-velocity | 375 | 15 | 45 | 120 |
| | High-velocity | 400 | 15 | 45 | 120 |

Studs and stud driver charges

| Length of stud, in. | Length of thread, in. | Cost per 100, $ |
|---|---|---|
| 1 1/16 | 3/16 | 45 |
| 2 | ¾ | 70 |
| 2⅜ | ¾ | 72 |
| 2⅝ | ¾ | 74 |
| 2⅞ | 1 | 75 |
| 2½ | 1¼ | 78 |
| 2⅞ | 1¼ | 80 |

| Stud driver, 22-caliber, charges | Standard | Heavy | Extra heavy |
|---|---|---|---|
| Cost per 100 | $24.00 | $25.00 | $32.00 |

**TABLE 21.8** Pipe Machines

| Item | Description | Purchase price, $ | Rental rate, $ | | |
|---|---|---|---|---|---|
| | | | Day | Week | Month |
| Polisher, joint preparer | Small mechanical buffer for copper pipe to 1 in., fittings to 2 in. | 400 | 16 | 45 | 140 |
| | Portable tripod mount buffer and deburrer, to 4-in. copper | 500 | 20 | 60 | 180 |
| Copper make-ready and finisher | Complete portable unit for cutting, reaming, deburring, and cleaning, to 4-in. copper | 3,500 | 140 | 500 | 1,500 |
| Pipe machine | Threader and cutter to 4-in. steel | 12,000 | 480 | 1,400 | 4,000 |

**TABLE 21.9** Sheet-Metal Duct-Making Machines

| Item | Description | Purchase price, $ | Rental rate, $ | | |
|---|---|---|---|---|---|
| | | | Day | Week | Month |
| Brake | 18 ga, 4 ft capacity | 2,250 | 90 | 260 | 800 |
| | 18 ga, 8 ft capacity | 3,000 | 60 | 320 | 900 |
| Lock seamer | 22 ga, electric | 500 | 20 | 60 | 180 |
| | 18 ga, pneumatic | 200 | 15 | 45 | 135 |
| Jump shear | 16 ga, 4 ft capacity | 5,500 | 25 | 400 | 1,800 |
| High-speed carbon-steel blades | — | 400 | | | |

**TABLE 21.10** Vertical Moving and Lifting Devices

| Equipment | Description | Purchase price, $ | Rental rate, $ | | | |
|---|---|---|---|---|---|---|
| | | | Hour | Day | Week | Month |
| Come-along or hand hoist | Wire rope, 6,000-lb capacity, general application | 425 | — | 15 | 40 | 100 |
| Hoist | Chain, manual: | | | | | |
| | To 1½ tons capacity | — | — | 30 | 90 | 270 |
| | To 2½ tons capacity | — | — | 35 | 105 | 315 |
| Portable lifting platform | Scissor, 4-wheel, self-propelled: | | | | | |
| | To ½ ton, 25 ft | — | — | 200 | 600 | 1,800 |
| | To 1 ton, 40 ft | — | — | 375 | 1,125 | 3,375 |
| | Self-erecting, gas-powered, 1½–2½ tons, 25 ft | — | — | 300 | 400 | 2,700 |
| Crane | Swinging boom, self-propelled: | | | | | |
| | To 2½ tons | — | 80 | 250 | 700 | 2,100 |
| | To 5 tons | — | 65 | 195 | 585 | 2,300 |
| | To 10 tons | — | 75 | 225 | 675 | 2,700 |
| | To 12 tons | — | 80 | 32 | 960 | 2,880 |
| Forklift trucks | 18-ft rise, to 1½ tons | — | — | 1,700 | — | — |
| | 28-ft rise, to 2 tons | — | — | 2,000 | — | — |
| Jack | Hydraulic, to 2 tons | 700 | — | 250 | — | — |
| | Hydraulic, to 4 tons | 1,225 | — | 450 | — | — |
| Winch | Hand-driven, 1-ton | 275 | — | 130 | — | — |
| | Hand-driven, 2-tons | 620 | — | 400 | — | — |

## TRENCHING AND DIGGING

Purchase prices and rental rates for trenching and digging equipment are given in Table 21.11.

## TRANSPORTATION EQUIPMENT

Trucks and other vehicles are usually rented at a flat rate (Table 21.12) plus a mileage penalty. Mileage varies between $0.60 and $1.00 per driven mile.

## WELDING EQUIPMENT, GENERATORS, AND CLEANING EQUIPMENT

Rental rates for welding equipment are listed in Table 21.13, and purchase prices and rental rates for generator sets are given in Table 21.14. Costs of purchasing or renting cleaning equipment are given in Table 21.15.

**TABLE 21.11**  Trenching and Digging Equipment

| Equipment | Description | Purchase price, $ | Rental rate, $ | | |
|---|---|---|---|---|---|
| | | | Day | Week | Month |
| Trencher, light-duty, 250 lb | Manually operated, trench to 3 in. × 1 ft, sprinkler systems, etc. | 3,500 | — | — | — |
| Trencher, crawler, 15-hp | Medium-duty, trench to 12 × 30 in. | — | 115 | 345 | 1,050 |
| Trencher, crawler, 20-hp | Medium-duty, trench to 15 in. × 5 ft | — | 180 | 540 | 1,620 |
| Trencher, digger, 30-hp | Heavy-duty, trench to 16 in. × 5 ft | — | 190 | 570 | 1,710 |
| Ladder trencher | Gas, 8 in. × 5 ft | — | 315 | 945 | 2,850 |
| | Diesel, 16 in. × 8 ft | — | 550 | 165 | 5,000 |
| Backhoe loader | 4-wheel, ½ yd | 5,000 | 215 | 650 | 1,950 |
| | 4-wheel, ¾–1 yd | 7,000 | 270 | 810 | 2,450 |

**TABLE 21.12**  Transportation Equipment

| Equipment | Description | Rental rate, $ | | |
|---|---|---|---|---|
| | | Day | Week | Month |
| Pickup truck | ½-ton | 65 | 150 | 540 |
| | ¾-ton | 65 | 190 | 370 |
| | 1-ton, with lift gate | 80 | 200 | 600 |
| Stake truck | 1½-ton, with lift gate | 80 | 240 | 720 |
| | 3-ton, with lift gate | 90 | 270 | 810 |
| | 5-ton, with lift gate | 100 | 360 | 1,080 |
| Trailer | Van, 32-ft | 39 | 150 | 450 |
| | Flatbed, 32-ft | 39 | 150 | 450 |
| | Office | — | — | 400 |

**TABLE 21.13**  Welding Machines

| Item | Description | Weight, lb | Rental rate, $ | | |
|---|---|---|---|---|---|
| | | | Day | Week | Month |
| Gas | To 250 amp | 350 | 40 | 120 | 375 |
| | 250–350 amp | 400 | 65 | 190 | 570 |
| Electric | 250–350 amp | 400 | 25 | 70 | 190 |
| | 350–500 amp | — | 60 | 180 | 540 |

**TABLE 21.14**  Generator Sets

| Item | Description | Purchase price, $ | Rental rate, $ | | |
|------|-------------|-------------------|-----|------|-------|
| | | | Day | Week | Month |
| Gas-operated | 5–7½ kW | 2,750 | 45 | 400 | 1,335 |
| | 5–10 kW | 6,000 | 80 | 240 | 720 |
| | 10–15 kW | 8,000 | 115 | 345 | 1,035 |
| | 20–25 kW | 7,000 | 80 | 290 | 965 |
| Diesel | 20–25kW | — | 85 | 235 | 705 |

**TABLE 21.15**  Cleaning Equipment

| Item | Description | Purchase price, $ | Rental rate, $ | | |
|------|-------------|-------------------|-----|------|-------|
| | | | Day | Week | Month |
| Industrial vacuum | Wet and dry pickup | 1,000 | 50 | 150 | 450 |
| Steam cleaner | 100 gph, 100 psi | 1,375 | 45 | 135 | 405 |

**TABLE 21.16**  Tubular Scaffolding Setups

Based on tubular steel scaffolding section modules, 7 ft long × 5 ft wide × 5 ft high, using standard end frames, crossbraces, and fast-locking connections with 2-in. planking on top. *Workhours* includes erection, leveling, tying in, and dismantling, but not trucking to and from jobsite. Costs shown are per single module and must be multiplied by the number of modules required in any direction. Rolling scaffold is interior high-caster type, 6 ft long × 2½ ft wide × 6 ft high, and is usually purchased rather than rented. Purchase price approximately $600.

| Description | Rent per month, $* | Labor workhours |
|-------------|--------------------|-----------------|
| Fixed scaffold, level floor | 10.00 | 1.0 |
| Fixed scaffold, floor not level | 10.00 | 1.5 |
| Rolling scaffold | 17.50 | 1.0 |

*For jobs under 25 frames. Rentals can go much lower on larger jobs.

## SCAFFOLDING

Rental rates for tubular scaffolding are given in Table 21.16.

## RECOMMENDED READING

*Building Construction Cost Data,* R. S. Means Co., Kingston, Mass. (Published annually.)

*Cost Reference Book for Construction Equipment,* Dataquest, San Jose, Calif. (Updated periodically.)

Dettman, S. S., "Estimating Operating Cost for Construction Equipment," *Cost Engineers Notebook,* C-3.300, American Association of Cost Engineers, Morgantown, W.Va.

*Rental Rate Blue Book for Construction Equipment,* 3 volumes, Dataquest, San Jose, Calif. (Loose-leaf—updated periodically.)

*Rental Rates Compilation for Construction Equipment,* Associated Equipment Distributors, Oak Brook, Ill. (Published annually.)

# CHAPTER 22
# INDOOR-AIR QUALITY (IAQ) AND ANTIPOLLUTION FILTRATION

## GENERAL DISCUSSION

Since the Clean Air Act of 1970 was passed, considerable progress has been made in the improvement of the outdoor ambient-air quality. This leads us to believe that the outdoor air available for ventilation is measurably cleaner. Unfortunately, however, there is still not enough information to prove the case. The National Research Council, for example, has found that virtually no testing has been done on the potential for neurobehavioral damage, birth defects, or toxic effects that might span several generations by passing from parents to offspring caused by the 50,000 industrial chemicals used in the United States. And the scientific meeting held at Wingspread, Wis., in summer 1991 presented fresh evidence that a wide assortment of environmental pollutants, constituting potential danger, were in the air, and called for an investigation to better assess the extent of *subtle* chemical damage to human health. According to an article in *Newsweek,* 2.4 billion pounds of toxins are emitted a year, but this does not include a large source of unmonitored toxins which could, said then Environmental Protection Agency (EPA) spokesperson, Chris Rice, "exceed 4.8 billion pounds annually."

Whether the outdoor ambient-air quality has improved during the last two decades remains a moot question. Nevertheless, during the same period, because of concern over energy conservation, buildings have been made tighter and ventilation rates have been reduced. As a consequence, many new contaminants have been detected or introduced into the indoor environment. Although the Occupational Safety and Health Administration published a signal report on the "sick-building syndrome" in 1984, and the American Society of Heating, Refrigeration and Air Conditioning Engineers (ASHRAE) published its significant Indoor Air Quality Position Paper in August the preceding year, it was not until the EPA released its two-volume, 1,221-page study (Nov. 10, 1988) that it became clear that volatile organic compounds in indoor white-collar workplace environments were as much as 100 times higher than outdoor levels. Finding the critical balance between human health, thermal comfort, and energy conservation—and doing it profitably—has been the goal of responsible leadership ever since.

As buildings become more energy-efficient they become less favorable environmentally; it is easy for energy efficiency control to go cross-purpose to environmental optimization.

Studies have revealed that there are three main sources of indoor-air contamination:

1. *Airborne allergens and pathogens called* bioaerosols: Bioaerosols cause Legionnaires' disease, respiratory infections, Q fever, and varicella that cause the loss of 150 million workdays and $59 billion a year, and allergenic reactions that cause 500,000 hospital emergency

room admissions per year with "house dust asthma." Toxic microbiological aerosols—fibers, combustion particles, and other microorganisms—contribute to the sick-building syndrome.

2. *Formaldehyde and other volatile organic compounds (mainly solvents, e.g., benzene):* Volatile organic compounds cause a variety of ailments, including asthma, severe mucous membrane irritation, menopsychological effects, and malignant disease.

3. *Combustion products:* Tobacco smoke and oxides of nitrogen cause respiratory disease, asthma, general morbidity, severe discomfort, pneumonia, and loss of lung function.

## INCREASED OUTSIDE AIR

The greatest problem has been traced to inadequate outside-air inducement for ventilation needed to offset the buildup of recirculating pollutants in the conditioned space. The logical response has been ASHRAE Standard 62-1989, *Ventilation for Acceptable Indoor Air,* which recommends ventilation rates much higher than those suggested previously. Table 22.1 compares the standard with the earlier standard for both smoking and nonsmoking spaces in several typical applications.

For all applications other than those in smoking areas, the rate has increased but because smoking has generally decreased, with separation between smoking and nonsmoking areas, the ventilation rates for smoking areas have been lowered as shown in Table 22.1. The immediate result of increased outside-air induction has caused an increase in cost as reflected in Table 22.2.[1]

---

[1] Tables 22.2 to 22.5 do not appear on the computer disk provided with this book.

**TABLE 22.1** ASHRAE Recommended Outdoor-Air Ventilating Rates in cfm per Person (Abbreviated Table)

| Application | 1981 Smoking | 1981 Nonsmoking | 1989 |
|---|---|---|---|
| Dining room | 35 | 7 | 20 |
| Office spaces | 20 | 5 | 20 |
| Beauty shops | 35 | 20 | 25 |
| Theater auditoriums | 35 | 7 | 15 |
| Transportation waiting rooms | 35 | 7 | 15 |
| Classrooms | 25 | 5 | 15 |
| Hospital patient rooms | 35 | 7 | 25 |
| Smoking lounges | — | — | 60 |

**TABLE 22.2** Increased Costs Caused by Increased Outside Air

| Item | Amount of increase |
|---|---|
| Central plant capacities, boilers | 10% |
| Central plant capacities, chillers | 20% |
| Annual energy increase, heating | 8% |
| Annual energy increase, cooling | 14% |
| HVAC first-cost increase, approx. | $0.35/ft² |

## SICK-BUILDING SYNDROME (SBS)

"Sick-building syndrome" (SBS) is described as that condition in a building where more than 20% of the occupants complain of headaches, fatigue, eye irritation, sore throat, and nausea. An independent survey conducted by Honeywell's Commercial Buildings Group discovered a number of causes of SBS. As many as 50% of building managers and owners interviewed felt they had "serious" problems of SBS. At the Clima 2000 International Conference held in London in 1993, it was pointed out that of the buildings observed by one firm, 30% were "inadequately ventilated" and only 23% were considered "satisfactory." According to IAQ expert Dr. Wallace Rhodes, 80–95% of the nonindustrial, nonresidential buildings in the United States have some kind of IAQ problem.

## COST OF IAQ REMEDIAL STRATEGY

There is neither a panacea nor a simple solution for IAQ-associated problems. Cross-discipline scientific work remains to be done. Questions need to be answered. Even ASHRAE 15 is under a barrage of questions and interpretations. There is no axiomatic generally recognized standard for acceptable indoor-air quality. Because every building is unique and the problems are often complex (but sometimes simple), no standard or rule of thumb can be applied. The IAQ specialist is a well-trained, experienced professional capable of performing a scientific investigation of an indoor-air environment, taking many air samples, gathering contamination data, and evaluating these data. A detailed report is then drafted with detailed, practical recommendations for remedial action.

The building, and its function in relationship to its occupants and their indoor environment, as well as the design of the HVAC system and its actual performance vis à vis the design, must be carefully appraised by the IAQ team—which must be multidisciplined in the fields of HVAC engineering and microbiology as well as chemistry and industrial hygiene. After a complete, in-depth survey of the building and mechanical systems and the accumulated complaints, an air-sampling test must be performed. The air samples may be analyzed by a professional on the team or sent out to an independent chemist or lab. The final step is a detailed report and a bill of recommendations and proposals to correct the condition(s).

For budget purposes, allow a two-engineer team 28 workhours at $300 per team hour ($8,400) for a complete survey and comprehensive report. This does not include tracking or expenses, nor does it include a complete microbial sampling. For moderate sampling, allow another $8,000 to $10,000. To cost-estimate a complete test for a typical 20-story building, see Table 22.3.

**TABLE 22.3** Indoor Air Quality Sampling and Testing

| |
|---|
| Test consists of |
| 50 microbial samples (yeast, mold, fungi, bacteria) at 25 selected locations |
| 20 carbon dioxide ($CO_2$) samples |
| 10 carbon monoxide (CO) samples |
| 10 nitrogen oxides (NO, $NO_2$) samples |
| 15 formaldehyde (HCHO) samples |
| 10 ozone ($O_3$) samples |
| 20 relative-humidity samples |
| Total cost for test, including all labor, lab work, and report—$15,500 |

**TABLE 22.4** Causes of Unacceptable IAQ

Based on a survey of 30 buildings, table illustrates the percentages of buildings exhibiting SBS and/or building-related illness (BRI) symptoms and the percentages of buildings with various contaminants, causes, and design problems.

| | Symptoms | | | Contaminants | | | | Causes | | | Design | |
|---|---|---|---|---|---|---|---|---|---|---|---|---|
| | SBS | BRI | Both | Temperature | Humidity | Chemical | Biological | Maintenance | Load changes | Energy conservation | System | Equipment |
| | 65 | 35 | 35 | 55 | 30 | 75 | 45 | 75 | 70 | 90 | 100 | 100 |
| **Chemicals** | | | | | | | | | | | | |
| Odors | | | | | | 75 | | | | | | |
| Particulates | | | | | | 5 | | | | | | |
| Other chemicals | | | | | | 5 | | | | | | |
| **Systems** | | | | | | | | | | | | |
| Inadequate outdoor air | | | | | | | | | | | 75 | |
| Inadequate supply air distribution | | | | | | | | | | | 65 | |
| Inadequate return and/or exhaust air | | | | | | | | | | | 70 | |
| Variable-air-volume systems | | | | | | | | | | | 25 | |
| Heat pump system | | | | | | | | | | | 10 | |
| Fan-coil system | | | | | | | | | | | 10 | |
| Induction unit systems | | | | | | | | | | | 5 | |
| **Equipment** | | | | | | | | | | | | |
| Lined ducts | | | | | | | | | | | | 45 |
| Humidifiers | | | | | | | | | | | | 20 |
| Drain pans and lines | | | | | | | | | | | | 60 |
| Inadequate access panels | | | | | | | | | | | | 60 |
| Inadequate filtration | | | | | | | | | | | | 65 |

SOURCE: Rask, Dean, "Indoor Air Quality and the Bottom Line," *Heating/Piping/Air Conditioning*, Sept. 1988, used by permission.

## CORRECTIVE MEASURES

Table 22.4 helps pinpoint some of the symptoms and causes of SBS and unacceptable indoor-air quality. In many cases IAQ problems are easily identified and inexpensively corrected. In other cases they may be quickly discovered but expensive to correct.

The solutions for poor maintenance and housekeeping—dirty-air intakes, clogged filters, scummy drain pans, fouled cooling coils, and contaminated ducts—are axiomatic.

A common problem is imposing new and unacceptable loads on perfectly good systems. Adding occupants, lights, computer terminals, and self-contained air-cooled vending machines, copy machines, and printers to a space and otherwise overloading the system while the air-conditioning system remains unchanged from the original design is a simple problem to identify but may be more difficult to solve—it's a management problem.

Bad design and/or installation, including poor distribution of conditioned air, inadequate outdoor-air intake arrangements, inadequate or malfunctioning controls, undersized equipment, improperly selected or installed (or *factory-shipped*) fans and cooling towers, etc., usually take longer to diagnose but are not very complex; a good test-and-balance technician can sometimes locate wrong-way rotation on a large system fan in five minutes. Leaky fresh-air or return-air ducts can be a lot more time-consuming to find. Leaking fresh-air ducts that deliver only 50% of the called-for outside air are not uncommon; 20 to 30% leakage is an everyday occurrence. Bad design or poor workmanship may require modest retrofit or major replacement.

Other corrective measures may require the addition of humidification and/or dehumidification or replacement and relocation of stats and controls. A good test, adjust, and balance (TAB) procedure could resolve many problems stemming from malfunctioning stats, controls, and dampers as well as outside-air, return-air, exhaust-air, and terminal-air distribution.

Contamination from off-gassing of window sealants, furnishings and wall coverings, book bindings, and even occupants' clothes as well as photomechanical smog caused by copy machines and the like may be very perplexing issues.

One easily diagnosed problem in contaminated buildings is dirt. This condition can be swiftly and inexpensively brought under control by initial cleaning and ongoing maintenance and proper air filtration. Duct cleaning costs for commercial and industrial buildings are unavailable. For residential duct cleaning, see Table 22.5. Coil and drain pan cleaning is not included in this table and depends on whether the section is removed. It was recently reported by one duct cleaning company that the average residential duct system yields 10 to 15 lb of dust, lint, mold, mildew, and "just plain dirt." In labor time, the average duct cleaning company can do three to four residential duct systems per day.

**TABLE 22.5**  Residential Duct Cleaning Service

| Item | Cost, $ |
|---|---|
| Duct vacuum, per outlet | 10–35 |
| Furnace, flue and stack | 35–50 |
| Fireplace and chimney | 50 |
| "De-germing" ductwork | 50 |

## OUTSIDE-AIR AND AIR FILTRATION

Two issues are basic and must receive careful attention: (1) outside air and (2) air filtration of both outside air and recirculating air. An elementary corrective strategy for existing buildings—and a design strategy for new buildings—is to bring the outside air up to ASHRAE

Standard 15. This is much easier talked about than accomplished or enforced, but that discussion is outside the scope of this book. Another critical question beyond the scope of this book is building pressures. Most buildings are designed to maintain 0.02- to 0.03-in. wg; very few operate in that range.

Filters fall into three general categories:

1. *Standard.* These are the least expensive. They are throwaway glass fiber or washable metal mesh. The capture efficiency for these filters is only 3 to 5%. They should be frequently checked and replaced or washed.

2. *Media.* These are capable of microscopic particle removal. They are 25 to 35% efficient and should be changed at least once a year.

3. *Electronic air cleaners.* These are the most complex, most expensive, and most efficient. At 95% capture velocity, they remove minute particles. Operating cost in kilowatts is equal to one 40-W light bulb. The aluminum collection plates can be washed in a laundry tub and reused repeatedly.

HEPA filters are used for special applications. They are 99.999% efficient but will not fit into standard air-handler filter frames. Frames need to be 6 to 12 in. deep.

## Mechanical Filters

Table 22.6 gives average first costs based on 520 fpm for clean high-velocity and 320 fpm for clean low-velocity filters. Workhours given in Table 22.7 include handling and moving up to 40 ft from the equipment, uncrating, and erecting. Table 22.6 gives data on mechanical filters; Table 22.7, on roll filters; and Table 22.8, on medium- and high-efficiency filters. Data on grease filters for kitchen exhaust systems are given in Table 22.9. Data for electrostatically charged exhaust systems are given in Table 22.10. These are not to be confused with electrostatic air-cleaner systems. Throwaway charcoal filters in a variety of sizes are available for replacement in various air-cleaner models and may be selected from Table 22.10.

## Mechanical Air Cleaners

Mechanical air cleaners are available in a range of sizes for both commercial and industrial application. These are fan-driven recirculating air packages that can accommodate a variety of mechanical filters, including charcoal, pleated, bag, and HEPA filters. They are very efficient and may be ceiling-hung, wall-mounted, or freestanding. Table 22.11 gives a typical industrial air cleaner with a 3,000-cfm capacity. Air-pollution control equipment for industrial application is covered in Table 22.12.

## Electronic Air Cleaners

Electrostatic air cleaners may be ceiling-hung, wall-mounted, or self-contained floor models. The residential type is usually plugged into a standard 110/220-V wall or ceiling receptacle. Other models are set in the return air of the air handler. Most residential models are washed manually; the elements are easily removed and washed in a laundry tub or bath tub. Large-type commercial systems have motor-driven automatic traveling washdown features and need to have plumbing connections. Table 22.13 shows prices for residential units and gives costs for commercial systems in a range of 3,000 to 16,000 cfm.

**TABLE 22.6** Mechanical Filters

| Description | Material cost per 1,000 cfm, $ | Workhours per 1,000 cfm |
|---|---|---|
| Low-velocity throwaways, 1–2-in. thick | 2.90 | 0.2 |
| High-velocity cleanable, 1–2-in. thick | 30 | 0.3 |
| High-efficiency, 24 × 24 × 6-in. deep | 80 | 0.6 |
| High-efficiency, 24 × 24 × 12-in. deep | 115 | 0.8 |
| Autoroll | 77 | 2.0 |

Trade prices for individual mechanical filters

| Description | Dollars per each |
|---|---|
| Throwaway replacement type | |
| 1 × 16 × 20 | 1.05 |
| 1 × 16 × 25 | 1.05 |
| 1 × 20 × 20 | 1.05 |
| 1 × 20 × 25 | 1.15 |
| 2 × 16 × 20 | 1.32 |
| 2 × 16 × 25 | 1.32 |
| 2 × 20 × 20 | 1.32 |
| 2 × 20 × 25 | 1.45 |

Trade prices for individual mechanical filters

| Description | Dollars per each |
|---|---|
| Washable aluminum type | |
| 1 × 16 × 20 | 9.45 |
| 1 × 16 × 25 | 10.40 |
| 1 × 20 × 20 | 10.40 |
| 1 × 20 × 25 | 11.00 |
| 2 × 16 × 20 | 13.95 |
| 2 × 16 × 25 | 14.90 |
| 2 × 20 × 20 | 14.90 |
| 2 × 20 × 25 | 17.50 |
| High-velocity washable | |
| 2 × 16 × 20 | 13.50 |
| 2 × 16 × 25 | 15.00 |
| 2 × 20 × 20 | 15.00 |
| 2 × 20 × 25 | 19.70 |
| Rollaway paper media, per roll | |
| 40 × 10 in. | 22.00 |

**TABLE 22.7** Automatic Roll Filter Replacements

Compatible with most models, 2-in. fiber-glass or 1-in. polyester and scrim backing. Length, 65 ft; media velocity, 300 fpm.

| Core width, ft | Material, $ |
|---|---|
| 3 | 75 |
| 4 | 92 |
| 5 | 115 |
| 6 | 130 |

**TABLE 22.8**   High- and Medium-Efficiency Filters

**High-efficiency, 99.97% absolute filters, HEPA**
Microglass media, aluminum separators, $\frac{1}{2}$-in. wood frames with
neoprene sealant and downstream gasket.

| Size, in., H × W × D | Capacity, cfm | Material, $ |
|---|---|---|
| 8 × 8 × 5$\frac{7}{8}$ | 50 | 47 |
| 12 × 12 × 5$\frac{7}{8}$ | 150 | 64 |
| 12 × 24 × 5$\frac{7}{8}$ | 325 | 100 |
| 24 × 24 × 5$\frac{7}{8}$ | 700 | 137 |
| 24 × 30 × 5$\frac{7}{8}$ | 900 | 175 |
| 24 × 36 × 5$\frac{7}{8}$ | 1,075 | 215 |
| 24 × 48 × 5$\frac{7}{8}$ | 1,450 | 255 |
| 24 × 60 × 5$\frac{7}{8}$ | 1,825 | 320 |
| 24 × 72 × 5$\frac{7}{8}$ | 2,200 | 390 |
| 30 × 60 × 5$\frac{7}{8}$ | 2,300 | 405 |
| 30 × 72 × 5$\frac{7}{8}$ | 2,775 | 470 |
| 36 × 72 × 5$\frac{7}{8}$ | 3,375 | 560 |

**Bag filters, borosilicate glass fiber, 95% efficiency**
**Final pressure drop 1-in. wg.**

| Size, in., H × W × D | Capacity, cfm | Material, $ |
|---|---|---|
| 24 × 24 × 36 | 2,500 | 92 |
| 24 × 24 × 29 | 2,000 | 62 |
| 24 × 24 × 21 | 1,500 | 64 |
| 24 × 12 × 36 | 1,250 | 47 |
| 24 × 12 × 29 | 1,000 | 42 |
| 20 × 20 × 22 | 800 | 46 |
| 24 × 12 × 21 | 750 | 35 |
| 24 × 12 × 18 | 500 | 30 |

**Cartridge filters, medium efficiency, 35%**
Double-ply polyester fiber medium. Does not include holding hardware.

| Size, in., | Capacity | Material, $ |
|---|---|---|

**TABLE 22.6**  Mechanical Filters

| Description | Material cost per 1,000 cfm, $ | Workhours per 1,000 cfm |
|---|---|---|
| Low-velocity throwaways, 1–2-in. thick | 2.90 | 0.2 |
| High-velocity cleanable, 1–2-in. thick | 30 | 0.3 |
| High-efficiency, 24 × 24 × 6-in. deep | 80 | 0.6 |
| High-efficiency, 24 × 24 × 12-in. deep | 115 | 0.8 |
| Autoroll | 77 | 2.0 |

Trade prices for individual mechanical filters

| Description | Dollars per each |
|---|---|
| Throwaway replacement type | |
| 1 × 16 × 20 | 1.05 |
| 1 × 16 × 25 | 1.05 |
| 1 × 20 × 20 | 1.05 |
| 1 × 20 × 25 | 1.15 |
| 2 × 16 × 20 | 1.32 |
| 2 × 16 × 25 | 1.32 |
| 2 × 20 × 20 | 1.32 |
| 2 × 20 × 25 | 1.45 |

Trade prices for individual mechanical filters

| Description | Dollars per each |
|---|---|
| Washable aluminum type | |
| 1 × 16 × 20 | 9.45 |
| 1 × 16 × 25 | 10.40 |
| 1 × 20 × 20 | 10.40 |
| 1 × 20 × 25 | 11.00 |
| 2 × 16 × 20 | 13.95 |
| 2 × 16 × 25 | 14.90 |
| 2 × 20 × 20 | 14.90 |
| 2 × 20 × 25 | 17.50 |
| High-velocity washable | |
| 2 × 16 × 20 | 13.50 |
| 2 × 16 × 25 | 15.00 |
| 2 × 20 × 20 | 15.00 |
| 2 × 20 × 25 | 19.70 |
| Rollaway paper media, per roll | |
| 40 × 10 in. | 22.00 |

**TABLE 22.7**  Automatic Roll Filter Replacements

Compatible with most models, 2-in. fiber-glass or 1-in. polyester and scrim backing. Length, 65 ft; media velocity, 300 fpm.

| Core width, ft | Material, $ |
|---|---|
| 3 | 75 |
| 4 | 92 |
| 5 | 115 |
| 6 | 130 |

**TABLE 22.8**    High- and Medium-Efficiency Filters

**High-efficiency, 99.97% absolute filters, HEPA**
Microglass media, aluminum separators, $\frac{1}{2}$-in. wood frames with
neoprene sealant and downstream gasket.

| Size, in., H × W × D | Capacity, cfm | Material, $ |
|---|---|---|
| 8 × 8 × 5⅞ | 50 | 17 |
| 12 × 12 × 5⅞ | 150 | 64 |
| 12 × 24 × 5⅞ | 325 | 100 |
| 24 × 24 × 5⅞ | 700 | 137 |
| 24 × 30 × 5⅞ | 900 | 175 |
| 24 × 36 × 5⅞ | 1,075 | 215 |
| 24 × 48 × 5⅞ | 1,450 | 255 |
| 24 × 60 × 5⅞ | 1,825 | 320 |
| 24 × 72 × 5⅞ | 2,200 | 390 |
| 30 × 60 × 5⅞ | 2,300 | 405 |
| 30 × 72 × 5⅞ | 2,775 | 470 |
| 36 × 72 × 5⅞ | 3,375 | 560 |

**Bag filters, borosilicate glass fiber, 95% efficiency**
**Final pressure drop 1-in. wg.**

| Size, in., H × W × D | Capacity, cfm | Material, $ |
|---|---|---|
| 24 × 24 × 36 | 2,500 | 92 |
| 24 × 24 × 29 | 2,000 | 62 |
| 24 × 24 × 21 | 1,500 | 64 |
| 24 × 12 × 36 | 1,250 | 47 |
| 24 × 12 × 29 | 1,000 | 42 |
| 20 × 20 × 22 | 800 | 46 |
| 24 × 12 × 21 | 750 | 35 |
| 24 × 12 × 18 | 500 | 30 |

**Cartridge filters, medium efficiency, 35%**
Double-ply polyester fiber medium. Does not include holding hardware.

| Size, in., H × W × D | Capacity, cfm | Material, $ |
|---|---|---|
| 16 × 20 × 9 | 800 | 21 |
| 20 × 20 × 9 | 1,000 | 21 |
| 16 × 25 × 9 | 1,050 | 21 |
| 20 × 24 × 9 | 1,200 | 21 |
| 20 × 25 × 9 | 1,225 | 21 |
| 24 × 24 × 9 | 1,500 | 25 |
| 20 × 24 × 15 | 2,000 | 32 |
| 24 × 24 × 15 | 2,500 | 37 |

**TABLE 22.9**  Grease Filters

Commercial kitchens, restaurants, etc. Material cost in dollars.

| Frame size, in. | Heavy-duty steel mesh galvanized | Aluminum mesh | Baffle-type* aluminum | Baffle-type* stainless | Erection, workhours |
|---|---|---|---|---|---|
| 16 × 20 × 1 | 23 | 7 | — | — | 0.2 |
| 16 × 25 × 1 | 27 | 9 | — | — | 0.2 |
| 20 × 20 × 1 | 27 | 9 | — | — | 0.2 |
| 20 × 25 × 1 | 31 | 9 | — | — | 0.2 |
| 16 × 20 × 2 | 35 | 11 | 25 | 67 | 0.7 |
| 16 × 25 × 2 | 39 | 14 | 28 | 81 | 0.7 |
| 20 × 20 × 2 | 39 | 14 | 28 | 81 | 0.7 |
| 20 × 25 × 2 | 41 | 16 | 32 | 88 | 0.7 |

*Add $2 per each for bail handles and $10 per each for lock handles. Labor shown for 2-in. filters includes bolting together in V bank.

**TABLE 22.10**  Washable and Throwaway Filters

**Electrostatic Charged, Washable Filters**

Replaces standard filters—no electrical hookup. Nonallergic media up to 500 fpm. Resistance at 1-in. thick, 0.18 wg; 2-in. thick, 0.26 wg—clean filter.

| Nominal size, in. | Cost, $ per 1-in. thickness | Cost, $ per 2-in. thickness |
|---|---|---|
| 16 × 20 | 38 | 44 |
| 16 × 25 | 40 | 47 |
| 20 × 20 | 40 | 46 |
| 20 × 25 | 45 | 55 |
| 24 × 24 | 53 | 61 |
| 25 × 25 | 55 | 80 |

**Charcoal replacement filters**

For ceiling-mounted, wall-mounted, or freestanding air cleaners.

| Dimension, in., H × W × D | Weight, lb | Cost, $ |
|---|---|---|
| 18 × 16 × ¾ | 2 | 42 |
| 20 × 20 × ¾ | 4 | 48 |

**TABLE 22.11**  Industrial Air Cleaners

For use in vocational schools, woodworking areas, printing shops, and general ventilation. Includes 95% bag-type primary filter and pleated, microglass prefilter. With forward-curved squirrel-cage blower, adjustable pulley 2-hp motor. Heavy-duty, ceiling- or platform-mounted. Covers 17,000-cu-ft area, 208/230/460-V, three-phase.

| Airflow, cfm | Size, in., L × W × H | Weight, lb | Cost, $ |
|---|---|---|---|
| 3,000 | 88 × 25½ × 26 | 325 | 2,200 |

**TABLE 22.12** Air-Pollution Control Equipment

Does not include fans, pumps, electrical connections, hoods, or ductwork.

| Description | 5,000 cfm, $ | Erection workhours | 10,000 cfm, $ | Erection workhours | 20,000 cfm, $ | Erection workhours |
|---|---|---|---|---|---|---|
| Bag house, mechanical shaker | 16,500 | 40 | 27,500 | 55 | 38,800 | 65 |
| Wet scrubber | 15,100 | 35 | 20,600 | 45 | 35,600 | 55 |
| Electrostatic precipitator, high-voltage | 10,300 | 15 | 18,600 | 25 | 31,600 | 35 |
| Bag house, pneumatic | 13,400 | 35 | 17,200 | 50 | 27,500 | 57 |
| Centrifugal cyclone | 8,100 | 20 | 12,500 | 25 | 23,800 | 30 |

| Description | 30,000 cfm, $ | Erection workhours | 40,000 cfm, $ | Erection workhours |
|---|---|---|---|---|
| Bag house, mechanical shaker | 56,300 | 75 | 73,800 | 85 |
| Wet scrubber | 51,600 | 60 | 63,300 | 70 |
| Electrostatic precipitator, high-voltage | 45,300 | 48 | 59,400 | 60 |
| Bag house, pneumatic | 38,400 | 67 | 49,700 | 75 |
| Centrifugal cyclone | 30,900 | 35 | 39,200 | 45 |

**TABLE 22.13** Electronic Air Cleaners

**Residential, furnace, and duct-mounted**

High-efficiency, 5-in.-deep collecting plates, twin prefilters, automatic disconnect. Calls manually removable for hand washdown, 95% efficiency; must be hard-wired; 120 V.

| Range, cfm | Duct size, in. | Cost, $ |
|---|---|---|
| 600–1,200 | 14 × 18 | 360 |
| 1,000–1,600 | 14 × 24 | 425 |
| 1,600–2,200 | 18 × 24 | 475 |

**Commercial type**

Freestanding, wet-wash system. Does not include wiring or plumbing; ¾-in. IPS water inlet and 2-in. drain connection. Allow 8 workhours per average unit for erection.

| Range, cfm | Cooling, tons | Heating, MBh | Material, $ |
|---|---|---|---|
| 3,000 | 7.5 | 300 | 2,340 |
| 4,000 | 10 | 400 | 2,470 |
| 5,000 | 12.5 | 500 | 2,730 |
| 6,000 | 15 | 600 | 3,120 |
| 7,000 | 17.5 | 700 | 3,450 |
| 8,000 | 20 | 800 | 4,000 |
| 9,000 | 22.5 | 900 | 4,260 |
| 11,000 | 25 | 1,000 | 4,880 |
| 12,000 | 30 | 1,200 | 5,980 |
| 14,000 | 35 | 1,400 | 6,960 |
| 16,000 | 40 | 1,600 | 7,570 |

## Activated Charcoal

Activated charcoal has been in use for decades. It is a powerful odor remover and operates by filtering the air through charcoal pellets. In this regard it has been used to conserve outside air long before the energy crisis of the 1970s. Where the odor is faint, 45 lb of activated charcoal will treat 1,000 cfm of circulating air. As the odor index increases, the weight of the charcoal must be increased. Recovery elements are available in cells, panels, and canisters of varying weights and are placed on the downstream side of the filtering device. The more compact the element, the greater the part of conversion to fresh air and the greater the resistance in the airstream. It is because of this resistance that the cost of arranging the elements in the airstream must be considered, too. For most jobs, activated charcoal may be estimated at $7.00/lb plus $5.40/lb to cover the cost of framing. Reactivation costs run about $3.50.

Table 22.14 is a rule-of-thumb selection chart to help determine the pounds of charcoal required for air treatment in lieu of outside air.

**TABLE 22.14**   Odor Index

| Application | Odor index | Space treated with 1 lb charcoal, cu ft |
|---|---|---|
| Churches | Faint | 1,000–3,000 |
| Residences | Faint | 1,000–3,000 |
| Public buildings | Light | 500–1,000 |
| Hotels | Light | 500–1,000 |
| Department stores | Light | 500–1,000 |
| Offices, general | Light | 500–1,000 |
| Restaurants | Medium | 300–900 |
| Theatres | Medium | 300–900 |
| Offices, private | Heavy | 100–500 |
| Bars and taverns | Heavy | 100–500 |
| Hospitals | Heavy | 100–500 |
| Laboratories | Saturated | 50–400 |

## RECOMMENDED READING

ASHRAE Standard 62-1989, *Ventilation for Acceptable Indoor Air.*

ASHRAE Standard 52.1 1992, *Gravimetric and Dust-Spot Procedures for Testing Air-Cleaning Devices Used in General Ventilation for Removing Particulate Matter.*

ASHRAE Standard 111-1988, *Practices for Measurement, Testing, Adjusting and Balancing of Building Heating, Ventilation, Air-Conditioning and Refrigeration Systems.*

ASHRAE Standard 113-1990, *Method of Testing for Room Air Diffusion.*

*Building Air Quality: A Guide for Building Owners and Facility Managers,* Superintendent of Documents, Washington, D.C.

Burge, H. A., and M. Hodgson, "Health Risks of Indoor Pollutants," *ASHRAE Journal,* July 1988.

Gladstone, J., "Sick Building Syndrome and the Florida Energy Code," *Florida Contractor,* Oct. 1989 (part 1), Nov. 1989 (part 2).

*IAQ 80: Engineering Solutions to Indoor Air Problems,* ASHRAE conference proceedings, Atlanta, Ga., April 1988.

*Indoor Air Pollution News,* Bureau of National Affairs, Inc. (published biweekly), Washington, D.C.

*Indoor Air Quality,* 1991 ASHRAE Annual Meeting papers.

*SMACNA Indoor Air Quality Manual,* 2d ed., 1993.

# CHAPTER 23
# MISCELLANEOUS CONSTRUCTION

Occasionally—on existing construction—the mechanical contractor is the prime contractor, and such items as lathing, furring, doors, and partitions become part of the contract. It is sometimes difficult and often slow to collect bids from subcontractors when only small areas are affected.

The cost figures given in Table 23.1 are reliable for the average job affecting small areas; they are total in-place dollar figures including labor and material at average value.

Table 23.2 provides cost figures for various demolition activities. When repairs and renovations must be done, the total cost is the demolition cost plus the cost of any new installation or construction.

**TABLE 23.1** Miscellaneous Construction Costs

| Item | Unit | In-place costs, $ |
|---|---|---|
| Gypsum plaster, wall or ceiling | sq ft | 2.00 |
| Ceiling tiles: | | |
|   Stapled to furring 12 × 12 × ½ in. | sq ft | 0.90 |
|   Stapled to furring 12 × 12 × ¾ in., plastic-coated | sq ft | 1.40 |
|   Add to above for furring, 1 × 2 in. strips wood | sq ft | 1.33 |
|   T-bar suspension system | sq ft | 1.15 |
|   Ceiling panels 2 × 4 × ¾ in. | sq ft | 1.05 |
|   Add to above for 2-hr fire rating | sq ft | 0.20 |
| Concrete floor with mesh, 6 in. thick, trowel finish slab on grade | sq ft | 2.50 |
| Cutting holes in walls and floors: | | |
|   6 in. round drilled up to 8 in. thick | Each | 48 |
|   12 in. round drilled up to 8 in. thick | Each | 100 |
|   Add 50% to above for 8 to 12 in. thick | | |
| Doors, including hinges, lock, and metal frame: | | |
|   Exterior metal: | | |
|     2'8" × 6'8" flush, 18 Ga. | Each | 615 |
|     3'0" × 6'8" flush, 18 Ga. | Each | 645 |
|   Louvered, wood: | | |
|     2'8" × 6'8", residential | Each | 390 |
|     3'0" × 6'8", residential | Each | 415 |
|   Metal-clad 3-hr fire rated including track and hangers: | | |
|     7 × 7 ft industrial sliding | Each | 1,800 |
|     Steel frame for 7 × 7 ft door | Each | 570 |
|     10 × 12 ft | Each | 4,700 |
|     Steel frame for 10 × 12 ft door | Each | 840 |
|   Rolling service door, including frame—manual operation: | | |
|     8 × 8 ft | Each | 1,200 |
|     10 × 10 ft | Each | 1,400 |
| Electrical: | | |
|   Two-lamp industrial fluorescent strip fixture 1' wide × 4' length | Each | 115 |
|   60 ft conduit and wire | Each | 145 |
|   100 ft conduit and wire | Each | 240 |
|   Switch or outlet | Each | 30 |
|   (Assumes add-on to existing circuit or panel) | | |
| Equipment pads—concrete 6 in. thick | sq ft | 3.25 |
| Floor tile—vinyl composition 3/32" | sq ft | 1.50 |
| Hatchways: | | |
|   Access to attic including folding stairs | Each | 270 |
|   Access to roof 2'6" × 3'0" watertight | Each | 475 |
|   Metal ladder | lin ft | 80 |
| Insulation: | | |
|   Building—fiberglass blanket: | | |
|     R-11 | sq ft | 0.50 |
|     R-19 | sq ft | 0.60 |
| Painting: | | |
|   Concrete and concrete block | sq ft | 0.68 |
|   Drywall, including preparation | sq ft | 0.60 |
|   Wood | sq ft | 0.73 |

**TABLE 23.1**   Miscellaneous Construction Costs  (*Continued*)

| Item | Unit | In-place costs, $ |
|---|---|---|
| **Partitions:** | | |
| Concrete block, ground face, lightweight: | | |
| 4-in. | sq ft | 7.50 |
| 6-in. | sq ft | 8.00 |
| 8-in. | sq ft | 9.50 |
| 12-in. | sq ft | 12.00 |
| Reinforcement | lin ft | 0.30 |
| Drywall, 10' high, ⅝" drywall both sides: | | |
| 3⅝-in. metal studs, 20 ga, 16-in. centers | sq ft | 3.00 |
| Load bearing add | sq ft | 4.00 |
| **Roofing:** | | |
| Repairs: | | |
| 10 sq ft or less | sq ft | 5.00 |
| 20 sq ft | sq ft | 4.75 |
| 50 sq ft | sq ft | 4.50 |
| Over 100 sq ft | sq ft | 4.00 |
| Insulation | sq ft | .70 |
| Pitch pockets | Each | 100 |
| Roof deck, corrugated metal, galvanized 24 ga. | sq ft | 2.50 |
| Steel supports, see Table 17.5 | | |
| **Windows:** | | |
| Industrial security sash | sq ft | 32 |
| Fixed industrial sash | sq ft | 26 |

**TABLE 23.2**   Demolition Costs

| Item | Unit | Cost, $ |
|---|---|---|
| Ceiling demolition | | |
| Drywall, on wood frame | sq ft | 0.38 |
| Drywall, on metal frame | sq ft | 0.40 |
| Drywall, on suspension system, including system | sq ft | 0.42 |
| Gypsum plaster, on gypsum lath | sq ft | 0.42 |
| Gypsum plaster, on metal lath | sq ft | 0.61 |
| Suspended ceiling, mineral fiber, 2 × 2 ft or 2 × 4 ft | sq ft | 0.20 |
| Suspended ceiling, on suspension system, including system | sq ft | 0.25 |
| Tile, wood fiber, 12 × 12 in. glued | sq ft | 0.34 |
| Tile, wood fiber, stapled | sq ft | 0.20 |
| Tile, wood fiber, on suspension system, including system | sq ft | 0.40 |
| Electrical demolition | | |
| Conduit to 15 ft high, including fittings and hangers—Rigid galvanized steel: | | |
| $\frac{1}{2}$–1 in. diameter | lin ft | 0.91 |
| $1\frac{1}{4}$–2 in. diameter | lin ft | 1.10 |
| 2–4 in. diameter | lin ft | 1.46 |
| Electric metallic tubing | | |
| $\frac{1}{2}$–1 in. | lin ft | 0.56 |
| $1\frac{1}{4}$–$1\frac{1}{2}$ in. | lin ft | 0.67 |
| 2–3 in. | lin ft | 0.93 |
| Wiremold raceway, including fittings and hangers | | |
| No. 3000 | lin ft | 0.88 |
| No. 4000 | lin ft | 1.01 |
| Channels, steel, including fittings and hangers | | |
| $\frac{3}{4}$ × $1\frac{1}{2}$ in. | lin ft | 0.71 |
| $1\frac{1}{2}$ × $1\frac{1}{2}$ in. | lin ft | 0.82 |
| Safety switches, 250 or 600 V, including disconnection of wire and pipe terminations | | |
| 30 A | ea | 17.90 |
| 60 A | ea | 25 |
| 100 A | ea | 30 |
| 200 A | ea | 44 |
| Pull boxes and cabinets, sheet metal, including removal of supports and pipe terminations | | |
| 6 × 6 × 4 in. | ea | 7.05 |
| 12 × 12 × 4 in. | ea | 9.45 |
| Junction boxes, 4 in., square and octagonal | ea | 2.75 |
| Handy box | ea | 2.06 |
| Switch box | ea | 2.06 |
| Receptacle and switch plates | ea | 0.86 |
| Wire, THW-THWN-THHN, removed from in-place conduit, ≤15 ft high | | |
| No. 14 | 100 lin ft | 3.38 |
| No. 12 | 100 lin ft | 4.00 |
| No. 10 | 100 lin ft | 4.84 |
| No. 4 | 100 lin ft | 8.30 |
| No. 3 | 100 lin ft | 8.80 |
| No. 1/0 | 100 lin ft | 13.25 |
| No. 2/0 | 100 lin ft | 15.05 |
| No. 3/0 | 100 lin ft | 17.60 |
| No. 400 MCM | 100 lin ft | 26 |
| No. 500 MCM | 100 lin ft | 27 |

**TABLE 23.2**   Demolition Costs  (*Continued*)

| Item | Unit | Cost, $ |
|---|---|---|
| Interior fluorescent fixtures, including supports and whips, ≤15 ft high | | |
| Recessed drop-in 2 × 2 ft, 2 lamps | ea | 12.55 |
| 2 × 4 ft, 2 lamps | ea | 13.35 |
| 2 × 4 ft, 4 lamps | ea | 14.65 |
| 4 × 4 ft, 4 lamps | ea | 22 |
| Surface mount, acrylic lens and hinged frame | | |
| 1 × 4 ft, 2 lamps | ea | 10 |
| 2 × 2 ft, 2 lamps | ea | 10 |
| 2 × 4 ft, 4 lamps | ea | 13.35 |
| 4 × 4 ft, 4 lamps | ea | 19.15 |
| Strip fixtures, surface mount | | |
| 4 ft long, 1 lamp | ea | 8.30 |
| 4 ft long, 2 lamps | ea | 8.80 |
| 8 ft long, 1 lamp | ea | 10.50 |
| 8 ft long, 2 lamps | ea | 11 |
| Flooring demolition | | |
| Brick with mortar | sq ft | 0.70 |
| Carpet, bonded, including surface scraping | sq ft | 0.15 |
| Tackless | sq ft | 0.03 |
| Composition, acrylic or epoxy | sq ft | 1.05 |
| Resilient, sheet goods (linoleum) | sq ft | 0.22 |
| Tile, 12 × 12 in. | sq ft | 0.30 |
| HVAC demolition | | |
| Air conditioner | | |
| Split unit, 3 tons | ea | 204 |
| Package unit, 3 tons | ea | 211 |
| Boiler, electric; | ea | 315 |
| Gas or oil, steel        <150 MBh | ea | 211 |
| Gas or oil, steel        >150 MBh | ea | 315 |
| Ductwork | | |
| 4 in. high, 8 in. wide | lin ft | 0.76 |
| 10 in. wide | lin ft | 0.80 |
| 14 in. wide | lin ft | 0.84 |
| 6 in. high, 8 in. wide | lin ft | 0.92 |
| 12 in. wide | lin ft | 1.01 |
| 18 in. wide | lin ft | 1.13 |
| 10 in. high, 12 in. wide | lin ft | 1.22 |
| 18 in. wide | lin ft | 1.32 |
| 24 in. wide | lin ft | 1.38 |
| 12 in. high, 18 in. wide | lin ft | 1.79 |
| 24 in. wide | lin ft | 2.03 |
| 48 in. wide | lin ft | 2.14 |
| 18 in. high, 24 in. wide | lin ft | 2.27 |
| 36 in. wide | lin ft | 2.41 |
| 48 in. wide | lin ft | 2.58 |
| 30 in. high, 36 in. wide | lin ft | 2.71 |
| 48 in. wide | lin ft | 2.87 |
| 72 in. wide | lin ft | 3.04 |
| Duct heater, electric strip | ea | 27.50 |

(*Continued*)

**TABLE 23.2** Demolition Costs (*Continued*)

| Item | Unit | Cost, $ |
|---|---|---|
| Furnace, electric | ea | 252 |
| Gas or oil | | |
| <120 MBh | ea | 98.50 |
| >120 MBh | ea | 131 |
| Heat pump | | |
| Package unit, 3 tons | ea | 170 |
| Split unit, 3 tons | ea | 204 |
| Mechanical equipment | | |
| Light items | ton | 455 |
| Heavy items | ton | 370 |
| Plumbing demolition | | |
| Piping, metal | | |
| ≤2 in. diameter | lin ft | 1.13 |
| ≤4 in. diameter | lin ft | 1.51 |
| ≤8 in. diameter | lin ft | 4.53 |
| ≤16 in. diameter | lin ft | 7.55 |
| Walls and partitions demolition | | |
| Brick, 4–12 in. thick | cu ft | 4.20 |
| Concrete block | | |
| 4 in. thick | sq ft | 0.93 |
| 8 in. thick | sq ft | 1.14 |
| Drywall | | |
| Nailed | sq ft | 0.15 |
| Glued and nailed | sq ft | 0.17 |
| Fiberboard | | |
| Nailed | sq ft | 0.17 |
| Glued and nailed | sq ft | 0.19 |
| Metal or wood studs, finish 2 sides | | |
| Fiberboard | sq ft | 0.91 |
| Lath and plaster | sq ft | 1.82 |
| Plasterboard (drywall) | sq ft | 0.09 |
| Plywood | sq ft | 1.05 |
| Plaster, gypsum or perlite | | |
| On gypsum lath | sq ft | 0.37 |
| On metal lath | sq ft | 0.51 |

SOURCE: *Means Repair & Remodeling Cost Data*, R. S. Means Co., Kingston, Mass., 1994.

# CHAPTER 24
# FIRE-CONTROL AND -ALARM SYSTEMS[1]

## GENERAL DISCUSSION

Fire-control systems include automatic sprinkler and other automatic and manual fire-suppression systems. Fire-alarm systems do not provide fire control but are fire-detection and signaling systems intended to provide early warning to aid evacuation and fire department response. Some specialized fire-control systems (such as preaction and deluge sprinkler systems) utilize fire-detection systems as an initiating means. The types of fire-protection systems and the national installation standards [published by the National Fire Protection Association (NFPA)] controlling their use are given in Table 24.1.[2]

Building codes generally specify the type of fire-protection systems required. Standpipe systems are required for large buildings that require internal firefighting capacity. Codes also commonly specify automatic sprinkler systems for high-rise buildings, large mercantiles, public assemblies, and other buildings considered hazardous to building occupants or firefighters. In a growing number of communities, automatic sprinkler systems are required in virtually all new construction, including single-family dwellings. Likewise, requirements for

---

[1] By Russell P. Fleming, PE, Vice President of Engineering, National Fire Sprinkler Association.

[2] Tables 24.1, 24.2, and 24.4 do not appear on the computer disk provided with this book.

**TABLE 24.1**  Fire-Control and -Alarm Systems

| System | Agent | NFPA Standard |
|---|---|---|
| Standpipe | Water | 14 |
| Automatic sprinkler | Water | 13 |
| Residential sprinkler | Water | 13D or 13R |
| Water spray | Water | 15 |
| Foam-water sprinkler | Water and foam additive | 16 or 16A |
| Carbon dioxide | $CO_2$ | 12 |
| Halon | Halon | 12A |
| Dry chemical | Chemical | 17 |
| Wet chemical | Chemical | 17A |
| Alarm and detection | None | 72 |

alarm and detection systems are commonplace in building codes. Water spray, foam-water, carbon dioxide, and dry and wet chemical systems are generally used for protection against special hazards or portions of occupancies where water would not be considered the most effective extinguishing agent. Like automatic sprinkler systems, these systems are often installed for insurance reduction purposes. Because of its adverse effects on ozone levels in the atmosphere, halon is being phased out as a fire-control agent.

This chapter addresses the two most common types of fire-control systems—sprinkler and standpipe systems—as well as alarm and detection systems.

The cost of sprinkler systems varies considerably with type, size (the basic valve costs are the same for a 1,000-sq-ft system as for a 50,000-sq-ft system), and water-supply requirements. The latter depend on the hazard classification of the protected occupancy as shown in Table 24.2. This table also includes standpipe system water-supply requirements. Where standpipes and sprinklers are fed from a common riser in a fully sprinklered building, the water supply is sized to meet the larger of the two demands. This is generally the standpipe demand. If the building is only partially sprinklered, part or all of the sprinkler demand must be added to the standpipe demand.

**TABLE 24.2**  Sprinkler Water-Supply Requirements According to Hazard Classification and Standpipe Water-Supply Requirements According to Class of Service

| Hazard classification | Examples | Typical minimum water supply | | |
| --- | --- | --- | --- | --- |
| | | Volume requirements, gpm | Flowing pressure requirements, psi | Duration, min |
| Dwelling (13D) | One- and two-family, manu-factured homes | 13–50 | 10–30 | 7–10 |
| Residential to 4-story (13R) | Apartments, motels, and dormitories | 50–100 | 10–30 plus 4 per story | 30 |
| Light | Offices, hotels, schools, nurs-ing homes, and auditoriums | 150–250 plus 100 for hose streams | 15 plus 5 per story | 30–60 |
| Ordinary | Factories, storage areas, and mercantiles | 300–900 plus 250 for hose streams | 20 plus 5 per story | 60–90 |
| Extra | Paint shops, refineries, and chemical works | 1,000–1,500 plus 500 for hose streams | 25 plus 5 per story | 90–120 |
| Class I or III standpipe systems (all hazards) | Fire department use ($2\frac{1}{2}$-in. outlets) | 500 for first standpipe plus 250 for each additional to maximum of 1,250* | 100 plus 5 per story† | 30 |
| Class II stand-pipe systems (all hazards) | Occupant use ($1\frac{1}{2}$-in. outlets) | 100 gpm | 65 plus 5 per story | 30 |

*In fully sprinklered buildings, maximum is 1,000 gpm.

†For fully sprinklered buildings, some codes permit standpipe systems to be maintained at sprinkler system pressures, with higher pressures supplied by arriving fire department personnel through the fire department connection.

Often the water-supply requirements can be met by the available municipal supply, resulting in considerably lower costs than when on-site supplies are required. On-site supplies include elevated tanks, pressure tanks, or fire pumps taking suction from ground storage tanks or open reservoirs. Building codes sometimes require secondary on-site water supplies for high-rise buildings, although these secondary supplies can often be smaller than the primary supplies. When the public supply can provide sufficient quantity to meet system water demand, but not at sufficient pressure, a fire pump is used as a booster pump to increase the supply pressure. This is frequently the case when standpipe systems are required because of their high pressure demands. Traditionally, NFPA 14 has required that the minimum flow at the highest outlet on fire department standpipes be available at a minimum pressure of 65 psi. In 1992 NFPA 14 was revised to require a minimum pressure at the highest fire department outlet of 100 psi.

Where comparison of Table 24.2 to public supply pressures indicates that additional water supplies will be needed, Chaps. 7 and 8 should be consulted. Pumps used for fire-control systems must be listed for fire service. This means that they must meet particular requirements established by product testing organizations, most typically Underwriters Laboratories or the Factory Mutual Research Corporation. Because of these special requirements, costs of fire pumps are approximately 10 to 15% higher than those of similar pumps intended for general use. Horizontal centrifugal or vertical turbine pumps are most commonly used. Pump control equipment for fire service costs approximately twice as much as pump control equipment for general use, except for the limited service fire pump controllers allowed for pumps up to 30 hp. In some cases, control equipment can represent up to two-thirds of the cost of a fire pump installation. A competent fire-protection engineer can evaluate available water supplies to determine their suitability.

## ESTIMATING

Standpipe systems are classified by type of service (fire department or brigade vs. building occupant) as well as water-supply arrangement (wet vs. dry types). For large jobs and those using prefabrications, the costs will run 15 to 25% less than those determined from Tables 24.3 and 24.4.

**TABLE 24.3**  Wet Standpipes

Wet standpipes are those in which the piping is normally filled with water and which are provided with an automatic water supply capable of serving fire hose streams. The number of standpipes is traditionally based on the need to reach all floor areas with 100 ft of hose and a 30-ft stream trajectory.

| Class of of service | Size, in. | Single floor (10 ft), $ | | | Additional floors, each, $ | | |
|---|---|---|---|---|---|---|---|
| | | Material | Install | Total | Material | Install | Total |
| I | 4 | 1,825 | 1,800 | 3,625 | 545 | 565 | 1,110 |
| | 6 | 3,025 | 3,125 | 6,150 | 865 | 885 | 1,750 |
| | 8 | 4,400 | 3,750 | 8,150 | 1,150 | 1,075 | 2,225 |
| II | 2 | 650 | 630 | 1,280 | 252 | 247 | 499 |
| | 2.5 | 935 | 930 | 1,865 | 291 | 287 | 578 |
| III | 4 | 1,875 | 1,800 | 3,675 | 460 | 475 | 935 |
| | 6 | 3,075 | 3,125 | 6,200 | 895 | 885 | 1,780 |
| | 8 | 4,450 | 3,750 | 8,200 | 1,175 | 1,075 | 2,250 |

*For Class II and Class III systems, add $240 (steel), $346 (aluminum), or $451 (stainless steel) per standpipe per floor for hose rack assembly, valve, and 100 ft of 1½-in. hose in cabinet for occupant use. For a fully sprinklered building, codes generally permit elimination of hose rack assembly and hose for Class III service.

**TABLE 24.4** Type of Standpipe Adjustment Factor

| Class | Type | Single-floor adjustment factor |
|---|---|---|
| I | Wet | 1.00 |
| | Dry with filling by opening hose valve | 1.20 |
| | Dry with filling by remote control device at hose station | 1.20 |
| | Dry with no automatic water supply (may be filled with water at some lower pressure) | 0.75 |
| II | Same as Class I<br>Note: Dry type with no automatic water supply not permitted | |
| III | Same as Class I | |

**TABLE 24.5** Wet-Pipe Sprinkler Systems

Wet-pipe systems are the most common and economical type of sprinkler system. The system is pressurized with water, which is discharged only from those sprinklers which are individually actuated by heat from a fire.

| Area, sq ft | Light hazard, cost per square foot, $ | | | Ordinary hazard, cost per square foot, $ | | | Extra hazard, cost per square foot, $ | | |
|---|---|---|---|---|---|---|---|---|---|
| | Matl. | Inst. | Total | Matl. | Inst. | Total | Matl. | Inst. | Total |
| Schedule 40 steel pipe; threaded | | | | | | | | | |
| One floor: | | | | | | | | | |
| 2,000 | 1.37 | 1.66 | 3.03 | 1.40 | 1.75 | 3.15 | 1.53 | 2.31 | 3.84 |
| 5,000 | 0.70 | 1.16 | 1.86 | 0.77 | 1.25 | 2.02 | 1.13 | 2.05 | 3.18 |
| 10,000 | 0.49 | 1.00 | 1.49 | 0.63 | 1.32 | 1.95 | 1.04 | 1.92 | 2.96 |
| 50,000 | 0.41 | 0.88 | 1.29 | 0.60 | 1.28 | 1.88 | 1.11 | 1.84 | 2.95 |
| Each additional floor: | | | | | | | | | |
| 2,000 | 0.43 | 1.13 | 1.56 | 0.48 | 1.24 | 1.72 | 0.65 | 1.81 | 2.46 |
| 5,000 | 0.33 | 0.96 | 1.29 | 0.50 | 1.18 | 1.68 | 0.56 | 1.60 | 2.16 |
| 10,000 | 0.31 | 0.90 | 1.21 | 0.45 | 1.22 | 1.67 | 0.65 | 1.44 | 2.09 |
| 50,000 | 0.37 | 0.85 | 1.22 | 0.44 | 1.11 | 1.55 | 0.64 | 1.37 | 2.01 |
| Schedule 10 steel pipe; grooved fittings | | | | | | | | | |
| One floor: | | | | | | | | | |
| 2,000 | 1.28 | 1.43 | 2.71 | 1.32 | 1.49 | 2.81 | 1.47 | 1.94 | 3.41 |
| 10,000 | 0.44 | 0.85 | 1.29 | 0.53 | 1.08 | 1.61 | 0.73 | 1.42 | 2.15 |
| Each additional floor: | | | | | | | | | |
| 2,000 | 0.36 | 0.92 | 1.28 | 0.40 | 0.98 | 1.38 | 0.60 | 1.47 | 2.07 |
| 10,000 | 0.26 | 0.75 | 1.01 | 0.35 | 0.98 | 1.33 | 0.52 | 1.26 | 1.78 |
| Type M copper tubing | | | | | | | | | |
| One floor: | | | | | | | | | |
| 2,000 | 1.35 | 1.42 | 2.77 | 1.41 | 1.61 | 3.02 | 1.60 | 1.96 | 3.56 |
| 10,000 | 0.55 | 0.86 | 1.41 | 0.64 | 1.01 | 1.65 | 1.13 | 1.53 | 2.66 |
| Each additional floor: | | | | | | | | | |
| 2,000 | 0.44 | 0.93 | 1.37 | 0.51 | 1.04 | 1.55 | 0.73 | 1.49 | 2.22 |
| 10,000 | 0.37 | 0.76 | 1.13 | 0.44 | 0.89 | 1.33 | 0.74 | 1.35 | 2.09 |

The cost figures for various types of automatic sprinkler systems in Tables 24.5 to 24.8 relate to interior piping only. Table 24.9 lists the costs of various alarm and detection system components. If the available water supply is not capable of meeting system demand, additional costs will be involved as described above. These cost figures assume all areas are open. Costs for large jobs and those using prefabrications will run 15 to 25% less than these.[3]

Dwelling and residential systems installed according to NFPA 13D and NFPA 13R are wet systems only, and can be estimated at approximately $1.00 to $1.25 per square foot. These systems are generally more economical for small residential buildings because sprinklers may be omitted from combustible concealed spaces as well as building areas statistically shown to have a low likelihood of fatal fires.

---

[3] All cost figures in this chapter are taken from the 1994 editions of *Means Building Cost Construction Data* and *Means Assemblies Cost Data*.

**TABLE 24.6**  Dry-Pipe Sprinkler Systems

In a dry-pipe sprinkler system, piping is pressurized with air or nitrogen, and water is held back until a sprinkler actuates. This type of system is used for unheated buildings.

| Area, sq ft | Light hazard, cost per square foot, $ | | | Ordinary hazard, cost per square foot, $ | | | Extra hazard, cost per square foot, $ | | |
|---|---|---|---|---|---|---|---|---|---|
| | Matl. | Inst. | Total | Matl. | Inst. | Total | Matl. | Inst. | Total |
| Schedule 40 steel pipe; threaded | | | | | | | | | |
| One floor: | | | | | | | | | |
| 2,000 | 1.67 | 1.84 | 3.51 | 1.74 | 1.94 | 3.68 | 1.94 | 2.51 | 4.45 |
| 5,000 | 0.90 | 1.24 | 2.14 | 1.00 | 1.33 | 2.33 | 1.18 | 1.87 | 3.05 |
| 10,000 | 0.64 | 1.04 | 1.68 | 0.82 | 1.37 | 2.19 | 1.21 | 1.75 | 2.96 |
| 50,000 | 0.51 | 0.89 | 1.40 | 0.78 | 1.34 | 2.12 | 1.27 | 1.68 | 2.95 |
| Each additional floor: | | | | | | | | | |
| 2,000 | 0.55 | 1.15 | 1.70 | 0.63 | 1.26 | 1.89 | 0.87 | 1.84 | 2.71 |
| 5,000 | 0.45 | 0.98 | 1.43 | 0.57 | 1.09 | 1.66 | 0.74 | 1.60 | 2.34 |
| 10,000 | 0.42 | 0.91 | 1.33 | 0.53 | 1.07 | 1.60 | 0.86 | 1.44 | 2.30 |
| 50,000 | 0.38 | 0.80 | 1.18 | 0.52 | 0.97 | 1.49 | 0.88 | 1.38 | 2.26 |
| Schedule 10 steel pipe; grooved fittings | | | | | | | | | |
| One floor: | | | | | | | | | |
| 2,000 | 1.59 | 1.62 | 3.21 | 1.66 | 1.68 | 3.34 | 1.88 | 2.14 | 4.02 |
| 10,000 | 0.59 | 0.89 | 1.48 | 0.72 | 1.13 | 1.85 | 1.00 | 1.48 | 2.48 |
| Each additional floor: | | | | | | | | | |
| 2,000 | 0.48 | 0.94 | 1.42 | 0.55 | 1.00 | 1.55 | 0.82 | 1.55 | 2.32 |
| 10,000 | 0.37 | 0.76 | 1.13 | 0.50 | 1.00 | 1.50 | 0.75 | 1.29 | 2.04 |
| Type M copper tubing | | | | | | | | | |
| One floor: | | | | | | | | | |
| 2,000 | 1.66 | 1.61 | 3.27 | 1.75 | 1.80 | 3.55 | 2.01 | 2.16 | 4.17 |
| 10,000 | 0.70 | 0.90 | 1.60 | 0.83 | 1.06 | 1.89 | 1.41 | 1.59 | 3.00 |
| Each additional floor: | | | | | | | | | |
| 2,000 | 0.56 | 0.95 | 1.51 | 0.73 | 1.09 | 1.82 | 0.95 | 1.52 | 2.47 |
| 10,000 | 0.48 | 0.77 | 1.25 | 0.59 | 0.91 | 1.50 | 0.97 | 1.38 | 2.35 |

**TABLE 24.7** Preaction Sprinkler Systems

A preaction system is similar to a dry-pipe system in that there is no water in the piping under normal conditions. In this system, however, water is allowed into the piping through the operation of a valve controlled by a separate detection system. The system then proceeds to act as a wet-pipe system, and actuation of a sprinkler will allow water to discharge onto a fire. This type of system is used where there is special concern for water damage resulting from mechanical damage to the piping or accidental discharge.

| Area, sq ft | Light hazard, cost per sq ft, $ | | | Ordinary hazard, cost per sq ft, $ | | | Extra hazard, cost per sq ft, $ | | |
|---|---|---|---|---|---|---|---|---|---|
| | Matl. | Inst. | Total | Matl. | Inst. | Total | Matl. | Inst. | Total |
| Schedule 40 steel pipe; threaded | | | | | | | | | |
| One floor | | | | | | | | | |
| 2,000 | 1.68 | 1.84 | 3.52 | 1.77 | 1.94 | 3.71 | 1.84 | 2.49 | 4.33 |
| 5,000 | 0.88 | 1.23 | 2.11 | 0.95 | 1.32 | 2.27 | 1.21 | 2.01 | 3.22 |
| 10,000 | 0.62 | 1.04 | 1.66 | 0.76 | 1.36 | 2.12 | 1.16 | 1.94 | 3.10 |
| 50,000 | 0.49 | 0.89 | 1.38 | 0.70 | 1.31 | 2.01 | 1.20 | 1.85 | 3.05 |
| Each additional floor | | | | | | | | | |
| 2,000 | 0.55 | 1.14 | 1.69 | 0.54 | 1.25 | 1.79 | 0.77 | 1.82 | 2.59 |
| 5,000 | 0.43 | 0.97 | 1.40 | 0.58 | 1.17 | 1.75 | 0.66 | 1.61 | 2.27 |
| 10,000 | 0.40 | 0.91 | 1.31 | 0.54 | 1.23 | 1.77 | 0.74 | 1.45 | 2.19 |
| 50,000 | 0.42 | 0.83 | 1.25 | 0.52 | 1.12 | 1.64 | 0.72 | 1.36 | 2.08 |
| Schedule 10 steel pipe; grooved fittings | | | | | | | | | |
| One floor | | | | | | | | | |
| 2,000 | 1.59 | 1.61 | 3.20 | 1.61 | 1.56 | 3.17 | 1.78 | 2.12 | 3.90 |
| 10,000 | 0.57 | 0.89 | 1.46 | 0.59 | 1.11 | 1.70 | 0.86 | 1.46 | 2.32 |
| Each additional floor | | | | | | | | | |
| 2,000 | 0.48 | 0.93 | 1.41 | 0.52 | 0.99 | 1.51 | 0.72 | 1.48 | 2.20 |
| 10,000 | 0.35 | 0.76 | 1.11 | 0.44 | 0.99 | 1.43 | 0.61 | 1.27 | 1.88 |
| Type M copper tubing | | | | | | | | | |
| One floor | | | | | | | | | |
| 2,000 | 1.66 | 1.60 | 3.26 | 1.72 | 1.79 | 3.51 | 1.91 | 2.14 | 4.05 |
| 10,000 | 0.68 | 0.90 | 1.58 | 0.77 | 1.05 | 1.82 | 1.26 | 1.57 | 2.83 |
| Each additional floor | | | | | | | | | |
| 2,000 | 0.56 | 0.94 | 1.50 | 0.56 | 0.97 | 1.53 | 0.85 | 1.50 | 2.35 |
| 10,000 | 0.39 | 0.76 | 1.15 | 0.47 | 0.83 | 1.30 | 0.83 | 1.36 | 2.19 |

**TABLE 24.8**  Deluge Sprinkler Systems

Deluge sprinkler systems utilize open sprinklers. If a fire is detected by a separate detection system, a valve is opened to allow all sprinklers to flow simultaneously. Water supply can therefore play a major role in determining system cost. This type of system is used only for special hazards where there is a danger of a fast-spreading fire. Some codes permit elimination of manual fire alarm boxes in fully sprinklered buildings.

| Area, sq ft | Extra hazard, cost per sq ft, $ | | |
| --- | --- | --- | --- |
| | Material | Installation | Total |
| Schedule 40 steel pipe; threaded | | | |
| One floor | | | |
| 2,000 | 2.28 | 2.46 | 4.74 |
| 5,000 | 1.24 | 1.81 | 3.05 |
| 10,000 | 1.16 | 1.73 | 2.89 |
| 50,000 | 1.21 | 1.68 | 2.89 |
| Each additional floor | | | |
| 2,000 | 0.76 | 1.78 | 2.54 |
| 5,000 | 0.65 | 1.57 | 2.22 |
| 10,000 | 0.75 | 1.47 | 2.22 |
| 50,000 | 0.77 | 1.42 | 2.19 |
| Schedule 10 steel pipe; grooved fittings | | | |
| One floor | | | |
| 2,000 | 2.22 | 2.09 | 4.31 |
| 10,000 | 0.94 | 1.42 | 2.36 |
| Each additional floor | | | |
| 2,000 | 0.71 | 1.44 | 2.15 |
| 10,000 | 0.60 | 1.23 | 1.83 |

**TABLE 24.9**  Alarm System Components

Alarm and detection systems can employ a variety of detection and alarm devices. Detectors are generally provided in all areas to be protected in accordance with their listed spacings. If manual fire-alarm boxes are required, at least one box is required to be on each floor, with boxes located within 200 ft and in the normal path of exit.

| Detection or alarm component | Material | Labor | Total | Total inc. O&P |
| --- | --- | --- | --- | --- |
| Smoke detector, ceiling type | 58 | 36 | 94 | 118 |
| Smoke detector, duct type | 232 | 69 | 301 | 360 |
| Rate-of-rise detector | 31 | 28 | 59 | 76 |
| Manual pull (break glass) box | 46 | 27 | 73 | 92 |
| Electromagnetic door holder | 71 | 55 | 126 | 161 |
| Combination holder and closer | 395 | 69 | 464 | 540 |
| Fire-alarm horn | 33 | 33 | 66 | 86 |
| Light and horn | 96 | 42 | 138 | 169 |
| Master box | 1,900 | 82 | 1,982 | 2,225 |
| Drill switch | 79 | 28 | 107 | 129 |
| Code transmitter | 630 | 55 | 685 | 780 |
| Control panel | | | | |
| 4-zone | 835 | 110 | 945 | 1,075 |
| 8-zone | 1,150 | 220 | 1,370 | 1,600 |
| 12-zone | 1,650 | 335 | 1,985 | 2,325 |
| Remote annunciator | | | | |
| 8-zone lamp | 221 | 122 | 343 | 425 |
| 12-zone lamp | 282 | 169 | 451 | 565 |
| 16-zone lamp | 345 | 200 | 545 | 680 |

# CHAPTER 25
# ENERGY MANAGEMENT[1]

Energy management and investments to save energy have been encouraged in recent years by utility demand-side management (DSM). Utility companies quite literally are paying customers to conserve energy. This is done through rebates from the utilities to their customers to help offset the investment costs of energy-conservation efforts. In some cases rebates are large enough to cover the majority of project costs.

One might ask why a utility company would pay a customer to use less of the company's product, energy. The reason is that energy demand continues to increase, and these incentives to encourage energy efficiency reduce the need to install additional power-generating capacity. Power plants represent extremely large capital investments, take a long time to build, and are increasingly difficult to license due to increasingly strict environmental regulations. Incentives to save energy can lead to postponement or even elimination of new electric power-plant construction, often saving far more money than the cost of the incentives.

Businesses that participate in DSM programs receive an additional benefit in reduced energy bills that, in the long run, can result in substantial life-cycle-cost (LCC) savings.

Energy management is an activity performed in existing buildings. To be effective, energy management must be given the same emphasis as management of any other cost/profit center. The energy management program should monitor energy supplies and costs to take advantage of fuel-switching opportunities and ensure that energy-using systems and equipment are purchased based on economics and the ability to perform the required functions, not simply on the lowest initial cost.

The steps in a program should include

1. An energy management plan
2. Detailed energy audits
3. Select energy-conservation opportunities
4. Design and implementation of energy-conservation measures
5. Training the energy management, operations, and maintenance staffs
6. Performing the follow-up energy audits

The basic stages in implementing an energy management program are

1. To conduct a planned comprehensive search to identify all possible opportunities for energy-conservation activities
2. To identify, acquire, allocate, and prioritize the resources necessary to implement and maintain energy-conservation opportunities
3. To accomplish energy-conservation measures in rational order
4. To maintain energy-conservation measures

---

[1] By David Rosoff, Building Economics Research Ltd., Alexandria, Va.

One of the first tasks of the energy management team is to determine the present energy end uses and to establish achievable goals for improving energy efficiency. These activities necessitate a careful accounting of energy flow and a reasonably comprehensive understanding of the characteristics of energy-using systems. The amount of measured data available for facilities is often limited, so initial program investments should be focused on overcoming these limitations by assembling the available data, identifying information gaps, and carrying out energy-use surveys and metering projects.

## ANALYSIS OF UTILITY BILLING DATA

In most cases utility billing data are the best place to begin the assessment. The following information should be assembled:

- Prior billing records for the past 3 to 5 years, including the quantities of energy consumed, the meter reading dates, and the utility rate structure
- Meteorological summaries for the facility indicating the daily minimum and maximum temperatures
- Salient characteristics and documents pertaining to the facility, such as the square footage of the buildings and construction documents; history of additions, demolitions, or other changes in the building stock or tenancy; central plant capacities and operation logs; and prior energy studies or conservation initiatives

These data should be assembled and summarized in an electronic spreadsheet for subsequent analysis. As the sensitivity of energy-use levels to weather and environmental parameters is explored, the billing records can be normalized for changes in climate. This is accomplished by matching the billing records to the exterior temperature conditions during the same period and conducting statistical regressions to explain historical variations in energy use. Once the baseline conditions are established, the aggregate performance of energy-conservation initiatives can often be determined and energy cause-and-effect relationships can be more duly understood.

## SCREENING FOR ENERGY-EFFICIENCY OPPORTUNITIES

The first task to be undertaken when screening a facility (or facilities) for energy-efficiency improvements is to assemble accurate information on the facility's characteristics and on conservation opportunities. The three types of audits that should be or could be undertaken are discussed in this section. The information to be gathered in each audit and analysis methods using the data will be detailed. Some of the more common energy-conservation opportunities (ECOs) will then be highlighted.

### Types of Energy Audits for Buildings

Most energy audits fall into three categories or types:

- Preliminary or walk-through audits
- Building and system audits
- End-use and equipment audits.

These are discussed in detail below.

## Preliminary or Walk-through Audit

The information to be gathered during the preliminary audit can be divided into four categories: overall facility information, information on major energy-using system and equipment, types of system and equipment contained in the building, and energy billing data. A complete list of information to be obtained in the preliminary audit is included in Table 25.1.[2]

---

[2] Tables 25.1 to 25.3 do not appear on the computer disk provided with this book.

**TABLE 25.1**   Information to be Gathered During Preliminary Audit

Overall facility information
  Floor area of building (sq ft) and of different functional parts (offices, warehouses, etc.)
  Volume of building (cu ft) and of different functional parts
  Age of building (date of construction, remodels, additions, and descriptions of changes)
  Blueprints of architectural, mechanical, and electrical systems
  Lighting types, amount, and operating schedule (interior and exterior)
  Insulation levels (type, amount, location)
  Building operating hours (seasonal, weekly, holiday changes)
  Occupancy (seasonal, daily, weekly changes)
  Any planned changes to the building
Major energy-using systems and equipment information
  Type, size, design, specs, age, etc.
  Fuel used for heating, cooling, and water heating
  Location noted on blueprints
  Operating hours and schedules
  Control schemes or equipment used
Types of systems and equipment to be considered
  HVAC distribution systems
  Heating systems (boiler, furnace, heat pump)
  Cooling systems (chiller, cooling tower, air conditioner)
  Water heater
  Freezer and refrigeration compressors
  Auxiliary equipment (pumps, fans, etc.)
  Other systems (food service, laundry, computers)
Energy billing data
  For all types of energy used (electricity, natural gas, oil, steam, etc.)
  For as many years as possible
  In as much detail as possible
  Per-unit cost (including any changes in cost per season, time of day, etc.)
  Demand changes

Of particular importance are the billing data, which are used to calculate the *energy-utilization index* (EUI), in Btu/ft$^2$. These data can be compared with other facilities under study to allow the focus to fall on the poorest performers in the group. Also, the EUI can be compared to EUIs for functionally similar buildings, such as offices and warehouses. The EUIs for one building can be compared over time to note any significant changes.

Conducting a walk-though audit of the building will allow the analyst to identify functional areas or zones of the building that will be useful for the next audit step. A zone consists of a portion of the building that shares common features such as

- Operating schedule
- Thermostat setpoint
- Similar loads (e.g., lighting watts per square foot)
- Type of HVAC system
- Outside wall and roof exposure

If possible, blueprints of architectural, electrical, and mechanical systems should be used for zoning. Ensure that all updates to the systems have been noted on the blueprints.

Also on the walk-through audit, a description and location of all major energy-using systems, including HVAC equipment, lighting systems, and control equipment, should be obtained. Any other major uses of energy in the building, such as computer, laundry, or food services, should also be noted. Additionally, the fuel and energy usage of the equipment should be noted, if possible.

### Building and System Audit

After gathering preliminary audit data, the energy manager must decide whether to proceed to the next audit step: the building audit. While the preliminary audit may be conducted by the building manager, the building audit may be more cost-effectively done by a professional audit company. In many areas of the country, the local utility may offer a free energy audit that includes a list of potential ECOs. The information gathered during the building audit will be used to model the energy use of the building, as well as to identify ECOs. The model used should be able to show the effect of implementing various ECOs.

A list of the information that should be gathered during a building audit is included as Table 25.2. This information is divided into the following five categories or types of data:

- Building envelope or shell
- Heating, ventilation, and air conditioning
- Lighting and electrical systems
- Central plant systems
- Weather

### End-Use and Equipment Audit

The final audit type, the end-use and equipment audit, should be undertaken only if the building audit shows a need for further information or that a particular ECO may be warranted. For example, a complete boiler analysis may be identified as a need in the building audit. In most cases, a professional boiler expert or engineer will need to perform this audit. Similarly, a professional HVAC engineer will be needed to evaluate the performance of the cooling plant components. Another method of gathering more detailed data for some systems (e.g., lighting and electrical) is to meter or monitor the end use of energy in the building. This allows the total energy use in the building to be disaggregated to a significant degree. This last audit step is very expensive and time-consuming and is usually only undertaken if it seems likely that significant savings will result from the identification of ECOs.

**TABLE 25.2**  Information to be Gathered During Building Audit

Building envelope or shell
   Floor area
   Number of zones and zone identification
   Area by zone
   Thermostat schedules and setpoints
   Occupancy schedules
   Sensible-heat and latent-heat gain from people
   Exterior walls (materials of construction)
   Roof
   Windows (type, area, weatherstripping, etc.)
   Shading and overhangs
   Doors (type, area, etc.)
   Underground walls
   Miscellaneous conduction (e.g., freezer walls)
   Insulation (type, location, area, etc.)
   Infiltration

HVAC data—required for both distribution systems and unitary equipment (e.g., heat pumps)
   System label and type
   Zone assignments to systems
   Heat source for systems (plant type)
   Cooling source for systems (plant type)
   System availability and schedules
   System-specific information as required, such as
      Deck temperature
      Controls
      Outside air and damper control
      Humidification
      Preheat and reheat
      Fan power and flow rate
      Loop temperature
      Backup heating
   Unitary system information as required, such as
      Design COPs for air conditioners and heat pumps
      Efficiency and parasitic losses for furnaces
      Unloading ratios for DX cooling systems

Lighting and electrical systems—most of this information is per zone
   Lighting levels (watts per square foot, footcandles)
   Control scheme for lights (switches, schedules)
   Location of fixtures
   Type and size of lights (fluorescent, incandescent, etc.)
   Motors (type, horsepower, amperage, etc.)
   Location and condition of transformers and switch boxes
   Power factor of building (if applicable)

Central plant systems—includes specifications of the primary energy-using systems such as boilers, chillers, cooling towers, circulating pumps, and water-heating systems
   Boiler specifications such as
      Fuel usage and cost
      Number of units
      Capacity
      Design efficiency

*(Continued)*

**TABLE 25.2**   Information to be Gathered During Building Audit  (*Continued*)

---

Central plant systems (*Cont.*)
    Controls
    Minimum part-load ratio
    Boiler pump kilowatts
    Standby or parasitic losses
  Cooling plant specifications such as
    Fuel usage and cost
    Number of units
    Capacity
    Design COPs
    Controls
    Unloading and part-load ratios
    Water temperatures and flow rates
    Load management system specifications
    Pump kilowatts
  Cooling-tower specifications such as
    Heat rejection capacity
    Number of cells
    Fan kilowatts per cell
    Water temperature and flow rates
    Pump kilowatts
    Approach temperature
    Controls
  Domestic water specifications such as
    Fuel usage and cost
    Heating capacity
    Average usage
    Inlet and supply temperature
    Circulation pump kilowatts and scheduling
    Design efficiency
    Standby losses

Weather data—auditor should select an available weather station which most closely corresponds to the location of the building being analyzed
  Air temperature (average daily and monthly)
  Relative humidity
  Wind speed
  Wind direction
  Insolation or cloud cover
  Average heating and cooling degree days (if average temperatures are not available)

---

## Energy-Conservation Opportunities (ECOs)

The most common ECOs found in existing commercial buildings fall into the following nine categories:

1. Building equipment operation
2. Building envelope
3. HVAC systems

4. HVAC distribution systems

5. Water-heating systems

6. Lighting systems

7. Power systems

8. Energy management control systems

9. Heat recovery and reclaim systems

An ECO may be realized either by implementing operation and maintenance (O&M) measures or by incorporating available technologies. Each of these energy-conservation areas is briefly described below.

## Building Equipment Operation

An enormous amount of energy is wasted because building equipment is operated improperly and unnecessarily. When the building is not occupied, the building systems should be turned off or their operation reduced to a minimum. Depending on building operations, the following systems' operating hours can be curtailed during slack time: HVAC systems, water-heating systems, lighting systems, escalators and elevators, and other equipment and machinery. Care must be taken to ensure that the reduction in hours has no adverse impact on building operations and systems.

## Building Envelope

The amount of heat (sensible and latent) supplied to or extracted from the indoors in order to maintain a comfortable indoor environment is directly proportional to the difference in temperature and humidity between indoors and outdoors. Consequently, one should lower the heating and raise the cooling temperature setpoint and/or lower the humidification setpoint and raise the dehumidification setpoint to minimize the space conditioning requirements. Another ECO is to set the heating setpoint back when the building is not occupied. Care must be taken to endure that the slight discomfort of the occupants does not reduce their productivity.

Energy is saved when the heat exchange between the building and the outside environment is reduced and/or solar and internal heat gains are controlled. The primary way to reduce heat conduction through ceilings/roofs, walls, and floors is by adding insulation. Another method is to install vapor barriers in ceiling and roofs and walls. To control or reduce solar heat gains through the roof or glazing areas, a reflective surface or film can be used. For glazing areas, the installation of interior or exterior shading will also help control solar heat gain. The installation of storm windows or multiple-glazed windows will also reduce heat conduction and long-wave radiation through glazing areas.

*Infiltration* is the unintended entry of unconditioned air into the building through doors, windows, and other openings in the building envelope. Infiltration can result in large increases in heating and cooling loads. Many infiltration control strategies are inexpensive and relatively simple to implement. Energy can be saved by sealing vertical shafts and stairways, caulking and weatherstripping doors and windows, or installing vestibules and revolving doors.

## HVAC Systems

The HVAC systems in the building are made up of energy-conversion equipment, which transforms electrical or chemical energy to thermal energy; and distribution and ventilation systems, which transport the thermal energy and supply fresh outdoor air to the conditioned space. Energy may be saved in HVAC systems by reducing ventilation requirements; improving the performance of space conditioning equipment such as boilers, furnaces, chillers, air conditioners, and heat pumps; using energy-efficient cooling systems; and reducing the occurrence of reheating or recooling.

## Water-Heating Systems

In general, heating and distribution of hot water consumes less energy than does space conditioning and lighting. However, for some cases, such as hospitals, restaurants, kitchens, and laundries, water heating amounts to substantial energy consumption. Water-heating energy is conserved by reducing load requirements, reducing distribution losses, and improving the efficiency of the water-heating systems.

## Lighting System

Lighting accounts for a significant fraction of electrical energy consumed in a building. Energy is saved and electric demand is reduced by reducing illumination levels, improving light system efficiency, curtailing operating hours, and using daylighting. Reduction of lighting energy can also increase the energy use of building heating and decrease cooling system consumption, since internal heat gains are reduced. However, this heat of light is often a relatively expensive method of heating a building. If the building cooling plant is to be replaced, implementation of lighting ECOs will reduce the required plant size.

## Power Systems

The inefficient operation of power systems stems mainly from a low power factor. Power-factor correction is cost-effective when utility penalties are imposed. Low power factors can be improved with power-factor correction devices and high-efficiency motors. Additional energy can be saved by installing energy-efficient transformers and replacing existing motors with smaller and/or higher-efficiency motors, or by installing variable-speed motor drives.

The peak power demand can be reduced by load-shedding, cogeneration, or cool storage systems that produce cold water or ice during off-peak hours. Load shedding may also reduce the total power consumption, as well as the demand. Cogeneration systems will increase the use of on-site energy but can also replace electricity consumption with less expensive fossil energy. Also, the waste heat from the cogeneration equipment can meet thermal loads. Cool storage systems sift the chiller demand to off-peak periods, reducing on-peak demand.

Evaluation of these ECOs requires a determination of the building demand profile. Several weeks of data in 15-min intervals should be taken with a recording meter. The measurements may have to be taken both in the cooling and heating season. Most electric utilities will provide this service at a nominal charge.

## Energy Management Control Systems

Energy can be saved by automating the control energy systems through the use of energy management and control systems (EMCSs). Rising energy costs and decreasing prices for computers and microprocessors have encouraged the use of EMCSs. An EMCS can efficiently control the heating, ventilating, air conditioning, lighting, and other energy-consuming equipment in the building. It selects optimum equipment operating times and setpoint as a function of electrical demand, time, weather conditions, occupancy, and heating and cooling requirements. The basic control principles for building energy conservation are

- Operate equipment only when needed.
- Eliminate or minimize simultaneous heating and cooling.
- Supply heating and cooling according to actual needs.
- Supply heating and cooling from the most efficient source.

About 100 companies manufacture EMCSs, and new technology is continually being developed. Potential users should be thoroughly familiar with currently available EMCSs.

## ANALYSIS OF ENERGY-CONSERVATION OPPORTUNITIES

All building energy consumption can be viewed conceptually as a rate of use multiplied by time (energy = rate × time). The maximum rate is specified or limited by parameter specifications of capacity or by intensity, such as wall $U$ value, lighting watts per square foot, or chiller tonnage. The rate over time is specified by the operating schedule or weather variable. The type of parameter and how it varies over time can be used to select the appropriate analysis technique. For example, an external lighting system uses energy at a constant rate, usually operates on a known schedule, and has no interaction with other patterns of building energy consumption. Therefore, a change in installed kilowattage (rate) or operating schedule (time) can be calculated manually with precision.

For most ECOs, however, an accurate calculation is not that simple. For example, the performance of heating and cooling systems is affected by internal heat gains and weather variables, which vary in a complex fashion over time. The efficiencies of the plant equipment and HVAC systems vary with percentage of load. Therefore, using an energy model rather than manual techniques offers the following accuracy improvements:

- Building parameters can be precisely scheduled.
- The impact of weather can be precisely determined.
- Equipment performance can be specified at part-load.
- Variable interactions, such as the effect of internal lighting reductions on heating and cooling loads, can be calculated.

Before personal computers were widely used, building energy analysts had limited choices of calculation methods for evaluating ECOs. Typically, they used manual calculation methods and nomographs. Those methods are simple and require a relatively low level of effort from the user. However, those methods are not as accurate and comprehensive as automated methods of calculation.

In the past, automated calculation methods were usually available only on mainframe computers and their use was costly, complicated, and time-consuming. However, those methods provided much greater accuracy and could evaluate building energy use hourly. With the advent of the personal computer, automated methods for analyzing building energy became accessible to a wider range of building professionals. Today, many software packages for analyzing building energy are available for the personal computer.

ASEAM[3] is such a model and was used to analyze the effects of several of the ECOs discussed above. ASEAM is a modified bin method program for calculating the energy consumption of residential and simple commercial buildings. ASEAM runs on an IBM-PC and compatible with at least 256 kilobytes (kbytes) of memory and two disk drives.

---

[3]ASEAM is a simplified energy analysis method, prepared as an account of work sponsored by the U.S. Department of Energy, Office of Federal Energy Management Programs.

Like most building energy analysis programs, ASEAM performs calculations in four segments:

- *Loads:* Thermal heating and cooling loads (both peak and "diversified," or average) are calculated for each zone by month and by outside bin temperature. Lighting and miscellaneous electrical consumption are calculated in this segment.

- *System:* The thermal loads calculated in the loads segment are then passed to the systems segment, which calculates "coil" loads for boilers and chillers. (The system coil loads are not equal to the zone loads calculated above because of ventilation requirements, latent cooling, humidification requirements, economizer cycles, reheat, mixing, etc.). Some building energy requirements are calculated in the systems segment (e.g., heat pump and fan electricity requirements).

- *Plant:* All the systems' coil loads on the central heating and cooling plant equipment are then combined, and calculations are performed for each central plant type. (Plant equipment can also impose loads on other plant equipment, such as cooling-tower loads from chillers and boiler loads from absorption chillers or domestic hot water.) The plant calculations result in monthly and annual energy consumption figures for each plant type.

- *Economic* (*optional*): Energy consumption from all the building end-use categories is then totaled and reported. If specified, the LCCs of the total energy requirement, combined with other parameters, are calculated and reported. In the parametric and ECO calculation modes, a base case may also be compared with alternative cases.

The ASEAM program is recommended as the initial energy-use assessment tool for residential and commercial buildings. It is relatively simple and inexpensive to use, does a good job of accounting for the complexities of energy use, and facilitates the examination of most ECO cost and benefits.

## SELECTION OF SUPPLEMENTAL METERING POINTS

An understanding of energy-use effectiveness is often severely constrained by a lack of scientific data on energy system performance. Measurements taken on a regular basis are most useful to assess energy-efficiency levels and the effects of operational or design changes. Measurements may be continuous, such as utility meters, or may be for short periods of time, such as combustion-efficiency tests. Some of the most critical measurements are listed below:

- Electrical consumption levels by type of day (working and nonworking days) and month of year
- Electrical demand levels by hour of day and season of year
- Interior lighting levels, efficacy, and schedules
- Interior temperature levels by hour of day and season of year
- Chiller and boiler efficiency levels under part-loads
- Makeup water requirements for steam and hot-water distribution systems
- Exterior temperature, humidity, and solar radiation
- Areas of heated, cooled, and unconditioned space
- Capacity rating and hours of operation for major equipment such as pumps, fans, and street lighting systems
- Thermal conductance (*U* value) of conditioned building envelopes
- Submetered electrical consumption for major buildings and equipment loads such as fans, pumps, lighting, and process equipment

- Submetered hot-water, chilled-water, and steam measurements for individual buildings and/or central plant headers
- Hours of operation and other facility production and/or use factors.

The analyst must verify the quality of the data before incorporating them into an analysis. Typically, this requires a skeptical attitude on the part of the user and a comparison of measurements and/or use of engineering calculations. While errors cannot always be found, inaccuracies in major items such as meter readings, motor capacities, square footage calculation, and meter multipliers and reading dates should be found and corrected.

## INFORMATION TO BE GATHERED DURING AUDITS

Table 25.1 contains information that should be gathered during the preliminary audit of a building and is divided into the following four categories: overall facility information, information on major energy-using systems and equipment, the types of systems and equipment contained in the building, and energy billing data. Table 25.2 contains information that should be gathered during the building audit and is divided into the following five data categories: building envelope or shell, HVAC systems, lighting and electrical systems, central plant systems, and weather.

## ENERGY MANAGEMENT SYSTEMS SAVINGS

A typical facility can save about 10% of its total energy use with an energy management system. This can range up to over 20% for an all-electric hotel or a building which is occupied only 50 hr a week but was operated full-time before getting the system. Savings can range down to zero for facilities that either are 24-hr operations with very low demand changes and/or use most of their energy for production purposes. Then the production process should be studied for potential energy savings. Table 25.3 illustrates the relative amounts of savings available. Many buildings are already turning their HVAC systems off nights and weekends.

**TABLE 25.3** Office Building Savings Available from Energy Management Savings

The total cost of energy for a building can be divided among HVAC, production, and lighting. Even with maximum energy management HVAC and lighting will have minimum costs. In addition, the production energy cost cannot be reduced by energy management. The center column shows the typical proportion of savings achievable with various strategies. The last column shows the remaining costs after management.

| Cost category | Strategy or minimum cost | Possible savings and minimum cost |
|---|---|---|
| HVAC | Off nights and weekends | Possible HVAC savings |
| | Cycle | |
| | Demand shed | |
| | Minimum | |
| Production | Computers and other office equipment | Minimum energy costs |
| Lighting | Minimum | Possible lighting savings |
| | Daylighting | |
| | Off nights and weekends | |

**TABLE 25.4** Energy Management Systems

Energy management system characteristics

| Items controlled | Points monitored | Printer | | Alphanumeric display | VDT or LCD* | Buildings | |
|---|---|---|---|---|---|---|---|
| | | Tape | Line | | | Single | Many |
| 1 | 0 | | | X | | X | |
| 4 | 0 | | | X | | X | |
| 8 | 0 | | | X | | X | |
| 16 | 0 | X | | X | | X | |
| 32 | 0 | | X | | | | X |
| 32 | 160 | | X | | X | X | |
| 64 | 0 | X | | X | | | X |
| 64 | 320 | | X | | X | | X |
| 128 | 0 | | X | X | | | X |
| 128 | 640 | | X | | X | | X |
| 256 | 0 | | X | | | | X |
| 256 | 1,280 | | X | | X | | X |
| 512 | 0 | | X | | X | | X |
| 512 | 2,560 | | X | | X | | X |
| 650 | 1,400 | | X | | X | | X |

Energy management system costs

| Items controlled | Points monitored | Cost, $ | | Installation per point workhours | Total system cost, $ |
|---|---|---|---|---|---|
| | | Per control | Per monitor | | |
| 1 | 0 | 80 | | 2 | 200 |
| 4 | 0 | 150 | | 3 | 1,000 |
| 8 | 0 | 150 | | 6 | 3,000 |
| 16 | 0 | 300 | | 10 | 10,000 |
| 32 | 0 | 500 | | 10 | 26,000 |
| 32 | 160 | 500 | 500 | 10 | 150,000 |
| 64 | 0 | 600 | | 12 | 60,000 |
| 64 | 320 | 600 | 600 | 12 | 400,000 |
| 128 | 0 | 800 | | 12 | 150,000 |
| 128 | 640 | 800 | 800 | 12 | 900,000 |
| 256 | 0 | 900 | | 12 | 300,000 |
| 256 | 1,280 | 900 | 900 | 12 | 2,000,000 |
| 512 | 0 | 900 | | 12 | 600,000 |
| 512 | 2,560 | 900 | 900 | 12 | 4,000,000 |
| 650 | 1,400 | 2,000 | 2,000 | 12 | 5,000,000 |

*Videodisplay terminal or liquid-crystal display.

## COST OF ENERGY MANAGEMENT SYSTEMS

Costs range from $80, plus installation of 1 workhour, for a programmable thermostat to $5 million or more for an entire system for a campus (Table 25.4). Systems are usually tailored to need, and purchased ones typically cost as much as the facility spends in 2 years for energy. Maintenance costs are typically 10% of the installed cost per year. It may not be practical to control individual items using less than 10 hp, 10 kW, or 100,000 Btuh. A system with 32 control points can be installed for about $26,000 or leased for about $15,000 per year.

## RECOMMENDED READING

*Architect's and Engineer's Guide to Energy Conservation in Existing Buildings,* U.S. Department of Energy, April 1990.

# CHAPTER 26
# COMPUTER-AIDED ESTIMATING

When the first edition of the *Mechanical Estimating Guidebook* was written in 1958, computers were in their infancy and estimates were generally prepared by hand with a slide rule or a bulky mechanical calculator. Very few companies had computers. Those computers were massive machines that required an air-conditioned, clean room for their 64 or 128 kbytes of mainframe memory. These machines also had an equally massive price tag, one so high that only multi-million-dollar corporations could afford them.

Today personal computers cost less than typewriters did a few years ago and have awesome computational capability in comparison to the computer dinosaurs of the past. Computers have become so inexpensive and simple to use that no contractor, large or small, can afford to be without them.

The last edition of this book was the first to discuss use of computers in any detail at all and listed some software that was available to facilitate estimating and design of mechanical systems.

Now so much software is available for computer-aided design and estimating that it is impossible to list it all in any chapter of any book. Indeed, new and improved software is coming onto the market at such a rapid rate that any listing of available software is obsolete before it is ever published. For this reason, no effort will be made here to describe specific software packages for mechanical estimating and/or design. Instead, it is suggested that those interested in current software contact one of the professional societies engaged in the cost engineering and/or HVAC disciplines for information on currently available software. Prominent societies with an interest in the field include the following:

AACE International (formerly the American Association of Cost Engineers)
209 Prairie Ave., Suite 100
P.O. Box 1557
Morgantown, WV 26507-1557
Phone: (800) 858-COST or (304) 296-8444
Fax: (304) 291-5728

Air-Conditioning and Refrigeration Institute
1501 Wilson Blvd., 6th floor
Arlington, VA 22209
Phone: (703) 524-8800

American Society of Mechanical Engineers
345 East 47th St.
New York, NY 10017
Phone: (212) 705-7722
Fax: (212) 705-7674

American Society of Professional Estimators
11141 Georgia Ave., Suite 412
Wheaton, MD 20902
Phone: (301) 929-8848
Fax: (301) 929-0231

American Society of Heating, Refrigeration, and Air Conditioning Engineers
1791 Tullie Circle, NE
Atlanta, GA 30329
Phone: (404) 636-8400
Fax: (404) 321-5478

Mechanical Contractors Association of America
1385 Piccard Drive
Rockville, MD 20850
Phone: (301) 869-5800

Sheet Metal and Air Conditioning Contractors National Association
8224 Old Court House Road
Vienna, VA 22180
Phone: (703) 803-2980

Another excellent way of examining and selecting a suitable software package is to use "DemoSource™," a proprietary product of the Means Company (R. S. Means Co., 100 Construction Plaza, P.O. Box 800, Kingston, MA 02364-9986). For a modest price, this package provides demonstration disks for a large number of commercially available estimating packages along with a copy of the Means database for mechanical costs (or any other Means database of the purchaser's choosing), thus permitting the purchaser to easily evaluate and compare the various software packages and to select the one that appears most suitable.

All the major software packages on the market can import data from *Lotus 1-2-3*[1] and other spreadsheet programs. The *Lotus 1-2-3* computer disk provided with this book is suitable for that purpose. It can also be used directly with *Lotus 1-2-3* spreadsheet calculations.

Most estimating programs are compatible with several major construction cost databases that are commercially available, including the databases of the R. S. Means Company, Richardson Engineering Services, the National Construction Estimator, the Mechanical Contractors Association of America, and the U.S. Army Corps of Engineers.

Another major source of computer assistance for the construction industry is the *AIA Online* information service of the American Institute of Architects. *AIA Online* is an information and communication network that enables construction people to access over 800 different databases with a modem-equipped computer and a local telephone call. Information about *AIA Online* may be obtained from the American Institute of Architects [1735 New York Ave., NW, Washington, DC 20006; phone (800) 864-7753 or (202) 626-7300].

In addition, information on specific software products may be obtained by calling software vendors directly. The following list gives telephone numbers for some vendors. This list includes only a small fraction of the many firms offering estimating software packages, and the inclusion or omission of any firm from the list should not be construed to imply endorsement or lack of endorsement for any particular product or vendor.

| | |
|---|---|
| AEC Data Systems | (800) 659-9001 |
| American Contractor | (800) 333-8435 |
| Building Systems Design, Inc. | (800) 857-0047 |

---

[1] *Lotus* and *1-2-3* are trademarks of Lotus Development Corporation.

| | |
|---|---|
| Computerized Micro Solutions | (800) 255-7407 |
| The Conac Group | (604) 273-3463 |
| Construction Computing | (800) 456-2113 |
| Construction Data Control, Inc. | (800) 285-3929 |
| Estimation, Inc. | (800) 275-6444 |
| G2 Inc. | (800) 657-6312 |
| HRS Systems, Inc. | (404) 934-8423 |
| ICARUS Corporation | (301) 881-9350 |
| Impaqt Data Systems | (800) 347-8805 |
| IQ Beneco | (801) 565-1122 |
| ISS | (416) 946-1880 |
| Management Computer Controls, Inc. | (800) 225-5622 |
| NoVA Technologies | (209) 434-0609 |
| Pinnacle Technology | (800) 346-4658 |
| Pro-Mation | (800) 521-4562 |
| SoftCOST, Inc. | (800) 955-1385 |
| Software Shop Systems | (800) 554-9865 |
| The TallySHEET Corporation | (213) 665-5891 |
| Timberline Software Corp. | (800) 628-6583 |
| Vertigraph, Inc. | (800) 989-4243 |
| Wendes Engineering and Contracting | (312) 593-2178 |
| WinEstimator, Inc. | (800) 950-2374 |

The last edition of this book said:

> Computer-aided estimating systems have been evolving along with computers and improvements in programming. As with any computer investment, the time to buy is when the product saves enough money in your operation to justify its cost. Computer-aided estimating will evolve toward more automated input, with quantities coming directly from the design and material and labor costs coming automatically from past experience of the firm.

Those predictions have come to pass, and today's computers and computer software easily justify their cost, even for the smaller mechanical contractor.

# CHAPTER 27
# LIFE-CYCLE COSTING[1]

## GENERAL DISCUSSION

Contractors and design professionals need practical methods and guidelines for evaluating the economic performance of mechanical systems in buildings. Life-cycle cost (LCC) analysis is one method for making such evaluations. LCC analysis is used to evaluate alternative systems which compete on the basis of cost. Thus only candidate systems which satisfy all performance requirements (e.g., code, safety, comfort, and reliability requirements) can be legitimately compared using the LCC method. The system alternative with the lowest LCC over the project study period is the most cost-effective choice.

An example of an appropriate use of the LCC method is choosing between an oil furnace and gas furnace for heating a building. To be candidate projects for an LCC analysis, each system must meet the minimum performance requirements for occupant comfort, and the fuel required for each system must be available at the site. The cost-effective choice will depend on which system has lower LCCs over the project study period, assuming other things equal.

Systems with the lowest LCC often have higher first costs than competing systems. This leads builders to ask why they should put out more money up front than is necessary, particularly when they plan to sell the building on completion. One answer is that the builder might expect a return on the cost-effective system that more than compensates for its extra costs. This happens, for example, if the owner-operator achieves sufficient net savings over time from reduced energy consumption to more than pay the builder's extra first costs and profit required for installing the cost-effective system.

This chapter describes how to measure LCCs and use the LCC method in choosing among alternative building systems. A sample problem using the LCC method shows how to find the cost-effective efficiency level of an air-conditioning system. And a sample problem using the savings-to-investment ratio (SIR), an evaluation method related to LCC, shows how to find the optimal combination of independent energy-conservation investments when there is too little money to do all the projects which return positive net savings.

The chapter also provides a brief overview of other measures of project worth, such as net savings and payback, and identifies circumstances when they might be appropriate. It has a section on how to treat uncertainty with sensitivity analysis. A list of definitions of economics terms is provided at the end of the chapter for your help whenever you see a term that is unfamiliar. Selected references conclude the chapter.

---

[1] By Harold E. Marshall and Stephen R. Petersen, National Institute of Standards and Technology, Gaithersburg, Md.

## HOW TO MEASURE AND APPLY LCC

Equation (27.1) shows that the LCC of a project alternative is the sum of its initial investment costs *I*, present value of replacement costs *R*, present value of energy costs *E*, and the present value of operation, maintenance, and repair (OM&R) costs, minus the present value of salvage *S*, which is sometimes referred to as *resale value* or *residual value*.

$$LCC = I + R + E + OM\&R - S \qquad (27.1)$$

Equation (27.2) is an alternative formulation that shows mathematically the discounting of future costs to present value and their summation into a single LCC calculation.

$$LCC = \sum_{t=0}^{N} \frac{C_t}{(1 + d)^t} \qquad (27.2)$$

where $C_t$ = sum of all relevant costs, less any positive cash flows such as salvage, occurring in time period *t*
$N$ = number of time periods in the study period
$d$ = investor's discount rate for adjusting cash flows to present value

### Steps in LCC Analysis

The following list shows the steps to follow in conducting an LCC analysis:

1. Identify acceptable alternatives.
2. Establish common assumptions (e.g., study period, discount rate, and base date).
3. Estimate all project costs and their timing.
4. Discount future costs to present value.
5. Compute total LCC for each alternative.
6. Identify alternative with lowest LCC.
7. Consider unquantifiable costs and benefits.
8. Consider uncertainty in input values.
9. Compute supplementary measures of relative economic performance (if necessary).
10. Select best alternative.

### Rules in Applying the LCC Method

To use the LCC method, you need to compute the LCC of a project alternative (sometimes called the *base case*) against which to compare the LCCs of your proposed design alternative(s). Usually the base case is the alternative with the lowest initial cost.

For each alternative you consider, you must use the same discount rate and the same study period (i.e., time over which you compare the alternatives). Only then can you determine which is more cost-effective. To come up with a common study period, you will sometimes have to include replacements in short-lived projects and account for salvage value in long-lived projects.

An implicit assumption in LCC analysis is that all the alternatives that you are considering for a particular project be capable of satisfying the minimum performance requirements for that project (e.g., safety, reliability, occupant comfort, and other building code requirements). Consider the extent to which any alternative exceeds such minimum performance requirements as additional benefits attributable to that alternative. If the additional benefits can be quantified in dollar terms (e.g., additional rental income), treat these benefits as negative costs in the years in which the benefits are realized. If the additional benefits cannot be quantified in dollar terms, include a description of these benefits in narrative form with the LCC analysis. Then use your own (or institutional) judgment to determine the extent to which the LCC penalty (if any) for a particular alternative is offset by such benefits. For example, air conditioner B costs $1,000 more initially than air conditioner A, but saves only $900 in present-value energy costs over air conditioner A. Air conditioner B, on the other hand, is significantly quieter than A. Thus air conditioner B could be the "economic" choice from the owner's standpoint, even though its LCC is $100 higher, if the owner considers this acoustic benefit as being worth at least the extra $100 in present-value LCC terms.

If project alternatives have substantial differences in performance that result in large positive cash flows, the LCC method may not be the most appropriate method of economic analysis. Instead, use net benefits or related methods of economic analysis that account explicitly for benefits as well as costs over the appropriate study period.

## LCC Applied to the Choice of an Air-Conditioning System

Suppose you are selecting a new central air conditioner for installation in a house with a design cooling load of 38.0 MJ/hr (i.e., 36,019 Btu/hr) in a region with approximately 1,500 full-load cooling hours per year. The system with the lowest initial cost that meets the Department of Energy's current energy performance standards has a *seasonal energy-efficiency ratio* (SEER) of approximately 10.55 kJ/Wh (10.0 Btu/Wh). Because the cooling load hours are above average, you will probably also want to consider systems with SEERs of 12.66 and 14.77 kJ/Wh (12.0 and 14.0 Btu/Wh), even though their initial costs are higher. The LCC method helps you determine which SEER will result in the lowest LCC over a 15-year study period.

Local electricity rates are currently $0.08/kWh (summer rates), with no demand charge, and are expected to increase at about 3% per year. Let's use an 8% discount rate to convert future costs (including price increases) to present value. All three systems have an expected life of 15 years and approximately the same maintenance costs.

Table 27.1[2] shows the computation of LCC for each alternative system, based on the sum of the initial cost and present value energy costs for each system. The BLCC computer program described at the end of this chapter will help you do the LCC Analysis. System B has the lowest LCC (Column 7, Table 27.1) and is therefore the economic choice, assuming that its reliability, maintenance, and sound characteristics are not worse than those of system A or C.

Note that if the local utility were to offer a cash rebate for selecting a higher efficiency air conditioner, the initial investment cost (Column 6, Table 27.1) should be reduced accordingly for systems B and C. Based on the rebates reflected in Column 8 (Table 27.1), system C becomes the most economic choice.

## Typical LCC Applications

Accept/reject decisions occur when you have to decide whether to do a project. Examples are the installation of solar water heating, storm windows, or a water-heater insulation kit. These can be evaluated as independent projects as long as an investment in one does not affect the savings of another. This would be true, for example, if they were in different buildings. The

---

[2] The tables in this chapter do not appear on the computer disk provided with this book.

**TABLE 27.1**   Computation of LCC for Three Air Conditioners

| (1) | (2) | (3) | (4) | (5) | (6) | (7) | (8) | (9) |
|-----|-----|-----|-----|-----|-----|-----|-----|-----|
| | | | | | Without utility rebate | | With utility rebate | |
| System | SEER Btuh/W | Annual kWh use | Annual kWh cost, $ | PV kWh cost, $ | Initial AC cost, $ | Total LCC, $ | Initial AC cost, $ | Total LCC, $ |
| (A) | 10.0 | 5,400 | 432 | 4,527 | 2,000 | 6,527 | 2,000 | 6,527 |
| (B) | 12.0 | 4,500 | 360 | 3,773 | 2,500 | 6,273 | 2,200 | 5,973 |
| (C) | 14.0 | 3,855 | 308 | 3,234 | 3,100 | 6,334 | 2,500 | 5,734 |

Explanation and computation of values (numbers in parentheses refer to column numbers):

(2)  from product literature

(3)  = 36,000 Btuh/SEER (Btuh/W) × 1,500 h/year

(4)  = (3) × $0.08/kWh

(5)  = (4) × 10.48, where 10.48 is the UPV* factor for an annually recurring cost increasing at a rate of 3% and discounted at 8% per year, based on the equation

$$\text{UPV*} = \frac{(1 + e)}{(d - e)} \left( 1 - \frac{(1 + e)^n}{(1 + d)^n} \right) \text{ (when } e \neq d, \text{ else UPV*} = n)$$

where $e$ = the annual rate of price increase

$d$ = discount rate, and

$n$ = number of time periods

(6)  estimated installed cost

(7)  = (5) + (6)

(8)  assumed rebate for SEER 12 = $300; assumed rebate for SEER 14 = $600

(9)  = (5) + (8)

LCC can help you decide if it pays to undertake any one of these projects compared to its base case. Accept the storm windows, for example, if their LCC is less than the LCC of the base case.

Efficiency level or size decisions occur when you must decide how much of something to invest in. Examples are choosing the seasonal efficiency rating of an air conditioner, the collector area for a solar energy system, or the level of thermal resistance for wall insulation. Make these types of decisions by choosing the level or size with the minimum LCC.

System or design decisions occur when you choose the most cost-effective of multiple alternatives for meeting an objective. For example, the LCC method can help you choose among oil, gas, or electricity for heating; among fiber-glass, foam, or cellulose for insulation material; and between a heat pump or electric resistance baseboard system. Choose the alternative with the minimum LCC as long as it satisfies system performance requirements.

## OTHER METHODS AND WHEN TO USE THEM

### Net Savings (NS) or Net Benefits (NB)

The NS method measures the amount of present value net savings earned over the study period from investing in a candidate project as compared to a base-case alternative. When an investment affects costs exclusively, a common approach to computing NS is to compare the LCC associated with the investment to the LCC of the base-case alternative. The NS for a heat pump, for example, is the difference between the LCC of heating and cooling a house to a target comfort level with the base-case system, say, an oil furnace with electric air conditioner, and the LCC of heating and cooling with the heat pump. If NS with the heat pump is positive, the investment makes money and is considered cost-effective; if NS is zero, the investment neither makes nor loses you money; if NS is negative, the investment loses money.

Use the NB method when positive revenues or benefits rather than savings accrue from the project. Either NS or NB is appropriate for accept/reject, size, or design decisions. For detailed information on how to calculate, apply, and interpret the NS and NB methods, see Ruegg and Marshall.[3]

### Savings-to-Investment Ratio (SIR)

Equation (27.3) shows that the SIR of a project alternative is the sum of its present-value (PV) savings divided by the sum of the present value of all investment-related costs attributable to that alternative over the base case.

$$\text{SIR}_{\text{A:BC}} = \frac{\sum_{t=1}^{N} S_t \big/ (1 + d)^t}{\sum_{t=0}^{N} I_t^* \big/ (1 + d)^t} \tag{27.3}$$

where $\text{SIR}_{\text{A:BC}}$ = the ratio of PV savings to additional PV investment costs of the alternative (A) relative to the base case (BC)
$S_t$ = PV savings in year $t$ in operating-related costs attributed to the alternative
$I_t^*$ = additional PV investment-related costs attributable to the alternative in year $t$

**Steps in SIR Analysis.**   The steps in performing an SIR analysis are similar to those shown under LCC analysis (above), except that for the SIR you need to calculate specific savings from each alternative rather than just its LCC.

**Rules in Applying the SIR Method.**   The main rule to remember in using the SIR is to place in the denominator of the SIR formula any investment-related cost on which you are seeking to measure your investment return. The placement of items in the numerator and denominator can alter the relative priority of a project within a group of cost-effective projects, but will not cause a project alternative with an SIR > 1.0 to fall below 1.0 or vice versa.

**Typical Applications of SIR.**   One use of the SIR is to make accept/reject decisions for single projects. Accept the project if the SIR > 1.0; reject it if the SIR < 1.0.

A second use of the SIR is to choose among cost-effective projects when the investment budget is limited. When money is not available to fund every building or system improvement that is cost-effective, try to allocate funds so that the overall net savings (total savings less total investment cost) are maximized from the project selection. An appropriate method for allocating limited funds among independent projects is to rank projects in declining order of their SIRs, and then fund them in that order until the budget is exhausted. The package of investment options selected by SIR ranking will generate the greatest net savings overall relative to any other package. This works for allocating a budget within a single building or

[3] Rosalie T. Ruegg and Harold E. Marshall, *Building Economics: Theory and Practice*, Chapman and Hall, New York, August 1990, pp. 34–47.

among many buildings to which a single budget applies. The projects must be functionally independent, however, for the SIR allocation method to work. That is, the savings from one project cannot significantly affect the savings from another.

The SIR ranking applies only to additional investments required by building system options which are expected to reduce future costs relative to the basic system. It is assumed that, at a minimum, the basic system must be installed for the building to function properly. For example, an SIR would not be calculated for the lowest first-cost (and presumably least efficient) air-conditioning system that meets the cooling requirements of a new building. But it would be calculated for the additional investment required to install a higher efficiency air conditioner. Furthermore, this SIR would only be compared to SIRs for other independent improvements (e.g., heating system improvements) to determine how to allocate a fixed budget among such improvements.

### SIR Applied to Choosing among Independent Projects When the Budget Is Limited.

Table 27.2 shows how to use the SIR in choosing among five building improvements for energy reduction in a new building. Each improvement is cost-effective because the SIR of each exceeds 1.0. But total investment costs for the improvements are $10,000, and only $5,000 is available to invest. In this case, the SIR ranking indicates that improvements A, B, and D should be selected. (Improvement C, while having an SIR higher than that of D, will break the budget, so you skip over it and choose D.) If $7,000 of funding were available, select improvements A, B, and C.

**TABLE 27.2**   SIR Ranking of Building Improvements

|  | Initial cost, $ | PV savings, $ | SIR |
|---|---|---|---|
| A. Improved lighting fixtures | 2,500 | 10,000 | 5.0 |
| B. Improved roof deck insulation | 2,000 | 7,000 | 3.5 |
| C. Higher-efficiency window systems | 2,500 | 7,500 | 3.0 |
| D. Higher-efficiency water heater | 500 | 1,250 | 2.5 |
| E. Automatic entry doors (to reduce uncontrolled air leakage) | 2,500 | 5,000 | 2.0 |

## Payback

*Payback* (PB) measures how long it takes to recover investment costs. If you ignore the time value of money when you compute the payback period (i.e., you use a zero discount rate), you have simple payback (SP). If you account for the time value of money by using a positive discount rate, you have discounted payback (DPB). The DPB is a more accurate measure of payback because the time value of money is taken into account.

Investors sometimes specify a maximum acceptable payback period (MAPP) for evaluating a building system. For example, a high-efficiency heat pump might be chosen over a conventional heat pump only if the higher first cost is returned through fuel savings in, say, 2 years (the MAPP). But we discourage using some arbitrary MAPP to select systems because it is an unreliable guide to cost-effective choices.

PB is easy to understand, however, and as a supplementary method, it may be helpful in screening potential projects quickly. It is also useful to determine how long it takes for a project to break even. But it is a poor measure of a project's profitability over the long run because it ignores cash flows after payback. And if you use SP, it will not even give you a reliable measure of the time to break even. So try to use LCC, NS, and SIR methods instead of PB when making economic decisions.[4]

## Uncertainty and Sensitivity Analysis

Long-lived investments such as building mechanical systems are characterized by uncertainties regarding project life, operation and maintenance costs, and other factors that affect project economics. Since values of these variable factors are generally unknown, it is difficult to make economic evaluations with a high degree of certainty. One approach to this uncertainty problem is to use sensitivity analysis. It is a simple, inexpensive technique for handling uncertainty that gives you some perspective of how far off your measures of project worth might be.

*Sensitivity analysis* measures the impact on project outcomes of changing one or more key input values about which there is uncertainty. For example, a pessimistic value, expected value, and optimistic value might be chosen for an uncertain variable. Then an analysis could be performed to see how the outcome changes as you consider each of the three chosen values in turn, with other things held the same. When computing measures of project worth, for example, sensitivity analysis shows you just how sensitive the economic payoff is to uncertain values of a critical input, such as the discount rate, project maintenance costs, and mechanical equipment service life. Table 27.3 provides ASHRAE service life data for many types of mechanical equipment.[5] Analysis reveals how profitable or unprofitable the project might be if input values to the analysis turn out to be different from what is assumed in a single-answer approach to measuring project worth.

Sensitivity analysis can also be performed on different combinations of input values. That is, several variables are altered at once and then a measure of worth is computed. For example, one scenario might include a combination of all pessimistic values; another, all expected values; and a third, all optimistic values. Note, however, that sensitivity analysis can in fact be misleading if all pessimistic assumptions or all optimistic assumptions are combined in calculating economic measures.[6] Such combinations of inputs would be unlikely in the real world.

Sensitivity analysis can be performed for any measure of worth. And since it is easy to use and understand, it is widely used in the economic evaluation of government and private-sector projects. Office of Management and Budget Circular A-94[7] recommends sensitivity analysis to federal agencies as one technique for treating uncertainty in input variables. And the American Society for Testing and Materials (ASTM), in its "Standard Guide for Selecting Techniques for Treating Uncertainty and Risk in the Economic Evaluation of Buildings and Building Systems,"[8] describes sensitivity analysis for use in government and private-sector applications.

---

[4] For more details on when to apply these methods, see the video and workbook *Choosing Economic Evaluation Methods,* Part III in a series entitled Least-Cost Energy Decisions for Buildings, National Institute of Standards and Technology, 1993.

[5] An analyst using equipment service lines, for example, as shown in Table 27.3, might want to calculate measures of worth for higher and lower values of project life in addition to the measure of worth based on the median life shown in the table.

[6] F. Hillier, "The Derivation of Probabilistic Information for the Evaluation of Risky Investments," *Management Science,* p. 444.

[7] Office of Management and Budget, revised Oct. 29, 1992. Circular A-94, "Guidelines and Discount Rates for Benefit-Cost Analysis of Federal Programs," pp. 12–13.

[8] American Society for Testing and Materials, "Standard Guide for Selecting Techniques for Treating Uncertainty and Risk in the Economic Evaluation of Buildings and Building Systems," E1369-93, *ASTM Standards on Building Economics,* 3d ed., Philadelphia, Pa., 1994.

**TABLE 27.3** Mechanical Equipment Service Life

*Service life* is a time value established by ASHRAE that reflects the expected life of a specific component. Service life should not be confused with useful life or depreciation period used for income tax purposes. It is the life expectancy of system components. Equipment life is highly variable because of the diverse equipment applications, the preventive maintenance given, the environment, technical advancements of new equipment, and personal opinions. The values in this table are a median listing of replacement time of the components. Service life can be used to establish an amortization period or, if an amortization period is given, service life can give insight into adjusting the maintenance or replacement costs of components.

| Equipment item | Median years | Equipment item | Median years |
|---|---|---|---|
| Air conditioners | | Coils | |
| Window unit | 10 | DX, water, or steam | 20 |
| Residential single or split package | 15 | Electric | 15 |
| Commercial through-the-wall | 15 | Heat exchangers | |
| Water-cooled package | 15 | Shell-and-tube | 24 |
| Computer room | 15 | Reciprocating compressors | 20 |
| Heat pumps | | Package chillers | |
| Residential air-to-air | —* | Reciprocating | 20 |
| Commercial air-to-air | 15 | Centrifugal | 23 |
| Commercial water-to-air | 19 | Absorption | 23 |
| Rooftop air conditioners | | Cooling towers | |
| Single-zone | 15 | Galvanized metal | 20 |
| Multizone | 15 | Wood | 20 |
| Boilers, hot water (steam) | | Ceramic | 34 |
| Steel water-tube | 24 (30) | Air-cooled condensers | 20 |
| Steel fire-tube | 25 (25) | Evaporative condensers | 20 |
| Cast iron | 35 (30) | Insulation | |
| Electric | 15 | Molded | 20 |
| Burners | 21 | Blanket | 24 |
| Furnaces | | Pumps | |
| Gas- or oil-fired | 18 | Base-mounted | 20 |
| Unit heaters | | Pipe-mounted | 10 |
| Gas or electric | 13 | Sump and well | 10 |
| Hot water or steam | 20 | Condensate | 15 |
| Radiant heaters | | Reciprocating engines | 20 |
| Electric | 10 | Steam turbines | 30 |
| Hot water or steam | 25 | Electric motors | 18 |
| Air terminals | | Motor starters | 17 |
| Diffusers, grilles, and registers | 27 | Electric transformers | 30 |
| Induction and fan-coil units | 20 | Controls | |
| VAV and double-duct boxes | 20 | Pneumatic | 20 |
| Air washers | 17 | Electric | 16 |
| Ductwork | 30 | Electronic | 15 |
| Dampers | 20 | Valve actuators | |
| Fans | | Hydraulic | 15 |
| Centrifugal | 25 | Pneumatic | 20 |
| Axial | 20 | Self-contained | 10 |
| Propeller | 15 | | |
| Ventilating roof-mounted | 20 | | |

*Data removed by TC 1.8 because of changing technology.

SOURCE: Obtained from a nationwide survey conducted in 1977 by ASHRAE TC 1.8 (RP 186).

**Sensitivity Analysis Application.**  The results of sensitivity analysis can be presented in text, tables, or graphs. The following illustration of sensitivity analysis applied to a programmable control system uses text and a simple table.

Consider a decision on whether to install a programmable time clock to control heating, ventilating, and air conditioning (HVAC) equipment in a commercial building. The time clock would reduce electricity consumption by turning off HVAC equipment that is not needed during hours when the building is unoccupied.

Using net savings (NS) as the measure of project worth, the time clock is acceptable on economic grounds if its NS is positive, that is, if its present-value savings exceed present-value costs. The control system purchase and maintenance costs are felt to be relatively certain. The savings from energy reductions resulting from the time clock, however, are not certain. They are a function of three factors: the initial price of energy, the rate of change in energy prices over the life cycle of the time clock, and the number of kilowatt hours (kWh) saved. Two of these, the initial price of energy and the number of kWh saved, are relatively certain. But future energy prices are not.

To test the sensitivity of NS to possible energy price changes, three values of energy price change are considered: a low rate of energy price escalation (slowly increasing benefits from energy savings), a moderate rate of escalation (moderately increasing benefits), and a high rate of escalation (rapidly increasing benefits).

Table 27.4 shows three NS estimates that result from repeating the NS computation for each of the three energy price escalation rates.

**TABLE 27.4**  Energy Price Escalation Rates

| Energy price escalation rate | Net savings, $ |
| --- | --- |
| Low | −15,000 |
| Moderate | 20,000 |
| High | 50,000 |

To appreciate the significance of these findings, it is helpful to consider what extra information you now have over the conventional single-answer approach where, say, you computed a single NS estimate of $20,000. Table 27.4 shows that the project could return up to $50,000 in NS if future energy prices escalated at a high rate. On the other hand, you see that the project could lose as much as $15,000. This is considerably less than breakeven, where the project would at least pay for itself. It is also $35,000 less than what you calculated with the single-answer approach. Thus sensitivity analysis alerts you that accepting the time clock could lead to an uneconomic outcome.

There is no explicit measure of the likelihood that any one of the NS outcomes will happen. The analysis simply tells you what the outcomes will be under alternative conditions. However, if there is reason to expect energy prices to rise, at least at a moderate rate, then the project very likely will make money, other factors remaining the same.

This adds helpful information over the traditional, single-answer approach to measures of project worth.

**Advantages and Disadvantages of Sensitivity Analysis.**  There are several advantages of using sensitivity analysis in engineering economics. First, it shows how significant any given input variable is in determining a project's economic worth. It does this by displaying the range of possible project outcomes for a range of input values. This shows decision makers the input values that would make the project a loser or winner. Sensitivity analysis also helps you identify critical inputs so that you can choose where to spend extra resources in data collection and in improving data estimates. Second, sensitivity analysis is an excellent technique to help you anticipate and prepare for the "what-if" questions that you will be asked when presenting and defending a project. When you are asked what the outcome will be if operating costs are 50% more expensive than you think, you will be ready with an answer. Generating answers to what-if questions will help you assess how well your proposal will stand up to scrutiny. Third, sensitivity analysis does not require the use of probabilities as do many techniques for treating uncertainty. Fourth, you can use sensitivity analysis on any measure of project worth. And finally, you can use it when there is insufficient information, resources, and time for more sophisticated techniques.

The major disadvantage of sensitivity analysis is that there is no explicit probabilistic measure of risk exposure. That is, while you might be sure that one of several outcomes might happen, the analysis contains no explicit measure of their respective likelihoods.

For techniques that go beyond sensitivity analysis and give you some measure of your risk of choosing an uneconomic project, see the video and workbook *Uncertainty and Risk*, Part II in a series entitled Least-Cost Energy Decisions for Buildings.[8]

## DEFINITIONS OF ECONOMIC TERMS

*Base case:* The base-case alternative is the alternative against which proposed alternatives are compared.

*Base date:* The date (usually the beginning of the study period) to which benefits and costs are converted to time equivalent values when using the present-value method.

*Breakeven:* A combination of benefits (savings or revenues) that just offset costs, such that a project generates neither profits nor losses.

*Cost effective:* The condition whereby the present-value benefits (savings) of an investment alternative exceed its present-value costs.

*Discount rate:* The minimum acceptable rate of return used in converting benefits and costs occurring at different times to their equivalent values at a common time. Discount rates reflect the investor's time value of money (or opportunity cost). *Real* discount rates reflect time value apart from changes in the purchasing power of the dollar (i.e., exclude inflation or deflation) and are used to discount constant dollar cash flows. *Nominal* or *market* discount rates include changes in the purchasing power of the dollar (i.e., include inflation or deflation) and are used to discount current dollar cash flows.

*Discounting:* A procedure for converting cash amounts that occur at different points in time to an equivalent amount at a common point in time.

*Life-cycle cost* (LCC): The sum of all discounted costs of acquiring, owning, operating, maintaining, and disposing of a building project over the study period. Comparing life-cycle costs among mutually exclusive projects of equal performance is one way of determining relative cost effectiveness.

*Measures of project worth:* Economic methods which combine project benefits (savings) and costs in various ways to evaluate the economic value of a project. Examples are life-cycle costs, net benefits or net savings, benefit-to-cost ratio or savings-to-investment ratio, and payback.

*Net savings:* The difference between savings and costs, where both are discounted to present or annual values. The net savings method can be used as a measure of project worth.

---

[8] *Uncertainty and Risk,* Part II in a series entitled Least-Cost Energy Decisions for Buildings, National Institute of Standards and Technology, 1992.

*Present value:* The time-equivalent value at a specified base time (the present) of past, present, and future cash flows.

*Risk exposure:* The probability that a project's economic outcome is different from what is desired (the target) or what is acceptable.

*Salvage value:* The residual or resale value, net of any disposal costs, of any system removed during the study period or remaining at the end of the study period.

*Savings-to-investment ratio (SIR):* The ratio of present-value savings to present-value investment costs. The SIR method is used to make accept/reject decisions for single projects and to choose among independent projects when the investment budget is limited.

*Sensitivity analysis:* A technique for measuring the impact on project outcomes of changing one or more key input values about which there is uncertainty.

*Study period:* The length of time over which an investment is evaluated, generally set equal to the life of the project or the time horizon of the investor, whichever is shorter.

*Uncertainty:* Uncertainty (or certainty) as used in this chapter refers to a state of knowledge about the variable inputs to an economic analysis. If the analyst is unsure of input values, there is uncertainty. If the analyst is sure, there is certainty.

## RECOMMENDED READING

American Society for Testing and Materials, "Standard Guide for Selecting Techniques for Treating Uncertainty and Risk in the Economic Evaluation of Buildings and Building Systems," E1369-93, *ASTM Standards on Buildings Economics,* 3d ed., Philadelphia, Pa., 1994.

Hillier, F., "The Derivation of Probabilistic Information for the Evaluation of Risky Investments," *Management Science,* April 1969.

Office of Management and Budget, revised Oct. 29, 1992, Circular A-94, *Guidelines and Discount Rates for Benefit-Cost Analysis of Federal Programs.*

Marshall, H. E., VHS tape and companion workbook, *Uncertainty and Risk,* Part II in a series entitled Least-Cost Energy Decisions for Buildings, National Institute of Standards and Technology, 1992.

Marshall, H. E., VHS tape and companion workbook, *Choosing Economic Evaluation Methods,* Part III in a series entitled Least-Cost Energy Decisions for Buildings, National Institute of Standards and Technology, 1993.

Petersen, S. R., *BLCC 4.0—The NIST "Building Life-Cycle Cost" Program User's Guide and Reference Manual,* NISTIR 5185, National Institute of Standards and Technology, Gaithersburg, Md., 1993.

Ruegg, R. T., and H. E. Marshall, *Building Economics: Theory and Practice,* Chapman and Hall, New York, August 1990.

## RECOMMENDED SOFTWARE

### Building Life-Cycle Cost (BLCC)

BLCC is a public-domain computer program developed at NIST for the economic analysis of buildings and building systems. It is designed to run on IBM PCs and compatibles. BLCC can compute the LCC for project alternatives and compare those LCCs to determine the most economic project alternative. It can compute the net savings, SIR, and payback period for any alternative relative to a base-case design. It can also generate an annual cash-flow report for each alternative and print out detailed or summary LCC analysis. [For a brochure with information on the BLCC program, contact the Office of Applied Economics at NIST, (301) 975-6132.]

# CHAPTER 28
# CODES, STANDARDS, AND LAWS

## GENERAL DISCUSSION

Those wishing to understand energy systems installation and design must understand the role, philosophy, and reasoning of the codes. There are 40,000 local jurisdictions in the United States. There is no mechanical project that can escape civil governance of some degree. Many cities and municipalities have their own local codes to which all construction must adhere; others have adopted one of the prevailing model codes—some in entirety, others in part—either with or without modifications. Varying code requirements may have a severe economic impact on any major job. Any contractor who has had to tear out yards of concrete, miles of pipe, insulation, or ductwork because the job could not pass local or federal specs *after* inspection, knows from bitter experience the importance of code literacy. The estimator must know the prevailing code in the territory where the project is going.

Two kinds of laws govern the installation of mechanical systems: immutable natural laws from which we derive our scientific and technical knowledge, and the constantly changing body of civil laws, codes, and regulations, whose chief purpose is usually safety. Code compliance may be voluntary, or when adapted by regional governments, may depend on code-writing agencies.

There are three major building code bodies in the United States. These are Building Officials and Code Administration International (BOCA), International Conference of Building Officials (ICBO), and Southern Building Code Congress International (SBCCI). Jointly, these three bodies sponsor both the Council of American Building Officials (CABO) One- and Two-Family Dwelling Code and the CABO Model Energy Code. Initially funded by the U.S. Department of Energy, the CABO codes are now maintained by CABO.

*BOCA:* BOCA codes are recognized and adopted by Kansas, Oklahoma, Missouri, Illinois, Wisconsin, Michigan, Indiana, Ohio, Kentucky, Virginia, West Virginia, Vermont, New Hampshire, Connecticut, Rhode Island, and parts of Pennsylvania. BOCA issues compliance reports that are recognized in BOCA jurisdictions to show conformance with appropriate standards and BOCA codes.

*SBCCI:* SBCCI codes are recognized and adopted in the southeastern part of the United States: Arkansas, Louisiana, Mississippi, Alabama, Tennessee, Georgia, Florida, North Carolina, South Carolina, and smaller towns in the state of Texas. They also offer the service of compliance reports to show compliance with appropriate standards and the "Standard" code.

*ICBO:* ICBO is the publisher of the Uniform Building Code and cosponsor of the Uniform Mechanical Code, which is recognized and adopted by California, Oregon, Washington, Nevada, Idaho, Montana, Wyoming, North Dakota, South Dakota, Colorado, Nebraska, New Mexico, Arizona, Utah, Minnesota, Maine, and the major cities in the state of Texas.

These standard codes are designed for adoption by state or local governments by reference. They are written in a language that makes them readily usable for insertion into local codes. Jurisdictions adopting them usually make additions, deletions, and amendments. Code writers must constantly introduce new technological advances and balance the triangle of *safety-economics-enforceability*. A continuing problem is the technological lag the code writers must inevitably face. The designers and builders, on the other hand, are confronted by the time lag between the code writer's incorporation of new information into the Standard Code—usually every year—and the time the jurisdiction adopts these changes and amendments into law, usually 3 to 5 years.

Code-writing bodies are made up of industry members and professionals representing a variety of viewpoints but the central idea in code formulation is the merging of the committee members' views into a solid consensus, i.e., not a mere majority but a very substantial, if not unanimous, agreement.

The BOCA Uniform Mechanical Code, the SBCCI Standard Mechanical Code, and the ICBO Mechanical Code all use reference standards as their foundations and may or may not cite the standard in the passage. The most important *referral* standards for HVAC are those of the following organizations:

American Gas Association (AGA)
1515 Wilson Blvd.
Arlington, VA 22209

American National Standards Institute (ANSI)
1430 Broadway
New York, NY 10018

American Society of Heating, Refrigerating and Air Conditioning Engineers (ASHRAE)
17791 Tullie Circle, NE
Atlanta, GA 30329

American Society of Mechanical Engineers (ASME)
345 East 47th St.
New York, NY 10017

American Society for Testing and Materials (ASTM)
1916 Race St.
Philadelphia, PA 19103

National Fire Protection Association (NFPA)
1 Batterymarch Park
Quincy, MA 02269

Sheet Metal & Air Conditioning Contractors National Association (SMACNA)
4201 Lafayette Center Drive
Chantilly, VA 22021

Underwriters Laboratories (UL)
333 Pfinsten Road
Northbrook, IL 60062.

As many as 60 different standards-writing organizations may be references in a single building code, but those listed above are the most common for mechanical systems designers, engineers, and estimators. Although most standards are voluntary, stricter inspections and regulation of systems is the trend in the United States and the world today. More states and local governments are adopting code standards and are demanding that contractors, engineers, and architects comply with these codes. Most recently energy-conservation and ecological issues are receiving equal attention to health and safety by standards and code writers. This trend is expected to continue into the future.

## RECENT DEVELOPMENTS

Codes and standards, by nature, impact costs. While federal health and safety laws such as OSHA have long been on the books, their effects on costs have been relatively moderate and, over the years, flat. The year 1990, however, began a marked rise in costs resulting from federal law. The 1990s may well be remembered as the decade of federal intrusion into the HVAC industry. It may be said that the natural conditions of planet Earth have made it necessary for governments to mandate the use, abuse, and conservation of certain natural resources as well as chemicals, and with these government actions comes a clearly defined increase in cost to the consumer in general and the HVAC industry in particular. Energy conservation, clean air, indoor-air quality, and CFCs all impact the industry at the cost-estimating level. Compliance with EPA-40 CFR Part 82, *Protection of Stratospheric Ozone, Refrigerant Recycling,* as well as ASHRAE Standard 15-1992 and ASHRAE Standard 62-1992, will certainly increase the cost of installing and servicing air-conditioning refrigerating machinery.

State and local building departments are writing more regulations that require more intricate and sophisticated permit and plans processing procedures as well as more tangible and specific code inspection and enforcement. Costs for building permits and plans processing have risen sharply across the country. Compliance with ASHRAE 62 translates into more outside air and increased refrigeration capacity per occupancy. Concern for indoor-air quality results in increased costs in several ways. ASHRAE Standard 15-1992 signals increased costs as the industry complies with revised machinery room requirements. Further, states that have never previously had contractor licensing requirements are joining the roster of those that have already mandated license examinations for HVAC contractors. Florida state HVAC contractor license candidates need to spend $800 to $900 just for the required books plus a $245 registration fee. They are also required to take biyearly CEU classes. Table 28.1[1] lists the licensing laws of all states as of 1994. Unfortunately, along with necessary industry standards and codes comes a burgeoning bureaucracy which, in many hidden ways, is responsible for still further costs to the consumer. No building code ever *reduced* costs.

The most percussive law affecting the HVAC industry is the U.S. Energy Policy Act of 1992. Public Law 102-486 mandates that every state shall have a code provision meeting or exceeding ASHRAE/IES Standard 90.1-1989.

### Energy Code for Commercial and High-Rise Residential Buildings Based on ASHRAE/IES 90.1-1989

In response to the increasing number of discrepancies between standards and model codes, ASHRAE recently developed a code language version of the original provisions cited in the Act into their building codes quickly and easily. Because of the nature of code language, many of the recommended or unenforceable provisions of the original standard have been deleted and other criteria needed for a model code added. See Table 28.2 for the cost of this new codified version of Standard 90.1-1998, as well as the helpful *User's Manual* and other impor-

---

[1] The tables in this chapter do not appear on the computer disk provided with this book.

**TABLE 28.1**   State HVAC License Requirements

This list does not include other trades, such as general contractors, electricians, asbestos abatement, etc. NR indicates that the state bond is required only for nonresident contractors.

| State | License required | Exam required | State bond required | Comments |
|---|---|---|---|---|
| Alabama | x | x | x | |
| Alaska | x | x | | |
| Arizona | x | x | x | |
| Arkansas | x | x | NR | |
| California | x | x | x | |
| Colorado | x | x | NR | Water and pumps only |
| Connecticut | x | x | | |
| Delaware | x | | | |
| District of Columbia | x | | x | |
| Florida | x | x | | |
| Georgia | x | x | | |
| Hawaii | x | | x | |
| Idaho | | | | |
| Illinois | | | | |
| Indiana | x | x | | Plumbing only |
| Iowa | | | NR | |
| Kansas | | | NR | |
| Kentucky | | | | |
| Louisiana | x | x | | |
| Maine | | | | |
| Maryland | x | | | |
| Massachusetts | | | NR | |
| Michigan | x | x | | |
| Minnesota | | | x | |
| Mississippi | x | x | | >$100,000 only |
| Missouri | | | | |
| Montana | | | x | Public works >$5,000 only |
| Nebraska | x | | NR | |
| Nevada | x | | | Exam may be required |
| New Hampshire | | | | |
| New Jersey | x | | | |
| New Mexico | x | x | | |
| New York | | | | |
| North Carolina | x | x | | |
| North Dakota | x | | x | |
| Ohio | | | | |
| Oklahoma | x | x | | Plumbing only |
| Oregon | x | | | Plumbing only |
| Pennsylvania | | | | |
| Rhode Island | | | | |
| South Carolina | x | x | | |
| South Dakota | x | x | | Plumbing only |
| Tennessee | x | x | | |
| Texas | x | x | | |
| Utah | x | | | Plumbing only |
| Vermont | | | | |
| Virginia | x | | | Exam may be required |
| Washington | x | x | x | |
| West Virginia | | | NR | |
| Wisconsin | | | NR | |
| Wyoming | | | | |

**TABLE 28.2**    ASHRAE Standards

| Standard number | Title | Date | 1994 list price, $ |
|---|---|---|---|
| 15 | *Safety Code for Mechanical Refrigeration* | 1992 | 31.00 |
| 34 | *Safety Classification of Refrigerants* | 1992 | 21.00 |
| | *Addenda, 34a* | 1993 | 12.00 |
| 55 | *Thermal Environment Conditions of Human Occupancy* | 1992 | 37.00 |
| 62 | *Ventilation for Acceptable Indoor Air Quality* | 1989 | 42.00 |
| 90.1 | *Energy Efficient Design of New Buildings except Low-Rise Residential Buildings* | 1989 | 98.00 |
| | *Addenda, 90.1* | 1989 | 12.00 |
| | *User's Manual, 90.1* | 1989 | 73.00 |
| | *Energy Code for Commercial High-Rise and Residential,* based on 90.1-1989 | | 98.00 |
| 100.2 | *Energy Conservation, Existing High-Rise Residential* | 1991 | 28.00 |
| 100.3 | *Energy Conservation, Existing Commercial* | 1985 | 28.00 |
| 100.4 | *Energy Conservation, Existing Industrial* | 1984 | 28.00 |
| 100.5 | *Energy Conservation, Existing Institutional* | 1991 | 28.00 |
| 100.6 | *Energy Conservation, Existing Public Assembly* | 1991 | 28.00 |
| Handbook | *HVAC Fundamentals* | 1993 | 119.00 |
| Handbook | *HVAC Systems and Equipment* | 1991 | 119.00 |
| Handbook | *HVAC Applications* | 1990 | 119.00 |
| Handbook | *Refrigeration* | 1990 | 119.00 |

tant ASHRAE standards. Other ASHRAE standards (15, *Safety Code for Mechanical Refrigeration;* 34, *Number Designation and Safety Classification of Refrigerants;* 55, *Thermal Environmental Conditions for Human Occupancy;* and 62, *Ventilation for Acceptable Indoor Air Quality*) will soon be published in code language.

### ASHRAE Standard 15-1992, *Safety Code for Mechanical Refrigeration*

Aside from the important new application rules for refrigerants, especially R-123 and R-134a, this standard contains new revised requirements for machinery rooms that will add considerably to job costs. These requirements include specific ventilation for the mechanical equipment room (MER), doors, passageway and access, long-term monitoring, vapor detectors, alarms, and self-contained breathing equipment. The estimator, as well as the designer, needs to be thoroughly familiar with this standard. Figures 28.1 and 28.2 illustrate the approved method for purging refrigerant from the equipment room. Compliance with these diagrams will increase costs.

## STANDARDS ORGANIZATIONS

The most important standards organizations affecting the heating, air-conditioning, ventilating, and refrigeration industries are described in the following paragraphs.

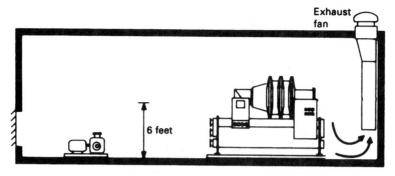

**Figure 28.1 SUGGESTED EXHAUST FAN LOCATION FOR MER TO MEET THE REQUIREMENTS OF ASHRAE 15-1992**
*Because refrigerant gas is heavier than air, the exhaust inlet should be located well beneath the breathing level. (SOURCE: The Trane Company, La Crosse, Wis.)*

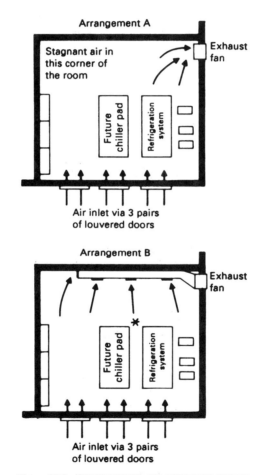

**Figure 28.2 CORRECTING AN EXISTING VENTILATION SYSTEM ARRANGEMENT TO MEET THE REQUIREMENTS OF ASHRAE 15-1992 FOR MER**
*In arrangement A the refrigerant is not thoroughly removed from the mechanical room. Arrangement B solves the problem. Note location of the refrigerant sensor(\*) in arrangement B. (SOURCE: The Trane Company, La Crosse, Wis.)*

## American National Standards Institute

ANSI is the largest publisher of standards in the world. There are over 8,000 ANSI standards. In many cases other organizations such as ASME, ASHRAE, or AGA may sponsor a particular standard and carry another designation number. Those numbers will read, for example, as ANSI/ASHRAE 15, or ANSI/NFPA 90A. If the sponsor does not employ a designation or if ANSI itself developed the standard, ANSI's acronym alone is used.

## American Society of Heating, Refrigerating and Air Conditioning Engineers, Inc.

ASHRAE publishes more than 75 standards in addition to handbooks, technical bulletins, and design guides. The four *Handbook* volumes are revised on alternating years; the standards are revised periodically. The most common standards listed in national or model mechanical codes as well as licensing examinations are shown in Table 28.2.

## American Society of Mechanical Engineers

ASME publishes more than 500 codes and standards and over 600 books. Of these, the most pertinent for the mechanical engineer and contractor are the ASME B31 Code for Pressure Piping, which consists of nine sections periodically revised to keep abreast of new technologies and materials; and the ASME Boiler and Pressure Vessel Code, consisting of 25 volumes which establish rules of safety governing the design, fabrication, and inspection of boilers and pressure vessels. Cost for the complete set is $4,753. Table 28.3 gives the most often cited boiler codes for heating and air-conditioning contractors and designers. Table 28.4 lists the pressure piping codes most frequently referenced in state and municipal codes.

**TABLE 28.3**  ASME Boiler Code

| Section number | Title | 1994 list price, $ |
|---|---|---|
| IV | *Heating Boilers* | 170.00 |
| VI | *Rules for Care and Operation of Heating Boilers* | 100.00 |
| VII | *Guidelines for Care of Power Boilers* (addenda issued every Dec. 31 between revisions; prices include update service through June 30, 1995) | 115.00 |

**TABLE 28.4**  ASME Piping Code

| Section number | Title | 1994 list price, $ |
|---|---|---|
| A13.1 | *Scheme for Identification of Piping Systems* | 18.00 |
| B31.1 | *Power Piping* | 131.00 |
| B31.2 | *Fuel Gas Piping* | 18.00 |
| B31.3 | *Chemical Plant and Petroleum Refinery Piping* | 189.00 |
| B31.4 | *Liquid Transportation Systems, Hydrocarbons, Liquid Petroleum Gas, Anhydrous Ammonia Piping* | 72.00 |
| B31.5 | *Refrigeration Piping* | 54.00 |
| B31.8 | *Gas Transmission and Distribution Piping* | 98.00 |
| B31.9 | *Building Service Piping* | 50.00 |
| B31.11 | *Slurry Transportation Piping* | 72.00 |

## National Fire Protection Association

The NFPA publishes more than 280 national fire codes and standards. Some of these are among the most frequently referenced in the construction industry as well as many other industries. The complete *1994 National Fire Codes* is available in 11 soft-bound volumes for $700 per set. The most commonly cited NFPA pamphlets for HVAC are shown in Table 28.5.

## Sheet Metal and Air Conditioning Contractors National Association

SMACNA publishes several important manuals that are often referenced in code books and appear on required book lists for contractor licensing examinations. Several of the most important SMACNA standards and design guides are listed in Table 28.6.

**TABLE 28.5**   NFPA Standards for HVAC

| Pamphlet number | Title | 1994 list price, $ |
|---|---|---|
| 13 | *Installation of Fire Sprinklers* | 24.50 |
| 13A | *Inspection, Testing, Maintenance of Fire Sprinklers* | 18.75 |
| 14 | *Standpipe and Hose Systems* | 18.75 |
| 17 | *Dry Chemical Extinguishing Systems* | 18.75 |
| 17A | *Wet Chemical Extinguishing Systems* | 15.50 |
| 31 | *Installation of Oil Burning Equipment* | 18.75 |
| 54 | *National Fuel Gas Code* | 22.00 |
| 58 | *Storage and Handling LP Gases* | 24.50 |
| 70 | *National Electrical Code* (looseleaf) | 38.50 |
| 82 | *Incinerators and Waste Systems* | 15.00 |
| 86 | *Ovens and Furnaces (Class A/B)* | 20.75 |
| 86C | *Industrial Furnaces (Class C)* | 20.75 |
| 86D | *Industrial Furnaces (Class D)* | 20.75 |
| 90A | *Installation of AC and Ventilation Systems* | 18.75 |
| 90B | *Installation of Warm Air & AC Systems* | 15.50 |
| 91 | *Exhaust Systems, Conveying Materials* | 18.75 |
| 92A | *Smoke Control Systems* | 18.75 |
| 96 | *Smoke and Grease Exhaust Commercial Kitchens* | 18.75 |
| 99 | *Health Care Facilities* | 29.75 |
| 101 | *Life Safety Code* | 33.75 |
| 204M | *Smoke and Heat Venting* | 18.75 |
| 211 | *Chimneys, Fireplaces, Vents, Appliances* | 18.75 |
| 214 | *Water Cooling Towers* | 15.50 |

**TABLE 28.6**   SMACNA Standards

| Title | 1994 list price, $ |
|---|---|
| *Accepted Industry Practice Industrial Duct Construction* | 32.00 |
| *Energy Recovery Equipment and Systems* | 86.00 |
| *Fibrous Glass Duct Construction Standard* | 85.00 |
| *HVAC Duct Construction Standard—Metal & Flexible* | 109.00 |
| *HVAC Systems—Duct Design* | 109.00 |
| *Installation Standards for Residential Heating & A/C* | 66.00 |
| *Round Industrial Duct Construction Standards* | 109.00 |

# RECOMMENDED READING

"Codes and Standards," *ASHRAE Handbook of Fundamentals,* American Society of Heating, Refrigerating and Air Conditioning Engineers, Inc., Atlanta, Ga., 1993, Chap. 38.

Cross, Wilbur, *An Authorized History of the ASME Boiler and Pressure Vessel Code,* American Society of Mechanical Engineers, New York, 1989.

*Directory of Building Codes and Regulations,* NCBCS Publications Department, 505 Huntmar Park Drive, Suite 210, Herndon, VA 22070.

Guckelberger, Dave, and Brenda Bradley, *Refrigeration System Equipment Room Design,* Pamphlet REF-AM-3, The Trane Company, La Crosse, Wis., August 1992.

# APPENDIX
# SELECTED CONVERSION FACTORS

**TABLE A.1**  Conversion Factors for the English Measurement System

| Multiply | by | to obtain |
|---|---|---|
| atmospheres | 29.92 | inches of mercury |
| atmospheres | 33.93 | feet of water |
| atmospheres | 14.70 | pounds per square inch |
| atmospheres | 1.058 | tons per square foot |
| barrels (oil) | 42 | gallons |
| boiler horsepower | 33,475 | Btu per hour |
| boiler horsepower | 34.5 | pounds water evaporated from and at 212°F |
| Btu | 778 | foot-pounds |
| Btu | 0.000393 | horsepower-hours |
| Btu | 0.000293 | kilowatt-hours |
| Btu | 0.0010307 | pounds water evaporated from and at 212°F |
| Btu per 24 hr | 0.00000347 | tons of refrigeration |
| Btu per hour | 0.00002986 | boiler horsepower |
| Btu per hour | 0.000393 | horsepower |
| Btu per hour | 0.000293 | kilowatts |
| cubic feet | 1,728 | cubic inches |
| cubic feet | 7.48052 | gallons |
| cubic feet of water | 62.37 | pounds (at 60°F) |
| cubic feet per minute | 0.1247 | gallons per second |
| feet of water | 0.881 | inches of mercury (at 32°F) |
| feet of water | 62.37 | pounds per square foot |
| feet of water | 0.4335 | pounds per square inch |
| feet of water | 0.02950 | atmospheres |
| feet per minute | 0.01136 | miles per hour |
| feet per minute | 0.01667 | feet per second |
| foot-pounds | 0.001286 | Btu |
| gallons (U.S.) | 0.1337 | cubic feet |
| gallons (U.S.) | 231 | cubic inches |
| gallons of water | 8.3453 | pounds of water (at 60°F) |
| horsepower | 550 | foot-pounds per second |
| horsepower | 33,000 | foot-pounds per minute |
| horsepower | 2,546 | Btu per hour |
| horsepower | 42.42 | Btu per minute |
| horsepower | 0.7457 | kilowatts |
| horsepower (boiler) | 33,475 | Btu per hour |

*(Continued)*

**TABLE A.1** Conversion Factors for the English Measurement System (*Continued*)

| Multiply | by | to obtain |
|---|---|---|
| inches of mercury (at 62°F) | 13.57 | inches of water (at 62°F) |
| inches of mercury (at 62°F) | 1.131 | feet of water (at 62°F) |
| inches of mercury (at 62°F) | 70.73 | pounds per square foot |
| inches of mercury (at 62°F) | 0.4912 | pounds per square inch |
| inches of water (at 62°F) | 0.07355 | inches of mercury |
| inches of water (at 62°F) | 0.03613 | pounds per square inch |
| inches of water (at 62°F) | 5.202 | pounds per square foot |
| inches of water (at 62°F) | 0.002458 | atmospheres |
| kilowatts | 56.92 | Btu per minute |
| kilowatts | 1.341 | horsepower |
| kilowatts | 3,415 | Btu |
| latent heat of ice | 143.33 | Btu per pound |
| pounds | 7,000 | grains |
| pounds of water (at 60°F) | 0.01602 | cubic feet |
| pounds of water (at 60°F) | 27.68 | cubic inches |
| pounds of water (at 60°F) | 0.1198 | gallons |
| pounds of water evaporated from and at 212°F | 0.284 | kilowatt-hours |
| pounds of water evaporated from and at 212°F | 0.381 | horsepower-hours |
| pounds of water evaporated from and at 212°F | 970.4 | Btu |
| pounds per square inch | 2.0416 | inches of mercury |
| pounds per square inch | 2.309 | feet of water (at 62°F) |
| pounds per square inch | 27.68 | inches of water |

**TABLE A.2**  Commonly Used HVAC SI Metric Conversions

| Unit of measure | *Multiply* | *by* | *to Obtain* | Symbol |
|---|---|---|---|---|
| Ductwork | | | | |
| Airflow | cfm | 0.0004719 | cubic meters per second | $m^3/s$ |
| | fpm | 0.00508 | meters per second | $m/s$ |
| | fpm | 0.508 | centimeters per second | $cm/s$ |
| | fps | 0.3048 | meters per second | $m/s$ |
| | mph | 0.447 | meters per second | $m/s$ |
| Pressure | inch of water ($H_2O$) | 0.25 | kilopascals | kPa |
| | inch $H_2O$ | 249 (use 250) | pascals | Pa |
| | inch $H_2O$ per 100 ft | 8.176 | pascals [newtons per square meter ($N/m^2$)] | Pa |
| | inch mercury (Hg) | 3.386 | kilopascals ($kN/m^2$) | kPa |
| Length and area | inch | 25.4 | millimeters | mm |
| | inch | 2.54 | centimeters | cm |
| | inch | 0.0254 | meters | m |
| | square inches (sq in) | 6.452 | centimeters squared | $cm^2$ |
| | feet | 0.3048 | meters | m |
| | $ft^2$ (sq ft) | 0.0929 | meters squared | $m^2$ |
| | $ft^3$ (cu ft) | 0.02832 | meters cubed | $m^3$ |
| Fan duty | cfm | 0.4719 | liters per second | L/s |
| | inch $H_2O$ | 249 (use 250) | pascals | Pa |
| | hp | 0.7460 | kilowatts | kW |
| | rpm | 0.10472 | radians per second | rad/s |
| | rpm | 60 | revolutions per second | rev/s |
| Pump duty | psf | 47.88 (use 50) | pascals ($N/m^2$) | kPa |
| | psi | 6,895 (use 7,000) | pascals ($N/m^2$) | Pa |
| | psi | 6,895 | kilopascals ($kN/m^2$) | kPa |
| | gpm | 0.00006309 | meters cubed per second | $m^3/s$ |
| | gpm | 0.06309 | liters per second | L/s |
| Energy, work, heat | Btuh | 0.2931 | watts | W |
| | Btuh | 0.0002931 | kilowatts | kW |
| | ton (ref.) | 3,516 | kilowatts | kW |
| | ton | 3,516 | kilowatts | kW |
| | Btu | 1,054 | joules (watts-second) | J |
| | kWh | 3.6 | megajoules | MJ |
| Thermal flow | Btu | 1,055.06 | joules | J |
| | Btu | 1.05506 | kilojoules | kJ |
| | $Btu/ft^3$ °F | 67,066 | joules per cubic meter ° Celsius | $J/m^3$ °C |
| | Btu/lb °F | 4,186.8 | joules per kilogram ° Celsius | J/kg °C |
| | Btuh | 0.2931 | watts | W |
| | $Btu/ft^2$ hr | 3.155 | watts per square meter | $W/m^2$ |
| | $Btu/ft^2$ °F(*U* value) | 5.678 | watts per square meter ° Celsius | $W/m^2$ °C |
| | temperature diff. °F | 0.555 | temperature diff. ° Celsius | Δ*t*°C |
| | *To obtain above* | *divide by above* | *starting with above* | |

Pressure conversion factors:

psi $\times$ 703.1 = mm $H_2O$

psi $\times$ 51.71 = mm Hg

psi $\times$ 0.0690 = bar

psi $\times$ 68.95 = m bar

psi $\times$ 0.06805 = atmosphere

bar $\times$ 1 $\times$ $10^5$ = $N/m^2$ (Pa)

atmosphere $\times$ 101,300 = $N/m^2$ (Pa)

*Notes:*

1. One pascal = 1 newton per meter squared ($N/m^2$).

2. All operating pressures should be stated clearly in terms of gage pressure, e.g., "gage pressure, 6 bar."

**TABLE A.3**   Conversion Factors for the SI Metric System

| Multiply | by | to obtain |
|---|---|---|
| meters | 100 | centimeters |
| centimeters | 10 | millimeters |
| kilopascals | 1,000 | pascals |
| meters squared | 10,000 | centimeters squared |
| meters cubed | 1,000 | liters |
| kilowatts | 1,000 | watts |
| kilojoules | 1,000 | joules |
| megajoules | 1,000 | kilojoules |
| kilograms | 1,000 | grams |
| *To obtain above* | *divide by above* | *starting with above* |

**TABLE A.4**   SI Metric Prefixes

| Prefix | Symbol | Factor | |
|---|---|---|---|
| tera | T | $10^{12}$ | = 1 000 000 000 000 |
| giga | G | $10^{9}$ | = 1 000 000 000 |
| mega | M | $10^{6}$ | = 1 000 000 |
| kilo | k | $10^{3}$ | = 1 000 |
| hecto | h | $10^{2}$ | = 100 |
| deka | da | $10^{1}$ | = 10 |
| deci | d | $10^{-1}$ | = 0.1 |
| centi | c | $10^{-2}$ | = 0.01 |
| milli | m | $10^{-3}$ | = 0.001 |
| micro | $\mu$ | $10^{-6}$ | = 0.000 001 |
| nano | n | $10^{-9}$ | = 0.000 000 001 |
| pico | p | $10^{-12}$ | = 0.000 000 000 001 |
| femto | f | $10^{-15}$ | = 0.000 000 000 000 001 |
| atto | a | $10^{-18}$ | = 0.000 000 000 000 000 001 |

The choice of the appropriate multiple of an SI unit is governed by the application. The multiple should be chosen so that the numerical values will be between 0.1 and 1 000 when practical; e.g.

| 23 kN | instead of 23 000 N |
|---|---|
| 5.86 mm | instead of 0.005 86 m |
| 8.72 kPa | instead of 8 720 Pa |

[*Note:* Numbers in metric notation do not include commas. Instead, blank spaces appear where commas are customary in the English system (e.g., "23,769,145" becomes "23 769 145" in metric notation).]

# INDEX

# ABOUT THE AUTHORS

JOHN GLADSTONE is a Fellow and Life Member of ASHRAE (American Society of Heating, Refrigerating, and Air-Conditioning Engineers) and a recognized authority in the fields of HVAC estimating and license examination preparation. He is the author of numerous articles and 17 books, including the new Third Edition of *Air Conditioning/Testing/Adjusting/Balancing* with David Bevirt, forthcoming from McGraw-Hill. Gladstone is a consultant and editor at *Engineer's Press*.

KENNETH K. HUMPHREYS, Ph.D., P.E., C.C.E., is a Fellow and former executive director of AACE International (American Association of Cost Engineers International). He is the author of several books and over 200 papers and has been recognized as a Certified Cost Engineer. He currently practices as a consultant engineer and editor. Humphreys is listed in *Who's Who in America*.

## INSTRUCTIONS FOR USE OF THE LOTUS 1-2-3[1] DISK
## ACCOMPANYING *Mechanical Estimating Guidebook, 6th edition*

This disk contains compressed files that must be expanded before use. You will need at least 2 megabytes of space on your hard drive. To load the files on your computer, complete the following steps:

1. Select a directory or create a new directory.
2. Copy the disk into the directory.
3. Type **GLADS** and press ENTER. (This will expand the files.)
4. Delete the file GLADS.EXE to save space.
5. Keep the original disk as a backup.

The expanded files are *Lotus 1-2-3* spreadsheets and are compatible with Release 2.2 and higher of *1-2-3*. The file names are similar to the table numbers in the book, with a hyphen substituted for the decimal point in the table numbers. Thus, for example, Table 1.5 has the file name **TAB1-5**, Table 2.3 has the file name **TAB2-3**, etc. All files have the standard *1-2-3* extension of **.WK1**.

These files are compatible for use with any spreadsheet estimating system or estimating database. The user can import the files, as desired, into a database and/or can modify and update them as appropriate to reflect differences in labor rates over time, area cost adjustment factors, price escalation, discounts, and contractor overhead and markups. Such adjustments can be made using the standard mathematical functions which are available with *Lotus 1-2-3*.

Except as otherwise noted in *Mechanical Estimating Guidebook*, 6th edition, these cost files are based on a U.S. average labor rate of $26.45 per hour. This figure includes all direct fringe benefits such as health care, insurance, vacation, and pensions, but does not include contractor's overhead. Labor costs can generally be updated by multiplying the cost figures in these spreadsheets by the current labor rate and then dividing by $26.45. Alternately, most tables provide labor requirements in terms of workhours. Thus, current labor costs can readily be determined simply by multiplying the workhours by the applicable labor rate at any specific location. An adjustment should also be made for local labor productivity conditions versus U.S. averages.

Adjustment of material costs may be made using *Producer Prices and Price Indexes*, which is published monthly by the U.S. Department of Labor, Bureau of Labor Statistics. These indexes are highly detailed, and individual indexes exist for most types of equipment. The index base used in *Mechanical Estimating Guidebook*, 6th edition, is mid-1994 unless otherwise noted. To update material costs on this disk, simply multiply the cost figure on the disk by the current value of the appropriate Producer Price Index and divide by the value for mid-1994. Past issues of *Producer Prices and Price Indexes* are available from the U.S. Government printing office and many libraries.

---

[1] *Lotus* and *1-2-3* are trademarks of Lotus Development Corporation.